TO THE BOOK REVIEW

Herewith is your review copy of the book de

Studies of Field Systems in the British Isles

Edited by A. R. H. Baker & R. A. Butlin

PUBLISHER Cambridge University Press

PLACE OF PUBLICATION New York (Cambridge and London UK)

PUBLICATION DATE   March 31, 1980

SIZE 5½ x 8½   PAGES   xxvi + 702

FRONT & BACK MATTER Preface, figures, tables,
        acknowledgements, abbreviations;
        selected bibliography, index

ILLUSTRATIONS   figures, tables

ISBN 0 521 20121 7   LC   72 91359

PRICE $24.95

Please retain this slip for checking details

We will appreciate receiving three copies of your
printed review: one for the author, one for our UK
office, and one for our files.

Publicity Department

_MBRIDGE ⬙ UNIVERSITY PRESS

STUDIES OF FIELD SYSTEMS IN
THE BRITISH ISLES

STUDIES OF
FIELD SYSTEMS
IN THE
BRITISH ISLES

EDITED BY

ALAN R. H. BAKER

FELLOW OF EMMANUEL COLLEGE AND
LECTURER IN GEOGRAPHY, UNIVERSITY OF CAMBRIDGE

AND

ROBIN A. BUTLIN

LECTURER IN GEOGRAPHY,
QUEEN MARY COLLEGE, UNIVERSITY OF LONDON

CAMBRIDGE
AT THE UNIVERSITY PRESS
1973

Published by the Syndics of the Cambridge University Press
Bentley House, 200 Euston Road, London NWI 2DB
American Branch: 32 East 57th Street, New York, N.Y.10022

© Cambridge University Press 1973

Library of Congress Catalogue Card Number: 72–91359

ISBN: 0 521 20121 7

Printed in Great Britain
at the University Printing House, Cambridge
(Brooke Crutchley, University Printer)

Contents

[v]

CHAPTER 2

Field Systems of Northwest England

By G. ELLIOTT, M.A.

Senior Research Officer in Geography, Schools Council Project,
University of Liverpool

CHAPTER 3

Field Systems of Northumberland and Durham

By R. A. BUTLIN

CHAPTER 4

Field Systems of Yorkshire

BY J. A. SHEPPARD, PH.D.

Lecturer in Geography, Queen Mary College,
University of London

CHAPTER 5

Field Systems of the West Midlands

BY B. K. ROBERTS, PH.D.

Lecturer in Geography, University of Durham

CHAPTER 6

Field Systems of the East Midlands

By J. THIRSK, M.A., PH.D., F.R.HIST.S.

Reader in Economic History, University of Oxford

CHAPTER 7

Field Systems of East Anglia

By M. R. POSTGATE, M.A., PH.D.

CHAPTER 10

Field Systems of North Wales

BY G. R. J. JONES, M.A.

Reader in Geography, University of Leeds

CHAPTER 11

Field Systems of South Wales

By M. DAVIES, c.b.e., m.a., ph.d.

CHAPTER 12

Field Systems of Scotland

By G. WHITTINGTON, ph.d.
Senior Lecturer in Geography, University of St Andrews

CHAPTER 13

Field Systems of Ireland

BY R. H. BUCHANAN, PH.D.

Senior Lecturer in Geography, The Queen's
University, Belfast

CHAPTER 14

Conclusion: Problems and Perspectives

BY A. R. H. BAKER AND R. A. BUTLIN

Preface

H. L. Gray's *English Field Systems*, first published in 1915 in Cambridge, Massachussetts, by Harvard University Press, remains after more than half a century of further investigations a classic but still very relevant work on the agrarian history of the British Isles. When reprinted in 1959 the book was referred to by H. P. R. Finberg as 'a standard work, containing much material of permanent value' and M. W. Beresford claimed that it would be a long time before students could afford to ignore the massive collection of evidence in Gray's book and that to bring its conclusions up to date would require not an essay but a multi-volume agrarian history.[1] Such a vast work is now fortunately in preparation under the general editorship of Professor Finberg and one volume, dealing with the period 1500–1640, has already been published.[2] The aims of this authoritative series are broad and its organisation primarily chronological. The purposes of this present book, by contrast, are more restricted and its organisation primarily geographical. It endeavours to examine, for a number of areas within the British Isles, 'the manner in which the inhabitants of a township subdivided and tilled their arable, meadow, and pasture land'.[3]

An enormous amount of research into British field systems has been undertaken by historical geographers, economic historians and others since Gray's book was published more than fifty years ago. Detailed local studies have been legion, generalised explanations of the origins and development of field systems few but influential in promoting further studies. The generalisations of Gray, like those of C. S. and C. S. Orwin put forward in 1938, have recently been challenged by Dr Joan Thirsk who has propounded an alternative model of the common fields.[4] The debate seems likely to continue for decades. The time is not yet ripe – perhaps it will never be ripe – for an ultimate

[1] H. P. R. Finberg, review note, *Agric. Hist. Rev.*, VIII, 1959, p. 51; M. W. Beresford, review note, *Econ. Hist. Rev.*, XIII, 1960, p. 282.

[2] J. Thirsk (ed.), *The Agrarian History of England and Wales*, IV, 1967.

[3] This definition of 'field system' is, of course, the one put forward in Gray, *English Field Systems*, p. 3.

[4] C. S. and C. S. Orwin, *The Open Fields*, 1938; J. Thirsk, 'The Common Fields', *Past and Present*, XXIX, 1964, pp. 3–25.

synthesis. But the editors share Marc Bloch's conviction: 'Dans le développement d'une discipline, il est des moments où une synthèse, fût-elle en apparence prématurée, rend plus de services que beaucoup de travaux d'analyse, où, en d'autres termes, il importe surtout de bien énoncerl es questions, plutôt, pour l'instant, que de chercher à les résoudre.'[1]

An introduction by the editors outlines the sources and methods of studies of field systems. There then follow twelve chapters concerned with the field systems of specific areas of the British Isles. The chapters deal with very differently sized areas, a reflection both of the differing complexities of the problems and of the differing position of field system studies from area to area. The book does not claim to be comprehensive in its spatial coverage of the British Isles – the whole of England is not covered by regional chapters. Nonetheless, the final chapter considers the problems and perspectives of field system studies in the context of the British Isles as a whole. This chapter is an attempt at generalisation in historical geography, generalisation in relation to both existing explanatory models of British field systems and putative problems which only further research can resolve.

We would like to express our gratitude to our contributors for their willing cooperation and patience, without either of which this book could not have been produced. Our thanks are also due to the carto-graphic draughtsmen of the Departments of Geography at the Universities of Cambridge, Durham and Leeds for drawing the maps and to the secretarial staffs of the Departments of Geography at the University of Cambridge, University College Dublin, the University of Nebraska and Queen Mary College, London, who have been so helpful in producing the edited typescript for the press. We are grateful to Mr B. M. S. Campbell for preparing the index. Our debt to the officials of the Cambridge University Press is also considerable.

July 1972   ALAN R. H. BAKER   R. A. BUTLIN
                   Emmanuel College   Queen Mary College
                   Cambridge   London

[1] M. Bloch, Les Caractères Originaux de l'Histoire rural Française, Oslo, 1931; quotation from reprinted edition, Paris, 1952, p. vii.

Figures

Tables

Acknowledgements

Chapter 2. The author is indebted to Lord Lonsdale and Sir W. Pennington Ramsden for permission to reproduce extracts from estate papers. Professor R. Lawton, University of Liverpool, made valuable comments on the text and his help was much appreciated by the author.

Chapter 3. The author wishes to acknowledge permission granted by His Grace the Duke of Northumberland to consult archives housed in Alnwick Castle. Dr B. K. Roberts furnished a copy of the map of Crawcrook, which was used as a base for Fig. 3.3. Mrs V. C. Chapman gave permission for a map originally compiled by her to be redrawn as Fig. 3.2 and Professor J. W. House gave permission for his map of physiographic regions of Northumberland to be used as a base for Fig. 3.1.

Chapter 4. The author is grateful to Dr A. Harris and Dr M. C. Storrie for kindly reading and commenting on the chapter, and to J. Harvey for making available material collected for his Ph.D. thesis.

Chapter 5. The author wishes to thank Mr D. J. Pannett for providing him with the majority of the material presented in this chapter concerning the later history of Warwickshire's field systems, as well as for many practical suggestions during the preparation of the chapter. The author is also indebted to Dr J. B. Harley and to Dr J. A. Yelling for permission to draw upon the conclusions of their unpublished theses and for comments and suggestions during the preparation of this essay.

Chapter 9. The author wishes to thank the following for permission to publish maps based on copyright material: Professor H. C. Darby for Fig. 9.1, Dr R. E. Glasscock for Fig. 9.2 and Dr P. F. Brandon for Fig. 9.7.

Chapter 10. The author is indebted to the Director of the Soil Survey of England and Wales for sanction to incorporate published and unpublished findings of the Soil Survey in this chapter and in Figs. 10.2, 10.4, 10.5 and 10.6. He is also particularly indebted to Sir George Meyrick, Bart., for permission to consult records in his private possession, and to the Rev. L. Parry Jones of Llanynys and Mrs I. Roger-Jones, formerly of Plas Llanynys, for facilitating access to records in their custody.

Chapter 13. The author is indebted to the following for permission to publish maps based on copyright material: P. Flatrès for Fig. 13.2, E. E. Evans for Fig. 13.3a, D. McCourt for Fig. 13.3b, the Ordnance Survey of Ireland for Figs. 13.4a, and 13.4c, the Ordnance Survey of Northern Ireland for Figs. 13.4b, and 13.4d, J. Otway-Ruthven and the Royal Society of Antiquaries of Ireland for Fig. 13.5a, and the Royal Irish Academy for Fig. 13.5c.

The authors and editors wish collectively to record their thanks to the many archivists in national, county and local record offices who gave invaluable assistance and advice.

Select List of Abbreviations

Advmt. Sci.   Advancement of Science
Agric. Hist.   Agricultural History
Agric. Hist. Rev.   Agricultural History Review
Amat. Histn.   Amateur Historian
Ann. Ass. Am. Geogr.   Annals of the Association of American Geographers
Arch. Camb.   Archaeologia Cambrensis
Br. Arch. Ass. Jnl.   British Archaeological Association Journal
B.M.   British Museum
Bull. Bd. Celtic Stud.   Bulletin of the Board of Celtic Studies
Bull. Inst. Hist. Res.   Bulletin of the Institute of Historical Research
CW1, CW2   Transactions of the Cumberland and Westmorland Antiquarian and
     Archaeological Society (Series)
Econ. Geogr.   Economic Geography
Econ. Hist. Rev.   Economic History Review
Econ. Jnl.   Economic Journal
Engl. Hist. Rev.   English Historical Review
Erdk.   Erkunde
Geogr. Annlr.   Geografiska Annaler
Geogrl. Jnl.   Geographical Journal
Geogrl. Mag.   Geographical Magazine
Geogrl. Rev.   Geographical Review
Geogrl. Stud.   Geographical Studies
Geogrl. Teach.   Geographical Teacher
Geogr. Z.   Geographische Zeitschrift
H.M.C.   Historical Manuscripts Commission
Ir. Geogr.   Irish Geography
Jnl. Brit. Stud.   Journal of British Studies
Jnl. R. Agric. Soc.   Journal of the Royal Agricultural Society
Jnl. R. Soc. Antiqu. Ir.   Journal of the Royal Society of Antiquaries of Ireland
Jnl. Soc. Archivists   Journal of the Society of Archivists
L.A.A.S.   Lincolnshire Architectural and Archaeological Society Reports and Papers
Nat. Lib. Wales Jnl.   National Library of Wales Journal
Proc. R. Ir. Acad.   Proceedings of the Royal Irish Academy
Proc. Soc. Antiqu. Scotland   Proceedings of the Society of Antiquaries of Scotland
Prof. Geogr.   Professional Geographer
P.R.O.   Public Record Office

Q. Jnl. Econ. *Quarterly Journal of Economics*
R.O. Record Office
Scott. Geogr. Mag. *Scottish Geographical Magazine*
Scott. Hist. Rev. *Scottish Historical Review*
Scott. Stud. *Scottish Studies*
Trans. Am. Phil. Soc. *Transactions, American Philosophical Society*
Trans. Inst. Br. Geogr. *Transactions, Institute of British Geographers*
Trans. R. Hist. Soc. *Transactions, Royal Historical Society*
V.C.H. *Victoria County History*

I

Introduction: Materials and Methods

BY ALAN R. H. BAKER AND R. A. BUTLIN

A. MATERIALS

I. MAPS

The available evidence on which reconstruction and analysis of field systems and associated settlement and field patterns may be based is abundant and varied in both character and date, but there can be little doubt that from the sixteenth century onwards maps constitute the most significant single body of evidence. Accurate topographic and cadastral maps are almost as essential a prerequisite for the detailed study of field systems of the past as they are for the study of contemporary geographical problems. The purpose, scale, detail, and accuracy of maps produced in the past vary widely, but in general they may be used both as charts which facilitate the study of the anatomy of field systems and as bases for the analysis of distributions which demonstrate regional variations in types of field systems. Modern topographic and cadastral maps, particularly at scales of six inches to one mile or larger, form useful starting points from which various features of the rural landscape may be traced back in time with the aid of historical maps, notably Ordnance Survey and earlier printed maps, the maps accompanying enclosure and tithe awards, and estate maps and plans. The use of such maps has been amply demonstrated in the work of historical geographers and economic and social historians. It is necessary, of course, to subject such map sources to a highly critical scrutiny before attempting to draw valid conclusions from the evidence they present. As a genus of historical evidence, the map *per se*, particularly in the pre-Ordnance Survey era, is often beset by as many limitations to use as any other document. Such limitations derive from the nature of a map itself and from scales, techniques of survey and reproduction, and the many idiosyncrasies, deficiencies and even dishonesties of land surveyors and map makers. A map is a two-dimensional spatial complexity, and it is necessary therefore to 'assess the proportion of total geographical reality which the cartographer has captured'.[1] On the one extreme, a map may be

---

[1] J. B. Harley, 'The Evaluation of Early Maps: Towards a Methodology', *Imago Mundi*, XXII, 1968, p. 75.

at best a caricature of landscape, a notional representation of what might be rather than what is, or on the other, a highly detailed and accurate representation, carrying in many cases the full weight of legal authority. The proportion of geographical reality portrayed by a map, which can vary in form from a crude sketch of a few parcels of land to a detailed cadastral and land use survey, can be assessed realistically in a number of ways, including studies of its immediate historical context, associated documents such as terriers, field books and enclosure and tithe awards, the purpose for which the map was produced, including commercial aspects and the techniques of production from the methods of survey to the production of the final manuscript or print. Special techniques of evaluation, including physical, mathematical and topographical tests may also be used. Given such critical appraisal, maps can then be used to give an added dimension, a spatial reality, not only to the landscapes they portray, but also to those which preceded them. All maps, regardless of scale, constitute points from which retrospective and retrogressive studies of the area portrayed may be made; hence the value of even the crudest of late medieval maps, which provides a feeble glimpse into a largely non-cartographic age. The earliest maps appear at a time when the rural landscape was already well on the way to assuming its modern aspect, and thus usually take up the story, with added perspectives from other documentary sources.

The single map gives a static picture of a landscape, but a series of maps of the same area at different points of time can add a dynamic aspect to such study; fortunate indeed is the scholar who can avail of complete sets of estate, enclosure, tithe and Ordnance Survey maps for his area, for his study will be immeasurably richer. The maximum value of historical maps derives, in the last analysis, from their study in relation to other types of evidence (such as other documents, field evidence and air photographs), and also thematic maps such as those of soil and land use. All forms of relevant evidence can, in fact, be synthesised and presented in readily digestible fashion on a carefully compiled summary map, which frequently suggests valid associations of various phenomena in terms of their location and distribution. The map, in fact, affords a vital perspective for the study of field systems.

(a) Ordnance Survey maps and their immediate predecessors

During the eighteenth century, initiative in the production of medium and large-scale topographic maps was taken by private surveyors in England, Wales, Scotland, and Ireland, in the absence of any general scheme or plan for the organisation and financing of mapping on a national basis. The rapid changes in industrial and rural economy

and the concomitant changes in society created a demand for a cartographic documentation of change, often with legal implications, which
was met by men who had been estate surveyors, and who were able
to provide accurate maps based on simple triangulation survey. The
'county' maps which they produced cover virtually every county in
the British Isles, but vary widely in scale, accuracy and content. Although
the first of these maps, that of Cornwall, appeared in 1700, they
become much more frequent and more detailed from the mid-
eighteenth century onwards. The scales of these maps varies from
approximately one-quarter to two inches to one mile, which means
that they do not provide detailed information of the type furnished
by the later large-scale Ordnance Survey maps, but they have been
widely used as a basis for studying general patterns of land use and
enclosure over large areas. Some of the best-known of such maps are
those produced by such practitioners as the Greenwoods, the Armstrongs,
Rocque, Andrews and Cary. The greatest deficiency of many of
these maps, in the context of studies of field systems, relates to the
dubious accuracy of the field patterns and field boundaries portrayed on
some of them, when comparison is made with later and more accurate
maps. In general, the field patterns which they record are much less
complex and more standardised than those on the large-scale Ordnance
maps, suggesting generalisation and, in some cases, known inaccuracy.
In the absence, for some areas, of alternative sources of evidence, they
do however provide a useful general picture of the rural landscape.

In addition to the county topographical maps, this period witnessed
the production of other large-scale maps, including General Roy's
military maps of Scotland, at a scale of 1:36,000, and the Grand Jury
maps of each county in Ireland, produced at scales of between one
and two inches to the mile, the latter inferior in many respects to
their privately made contemporary county maps, being rarely based
on accurate theodolite triangulation.

The foundation of the Ordnance Survey in 1791 on the initiative
of the Duke of Richmond, Master-General of the Ordnance, does
mark a complete break with the cartographic methods of the eighteenth
century, for the earliest one-inch O.S. map of Kent, published in
1801, was the work of a surveyor employed for the purpose, and the
choice of the one-inch scale was undoubtedly influenced by the
popularity of this scale on the county maps. The surveys for the
one-inch series began in 1792 and 'by 1840 maps had been produced
to cover the whole of England and Wales south of a line through
Preston and Hull'.[1] It has been suggested that great care should be

[1] J. B. Harley, 'A Guide to Ordnance Survey Maps as Historical Sources. I: The One-
Inch to the Mile Maps of England and Wales', *Amat. Histn.*, v, no. 5, 1962, p. 131.

exercised in the use of these maps, for 'in terms of accuracy it is probable that this group of maps is the least reliable of those published by the Ordnance Survey, notwithstanding the great improvement they represent over the privately produced maps contemporaneous with them',[1] and the printed date on them may well be inaccurate by up to forty years.

In 1824, the need for a detailed survey of Ireland was outlined by the Spring Rice Committee, investigating local taxation, who concluded that a map was needed which would show the outline of every Irish townland – the basis of taxation – and the decision was taken to bring the Ordnance Survey to Ireland to survey the country on the scale of six inches to one mile. This survey was extended to northern England and Scotland in 1840, and subsequent one-inch maps were reductions from this scale. The subsequent history of Ordnance mapping in these islands has been well documented, and need not be recapitulated here. The general significance of this period, however, cannot be overstressed, for in the period from 1801 to the present there is available, in various editions of the one-inch, two-and-a-half-inch, six-inch, and twenty-five-inch maps of these islands an unique body of cartographic evidence which records, with a generally high degree of accuracy, landscape changes of the nineteenth century.

There can be little doubt however of the overriding importance of the six-inch and twenty-five-inch maps in studies of field systems, both in relation to studies of present field patterns, settlement patterns, field names and areas, and to studies of these features in the nineteenth century, at a time when many areas, particularly of Ireland, were still characterised by ancient conventional farming practices. The Irish survey was carried out in the period 1825–41, and over 900 sheets were published by 1841. The earliest six-inch maps, produced from surveys carried out between 1840 and 1854 in England and Scotland, covered Lancashire, Yorkshire and some Scottish counties. After considerable controversy and temporary abandonment of the six-inch scale in Scotland, the twenty-five-inch scale was accepted as the best scale for large-scale maps, and from 1853 onwards the twenty-five-inch series was extended to cover the whole of the country, except for moorland and uncultivated areas (where the six-inch survey scale remained). Six-inch maps were therefore produced by reduction from the twenty-five-inch scale.

A brief description of the content of these maps reveals their value in an investigation of evolving field systems and field patterns. On the twenty-five-inch maps, roads, fields and field boundaries, rivers and streams and buildings and settlements are portrayed,

[1] *Ibid.*, p. 133.

'non-agricultural land is distinguished by ten different symbols for categories of woodland, marsh and rough pasture; quarries, sand, gravel and clay pits are depicted separately; all administrative boundaries, civil and ecclesiastical, are shown...hundreds of minor place-names, including field names until 1888, appear on a map for the first time...on occasions the remaining strips and other vestiges of open fields and open meadows may be recorded.'[1]

The six-inch maps omit some of the detail of the twenty-five-inch, including numbers and size of enclosures, but they do have contours which were not used on the twenty-five-inch maps. One of the difficulties attached to the early six-inch maps, however, relates to the definition and delimitation of fields and their boundaries. This is particularly true of Ireland, where ignorance of the prevalent agrarian system and confusion in objective led to the omission of field boundaries in some northern counties, where the survey had started, and the inclusion of only 'leading fences' (a phrase variously interpreted by surveyors) in the Midlands, though all fields were recorded in the south. Thus, for some areas an open field appears as a single property unit with the tenurial strips omitted, and the presence of a clustered settlement the only indication of a possible open field or 'rundale' system.

Additional material for the agrarian historian is provided by the area books and books of reference which accompanied the twenty-five-inch series from 1855 to 1886, wherein the reference serial number of each enclosure on the map is printed and details of land use, such as arable or pasture, given though inaccuracies have been established in some cases. Roughly similar information is provided by the drawings prepared for the first edition of the one-inch maps. These are at scales of two, three, and six inches to one mile and were produced from the late eighteenth to the mid-nineteenth century. Land use and field boundary details are shown by the six-inch and three-inch scale drawings, and to a lesser extent by those of two-inch scale. These are deposited in the British Museum and constitute a valuable supplementary source of information.[2]

(b) Tithe maps and documents

The Tithe Commutation Acts of 1836–60 provided for the substitution of a money rent, based on average corn prices for seven years, to be

[1] J. B. Harley, 'A Guide to Ordnance Survey Maps as Historical Sources. III: The Maps of England and Wales at the Six Inch and Twenty-Five Inch Scales', *Amat. Histn.*, v, no. 7, 1963, p. 210.

[2] J. T. Coppock, 'Maps as Sources for the Study of Land Use in the Past', *Imago Mundi*, XXII, 1968, pp. 37–49.

paid by landowners for the commutation of tithes paid to the Church. In some areas this process had already been effected in the course of Parliamentary enclosure, but in others the anachronistic payment remained. The implementation of commutation was the duty of Tithe Commissioners, under whose authority maps and awards or apportionments were prepared, mostly in the period 1836 to 1841. Some 11,800 parishes in England and Wales were surveyed – roughly three-quarters of the total land area – and an equivalent number of maps prepared. One copy of each of the apportionments and plans was deposited with the Tithe Commissioners, one in the Diocesan Registry, and one with the incumbent. The extent of land covered by these maps and documents varies from place to place, according to the degree of tithe commutation already achieved and of exemptions from tithe payment. Extensive coverage is afforded for counties little affected by Parliamentary enclosure, whereas only small areas of the east Midlands were surveyed. For each parish affected by the Commutation Act, a large-scale map and an appended apportionment were made. The maps, which were made by the Ordnance Survey and by local surveyors, are mostly at scales of twelve or twenty-five inches to one mile, and show in detail the fields of each parish, each field being numbered for reference to the accompanying schedule or apportionment roll. In some cases land use is distinguished by a colour wash on the map, this method being used also to distinguish land not subject to tithes, though in many instances land use is only recorded in the apportionment roll, thus necessitating the plotting of land use categories for each parcel on the map from the roll. The index of the apportionment roll attached to the map is divided into a series of columns giving, for each numbered parcel of land, details of ownership, occupier, name and description of the field of parcel, including land use, its state of cultivation, acreage, and the tithe rent charge apportioned to it. Shortened schedules appear at the end of the roll detailing land owned or occupied by each proprietor or tenant, and there is also a preliminary schedule giving summary details for the whole parish.[1]

The information provided by the maps and apportionments sometimes includes the names of common fields. The field names given in these surveys are invaluable sources of reference for reconstruction of field systems of earlier periods, and the land use data facilitate analysis of the relationship between field patterns and types of culti-

[1] See: H. C. Prince, 'The Tithe Surveys of the Mid-Nineteenth Century', *Agric. Hist. Rev.*, VII, 1959, pp. 14–26; H. G. Richardson, 'The Records of the Tithe Redemption Commission', *Jnl. Soc. Archivists*, I, 1959–60, pp. 132–9; L. M. Munby, 'Tithe Apportionments and Maps', *History*, LIV, 1969, pp. 68–71.

vation. The maps generally attain a high degree of accuracy (attested by the fact that those maps sealed by the commissioners are legally accepted as proof of tithe), though in some cases the map information and apportionment roll data differ for a particular parcel, a fact partially explicable by difference in dates of collection of information. A comparison of tithe maps with the earlier Ordnance Survey maps for an area is an instructive exercise. It is also interesting to note similarities of the tithe maps and the French *anciens cadastres*[1] of c. 1830–50: Marc Bloch made considerable use of the latter as a basis for his studies of medieval field systems. A valuable supplementary source of material is that contained within the tithe files, one of which should exist for every parish surveyed by the commissioners. These contain the reports of the Assistant Commissioner who carried out the commutation, and the draft Award. 'They also throw light on the nature of tithes and exemptions from payment, enclosures, boundary disputes, the condition of the clergy and the attitude of their parishioners.'[2] Of particular importance are the details of agriculture, ownership, tenancy, and rent given in the replies to printed question-naires circulated in each tithe district.

A similar type of information is available for Ireland in the Tithe Composition Applotment Books, compiled between 1823 and 1838 as a result of the Irish Tithe Composition Acts. The 1823 Act provided for a voluntary commutation of tithes, which was availed of by 1,353 out of 2,450 parishes, and two commissioners for each parish, representing the diocesan authorities and parishioners respectively, arranged the commutation by valuation or agreement, in the former case being empowered to make a survey. 'By the act of 1832 the privilege of making a composition by agreement was removed, and a single commissioner for each parish was appointed by the Lord Lieutenant. Under this act, the survey was completed for the whole country.'[3]

In general terms, the Irish tithe material compares unfavourably with its English counterpart. Fewer details of land use are given in the Irish surveys, because of the lack of comprehensive instructions given to land surveyors. There are few accompanying maps and descriptions of land use in the applotment books are often vague. It has been suggested that the value of this source 'lies in sample studies which

[1] H. D. Clout and K. Sutton, 'The "Cadastre" as a Source for French Rural Studies', *Agric. Hist.*, XLIII, 1969, pp. 215–23.

[2] E. A. Cox and B. R. Dittmer, 'The Tithe Files of the Mid-Nineteenth Century', *Agric. Hist. Rev.*, XIII, 1965, pp. 1–16.

[3] J. H. Johnson, 'The Irish Tithe Composition Applotment Books as a Geographical Source', *Ir. Geogr.*, III, 1958, pp. 254–62.

can be drawn from the more fully covered parishes, rather than in any general picture which might be reconstructed from them'.[1]

(c) Enclosure maps and awards

The enclosure of open and common land, by a variety of processes and for a variety of motives, is a feature of agrarian change in these islands which can be traced back at least to the early Middle Ages. The record of enclosure varies from a complete absence of documentation in some instances to the highly detailed enclosure acts, awards and plans, characteristic of the great wave of Parliamentary enclosure in the eighteenth and nineteenth centuries. These maps and awards produced by the commissioners responsible for the implementation of the act of Parliament which decreed enclosure, particularly where they relate to large remaining areas of open field and common land, constitute an extremely valuable record of former field systems on the eve of their transformation by reallocation and enclosure into farms and fields of modern aspect. It has been estimated that in the period from 1700 to 1900 six and a half to seven million acres of land were enclosed, comprising about 3,200 acts relating to 2,300,000 acres of waste. Tate states that in England during the eighteenth and nineteenth centuries some 5,400 individual enclosures were effected by nearly 4,200 acts and more than seven million acres were enclosed under the various general enclosure acts.[2] The commissioners responsible for the implementation of the act frequently – though not always – appointed a surveyor to survey the land to be enclosed and produce a terrier and map.[3] On the basis of the survey the allocation of land would be made and stated on the award. The most useful awards are those which are accompanied by two maps, the one showing the proposed allotment and layout of property after enclosure, the other showing the layout of the common fields before enclosure, including the distribution of holdings and strips of land in the common open fields. These maps were drawn by the appointed surveyor, usually a local surveyor, who was instructed to make a true and exact plan and admeasurement of the land. The large-scale plan has a scheme of reference numbers for each allocated parcel, which correspond to the allocation schedule in the award, the legal document which contains details of the reallocation to all those entitled to land. The plans themselves are generally very accurate, and like some of the awards are legally binding proofs of titles. In addition to details of landholding

[1] *Ibid.*, p. 259.
[2] W. E. Tate, *The English Village Community and the Enclosure Movements*, 1967, p. 88.
[3] J. B. Harley, 'Maps for the Local Historian: a Guide to British Sources. III: Enclosure and Tithe Maps', *Amat. Histn.*, VII, no. 8, 1967, pp. 265–74.

and the layout of fields, the awards and plans give details of field names, aspects of land use and roads and footpaths. The extent to which a particular parish or township was affected by enclosure of this kind varied greatly according to location and previous enclosure history. There are some counties, like Kent, Cornwall and Lancashire for which there are few awards dealing with common fields, whereas the awards for some of the Midland counties contain much detail of the enclosure of these fields. A careful study of the plans and awards, where available, for a particular region thus becomes an essential prerequisite for an analysis of the development of field systems in that region. Of equal significance, in this context, are areas which were *not* subject to enclosure, many by virture of having been enclosed at an earlier date. The plans and awards constitute an important point from which a retrogressive study can be made of agrarian arrangements in earlier times.

Further details of field systems and field patterns are provided by the records relating to enclosures in the pre-Parliamentary enclosure era. Some of these sources will be dealt with later, but it is worth noting here that some awards relating to enclosures 'by agreement' and private enclosures in the sixteenth, seventeenth and early eighteenth centuries, have plans and maps, sometimes in the form of rough sketches, appended to the awards and agreements, providing an inferior but nevertheless useful equivalent to the Parliamentary award plans. Such documents are to be found in estate paper collections, Chancery, Exchequer, and Star Chamber records.[1]

Scotland, Ireland and Wales were not generally subject to enclosure by act of Parliament, for in these countries there were no equivalent common rights to be extinguished by law, and landowners could enclose land without resort to Parliamentary authority. In these countries the cartographic record of enclosure, where it exists, occurs in the form of estate maps and plans, which, as demonstrated below, occasionally furnish evidence of old field systems equivalent to that of the English awards and plans.

(d) Estate maps and surveys

The term 'estate maps' is used here, with the connotation of a map, or plan, or perspective sketch of an 'estate', and can thus vary in quality and content from an exact survey of a large estate in the eighteenth century to a crude sketch of the small holding of a Tudor

---

[1] M. W. Beresford, 'Habitation versus Improvement. The Debate on Enclosure by Agreement', in F. J. Fisher (ed.), *Essays in the Economic and Social History of Tudor and Stuart England*, 1957, pp. 40–69.

yeoman.[1] An estate map is a cartographic record of the extent of all
or part of an estate, and thus is capable of providing invaluable
evidence for a study of the development of field systems. The estate
map as a form of estate record stems initially from large-scale changes
in landholding and changes in surveying techniques in the sixteenth
and seventeenth centuries.[2] The most important developments in
surveying technique, beginning in the late fifteenth century, were
'the advances in, and wider dissemination of, arithmetic and geometry;
the invention of simple instruments for surveying; and the addition
of a "plot" or plan to the written record of a survey'.[3] The social
and economic changes which stimulated the development of this new
form of land inventory included large-scale transference of land to
new ownership, notably after the dissolution of the monasteries and
in the mid- and late seventeenth centuries, the widespread leasing of
land, a desire for improvement of agriculture by engrossing and
enclosing open field strips and the inevitably consequent disputes over
ownership and boundaries. The older medieval surveys were written
surveys, primarily concerned with the valuation of land, but the new
estate maps comprised a much more exact definition and delimitation
of land and formed a valuable supplement to the written extents, surveys, rentals and similar documents. Many of the estate maps were
produced in the period c. 1550–1850, increasing in number and quality
after 1700, the period from 1700 to 1850 being 'the golden age of the
local land surveyor'.[4]

Estate maps of the sixteenth and seventeenth centuries vary in
scale, quality and content, but generally derive from the desire of
great landowners to have an accurate record of the extent, quality and
modes of tenure of their land, which thus 'enabled the landowner
to consider his lands as a whole, and to weigh the advantages of
some fresh disposition of the fields, or of some intended sale or
purchase'.[5] Extensive patronage by such landowners with very large
estates, of surveyors such as Norton, Norden, Saxton, Symonson and
Senior resulted in the production of many estate maps and plans.
Their scale is usually between ten and forty inches to the mile. Land
use and ownership are frequently shown by colour, and five or six

[1] See: J. B. Harley, 'Maps of the Local Historian: A Guide to British Sources.
II: Estate Maps', *Amat. Histn.*, VII, no. 7, 1967, pp. 223–31. Also: A. R. H. Baker,
'Local History in Early Estate Maps', *Amat. Histn.*, V, no. 3, 1962, pp. 66–71 and
F. G. Emmison, 'Estate Maps and Surveys', *History*, XLVIII, 1963, pp. 34–7.
[2] See: H. C. Darby, 'The Agrarian Contribution to Surveying in England', *Geogrl.
Jnl.*, LXXXII, 1933, pp. 529–35.
[3] E. G. R. Taylor, 'The Surveyor', *Econ. Hist. Rev.*, XVII, 1947, p. 124.
[4] Harley, *Amat. Histn.*, VII, no. 7, 1967, p. 227.
[5] Taylor, *Econ. Hist. Rev.*, XVII, 1947, p. 131.

categories of land use are normally shown, including, arable, pasture, meadow, woodland and waste, together with various types of parkland and other features. Land quality is sometimes indicated by special markings, as on the Norton maps of the Percy estates, which indicate quality by use of portions of a Maltese cross, the portions (of a maximum number of four) decreasing with decreasing quality. The detailed picture afforded by the best of these maps includes an accurate portrayal of open fields with furlongs and strips, the closes, tofts and crofts, the houses and other buildings in the village, natural and ornamental woodland, gardens, mills, fishponds, types of field boundary, field shapes and names, roads and footpaths and even the presence of such minerals as coal and limestone. The area covered by these maps depends of course on the immediate objective of the survey – whether, for example, it is a survey of one holding or part of a township, or perhaps part of a large-scale survey of all the landowner's estate, in some cases ranging over several widely separated counties. In marked contrast to the detailed surveys described above, some of the maps produced even by notable surveyors are merely outline maps of estate, administrative, or tenurial boundaries, and as such show little or nothing of the complex mosaic of fields and holdings.

A valuable supplement to the early estate maps is the terrier, field book, or book of reference, which in many cases contains details of the size of each unit of land, ranging in size from the smallest toft or croft or strip in the open fields to large areas of moor, heath, woodland or parkland. In addition, information may be given of the name of each landowner or landholder, his tenurial status, rent, labour and other customary dues and common rights, the size of his holding and the location and nature of its component units, and possibly regulations relating to the cultivation of land and crop rotations. Appended notes and comments by the surveyor may shed light on such processes as assarting from the waste and enclosure. If a reference scheme is adopted in the map, or the descriptions in the field book are sufficiently clear to enable definite location of each unit of a holding on the map, valuable reconstructions can be made, for example, of the distribution of land among tenants in the common fields, and many aspects of the workings of the field system determined.

From 1700 onwards estate maps increased in number and in accuracy, as a result of the growing demand for accurate cartographic records of land which was being enclosed, leased and sold, on which new roads and settlements were being built, and under which there existed in some places deposits of coal, exploitation of which was gradually increasing. The quality of these maps is far superior to those produced earlier, for surveying techniques and instruments became more accurate and precise, the quality of map drawing improved, and the reproduction of maps was facilitated, in the early nineteenth century, by the use of lithographic reproduction. The work of cartographers in this period played a significant role in the foundation of the Ordnance Survey, with eighteenth-century surveyors providing initial surveys for the map of Kent. The Duke of Richmond, the founder of the Ordnance Survey, had in fact employed surveyors, Thomas Yeakell and William Gardner, to produce surveys of his estate around Goodwood in west Sussex. These terriers and maps, produced from c. 1765 onwards, were initially produced at scales of twenty inches to the mile (in manuscript terriers), reduced subsequently to six-inch and two-inch scales, and are recognised as epitomising the highest standards of eighteenth-century cartography.

The history of estate surveying in Ireland, Scotland and Wales is rather different from that of England, particularly in the pre-Hanovarian period. In Ireland in the latter part of the sixteenth century, surveys were undertaken of land confiscated and reallocated to English speculators and settlers under the plantation schemes for Leix and Offaly in 1556 and the Munster plantation of 1586. These comprised general surveys of confiscated territory by men such as Lythe and Jobson, and more rarely, larger-scale maps of estates such as those of Sir Walter Raleigh in Cork and Waterford. The turbulent political and social history of Ireland from about 1580 to 1690 discouraged the presence and interest of qualified English surveyors, with the result that there are few examples of estate surveys and maps in the seventeenth century, and these are generally of poor standard, often comprising a simple outline map of estate boundaries, executed by local surveyors. Information relating to agrarian practice in the seventeenth century in Ireland can be obtained from maps commissioned to show the apportionment of confiscated land and the location of fortifications and military strongpoints. These include Barthelet's maps for Mountjoy's campaigns in Ulster at the turn of the century, the maps by Bodley, Pynnar and Raven of the Ulster plantation starting in 1608 and the maps of Petty's Down Survey of 1654.[1]

Scotland, like Ireland, exhibits a similar dearth of detailed estate plans in the sixteenth and seventeenth centuries. The Scots rural economy, like the Irish, was based on a rudimentary infield–outfield system, and associated with extensive use of land of marginal quality, in an environment of slow economic development and change which afforded little stimulus to the activity of surveyors and map makers. Some plans associated with military activities were produced in the

[1] J. H. Andrews, *Ireland in Maps*, Dublin, 1961; and, 'Ireland in Maps: a Bibliographical Postscript', *Ir. Geogr.*, IV, 1962, pp. 234–43.

sixteenth century, and a few large-scale plans were produced in the seventeenth, but 'the few examples that are known, dating from the closing years of the century, are simply crude diagrams similar to those made in England nearly two hundred years earlier'.[1] The situation was somewhat similar in Wales where estate maps were rare prior to the mid-eighteenth century.

The occurrence of estate survey and map material in these three countries increased dramatically in the eighteenth century. In Ireland, the eighteenth century was marked by the social dominance of the landlords or estate owners, many of whom employed surveyors to produce maps of their property. In the earlier part of the century, estate maps continued in the tradition of the Petty and Cromwellian surveys, generally including only townland or tenurial boundaries and the acreage of a holding. Details of land use variation, fences, type of cultivation and topography were generally omitted, giving rise to maps of an attenuated style. Such a style could be understood as a response to seventeenth-century conditions, including 'the need to get through a great quantity of work in a short time, and the paucity of mappable detail in a war-torn (and in any case never well developed) countryside',[2] but not in relation to the improvement in agriculture attempted in the eighteenth century. This conservative tradition of Irish surveyors was broken by the use of foreign surveyors, notably John Rocque and Bernard Scalé. Rocque introduced many innovations into Irish estate cartography from 1754 to 1760, and produced 'some of the most remarkable manuscript estate surveys ever made in Ireland', notably those of the Earl of Kildare's estate in County Kildare. His maps distinguish various topographic features, types of land use, types and forms of field boundaries, some field names, buildings, townland and tenurial boundaries, and the size of holdings. Scalé, Rocque's pupil and brother-in-law, produced estate maps of high quality in Ireland from 1759 to 1782, including maps of the Devonshire estate in Cork and Waterford. The traditions of the 'French school' of surveyors were continued by pupils of Scalé, notably Sherrard and Brownrigg, who produced large numbers of estate maps until the end of the nineteenth century, when the private surveyors were ousted by the 1:2,500 survey of Ireland.[3]

The eighteenth century witnessed similar developments in Scotland,

---

[1] I. H. Adams, 'Scottish Large-Scale Plans: Their Value for Studying the Evolution of the Scottish Rural Landscape', paper presented to the History of Cartography conference, London, 1967, p. 24.

[2] J. H. Andrews, 'The French School of Dublin Land Surveyors', *Ir. Geogr.*, v, 1967, pp. 277–8.

[3] *Ibid.*, pp. 275–92.

during a period when agricultural improvement was effected and extensive mapped surveys made to facilitate such improvement. The anachronistic run-rig system, associated with intermixed parcels of land and joint tenancies was gradually replaced by tenure and cultivation in severalty, but before this was possible, plans had to be made which showed the location of the fragments of each holding and, subsequently, which showed the new layout of holdings, fields and settlements. The process of consolidation and enclosure of run-rig and common land produced, before 1745, a number of mapped surveys, including those of the Duke of Buccleuch's Liddesdale lands in 1718, though surveys at this time were usually of 'small well-situated estates whose lairds had achieved a certain prosperity either due to the inherent fertility of their lands or to a fortune made in the cities or industrial areas'.[1] After the 1745 rebellion, forfeited estates, annexed to the Crown, were subject to various improvements, implemented with the assistance of commissioned surveys which in turn attracted surveyors to the Highlands. From 1765 onwards, particularly from 1765 to 1775, large numbers of estate maps and plans were produced by competent and skilled surveyors, employed by landowners with the capital to effect improvements. Men like John Ainslie produced many estate maps and plans in the late eighteenth and early nineteenth centuries – an indication of the important role of the surveyor at this time of profound change. The plans produced vary in scale and detail, but the most detailed provide an extremely instructive picture of arable fields, rigs, meadows, moorland, pastures, settlements, roads, paths, mills and other features, and often form parts of sequences of maps which enable the rapid transformation of the rural landscape, with accompanying social ramifications such as clearance and eviction, to be traced in detail. Another significant development at mid-century was Roy's topographic survey of Scotland, commenced in 1747. Estate surveying continued in the nineteenth century, and further surveys for clearances were carried out in Sutherland between 1806 and 1820, producing plans, some of doubtful accuracy, of clearance and reception areas.[2] As in Ireland, the advent of the 1:2,500 plan survey marks the effective termination of the production of maps by private surveyors.

In Wales, estate maps increased significantly in number in the second half of the eighteenth century, 'and provide a good coverage of some areas. In the National Library of Wales, for example, the

[1] B. M. W. Third, 'The Significance of Scottish Estate Plans and Associated Documents', *Scott. Stud.*, I, 1957, p. 41.
[2] H. Fairhurst, 'The Surveys for the Sutherland Clearances of 1813–20', *Scott. Stud.*, VIII, 1964, pp. 1–18.

Bute and Dunraven collections contain nearly 300 post-1767 estate maps, mainly relating to Glamorganshire; and the Gogerddann collection contains 160 post-1737 maps of mid- and north Cardiganshire.'[1]

(e) Limitations

While there can be little doubt of the great value of estate maps, plans and associated documents to studies of field systems these documents have definite limitations of use. Some of the early estate maps of the sixteenth and seventeenth centuries were produced by surveyors who were using rather unsophisticated methods and instruments and who themselves may have had little training. In some instances, the plans are rough perspective sketches of a piece of land, with little indication of accuracy. Such early maps must always be carefully scrutinised to establish the authenticity and accuracy of their depiction of land, both in relation to scale and to inserted detail. Generally speaking, estate maps and plans increase in accuracy of scale, land area measurement and depiction of detail during the eighteenth century, and thus become relatively more useful than their earlier counterparts. Nevertheless, the efficiency, accuracy and honesty of individual surveyors varied widely at this time, and care must again be taken to check accuracy against contemporary and later plans and maps, air photographs and other documents, and in the field where possible. Particular care must be exercised with plans and surveys that relate to periods of confiscation and alienation of land, as in Ireland in the sixteenth and seventeenth centuries, and in Scotland in the eighteenth, for it is at such times that the unscrupulous surveyor became active, being able to derive considerable financial and territorial benefit from deliberate under- and over-estimation of land area.

Even in cases of maps produced by cartographers whose general competence is not easily disputed, it may be necessary to examine a map carefully in order to distinguish those features which have been added by eye. It has been generally established, for example, that the field boundaries shown on John Rocque's maps are highly unreliable, as some 'were merely sketched in and in some cases [were] purely fictitious'.[2] It has been suggested that 'it seems unlikely that the fields on his Irish county maps are intended to be taken literally',[3] for they do not compare favourably with later, accurate, estate maps. Similar judgements may doubtless be made of many of the other surveyors.

---

[1] Harley, Amat. Hist., VII, 1967, p. 228.
[2] G. R. Crone, E. M. J. Campbell and R. A. Skelton, 'Landmarks in British Cartography', Geogrl. Jnl., CXXVIII, 1962, p. 429.
[3] Andrews, Ir. Geogr., V, 1967, p. 280.

Perhaps the greatest limitation of estate maps in general is the frequent lack of detail, relating to such features as types of land use, cultivation, field boundaries and the distribution of holdings. For a variety of reasons, much detail may be withheld, and evidence, for example, of communal cultivation and use of land may at best be indirect, even where large collections of maps are involved. Thus 'Of one hundred and twenty-four estate maps of Kent for the period 1588–1699, only three show any "common marsh", four any "common mead", and four any "common field" which was probably arable. For the arable "common fields" the maps supply no evidence about common rotations or common grazing rights after the harvest.'[1] Such limitations may partly be circumvented by the use of supplementary documentary and field data. In the last analysis, however, there can be no effective substitute for a series of accurate estate maps and plans as *prima facie* evidence for agrarian practice and the nature of the rural landscape of a region. Cartographic evidence is thus particularly useful in relation to the morphology of field and settlement patterns – maps provide visual representation of spatial relationships and descriptions of the size, shape and spacing of settlements of fields and tenurial units. In themselves, however, they usually convey little information on either agrarian function or genesis. Their second useful role is therefore that of raising questions that need to be answered, and hypotheses that need to be tested, by study of the earlier and non-cartographic evidence. It is worth noting, in this context, that the most eminent of agrarian historians, such as Maitland, Seebohm and Bloch, almost invariably commenced their studies with reference to maps.

2. DOCUMENTARY AND PRINTED SOURCES AFTER 1500

(a) The sixteenth and seventeenth centuries

The sixteenth century may in a sense be seen as a watershed in the documentary history of agriculture and field systems, in that rapid changes in the nature of society and in land ownership gave rise to new types of survey and a new type of documentation of social and agrarian change. The transition from medieval to modern was gradual, and many of the medieval documents described below continue into the sixteenth and seventeenth centuries and beyond. Manorial extents and surveys, for example, have been used to determine regional variations in farming practice, including the form and function of field systems in the sixteenth and seventeenth centuries, with supple-

[1] Baker, *Amat. Histn.*, v, 1962, p. 68.

mentary information provided from court rolls. A number of new documents, however, which fill in much of the detail afforded by the manorial surveys, become available at this time, and it is to these that this section is primarily devoted.[1]

Probate inventories, listing the possessions of a person who had died and left a will, furnishing details of household possessions, implements, animals and crops, and amounts of grain, wool, hay and other items, are extant for the period 1530 to 1830, but reach maximum frequency in the sixteenth and seventeenth centuries.[2] They relate to peasant and yeoman holdings, and thus partially redress the imbalanced picture afforded by demesne surveys. These documents comprise assessed inventories of all the possessions of the deceased, and 'although more of the inventory is invariably given up to valuing the household goods than the farm stock (which nevertheless usually represent a much larger proportion of the total), considerable information is usually provided under the headings of: Crops (in barn or granary, and growing), cattle, sheep, horses, pigs, poultry, bees, gear, sundries'.[3] The type and quality of information given in an inventory 'depends on the type of farm, the conscientiousness of the appraisers, and to some extent on the month in which the inventory was made, those made between seed-time and harvest usually providing useful information on cropping which those made at another time of the year necessarily lack'.[4] The study and synthesis of the details of large numbers of these documents[5] can assist in the determination of regional variations in farming types, including significant crops, though attempts to deduce crop rotations in the open fields from inventory data are fraught with difficulty, usually because of the disproportionate amount of the peasant's land under winter and spring crops or the fact that part of his land was enclosed.

[1] A general survey of documentary evidence for this period is: J. Thirsk, 'The Content and Sources of English Agrarian History after 1500', *Agric. Hist. Rev.*, III, 1955, pp. 66–79.

[2] F. W. Steer, 'Probate Inventories', *History*, XLVII, 1962, pp. 287–90; O. Ashmore, 'Inventories as a Source of Local History: II. Farmers', *Amat. Histn.*, IV, 1960, pp. 186–95.

[3] H. Long, 'Regional Farming in Seventeenth Century Yorkshire', *Agric. Hist. Rev.*, VIII, 1960, p. 103.

[4] *Ibid.*, p. 103.

[5] See, for example: J. Yelling, 'The Combination and Rotation of Crops in East Worcestershire, 1540–1660', *Agric. Hist. Rev.*, XVII, 1969, pp. 24–43; Yelling, 'Probate Inventories and the Geography of Livestock Farming: a Study of East Worcestershire, 1540–1750', *Trans. Inst. Br. Geogr.*, LI, 1970, pp. 111–26; F. V. Emery, 'The Farming Regions of Wales', chapter II of J. Thirsk (ed.), *The Agrarian History of England and Wales*, 1967, pp. 113–60.

Less representative, but nevertheless potentially valuable sources of information, are the glebe terriers – surveys of the glebe land or church property, including buildings, land, tithes and other perquisites of the Church. The most detailed of these may afford evidence of types of open field and the progress of enclosure on a 'sample' basis.[1] Glebe terriers occur from the end of the sixteenth century to the eighteenth century.

This is also a period when there were numerous Crown surveys of escheated or confiscated land, and of private surveys of estates or manors. These have already been discussed in the section dealing with estate maps. Large numbers of these surveys have been used in the reconstruction of agrarian arrangements in the early modern period. The Crown surveys are housed in the P.R.O., and local surveys in both public and local muniment collections.

A vital feature of the changing agriculture and field systems of this period is the occurrence and effect of enclosure, which effectively modified or completely altered the old order. Records of enclosure vary according to the method of enclosure: in some cases there is a full record, notably where litigation or lengthy dispute were involved, in others there is no record at all, especially where enclosure was autocratically imposed. Methods of enclosure included piecemeal enclosure, enclosure by private acts of Parliament (the earliest being in the reign of James I), by agreement, with the agreement sometimes being enrolled in Chancery, though in other cases such agreements were made by authority of a commission from the court of Exchequer, and others made privately between landowners without recourse to the authority of the courts. 'Some were accomplished by a still simpler process; the lord consolidated all the common fields into his own hands and inclosed without an agreement of any kind.'[2] In the sixteenth and early seventeenth centuries, the records of the enclosure commissioners of 1517, 1548, 1565 and 1607 form valuable evidence of enclosure, particularly of the 'depopulating' variety, but in the seventeenth century the documents of enclosure 'by agreement' become more significant. In addition to documents dealing specifically with enclosure, incidental information is also afforded by surveys, terriers and various types of lawsuit.

While the detailed structure and development of field systems can only be reconstructed from documents such as those described above, which relate to specific manors and townships, valuable background

[1] M. W. Beresford, 'Glebe Terriers and Open-Field Buckinghamshire', *Records of Bucks.*, xv, 1951–2, pp. 283–98 and xvi, 1953–4, pp. 5–28.
[2] E. M. Leonard, 'The Enclosure of Common Fields in the Seventeenth Century', *Trans. R. Hist. Soc.*, xix, 1905, p. 110.

and supplementary material is afforded by other types of documentary
and printed material, including the topographic descriptions of anti-
quarians, and the surveys produced after the Restoration, symptomatic
of a revived spirit of scientific enquiry into a wide variety of natural
features, including agriculture and soils.

It has been suggested that the development of a strong tradition of
topographical writing was one of the significant features of English
literature from 1500 onwards and this is substantiated by consideration
of the work of such people as Leland, Camden, Fiennes, Defoe, and
the authors of the county histories and natural histories of the seventeenth century. John Leland, 'a pioneer of the method of direct
enquiry and observation' compiled extensive notes for a 'Description
of the Realm of England', in the first half of the sixteenth century,
which was never composed, but the notes of this extensive traveller,
which were collected and edited in the eighteenth century, under the
title of 'Itinerary', 'unco-ordinated and incomplete though they
remain, they afford us a picture of Early Tudor England which is as
revealing by what it omits as by what it emphasises'.[1] Although
Leland's descriptions of farming and agricultural landscapes are not
highly detailed, he distinguished between open and enclosed land, and
gives some idea of regional variations in cropping and husbandry
practices. William Camden, born in the mid-sixteenth century,
journeyed throughout England in the reign of Elizabeth, seeking
material for a reconstruction of Roman Britain, which was published
as 'Brittania' in 1586, from which 'it is possible to extract...an
outline geography of Elizabethan England, and to discern especially
the elements of permanency in the rural scene'.[2] He also distinguishes
in places between open field and enclosed land, and facilitates, often
by reference to soil types, the determination of regional variations in
agricultural practice, as, for example, in Sussex, where the 'three
belts, the chalk country...the mingled sands and clays of the Weald,
and the timbered forest ridges, are recognisable today'. Later itineraries
affording similar information are those of Celia Fiennes, described in
her diary, and of Daniel Defoe, though the authenticity of the sources
of his Tour have been seriously called in question.[3]

In addition to these itineraries, a number of works relating to
individual counties afford details of regional variations in agriculture

[1] E. G. R. Taylor, 'Leland's England', in H. C. Darby (ed.), *An Historical Geography of England before 1800*, 1951, p. 330.
[2] E. G. R. Taylor, 'Camden's England', in Darby (ed.), *Historical Geography of England*, p. 354.
[3] J. H. Andrews, 'Defoe and the Sources of his "Tour"', *Geogrl. Jnl.*, cxxvi, 1960, pp. 268–77.

and landscape. Most of these date from the middle or late seventeenth century, and reflect the new methods and aims of scientific enquiry prevalent at this time. Such works as Dugdale's *Warwickshire* (1656), Aubrey's *Natural History of Wiltshire* (1685), and Plot's *Natural Histories of Oxfordshire* (1677) and *Staffordshire* (1686), were based on field investigation, printed and circulated questionnaires or 'enquiries' (a method promoted by the Royal Society), and employ geological, physiographical, and soil characteristics in the definition of regions and regional variations in agricultural practice.[1] These works are more scientifically based than the general itineraries, and their regional definitions are clear and valid. Plot, for example, in his Staffordshire volume, distinguishes three main regions: the Moorlands and the Pennine fringe; the rich agricultural area to the west and south of the Trent; and the Woodlands or Middle Part of Staffordshire. His description of agriculture suggests that where enclosure had not taken place, the clay lands were managed under a three-course rotation, and possibly on the basis of three common arable fields. Elsewhere on poorer soils, common land may well have been farmed on a system approximating to an infield–outfield system, with periodic reclamation of waste land for supplementary arable. He gives the impression that agriculture in Staffordshire was in a period of transition, from the common management of open fields and commons, to improved farming practised in enclosed fields. Such county volumes continued into the eighteenth century, and were eventually superseded by the County Reports to the Board of Agriculture.

(b) The eighteenth and nineteenth centuries

The major sources for this period are the enclosure acts and awards, private and Parliamentary, the tithe awards and plans, rentals, land tax assessments, and crop returns. The first two items have already been discussed and little more need be said, other than that private enclosure acts and awards and enclosures by agreement continue to dominate as methods of enclosure until the later part of the eighteenth century, when they are ousted by Parliamentary acts of enclosure.

Enquiries initiated by the Home Office into the high grain prices of the late 1790s and early 1800s led to enquiries into acreages of sown crops, but only the returns of 1795 and 1801 provide a suitable basis for analysis and reconstruction of cropping practices and yields. The 1795 returns do not give complete coverage, even for individual counties, and are comparatively unused. The 1801 returns were made by the clergy of England and Wales to the Home Office, and theoreti-

[1] R. A. Butlin, 'Plot's Natural History of Staffordshire: a Reappraisal', *N. Staffs. Jnl. of Field Stud.*, II, 1962, pp. 88–95.

cally return the acreages in each parish under wheat, barley, oats, rye, turnips, rape, peas, beans and potatoes. In spite of apparent under-estimation of acreages, and lack of information on the forms of land use, they may be used to reconstruct variations in emphasis of the use of different crops.[1] Various attempts were made to collect similar returns from different areas during the nineteenth century, but these were supplanted by the beginning of systematic collection of data by the Board of Trade from 1866 onwards.

Patterns of landownership can be constructed from the Land Tax Returns, made from *c.* 1770 to 1832, 'which allow the proportion of farms which were owned by their occupiers and those which were rented to be calculated for each parish'. Maps using such data 'suggest that there were very marked regional differences in the relative importance of tenants and occupier owners and that their distribution often coincided with differences in land use and soil type'.[2]

Apart from these new sources in this period, additional information on agriculture and field systems is afforded by estate surveys and rentals and farm accounts, supplemented by crop books and corre-spondence between agents and owners.

Among the most valuable printed sources for this period are the tours of individuals, the county reports to the Board of Agriculture, the reports and prize essays in the *Journal* of the Royal Agricultural Society of England, and the Parliamentary Papers. The two most significant agricultural writers of the late eighteenth and early nine-teenth century undoubtedly were Arthur Young and William Marshall. Young made a number of tours[3] in the British Isles in the 1760s and 1770s, and recorded, in a way far superior to that of the older topo-graphies, the changes which were taking place in agriculture. There is little doubt that his writings must not be accepted uncritically, either in the *Tours* or the *General Views* which he wrote, which like contemporary writings tended to emphasise new methods and the

[1] See, for example, W. E. Minchinton, 'Agricultural Returns and the Government during the Napoleonic Wars', *Agric. Hist. Rev.*, I, 1953, pp. 29–43; D. T. Thomas, 'The Statistical and Cartographic Treatment of the Acreage Returns of 1801', *Geogrl. Stud.*, v, 1958, pp. 15–25; H. C. K. Henderson, 'Agriculture in England and Wales in 1801', *Geogrl. Jnl.*, cxviii, 1952, pp. 338–45.

[2] D. B. Grigg, 'The Changing Agricultural Geography of England: a Commentary on the Sources Available for the Reconstruction of the Agricultural Geography of England, 1770–1850', *Trans. Inst. Br. Geogr.*, xli, 1967, p. 89. See also: D. B. Grigg, 'The Land Tax Returns', *Agric. Hist. Rev.*, xi, 1963, pp. 82–94; G. E. Mingay, 'The Land Tax Assessments and the Small Landowner', *Econ. Hist. Rev.*, xvii, 1964, pp. 381–8.

[3] Arthur Young, *A Six Weeks' Tour Through the Southern Counties of England and Wales*, 1768; *A Six Months' Tour Through the North of England*, 1770; *A Farmer's Tour Through the East of England*, 1771.

improved farming areas rather than general levels and standards, but the fact remains that Young's observations are a mine of information on contemporary agricultural practice and the changing order. William Marshall (1745–1818) described the rural economy of England and its regional variations in his books on the rural economies of the West of England (1796), Yorkshire (1788), Gloucestershire (1789), the Midland Counties (1790) and the Southern Counties (1798). In the period 1808–17 he produced reviews and abstracts of the Board of Agriculture reports, and the reviews were published in 1818. The significance of Marshall's rural economies and reviews and abstracts as sources of agricultural history is enhanced by their arrangement on a regional basis.

The county reports of the Board of Agriculture comprise a series of surveys of the agriculture of the individual counties of England, Wales and Scotland, which appeared from 1793 (the date of establishment of the Board) to 1815.

'Two reports for each county were produced. The earliest reports were published in 1793–96, and the pages generally have wide margins and are often called the Quarto series; they were supposed to be circulated among local farmers and landlords to allow comments to be made upon them. The second edition was sometimes written by the original author, but more commonly another writer was found; this edition is often described as the Octavo. The original authors were not always pleased by this.'[1]

They were published under the title of *A General View of the Agriculture of ——*, and have a commendable disposition to the use of regions as a basis. They have notable limitations as a genus of documentation, including, in some instances: a natural tendency to emphasise the best farming standards; cursory field survey; the assessment of improvements by local rather than national standards; fabrication of information; and plagiarism. They do, however, describe the progress of enclosure, in rather general terms, and often indicate those areas which were still unenclosed and being farmed under archaic methods, including whole-year fallows and old rotations, and occasionally make retrospective reference to systems of cultivation recently replaced by newer methods. The maps which accompany many of these reports attempt to portray the regional diversities in topography, soils, and farming practice, and constitute, 'the first large-scale attempt to indicate the regions of England'.[2]

---

[1] Grigg, *Trans. Inst. Br. Geogr.*, XLI, 1967, p. 77.
[2] H. C. Darby, 'Some Early Ideas on the Agricultural Regions of England', *Agric. Hist. Rev.*, I, 1953, p. 37.

County reports were also printed by the Royal Agricultural Society in its *Journal* in the form of essays, for which prizes were offered. Forty-five county prize reports, one for each English county, were published between 1845 and 1870, and most of these contain maps of the regional divisions of the counties concerned. They vary, of course, in quality, but represent an improvement on the reports of the Board of Agriculture. In the second half of the nineteenth century when these reports were published open fields had largely been extinguished by the enclosure acts and awards, but a few relict survivals are mentioned. Additional information may be obtained from other journals, including *The Farmers' Magazine* and the *Annals of Agriculture*.

The general development of agricultural change in the nineteenth century is well documented in the Parliamentary Papers. The reports and evidence of select committees deal with such topics as agricultural distress, enclosures, agricultural customs, and the corn trade, and accounts and papers give statistical information for many topics, including income tax and corn sales.[1]

Ireland, Scotland and Wales are well covered by the agricultural writers of the eighteenth century. Arthur Young in his *Tour of Ireland in 1776, 1777 and 1778* describes the agricultural scene in both detailed and general terms, the former based on several journeys made across Ireland. In spite of the limitations in his work relating to his pre-occupation with improvement, a reasonably balanced picture of Irish agriculture is given, including the low state of the agricultural labourer. Ireland was not included in the Board of Agriculture county report scheme, but developed a similar scheme in the form of the Royal Dublin Society's *Statistical Surveys*, published on a county basis for twenty-three of Ireland's thirty-two counties between 1801 and 1832, and very similar in form and content to the Board of Agriculture Surveys. In some cases the surveys were never completed, and in at least two others the manuscripts were lost. Again, there is an uneven-ness of quality in these surveys, but they do provide much valuable information on regional variations of agriculture, industry and society, and contain invaluable accounts of the survival of the infield–outfield system in the north and west. For the nineteenth century, the sources of information are similar to those for England, and Parliamentary Papers in particular offered much valuable detail on the state of agriculture. The most significant documents are the 'Devon Digest' (Digest of evidence taken before H.M. Commissioners of inquiry into the state of law and practice in respect to the occupation of land in Ireland) (1847), the Report of the Select Committee of the House of Lords on colonisation from Ireland, together with minutes of evidence

[1] See: P. and G. Ford, *Select List of British Parliamentary Papers, 1833–1899*, 1953.

(1847), the Report of the markets and fairs commission (1853), and the Reports of the Poor Law Enquiry of 1835. The base-line reports of the Congested Districts Board (c. 1891) and in more recent times of the Land Commission contain detailed descriptions of the re-organisation of open field land.[1]

Information on Scottish agriculture may be derived from the Board of Agriculture county reports, the Old and New Statistical Accounts of Scotland, and various commission reports, including the Scottish Congested Districts Board (1887–1911), the Napier Commission (1884) and the Crofters Commission.

Wales at this time is described in a number of tours, including Arthur Young's *Six Weeks' Tour of the Southern Counties of England and Wales* (1768), by the county reports of the Board of Agriculture, and by a number of Parliamentary commissions and surveys.

3. DOCUMENTARY SOURCES BEFORE 1500

The difficulty of reconstructing field systems and general agrarian arrangements up to the end of the medieval period stems partly from the fact that this was a time when few maps were produced. The main problem for the historical geographer is thus to utilise an extensive and varied body of material – the by-product of lay and ecclesiastical administration and management at a variety of levels – as a basis for mapping, and thus give it a spatial, locational and distributional sig-nificance. This task involves, of necessity, the use of special mapping techniques, and a thorough knowledge of the nature and limitations of the sources of documentation. The grossest of errors may be perpetrated by uncritical and unselective use of statistical material of highly dubious authenticity, particularly when endowed with apparent respectability by being presented in map form. In spite of obvious limitations to use, much medieval material has been used to throw light on certain aspects of agrarian society and economy, and a brief outline of the more significant types of material follows below.[2]

(a) England

Early agrarian history depends to a large extent for its source material on archaeological evidence, of which the more important elements will be discussed later, but early evidence of the existence and manage-

---

[1] Most of these sources are used in: T. W. Freeman, *Pre-Famine Ireland*, 1957.
[2] A resumé of the evidence for this period is to be round in: R. H. Hilton, 'The Content and Sources of English Agrarian History before 1500', *Agric. Hist. Rev.*, III, 1955, pp. 3–19. See also: J. Z. Titow, *English Rural Society 1200–1350*, 1969, pp. 15–42.

ment of strips in the arable fields and meadows is afforded by the laws of King Ine of Wessex (688–726), and evidence for the later Anglo-Saxon period by landbooks, leases and charters which record land grants. The charters or landbooks are documents which record the conveyance of property and also of rights over that property from the King to another person, or body of persons, frequently to a religious order or house. They include details of topographic features, boundaries, field names and place-names. They also refer to the distribution of land holdings, including intermingled strips, and the development of large estates.[1]

The other major documentary source for this period is the Domesday Survey of 1086, the main purposes of which were to discover the distribution of feudal estates, the value of land for tax purposes, and the numbers of persons of various social classes. The nature of the survey itself and difficulties of its interpretation have been well covered by a number of authorities, and need not be recapitulated here.[2] It is sufficient to emphasise that this survey is an extremely important source of information for social and economic conditions in the years between 1066 and 1086. To the agrarian historian, the work of Professor H. C. Darby and his collaborators is particularly important, in that it has demonstrated some of the regional variations in economic and social conditions which prevailed at the time.[3] Little evidence of field systems is afforded by the survey, but general detail is afforded of the relative significance of various types of land and land use which may be linked with other forms of evidence to give a more accurate reconstruction of agrarian arrangements.

The period from 1086 to the late thirteenth century may profitably be studied with particular reference to land charters, describing transfer of land or privilege, many of which survive in the form of the collections of chapters or cartularies of religious orders. These charters frequently contain sections which describe the land transferred in minute detail, including the location of strips of land in the village fields, and the rights of common associated with a holding.

[1] See: H. P. R. Finberg, *Early Charters of the West Midlands*, 1961; Finberg, *Early Charters of Wessex*, 1964; C. R. Hart, *Early Charters of Eastern England*, 1966.
[2] F. W. Maitland, *Domesday Book and Beyond*, 1897; R. V. Lennard, *Rural England 1086–1135*, 1959; V. H. Galbraith, *The Making of Domesday Book*, 1961; R. W. Finn, *An Introduction to Domesday Book*, 1963.
[3] H. C. Darby, *The Domesday Geography of Eastern England*, 1952; Darby and I. B. Terrett (eds.), *The Domesday Geography of Midland England*, 1954; Darby and I. S. Maxwell (eds.), *The Domesday Geography of Northern England*, 1962; Darby and E. M. J. Campbell (eds.), *The Domesday Geography of South-East England*, 1962; Darby and R. W. Finn (eds.), *The Domesday Geography of South-West England*, 1967.

Documents for the twelfth, thirteenth and fourteenth centuries which also afford the detailed evidence of agrarian structures and practices are those which were produced in connection with the administration of estates, lay and ecclesiastical. Careful control was exercised in the management and administration of these estates, particularly with the increase of money income, money rents and labour rents. Estate surveys, giving details of the demesne lands and rents and services, commence in the twelfth century, and in the thirteenth century further details of estates are provided by the manorial accounts of bailiffs and other officials and the records of local manorial and central courts. The accounts, in addition to details of income and expenditure, also contain, in some instances, details of grain and livestock, including acreages of crops sown, field names, yields, income from sales of grain and livestock and other commodities. Thus it is possible to determine crop rotations, fluctuations in area of land under a particular crop, and the size, grouping and general management of fields. The prime limitation of their accounts is that they relate almost entirely to demesne land.

Custumals, giving details of customs which the tenants in a manor had to observe, often include facts relating to the management and cultivation of land. The records of the manor courts, contained in the court rolls, afford details of the social and economic life of the manor, for 'the offence with which the court dealt in its judicial capacity were chiefly concerned with tenure, services and dues within the manor'.[1] These records are most common in the thirteenth and fourteenth centuries, though they relate principally to the large estates. Valuable information on the regulation of the use of land in the manor is frequently given in the court rolls, usually in the instance of a villager having broken one of the regulations, e.g. relating to the grazing of animals on common land. In the case of a village's lands being located in more than one manor, 'there was a strong tendency for the village meeting to be the active governing body rather than the manor court', producing 'interesting collections of village by-laws, governing every detail of the management of the fields, arable, meadow, pasture and commons'.[2] Inquisitions Post Mortem and manorial extents are records of the property of tenants holding land under the Crown, made at death, which sought to establish possible obligation to the Crown and the question of wardship. The Inquisitions give details of the type of tenure, value of the land, attendant services, and

[1] J. West, *Village Records*, 1962, p. 30.
[2] W. G. Hoskins, *Local History in England*, 1959, p. 47; W. O. Ault, 'Open-Field Husbandry and the Village Community: A Study of Agrarian By-Laws in Medieval England', *Trans. Am. Phil. Soc.*, IV, part 7, 1965.

of successions. They may often include 'extents' or detailed description of the land of the deceased. These are not accurate, measured surveys, but were based on information given by local testimony. The extents were the normal form of medieval survey. Nevertheless, they furnish valuable detail of the extent and resources of (demesne) land, including crop rotations, field names, acreages and value of various types of land, and the nature of tenants, tenancies, rents and services, and thus enable a picture of rural society and landscape to be built up at least for areas which are well endowed with these documents. The Inquisitions and extents occur from the thirteenth to the seventeenth century, with the earlier ones less detailed but more accurate than those, for example, of the sixteenth century.

The Hundred Rolls furnish information about royal rights and estates in the later part of the thirteenth century. The rolls for 1274 are of little assistance in agrarian history, being concerned with encroachments of royal rights, but the 1279 rolls provide details of the royal estates in Bedfordshire, Buckinghamshire, South Cambridgeshire, Huntingdonshire, Oxford, Suffolk and Leicester, and include information on the character and size of property holdings, rents, services, and the rolls illustrate the complex nature of agricultural organisation and society at this time. Detailed studies of these documents have been made by H. M. Cam, E. A. Kosminsky, and others, while J. B. Harley has demonstrated their geographical significance.[1]

In the early part of the fourteenth century the acreage of arable land in England began to decline, and an important record of this decline is provided for certain parts of England by the *Nonarum Inquisitiones* of 1342. These relate to a grant by Parliament to Edward III in 1342 to assist him in his wars, of one-ninth of the value of corn, wool and lambs produced in the realm, in fact in 1341. These returns have been used by historical geographers to demonstrate varying regional emphasis on corn producing or sheep rearing, the relationship between soil fertility and valuation, and the contraction of arable land. They can be compared with the evidence of Domesday Book and the taxation of Pope Nicholas IV to demonstrate changing land values and land utilisation.[2]

[1] H. M. Cam, *Studies in the Hundred Rolls*, 1921; E. A. Kosminsky, *Studies in English Agrarian History in the Thirteenth Century*, 1956; J. B. Harley, 'Population Trends and Agricultural Developments from the Warwickshire Hundred Rolls of 1279', *Econ. Hist. Rev.*, II, 1958, pp. 8–18, and 'The Hundred Rolls of 1279', *Amat. Histn.*, v, 1961, p. 16.

[2] See: E. M. Yates, 'Medieval Assessments in North-West Sussex', *Trans. Inst. Br. Geogr.*, xx, 1954, pp. 75–92; and A. R. H. Baker, 'Evidence in the *Nonarum Inquisitiones* of Contracting Arable Lands in England during the Early Fourteenth Century', *Econ. Hist. Rev.*, xix, 1966, pp. 518–32.

Commutation of labour services and widespread leasing of demesne land, conspicuous from the later part of the fourteenth century onwards, removed much of the former detail from state surveys, and thus necessitates increased dependence on rentals and surveys as sources of information. Legal records are also important sources of information, notably in the form of the records of the courts of Chancery, Star Chamber, and the Court of Requests, which all dealt with disputes which had an agrarian bias,[1] and give vital evidence of the nature and chronology of enclosure in particular. Another type of record stemming from litigation over land is the final concord, which is 'a legal instrument by which land was conveyed or transferred, in the form of a compromise or agreement made between two parties who had been litigating at the King's Court'.[2] The concords, or feet of fines, in time came to relate to the amicable settlement of fictitious suits in the court of Common Pleas to secure transfer or settlement of freehold property. Thus the concord became in effect a popular mode of conveyance. These records are extant from the thirteenth to the eighteenth century, and the details of land which was transferred, although generally given as a round figure, have been used to produce maps which endeavour to show regional variations in land use, by means of quantitative assessments on a sample basis.[3]

(b) Ireland, Wales and Scotland

The documentary sources outlined above have been used extensively in studies of the changing economic, social, and geographical character of England in the medieval period, though problems arise from the fact that the areas covered by these documents vary widely both regionally and chronologically. While some of the documentary sources already mentioned, which were produced by manorial administration, are available for feudalised areas of Ireland, Wales, and Scotland, there are areas and periods for which, for a number of reasons, entirely different sources of evidence must be utilised.

Much of the evidence for early Irish agriculture is archaeological, but literary and documentary evidence does shed some light on this subject. The earliest writing about agriculture is contained in the Ancient Laws of Ireland, or the Brehon Laws, treating of social organisation, ethics and agriculture, though not in a systematic or itemised way. These were preserved orally until the seventh or eighth

[1] Hilton, *Agric. Hist. Rev.*, III, 1955, p. 17.
[2] W. Farrer (ed.), 'The Final Concords for the County of Lancaster', *Record Society of Lancashire and Cheshire*, XXXIX, 1899, p. vii.
[3] H. B. Rodgers, 'Land Use in Tudor Lancashire: The Evidence of the Final Concords, 1450–1558', *Trans. Inst. Br. Geogr.*, XXI, 1955, p. 79.

century, when they were written down. While they thus obviously preserve details of life in prehistoric Ireland they also reveal much about Irish society in the eighth century. They represent a legal system based on the power of traditional custom, formulated and applied by a learned professional caste, and include references to and explanations of, land ownership and land tenure, social rank, livestock husbandry, tillage, enclosures, and farm implements.[1] While it is true to say that the laws represent a schematic and somewhat idealised picture of society and economy at this time, it must be recognised that

'agriculturally the Laws exhibit complete sanity and rationality and the content, while lacking entirely the quality of accurate accounting or recording, exhibits an approach to farming characterized by wisdom and reality and at times is startingly well-informed. Perhaps the two most outstanding features of the farming as viewed from present-day standards are the effort to provide agricultural education or training and the provisions made for controlling the quality of various livestock and of food and drink products.'[2]

In the medieval period, additional information is afforded, though usually in indirect and oblique form, by references in lives of the Celtic saints, annals of the exploits of gaelic chieftains, and commentaries on the law tracts. From the twelfth century onwards, however, with the advent of the Normans and the feudalisation of parts of eastern, southeastern, and southwestern Ireland, documentary evidence in the form of manorial surveys, accounts, extents, court rolls, *inquisitiones post mortem* and the like, becomes available, and has been used to build up an outline picture of rural society and landscape at this time.[3] The great surveys, such as Domesday Book and the Hundred Rolls, do not cover Ireland, and additional difficulty is afforded by the dearth of much of the normal manorial documentation, a result of the destruction of a large amount of Irish material in the Public Record Office in Dublin in 1922. The picture of Irish medieval agricultural systems is at best a hazy one, and hedged about with uncertainty. Further study of extant manorial records and careful study of Irish literature may add more detail.

The evidence for the nature and development of field systems and

[1] See: J. O'Loan, 'A History of Early Irish Farming', *Journal, Department of Agriculture* (Dublin), LX, 1963, pp. 131–97.
[2] *Ibid.*, p. 62.
[3] J. Otway-Ruthven, 'The Organisation of Anglo-Irish Agriculture in the Middle Ages', *Jnl. R. Soc. Antiqu. Ir.*, LXXXI, 1951, pp. 1–13, and *A History of Medieval Ireland*, 1968.

agricultural systems in medieval Wales is essentially similar to that for Ireland, comprising the texts of the Welsh laws together with manorial and Crown survey material. The evidence of the Welsh laws, however, provides a more highly detailed picture of agrarian organisation than does that of the Brehon Laws of Ireland. The reasons for this include the later date of the Welsh law tracts, making them more readily intelligible, their apparently greater detail of agrarian organisation, and the intensive research by Welsh scholars into their meaning and interpretation. These tracts are described in Chapter 10, where it is shown that the general impression created by a study of the laws is then of an old-established practice of mixed farming organised in the main on an open field basis with a degree of communal control. This evidence can be tested against other material, notably the extents of parts of North Wales compiled in the time of Edward I, and surveys of the fourteenth century. Domesday Book also furnishes limited information for parts of the Welsh borderland. General, though in places misleading, evidence is provided by the description by Geraldus Cambrensus in the twelfth century.

The evidence for the agricultural systems and rural society of medieval Scotland takes a variety of forms: archaeological, geographical, documentary and onomastic. The documentary evidence includes land grant charters, law codes, estate rental books (notably those of the estates of the Crown and the larger abbeys) and fiscal and legal records somewhat similar to those described above for medieval England. The study of early Scottish agriculture from documentary sources has been likened to 'palaeontologists trying to reconstruct the whole body of an extinct form of life from a chance survival of imperfect fossils', but sufficient material exists on which to base a general picture of the agrarian landscape and society of Scotland at this time.[1]

4. FIELD EVIDENCE

Extensive documentation can form an invaluable basis for the investigation of changing field systems and agricultural techniques but knowledge so derived can frequently be considerably improved by a consideration of field evidence. In 1883 the historian J. R. Green pointed out that 'the ground itself, where we can read the information it affords, is, whether in the account of the Conquest or in that of the Settlement of Britain, the fullest and most certain of documents'.[2]

---

[1] See: J. A. Symon, *Scottish Farming Past and Present*, 1959; and G. W. S. Barrow, 'Rural Settlement in Central and Eastern Scotland: The Medieval Evidence', *Scott. Stud.*, VI, 1962, pp. 123–44.

[2] J. R. Green, *The Making of England*, 1883, p. vii.

Since Green wrote, a number of historians, notably M. W. Beresford and W. G. Hoskins, have married work in the archives to investigation in the field.[1]

For historical geographers, the present-day landscape has a dual importance. First, its component parts are of interest in their own right, as survivals from a past period, for *sensu lato* all elements in the present landscape are relict features. Secondly, relict features may be studied as primary documents, as a source of invaluable evidence for the reconstruction of past geographies which are to be explained by historical study.[2] It is in this latter sense that present-day rural settlements and field patterns can be studied for the light which they throw upon former field systems. Such an approach has been adopted most notably in Germany and Sweden and it has been termed morpho-genetic study of the agrarian landscape. While such an analytical method is not without its merits, its limitations have frequently been overlooked. By an examination of field evidence and of the earliest extant cadastral maps and plans, such morphological studies try to establish the relationship of field patterns to settlement, relief, soils and drainage. Then follows an attempt to reconstruct the most likely relative order in which the various elements of the field pattern were introduced. For example, small furlongs at the edge of village territory may be thought to be later in origin than a large nucleus of arable land or more easily accessible and fertile, well-drained soils nearer to the centre of the settlement. There exists here a real danger, not always avoided, of entering into a type of circular argument which results from interpreting landscape features in terms of themselves. Such a danger can and must be avoided by recourse to documentary evidence.[3] On its own, field evidence can easily be misinterpreted if two basic principles of landscape formation are ignored: the principle of equifinality, which means that field structures similar in form at one moment in time can have had very different functions in earlier times and have originated in different ways; and the principle of indeterminacy, which means that similar processes operating in different areas and at different times can result in different field structures. Provided that these reservations are borne in mind, an examination of field evidence can be of value. The short sections which follow are

[1] M. W. Beresford, *History on the Ground*, 1957; W. G. Hoskins, *Fieldwork in Local History*, 1967.
[2] H. C. Prince, 'Relict Features: the Past in the Present', a paper read to the Agrarian Landscape Research Group of the Institute of British Geographers, 1 January 1969, summarised in *Area*, no. 1, 1969, pp. 29–30.
[3] C. T. Smith, 'Historical Geography: Current Trends and Prospects', in R. J. Chorley and P. Haggett (eds.), *Frontiers in Geographical Teaching*, 1965, pp. 118–43, and *An Historical Geography of Europe before 1800*, 1967, pp. 224–5.

intended only as brief reviews of those aspects of relict features which are most relevant to the study of field systems.

(a) Field patterns and field names

The forms and patterns of fields and field boundaries are of importance in a study of field systems, in the sense that such features can sometimes be associated with a particular phase of agrarian change and may also preserve in fossil form the outline of, for example, a furlong in an open field. A basic distinction may perhaps be made between regular and irregular forms of field pattern and boundary, with regular forms, notably as squares or rectangles or shapes with straight sides, frequently resulting from organised statutory forms of enclosure, and irregular forms, with completely irregular or perhaps curving sides, from earlier forms of enclosure, frequently on a small scale. To the student of field systems, one of the most indicative field forms is the curvilinear boundary: the linear field with 'aratral' curved sides, which provides evidence of medieval (large plough-teams) ploughing, and probably indicates the existence of former open fields. It has been shown that the reversed S-shape of an elongated field is one of the most common of field patterns in many parts of England, and that this form was strongly influenced by the technique of medieval ploughing. From their shape the inference has been drawn that the fields with such distinctive boundaries were once parts of open fields, and that wherever such field boundaries occur it would appear therefore that they are evidence of piecemeal enclosure of former open fields.[1] The recognition of such forms in the field and on maps can thus form an important and integral part of the process of reconstruction of past field systems. Such forms or shapes often contrast markedly with more regular shapes, and this may enable a relative chronology of enclosure to be established. Not all open fields were, of course, enclosed in piecemeal fashion, and the absence of such shapes does not necessarily imply a former absence of open fields. Enclosure by agreement and enclosure by statute, characteristic of the seventeenth and eighteenth centuries, imposed a regular pattern over many townships in England and Wales, with regularly shaped fields covering, for example, both areas of arable and rough pasture and waste. In this context the size as well as the shape of fields is important, for almost invariably the fields of the poorer lands of the upper slopes of a valley or hill are much larger than those of the better quality arable, meadow and pasture normally found near the settlement. Fields of Tudor enclosures for pasture were also very large. Similarity of field shape and pattern over the whole

[1] S. R. Eyre, 'The Curving Plough-strip and its Historical Implications', *Agric. Hist. Rev.*, III, 1955, p. 86.

of a township area normally indicates near-contemporaneous enclosure, whereas contrasting patterns indicate, in all probability, different phases of enclosure for different types of land and different holdings. Studies of field patterns must, of course, be related also to the patterns of settlements, of topography and soils, to the documentary evidence available, and to other relict features, including ridge-and-furrow. The nature of field boundaries themselves should also be considered, for in the British Isles 'they are characterized by an intensity of occurrence, a regional and local variation, a historical significance and a changing contemporary revaluation, that are equalled in few parts of the world'[1] and a careful study of their form and composition may reveal evidence, for example, of old intake or forest clearance. Many field boundaries, of course, are little more than two hundred years old, but nevertheless can afford detailed testimony of the process and methods of enclosure.

The names given to fields, both at present and in historic documents such as tithe and enclosure maps and awards, manorial surveys and estate surveys, also offer fragmentary evidence of their former state of cultivation, tenure, and location in open fields of one kind or another. Such evidence is impossible to use in isolation, for the danger of anachronistic interpretation is great, and field names like other toponyms tend to be retained long after their descriptive names have been rendered inaccurate by agrarian and social change. Perhaps the greatest difficulty of interpretation derives from the nomenclature and terminology of medieval Latin, and much debate has certainly revolved around such terms as *campus*, which in some instances referred to open field land, but in other to enclosures, and even the more explicit *in communi campo* or *in communibus campis*.[2] Similar difficulties attach to the use of terms such as *town field*, *mean field* or *common field*, which of themselves do not always provide evidence of open and common fields. The elements *butt*, *dole*, *selion*, *furlong*, *shott*, *flatt*, *rigg*, *gore*, and others may be indications of former open fields, as such terminology is usual in open field areas, but this use was not exclusive to open fields, and substantiating evidence must be sought in the form of intermixed holdings, general descriptions and, where possible, maps. Field names associated with former wood or waste, such as *intake*, *-ley*, or *hurst* are prominent in many areas, but considerable difficulty may be experienced in dating their origin. In spite of these difficulties, it must be admitted that the great advantage to be derived from a careful study of field names, usually in retrogressive fashion,

[1] W. R. Mead, 'The Study of Field Boundaries', *Geogr. Z.*, LIV, 1966, p. 101.
[2] A. R. H. Baker, 'Some Terminological Problems in Studies of British Field Systems', *Agric. Hist. Rev.*, XVII, 1969, pp. 136–40.

is that they provide topographic reference points by means of which changes in field systems and enclosure can be based, assessed or measured, albeit only in relative terms.[1] Thus tentative reconstruction of the location of (early) medieval fields can be made with reference to field names and abuttals, and diagrams produced which considerably facilitate analysis of early agrarian arrangements.[2]

(b) The evidence of ridge-and-furrow

One of the most interesting arguments to have arisen among agrarian historians in recent times is that dubbed the 'ridge-and-furrow controversy'.[3] In simple terms, this has resolved around the contention of M. W. Beresford, that 'the ridge-and-furrow pattern visible in Midland fields, and elsewhere, is in fact the pattern of strips of the open field, fossilized, as it were, and unobliterated by the newer alignment of hedges or by the ploughing demands of three wars'.[4] This argument was challenged by E. Kerridge, who contended that such features continued to be produced by ploughing *after* enclosure, even on land ploughed for the first time during the Napoleonic wars, and who argued that most of English ridge-and-furrow was nineteenth-century rather than medieval in origin.[5] It transpired, however, that Beresford and Kerridge were discussing different types of ridge-and-furrow – the former, types which were curvilinear and medieval, and the latter types which were straight and probably of early modern date. This debate has continued, with reference to drainage practice, water meadows, and increases in the surface area of a farm, but perhaps the most significant outcome has been the response to the debate by geographers in particular, by way of detailed mapping of these ridges-and-furrows, or high-backed, grassed-over sinuous ridges which are so conspicuous in many fields. In such exercises, a successful combination of field survey, mapping from air photographs, and the use of old maps and surveys has been employed.[6] As yet, too few areas have

[1] See, for example, J. A. Sheppard, 'Pre-Enclosure Field and Settlement Patterns in an English Township (Wheldrake, near York)', *Geogr. Annlr.*, Ser. B, XLVIII, 1966, pp. 59–77.

[2] A. R. H. Baker, 'Open Fields and Partible Inheritance on a Kent Manor', *Econ. Hist. Rev.*, XVII, 1964, pp. 1–22.

[3] A summary of this debate appears in J. C. Jackson, 'The Ridge-and-Furrow Controversy', *Amat. Histn.*, V, 1961–2, pp. 41–53.

[4] M. W. Beresford, 'Ridge and Furrow and the Open Fields', *Econ. Hist. Rev.*, I, 1948, pp. 34–45.

[5] E. Kerridge, 'Ridge and Furrow and Agrarian History', *Econ. Hist. Rev.*, IV, 1951, pp. 14–36.

[6] W. R. Mead, 'Ridge and Furrow in Buckinghamshire', *Geogrl. Jnl.*, CXX, 1954, pp. 34–42; M. J. Harrison, W. R. Mead and D. J. Pannett, 'A Midland Ridge and Furrow Map', *Geogrl. Jnl.*, CXXXI, 1965, pp. 366–9.

been mapped and studied in detail, and substantial evidence to support
Beresford's theory about the pre-enclosure origins of much ridge-and-
furrow has not yet been forthcoming. It cannot be disputed, however,
that ridge-and-furrow does in some cases preserve an old pattern, and
is thus worthy of investigation, and also (and perhaps more important)
that it could be in many areas the sole indication of extensive arable
cultivation, possibly in common fields. The study of the presence and
form of ridge-and-furrow can therefore provide an invaluable indication
of the possibility of there having been open fields in an area. Ridge-
and-furrow *per se* (in a rather similar way to field names and shapes
per se) proves nothing more than the former existence of arable
cultivation by means of a mould-board plough (but not necessarily
a *fixed* mould broad), but, as an initial basis for further investigation,
its study constitutes an important and useful research technique, which
may be considerably enhanced and supplemented by the study of
related phenomena such as settlements, notably deserted villages, trackways, field and parish boundaries and shapes, and field names. A similar
technique may be applied to the study of relict spade ridges, characteristic of many marginal farming areas of Ireland and Scotland,
notably those dating from the mid-nineteenth century, which frequently
indicate the extension of cultivation limits in times of crisis and pressure
on the land, and in some instances of the former existence of infields
and outfields.

(c) Other field evidence of former cultivation

The general evidence of 'ancient fields', their forms and origins, has
been admirably summarised by H. C. Bowen in his book of that
title.[1] In this category are included the so-called 'Celtic fields', and
various forms of lynchet. The term 'Celtic field' covers 'all those
fields of regular shape which were laid out before the Saxons established
themselves in this country'.[2] Such fields are characteristically small
in size, rectangular in shape, and often bounded by lynchets resulting
from one-way ploughing. They appear to 'represent the first imposition
of a regular cultivation pattern on the landscape in this country'[3],
and as such merit attention and study, with particular reference to the
Romano-British period, together with associated earthworks such as
long and round barrows, isolated platforms or enclosures, ponds,
marl-pits, sunken tracks, and cross-ridge dykes. Where there is a
dearth of documentary material, this field evidence becomes of
paramount importance.

Strip lynchets are long, narrow, terraces found on slopes, comprising

[1] H. C. Bowen, *Ancient Fields*, 1962.
[2] *Ibid.*, p. 2. [3] *Ibid.*, p. 14.

a flat arable area, or 'tread', and a scarped side, or 'riser'. These may occur singly or in 'flights', and may be distinguished from linear types of 'Celtic field' by ends which are either open, or if closed are curved and drawn out, by attenuated proportions and arrangement in bundles. They are often found near nucleated settlements, but occasionally at greater distance from them. It has been suggested that 'the vast majority surely represent but one form of the strips of open fields, and documentary evidence, though sparse, shows that a communal system of agriculture was practised in Wessex certainly by the end of the seventh century'.[1] They could, therefore, date from any time from the seventh to the nineteenth centuries. Their origin appears to have been similar to that of the 'Celtic' lynchets, 'with the important difference that the vast bulk of them would have been accelerated in their formation by the use of a heavy plough always turning the slice downhill'.[2] As a genus of evidence they appear to be in a similar category to that of ridge-and-furrow. Their distribution within these islands has not yet been ascertained in detail, but more field mapping and interpretation by means of documents and maps will certainly shed much light on the origins and development of field systems.[3]

(d) The relevance of aerial photography

The development of air photography during and since World War I has provided archaeologists, historians, geographers and others with one of their most important research aids. Oblique and vertical photographs offer a basis for initial recognition of relict features in the landscape which are not always visible or comprehensible from ground level, for measurement and mapping by photogrammetric methods and for further investigation in the field. The relevance of air photographs to field systems study need not be developed at length, for it has already been amply demonstrated in a number of works, notably in *Medieval England* by M. W. Beresford and J. K. S. St Joseph.[4] The main application is to subjects such as ridge-and-furrow, Celtic fields, lynchets, strip lynchets and other agrarian earth works, and also to deserted settlements, vegetation and soil patterns (including patterns of disturbance), field shapes and patterns. The use of air photographs from a variety of sources adds a necessary dimension to field system studies, from which they invariably derive considerable benefit.

[1] *Ibid.*, p. 45.   [2] *Ibid.*, p. 42.
[3] G. Whittington, 'The Distribution of Strip Lynchets', *Trans. Inst. Br. Geogr.*, XXXI, 1962, pp. 115–30.
[4] M. W. Beresford and J. K. S. St Joseph, *Medieval England, an Aerial Survey*, 1958.

B. METHODS AND APPROACHES

In a volume such as this, dealing in a selective way with a number of problems which the editors and authors consider important and outstanding, it may well be thought that there are represented as many differing approaches to these problems as there are authors, in the sense that each author has an unique way of looking at the study of field systems, and that each area, notably in respect of the amount of attention devoted to it by scholars past and present, presents a more or less formidable task when a generalised account of its agrarian development is attempted. Nevertheless, there are two basic methodological themes which are relevant to most, if not all, of the contributions to this volume, and it is perhaps fitting that they be developed here. The themes are: first, the nature and relevance of a geographer's contribution to studies of field systems; second, the general question of whether the direction of approach is either progressive or retrogressive.

I. GEOGRAPHY AND THE STUDY OF FIELD SYSTEMS

No single formal intellectual discipline can provide a comprehensive solution to the problem of so complex a subject as the past structure and organisation of field systems. The value of multi-disciplinary contributions is indisputable, but of equal significance is the contention that each discipline or subject can bring to the study a particular expertise or approach which will often provide or stimulate new ideas about form, function, and formation. In this volume, all the contributors save one are trained geographers, with particular interests in the field of historical geography. It is pertinent, therefore, to consider briefly the essential features of what might be termed the geographical viewpoint of field systems study. In essence geography is primarily concerned with spatial organisation, with the description and analysis of locations and distributions of largely anthropocentric features of the earth's surface, including all forms of production, agricultural and industrial, transport and communications, settlements, and less tangible elements such as social structure and form, and, not least, with the many aspects of population study. Such phenomena are studied by geographers with particular reference to form, function, development, location and distribution, with cartographic analysis playing an important role. The production and use of specialist maps is very much part of the geographer's craft, which may be applied equally to problems of contemporary industrial location or urban redevelopment as to problems of past forms and structures of settlement and agriculture.

Studies of past landscapes simply transfer present geographical purposes and techniques to past problems, insofar as the historical source materials allow this, so that in any study of the development of field systems by historical geographers, the use of existing manuscript and printed maps together with special maps produced by the geographer himself is given great emphasis. It is, in fact, exceedingly difficult to study past agrarian systems without reference to the location and geographical environment of the region being studied; and to the precise details of the anatomy of its fields and farmsteads. A geographical approach, therefore, is usually characterised by an emphasis on spatial analysis, normally of two kinds. The first involves the use of existing maps, including manuscript and printed estate maps, topographical maps, geological and soil maps, which furnish detailed information and facilitate the task of description and analysis. The second involves the construction of maps, from a wide variety of sources, for a similar purpose. Of particular significance in this respect is the production of maps based on documents originating in a largely pre-cartographic age, such as medieval land charters, surveys, extents, rentals and accounts, on air photographs, and on field survey. The inherent danger in this latter process, as in all forms of cartography, is that it can give an air of authenticity and respectability to material of dubious reliability, accuracy, and coverage, especially that derived from early documents, but providing data limitations are fully recognised, the technique is of inestimable value. Analysis by geographers of the features portrayed in these maps usually accords full weight to environmental factors, both physical and social, including geological, pedological, topographical, demographic, social, technological and institutional considerations. Traditional emphasis on field study and survey within geographical studies is often reflected in the particular attention paid to relict features in the landscape, which are studied because they facilitate reconstruction of past landscapes and societies and the processes of development of present landscapes, these being fundamental aspects of historical geography.

Omniscience is no more characteristic of geography than of any other discipline, and it would be presumptuous to pretend that the geographical approach provided answers to all problems. Such an approach may, in some instances, underestimate the influences of economic and institutional change, in the form of fluctuations in prices, forms of exchange, the changing nature of feudal and later societies, the influence of political decisions, and the complexities of land tenure, but against such possible limitations must be weighed the advantages of what is essentially an approach from a spatial viewpoint. Such an approach has undoubtedly furthered knowledge even in fields well-trodden by economic and other historians, notably in Darby's studies of Domesday Book, and will doubtless continue to produce significant contributions to other aspects of historical study, including the study of field systems. It is certainly no accident that much of the literature on field systems in the past two decades has come from geographers. It is hoped that this present volume will serve to demonstrate, *inter alia*, the value of the geographical contribution to this important and perplexing subject.

2. PROGRESSIVE AND RETROGRESSIVE APPROACHES

There are two basic methods by which historical research may be conducted and presented: one may be termed progressive, the other retrogressive. The former consists of finding a convenient point or period in time as a starting point, and then adopting an order for enquiry and presentation which corresponds to the chronological sequence of events, i.e. proceeding towards the present from the past. This method has been employed in countless studies, including some of the chapters in this volume, and perhaps in some senses it is hallowed by tradition, but it has not been without its critics, and alternative approaches have been proposed and used. Paramount among these is the retrogressive method, advocated notably by Marc Bloch, which emphasises the frequent necessity of reading history backwards. Bloch argued that the paucity of documentation for the early stages of development of the rural landscape necessitated a thorough study of more recent phases, including the present, before moving backwards to study their antecedents, and makes this telling point in both his *Historian's Craft*, and *French Rural History*:

'In certain of its fundamental features, our rural landscape...dates from a very remote epoch. However in order to interpret the rare documents which permit us to fathom its misty beginnings, in order to ask the right questions, even in order to know what we were talking about, it was necessary to fulfil a primary condition: that of observing and analysing our present landscape. For it alone furnishes those comprehensive vistas without which it was impossible to begin. Not, indeed, that there could be any question of imposing this forever-static picture, just as it is, at each stage of the journey upstream to the headwaters of the past. Here, as elsewhere, it is change which the historian is seeking to grasp. But in the film which he is examining, only the last picture remains quite clear.

In order to reconstruct the faded features of others, it behoves him first to unwind the spool in the opposite direction from that in which the pictures were taken.'[1]

Prior to Bloch's exposition, similar theses had been expounded by Landau, Seebohm and Maitland, the last of these having referred to the 'retrogressive method' in his *Domesday Book and Beyond*.[2]

Considerable difficulties attach to the use of the retrogressive method, but it is worth noting that this was the method employed by H. L. Gray, which of itself commends its more widespread use in the future:

'...the plan has been to seek first the characteristics of the field system of a region in those descriptions which, though relatively late, are most nearly complete...Earlier evidence is then adduced to discover whether the thirteenth century situation was a prototype of that of the eighteenth century, or whether there had been change ...This method of trying to ascertain early conditions largely through the use of late evidence is not without danger, and from its effects neither Seebohm's nor Meitzen's works are free. Yet there seems to be no other way of approaching clearly the subject in hand, while it is often only by the aid of late survivals that the earlier phenomena can be interpreted at all.'[3]

[1] M. Bloch, *Les Caractères Originaux, de l'Histoire Rurale Française*, Oslo, 1931, new edition, Paris, 1952, pp. x–xiv; Bloch, *The Historian's Craft*, 1954, pp. 45–6.
[2] For a discussion of the uses, merits and limitations of the retrogressive method and of what differentiates it from retrospective human geography, see: J. L. M. Gulley, 'The Retrospective Approach in Historical Geography', *Erdkunde*, xv, 1961, pp. 306–9; A. R. H. Baker, 'A Note on the Retrogressive and Retrospective Approaches in Historical Geography', *Erdkunde*, xxII, 1968, pp. 244–5; H. Jäger, 'Reduktive und progressive Methoden in der deutschen Geographie', *Erdkunde*, xxII, 1968, pp. 245–6.
[3] Gray, *English Field Systems*, p. 16.

2
Field Systems of Northwest England

BY G. ELLIOTT

The researches of T. Hesketh Hodgson in Cumberland and W. B. Kendall in Furness indicated affinity with Seebohm's belief that there was a uniformity in common field arrangements throughout England, and what was typical of the Midlands could also be found in the Northwest.[1] Both papers helped to start a new line of enquiry into the early organisation of agriculture which had been ignored at a regional level up to that date, and by the time H. L. Gray published his important work on English field systems, the county historical societies had published papers which were beginning to reveal a variety of past field arrangements and cropping systems in the Northwest.[2] Most writers of local history have accepted Gray's view that common arable fields were of some importance in the early agrarian history of the Northwest and disagreed with the Orwins' conclusions that the basis of farming had always been the efforts of individuals working from ring fence farms, probably paying more attention to pastoralism than crop growing and only rarely combining to assart land from the waste and dividing it up into unfenced shares.[3] But while the most recent work has confirmed Gray's findings on the importance of common arable fields, it has taken the emphasis away from one of his chief lines of reasoning regarding their evolution, namely that an ethnic element played an important part in the evolution of English field systems. Because of their nearness to the Scottish border, Cumberland and Lancashire were assumed to have many similarities with Scotland, and these were attributed to Celtic influence. Similarly, Cheshire was thought to be influenced by equally strong Celtic

[1] T. Hesketh Hodgson, 'The village community in Cumberland as instanced at Halltown near Rocliff', *Transactions of the Cumberland and Westmorland Antiquarian and Archaeological Society*, Old Series (hereafter *CW1*, and New Series *CW2*), XII, 1891, pp. 133–42; W. B. Kendall, 'Cocken; The History of a Furness village', *Proceedings of Barrow Naturalist Field Club* (hereafter *P.B.N.F.C.*), 1896, pp. 2–21.

[2] T. H. B. Graham, 'The Townfields of Cumberland', *CW2*, X, 1910, pp. 118–34; W. B. Kendall, 'The History of the Hamlet of Salthouse', *P.B.N.F.C.*, VI, 1948, pp. 21–40; R. Stewart-Brown, 'The Townfield of Liverpool 1207–1807', *Transactions of the Historic Society of Lancashire and Cheshire* (hereafter *Trans. Hist. Soc. Lancs.*), LXVIII, 1917, pp. 35–67; H. L. Gray, *English Field Systems*, Cambridge, Mass., 1915; G. Slater, *The English Peasantry and the Enclosure of the Common Fields*, 1907.

[3] C. S. and C. S. Orwin, *The Open Fields*, 1954, p. 65; Slater, *The English Peasantry*, p. 274.

traditions, and its nearness to the Welsh border was stressed as a factor of some importance. By describing Scottish, Welsh and Irish common field practices in detail Gray hoped to make 'phenomena otherwise perplexing...become intelligible'.[1] But Gray's work did not rely entirely on the comparative method. Some of his conclusions were based on the absence of Parliamentary enclosure of common fields; the small size of townships and their common fields; the existence of infield and outfield in Cumberland; and, 'that, if a Cumberland hamlet had two openfields, the acres of the holding were not divided between them but lay distributed throughout one of them'. Lancashire and Cheshire he assumed to be similar, stressing the importance of piecemeal enclosure in destroying the common fields. While Gray's work revealed some elements of diversity in organisation and farming practice within the common fields of the Northwest, it is evident that he implied a degree of unity of field arrangements which is worth examining in more detail.

A. THE COMMON ARABLE FIELDS

I. THE SIZE OF THE COMMON ARABLE FIELDS

Gray considered that a unifying feature of common fields in Celtic areas was their small size and association with small settlements. He estimated that 'the open fields were seldom 300 acres in extent and often not above 50 or 100 acres'. But in both Cheshire and Cumberland the common fields were larger than Gray thought. The average size of townships in Cumberland was 3,000 acres, and if common fields only covered one-tenth of their area then the average size would have been significantly in excess of Gray's figure. The Cheshire common fields were even larger and Miss Chapman estimated that they covered three quarters of the township area in the western part of the county.[2] Such variety implies that factors other than their location in 'Celtic' areas affected the size of common fields. This is emphasised by variations in field size within counties and reveals the necessity of taking into account local factors, e.g. physical location, complexities of reclamation and varying impact of enclosures in analysing the field systems of the Northwest.

[1] Gray, *English Field Systems*, pp. 157–205, 227–58, 412.
[2] D. Sylvester, 'The Open Fields of Cheshire', *Trans. Hist. Soc. Lancs.*, CVIII, 1956, p. 16; G. Elliott, The System of Cultivation and Evidence of Enclosure in the Cumberland Open Fields in the Sixteenth Century', *CW2*, LIX, 1959, pp. 85–104; V. Chapman, 'Open Fields in West Cheshire', *Trans. Hist. Soc. Lancs.*, CIV, 1952, p. 53.

2. THE DIVISIONS WITHIN THE FIELDS

Even though the total area of common arable fields varied, a typical feature was that they were made up of a number of small units referred to as furlongs (locally called flatts, shoots, rivings, brakes or fields), similar to the furlongs of Midland fields but in no way comparable to those Midland fields which were groups of furlongs. It is consequently misleading in view of the interchangeability of the term furlong and field in Northern common field terminology to speak of 'multi-field townships' unless clear evidence occurs that the 'fields' referred to are groups of furlongs. A small extract from the map accompanying an early seventeenth-century Field Book of Hayton (Cumb.) shows some typical furlongs (Fig. 2.1). The numbers are listed in the Field Book under the heading 'furlong', e.g. '14. Another furlonge of lands and tenemts. there more easte betwene the highwaie weste and the Comon pasture easte.' This particular example contained 36 parcels shared among 22 tenants and there was no evidence to suggest a grouping of these furlongs into the fields of the Midland type.[1] Such evidence is important because in the abbreviated type of reference found in most deeds and surveys the term 'furlong' is either omitted or alternative location names, e.g. 'Ranylandes', 'Langrigg', 'Watelands', are used to locate strip holdings. Where these occur they are best interpreted as furlongs rather than fields. Such an interpretation could apply to the descriptive location names used in Lancashire, e.g. 'Peselandis', 'Langlandis', 'Lynebuttes', and 'Lanrige'; and small units termed 'fields' at North Scale, Farrington, Melling and Little Crosby. The fact that 'Baxtelands', 'Twingates', 'Plentie lands' and 'Clayfielde' were all part of 'Little Crosby Field' must be additional proof of the interchangeability of 'field' and 'furlong' in this area and the fact that Little Crosby had 'a second common field as large, if not larger, than the one near the village and consisting of Seafield, Highfield, Short Field and Hook Field' each consisting of groups of butts is an exact parallel to a Midland field made up of its constituent furlongs.[2] Equally important is the reference at Stalmine to 'campo dicitur Morfurlong' and, as Youd suggests, this interchangeability of field and furlong in North-western common field terminology helps to explain the presence of 'ten or more fields' at Speke and Garston in south Lancashire for, as

[1] T. H. B. Graham (ed.), *The Barony of Gilsland, Lord William Howard's Survey*, taken in *1603*, 1934, p. 143.
[2] G. Youd, 'The Common Fields of Lancashire', *Trans. Hist. Soc. Lancs.*, CXIII, 1961, p. 8; F. Tyrer, 'The Common Fields of Little Crosby', *Trans. Hist. Soc. Lancs.*, CXIV, 1962, pp. 37 and 39.

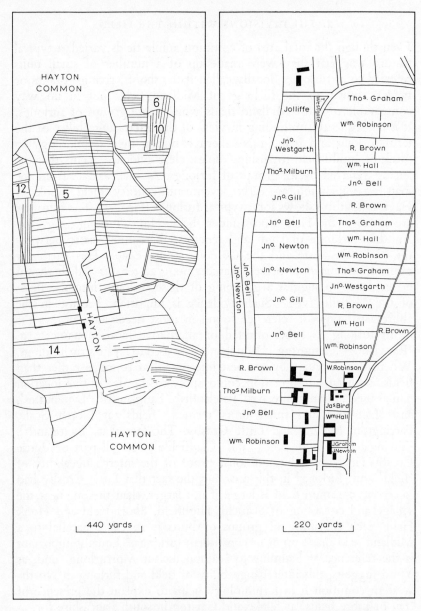

Fig. 2.1 Part of the common arable fields of Hayton (Cumberland),
before and after enclosure.

Sources. Carlisle City Library, Tullie House, Copy of Map of Gilsland Barony 1604.
T. H. B. Graham, 'The Common Fields of Hayton', *Transactions of the Cumberland
and Westmorland Antiquarian and Archaeological Society*, VIII, 1908, p. 344. Furlong
numbers indicated on the map correspond to those listed in T. H. B. Graham (ed.),
The Barony of Gilsland, Lord William Howard's Survey, taken in 1603, 1934.

at Stalmine, these 'fields' are again really 'furlongs'.[1] The Cheshire evidence is equally convincing. At Manley 'four selions in Aspone – furlong in the territory of Manley of which one is called Aleynes Heddeland...another in the same field', reveals the validity of Gray's statement that 'Such fields as occasionally appear in other terriers are likely to be co-ordinate with furlongs'.[2] This clarification of terms is important in view of the previous discussion on field size and in later discussions on methods of cultivation.

3. THE SIZE OF FURLONGS

The size of furlongs varied. The smallest, held by one tenant, are comparable with those mentioned by Gray in Cumberland. This in itself is a point of contrast between the Midlands and Northwest and where this individuality of ownership is accompanied by small size, it must represent a peculiar local usage of the term 'furlong', e.g. 'Jo. Tiffin...one flat or furlong lying on the south side of Kirkrode in Kirkland feild betwixt 2 balks con. one acre 2 Ro...'[3] At the other extreme were furlongs typified by those in Hayton common field where furlong 14 contained 36 parcels totalling 170 acres. This variability in size and composition is a puzzling feature, especially if the furlong is regarded as a unit of reclamation in the expansion of common fields into the waste – a concept suggested by T. A. M. Bishop for certain areas of Yorkshire and for which there is evidence in the Northwest.[4] Gray regarded some of the Cumberland evidence as an indication of the 'improvement of the waste in which many tenants had shared' taking the 'equality of partition and character of the names' as his chief source.[5] A similar type of evidence exists in Cheshire and Lancashire. Field names such as 'whyndalmor', 'ridding' and 'brand earth' are indicative of 'an expansion in common field cultivation'; riddings and assarts were created in medieval Cheshire, and in some townships there is a clear distinction between the anciently cultivated areas (oxgang land) and newly reclaimed areas (Rodeland).[6] This reclamation on a communal basis was still going on in Cumberland in the sixteenth and seventeenth centuries, long after it had ceased

[1] Youd, *Trans. Hist. Soc. Lancs.*, CXIII, 1961, p. 8.
[2] Sylvester, *Trans. Hist. Soc. Lancs.*, CVIII, 1956, p. 21; Gray, *English Field Systems*, p. 266.
[3] P.R.O., M.B. Exch. K.R., vol. 37, fo. 48.
[4] T. A. M. Bishop, 'Assarting and the Growth of the Open Fields', *Econ. Hist. Rev.*, VI, 1936, pp. 13–29.
[5] Gray, *English Field Systems*, pp. 233–4.
[6] Youd, *Trans. Hist. Soc. Lancs.*, CVIII, 1961, p. 9; Sylvester, *Trans. Hist. Soc. Lancs.*, CVIII, 1956, p. 26; W. Farrer, *Court Rolls of the Honor of Clitheroe*, 1912, II, p. 48.

further south. It is an essential feature of an evolving field system and led to an addition of at least 1,700 acres of new land to common arable fields in east Cumberland in the sixteenth century, in spite of the fact that some of these areas formed part of the Forest of Inglewood and were subject to restrictions imposed by Forest Law. Such evidence may lend weight to the impression of broad regional differences in the history of reclamation in the Northwest and indicates that what had happened in fifteenth-century Cheshire was taking place in parts of Cumberland in the late sixteenth century.[1]

4. TOWNFIELDS

One of the commonest names given to common arable fields in the Northwest was 'Townfield'. In Cheshire alone there are sixty-eight references to 'the former existence of a townfield with strip cultivation'.[2] It is frequently used as a term for the location of tenants' holdings, e.g. 'The fflatt and aycre by estim. three Ackres adjoining to Loine and on the eastern side of the same one ackre of ground in the Towneffield situate on the east side of the highway betwixt Tunstall and Melling'.[3] That these references begin as early as the fourteenth century is indicative of the antiquity of the feature and militates against the explanation of it in terms of a small surviving area of common field arable which remained after the rest of the township's common fields had been enclosed. Such an explanation would fit the bulk of references to it in the eighteenth and nineteenth centuries but not the earlier ones.[4] In certain cases it may represent an alternative name used in single field townships. All eighteen tenants of Wasdale Head (Cumb.) held shares in a single common arable field – Wasdale Head Field – and in other townships it is referred to simply as 'the common feilde'. 'In Lancashire it was ubiquitous throughout the western arable belt...in the Ribble and Lune Valleys and Furness.' Within former Forest areas its use is more restricted but in general it

[1] Cumberland R.O., Survey of Inglewood Forest, 1619; C. S. Davies, *The Agricultural History of Cheshire 1750–1850*, Chetham Soc., x, 1960.
[2] Sylvester, *Trans. Hist. Soc. Lancs.*, cviii, 1956, pp. 21–2; Chapman, *Trans. Hist. Soc. Lancs.*, civ, 1952, p. 58.
[3] Lancashire R.O., DRB/3/18, Glebe Terrier for Melling 1663.
[4] Youd, *Trans. Hist. Soc. Lancs.*, cxiii, 1961, p. 3; G. A. Stocks and J. Tait (eds.), *Dunkenhalgh Deeds*, Chetham Soc., N.S. lxxx, p. 52; J. Twemlow (ed.), *Liverpool Town Books*, 1918, i (1550–1571), pp. 4–7; J. H. Lumby (ed.), *A Calendar of the Deeds and Papers in the possession of Sir James de Hoghton Bart.*, Lancashire Record Society, lxxxviii, 1936, p. 15; J. Brownbill (ed.), *A Calendar of that part of the Collection of Deeds and Papers of the Moore Family...*, Lancs. Rec. Soc., lxvii, 1913, pp. 1–3.

seems to have been used as a generic term covering all the common field arable land in a township.[1] At Kirkham it was used to describe a common arable field of at least 580 statute acres, and in most townships for which the term is recorded the holdings were frequently located within the townfield by descriptive names which may have been field divisions equivalent to furlongs or in extremely small townfields, the names of individual riggs or dales.[2]

5. RIDGES, REANNS AND RING DYKES

Local evidence suggests that stony soils such as were found in the fields of Warton (Lancs.) gave rise to ridges which 'one would rather take...for so many causeways to walk on' in newly ploughed fields.[3] Many of these ridges have been preserved, particularly in marginal areas where the land has subsequently gone out of cultivation, but no systematic research linking their distribution to cartographic evidence of common fields has been undertaken for this region. Late survivals of the feature were noted by Eden and Housman, but neither commented on their purpose which has been presumed to be to facilitate drainage in the arable lands.[4] Local names were evolved to describe them and included 'butt', 'dale', 'land', 'lound' (a half land was abbreviated to 'halland'), 'lount', 'ridge', 'rigg' and 'selion'. They consisted of a group of furrows and varied considerably in size even within a single township (Table 2.1). In some townships the water running off the ridges was channelled into water furrows which separated them and Youd quotes the modern Lancashire word 'reann' to describe this feature.[5] Reann (rein) was also used to describe unploughed balks in the common fields, e.g. at Kirkandrews (Cumb.) 'no ranes betwixt neighbour and neighbour cutt nor eater with cattell or horses nor mares and cowes'.[6] The frequent use of the common

[1] P.R.O., Misc. Books, Exch. K.R., vol. 37, fos. 83–6, 78–9, 53–5, 57–9; Youd, *Trans. Hist. Soc. Lancs.*, CXIII, 1961, p. 3; R. Cunliffe Shaw, *Royal Forest of Lancaster*, 1956, p. 312.

[2] Cunliffe Shaw, *Trans. Hist. Soc. Lancs.*, CXIV, 1962, p. 24; Tyrer, *Trans. Hist. Soc. Lancs.*, CXIV, 1962, pp. 37–41; Westmorland R.O., Musgrave D.P. Court Rolls.

[3] J. Lucas, *The History of Warton Parish*, ed. J. Rawlinson Ford and J. Fuller Maitland, 1931, pp. 134–9.

[4] Sir F. M. Eden, *The State of the Poor*, 1797, II, 65–8; W. Hutchinson, *A History of the County of Cumberland*, 1794, I, pp. 181, 203, 212; Chapman, *Trans. Hist. Soc. Lancs.*, CIV, 1952, pp. 58–9.

[5] Youd, *Trans. Hist. Soc. Lancs.*, CXIII, 1961, p. 17.

[6] Cumberland R.O., D/Sen. Burgh Court Rolls 1703, cf. E. Kerridge, 'A Reconsideration of Some Former Husbandry Practices', *Agric. Hist. Rev.*, III, 1955, pp. 26–40. H. Beecham, 'A review of Balks as Strip Boundaries in the Open Fields', *Agric. Hist. Rev.*, IV, 1956, pp. 22–44.

Table 2.1. Variations in size of ridges

	Township	Size of ridge	Date
CUMBERLAND	Drigg	2 dales = 3 acres	1587
		3 dales = 1 acre	
		1 dale = 1 acre	
		7 dales = 2 acres	
	Orton	11 riggs = 3 acres	1704
		4 riggs = 1 acre	
LANCASHIRE	Tarleton	7 ridges = ½ acre	18th c.
	Liverpool	3 ridges = 1 acre	18th c.
CHESHIRE	Sale	1 dole = 30 perches	1728
		1 dole = 20 perches	
	Cheadle	1 dole = 3 roods	1709
		1 dole = 30 perches	
		1 dole = 24 perches	

Sources: P.R.O., Misc. Books, Exch. K.R., vol. 37, fos. 78–9; W. Nicolson, *Miscellany accounts of the Diocese of Carlisle...*, ed. R. S. Ferguson, 1877, pp. 165–6; Youd, *Trans. Hist. Soc. Lancs.*, CXIII, 1961, pp. 12–13; Cheshire R.O., EDV/8.

arable fields in summer for grazing was made possible by the existence of these areas on which sufficient grass grew to feed the stock and which were wide enough to tether them.[1] But the frequent trespass to which this gave rise caused some townships to abandon the practice and the decision is recorded in 'paines' which among other things set down the rules for the management of the common fields.[2] Where a reann was shared between two tenants, marks or merestones had to be placed along it to divide one holding from another and the removal of them or the ploughing up of reanns was often punished by manorial courts.[3]

The 'ring dyke' or ring fence was an important feature of the common arable fields, particularly in the northern counties. Its function was to protect growing crops from the trespass of stray stock but in areas that were frequently subjected to raids it also served as the first line of defence against marauders.[4] Its base was usually a raised mound

[1] Cumberland R.O., D/Sen. Burgh Court Rolls 1709, Oughterside Court Rolls 1696; W. Hutchinson, *A History of the County of Cumberland*, I, pp. 181, 203, 212.

[2] J. Whiteside, *Shappe in Bygone Days*, 1904, p. 196; Cumberland R.O., D/Sen. Burgh Barony Court Rolls, 1703 and 1709; D/Lon., Great Strickland Court Rolls 1727.

[3] P.R.O., Misc. Books, Exch. K.R. vol. 37, fos. 53–5, 57–9; Cumberland R.O., DX/128/7/1, Cumwhinton Court Rolls 1601; Youd, *Trans. Hist. Soc. Lancs.*, CXIII, 1961, pp. 10–18.

[4] W. Hutchinson, *History of Cumberland*, I, p. 55; E. King, 'Notes from the Penrith Registers', *Trans. R. Hist. Soc.*, x, 1882, p. 102.

of earth on to which was built other protective structures and in some cases it is fossilised in the landscape and commemorated by the name of daughter settlements which were built along its edge as cultivation was extended into the common waste, e.g. Salkeld Dykes, Bascodyke (Cumb.). Access to the common waste was through gates at selected places in the dyke and this line of access frequently survives as a green road and has again given rise to settlement names, e.g. Aiketgate, Hornsbygate (Cumb.). In those townships where outfield management necessitated the ploughing up of a new piece of land at the end of a period of cultivation, the start of a new cropping course would be initiated by the erection of a head dyke around the rivings.

As the system developed it may have reached a stage where the number of rivings became relatively static, and in this case the tendency would be to leave the ring hedge, particularly as in some cases it was built of stone, at the end of the period of cultivation. In this way the riving which went out of cultivation may then have become common pasture again, but because it was provided with a fence it could have had a special place in feeding stock, e.g. as pasture for plough oxen. This explanation would fit in with a description given to Scotby Ox Pasture which was enclosed from the waste 'and yet sometimes they plow the same'.[1]

6. SPECIAL CLOSES

In some townships special closes were kept for common grazing of stock (e.g. Colt Park, Ox Park), but at times they were converted into common arable fields. There is a parallel between these closes and those described by J. Murray in Dumfriesshire, 'and their cattle were confined during the night, together with some of the milk cows, in small inclosures or folds, formed either of turf taken from the ground, or moveable wooden fences, which were thus manured with the dung of the beasts shut up during the night, and ploughed and cropped for as long a time as they would produce grain'[2]. Although not outfield farming *in sensu stricto* this closely resembles it and was another aspect of a pastoral bias in the farming economy of the Northwest. A late survival of this feature has been identified in Arlecdon (Cumb.).[3] This emphasis on stock farming is frequently

[1] Cumberland R.O., Survey of Inglewood Forest 1619.
[2] Dr Singer, *General View of the Agriculture in the County of Dumfries*, 1812, p. 504.
[3] E. H. Sugden, *History of Arlecdon and Frizington*, 1918, p. 8. Hog's Heys in Fig. 2.6 is another type of close kept for stock. There is no evidence that it was ploughed.

indicated in inventories where stock values outweigh those of crops, and even in south Lancashire large numbers of stock were reared, many of which would participate in grazing the common field stubble.[1] To many stock owners, this right was of less significance to their large-scale organisation of pastoralism than the extensive common wastes. The 404 sheep, 18 cattle and 3 work horses which Henry de Holand kept on the demesne at Woolton (Lancs.) was only a fraction of his total stock holding, most of which was reared outside the common arable field belt. In part it is an organisation which reflects pastoral use of rough land that was difficult to assart and only slowly won over to more intensive farming in the latter part of the eighteenth century and is in part a reflection of the changing use of forest land. It is represented in the eastern Fylde by a marked transition from predominantly common field arable townships in the west, to a more specialised and extensive pastoralism in the uplands of Bowland and the Pennines.[2] Upland wastes were grazed by stock from farms scattered along valley floors and this had its counterparts in other parts of the Northwest. The northern edge of Inglewood Forest (Cumb.) marked a similar transition from the common field townships of the Solway Plain to the pastoral uplands on the northern fringe of the Lake District. Some lowland settlements sent cattle to the forest during summer, leading to the growth of 'scales' or temporary settlements which had their counterpart in Lancashire 'booths'.[3] Within Cheshire the belt of common arable field townships in the centre of the county were bordered on east and west by two important forest areas (Macclesfield and Delamere) in which pastoralism predominated and individual assarts were more numerous than common field strips.[4]

7. THE DISPERSAL OF HOLDINGS

In his account of the field systems of the Northwest, Gray stressed that individual holdings formed a consolidated group of strips in parts of the common fields which he distinguished from the Midland system, characterised by a wide dispersal of parcels, and inferred that

[1] Cunliffe Shaw, *Royal Forest of Lancaster*, pp. 340–5; G. Tupling, *The Economic History of Rossendale*, Chetham Soc., N.S. LXXXVI, 1927, pp. 15ff.
[2] Cunliffe Shaw, *Royal Forest of Lancaster*, pp. 350–80.
[3] A. L. Rowse, *The England of Elizabeth*, 1950, p. 78; J. Nicholson and R. Burn, *The History and Antiquities of the Counties of Westmorland and Cumberland*, 1777, p. 141.
[4] H. J. Hewitt, *Medieval Cheshire – An Economic and Social History*, Chetham. Soc., N.S. LXXXVIII, 1929, pp. 48–51; M. B. Husain, 'Delamere Forest in late-medieval times', *Trans. Hist. Soc. Lancs.*, CII, 1952, pp. 23–9; C. S. Davies, *The Agricultural History of Cheshire 1750–1850*, Chetham Soc., 3rd Ser. X, 1960, pp. 5–8.

it was a feature common to the Celtic system in England.[1] His chief evidence from descriptive surveys referred to Ainstable (Cumb.) where there were

'some half-dozen tenants, with holdings of about ten acres apiece in the respective hamlet fields of "Southeranraw", Ruckroft and Castle-dyke...but regarding the position of these acres we learn nothing. The remaining tenants seem to belong to the hamlet of Ainstable proper. Although sometimes the holdings here are not located at other times they are said to have lain largely in Southfield or Kirkfield. When this is the case, each was, except in one instance, entirely within one or the other of these fields. Sometimes too, the acres of a tenant of one of the other hamlets lay wholly or partly in Southfield. Now, Southfield and Kirkfield were pretty clearly not hamlet-fields attached to different hamlets, but were the two fields of a single township...if a Cumberland hamlet had two open fields, the acres of the holdings were not divided between them but lay distributed throughout one of them.'[2]

The validity of this thesis can be reviewed against the evidence contained in five charters granting land in Ainstable to Wetheral Priory where there are indications of great fragmentation of holdings and the use of a multiplicity of location names. Two acres granted by William de Terribi consisted of eleven parcels in such diverse locations as 'in Alderrnccrofte, in Lincora, in Wyterays in Ssarrait, Apud Boream, juxta Langthorrave, in Witelandes'. The first example probably refers to land in the hamlet of Ruccroft, and the exact location of the rest is unknown. This contrast, between the evidence from the thirteenth century which is indicative of a wide scatter of holdings and the later evidence quoted by Gray which indicates a tendency for holdings to consist of blocks of strips, is probably the result of exchange and consolidation of strip holdings within the common fields. As such, the evidence from Ainstable in the sixteenth century is not typical of common field townships in other parts of Cumberland and Westmorland. In Hayton and Cumrew – the only area for which contemporary map and survey evidence is available – there is a wide scatter of holdings through several furlongs.[3] In west Cumberland the demesne lands of Bromfield manor were widely scattered. Not only did the lord have numerous acres in a large number of furlongs in Bromfield townfields but he also held lands in the fields of Ethrigg, Kelsicke, Dunrowe, Langrigg, and Allonby. The

---

[1] Gray, *English Field Systems*, pp. 234–5.
[2] *Ibid.*, p. 235.
[3] Graham (ed.), *The Survey of Gilsland Barony 1603*, pp. 97–119, 132–60.

last example is interesting, for Gray quoted later evidence from Allonby to supplement that on Ainstable. He pointed out how the riggs of Janet Shaw and Michell Fawcon were grouped together in the Eastfield,[1] yet the lands in Allonby belonging to Bromfield manor were rented to Cuthbert Shaw and consisted of '...2 cross Riggs one in the East Close and the other in the West Close containing 2 acres'.[2] In Westward on the northern edge of Inglewood Forest the common arable fields were associated with a large number of small hamlets, hamlet fields and isolated common fields as in Ainstable. But there was a wide dispersal of holdings.[3] The problem of the concentration of a strip holding into a single field is obviously not explicable in terms of agricultural policy within settlements, but is related also to the size of settlements, history of reclamation and progress of consolidation. This is confirmed by evidence from Lancashire and Cheshire. Gray's interpretation as it affected Thistleton (Lancs.) has been examined and doubt cast on its validity in the light of evidence from other charters.[4] In Cheshire there is a tendency to a similar scattering of common field strips except where consolidation had altered the pattern and this type of land distribution would be implicit in the organisation of a three-field system for which evidence has recently been discovered in the county.[5]

8. VARIETIES OF TENURE

There were significant variations of tenure by which land was held in the Northwest. In Cumberland and Westmorland the tenants held their land by 'a customary tenant-right varying somewhat from one manor to another but a tenure tantamount to freehold'.[6] This may have been modified from time to time. During the sixteenth century the steep rise in prices resulted in tenant right being the subject of litigation between the Crown and tenantry of Westmorland. One of its aspects, that of Border Service, was particularly onerous in that not only had relatively poor men to find horse and armour but the call to active service was frequent during times of trouble between

[1] Gray, *English Field Systems*, p. 235.
[2] B.M., Add. Mss. 27409.
[3] P.R.O., Misc. Books, Exch. K.R., vol. 37, fos. 76–9.
[4] Gray, *English Field Systems*, p. 248; R. Cunliffe Shaw, *Kirkham in Amounderness*, 1949, pp. 234–6, 349; W. H. Chippendale (ed.), *A Sixteenth Century Survey of Hornby Castle*, Chetham Soc., N.S. CII, 1939, pp. 41–3.
[5] Sylvester, *Trans. Hist. Soc. Lancs.*, CVIII, 1956, pp. 21–3; D. Sylvester, 'A Note on Medieval Three-Course Arable Systems in Cheshire', *Trans. Hist. Soc. Lancs.*, CX, 1958, pp. 183–6.
[6] C. M. L. Bouch and G. P. Jones, *A Short Economic and Social History of the Lake Counties 1500–1830*, 1961, p. 65.

England and Scotland. Its implications in relation to the important problem of enclosures however were outweighted by the influence of a few landlords whose estates covered the greater part of Cumberland. The division of most of the county into large baronies created a group of paramount lords whose influence up to the end of the sixteenth century was virtually complete. Their lack of interest in enclosure is reflected in the state of the common fields at the end of the century as recorded in detailed estate surveys. To a certain extent exchange of lands between individuals was permitted within manors on these baronies but the general impression is that where common arable fields existed the lords saw no purpose in enclosing them; indeed in an extreme case it was suggested by the tenantry of the Royal Forest of Inglewood that the Dacres of Gilsland deliberately opposed enclosure because it would impede the raids made by their lawless tenantry into the farms of central and south Cumberland.[1] The pattern in Westmorland is very similar, and while north Lancashire may not have been as troubled by border strife by the sixteenth century as its two northern neighbours, there appear to have been similarities at an earlier date. In 1324 land in the manor of Carnforth 'is worth... yearly 6d and no more because it was destroyed and burnt by the Scots'.[2] The impact of these conditions was felt throughout the estates of the earl of Lincoln as far south as Halton (Ches.), but as national conflict gradually gave way to border feuding, the importance of these retarding factors lessened in Lancashire. In Cheshire, the problem was on the Welsh border and, although subject to unstable conditions in the early Middle Ages, its pacification seems to have been more successful.[3] There is an earlier appearance in both Cheshire and south Lancashire of lords holding manors from paramount lords, e.g. Molyneux, Halsalls, Lathoms in South Lancashire. As they increased their influence and improved their status the consolidation of holdings and the emparking of estates would bring in their train the gradual disappearance of common arable fields. This was especially the case in parts of Lancashire where the extension of the lord's demesne could not be at the expense of the waste because it was poorly drained mossland, e.g. Halsall, Scarisbrick, Rufford.

The problem of inheritance of estates is not easy to disentangle from the mass of conflicting evidence – partible inheritance and primo-

---

[1] B.M., Lansdowne Mss. 105, no. 8; J. M. Bean, *The Estates of the Percy Family 1416–1537*, 1958, p. 68; Bouch and Jones, *The Lake Counties*, pp. 74–8. P.R.O., Misc. Books, Exch. K.R., vol. 37, fos. 4–91; vol. 38, fo. 250; vol. 42, fos. 1–79.
[2] W. Farrer (ed.), *Lancashire Inquests and Extents*, Lancashire and Cheshire Record Society, LIV, part 2, 1907, pp. 107, 148, LXX, p. 6.
[3] Sylvester, *Trans. Hist. Soc. Lancs.*, CVIII, 1956, p. 11.

geniture are both represented in manorial records from the early Middle Ages and the question of their effect on common arable fields is very difficult to assess. Where partible inheritance did exist there must have been some subdivision of holdings and it has recently been suggested as one important factor leading to a very complex field system in parts of Lancashire.[1]

As early as the fourteenth century the growth of villages into small towns had its effect on the structure and cultivation of common arable fields. There are signs of burgage tenements as early as 1400 and the common arable fields of Carlisle were subdivided into a great complexity of holdings by 1601.[2] In both these cases growing urban settlements created new demands on land and added to land values. This may not have represented conditions in the countryside and even small towns retained their common fields little disturbed by engrossing and enclosure until the eighteenth century. Penrith, Workington, Whitehaven and Wigton in Cumberland; Kendal and Kirkby Stephen in Westmorland; Dalton, Ulverston, Clitheroe and Prescot in Lancashire; Stockport, Wilmslow, Macclesfield and Sandbach in Cheshire all had flourishing markets, fairs and small-scale industry in the sixteenth century but retained their functions as agricultural communities farming common arable fields.[3]

9. HALF-YEAR LANDS

Where outfield on its own, or infield–outfield, do not occur they are replaced by a variety of terms used in the location of common field strips. In many cases there is reference to 'Townfield(s)' or simply the settlement name plus 'Field(s)', e.g. 'Rosuen field', 'the fields of Clitheroe', 'Heswall field'. Within these units individual holdings are located by descriptive or topographic names. A good example of this type is Aston Townfield (see Table 2.5). It shows a townfield that has not been greatly affected by either consolidation or enclosure and in this sense it may not be typical of seventeenth-century Cheshire.

[1] Cunliffe, Shaw, *Trans. Hist. Soc. Lancs.*, CXIV, 1962, pp. 26–7; Sylvester, *ibid.*, CVIII, 1956, p. 12.
[2] Stewart-Brown, *The Townfields of Liverpool*, pp. 30–9; Twemlow (ed.), *Liverpool Town Books*, pp. 419–21; Brownbill (ed.), *Calendar of Moore Papers*, pp. 15–18; P.R.O., Land Revenue Misc. Books, vol. 212, fos. 129–58.
[3] Bouch and Jones, *The Lake Counties*, pp. 25, 93, 108; F. A. Bailey, *A Selection from the Prescot Court and Other Records, 1447–1600*, Lancs. and Ches. Rec. Soc., LXXXIX; J. F. Curwen (ed.), *Records relating to the Barony of Kendall by W. Farrer*, 1924, I, pp. 54–79; Cumberland R.O., Survey of Inglewood Forest 1619; J. D. Marshall, *Furness and the Industrial Revolution*, 1958; Cheshire R.O., EDV/8, Glebe Terriers for Stockport 1662, Sandbach 1661.

The field is split into a number of divisions which are used as location features but which are frequently very small and may only contain one holding. Brick Butts is of this type. It clearly represents what is the most frequent form of field layout in the Northwest in which there is no clear-cut division into a small number of fields, or if 'fields' do occur they are synonymous with furlong. The maps and field books of the Barony of Gilsland (1603) show this layout but in the formal language of the surveyor all descriptive location names are omitted and the field divisions are called furlongs. In both these cases we know exactly where every acre lay in the common fields, where strips were enclosed, which were headlands, which was arable and which meadow, but we are given no indication how the fields were cultivated. In the case of Hayton, Graham has suggested a three-field system but his conclusions are largely conjectural.[1] In both townships, however, the pattern of holdings could be fitted into a system of cultivation practised in south Lancashire which Youd has called 'half-year lands', and in which spring-sown cereals with oats pre-dominating formed the basis of cultivation. After harvest stock were allowed to graze the stubble until the following spring when the land was once again prepared for the next cereal crop. Six months in crops followed by six months grazing was the system of cultivation.[2] If this system is applied to manors of the barony of Gilsland, e.g. Hayton, which is the only area in the Northwest for which contemporary map and field book evidence exists, the continuous cropping of the 569 acres of Hayton common field would represent high-intensity cultivation. It is the equivalent of infield farming over the whole of the township's common arable lands. Whether the land could withstand this succession of white crops year after year is a critical question. Youd's positive evidence hinges on the statement made in the court orders of Leyland (Lancs.) relating to grazing. This states that the tenants were to 'take all their Cattle out of the said Townefeildes yearely at or before...Lady Day'. He has interpreted 'yearely' as every year and 'Townefeildes' as the equivalent of all the common arable land in the township. In the absence of contradictory evidence from other townships of lowland Lancashire he has assumed that the cropping was continued every year without a reversion to grass at the end of a cropping cycle as would occur under typical outfield conditions. Corroborative evidence from late seventeenth-century sources, e.g. Little Crosby, states that the land was 'very much bared

[1] Graham (ed.), *Survey of Gilsland Barony 1603*, pp. 98–161; T. H. B. Graham, 'An old map of Hayton manor', *CW2*, VII, 1907, pp. 43–53; Graham, *CW2*, x, 1910, pp. 118–34.
[2] Youd, *Trans. Hist. Soc. Lancs.*, CXIII, 1961, pp. 21–7.

by reasons of long tillage' and the indication that many townships had 'fence' days when stock were put or taken off the fields, was included to support his argument.[1]

Three questionable points seem to emerge from this interpretation of the evidence. The utilisation of stubble during periods of cultivation was equally a characteristic feature of outfield cultivation. Not only were the 'beast gates', which gave tenants a restricted grazing right, attached to the outfield lands of Aspatria (Cumb.), but in Dean (1753) the eleven tenants who shared the outfield held arable strips in proportion to the number of 'cowgrasses' or stints to which each tenant was entitled. The vicar's share is stated 'In the Outfield south east of Greysouthen Moor, twelve grasses or stints with arable ground proportionable'.[2] The whole emphasis is a pastoral economy in which a temporary cultivation of parts of the waste was subsidiary. This must have been the case in many other parts of Northwest England where even today the growing of cereals is made difficult by soil, drainage and climatic considerations. The date for freeing this land in preparation for the spring sowing was, as in south Lancashire, about mid-March. But the absence of the term outfield does not rule out a long ley system of farming. In Arlecdon the outfield was referred to as 'High Leys', and the Dean 'Outfield' was divided up into a number of units, e.g. 'Lock Dales', 'Corney Flat', 'New Close' or 'Middle Break', 'Rampra Banks' and 'Wood Heads' and these were frequently used for locating parcels without any reference to the outfield in which they lay.[3] Yet these two types of descriptive locations of arable land within common field areas are common in the Northwest and could be synonymous with long ley farming. The 'townfield' of Lancashire, as Youd has indicated, was a relic of a formerly more coherent common field system and by the seventeenth century the 'Townfield of Leyland' may have been only a small remnant of the common fields. Thus its part in the cultivation of any holding or farm was probably relatively unimportant and was neither representative of other cultivation in the rest of the arable land of the township nor reflected an earlier system in which common arable fields were more extensive. Such a situation is revealed in the bulk of seventeenth- and eighteenth-century glebe acreage. The problem of interpreting 'yearely' literally is one of emphasis. Cunliffe Shaw would prefer an interpretation which allowed the arable lands 'a reasonable period

[1] *Ibid.*, p. 23.
[2] Elliott, *CW2*, IX, 1960, pp. 99 and 106; Dean Church Papers 1753, in the custody of Mr Dickinson, Red How, Lamplugh; Cumberland R.O., DRC 9, Dean Glebe Terrier 1698.
[3] Dean, *op. cit.*

for resuscitation'. In disagreeing with Youd's interpretation he quotes a nineteenth-century lease for a farm in the Fylde and believes it is on 'traditional lines', comparing it in its essentials with the three years corn followed by six years pasture of the Huthwaits at Carnforth.[1] If these parallels are valid they would push the boundary of outfield types of cultivation south to the Ribble and if Youd's interpretation is correct, the 'half-year land' type of cultivation would represent a highly distinctive enclave of intensive land utilisation in south Lancashire, with the evidence for Cheshire land use being too thin on which to base firm conclusions.

10. THE THREE-FIELD SYSTEM

There are only two references which would indicate a probable three-field system. One is from south Lancashire and the other from west Cheshire. After summarising the evidence for Cheshire Miss Sylvester originally concluded that 'the evidence for there having been a genuine three-field arable system in this part of England was inconclusive'.[2] The Lancashire evidence is later in date and presents more problems of interpretation.[3] In his analysis of 'a system of share-cropping' at Speke near Liverpool in 1694 Youd states

'The orders for cultivation were:
"1. The lower eleven Acer being 12 Acers to fallow for wheat.
2. The Hier sute in Mill field 8 Acers to fallow for wheate.
3. My one Teame to fallow for Wheate all the lower sute in the Mill field and to plow and sowe with Oates and Barley all the nerer Mill field.
4. The three crofts being 7 Acers to be sowed with oates."'

This was a township with at least five 'fields' or furlongs. What at first sight appears a three-course rotation of wheat, oats and fallow is open to other interpretations. If the quotation is a statement of intent for the year 1694 (it must have been written in the early months of that year as it refers to the spring sowing of oats) then the wheat may not have been sown until the autumn after 'My one Teame' had suitably prepared the ground by spring and summer ploughings. This indicates that no wheat would be sown in these fields in that year, nor is there reference to any having been sown on part of them the previous year. This interpretation of the evidence would put three fields fallow and two in oats in 1694. An inventory of 9 July

[1] Cunliffe Shaw, Trans. Hist. Soc. Lancs., CXIV, 1962, pp. 33–6.
[2] Sylvester, Trans. Hist. Soc. Lancs., CX, 1958, p. 183.
[3] Youd, Trans. Hist. Soc. Lancs., CXIII, 1961, pp. 27–8.

1700 for Speke Hall does not add much to the evidence but it does indicate the possibility of a three-course rotation in the manor:[1]

'Five Acres of Wheatt in the Bankfield at £5. 10s.
  per Ac.   £27. 10. 0
Fourteen Acres of Oats in the Three Crofts at
  £2. 15s. per Ac.   £38. 10. 0
Beanes one acre in the further three Crofts   £ 4. 0. 0
Four Acres of oats in the Long Cross and
  Oglet Fields   £ 8. 0. 0'

As 'Three Crofts' is the only field mentioned in both sources it is the only basis for comparison and deduction. It follows that under a three-course rotation the Three Crofts which carried oats in 1694 would also carry oats in 1700. But it must be noticed that only 7 acres are mentioned in the first survey and 14 acres are listed in the inventory. As this is the only 'direct evidence' for Lancashire and none exists for Westmorland or Cumberland it must be assumed that the three-field system was marginal to the Northwest. Other evidence generally indicates a flexible form of field arrangement and evidence of a three-course rotation is frequently inconclusive. References such as those contained in the Stretford court rolls are problematic. A 'Wheat Croft' shared among some tenants cannot add much to the incomplete picture of farming except indicate that wheat was grown in the Northwest.[2] But 'Wheat Croft' is a fairly common field name even in Cumberland and Westmorland where wheat was never important as a field grain. If indirect evidence of this type is accepted then the probability of the former existence of three-course rotation is outweighted by data which emphasise the overwhelming importance of oats as the major cereal crop from early medieval times. In the township of Woolton which borders Speke on the north, a list of the demesne lands of Thomas de Halton compiled in 1324 lists 'six acres sown with wheat, one and a half acres with beans and peas, thirty three acres with oats collected and put in the grange'. His demesne lands in Hale produced '15 quarters 5½ strikes of wheat and 174 quarters 7 bushels of oats'.[3] This ratio of almost 13:1 does not seem synonymous with a three-course rotation. Further north the references to wheat are fewer and Singleton would invoke 'geographic rather than ethnic factors' for the distribution. While one would query his assumption that a map of twentieth-century crop distributions can be projected back to mirror medieval conditions the documentary

[1] Liverpool R.O., Norris Papers 2/520A.
[2] H. T. Crofton, *A History of the Ancient Chapel of Stretford*, 1893, p. 35.
[3] Farrer (ed.), *Lancashire Inquests and Extents*, part 2, pp. 211 and 213.

evidence does suggest that wheat growing has always been marginal in the Northwest and wheat has always been subordinated to oats and bigg as a cereal crop.[1]

II. CROPS AND PASTURE IN THE COMMON ARABLE FIELDS

While one of the chief functions of the common arable fields was to supply grain, it was not the only one. Other crops such as peas and beans could be grown. Mention has been made of these at Speke in the late seventeenth century, but as early as 1324 they were grown at Hale and there were orders in the town books of Liverpool relating to their gathering.[2] Such crops would have been easier to introduce into the flexible field arrangements of the Northwest than into the greater rigidity implied by the three-field system of the Midlands. Hemp and flax were also introduced at an early date and although they were probably grown in enclosed fields, as the frequency of Hemp Garth as a field name testifies, they and other crops, e.g. potatoes, vegetables, could be grown on the common arable lands, especially where these survived into the eighteenth and nineteenth centuries and especially where rapidly growing urban centres created a demand for them.[3] Some parts of the common arable fields were regarded as meadow and were cut for hay. Of 270 acres of infield at Aspatria 119 acres were classified as meadow and one of the peculiar features of references to riggs and dales in the Northwest is the frequency with which they are listed 'arable meadow and pasture' within the same field. This would seem to indicate changing use but it is not clear how this fitted in to crop rotations. Where the reanns formed unploughed strips they were grazed by tethered stock. This facility was especially used for cattle and horses, and the origins of the unploughed strip (balk) may lie in their usefulness during the ploughing season for this purpose. Otherwise it is difficult to understand why some are said to 'belong' to a particular tenant and why merestones should be set along them to divide one tenement from another.[4] At best they represent access strips along which footpaths may be made

[1] F. J. Singleton, 'The Influence of Geographical Factors on the Development of the Common Fields of Lancashire', *Trans. Hist. Soc. Lancs.*, CXV, 1963, pp. 31–40; Elliott, *CW2*, LX, 1960, p. 102 fn.

[2] Farrer (ed.), *Lancashire Inquests and Extents*, part 2, p. 213; Twemlow (ed.), *The Town Books of Liverpool*, p. 247.

[3] B. Dickens (ed.), *The Place-Names of Cumberland*, English Place-Name Society, vols. XX, XXI, XXII, 1950; M. C. Fair, 'The Townfields of Drigg', *CW2*, XXXIV, 1934, pp. 41–3.

[4] Cumberland R.O., D/Lons., Rosgill Court Verdicts 1690, Burgh Court Verdicts 1710, Kirkandrews Court Verdicts, 1703, 1707, 1710.

but at worst they represent a waste of arable land and a harbour for weeds. In order to graze the reanns stock had to be tethered and increasing concern over the disadvantages of this system, especially trespass of tethered cattle on to growing crops, led to frequent mention of such offences in the court rolls of the seventeenth and eighteenth centuries and a move on the part of some townships to further regulate and revise the whole system and occasionally to its abandonment.[1] Stubble provided grazing for stock after harvest and, in an attempt to rationalise this, manor courts resorted to the creation of stints or beast gates relative to each tenement. To equalise shares sheep, cattle and horses were graded according to the amount they could eat. The stints of Seaton (Cumb.) were 12 sheep per oxgang, and in Musgrave (Westmorland), 'for the good of the Townfield of Great Musgrave being sore abused and misorderly eaten for the future to have a pounder every year... and to be payed by tenants... for every horse lawfully taken in any of the feilds two pence every other beast one penny every seven sheep one penny'. In some areas swine were allowed in to the fields but it is generally stipulated that they must be ringed.[2] In Aspatria and Dean parts of the fields were quarried for stone and at Orgrave in Furness iron mines were eventually worked in the Townfields.[3] The maintenance of fertility was always one of the major problems in the cultivation of common arable fields, and the barrenness of Little Crosby in 1659 was not the only reflection of inadequacies of cultivation and management which characterised many areas of the Northwest by the seventeenth century. Where they were available, local products were used to maintain fields in good heart. From the twelfth century marl was used in Lancashire and Cheshire although its use does not seem to have reached the two northern counties until the late eighteenth century. One source particularly emphasises the marling of land before wheat was sown, and its value in improving a variety of soils together with its ready availability from many types of drift deposits made it an important part of land improvement programmes in Lancashire and Cheshire.[4] In coastal areas sea sand and seaweed were spread on fields. Known locally as 'tangle', the seaweed found on the south Cumberland coast

---

[1] Westmorland R.O., Musgrave D.P., Court Rolls 1704 and 1706; *Whiteside, Shappe in Bygone Days*, p. 196; Cumberland R.O., D./Lons., Kirkandrews Court Rolls 1703.
Westmorland R.O., Musgrave D.P., Court Rolls 1706; Cumberland R.O., D/Lons., Workington Court Rolls 1704, Seaton 1703, Blindcrake 1720.

[3] W. Farrer and J. Brownbill (eds.), *V.C.H. Lancashire*, 1914, III, 308; Elliott, *CW2*, IX, 1960, p. 107.

[4] R. W. Dickson, *General View of the Agriculture of Lancashire*, 1815, pp. 489–501; Davies, *The Agricultural History of Cheshire*, pp. 18, 51, 112.

was carefully divided among tenants, shares being called 'tangle dales' in Drigg (Cumb.).[1] But frequently the whole rhythm of the agricultural environment was broken by forces outside the cultivators' control. The impact of warfare between England and Scotland was frequently manifested by raids followed by a scorched earth policy. Border estates in particular suffered and the depressed value of agricultural land in the fifteenth and sixteenth centuries is attributed directly to raids by the Scots. In 1485 Humphrey Dacre received a rent of £3 2s. 6½d. from a group of manors which extended ten miles along the foot of the Pennines – the equivalent in value of 12 oxen. The low financial return from these manors was paralleled by the miserable condition of the tenants. Not only did they frequently lose crops and stock but occasionally their lives. The problem was so great that many townships were wasted and ploughs lay idle.[2] These conditions obtained in Lancashire in the fourteenth century and in the previous century the unsettled state of the Welsh border was brought to the notice of the Pope by the Bishop of Coventry.[3] Little is known of the impact on the field systems of such variable and local factors as the weather, changes in prices, bouts of plague, floods, cattle sickness and harvest failures. Occasionally documents throw shafts of light on the problem but the general patterns cannot be picked out. Some indicate gain, others loss.[4] Lord Edward Hanley returned from wars in Scotland and gave his tenants of Wray liberty to enclose 3 acres each from the common waste. But, in both Drigg and Holm Cultram, land was lost through being 'over blown with the sea sands'. Such references are indicative of factors affecting cultivation in common arable fields but are never sufficiently numerous for trends to be observed.[5]

B. THE COMMON MEADOWS

The management of common arable fields in the Northwest cannot be isolated from other aspects of land use, of which common meadows and waste were the most important. This integration of land resources

[1] P.R.O., M.B. Exch. K.R., vol. 37, fos. 78–9. This practice continued to the midnineteenth century: W. Dickinson, 'The Agriculture of Cumberland – Prize Report', *Jnl. R. Agric. Soc.*, XIII, 1853, p. 33.

[2] *Calendar of Inquisitions Post Mortem, Henry VII*, I, 67; *State Papers Henry VIII*, part IV, Correspondence relative to Scotland and the Borders 1513–1534, 1894, p. 492.

[3] Sylvester, *Trans. Hist. Soc. Lancs.*, CVIII, 1956, p. 9.

[4] Chippindall (ed.), *Hornby Castle Survey*, p. 37.

[5] P.R.O., M.B. Exch. K.R., vol. 37, fos. 78–9; Grainger and Collingwood, *Register and Records of Holm Cultram*, p. 170.

is typified by the way in which stock were moved from one type of land to another during the year. The role of the common meadows in this system was a dual one. During the summer they were cut for hay but in autumn the aftermath was grazed by stock, and it was a combination of these elements which kept the stock alive during the winter. In many townships 'meadow' is a term frequently used for parts of common arable fields ranging from 'a pece of medowe ground in the forme of a harpe...with narrow goringe points at the north and south endes... 2a. or. 10p.' to the larger areas of grass on balks which were grazed and cut for hay.[1] But in most townships there were areas of common meadow frequently divided into long narrow dales and normally situated on alluvial flats. They are referred to as Holm land or given a descriptive name, e.g. The Fittes, Benwray Flats, Willow Holm, some of which remained unenclosed until the nineteenth century. The seasonal use of alluvial flood plains within a township reflects a system which was dovetailed into the potentialities of the environment and is marked in particular by the concentration of use when the land would be least subject to flooding. This was emphasised where meadows were extensive enough to take on a special regional significance, e.g. along the lower Alt valley (Lancs.) and on the marshland fringes of the coast. Here large tracts of grassland, much of which was poorly drained, provided the regional framework for an intensification of stock farming. The Alt meadows were used for hay and for sheep grazing, and it is significant that one of the few medieval settlements in the marsh was Altcar which in 1232 was a grange of the Cistercian abbey of Merivale (War.). The use of the meadows along the Mersey enabled the Norris family of Speke to fatten cattle sent down from Rydal in the Lake District in the seventeenth century.[2] This regional integration of resources with the upland farms acting as suppliers of stock to be fattened on the richer lowland pastures had developed during the Middle Ages in the forest areas. During the twelfth century Wyresdale and Quernmore on the western edge of the Forest of Bowland (Lancs.) supplied the demesne arable areas of lowland Amounderness with stock. Macclesfield and Inglewood Forests were equally important for stock rearing, the expansion of which during the fourteenth century depended in part on the utilisation of riverine lowlands for grazing and hay. The value of this meadow was expressed in its high rentals. Even in lowland manors meadow was frequently more valuable than arable and in comparison to upland pasture it could be as much as sixteen times the

---

[1] Graham (ed.), *Survey of Gilsland Barony 1603*, p. 160.
[2] Cunliffe Shaw, *The Royal Forest of Lancaster*, p. 157; M. Armitt, *Rydal*, ed. W. F. Rawnsley, 1916, p. 245.

value. As early as 1283, demesne arable in Grasmere was let at 12*d*. per acre whereas meadow was let at 2*s*. 6*d*. per acre.[1]

The development of meadows was closely related to the economic development of the region in which they were located. Townships located on drove roads used by cattle on their way south from Scotland benefited by the expansion of this trade during the eighteenth century, and meadows were enclosed as land was brought up to meet the demands of an expanding market for stock food.[2] The growth of demand for pack horses in the West Cumberland coal-field increased the value of meadows in that area, and meadow land in Walton and Stretford (Lancs.) increased greatly in value during the eighteenth century as demands for hay increased in Liverpool and Manchester. But enclosure of common meadows was a slow process which proceeded in piecemeal fashion up to the beginning of the present century and was only rarely affected by the Parliamentary enclosure movement where an act was used to complete an enclosure. This tidying up process was generally part of legislation dealing with common waste and this type of enclosure became more common after the General Act of 6 William IV.

C. OUTFIELD CULTIVATION

Court rolls, miscellaneous deeds and estate papers are the chief sources of evidence for the cultivation of the common arable fields in the Northwest. Where outfield cultivation existed land was subject to a form of long ley farming which persisted in little modified form through to the nineteenth century in some areas. Bailey and Culley commented on the system in their report on the agriculture of Cumberland and were convinced that nine to twelve years of a rotation of oats, oats, barley, oats followed by seven to nine years in grass even on newly enclosed ground whose fertility had not been sapped by centuries of such farming 'remains a spectacle of the bad effects of such culture'.[3] Pringle remarked on a similar feature in Westmorland where the length of cultivation was four years followed by seven years in grass.[4] The variable length of this rest period can be traced back through the eighteenth century where it is associated

---

[1] J. C. Curwen (ed.), *Records of the Barony of Kendale*, 1924, I, p. 2.
[2] Eden, *State of the Poor*, 1797, p. 158; Cumberland R.O., Dean and Chapter D.P., Renewal of Leases 1672–1670.
[3] W. Bailey and G. Culley, *General View of the Agriculture of the County of Cumberland*, 1813, pp. 185–6.
[4] A. Pringle, *General View of the Agriculture of Westmorland*, 1797, pp. 270–1.

Table 2.2. Length of period of tillage in outfield cultivation

	Township	Period of cultivation (Years)	Period of fallow (Years)	Date
CUMBERLAND	Holm Cultram			
	(a) Hards of Holm	3	9	1780
	(b) Colt Park	3	6	
	Arlecdon	2	?	?
LANCASHIRE	Carnforth	3	6	1745
	Hornby	?	6	1584
	Biggar	5	5	?

Sources: Cumberland R.O., Mounsey–Heysham D.P., fo. 325; E. H. Sugden, *A History of Arlecdon and Frizington*, 1912, p. 8; Youd, *Trans. Hist. Soc. Lancs.*, CXIII, 1961, pp. 30–1; G. H. Pearson, 'The Town Books of Biggar', *CW2*, XI, 1911, p. 191.

with lands farmed in common arable fields (Table 2.2). It can only be explained in terms of local preference probably based on trial and error and possibly subject to change as intensification of land use cut down the length of a fallow period. Graham has suggested that this could have led to the creation of a one-field system.[1] This possibility is a mark of the versatility of outfield cultivation but there is no definite evidence that this actually happened. Rationalisation of an outfield most probably took the form of the systematisation of cropping units, land division within them, and where possible, a decrease in the length of a fallow period. By the sixteenth century the outfield was clearly divided up into a number of brakes or rivings and the plough was moved around each in turn, returning after a suitable rest period. This would imply a reallocation of land when an arable cycle was begun in those townships where primitive forms of land distribution persisted. Here the choice of a piece of common waste suitable for ploughing would be made, the land divided and ploughing begun. If the ridging of lands was a common feature of ploughing practice, each tenant could return to his own acre strips which would be still clearly marked from previous ploughings. The only definite reference to a pattern of holdings emerging at an early date in the outfield occurs in Mansergh (Westmld.) where the strips may have been distributed on the 'solskifte' principle. One of its characteristics – the location of holdings by reference to the sun – is clearly stated in a charter in the Chartulary of Cockersand Abbey where a tenant's acres are described '...and one acre, half of which lies towards the sun in

[1] Graham, 'The Townfields of Cumberland', *CW2*, X, 1910, p. 133.

Table 2.3. Samples of holdings in infields and outfields

Township		Outfield				Infield			
Aspatria	Size of holding (acres)	1	2	3	4	Very complicated (see Elliott, CW2, LX, 1960, p. 106)			
	No. of tenants	3	7	1	13				
Mockerkin	Size of holding (acres)	5	8	12	16	6	9	10	12
	No. of tenants	4	7	2	1	7	2	4	1
Fingland	Size of holding (acres)	10				21			
	No. of tenants	8				8			

Sources: P.R.O., Misc. Books, Exch. K.R., vol. 37, fos. 11–15, 35; vol. 42, fo. 20.

Siward's ridding and the other towards the sun in Gilbert's scale'. Other acres in the same township are described as 'versus boream' 'in occidente' and 'versus australem'.[1] This type of description is rare and if such orderly arrangement had previously existed in other townships it had been greatly changed by the time written evidence is complete enough to interpret patterns of holdings in the majority of townships. What is striking, however, is the relative equality of size of holdings in outfields. All eight tenants of Fingland (Cumb.) had an equal share of the eighty acres of outfield. In Aspatria the range in size is greater but does not compare to the complexity of holdings in the infield (Table 2.3). The township of Mockerkin (Cumb.) seems to be an intermediate type between the rigidity of Fingland and flexibility of Aspatria. If Fingland represents an earlier and simpler type of organisation then Aspatria shows what great changes could and did take place by exchange, sale or partible inheritance without destroying the coherence of the outfield. The outfield of some townships was not associated with an infield as such, but no doubt the method of cultivation employed on it would be the normal long ley farming with the emphasis on grass and pastoralism. Beckermet is a good example of this type, and even here the subdivision is marked by its uniformity (Table 2.4). When a period of cultivation in one part of the outfield was terminated the land was allowed to grass over naturally and became part of the common

[1] W. Farrer (ed.), Cockersand Chartulary, vol. III, part 2, Chetham Soc., N.S. LVII, 1905, pp. 1031–6. For a late survival of this see H. T. Crofton, History of the Ancient Chapel of Stretford, Chetham Soc., N.S. XLV, 1893, p. 34; Cunliffe Shaw, Royal Forest of Lancaster, p. 293; J. E. Prescott, Register of Wetheral, 1897, p. 367.

Table 2.4. An analysis of a survey of Beckermet (Cumberland) 1587

Above St Brides Church (acres)	Between Red Car Band and the Sea (acres)	The Outfield (acres)	Common Meadow (roods)	Red Car Meadow (acres)	Crofts (dales)	Peat Moss (fraction)
2	1	10	2	3	1	$\frac{1}{13}$
1	1	11	$\frac{1}{2}$	2	—	$\frac{1}{13}$
1	1	11	$\frac{1}{2}$	2	—	$\frac{1}{13}$
2	1	10	$\frac{1}{2}$	3	1	$\frac{1}{13}$
1	1	12	—	3	1	$\frac{1}{13}$
1	1	11	$\frac{1}{2}$	2	—	$\frac{1}{13}$
2	1	10	$\frac{1}{2}$	3	1	$\frac{1}{13}$
4	1	9	$\frac{1}{2}$	3	1	$\frac{1}{13}$
Total 14	8	84	5	21	5	$\frac{8}{13}$

Source: P.R.O., Misc. Books, Exch. K.R., vol. 37, 7.76.

waste. While it was under cultivation stock were allowed on to a riving during the winter months. 'After the last sheaf of corn has been Inned' is the day normally referred to in court rolls for the start of the grazing season, and the stock were removed in early spring to allow the land to be prepared for the following season's crop of oats or bigg.[1] This concentration on spring sown cereals was essential for the integration of pastoral and arable farming on the outfield. Without a supply of manure provided by grazing stock the length of period that an outfield was maintained under crops would have been further curtailed. Yet without the additional supply of fodder which the cereal stubble provided the stock could not have been kept through the winter.

The firmest evidence relating to outfield cultivation is from Cumberland. This may reflect the fact that it was well developed only in this county, but more likely reflects the incompleteness of information on methods of cultivation in the Northwest. Youd has however quoted Lucas's detailed description of Warton and found evidence from Hornby in the Lune valley of a long ley associated with fields held in strips. There are also references to infield but these are not associated with any evidence of an outfield in the same township. The importance of the Warton evidence lies in the fact

[1] Elliott, CW2, LIX, 1959, p. 91; Cumberland R.O., D/Sen. Court Rolls, Burgh 1709, Kirkandrews 1703. DX/128/7/1 Court Books, Aglionby 7 Edw., VI, Cumwhinton 43 Eliz.

that a description which obviously refers to outfield practice does not include the term outfield, but refers to divisions called 'thwaites'. These are the equivalent of Cumberland rivings, and indicate that in many townships where there is a complete field survey but no reference to outfield there could still be a form of long ley farming.[1]

Miss Sylvester has suggested this as a possible solution to the problem of cultivation in parts of Cheshire where 'the term outfield has never been encountered' but where the numerous 'riddings' may have served the same purpose.[2] This is strongly suggested in the survey of the demesne lands of Aston (Cheshire) where the twenty-eight tenants' holdings were dispersed among small divisions of the Town-field (Table 2.5) but where there was also 'the new marld field called the Great Brake (23 acres), Willows Ridding and the heath field'. We are not sure if the first two were shared by tenants or held in severalty, but most tenants had 'His acre on the heath' and the frequent reference to 'his part in the new hay' may refer to the Great Brake or Willows Ridding, 'hay' being used here in the sense of enclosure.[3]

D. THE COMMON WASTE

The common waste formed the largest single division of land in the Northwest, but within it there was a wide variety of terrain including both lowland and upland, mosses, moors and heaths. In a sense this waste represents the residue of land left after the processes of reclamation had gradually eaten into the more favoured areas, particularly on the plains and in the valleys. It was, however, an essential adjunct to common field farming for it represented the summer grazing for the townships' stock which was as carefully controlled as the manorial courts could make it. There gradually evolved a routine which enabled the courts to fix dates for the start and finish of a grazing season, allocate repair and maintenance of walls and hedges to keep stock from growing crops, limiting or banning foreigners' stock, and in some townships the number and type of stock grazing the common wastes was controlled by stints ('beast gates', 'stintins'). This develop-ment was probably more influenced by a township's inability to feed stock during the winter when they were brought on to the common arable, than any shortage of summer pasture on the wastes. The improvement of technical knowledge which could be applied to problems of land reclamation led to the enclosure of many lowland

[1] Youd, Trans. Hist. Soc. Lancs., CXIII, 1961, pp. 29–32.
[2] Sylvester, Trans. Hist. Soc. Lancs., CVIII, 1956, p. 7.
[3] Liverpool R.O., 920 MD 171, Survey Book of Sir Thomas Ashton 1636.

Table 2.5. The arrangement of holdings in Aston Townfield (Cheshire) 1636

	Tenant	Rabbit Land	Burton Hedge	Brick Butts	Beyond the Chappell	Dale Lands	Hang-mans Land	Ash-lands	Amidst the Chappell	New Marl	Christen-ing Lands	Wind-mill Land	Gum-bolte Stile	Total
1	John Hall		30p.		30p.									1r. 20p.
2	Rich. Higginson	½r. 21p.	½r. 11p.			½r. 29p.		¼r. 8p.	¼r.				¼r. 19p.	4r. 18p.
3	George Best				15p.									15p.
4	Thomas Harper				¼r.	½r. 2p.	¼r. 4p.		¾r. 13p.	¾r. 10p.		¼r.	¼r. 23p.	4r. 12p.
5	Thom. Birlainge				¼r. 4p.									14p.
6	Thom. Ratliffe				½r. 21p.	29½p.	18p.							2r. 8½p.
7	Henry Harper						¼r. 11p.				½r. 11p.			1r. 12p.
8	Thom. Mollat			¼r. 25p.			¼r. 1p.		35p.					2r. 1p.
9	John Harriman				37p.	34p.					¼r. 26p.	½r. 30p.		3r. 37p.
10	Thom. Pikeringe				39p.		½r. 10p.							1r. 29p.
11	Thom. Harper				¼r. 7p.				¼r. 22p.				30p.	1r. 9p.
12	John Hall								¼r. 28p.		26p.	¼r. 24p.	¾r. 26p.	3r. 34p.
13	John Jackson					¼r. 16p.		15p.			¼r. 36p.		19p.	2r. 26p.
14	Thom. Ffenells					¼r.				¼r. 16p.				36p.
15	Thom. Ashton					¼r. 15p.								25p.
16	John Bell	¼r. 1p.				31p.	¼r.							1r. 12p.
17	George Eeste					15p.								15p.
18	Thom. Ashton (2nd.)					¼r. 35p.								1r. 5p.
19	Mr Martin	1½r.								½r. 34p.			35p.	3r. 29p.
	Total	2r. 32p.	1r. 21p.	35p.	5r. 3p.	7r. 6½p.	2r. 24p.	33p.	3r. 38p.	1r. 26p.	3r. 19p.	2r. 14p.	5r. 2p.	37r. 13½p.

Source: Liverpool R.O., 920 MD 171, Survey Book of Sir Thomas Ashton 1636; r = rood, p = perch.

wastes in the seventeenth and eighteenth centuries before the period of Parliamentary enclosure which in the Northwest was more concerned with marginal land, upland moors, heath and mosses (Figs. 2.2 and 2.3). The relative lack of Parliamentary enclosure in Cheshire compared to the other three counties is as much a reflection of the physical environment as it is of the progressiveness of the county's landlords. It indicates that piecemeal enclosure of the waste had been very important in the county and other sources show that this had been proceeding steadily from the Middle Ages. In upland Cheshire, farms were established in valleys and along the foot of the hills. Sheep were grazed on the upper slopes and some valley land was enclosed for their use. This was followed by private enclosure of hill pastures and establishment of new farms in former grazing areas. In lowland Cheshire much early settlement dates back to medieval grants of land from the Crown. This resulted in the establishment of small freehold estates surrounded by assarts. During the Tudor period larger estates were established as sheep farms. These acted as the core from which further enclosure took place. As Mrs Davies has emphasised, however, this general sequence of colonisation and enclosure cannot be separated from local factors of soil, altitude and forest administration which affected the detail of the pattern.[1] In general terms it is also representative of the probable course of events in the other three counties. The enclosure of the Royal Forests of Lancaster and Inglewood owed much to the efforts of medieval lord and tenant, but in the latter case it left 28,000 acres to be enclosed by act in 1819, in spite of 1,994 acres having been improved between 1578 and 1619.[2] The large acreage still remaining as waste in the two northern counties was a measure of the amount of difficult land in the area and while 'the geological map' is not 'entirely the key'[3] to the enclosure history of the Northwest, physical factors certainly influenced both the location of the common wastes and the period when they were enclosed (Figs. 2.2 and 2.3).[4] This enclosure activity during the eighteenth and nineteenth

[1] Davies, *Agricultural History of Cheshire*, pp. 5–7.
[2] Cunliffe Shaw, *The Royal Forest of Lancaster*, pp. 321, 417, 437, 445; Tupling, *An Economic History of Rossendale*, pp. 23ff.; F. H. M. Parker, 'Inglewood Forest – Part IV', *CW2*, IX, 1919, p. 35; Parker, 'Inglewood Forest – Parts V and VI', *CW2*, X, 1910, pp. 1–29; Cumberland R.O., Survey of Inglewood Forest 1619. Enclosure Award, No. 135 – Inglewood Forest, 1819; W. Farrer (ed.), *Court Rolls of the Honor of Clitheroe*, III, 319, 417–19, 459–60.
[3] Lord Ernle, *English Farming Past and Present*, 1927, p. 167.
[4] G. Elliott, 'Some Aspects of the Changing Agricultural Landscape in Cumberland,' M.A. thesis, Liverpool University, 1956; G. Youd, 'Common Lands and Enclosure in Lancashire', M.A. thesis, Liverpool University, 1958; T. W. Fletcher, 'The Agrarian Revolution in Arable Lancashire', *Transactions of the Lancashire and Cheshire Antiquarian Society*, LXXII, 1962, pp. 93–123.

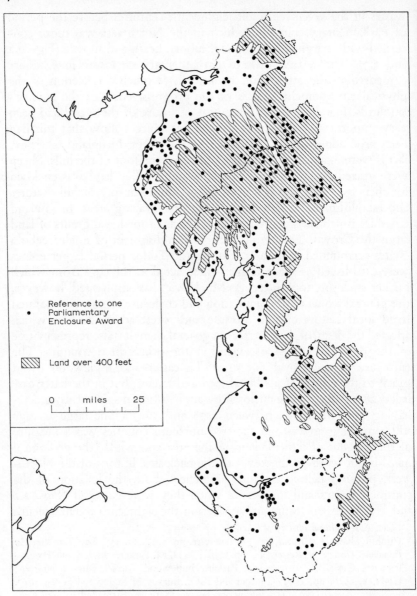

Fig. 2.2 The location of areas of common waste enclosed by Act of
Parliament 1750–1900 in Northwest England.
Sources. Cheshire R.O., Lancashire R.O., Cumberland R.O., Handlists of Enclosure
Acts and Awards. F. W. Garnett, *Westmorland Agriculture 1800–1900*, 1912, pp. 75–8.

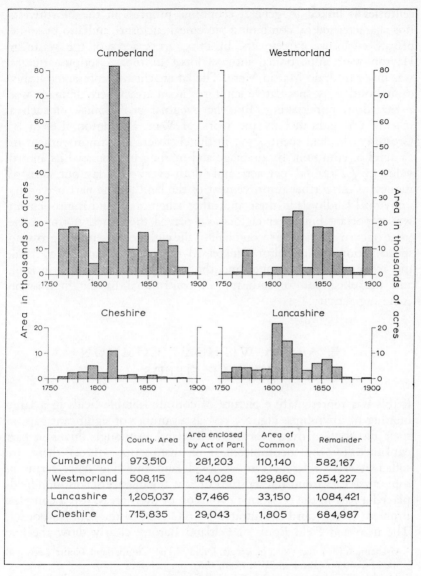

	County Area	Area enclosed by Act of Parl.	Area of Common	Remainder
Cumberland	973,510	281,203	110,140	582,167
Westmorland	508,115	124,028	129,860	254,227
Lancashire	1,205,037	87,466	33,150	1,084,421
Cheshire	715,835	29,043	1,805	684,987

Fig. 2.3 The chronology of enclosure of common waste by Act of
Parliament 1750–1900 in Northwest England.

Sources. G. Elliott, 'Some Aspects of the Changing Agricultural Landscape in
Cumberland', M.A. thesis, University of Liverpool, 1956. Garnett, *Westmorland
Agriculture 1800–1900*, pp. 75–8. G. Youd, 'Common Lands and Enclosure in
Lancashire', M.A. thesis, University of Liverpool, 1958. Cheshire R.O. Handlist of
Enclosure Acts and Awards.

centuries is linked to general economic progress in the Northwest. It is characterised by continuing piecemeal enclosure and also by some private enclosure agreements. In 1704, 2,125 acres of the waste in Hayton were apportioned into 88 lots.[1] In 1692 a serious attempt was made to drain Martin Mere. The latter scheme represented heavy capital outlay by speculative landlords in an area where drainage was a hazardous undertaking. But the eventual profitability of such a scheme was indicated by the work of Wm. Pilkington, Rector of Croston, who had spent £537 in the enclosure and improvement of 21 acres of common. By drainage and marling he increased its annual value to £2 12s. 6d. per acre and 'doth every year lay out sums of money in the further improvement of the land'.[2] The part played by individual landlords in these and other schemes of land improvement was important but other factors also played their part. A rise in the price of corn during the second half of the eighteenth century, growing specialisation in agriculture, increased returns from improved land, the accumulation of capital and the willingness to invest it in land, and the expansion of industry all contributed to the increase in enclosing activity.[3]

E. AREAS WITHOUT COMMON ARABLE FIELDS

If this is a representative picture of common arable fields in a large number of townships, Fig. 2.4 reveals a number of significant gaps in their distribution over Northwest England. Although this is in part explained by the incompleteness of manuscript sources there are sufficient early references to enclosed land and ring fence farms in some areas to warrant a closer study of how the absence of common fields played a part in the economic evolution of these areas. It is a complex problem which can be illustrated by reference to the Scottish border. The map and Field Book of Gilsland Barony clearly show the line

[1] Graham, *CW2*, VII, 1907, p. 43; R. Dilley, 'The Cumberland Court Leet and use of Common Lands', *CW2*, LXVII, 1967, pp. 125–51.
[2] Fletcher, *Trans. Lancs. and Cheshire Ant. Soc.*, LXXII, 1962, pp. 97–9; R. Millward, *The Making of the English Landscape – Lancashire*, 1955, pp. 52–3; Lancashire R.O., DRB/3, Croston Glebe Terrier 1728.
[3] Fletcher, *Trans. Lancs. and Cheshire Ant. Soc.*, LXXII, 1962, pp. 93ff.; W. E. Tate, 'A Handlist of English Enclosure Acts and Awards', *CW2*, XLIII, 1943, pp. 175–98; J. C. Curwen, *President's Report to the Workington Agricultural Society*, 1809, p. 82; Cumberland R.O., Mun. D.P. Correspondence Lord Muncaster and his agent 1745–1751; G. E. Fussell, 'Four Centuries of Cheshire Farming Systems, 1500–1900', *Trans. Hist. Soc. Lancs.*, CVI, 1954, pp. 57–79.

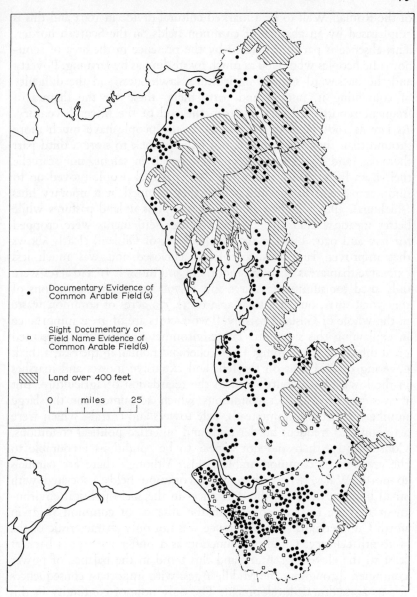

Fig. 2.4 A summary of evidence for common arable field(s) in
Northwest England.

Sources. G. Elliott, 'The System of Cultivation and Evidence of Enclosures in the
Cumberland Open Fields in the Sixteenth Century', *Trans. Cumberland and Westmorland
Antiq. and Arch. Soc.*, LIX, 1959, pp. 85–104. D. Sylvester, 'The Open Fields of
Cheshire', *Trans. Hist. Soc. Lancs.*, CVIII, 1956, pp. 1–33. G. Youd, 'The Common
Fields of Lancashire', *Trans. Hist. Soc. Lancs.*, CXIII, 1961, pp. 1–40.

of the Roman Wall to be a marked cultural divide in 1603 and this is emphasised by an absence of common fields on the Scottish border. This absence is partly explained by the presence in the area of semi-nomadic peoples who lived as much by stealing as by farming. Poverty and the backward state of agriculture, lawlessness and the difficulty of containing it, raiding and petty theft – these are the themes of frequent reports and surveys from the end of the fifteenth century. As late as 1601 poverty was so acute 'the people have much more ground than they can manage, not having stock to store a third part thereof...and could never keep their goods in safetie, nor scarcelie their own lives'. During summer these pastoral people moved up to summer pastures in the hills where they camped in temporary huts (shielings), allowing their stock to graze poor upland pastures while better meadow lands around their winter settlements were cropped for hay and oats. But the 1603 Field Book of Gilsland clearly shows that improved land was completely enclosed and was much less extensive than areas of rough moorland and mosses: 16,480 acres were only used for summer pastures and 13,798 acres were 'commons of the worst sort', out of a total area of 32,770 acres of common waste in the whole of Gilsland barony. Two factors are of great importance in explaining this situation. The environmental conditions presented great difficulties to farming. High relief and rainfall in the east, a thick covering of acid peat on the fells and extensive mosses and marshes in the lowlands all contributed to the retardation of agriculture. But it was unsettled border conditions which accounted for the large number of fortified homesteads, pele towers and corrals, which were a response to frequent border raids and unsettled political conditions. Consequently, there did not appear to be conditions favourable to the creation of common arable fields. Although there are parallels to north Wales, where there were common fields associated with small bond settlements, the differences in the socio-political environment may be the key to explain the absence of common fields in north Cumberland.[1] This difference was not only characteristic of the sixteenth century. Cumbria's function as a buffer zone goes back at least to the eleventh century and this trend in the balance of power continued throughout the Middle Ages, with important consequences for its agricultural development. The only note of continuity in this

[1] R. P. Sanderson (ed.), *A Book of the Survey of the Debatable and Borderlands, 1604*, 1891; J. Bain (ed.), *Calendar of Letters and Papers relating to the affairs of the Borders of England and Scotland*, 1894, I, 9; R. B. Armstrong, *The History of Liddlesdale, Ewesdale, Eskdale, Wauchopedale and the Debatable Land*, 1883, pp. 10, 66, 75; J. V. Harrison, 'Five Bewcastle Wills', *CW2*, LXVII, 1967, pp. 93–112; D. Tough, *The Last Years of a Frontier*, 1928, pp. 31–111; G. R. J. Jones, 'Some Medieval Rural Settlements in North Wales', *Trans. Inst. Br. Geogr.*, XIX, 1953, pp. 51–64.

period of flux was a continuing emphasis on pastoralism. The feudal lord was as much a 'cattle baron' as his tenants were 'Celtic cowboys', and it seems that if there were any similarities in agricultural practices between medieval north Wales and the Scottish border they were to be found in the area south of the Roman wall, where common arable fields played a part in the farming system.[1]

The other major gaps in the distribution of evidence for common arable fields are in the upland areas. Even today the bulk of the Lake District and Pennines are uncultivated and in the Middle Ages land utilisation was predominantly grassland with only small patches of arable. Common fields, where they existed, occupied patches of better soils in the dales. These areas were inhabited by small farms whose occupiers had frequently to combine farming with other occupations.[2] The holdings were minute. Forty-one holdings rented from Furness Abbey by tenants in Borrowdale only realised £28 10s. 0d. per year. The largest farm was ten acres and shortage of capital among the tenants is clearly expressed by the fact that the abbey had '40 kyne letten to farm to the tenants of Borrowdale after the rate of 2d. the cow'.[3] This pattern is repeated throughout the Lake District and is typical of many Pennine manors.[4] It is as typical of the Upper Irwell valley in Lancashire as of Eskdale in Cumberland. It is not surprising that extensive tracts of these uplands were created Forest areas in early medieval times, and in spite of attempts to expand crop cultivation with the declining importance of the Forests as sources of venison their whole economy was geared to cattle and sheep farms (vaccaries, herdwicks, berecaria) as the chief means of utilising rough hill pastures.

Apart from these two major zones there is a fairly even scatter of evidence for common arable fields over the rest of the area. Parts of the lowland resisted the expansion of farming until the eighteenth century because they were very light soiled or badly drained. These obviously were not common field areas yet even in the most difficult terrain a slight amelioration of conditions frequently led to the establishment of a common field settlement. This is especially noticeable in the poorly drained lowlands which border the Irish Sea from the Dee estuary to the Solway. Islands of boulder clay, raised beaches,

[1] D. P. Kirby, 'Strathclyde and Cumbria: a Survey of Historial Development to 1092', *CW2*, LXII, 1962, pp. 90–4; *Calendar of Inquisitions Post Mortem, Henry VII*, 1898, I, 67; *State Papers Domestic, Additional Volume Part I, Henry VIII*, 1902, p. 329; G. R. J. Jones, 'The Pattern of Settlement on the Welsh Border', *Agric. Hist. Rev.*, VIII, 1960, pp. 66–9.

[2] J. Thirsk (ed.), *Agrarian History of England*: IV, 1967, p. 20.

[3] B.M., Additional Mss. 24764, fos. 6 and 15.

[4] Cunliffe Shaw, *Royal Forest of Lancaster*, 1956, pp. 353–79; P.R.O., Misc. Books, Exch. K.R., vol. 37, fos. 23–8, 32–4, 35–8, 83–90.

old storm beaches, patches of lighter sands on heavy soils, outcrops of solid rock creating a dry point site within a marsh – all were utilised as settlement sites, and from them the farmers expanded their common fields to the limits of their technical knowledge in areas which were frequently badly drained, often inaccessible because of floods, occasionally overblown with sand and in extreme cases destroyed by high tides.[1] Such a pattern is indicative of the fact that one must approach with caution the concept that 'many of the mossland areas probably never had common fields'. It is evident that large areas on the coast plain remained waste until the eighteenth century or were reclaimed by the process of individual reclamation, but the bulk of the mossland townships had a core of common arable fields which represented very early colonisation and were the basis for later piece-meal reclamation. In many ways they were probably similar to the 'small islands of slightly higher elevated, better drained, sandy soils ...called *Esch* which are found in the lowlands of northwest Germany and on which common arable fields were developed in the Middle Ages'.[2]

F. ENCLOSURE HISTORY

I. CUMBERLAND

Up to the end of the sixteenth century the area of common fields in Cumberland continued to expand. Piecemeal enclosure had taken place in some townships prior to this date but it was on such a small scale that it had not greatly altered the form of the common fields nor interfered significantly with their use on a communal basis. It had consisted of occasional engrossing and fencing of individual holdings rather than a systematic replacement of common fields by individual closes.[3] By the middle of the eighteenth century however, there were clear signs that the impact of piecemeal enclosure which had been proceeding steadily for a century was being felt. This movement gained momentum during the second half of the eighteenth century and was responsible for the gradual eradication of the common arable fields. The evidence from glebe terriers provides a useful summary of conditions in the majority of cases by 1704 (Fig. 2.5) and indicates that the enclosure movement pre-dates the Act of Union (1707)

[1] Cunliffe Shaw, *Trans. Hist. Soc. Lancs.*, CXIV, 1962, p. 30; Grainger and Collingwood, *Register and Records of Holm Cultram*, pp. 170–2.
[2] H. Uhlig, 'Old Hamlets with Infield and Outfield Systems in Western and Central Europe', *Geogr. Annlr.*, XLIII, 1961, pp. 285–9.
[3] Elliott, *CW2*, LIX, 1959, pp. 100–3.

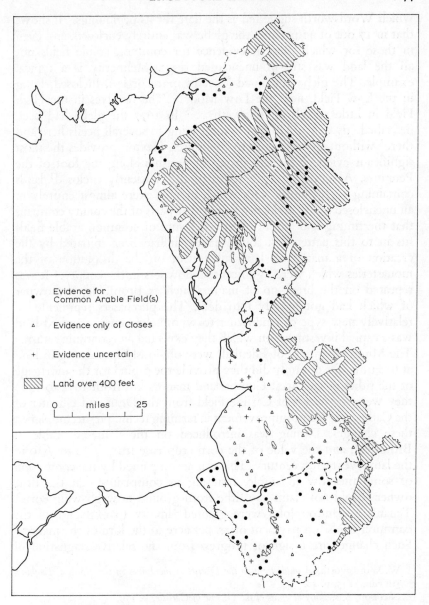

Fig. 2.5 Indications of common arable fields and enclosures in Northwest
England from information in glebe terriers, 1660–1830.

Sources. Cheshire R.O., EDV/8. Lancashire R.O., DRB/3, DRC/3, DRL/3, DRM/3.
Westmorland R.O., Glebe Terriers Ambleside – Preston Patrick. Cumberland R.O.,
DRC/9, DD/79. W. Nicolson, *Miscellany Accounts of the Diocese of Carlisle*, Ed.
R. S. Ferguson, 1877, pp. 159–241.

which Wordsworth suggested as the date for its beginnings.[1] It shows that in 17 out of 42 parishes the glebe was entirely enclosed, and even in those for which there is evidence for common arable fields not all the land was still in unenclosed riggs. Melmerby is a typical example. The glebe contained '2 acres more or less, Inclosed, lying in the Low Field, next the Low Moor...The rest lyes in the High Field in little parcels as followeth...'[2] In 1677 the glebe had been described 'tis worth 8 lb. per annum lying in severall pcells here and there' without any reference to enclosures. Hayton provides the most significant evidence for this group of parishes along the foot of the Pennines. A survey of 1710 refers to the 'anciently enclosed' lands containing 1,478 statute acres which in 1603 were almost entirely in an unenclosed state.[3] Evidence from other parts of the county confirms that the timing and nature of the enclosure of common arable fields fits in to this pattern. In some manors it had been initiated by the creation of a market in land subsequent on the dissolution of the monasteries which were significant landowners in the county.[4] It was repeated on the break-up of manors such as Bromfield, the owner of which had got heavily into debt. The purchasers represented a relatively new type of landowner to whom the newly acquired land was a capital investment on which they expected an economic return.[5] The Musgrave family of Edenhall were obviously speculating in land at this time, for not only did they provide the capital for the mortgage of the tithes of two west Cumberland manors but from 1674 to 1702 they were the lessees of Carlisle Field from the Dean and Chapter of the Cathedral.[6] Some improvement in farming techniques accompanied these changes. Liming was introduced on the demesne arable at Bromfield, and the value of the corn crop rose from £20 to £30 in the late seventeenth century. This was accompanied by the conversion of some meadow to arable, resulting in complaints that the tithe owner 'could not claim hay tithe from ground now growing corn'. Tenants at Hutton John were granted 'liberty to exchange in the common fields' on payment of 2s. per acre to the lord of the manor.[7] Such changes are a sign of progress from the relative stagnation of

[1] W. Wordsworth, *A guide through the District of the Lakes in the North of England*, 5th edn, 1835, p. 46.
[2] Nicolson, *Miscellany accounts of the Diocese of Carlisle*, p. 179.
[3] Graham, *CW2*, VII, 1907, p. 53; Graham (ed.), *Survey of Gilsland Barony*, p. 132.
[4] Grainger and Collingwood, *Holm Cultram*, pp. 159–63, 167; Bouch and Jones, *The Lake District*, pp. 55–6; Jackson Collection, Tullie House, Carlisle, Documents relating to Abbey Holm 1628, 1646.
[5] B.M., Add. Mss. 27409.
[6] *Ibid*. Cumberland R.O., Renewal of Leases Dean and Chapter 1674 and 1682.
[7] Cumberland R.O., Hutton John D.P.

Table 2.6. Enclosure of common arable fields by
private agreement in Cumberland

Township	Date of agreement	No. of shares
Arlecdon	1697	8
Bothel	1726	4
Dean	1753	11
Aspatria	1758	24
Aspatria	1759	22
Seascale	1764	13
Oughterside	1776	18
Whitrigg	1776	11
Beaumont	1781	?
Haverigg	1797	23

Sources: Dean Church Papers 1753; W. Sugden, History of Arlecdon, p. 8; Elliott, CW2, LX, 1960, pp. 107 and 108; Cumberland R.O., Seascale D.P., Private Enclosure Agreement 1764; Mounsey–Heysham D.P., Private Enclosure Agreement for Beaumont 1781; DX/104, Private Enclosure Agreement of Haverigg 1797; Mounsey–Heysham D.P., Private Enclosure Agreement for Bothel 1726.

the previous century. They were particularly marked in west Cumberland where the increasing development of coal led to a variety of changes. Land values increased as the prospect of finding coal extended. There was a great demand for pack horses and many farmers became carters taking coal and lime down to the ports.[1] But the Court Rolls of the Lawson, Lowther, Pennington and Senhouse manors, which cover the major part of west Cumberland from the Solway to the Duddon, indicate that although change was evident in the first half of the eighteenth century, the enclosure of common arable fields was not tackled systematically until the second half. Up to 1750 the process of piecemeal enclosure was proceeding but after 1750 a number of private enclosure agreements were made between lords of the manor and tenants, which besides completing the redistribution and fencing of strips also reveals that this method was much quicker and cheaper than Parliamentary enclosure (Table 2.6).

Preceding this type of organised enclosure, there had been some attempt to rationalise the common arable fields in the county. In 1731 the glebe land of Aspatria is described: 'There is to the vicar about 4 acres of plowing ground in the East Outfield and as much in the west Outfield except when the Hall Banks is plowed and then he has

---

[1] Cumberland R.O., Lawson D.P. Proposals for letting Oughterside Colliery 1760; Hutchinson, History of Cumberland, II, pp. 93, 99, 100.

scarce one acre four years.' This indicates that the outfield as described in 1576 was now split into two parts, each of which was organised quite separately. If interpreted literally the 'four years' would refer to a four year period under crops and when the fields of Aspatria were eventually enclosed in 1758/9 these two divisions were the subject of separate agreement.[1] Advantages of such a rationalisation had been envisaged as early as 1640 when the tenants of Brigham had reallocated their land 'for the better lying it together' and put it in three groups – Eastfields, the Craggs and Wood. These were still managed as common arable fields but their management had been simplified by this redistribution.[2] Eventually the new riggs and dales were fenced and the whole process completed by piecemeal enclosure. In central Cumberland there was a parallel emphasis on stock but the references here are to sheep and cattle which were annually driven south from Scotland. One of the great drove routes lay through Hesketh and Plumpton and 'Drovers Lane' is still a street name in Carlisle and Penrith. Arable was converted to grass in these areas to provide sufficient herbage for the thousands of stock that passed through each year. This trade must have been affected, as was a large area of the Northwest, by the cattle plague of the mid-eighteenth century. Bans were imposed on the movement of cattle, fairs were closed for three to nine months. Many cattle were either sold off just before the plague struck or were killed by the disease when it swept through the area. Landlords and tenants felt the effects. Sir J. Pennington could not let his park land for grazing and many tenants had not the cattle to fill their stints.[3] Bell suggested that it encouraged conversion to arable and was a powerful force in enclosure.[4] As it was immediately followed in Cumberland by a period when the value of stock products fell and the price of grains rose this may well have applied.[5] Although there is no record of its impact this may have been another contributory factor to the known upswing in the curve of enclosure of common arable fields in the second half of the eighteenth century. Others which could be cited would include an expanding population, particularly in west Cumberland; the development of military and later turnpike roads, the expansion of the textile industry in Carlisle which encouraged

[1] Elliott, *CW2*, IX, 1960, pp. 100 and 107.
[2] Jackson Collection, Tullie House, Carlisle, Brigham Paine, *c.* 1640.
[3] J. F. Curwen, *The Later Records of North Westmorland*, 1932, p. 225; Cumberland R.O., Pennington D.P., Correspondence Sir J. Pennington and his agent 1750.
[4] J. Bell, 'The Cattle Plague in Westmorland and Cumberland 1745–54', 1883, p. 6; Sir Lees Knowles, *Records of the Manor Court of Thurton 1737–1850*, 1909, p. 29.
[5] Cumberland R.O., Pennington D.P., Correspondence Sir J. Pennington and his agent 1750–52.

an expansion of hemp and flax growing in the north of the county, and the influence of individual landlords.[1] By 1789 Clarke could write of the 'wonderful changes' enclosure was making in the Lake Counties and as the enclosure of the wastes was just beginning he probably was referring in part to the enclosure of arable.[2] Both Housman and Eden were more specific in their references to this, and, besides giving impressions of the common arable fields which still remained, referred to enclosures in some parishes. No extensive area of common field arable was dealt with by Parliamentary enclosure acts and this led Slater and Gonner to assume that the common arable fields had never been important.[3] Such an assumption does not accord with the documentary evidence, and it is the importance of piecemeal enclosure and private agreement which explain this absence. Those common fields which were dealt with by act were included as part of an act for the enclosure of common waste or they were small parcels of common meadow. The natural result of the predominance of piecemeal enclosure is that the common field strip became fossilised in the enclosed landscape. Fragmentation of holdings persisted until the twentieth century; there were many 'quilleted holdings' remaining as a result of the inclusion of isolated riggs in closes created by tenant/ owners of common field land; and the line of bank and hedge in the present landscape often represents the line of a reann from the common fields it has replaced T. H. B. Graham made a valuable survey of such survivals in Cumberland and his work was followed by more detailed reports from Drigg and Threlkeld of fields still divided into 'rig an' reann'.[4]

---

[1] G. P. Jones, 'Some Population Problems relating to Cumberland and Westmorland in the Eighteenth Century', *CW2*, LVIII, 1958, pp. 123–39; R. Maxwell, *The Practical Husbandman, A Collection of miscellaneous papers on husbandry*, 1757, p. 248. Grainger and Collingwood, *Holm Cultram*, p. 247.

[2] J. Clarke, *A Survey of the Lakes of Cumberland, Westmorland and Lancashire*, 2nd edn, 1789, p. xxiv; T. H. Bainbridge, 'Eighteenth Century Agriculture in Cumbria', *CW2*, XLII, 1942, pp. 56–66.

[3] Hutchinson, *A History of Cumberland*, 1794, I, pp. 143, 180, 181, 203, 212; Eden, *The State of the Poor*, 1797, II, pp. 45, 65, 67, 68. Tate, *CW2*, XLIII, 1943, pp. 175–98; Elliott, 'Changing Agricultural Landscape in Cumberland', pp. 81–3; Slater, *The English Peasantry and the Enclosure of the Common Fields*, p. 274; E. C. K. Gonner, *Common Land and Enclosure*, 1912, pp. 124–30.

[4] Dickinson, *Jnl. R. Agric. Soc.*, XIII, 1853, p. 34; L. D. Stamp (ed.), *Land Utilisation Survey of Britain. Part 49. Cumberland*, 1943, pp. 310, 312, 315; T. H. B. Graham, 'The Townfields of Cumberland, Part 2', *CW2*, XIII, 1913, pp. 1–30.

2. WESTMORLAND

Documentary evidence points to a close similarity between the enclosure history of Cumberland and Westmorland, although the latter county has not yet received the same attention in published work. There is the same absence of Parliamentary enclosure of common fields which, from the list in Garnett's *History of Westmorland Agriculture*, was only responsible for the enclosure of 500 acres.[1] 'Only a very few open fields on the east side of the river Eden' remained when Pringle wrote his Report for the Board of Agriculture (1797) and this impression is corroborated by evidence from the Lonsdale and Musgrave archives which cover much of north Westmorland.[2] Eighteenth-century estate maps, surveys and court rolls indicate that in most cases the common arable fields had been subjected to steady attrition, leaving the characteristic features of piecemeal enclosure that were found in Cumberland. Riggs and dales still remained but they were mostly in small isolated blocks. An exception could be found in a 1764 estate map of Murton where there were three large unenclosed fields – North Field, Murton Moor Field and Murton Little Field – split into 231 riggs.[3] This evidence is in contrast to that for the beginning of the century when only two of the twenty-four areas of glebe were definitely enclosed. Many of the surveys reveal that even consolidation had not proceeded very far, e.g. Ormside, Warcop and Appleby, although part of the glebe in the latter parish had been enveloped by the enclosure of Christopher Gregson in which the vicar still retained his half-acre.[4] The management of the fields still appeared to be on traditional lines but most references in court rolls are to the management of stock rather than to the cultivation of the land. This was a reflection of the pastoral bias in the area, but it may also be related to the fact that stock management in common arable fields was the most likely cause of offences to be tried at manorial courts. Townships along the eastern side of the Eden valley carried large flocks of sheep which grazed stubble in winter when their diet was supplemented by hay, and in summer they were driven to high pastures on the Pennines. In some cases complex regulations were evolved to deal with the handling of sheep in the lowlands after the

[1] Garnett, *History of Westmorland Agriculture 1800–1900*, pp. 71–2, 75–8.
[2] A. Pringle, *A General View of the Agriculture of the County of Westmorland*, 1797, p. 269; Cumberland R.O., D/Lons. Court Rolls Bampton 1747–1760, Crosby Ravensworth and Maulds Meaburn 1729–1828, Great Strickland and Melkinthorpe 1703–1724, Lowther 1732–1839; Plans 117, 134, 141, 161, 162, 164, 168, 190, 195, 243; Westmorland R.O., Musgrave D.P., Court Rolls 1631–1730.
[3] Cumberland R.O., D/Lons., Plan 198.
[4] Nicolson, *Miscellany Accounts of the Diocese of Carlisle*, pp. 185–8.

common arable fields had been sown with oats and before the sheep could be sent on to the fell pastures which, because of their altitude, could not support sheep until June. The townships made full use of any low common at this time, but some were so short of lowland pastures that sheep were allowed to remain in the lanes (lonning) which surrounded the settlements and linked them to the high pastures to which the sheep were sent after lambing, and to which they were brought for shearing in June.[1] It is clear that in this type of environment, the management of sheep with a common field arable system precluded the use of winter sown crops and led to heavy demands on any available winter pasturage. The long narrow parishes stretching some five miles from the upper Pennines to the Eden valley are a form of adaptation to these conditions and the heavy demands on winter grazing led to the necessity of stinting the common arable fields. Occasionally these stinting rules were broken, resulting in the 'Townfield...being sore abused and misorderly eaten'.[2] The remedy was to employ a pounder who had to make sure the stints were carefully maintained. This form of stock management was paralleled in some Lake District manors. The tenants of Shap combined to reclaim the waste in 1621 and the 'new Intake' which they made had to be separated from a neighbouring close by a wall five feet high. By 1671 the land had decreased in quality and the stint had to be reduced from five beast gates to three.[3] Cattle were also reared in these fell townships. In Kentmere each quarter into which the manor was divided had its common Cow Pasture in the valley and access to vast areas of upland grazing. Parts of the Cow Pasture were broken up and ploughed as in other northern manors but the emphasis was on pastoralism rather than cultivation.[4] Consequently the cattle plague of the mid-eighteenth century, which caused the stoppage of Kirkby Stephen fair in 1746 and the cessation of trade in cattle, hit Westmorland as hard as Cumberland.[5] This was not the first time the area had been hit. In 1631 'the sickness' was rife in Walney and the Flemings of Rydal bought no cattle at Ravenglass that year.[6] By 1689 they had by judicious management improved the quality of their estate and the increased revenues from agisted cattle point to a lucrative and well managed form of pastoral husbandry.[7] Yet management of this type and on this scale was rare, and as in the Cumberland part of the

[1] Westmorland R.O., Musgrave D.P., Court Rolls 1697.
[2] Westmorland R.O., Musgrave D.P., Court Rolls 1695.
[3] Whiteside, *Shappe in Bygone Days*, p. 197.
[4] Westmorland R.O., Musgrave D.P., Kentmere Court Rolls 1837 and 1847.
[5] Curwen, *The Later Records of North Westmorland*, p. 225.
[6] Armitt, *Rydal*, p. 245.   [7] *Ibid.*, p. 250.

Lake District, a few acres of valley land and a right to graze stock on the common pasture was more usual. Factors such as a decline in stock prices from 1750 to 1790 would slow down the rate of economic growth in the mountain townships and it was not until the middle of the nineteenth century that there are clear signs of enclosing activity of common fields. References such as 'any who inclose ground in Rosgill Field' are relatively rare, and the indications of a market in land in the Lowther area in the mid-eighteenth century represent the greater potential of this area on the northern edge of the county.[1] The result was that although piecemeal enclosure, supplemented by a tidying up process in the form of thirteen Parliamentary awards affecting common fields, gradually created an enclosed landscape in the mountain valleys there occasionally remained the small bundle of strips as recorded in Rydal as late as 1916. 'The Townfield towards Easedale, is known, and yet unenclosed in parts, while the mere stones which divide one man's balks or strips from his neighbours, are not all gone.'[2] In contrast to the Lake District, the area of Westmorland lying south of Kendal is lower and more fertile. Celia Fiennes noted enclosed 'Lands...very rich good Land enclosed – Little round green hills flourishing with Corn and grass as green and fresh.'[3] Such a description of the drumlin country indicates in general terms the progress of enclosure in this area by 1700, and although glebe terriers indicate scattered survivals of common arable fields (Fig. 2.5) court rolls and estate plans of extensive Lonsdale Estates in south Westmorland confirm Celia Fiennes' dating of enclosures. By 1750 only a few scattered references are made to dales in common fields.[4]

3. LANCASHIRE

Enclosure of common fields in Lancashire and Cheshire took place earlier than it did in the two northern counties. In a detailed review of the evidence Youd saw both piecemeal enclosure and enclosure by agreement contributing to this. He could find no evidence that would support Millward's assertion that the sixteenth century was a period of more rapid enclosure and he summarises the movement as being closely associated with reclamation and enclosure of common waste

---

[1] Bouch and Jones, *The Lake Counties*, p. 234; Cumberland R.O., D/Lons., Rosgill Court Rolls – Verdicts 1690, Great Strickland and Melkinthorpe Court Rolls 1735, Helton Fleckett Court Rolls 1740.
[2] Armitt, *Rydal*, p. 58.
[3] Bouch and Jones, *The Lake Counties*, p. 97.
[4] Cumberland R.O., D/Lons., Court Rolls Grayrigg/Lambrigg 1704–1808, Barony of Kendal 1650–1660, Kirkby Lonsdale 1702–1797. Plans 207, 214.

Table 2.7. Evidence of enclosure from glebe terriers
1660–1830

County	No. of references	Evidence only of closes	Evidence of common arable fields	Uncertain evidence
Cumberland	32	17	13	2
Westmorland	24	2	18	4
Lancashire	55	30	11	14
Cheshire	56	18	35	3

Sources: Cheshire R.O., EDV/8; Lancashire R.O., DRB/3, DRC/3, DRL/3, DRM/3; Westmorland R.O., Terriers, Ambleside – Preston Patrick; Cumberland R.O., DRC/9, DD/79; Nicolson, *Miscellany Accounts of the Diocese of Carlisle*, pp. 159–241.

which proceeded steadily from the fourteenth to the eighteenth and nineteenth centuries.[1] The evidence from glebe terriers for the period 1680 to 1880 indicates that few common field strips remained in Lancashire by the middle of the eighteenth century and of the 55 parishes for which glebe terriers produce any evidence, in 30 cases the glebe is in closes and 14 are doubtful cases (Table 2.7). The striking concentration of common arable land in south Lancashire where half the Lancashire evidence for this type of cultivation occurs is a particular feature of this distribution (Fig. 2.5). It is not only the quantity but the relatively complete nature of the eighteenth-century evidence for south Lancashire which, when taken in conjunction with evidence from other sources, yields a fairly complete picture of the later stages in the break-up of some Lancashire common fields. A well-documented case exists in Walton (Liverpool). The glebe terrier of 1686 lists nine tenants holding scattered strips of glebe land in four common fields, Heatherlow, Spellow Field, Church Field and Hatch Field. One tenant also had 'one acre and a roodland by the Midland side'. As far as can be inferred from the glebe evidence this parish situated on a sandstone ridge overlooking the River Mersey was being cultivated as it had been since the Middle Ages. Earlier evidence points to the continuity of common field arrangements. 100 acres of arable and 20

[1] Youd, *Trans. Hist. Soc. Lancs.*, CXIII, 1961, p. 40; Millward, *Lancashire*, pp. 48–9. For late survivals see: T. Ellwood, 'The Reanns of High Furness', *CW1*, XI, 1891, pp. 361–7; R. E. Porter, 'The Townfields of Coniston', *CW2*, XXVIII, 1928, pp. 273–7; W. Butler, 'The Townfields of Broughton- and Subberthwaite-in-Furness', *CW2*, XXVIII, 1928, pp. 293–302; H. Williams, The Halmote Court Rolls of the Manor of Crosby, 1452–1880, 2 vols., Mss. in Bootle Public Library (typescript copy).

acres of pasture mentioned in a survey of 1586 can be roughly equated with the 138 acres which the common or 'Townfields' covered in 1639 when they were shared between 6 landlords:

Richard Chorley (lord of the manor)	46 acres
Robert Fazakerley	30 „
Roger Breeres	30 „
Dr A. Clare, Parson of Walton	20 „
Richard Lord Mollineux	8 „
Nicholas Walley	4 „
	138 „

This 138 acres together with 1,200 acres of common waste made up the bulk of the township land. But the picture was not static. The 1638 survey mentioned encroachments on the waste by Mr Fazakerley of Spellow House and his tenants, and by the latter part of the eighteenth century two significant changes had taken place. In 1761 the common waste was enclosed by act of Parliament adding 19 acres and 32 perches to the glebe in three parcels. In spite of a refusal on the part of the rector to pay his enclosure expenses, the land being mortgaged to Sir Thomas Heathcote until they were paid, this newly enclosed land was rapidly improved by marling.[1] Eight acres 10 perches called 'the Fazakerley allotment' had their value increased to £18 and with this rate of progress it was estimated the glebe would be free of mortgage in ten years. Another parcel of 4 acres 3 roods 19 perches (Walton Breck) was let for £20 2s. 0d. per year. At the same time changes were taking place in the common fields. By 1763 Spellow Field had become Spellow Crofts and was enclosed. Whereas in 1686 the glebe had five tenants there, by 1763 the number had been reduced to one.[2] Replacing the 5 ridges (lands) were 2 crofts, one acre called Spellow Field Hey, and the remains of 2 ridges. This was obviously a case of piecemeal enclosure which was not accompanied by a serious attempt to consolidate the scattered ridges into blocks and they were recorded in the schedule accompanying the Tithe Award for Walton (Table 2.8).[3] In Hatchfield 1½ hallands had been enclosed, Church Field had disappeared but Townfield replaced it as a location name in which holdings were still unenclosed apart from 'one and a half halland inclosed'.[4] Other location names which occur in 1763 but were not in the 1686 glebe terrier are 'at the side of Bottle Road'

---

[1] Lancashire R.O., DRL/3, Walton Terriers 1686 and 1761; R. D. Radcliffe (ed.), *The Chorley Survey...1652*, Rec. Soc. Lancs. and Ches., XXXIII, 1896, pp. 33–54.
[2] Lancashire R.O., DRL/3, Walton Terrier 1763.
[3] Lancashire R.O., Tithe Map and Schedule, Walton.
[4] *Ibid.*

and 'Near Bootle Gate', Bootle being a neighbouring township. The number of tenants had increased to 13 and only three surnames were common to each list indicating probable changes in tenancy. The appearance of Townfield as a field name within Walton is of interest because it reveals the changing character of the common fields but it has obviously not the same connotation as the 'Townfield' of the 1638 survey which applied to the whole of the parish's common arable fields. By 1840 the glebe was completely enclosed but the persistence of earlier field names marked a link between the closes and the common fields they had replaced (Table 2.8). Taken in conjunction with fields in other ownership and linked to evidence from the Tithe Map they give a fairly accurate idea of the exact location and former extent of the common fields. But by this time there were signs of the village coming under the influence of the growing port of Liverpool and successive Ordnance Survey plans show the gradual obliteration of the former townfields under the spread of late nineteenth and early twentieth-century urban expansion. The only survival of earlier conditions is the use of Spellow Lane as a street name in the parish.

Liverpool's own Townfield had been engulfed by urban expansion in the mid-eighteenth century. Its evolution has been traced in detail and Fig. 2.6 shows how the layout of furlongs in the townfield can still in places be traced in the city's street plan. The survival of the townfield into the eighteenth century runs counter to the idea that the ease with which burgage tenements could be transferred by gift, sale or bequest greatly facilitated early piecemeal consolidation and enclosure of such land.[1] The evidence in Liverpool points to this process leading to an increasing complexity of holdings from the fourteenth century. Burgage tenements were split into small lots and the increasing number of holders allied to the increasing value of land made consolidation very difficult.[2] But the burgesses were not the only holders of lands in the townfield. Whether by grant or purchase of former burgage land the tenantry of the townfield became diverse and in this respect there was an important difference between Liverpool and Kirkham where the rentals show 'subdivision...did not happen' and the fields were enclosed in the sixteenth century.[3]

[1] Stewart-Brown, Trans. Hist. Soc. Lancs., LXVIII, 1917, pp. 30–4; Cunliffe Shaw, Trans. Hist. Soc. Lancs., CXIV, 1962, pp. 24–5.
[2] Twemlow (ed.), Townbooks of Liverpool, pp. 419–29; Brownbill (ed.), Moore papers, pp. 62–76.
[3] Cunliffe Shaw, Trans. Hist. Soc. Lancs., CXIV, 1962, p. 25.

Table 2.8. Rector's glebe land in the Tithe Schedule for Walton (Lancashire) 1840

Field no. (refers to Tithe Map)	Field name	Use	Area		
			a.	r.	p.
346	Spellow Field	Potatoes Vegetables	3	—	1
322				2	10
283	2 cottages and 3 gardens		—	—	25
282			—	—	19
56	Rector's Hey	Clover Meadow	5	3	13
56a	Rector's Hey	Clover Meadow	1	2	32
425	Heatherlow	Meadow	5	1	38
427	Heatherlow	Meadow	1	3	16
372	2 cottages and gardens		—	3	11
319	Garden		1	—	27
280	Rectory		1	3	18
283a	Garden		—	2	28
279	Lawn	Pasture	4	—	3
284	Hatch Field	Pasture	3	2	12
312	Grave Yard		1	3	4
315	School		1	2	8
198	Church Field	Meadow	1	3	37
281	Farm		—	1	2
300	Little Church Field	Wheat	4	1	16
311	Church Field	Clover Meadow	12	3	31
321	House and garden		—	2	2
349	Mill Lane Field	Clover Meadow	3	1	32
423	Part of Hetherlow	Meadow and Wheat	9	—	22
426	Hetherlow	Meadow and Wheat	6	2	18
344	Spellow Field	Pasture	1	3	31
347	Spellow Field and Higher Spellow Field	Meadow	7	—	31
192	Hatchfield	Mangold Wurzel	2	2	19
			51	—	1

Source: Lancashire R.O., Tithe Schedule: Walton.

4. CHESHIRE

Recent studies reveal a fossilisation of former common fields in the rural landscape of west Cheshire.[1] Tithe maps and schedules have been related to earlier documentary evidence to show that many

[1] Chapman, *Trans. Hist. Soc. Lancs.*, CXIV, 1953, pp. 35–61.

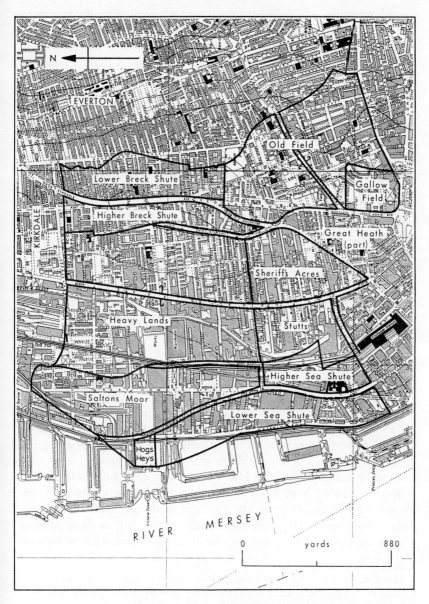

Fig. 2.6 The Townfield of Liverpool.
Sources. R. S. Brown, 'The Townfield of Liverpool 1207–1807', *Trans. Hist. Soc. Lancs.*, LXVIII, 1917, p. 36. Base-map reproduced from the Ordnance Survey Map with the sanction of the Controller of H.M. Stationery Office, Crown Copyright reserved.

complex tenurial and field patterns have been created by the piecemeal enclosure of common arable land, with an occasional survival of 'quilleted holdings' marking the penultimate stage in the transfer to a fully enclosed landscape. The relative fertility of Cheshire soils and the former importance of common field farming is indicated by Miss Chapman's statement: 'In a number of townships strip-like field shapes alone suggest that open fields once covered three-quarters or more of the total area of the township.'[1] This contrasts with the estimate of one-seventh for Cumberland and one-tenth for Lancashire and suggests that smallness cannot have been a factor facilitating their early enclosure.[2] Yet by 1794 Wedge estimated that only 1,000 acres of common field remained in Cheshire and the fact that only two common fields were enclosed by act of Parliament (Chester and Frodsham) indicates large-scale enclosure some time before the end of the eighteenth century.[3] Some evidence has been quoted to show the earliness of the start of this process but most of it is of such a fragmentary nature that the detail and trends are still relatively unknown.[4] Other work on Cheshire has concentrated on medieval sources to show the character and organisation of Cheshire field systems.[5] Consequently the period from 1500 to 1800 has been neglected in tracing the decay of the common fields. Evidence from glebe terriers helps to fill in the gap from 1650 to 1800, and Fig. 2.5 shows that 35 cases of existing common fields can be found in eighteenth-century evidence and their distribution is wide enough to represent any regional variations in the history of enclosure within the county. It is obvious that the enclosure movement which affected Lancashire up to the eighteenth century did not effect Cheshire to the same extent. Moreover many of the parishes for which glebe terriers indicated common arable fields in the eighteenth century were not only large parishes with a number of fields but also 'small settlements' where conditions have been assumed to be conducive to early enclosure.[6] From these terriers there is firm evidence that enclosure was only being considered in the eighteenth century and in those parishes for which a series of terriers survive there is a clear commentary on

[1] Ibid., p. 53.
[2] Elliott, CW2, LIX, 1959, p. 89; Youd, Trans. Hist. Soc. Lancs., CXIII, 1961, p. 10.
[3] Cheshire R.O., Enclosure Awards, St Marys on the Hill, Chester, 1805 (?), Frodsham Townfield 1784.
[4] Sylvester, Trans. Hist. Soc. Lancs., CVIII, 1956, p. 17; Chapman, Trans. Hist. Soc. Lancs., CIV, 1953, p. 57; Davies, Agricultural History of Cheshire, p. 5.
[5] Sylvester, Trans. Hist. Soc. Lancs., CVIII, 1956, pp. 6–17; Chapman, Trans. Hist. Soc. Lancs., CIV, 1953, pp. 47–8.
[6] Sylvester, Trans. Hist. Soc. Lancs., CVIII, 1956, pp. 31–2; Chapman, Trans. Hist. Soc. Lancs., CIV, 1953, p. 57; Davies, Agricultural History of Cheshire, p. 5.

picemeal consolidation and enclosure. The glebe terrier for Eastham (1696) describes 'one pasture field of 3 Acres. One loont in the Town field next the wen – half an acre. One loont in the same field of 3 measures sowing of barley one other in the same field of 2 measures sowing one other of which hath been exchanged with Jn. Grieve tenement of Eastham.' In 1716 there is also a reference to a field 'called the Hen Hey' which had been 'changed for some butts belonging to the vicar in the townfield'.[1] Similar evidence of exchange and enclosure comes from Handley (1858), Marbury (1778), Wallasey (1733), Grappenhall (1709) and Nether Knutsford (1663).[2] The evidence for Knutsford is one hundred and fifty years later than the last manuscript reference to common arable fields in this township quoted in Miss Sylvester's study of Cheshire field systems. It is indicative of the difficulties inherent in tracing the history of enclosure in regions of piecemeal enclosure where sources for its reconstruction in a manor may be lost or widely scattered.[3] In this period the attitude to enclosure was obviously one of acceptance, although the rate at which enclosure was accepted must have been conditioned by difficulties that had to be overcome in order to put it in to practice. It was welcomed in Northenden but it took the vicar from 1705 to 1754 to exchange all but one of his strips in the common field to the 'great advantage' of the glebe estate.[4] In some Wirral parishes however (e.g. Woodchurch) the glebe did not alter throughout the eighteenth century. The survey of 1697 shows a large number of unenclosed strips scattered through the townfields and in 1778 the position is exactly the same.[5] The evidence from Pulford besides showing how some lands were consolidated before enclosure also shows the danger of accepting the term 'Townfield' on its own as an indication of common field farming. In 1663 the vicar had two strips of ground called 'the crooked hadland one butt in the white Lound'. In 1705 this was measured as 'sowing of 3 measures of barley'. By 1785 it was 'a field called the Townfield' and contained 'about 1 Cheshire acre'.[6] When the effect of growing urbanism on the structure of common fields is studied in relation to Stockport it reveals a close parallel to developments in Walton (Liverpool). In 1662 Stockport was a large parish which combined the function of agricultural settlement and local market centre. There were 'mean fields' which the rector leased for periods ranging from

[1] Cheshire R.O., EDV/8, Glebe Terriers for Eastham 1696 and 1716.
[2] Cheshire R.O., EDV/8, Glebe Terriers for Handley (1858), Marbury (1778), Wallasey (1733), Grappenhall (1709), Nether Knutsford (1663).
[3] Sylvester, Trans. Hist. Soc. Lancs., CVIII, 1956, p. 15.
[4] Cheshire R.O., EDV/8, Glebe Terriers for Northenden 1705 and 1754.
[5] Cheshire R.O., EDV/8, Glebe Terriers for Woodchurch 1697 and 1778.
[6] Cheshire R.O., Glebe Terriers for Pulford 1663, 1705 and 1785.

one to seven years, and the 20 cottages in Church Gate with their appendant doles or shares in parts of the 'mean fields' represented a flourishing agricultural community.[1] By 1772 these 'mean fields' had been enclosed by private agreement and the rector exchanged part of his share for a larger acreage of land owned by Sir George Warren. This enclosure was probably influenced by industrial growth in the area and a demand for the former common field land for industrial and housing developments. It brought significant gains to the rector, for the £6 19s. 0d. per annum rent he received for the cottages in Church Gate was pushed up to £201 10s. 4d. chief rent from properties which developed on the enclosed fields.[2] A similar change occurred a century earlier in the growing salt-town of Sandbach. Land which was described as 'open field dales' in 1661 was covered by houses and gardens in 1714.[3] In the middle of this change it is interesting to note how a settlement developed from a field. In 1712 the vicar of Wallasey had 'Six Cowgarths and a half in a parcel of land now Inclosed by Wallasey Leasow'. 'Leasow' was a dialect term for pasture ground and is probably the 'Ox Park' of other Northwest townships. It lay on poorly drained lowlands in the Birket valley on the northern edge of the Wirral peninsula, and was quite distinct from both the townfield and the common waste.[4] Although no detailed records of the change exist it is obviously the area on to which pressures of urban population forced the borough of Wallasey to expand. It is another example of the absorption of a unit of the common field system by growing urban areas in the Northwest and in this case it has given its name to a part of the expanding conurbation.

[1] Cheshire R.O., Glebe Terriers for Stockport 1662 and 1772; S. Giles, 'Stockport Enclosure', *Trans. Lancs. and Cheshire Antiq. Soc.*, LXII, 1953, p. 46.
[2] Cheshire R.O., Glebe Terriers for Stockport.
[3] Cheshire R.O., EDV/8, Glebe Terriers for Sandbach 1661 and 1714.
[4] Cheshire R.O., EDV/8, Glebe Terrier for Wallasey 1712.

3
Field Systems of Northumberland and Durham

BY R. A. BUTLIN

A. INTRODUCTION

Landscapes of Northumberland and Durham derive much of their present character from intensive industrialisation and urbanisation in the nineteenth and twentieth centuries, based on the working of extensive mineral deposits, notably coal and iron. Some areas within this region, however, escaped 'the old and somewhat localised scars of Carboniferous capitalism',[1] and their predominantly rural landscapes have evolved over a much greater period of time. Even the industrialised parts of the Northumberland and Durham coalfield bore, up to the eighteenth century at least, an agrarian aspect which faithfully reflected the various forms of economic change which were then in progress. By 1800 enclosures, which had operated with notable intensity in the seventeenth and eighteenth centuries, had effected the almost total disappearance of the open and common fields, meadows and pastures, leaving only a few small remnants in the lowlands and various moorland and fell commons to be enclosed in the nineteenth century. While the processes of change which operated within this region in the eighteenth century may be described and analysed with a relatively high degree of accuracy, the fact that the common fields were largely enclosed by methods other than private or general acts of Parliament means that there are only relatively small numbers of enclosure awards and maps which may be used as essential starting points for investigations of the development of field systems.

The most important evidence of agrarian systems of the region before the eighteenth century are the maps, surveys, and related documents of the estates of the principal landowners, subject only in fairly recent times to detailed scrutiny. These documents, including numerous private enclosure agreements, reveal a situation totally different from that at the end of the eighteenth century, for they portray a system of cultivation of essentially medieval characteristics being changed and broken up by population pressure, increasing market demands for beef and butter, and a general intolerance of the deficiencies of the old system. The sixteenth and seventeenth centuries from the point of view of an investigation of former field systems

[1] A. E. Smailes, *North England*, 1960, p. 7.

[93]

thus form a key period and most of this chapter will be devoted to a detailed consideration of its dominant agrarian characteristics. Antecedents of the late medieval and early modern systems are very difficult to establish, partly on account of the relative paucity, for Northumberland at any rate, of the more important documentary sources, notably court rolls and ministers' accounts, and partly as a result of the consequent lack of detailed investigation of the medieval economic geography and history of this region.

H. L. Gray considered that Durham, as far north as Durham City, comprised the northern limit of the zone characterised by the three-field system:[1] Northumberland he considered to be transitional in its field systems between 'Celtic' and 'Midland' areas. Similar opinions have been voiced by other scholars. Before proceeding to an analysis of the evidence and hypotheses relating to the field systems of Northumberland and Durham, it is necessary to discuss two main groups of factors which have undoubtedly influenced agriculture and settlement in this region in the past, namely its physiography and its social, economic, and political history.

B. THE PHYSICAL GEOGRAPHY OF
NORTHUMBERLAND AND DURHAM

The most significant physiographical contrasts are afforded by three major types of region. First, the high hills and fells of the Cheviots, the Border and Bewcastle Fells and the North Pennine scarp. Second, the plateaux and scarplands, including the Fell Sandstone scarps and transitional low plateau of Northumberland, the sandstone plateau and Magnesian Limestone scarp of Durham. Third, the lowlands, comprising the coastal plain of eastern Northumberland and Durham, the lower Wear valley, the Tees lowland and estuary and the Northallerton lowland. Considerable extensions of relative lowland are effected by the valleys of a number of major rivers, notably those of the Till and Breamish which have eroded marked valleys in the cementstones (Lower Carboniferous), the North and South Tyne and Rede, the Wear and the Tees.

The high hills and fells of the northwest and the high fells and dales of the North Pennine block, rising to heights of 2,500 to 3,000 feet, are open and desolate, difficult of access, clothed in acid peat and characterised by an average annual rainfall often in excess of 60 inches, and a very short growing season. These regions, described in the Reports to the Board of Agriculture of the nineteenth century as

[1] H. L. Gray, *English Field Systems*, Cambridge, Mass., 1915, p. 62.

'mountainous heathy wastes', have traditionally been associated with temporary summer grazing of cattle at an extensive level, and also with the nefarious activities of the moss-troopers in times past, and with extensive reafforestation schemes at the present. These areas are drained by rivers which have excavated the 'border dales' of North-umberland and the 'lead dales' of the Pennine block, namely Redesdale, Upper North Tynedale, Upper Coquetdale (the 'border dales'), Allendale, Upper Teesdale and Upper Weardale (the 'lead dales'). The border dales form significant breaks in an inhospitable environ-ment, and afforded potential for arable and meadow land in con-junction with the extensive pastoral use of the fells and hills, in contrast to the narrower vales of the 'lead dales', where arable farming was never important, and agricultural colonisation closely associated at a late date with lead mining.

The scarps, plateaux and vales which are transitional between the high uplands and coastal lowlands are physically varied, which partially accounts for their varied agriculture in the past. The Fell Sandstone scarps of Northumberland contrast markedly in appearance and use with the fluvio-glacial and alluvial lowlands drained by the Till and Breamish at the foot of the Cheviots and the vales and coastal lowland, and comprise high barren moorlands, affording extensive wasteland traditionally utilised as a complement to the arable, meadow and pasture land of the vales and plains, whence extensive assarting could be effected. The area of scarplands and vales, drained by the Rede and North Tyne and breached by the North Tyne in its lower course, affords a complex and varied pattern of relief, much modified by the presence of glacial drift. The transitional plateau between the scarps and the coastal plain, which broadens southwards towards the Tyne valley, is low in altitude, drift-covered, and slopes gently east-wards. Rainfall here, as in the scarpland and vales to the west, is lower than that of the high fells – c. 30 to 40 inches per annum – and has enabled, with the 'moist loams' which cover its surface, a mixed form of husbandry to be practised in the past, based on villages commonly sited on outcrops of grits and limestones. The southern counterparts in Durham of the scarps and plateau of Northumberland are the sandstone plateau and the grit-capped moorlands of the Pennine block, each crossed by the valleys of the Upper Wear and Upper Tees, and the Magnesian Limestone scarp, constituting the East Durham Plateau, rising to 600 feet, sloping eastwards under glacial drift. The plateau and moorland vales bear the imprints of mining. The boulder clay which covers the East Durham plateau is modified by patches of sand and gravel, and the soils of this region, though varied, have afforded opportunity for intensive cultivation in the past, as also have the drift-covered valleys of the Middle Wear and Tees, particularly in regions of adequate drainage.

The third region comprises the coastal lowlands of Northumberland and Durham, the lower Wear and lower Tees valleys, and the Tyne valley. The undulating Northumbrian coastal lowland broadens southwards, its heavy clay soils being modified by patches of alluvium and sand and gravel, which, together with the sandstone knolls, have been extensively adopted as preferred sites for villages. More extensive outcrops of sandstone occur farther south towards the Tyne, taking the form of low plateaux which are separated in places by alluvial lowlands. The valley of the Tyne itself broadens below Hexham, with extensive alluvial meadow land, but narrows again between Newcastle and the sea. The broad lower valleys of the Wear and the Tees consist of undulating drifts and alluvium-covered lowlands, with patches of sands and gravels on the boulder clay which have been utilised for tillage. These lowlands are the driest and warmest parts of the north-east, for annual rainfall averages 25 to 30 inches, though the influence of local topography can effect substantial variations from this norm.

C. SETTLEMENT HISTORY

Physiography appears to have played a fundamental role in the development of varying field systems in Northumberland and Durham in the past. Social and economic factors, however, have obviously had an equally profound effect on the form and functions of agrarian systems and associated settlements. The first significant settlement dates from the second millennium B.C., with the entry of the Beaker folk, who colonised river valleys and higher slopes up to 800 feet. In the later Bronze Age further expansion of the settled areas took place, notably on to the moorlands, giving rise to predominantly high settlement densities in the Tyne valley, on the Cheviot slopes, the Wear valley and the Cleveland area. A conspicuous type of settlement form in this region is the stone-built ring-fort farmstead, located on the uplands and occurring both singly and in village clusters. These have been termed 'British' settlements, for it has been suggested that they are the settlements of Britons who were gradually forced up into the hills and moorlands by alien invaders. The occupants of the ring-forts practised a mainly cattle keeping economy, supplemented with a small amount of arable cultivation. It appears that this essentially Bronze Age way of life persisted over large areas of northeastern England until the Anglian and Scandinavian settlements, for even the Roman colonisation of this essentially military border region, outside the civil zone, left little impact, save perhaps for the extended use of iron implements, and the construction of defensive walls, notably Hadrian's Wall, and strategic roads.

The Anglian colonisation began in the mid-sixth century, with the establishment and development of the Kingdom of Bernicia. Initially, this comprised a small coastal area, but by 600 the Kingdom of Bernicia had been extended to include most of the coast from the Tees to the Forth and the Tyne and Tweed and other valleys. It then expanded westwards and also united with the Kingdom of Deira to the south, and these two kingdoms became Northumbria. Although the initial strongholds of the Anglians were essentially similar in location to those of earlier invaders, notably in coastal areas, they soon expanded into the forested lowlands, establishing villages and hamlets with stronger arable traditions than had hitherto been experienced. The political power of the kingdom of Northumbria waned after c. 700, but did not cease to exist until 867, when the Northumbrians were defeated by the Danes at York. Although the northern parts of Northumbria were invaded, they were not settled by the Danes and thus preserved essentially Anglian traditions and institutions; the land south of the Tyne, although part of the Danelaw, only experienced Danish settlement in south Durham. There may also have been small pockets of Norse settlement, spreading from the west, in the Tyne valley and elsewhere. Modern County Durham appears in the early medieval period as a thinly populated wasteland, with fewer settlements than the land to the north. In the sixth century it was described as 'a deserted waste...and thus nothing but a hiding place for wild and woodland beasts'.[1] With bleak uplands comprising the greater part of the country east of the Roman road from Piercebridge to Gateshead, conditions were not conducive to intensive settlement, and therefore 'it is not surprising that, when the Normans sent a reconnaissance north over the Tees, they found no one, for the inhabitants had taken to the woods'.[2] After the Norman conquest in the eleventh century, and the harrying of the north, northeastern England was devastated and wasted by Normans and Scots, and was left as a thinly populated zone. Northumberland then 'assumed its medieval character – a frontier province organised for defence, including wide feudal liberties where the King's writ did not run'.[3] The remoteness of Northumberland and Durham from the seat of government and its proximity to Scotland strongly influenced its social, economic and political development

[1] *Life of St Oswald*, cited by Smailes, *North England*, p. 88.
[2] W. S. Angus, 'Anglo-Saxon and Medieval Settlement', in P. C. G. Isaac and R. E. A. Allen (eds.), *Scientific Survey of North-Eastern England*, 1949, p. 72.
[3] *Ibid.*, p. 72.

from the eleventh to the seventeenth century, when violence was endemic and power concentrated in the hands of powerful military aristocrats and prince–bishops. Physical security was of paramount importance, a fact reflected in the great castles and strongholds, the ubiquitous pele towers, and the widespread adoption of 'border tenure'. With the termination of border warfare in the seventeenth century, agrarian reforms proceeded rapidly, via enclosure and improved farming methods, to a modern agrarian and industrial society.

There can be little doubt that the changing social and economic structures and conditions of this region throughout the greater part of historic time, operating in a strongly influential physiographic milieu, effectively conditioned the development of various types of field systems. Their precise effects will now be considered in the specific context of changing field systems and agrarian structures, commencing with late survivals and then moving retrogressively to earlier arrangements and origins.

D. FIELD SYSTEMS AND ENCLOSURE,
1740–1850

The enclosure of open and common fields and commons in Northumberland and Durham by private and general acts of Parliament in the period c. 1740–1850 represent the terminal phase of an enclosure movement which had effectively commenced much earlier. The Orwins concluded that in Northumberland 'there was much inclosure in the seventeenth and in the early part of the eighteenth centuries, but Parliamentary inclosure appears limited to a few Acts and Awards', and that in Durham, enclosure was also widespread in the seventeenth century, 'and by the end of the eighteenth, only some six parishes had any open field'.[1] The work of other scholars[2] and the testimony of the enclosure acts, awards and plans substantiate the accuracy of this conclusion. In Northumberland, only a very small proportion of the land enclosed by means of private and general acts during the

[1] C. S. and C. S. Orwin, *The Open Fields*, 3rd edn, 1967, p. 66.
[2] E.g. W. E. Tate, 'A Handlist of English Enclosure Acts and Awards, Part 26. Durham', *Proceedings Society of Antiquaries of Newcastle upon Tyne* (hereafter = *Proc. Soc. Antiqu. Newcastle*) 4th Ser., x, no. 3, 1943, pp. 119–40; and 'A Handlist of English Enclosure Acts and Awards, Part 26. Northumberland', *Proc. Soc. Antiqu. Newcastle*, 4th Ser., x, no. 1, 1942, pp. 39–52; and E. M. Leonard, 'The Inclosure of Common Fields in the Seventeenth Century', *Trans. R. Hist. Soc.*, xix, 1905, pp. 101–46; R. I. Hodgson, 'The Progress of Enclosure in County Durham', a paper presented to a symposium of the Agrarian Landscape Research Group of the Institute of British Geographers, May 1970.

eighteenth and nineteenth centuries was arable: the greater part of the enclosed areas comprised the extensive pastures and moorlands of the Fell Sandstone Uplands, the moors of the upper North Tyne and Redesdale, the western scarplands and the north Pennines. In this period there were some fifty-four private enclosure acts affecting Northumberland, of which only nine included areas of common arable field. The General Acts of 1845 and after include no such areas. Approximately 15 per cent of the total area of Northumberland was enclosed by private and general acts, and only 3 per cent of the total area enclosed in this fashion, or 0.5 per cent of the total area of the county, included common arable. Of some forty-one acts of enclosure for Durham in this period, only six relate to the enclosure of common arable, that is c. 3.3 per cent of the total area of the county enclosed by act or c. 0.5 per cent of the total area of the county.

In Durham, common arable was included in the enclosure acts for Walsingham (Act 1769, Award 1770), Thornley (1769, 1772), Bolam (1782, 1786), Barnard Castle (1783, 1785), Crawcrook (1794, 1800), and Gateshead (1814, 1818), located in the valleys of the Tyne, Tees, and Wear (Fig. 3.1). Bolam, sited below the rim of the Tees basin, immediately prior to enclosure had on a small scale an almost classic layout of the three-field system[1] (Fig. 3.2), comprising Dunwell Field (270 acres), West Field (209 acres) and North Field (178 acres). Old enclosures occupied the northern, western and southwestern extremities of the township. The subdivision of the fields is not shown on the award, though 'the name Kiln Riggs used for a part of Dunwell Field does, however, suggest that the strips may have lain in ridge and furrow'.[2] Eleven properties were involved in the enclosure, of which the largest was 314 acres, mainly reallocated by division between the North and West fields, and the smallest was 14 acres. The allocation of land in the award is not particularly helpful for reconstruction of former tenurial arrangements, but the significance of this township derives from the fact that it represents a late survival of a form of three-field system. It is interesting to note in this context, the terrier for Bolam, dated 1606, which Gray reproduced: 'Terrier of seven holdings. Each has an almost equal amount of arable and meadow in East Field, West Field and North Field' (East Field being the Dunwell Field of 1786).[3]

At Barnard Castle, also in the Tees basin, six 'town fields' were enclosed by an act of 1783, together with the stinted town pasture.

[1] V. C. Chapman, 'The Fields of Bolam', *Trans. Archit. and Arch. Soc. of Durham and Northumberland*, XI, parts 5 and 6, 1965, p. 446.
[2] *Ibid.*, p. 448.
[3] Gray, *English Field Systems*, p. 462.

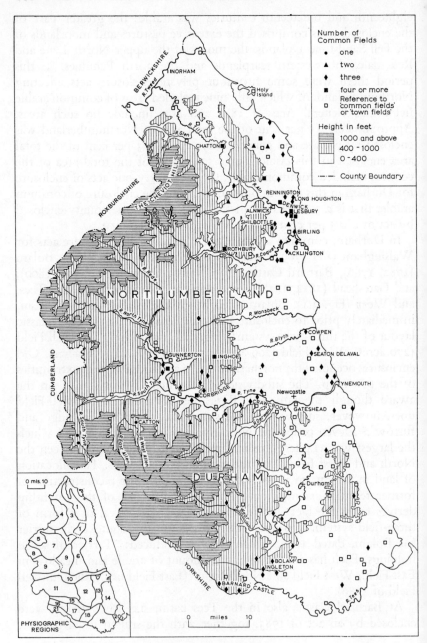

Fig. 3.1 (*see opposite*)

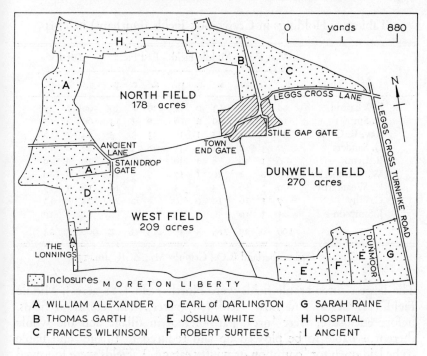

Fig. 3.2 The common fields of Bolam (Durham) in 1786.
Source. V. Chapman, 'The Fields of Bolam', *Trans. Archit. and Arch. Soc. of Durham and Northumberland*, XI, 1965, p. 447.

Fig. 3.1 Common fields of Northumberland and Durham, *c.* 1550–1800.
Key to physiographic regions: 1, Fell Sandstone Scarps; 2, Coastal Plain; 3, Cementstone Vales; 4, Cheviot Hills; 5, Border Fells; 6, Low Plateau; 7, Upper North Tyne and Redesdale; 8, Bewcastle Fells; 9, Scarp; 10, Tyne Valley; 11, Northern Dales; 12, Sandstone Plateau; 13, Lower Wear Valley; 14, Magnesian Limestone Scarp; 15, Upper Weardale; 16, High Fells; 17, Grit-Capped Moorlands; 18, Sandstone Plateau; 19, Tees Lowland; 20, Tees Estuary; 21, Upper Teesdale.
Sources. Alnwick Castle archives, classes A, J and O; Enclosure awards and acts, Northumberland R.O. and Durham R.O.; R. A. Butlin, 'The Evolution of the Agrarian Landscape of Northumberland, 1500–1900', M.A. thesis, University of Liverpool, 1961; W. E. Tate, 'A Handlist of English Enclosure Acts and Awards, Part 26, Durham Field Systems and Enclosure Movements', *Proc. Soc. Antiqu. Newcastle*, x, 1943, pp.119–40; E. M. Leonard, 'Enclosure of Common Fields in the Seventeenth Century', *Trans. Roy. Hist. Soc.*, XIX, 1905, pp. 101–46.

Table 3.1. Holdings in Crawcrook Fields (Durham) in 1794

Proprietor	West Field			Middle Field			East Field			Total		
	a.	r.	p.	a.	r.	p.	a.	r.	p.	a.	r.	p.
J. Wharton	99	3	5	83	0	1	126	1	39	309	1	5
C. Surtees	19	1	28	29	2	16	20	3	13	69	3	17
Rev. R. Croft	35	0	24	25	1	37	33	3	5	94	1	16
G. Sanders	7	3	2	11	1	31	8	1	20	27	2	13
R. Lynn	6	1	36	8	1	30	5	3	23	20	3	9
W. Weatherby	14	2	4	10	1	17	7	3	19	32	3	0
C. Weatherby	6	3	16	5	2	23	3	3	16	16	1	15
C. Jolly	7	1	16	12	0	10	8	2	27	28	0	13
J. Simpson	1	3	16							1	3	16
	199	0	27	185	3	35	215	3	2	600	3	24

Source: Northumberland R.O., Griffiths Ms., ZGR, dm. 13.

The largest three arable fields were North Field (121 acres), Middle Field (112 acres) and Low Field (107 acres). The common fields, before enclosure, were 'great part thereof in tillage and the whole thereof...liable to be plowed up and reduced to tillage' and liable to be laid open for 'common or winter eatage'.[1] 'Fields were followed in summer in rotation: from 5th April to 8th June no depasturing was allowed; after 8th June for four weeks exclusive right of eatage was allowed to those who had stints or cattle-gates in the town pasture; after that the fallow field was open as common pasture until 10th October.'[2] The three smaller fields, the Crook (45 acres), the Lugs (59 acres) and New Field (79 acres), which appear to be later intakes from the waste land, were probably used in a more flexible way.

The most detailed maps and terriers for the late survivals in Durham are those for Crawcrook, a township in the Tyne valley. *A Survey of Crawcrook open fields in the Parish of Ryton in the County Palatine of Durham* was produced by R. Burton in 1794, on the eve of enclosure, and this, with the accompanying map by J. Mowbray (Fig. 3.3) affords valuable details of the field system.[3] There were, at this time, three large open and common arable fields. The total area of the proprietors' holdings in each field is shown in Table 3.1 and the distribution of sample holdings in Fig. 3.3. The holdings were

[1] V. C. Chapman, 'Barnard Castle: the Enclosures', in T. H. Corfe, R. W. Davies, and A. Walton (eds.), *History Field Studies in the Durham Area*, 1967, p. 93.
[2] *Ibid.*, p. 93.
[3] Northumberland R.O., Griffiths Ms., ZGR, dm. 13 (copy).

in fact distributed throughout the fields in proportion directly related to the size of the fields, giving a close approximation to an equal distribution. The survey itself provides no information about the method of cultivation and crop rotation, but demonstrates the presence at least of structural elements of the system: three large open and common arable fields, subdivided into strips and blocks of varying sizes, but with large areas showing the quilletted pattern of small strips. The larger blocks presumably represented engrossing of smaller holdings. There were few closes. The interesting feature of this arrangement is that it mirrors, quite faithfully, the field layout and distribution of holdings which were characteristic of many townships in the seventeenth century.

The evidence for Northumberland comprises some nine enclosure acts, namely those for Gunnerton (Act 1740, Award 1741), West Matfen (1757), Norham (1761, 1762), Corbridge (1776, 1779), Elrington (1784), Thorneyburn, Greystead and Stannersburn (1804, 1816), Smiddywell in Simonburn (1809, 1818), Ovingham, Bywell St Peter and Bywell St Andrew (1817, 1817) and Haltwhistle (1844, 1849). The Northumberland acts and awards do not demonstrate the survival of old field systems quite so clearly, but they do provide indications of regional variations.

Perhaps the most important of the townships enclosed by act was Corbridge. The medieval borough of Corbridge – successor to the Roman stronghold Corsitopium – formed the centre of Corbridge township, which included land to the north and south of the River Tyne, with the borough itself on the north bank of the river. The township included much agricultural land of high value, including the rich alluvium of the valley, and the drift-covered south-facing slopes north of the river have traditionally been conducive to the growing of corn. The act for enclosure of the fields around Corbridge is dated 1776, and the enclosure award 1779.[1] The details in the act and award are supplemented by a detailed map of the township by John Fryer, which outlines the pre-enclosure pattern of fields and holdings[2] (Fig. 3.4). The total area of open common field arable was 964 acres, 14 perches, divided into five parts.[3] The East Field consisted of 374 parcels, West Field comprised 365 parcels, North Field 201, Little Field 102, and the Eales 30 parcels. In each case, the size and form of the individual parcels in the fields varied widely, and included long and short strips, gores and butts, mostly of one acre or less in size, and closes, representing engrossed holdings. The distribution of

[1] Alnwick Castle Ms., A.VI, 18, 19.
[2] Northumberland R.O., ZAN. MSM. 10.
[3] Alnwick Castle Ms., A.VI, 18.

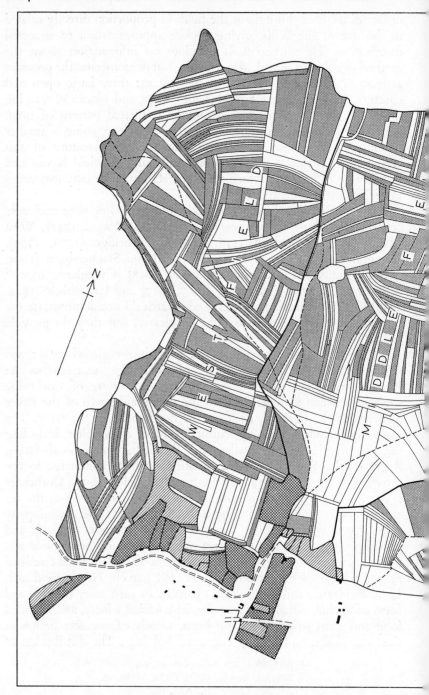

Fig. 3.3 The common fields of Crawcrook (Durham) in 1794.
Source. John Mowbray's map, Northumberland R.O., ZGR (Griffiths Mss.) dm.
(copy).

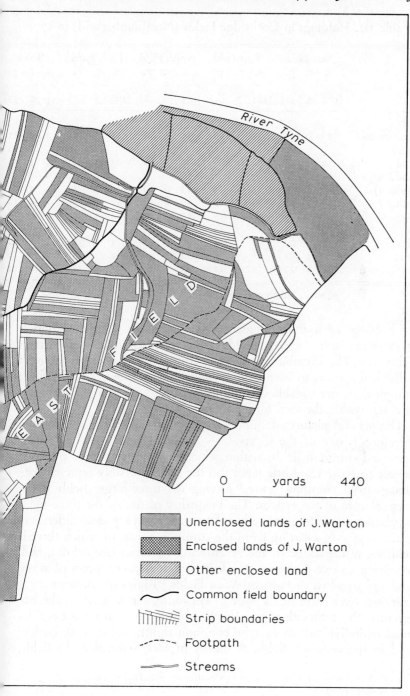

River Tyne

FIELD

EAST FIELD

0   yards   440

Unenclosed lands of J. Warton

Enclosed lands of J. Warton

Other enclosed land

Common field boundary

Strip boundaries

Footpath

Streams

Table 3.2. Holdings in Corbridge Fields (Northumberland) in 1777

	East Field a. r. p.	West Field a. r. p.	North Field a. r. p.	Little Field a. r. p.	Eales a. r. p.
	(402 3 33)	(434 3 11)	(275 0 28)	(109 3 1)	(41 2 37)
Duke of Northumberland	80 0 36	35 3 9	58 1 4	17 0 23	4 1 22
Greenwich Hospital	50 1 0	88 1 6	15 1 37	22 2 4	4 2 32
Dean and Chapter (of Durham)	12 3 0	23 1 5	15 0 3	16 2 13	2 2 25
B. Winship	21 3 13	29 0 17	26 2 24	8 1 16	1 1 32
J. Gibson	21 2 16	32 2 35	17 2 8	3 3 12	
P. Hall	19 3 5	19 3 15	11 2 20	4 1 15	1 3 33
J. Walker	25 2 24	60 3 39	8 0 1	1 2 36	1 2 4
R. Sparke	12 2 32	18 3 2	12 2 22	2 1 37	
C. Potts	14 1 37	15 1 11	11 3 33	5 3 34	3 0 14

Source: Northumberland R.O., ZAN. M17.127.

the holdings of four landholders is shown in Fig. 3.4. The division
of these and other selected holdings between the fields is shown in
Table 3.2. The distribution of the common field holdings of each
individual appears to be roughly proportional to the size of the field,
though there are notable exceptions, usually caused by the inclusion
of closes within the total for a particular field.

The general picture of the field system at Corbridge at this time
therefore is one of the survival, in modified form, of five largely
open and common fields, within which holdings formed a confused
mosaic pattern. The Little Field and the Eales probably represent late
intakes from common waste,[1] leaving the three larger fields as the
essential core of the system. The inequality of size of the three fields
may be accounted for in a number of ways: this may represent differences
in the degree of assarting from the common waste, of which there is
evidence in the sixteenth and seventeenth centuries (see below), and,
according to one authority, the fact that there were pieces of waste
land and meadow in East and West Fields.[2] Rights of common were
exercised over these fields prior to enclosure, but as early as the late
seventeenth century there was much confusion over the exact entitlement of individuals to exercise common rights, and even to enclose
land in the common fields. A survey of 1664 states that the fields,

[1] Northumberland County History (hereafter = N.C.H.), x, 1914, p. 140.
[2] Ibid., p. 140.

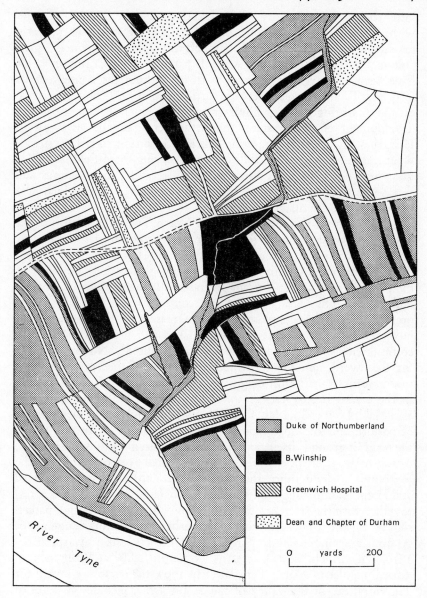

Fig. 3.4. Part of East Field in Corbridge (Northumberland) in 1777.
Source. John Fryer's map, Northumberland R.O., ZAN. MSM. 10.

'after the corne and hay are off, are laid open, and are eaten, sometimes with, sometimes without stint, but how many beasts or sheep everie tenement may keep is uncertain and left as ye Neighbours may agree among themselves; And that severall parcells of ye Common fields have been inclosed, but whether with or without the consent of ye lord and Tennants wee refere to further enquiry.'[1] The significance of the Corbridge fields, however, in the general context of the development of field systems in northeastern England, is twofold. First, they again demonstrate the existence of a type of field system – what might be termed a 'modified and decaying three-field system' – in an area beyond Gray's northern limit; secondly, they demonstrate that some common fields of the region contained land which was not entirely under tillage.

At Gunnerton, in the valley of the North Tyne, the enclosure act refers to 'several common fields of arable and pasture land, called or known by the name of the In-grounds', and 1,300 acres in total area, in addition to the common wastes or 'out-grounds'.[2] The lands of the proprietors lay 'dispersed in several small parcels', and 'soil of the said arable lands hath, by long and constant usage in tillage, been greatly impoverished, and cannot, by reason of the distance and inconvenient situation of the several lands and grounds in the said common fields, be properly cultivated and manured'.[3] No plan survives for the award, and the form and disposition of the common fields thus becomes a matter for conjecture. The total area of land reallocated in the award is 2,630 acres, and includes fields with such names as East Field, Low Field, New Intack, New Law, together with a number of pasture and meadow closes, garths and the town green. While the term 'inground' itself cannot be used synonymously with 'infield', in the sense of an intensively cultivated small area of arable (as the ingrounds include more than the arable land), the small scale of arable cultivation suggested by the award (approximately 100 acres) together with the reference to continuous cultivation and small parcels suggests a genus of field system related perhaps to Scottish arrangements. A similar arrangement is suggested by the enclosure award, dated 1816, which includes 71½ acres in 'common fields' at Stannersburn, a small hamlet in North Tynedale.[4] In 1797, the enclosure award for Thorngrafton, in the valley of the South Tyne, includes 39 acres of common fields at Thorngrafton, 11 acres at Birkshaw and 58 at Millhouse. The award for Tarretburn Common, and Smiddywell

[1] Alnwick Castle Ms., A.vi, 26 (ii), 6.
[2] Alnwick Castle Ms., A.iv 9(6); Northumberland R.O., Q.R.A. 25 (1741/2).
[3] Ibid.
[4] Northumberland R.O., Q.R.A. no. 55.

Rig, in Simonburn[1] (1815) includes 'certain common fields called Smiddywell Rig, Blackmiddings, Hatheryhurst, Sheep Gatehouse, Greenheald, Shiply Shields, Dunstead, Cleenlea, and Newbiggin, totalling *c.* 300 acres', and the 1849 award for Haltwhistle includes parcels known as 'the Rig and Dale Lands and respectively being dispersed and intermixed and uninclosed from each other', totalling *c.* 120 acres.[2] Although suggestive of small-scale intensive agriculture of the infield–outfield, or runrig type, these instances afford inadequate bases on which to base generalisations on the type of field system which they represent, for in most cases the common field land comprises only a late and partial survival of what must have been more extensive common land: indicated by the 'ancient enclosed lands' which are located near the settlements on the enclosure award plans. Similarly, caution must be exercised in respect of evidence afforded by the enclosure award and plan for Henshaw, in the Parish of Haltwhistle (1787),[3] which includes, *inter alia,* reference to 'certain townfields called and known by the names of High Townfield and Low Townfield', and the Townfield in nearby Melkridge, whose areas were 15a. 1r. 36p., 94a. 1r. 10p., and 124a. 1r. 5p., respectively. At Catton, three common fields were enclosed in 1880, but the award gives little indication of the extent of previous enclosure of arable land.[4]

Two further acts and awards, in fact relating to land which was formerly part of Durham, use the term 'infield', namely those for Norham and Holy Island. An act of 1761 and an award of 1762 describe the enclosure of Norham infield and moor,[5] and an act of 1791 and an award of 1793 the enclosure of the infields of Holy Island.[6] The Holy Island enclosure act refers to 'a certain large open tract of land called or known by the name of Holy Island Common', which was in fact 1,023 acres in size. This was a stinted common pasture, and the petition for enclosure required its division and enclosure and the extinction of rights of common or 'eatage' over certain old infield lands. The commissioners 'estimated ascertained and settled the number of the several ancient freehold burgage and tenements and other estates in respect whereof any persons are entitled to right of common or stints upon the said tract of land'. The award makes no reference to the size of the infield lands nor to their quality and

[1] Northumberland R.O., Q.R.A. no. 54.
[2] Northumberland R.O., Q.R.A. no. 33.
[3] Northumberland R.O., Q.R.D. no. 33.
[4] Northumberland R.O., Q.R.D. no. 31.
[5] Lit. and Phil. Soc. of Newcastle upon Tyne, Collections of Local Acts, XII, no. 10.
[6] *Ibid.,* XIV, no. 10.

use. A similar situation appears to have obtained at Norham, for the act and award (which like those for Holy Island have not retained an accompanying map) describe the existence of 'several large open and common arable, meadow and pasture grounds, called and known by the general name of "Norham Infields"', whose area was 437 acres, and Norham Moor or Common, of an area of 1,500 acres, with no indication of the actual farming system practised. It seems, however, that the term 'infield', in these places, as elsewhere in Northumberland at this time, was being used as a general term describing land which was located near the main settlement and which presumably was subject to a more intensive utilisation than the 'outfield' land. Support for this assumption appears in the 1841 essay of John Grey of Dilston: 'A view of the past and present state of agriculture in Northumberland'.[1] Referring particularly to the sandy soils of the Till vale, he writes of:

'Most farms being divided into what was called the "infield" and "outfield" land; the former being subjected to a severe course of cropping, with very inadequate cultivation; the latter left to its native produce as a pasture for young sheep and cattle, or if choice portions of it were occasionally broken up, it was to rob it of its fertility by the production of a succession of corn crops, and then to leave it to recruit itself by several years of pasture.'[2]

The evidence thus afforded by enclosure acts and awards for Northumberland and Durham, although comparatively meagre, affords a number of valuable pointers to variations in the form and use of arable fields. The most significant facts which emerge are as follows. First, that if there had once been extensive open and common fields in this region, they had largely disappeared by about 1750. Secondly, that the surviving examples suggest a logical variation between large-scale arable farming in favoured lowland areas, such as the valleys of the Lower Tyne, the Wear and the Tees, and a smaller scale of cultivation on the upper reaches of the Tyne, Upper Tyne and Rede. This theme of regional variation in agrarian practice will be considered, using the retrogressive method, in the following section.

[1] *Jnl. R. Agric. Soc.*, II, 1841, pp. 151–92.
[2] *Ibid.*, p. 153.

E. FIELD SYSTEMS AND AGRARIAN CHANGE
c. 1550–1740

I. THE DISTRIBUTION AND FORM OF THE COMMON FIELDS

Fig. 3.1 represents in summary form the evidence for the distribution of open common fields within the two counties. It demonstrates fairly conclusively that the management of arable cultivation on the basis of two, three, four or more open, and usually commonable, fields, was a normal feature in both counties in the period under consideration. Of a total number of 175 townships represented on the map, three had one such field, five had two, sixty-three had three, thirteen had four or more, and for ninety-one there is documentary evidence for 'town fields' or 'common fields', with no actual reference to numbers. The greatest density of common fields occurs in what were essentially the physiographic regions most favourable to arable farming, namely the coastal plain, cementstone vales, scarplands and transitional low plateaux of Northumberland, the Tyne valley, and the sandstone plateaux of the North Pennine block, the middle and lower valleys of the Wear and Tees and the Magnesian Limestone scarp in Durham. These were also the most densely populated areas. The absence of such features is most marked in the bleak, inhospitable, and thinly populated regions of the Cheviots, Border and Bewcastle Fells, Upper North Tyne and Redesdale, in Northumberland, and the Northern dales and high fells of Durham.

(*a*) *Northumberland: the coastal plain*

The coastal plain of Northumberland runs the whole length of the county. Enclosure of common fields in this region in the late seventeenth and eighteenth centuries was widespread. Although the enclosure agreements themselves do not always provide a detailed picture of the form and function of the common fields, extensive evidence is provided by a remarkable series of estate surveys, including maps, undertaken for the earls of Northumberland, notably from *c.* 1580 to 1630.[1] The township of Denwick, northwest of Alnwick, was once part of the demesne land of the earl of Northumberland, but by the late sixteenth century this was no longer the case. The 1618 survey[2] shows

---

[1] Alnwick Castle Ms., A; O; *cf.* R. A. Butlin, 'Northumberland Field Systems', *Agric. Hist. Rev.*, XII, 1964, p. 120.
[2] Alnwick Castle Ms., A.IV, 8 (1618).

'there is in Denwick fower severall fields named the South Field, West Field, East Field and North Field, wherein every whole tenement is to have twenty-eight beast stints yearly and every half farm eighteen beast stints, viz. the summer halfe year in the out pasture and the winter halfe year in the corne fields after the corne and hay be carried away'. The accompanying map (Fig. 3.5) and terrier show that South Field contained 209 acres of arable, West Field 67 acres, East Field 97 acres and North Field 142 acres. A large part of South Field was meadow land, comprising part of the alluvial flood-plain of the River Aln. Beyond the North Field the common waste rose steeply to the northeast. The common fields were located in what were the most favourable topographic and pedological situations. The holdings of the tenants in each field were almost directly proportioned to the size of the field: thus South Field and North Field, which were almost equal in size, show an average holding size of $9\frac{1}{2}$ acres, the corresponding figure for West Field and East Field being 4 and 6 acres respectively. At Rennington, to the north, there were three common arable fields in the early seventeenth century (Fig. 3.6).[1] These were located on soils derived from boulder clay and river alluvium which Clarkson the Surveyor had described as good corn soil 'if the same were used with good husbandry'.[2] The fields lay to the south, west and north of the village, on land of low altitude, in contrast to the moor – at a much higher elevation to the south of the village. The distribution of the holdings of copyhold tenants between the fields shows a markedly proportional relationship to field size, a fact denied by Gray who was using the specifications of the holding of Trestram Phillipson,[3] printed in the *History of Northumberland*, which was definitely untypical of the majority of holdings in Rennington. The inequality of field size may have been caused by disproportionate expansion by assarting from common waste, of which there is evidence (Fig. 3.6) in the form of new strips on the common. At Shilbottle in 1618 (Fig. 3.7) the arable land comprised four sectors: the North Field, Middle Field, South Field and the 'Four farms at the head of Shilbottle'.[4] This latter part of the township had been separated from the rest by four tenants in the sixteenth century, as Clarkson stated: 'for they have ther arable land and medowe lying together with a certain parcell of pasture ground enclosed with hedges within themselves which is more comodyous to them than if it lay as thother doth'.[5] The land of the

[1] Alnwick Castle Ms., A.IV, 8 (1618); A.V, 4 (1622).
[2] G. Clarkson, *A description and survey of divers of the possessions of the Right Honorable the Earl of Northumberland...1566* (1567). Alnwick Castle Ms., A.I, 1f.
[3] Gray, *English Field Systems*, p. 213.
[4] Alnwick Castle Ms., A.IV, 7 (1618), A.V, 2 (1622).   [5] Alnwick Castle Ms., I.I, 1e.

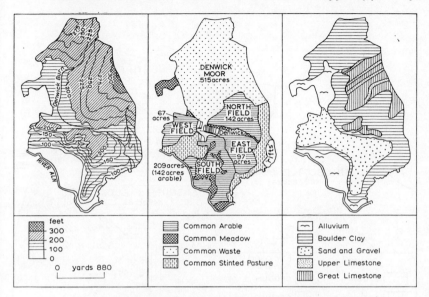

Fig. 3.5 The township of Denwick (Northumberland) *c.* 1624.
Source. Alnwick Castle Ms. maps, O.III, 1 (*a–d*) 2.

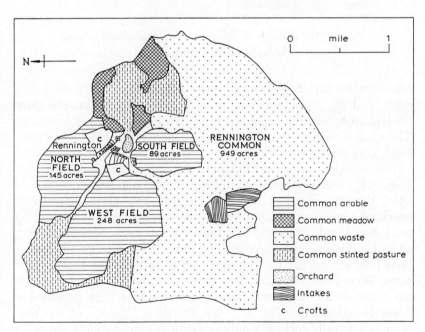

Fig. 3.6 The township of Rennington (Northumberland) *c.* 1624.
Source. Alnwick Castle Ms. maps, O.VIII, 1 (*a–d*).

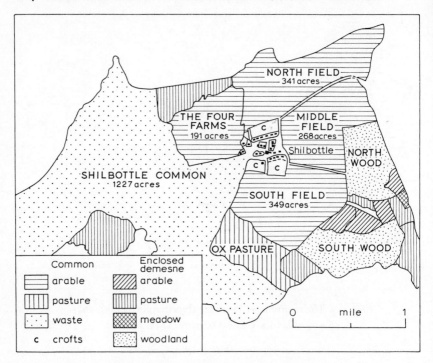

Fig. 3.7 The township of Shilbottle (Northumberland) *c.* 1624.
Source. Alnwick Castle Ms. maps, O.IV, I (*a–e*).

other tenants lay in intermixed strips in the three common arable fields, and the equal distribution of tenant holdings between three fields of approximately equal size suggests a type of three-field system. The median sizes of tenant holdings in the three fields were: North Field, *c.* 14 acres, Middle Field, *c.* 13 acres, South Field, *c.* 15 acres.

The situation at Long Houghton, to the northeast of Alnwick (Fig. 3.8), was extremely interesting. Before Clarkson's survey of 1567, the township had been divided into two parts, in order to restrict the area over which the strips of arable land of any one holding were distributed. A map of 1619 shows that the new boundaries cross an older division into three arable fields. When the two halves of each field are added, the respective areas become: South Field 375 acres, West Field 181 acres, East Field 544 acres.[1] Gray's conclusion from this arrangement was 'that no three-field system prevailed at Long Houghton in 1619, and that the three "fields" of the map were never really such, but only convenient topographical names for

---

[1] Alnwick Castle Ms., O.VII (*c*): map by Robert Norton (1619).

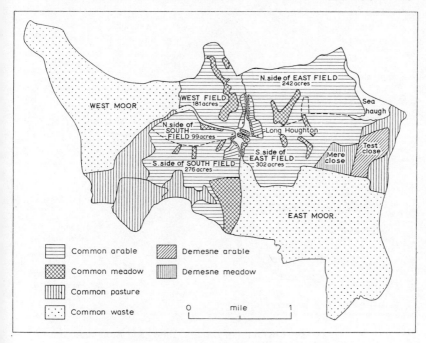

Fig. 3.8 The township of Long Houghton (Northumberland) *c.* 1619.
Source. Alnwick Castle Ms. maps, O.vii, 1 (*a*).

different parts of the township's arable'.[1] It is certainly difficult to
ascertain the form and management of the three fields prior to division,
but the new holding distributions shed some light on the system
which replaced it. The tenants of the south side had their arable
land in two fields, South Field and East Field. Their part of South
Field comprised 276 acres, and of East Field 302 acres, and the
approximate mean size of holding in each field was 15½ acres and
17 acres respectively, suggesting the operation of a form of two-field
system. The distribution of holdings of the tenants of the north side,
however, was markedly different. The mean sizes of holdings in the
north sides of South Field (99 acres), West Field (181 acres) and East
Field (242 acres) being 5, 8½ and 16½ acres respectively. A combination
of the acres of each holding in West Field and East Field would provide
a theoretical basis for a type of system based on two units, but there
is no evidence to substantiate this supposition.

Other townships of the central coastal plain, notably those between
the Aln and the Coquet – Lesbury and Bilton (see Fig. 3.9), for

[1] Gray, *English Field Systems*, p. 211.

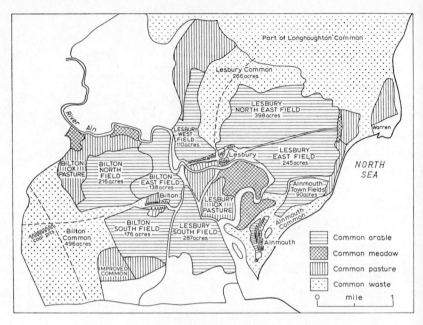

Fig. 3.9 The townships of Lesbury, Bilton and Alnmouth
(Northumberland) 1624.
Source. Alnwick Castle Ms. maps, O.vi, 1 (*a–e*) 2 and 3.

example – reveal different patterns of field layout and organisation.
The township of Lesbury, sited on the Aln near the sea, described in
1567 as having good corn soil enriched by the use of seaweed as
manure, had at this time four common arable fields: West Field,
North East Field, East Field and South Field.[1] The distribution of
tenant holdings between these fields is directly proportional to their
size, with mean holding sizes of 13, 3, 7 and $7\frac{1}{2}$ acres respectively.
Gray felt that 'no combination here would evolve into anything like
a three-field arrangement except the union of West Field with East
Field, and even this, apart from the situation of the two, does not
obviate considerable discrepancy'.[2] An added complication in this
place, as in other places in Northumberland and Durham, is the
presence of large quantities of meadow land in two of the fields:
53 acres in North East Field and 65 in South Field, allocated on a
pro rata basis, according to the number of 'farms' or tenements held.
No clear idea of the basis of management of the four common fields

[1] Alnwick Castle Ms., A.iv, 3 (1614); A.v, 3 (1622).
[2] Gray, *English Field Systems*, p. 212.

emerges from a study of their size and of the distribution of holdings between them.

The 1624 map of Bilton (Fig. 3.9) shows three common arable fields: South Field, East Field and North Field. These fields include meadow land, namely 39 acres in the South Field, 53 in the East Field, and 28 in the North Field. The land in these fields was held as copyhold, freehold and demesne land. By the late sixteenth century, it appears that the extent of the demesne land was not accurately known, being intermixed with copyhold land, and a survey was undertaken to determine its extent. By the early seventeenth century, 66 acres of demesne land were being farmed by Thomas Slagg, and the remnant by the copyhold tenants, in addition to their own tenements. Perhaps the most interesting feature of the distribution of the freehold, demesne and copyhold land was the similarity of areas of copyhold land in each of the three fields, namely 90 acres in East Field, 95 acres in South Field, and 109 acres in North Field. Demesne arable land in these fields comprised 4 acres in East Field, 33 in South Field and 67 in North Field. The amount of freehold arable was very small. The equality of distribution of copyhold land between the three fields (with individual tenements showing a mean distribution of about 11 acres in North Field, 9 acres in East Field and 11 in South Field) suggests a three-field system.

The township of Guysance in 1618 had three common arable fields: East Field (113 acres), North Field (121 acres) and West Field (77 acres).[1] Clarkson in his 1567 survey had recommended division of the township, owing to the uneven distribution of the arable, but no mention of this division is made in the 1618 survey. The normal size of tenant holdings in each of the fields was of the order of 16 acres (East Field), 16 acres (North Field) and 15 acres (West Field). In addition, each tenant held between 2 and 6 acres of demesne land. The three fields obviously formed the basis of arable management (though again there was meadow land in each), and the unequal size may perhaps be explained by the ease with which supplementary arable could be ploughed from the common waste, a practice referred to by Clarkson at Guysance, where tenants had 'every xvi[th] rigge in every rifte which is to be made arable and which before was lee or pasture grounde'.[2] Similar expansion of the common arable was also practised at Acklington where, in 1616, there were three common fields (Fig. 3.10), South Field, East Field and North Field.[3] For each of the two larger fields, the 1616 survey makes reference to land

[1] Alnwick Castle Ms., A.iv, 7 (1618); A.v, 2 (1624).
[2] Alnwick Castle Ms., A.i, 11.
[3] Alnwick Castle Ms., A.iv, 4 (1616); A.v, 6 (1624); O.xvi, 1d.

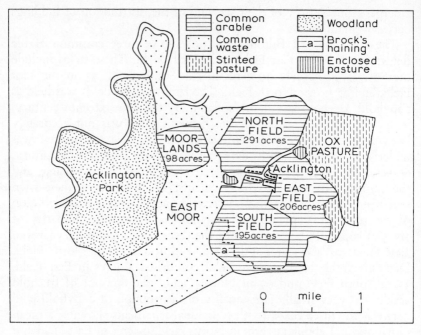

Fig. 3.10 The township of Acklington (Northumberland) in 1616.
Source. Alnwick Castle Ms. maps, O.

newly ploughed from the common or waste, for example, Deanes
Flatt, in East Field, a flatt of 23 acres: 'this furshotte last goienge
before was common pasture and now lately plowed upp, and devided
among the tenants themselves'. Some of the Moor lands, totalling
98 acres, in the North Field had also been newly ploughed from the
waste: 'some of this field called Moore lands, being all lately taken
of the common, and converted to arable'.[1] The strips of this field
were allocated on a strict rotation; Henry Jackson, for example, being
given the first, twenty-first and forty-first strips. This practice is
interesting for it demonstrates how arable fields of unequal size might
develop. It is also clear that at Acklington the reverse process also
operated, for several pieces of land which were formerly common
arable had been allowed to revert to pasture.[2] Brocks Haining, as it
was called – some 34 acres in extent – was described as being pasture
land which had formerly been arable, but laid to pasture 'as it is
said because of its barrenness'. This mechanism of conversion and
reversion effectively maintained a reasonable balance between the size

[1] Alnwick Castle Ms., A.IV, 4.
[2] *Ibid.*

of the three fields, between which the copyhold tenant holdings were evenly distributed.

The townships of the southern coastal plain in southeast Northumberland exhibit features similar to many of those described above. At Hartley in 1536, there were three common fields.[1] The distribution of tenant holdings between these fields is revealed in a deposition of 1596 made against Robert Delaval, who had obtained control of the whole township and evicted some of the tenants. The deponent states that before 1596 there were 15 tenants and 15 ploughs in the township, '60 acres of arable land at least to every plough, 20 acres in each field'.[2] Similar evidence is given for Seaton Delaval in 1596: 'the seven farmholds displaced had to every one of them 60 acres of arable land, viz. 20 in each field at the least'.[3] Gray did not regard this as reliable evidence of a three-field system. He thought that the author, 'speaking as it were parenthetically, may have been referring to a three-course rotation of crops. This method of tillage might appear where open field furlongs were not grouped into three compact fields...even in the most typical of midland townships the acres of the copyholds were not divided with this precision among the fields'.[4] That this was an idealistic or notional appraisal is not questioned, but the existence of three fields at Seaton and in neighbouring townships gives good reason for assuming that the deponent was in fact referring to a three-field system. In the township of Tynemouth there were three common fields in the early seventeenth century named in petitions for enclosure: North Field (258 acres), Middle Field (286 acres) and South Field (188 acres). The nearby township of Preston, when enclosed in 1649, had two such fields, North Field (183 acres) and West Field (137 acres): only the land which was to be enclosed was described in the Preston and Tynemouth survey, and it is possible that other common fields may have been previously enclosed.[5] Of the township of Seghill, the same deponent in 1596 stated that there had been '10 tenements – 10 ploughs, 60 acres of land to each plowetilt, viz. 20 acres in each field at the least'.

At Cowpen, there were at least two common fields in the seventeenth century, evidenced by articles of agreement for the division of the township into two parts in 1619,[6] which refers to a North Field and an East Field being allocated to the first part: presumably there was at least one other common field in the second part. An interesting

---

[1] *N.C.H.*, IX, 1909, p. 22.   [2] *Ibid.*, p. 124.
[3] *Ibid.*, p. 201.
[4] Gray, *English Field Systems*, p. 221.
[5] Alnwick Castle Ms., J.IX, no. 1 (*c*), 3.
[6] Northumberland R.O., ZMD 117*a*, *b*.

aspect of the management of the arable is contained in an account of the queen's demesne at Cowpen in 1599.

'At the layenge forth of any decayed or wasted corne feilde, and takinge in any new feildes of the common wastes in liewe thereof, everie tenawnte was and is to have so much lande in everie newe feilde as everie of them layde forth in everie wasted or decayed corne feilde, or accordinge to the rents of everie tenawnte's tenement in such place and places as did befall everie of them by their lott.'[1]

This describes the practice of reclaiming waste land as supplementary arable, and which, as already shown, was widespread in Northumberland. Its implications were examined by Gray,[2] who concluded that the 'abandonment of furlongs *within* the arable area would under any circumstances make impossible the existence of *compact* arable fields', and suggests that 'there is no reason why the term "field" should have been used in Northumberland with its midland significance'.[3] The broader implication of this practice will be discussed later, but the point may be made that given a large area of waste or common in close proximity to the common arable of a township, reclamation and reversion to and from arable, if confined to the outer furlongs of a field, could still maintain a fairly compact common field area.

(b) Northumberland: the scarplands, plateaux, interior vales and the Tyne valley

In general terms, the agrarian practices of townships in these regions in the seventeenth century were very similar to those of the coastal plain, the main feature being three or four large common arable fields, between which the holdings of the copyhold tenants were distributed in direct proportion to the size of the fields.

In 1567, Clarkson described the lordship of Chatton, situated on the west bank of the River Till, as being 'marvellously sited on the River Till, and the arable land is very good, specially about the town and river'.[4] A map produced to accompany the 1616 survey shows the farmsteads concentrated in the village,[5] sited on the west bank of the Till on an extensive spread of sand and gravel. The common arable fields lay to the west of the Till, and were bounded to the north by a southerly bend in the river to the north of the village. These fields were sited on surface deposits of sand and gravel, terrace

[1] N.C.H., IX, 1909, p. 334.
[2] Gray, *English Field Systems*, pp. 223–4.   [3] *Ibid.*, p. 224.
[4] Alnwick Castle Ms., A.I, 1g.
[5] Alnwick Castle Ms., O.x, 1 (1616).

gravels, alluvium and boulder clay – all widespread to the west of the town. To the east of the Till, beyond the common pasture, the land rises steeply from 200 to 700 feet, the location of Chatton Common and the former Chatton Park. Clarkson, in his survey, says that the township had been divided because of the large quantity of arable land and the consequent inaccessibility of the strips. Several divisions in fact took place, and by 1616 the arable land comprised five 'fields': Milneside Quarter (248 acres), Peppott Quarter (255 acres), Henlaw Quarter (246 acres), Gorbutt Quarter (85 acres) and East Field (183 acres). East Field was held by one tenant, and eight cottagers. The other 'fields' or quarters resulted from a division but the important feature is the near-equal size of the three large fields and the equal distribution of copyholders' holdings between them.[1] This suggests that although division and reallocation of land had taken place, a modified three-field system of management operated which may have been the system prior to division. The proportion of each holding in each field was of the order of: 10 acres in each of the three large fields and 3 acres in Gorbutt Quarter.

At South Charlton, north of Alnwick, there were four common arable fields in the early seventeenth century: North Field (142 acres), East Field (113 acres), Middle Field (58 acres) and West Field (147 acres).[2] Apart from the Middle Field, the similarity of size of the other three would suggest some kind of three-field arrangement: 'by combining the arable of the East Field and Middle Field we should get a total greater by only 30 than the area of each of the other fields, a not impossible three-field arrangement'.[3] Again, meadow land was included in each of these fields. The distribution of copyhold tenant holdings between the North, East, Middle and West fields was of the order of 9 acres, 7, 4 and 9. At Newham at this time there were, in contrast, two common arable fields, West Field (225 acres) and East Field (302 acres).[4] An interesting feature of this township was the fact that most of the tenants had twice as much arable in the East Field as in the West Field, and that one-third of the West Field was 'waste' land.

Between the Coquet and the Tyne, on the scarplands and within the Tyne valley itself, there is a great deal of evidence of common fields in the seventeenth century. References to 'common fields' are widespread (cf. Fig. 3.1) in this region, and combinations of three, four or more fields were commonly experienced, though the form

[1] Alnwick Castle Ms., A.iv, 5 (1616); A.v, 5 (1624).
[2] Alnwick Castle Ms., A.iv, 11 (1620); A.v, 5 (1622).
[3] Gray, *English Field Systems*, p. 212.
[4] Alnwick Castle Ms., A.iv, 14 (1620).

of arable management is not always clear. A map of Inghoe, dated
c. 1629 (Fig. 3.11)[1] shows four common arable fields. No terrier of
holdings is extant and it is thus difficult to assess the system of management. The proximity of two of the fields to the common does indicate,
however, the relative ease with which the arable area could be expanded
or contracted, with consequent inequalities in field size. The fields
survived in this form until the end of the seventeenth century, when
a division was agreed.[2] At Kirkwhelpington, a request for similar
agreement for division of the common fields, dated 1707, refers to
lands lying intermixed in the High Field, East Field and South Field.[3]
The townships of Clarewood and Halton Shields, just north of
Hadrian's Wall, both had three common fields in the seventeenth
century.[4] The fields at Clarewood were the East Field, West Field
and Pontacre Field, and at Halton the West Field, Middle Field and
South Field. A similar three-field arrangement appears to have existed
at Fallowfield, a settlement south of Hadrian's Wall just to the east
of the valley of the North Tyne. Beresford has described the features
of this deserted village, and the location of its common fields as
indicated by an Elizabethan plan and by surviving ridge-and-furrow.[5]
At Acomb, a township bordering Fallowfield on the south, there were
common fields in the seventeenth century, which were divided in
1694, but the number is not certain.[6] Great Whittington, a township
to the west of Clarewood, was divided and enclosed by articles of
agreement in 1687,[7] and the survey mentions three common fields.
A deed of sale of a holding in Aydon township in 1562 describes the
holding as comprising a messuage with a house, barn and garth on
the south side of the village, two houses at the west and a little garth
at the east end; and eight acres of arable in each of the three common
fields.[8] The fields of Corbridge, as has already been shown, survived
until the late eighteenth century, albeit in modified form. A survey
of 1664 describes the common fields which are known to have existed
a century later:[9]

'the names of common fields within this manor are as followeth.
The East Field, the North Field, Little Field, Low Farnelaw, West
Field and ye Eales. Which saide fields, after the corne and hay are
off, are laid open, and eaten, sometimes with, sometimes without,

[1] Alnwick Castle Ms., O.xviii, 3.
[2] Alnwick Castle Ms., J.iv, 6(h).
[3] Alnwick Castle Ms., J.iv, 3(k).   [4] N.C.H., x, 1914, p. 387.
[5] M. W. Beresford, 'Fallowfield, Northumberland: an early cartographic representation of a deserted village', Medieval Archaeology, x, 1966, pp. 164–7.
[6] N.C.H., iv, 1899, p. 140.   [7] N.C.H., x, 1914, p. 424.
[8] Ibid., pp. 367–8.   [9] Ibid., p. 140.

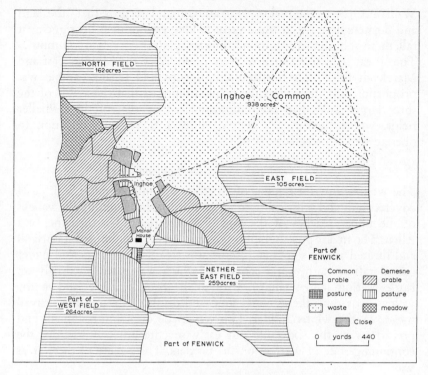

Fig. 3.11 The township of Inghoe (Northumberland) c. 1629.
Source. Alnwick Castle Ms. maps, O.xviii, 3.

stint. But how many beasts and sheep everie tenement may keep is
uncertain and left as ye Neighbours may agree among themselves;
and that severall parcels of ye common fields have been inclosed.'

Low Farnelaw was an improvement from the common. At Dilston,
on the opposite bank of the Tyne, there were three arable fields,
described in a series of leases made to tenants in 1632.[1] At Ovington,
on the north bank of the Tyne, there were three common arable
fields in the seventeenth century: Low Field, Middle Field and North
Field, totalling 600 acres in area.[2] These fields were divided by commissioners appointed by the freeholders in 1708. North of Ovingham
is Horsley, which had six common arable fields in the early seventeenth
century: East Field (197 acres), Nether East Field (67 acres), Middle
Field (142 acres), Gallow Field (46 acres), Morbridge Field (42 acres)
and Mareletch Field (141 acres).[3] In 1622, a certificate of survey from

[1] Ibid., p. 276.   [2] N.C.H., xii, 1926, p. 239.
[3] Alnwick Castle Ms., A.v, 7 (1624).

William Orde to the earl of Northumberland records that 'the land and farmers here lye in three great fieldes, everye man his rigge as it falleth, so as both ther common fieldes and pasture lye yett in common'.[1] The 'great fieldes' referred to were presumably the Middle, East and Mareletch fields. The distribution of copyhold tenants' arable was proportional to the size of the fields. It appears that the arable of the three larger fields had been supplemented by that of three smaller fields, which theoretically would allow a three-course rotation to operate without difficulty.

(c) Northumberland: the highland west

The western interior regions of Northumberland comprise high peat-covered hills and fells, rising to c. 3,000 feet, penetrated by the valleys of the upper reaches of the Aln, Coquet, Rede, North Tyne, and Allen. The major physiographic contrast between unlimited moorland and limited valley slopes and floors was reflected in the period under consideration in the rural economy, which was based essentially on cattle rearing (and stealing), with small areas of arable land in the valleys providing the essential food and drink grains and the alluvial meadows the winter fodder. Life was made even more difficult and precarious in the sixteenth and early seventeenth centuries by the continuing state of warfare on the borders. The society of these areas was

'one where the strong lived on the weak, and where "reiving", with its attendant arts of blackmail and murder were not thought of as a crime, but as the expression of a way of life. Violence was stimulated by the border, and by a mounting population pressure on available resources.'[2]

The border clans, according to a sixteenth-century survey, 'doe inhabit in some places three or fower household, soe that they cannot uppon soe small fermes without any other craftes live truely but either be stealing in England or Scotland'.[3] Violence was also conditioned by the strong blood and kinship ties of the border clan families,

'and in the archaic communities of Redesdale, Tynedale and Coquetdale in the upland of the East and Middle Marches, and in Bewcastle

[1] N.C.H., XII, 1926, p. 191.
[2] M. E. James, A Tudor Magnate and the Tudor State, Borthwick Papers No. 30, 1966, p. 10.
[3] Sir Robert Bowes, 'A book of the State of the Frontiers and Marches', printed in J. Hodgson, A History of Northumberland, pt. III (ii), 1828, p. 243, and cited by James, A Tudor Magnate, p. 11.

and Eskdale in the West, the joint family seems to have survived until well into the Tudor period, centring on the "stronge houses" built of "great sware oke trees strongly bounde and joined together with great tenors of the same" occupied by the headsmen of the "graynes" or clans'.[1]

A number of characteristic features of rural society and economy in these regions are described in the 1604 survey of the borders.[2] The most notable features are: the small size of the settlements and the small quantity of arable land; the predominance of cattle rearing, and the practice of transhumance; and the practice of partible inheritance.

The arable land of the isolated farms, hamlets and small villages was located in closes or in small common fields, and the border survey, with reference to the common fields, describes how the tenants in the manor of Harbottle 'soe, reape and moae each man his knowne grownd, and after the first crops they eate all in common without either stynt or number'. In the manor of Wark, which included land in North and South Tynedale, 'they till, reape and moe each their knowne grownde particularly, and often the first crope they eate all in common without stint or number, except in some places where the tenement lyeth in severall'. The most common crops in order of importance were: oats, four-rowed winter barley or 'bigg', rye, and wheat. Pulses were also grown for cattle food. In these districts, the form taken by the common arable fields appears to have varied from small single fields or groups of flatts, cultivated by the tenants of hamlets, to larger fields, occurring in groups of two or three, associated with the larger settlements, for example, of lower North Tynedale. Table 3.3 gives some idea of the relative proportion of land uses of each type in three small settlements in North Tynedale.

In North Tynedale in 1604 there were: sixty-seven farmhouses with eighty outhouses: 468 acres of meadow, 841 acres of arable, 1,140 acres of pasture, and 9,750 acres of waste or common. The larger settlements stand out from the small hamlets and single farms; Wark, for example, having eighteen customary tenants with 111 acres of arable, 183 acres of pasture, and 97 acres of meadow. There can be no doubt, however, that 'the highland farmer's main business was the breeding of cattle,

---

[1] M. E. James, *Change and Continuity in the Tudor North*, Borthwick Papers No. 27, York 1965, p. 6, citing Bowes and Ellekers 'Survey of the Borders, 1542', printed in Hodgson, *A History of Northumberland*, pt. III (ii), 1828, p. 232.

[2] R. P. Sanderson (ed.), *A Book of the Survey of the Debateable and Border Lands Adjoining the Realm of Scotland and Belonging to the Crown of England, 1604*, 1891.

Table 3.3. Land holdings in North Tynedale (Northumberland)
c. 1604

Place	Tenant's name	Rent (£ s. d.)	Buildings House	Out-(house)	Meadow (acres)	Arable (acres)	Pasture (acres)
The Nuke (Nook)	John Stokey	1 6	1		3	4	10
	Roman Charlton	1			4		6
	Edward Stokey	6		1	1	2	1
Total		3 0	1	1	8	6	17
The Shawe	George Dodd	2 8	1		6	7	4
	John Dodd	8	1		1	3	1
Total		3 4	2		7	10	5
							(roods)
Dunterley	Jarrat Charlton	8 4	1	1	4	6	25
	John Charlton	12 6	2	2	6	10	40
	John Charlton	3 2	1	1	3	4	18
	Henry Charlton	3 4	1	1	2	2	10
	Thos. Charlton	1 0				2	5 3
Total		1 8 4	5	5	15	24	98 3

Source: R. P. Sanderson (ed.), A Book of the Survey...1604, 1891.

which were sold as stores into more southerly counties, and the
keeping of sheep, which were pastured on the hills and were kept
for their wool'.[1] Other animals mentioned in records of the time were
horses, goats, pigs, and geese. An essential part of the animal husbandry
practised in these regions was the 'summering' of animals, or transhumance, on the sheilings of the high pastures. This practice was
a carefully controlled affair: the 1604 survey, referring to the North
and South Tynedale tenants, states that 'for their sheiling grownds
they doe begyn and end by agreement among themselves according
as the season falleth out'.[2] In the manor of Harbottle, there were
eighteen places or 'high landes called Summer growndes', totalling
21,200 acres.[3] 'The aforesaide growndes are used as summer and
sheildinge grounds by the inhabitants of the Manor, wherein each
man knoweth his sheildinge steed; and they sheylde together by
surnames, not keepinge catle according to the proporcion of the

[1] J. Thirsk, 'The Farming Regions of England', The Agrarian History of England
and Wales: IV, 1967, p. 22.
[2] Sanderson, Survey of the Border Lands, p. 51.
[3] Ibid., p. 104.

rent, but eatinge all in common without stint or number.'[1] The 'summering' season normally lasted until August, but could be terminated by unseasonable weather, or the activities of the Scots or of neighbouring clans.

The practice of partible inheritance was a significant factor in the rural life of these regions. This process of equal subdivision of a man's estate among all his sons, either at his death or at an earlier date when the sons were capable or desirous of owning their own land, is frequently mentioned in documents referring to life in these border areas. A certificate of the musters of the middle marches for 1580 contains a statement that the men of North and South Tynedale 'have ever had a custom, if a man have issue ten sons, eight, six, five or four, and sits on a holding but of six shillings rent, every son shall have a piece of his father's holding'.[2] This practice undoubtedly gave rise to high population pressure on the better quality land. In 1542 Tynedale and Redesdale were described as being 'overcharged' with inhabitants, and there can be no doubt that the physiographic population density of these areas was high, and that they were, under the existing conditions, overpopulated. The effects of partible inheritance are clearly seen in the small-sized holdings of tenants – members of the same family – who inhabited the hamlets of North and South Tynedale and Redesdale. Table 3.4 provides illustration of this fact, giving details of the holdings in Carrick, Headshope and Landshot, three small settlements in Redesdale in 1604.

(d) Durham

The existence of large common arable fields in County Durham in the late eighteenth century has already been demonstrated from the evidence of enclosure awards. The evidence for the earlier period under consideration confirms the fact that the management of arable land on the basis of three or more large common fields was a practice widespread in Durham in the sixteenth, seventeenth and eighteenth centuries. Most common arable fields were located in the east and south of the county, with few in the west (Fig. 3.1). Jacobean surveys of south Durham, cited by Gray, record the existence of fourteen three-field townships.[3] Bolam, whose common fields survived until the eighteenth century, in 1606 had three common fields, East Field, West Field and North Field, with both arable and meadow in each of the fields and the holdings divided almost equally between them.

[1] Ibid., p. 104.
[2] J. Bain (ed.), Calendar of Letters and Papers relating to the Affairs of the Borders of England and Scotland, vol. 1, 1894, p. 50.
[3] Gray, English Field Systems, p. 36, and App. III, p. 462.

Table 3.4. Land holdings in Redesdale (Northumberland)
c. 1604

Place	Names	Rent (£ s. d.)			Buildings Houses	Out-houses	Meadow a.	r.	Arable a.	r.	Pasture a.	r.
	Robert Pott Snr		2	4	1		3	2	3	2		
	John Pott		2	4	1		3	2	3	2		
	Reynold Pott		4	8	1	1	2		3	2		
Carrick	Robert Pott Jnr		8	2	1		5		4			
	George Pott		3	6	1		2	2	3			
	James Pott		1	9	1	1	2	2	7			
	Marke Pott		3	6	1	1	5		14			
	Anthony Pott		1	9	1		2	2	7			
Total		1	8	0	8	3	26	2	45	2	85	
	Jasper Pott		1	3	1	1			3	2		
	Robert Pott		1	3	1	1			3	2		
Headshope	Thomas Pott			11¼	1	1			2	2		
	Thomas Pott			11¼	1	1			2	2		
	Gregory Pott			7½	1				1	3		
Total			5	0	5	4			13	3	56	1
	John Hedley Snr		2	6	1		5		6			
Landshot	Anthony Hedley		2	6	1		5		6			
	William Hedley		2	6	1		5		6			
	John Hedley Jnr		2	6	1		5		6			
Total			10	0	4		20		24		36	

Source: R. P. Sanderson (ed.), A Book of the Survey...1604, 1891.

Gainford,[1] a village sited on a narrow gravel terrace of the Tees valley, had three common fields, West Field, Middle Field and East Field, mainly arable, and with the tenant holdings equally distributed. Three common arable fields were also recorded at Ingleton, Langton, Long Newton, Raby, Shotton, Summerhouse, Wackerfield, Wellington, Whitworth, Whorlton, West Wick and Wolviston.[2] Holdings in most places were evenly distributed among the three fields, although the relative proportions of arable and meadow in each varied. The location of these three-field townships is interesting: they occupied favourable physiographical locations, namely the gravel terraces of the middle Tees, notably between Barnard Castle and Darlington, the alluvial flat of the lower Tees, the terraces of the Wear, and the Magnesian

[1] Ibid., p. 462. [2] Ibid., pp. 462-3.

Limestone Plateau. The soils of these districts were variously described on the map accompanying Bailey's agricultural survey of Durham[1] as: 'Mostly dry, intermixed with clayey and moist loam', 'fertile strong clayey loam', 'clayey loam', 'dry loam on magnesian limestone', and 'moist soft loam on ochery clay'. Gray emphasises the importance of physiography on the field systems of these manors, 'situated for the most part where the moors slope eastward toward the valleys of the Tees and Wear. Those townships lying in the plain of the Tees were the ones in which the three-field system was most intact.'[2] Further indications of the existence of three-field townships are contained in records of the enclosure of many of the common fields of Durham in the seventeenth century.[3] In 1638, the North, South and East Townfields together with the Oxclose in Middridge, were enclosed by agreement. A similar process effected the enclosure of the Hither, Middle and Far Townfields in Bishop Auckland in 1651, Corn Pool Field, Millfield, Toft and Down Hill Field in East and West Boldon c. 1658, West Field and Croft, East Field and Croft, Hedge Field and Church Dean in Ryton, c. 1690, The East, West, and North Townfields in Newbottle c. 1700, and East Field, West Field, and South Field in Whitburn in 1718.[4] The numerous references to the enclosure of 'townfields' in Durham township in the seventeenth century suggest that a pattern of cultivation based on a three-field system, or limited variations of it, were widespread at that time. It is quite likely, however, that many of the examples quoted and of those which appear on Fig. 3.1 did not conform to an ideal pattern or model. Gray himself indicates that members of the manor of Brancepeth, lying to the west of Durham City and partly on the uplands, showed greater areas of pasture land and enclosures, for example, Crook and Billy Row, Thornley, Helme Park and Cornsey.[5] He considered that the large amount of meadow in the common fields at East Brandon, Eggleston, Westwick, Whorlton, Bolam and Willington, indicated an 'interesting departure from the normal system'.[6] The statistics reproduced by Gray for East Brandon[7] and Eggleston are certainly not indicative of 'model' three-field townships, and the fact that enclosure of the common fields in East Brandon took place in 1658 and, in all probability at Eggleston before the

---

[1] J. Bailey, *A General View of the Agriculture of Durham*, 1794.
[2] Gray, *English Field Systems*, p. 105.
[3] W. E. Tate, *Proc. Soc. Antiqu. Newcastle*, x, 1943, pp. 119–40; Leonard, *Trans. R. Hist. Soc.* XIX, 1905, pp. 101–46.
[4] Tate, *Proc. Soc. Antiqu. Newcastle*, x, 1943, pp. 125–40.
[5] Gray, *English Field Systems*, p. 105.
[6] *Ibid.*, p. 107.   [7] *Ibid.*, pp. 534–5.

end of the seventeenth century, might indicate a late stage of development and modification of the field systems there.

Observations made by topographers and travellers through Durham in the seventeenth century give a general impression of the east and south of the county having the greatest amount of arable in common fields. East Durham was described as the 'richest and most champion' part of the county. Blome, in 1673, described east Durham as the most champion part of the county, and the south as the most fertile part. Ogilby, in his *Intinerary*, in 1675, showed the county in open arable along the road from Whitby to the North.[1] In contrast, the highlands and moors of the west of the county had very little arable. The upper reaches of what have been termed the 'lead dales' of the northern Pennines differ in many respects from the 'border dales' to the north: apart from Teesdale, they are higher in altitude; their sides do not have the same continuous drift cover as the border dales; and there was no parallel social organisation based on the kinship group such as was found in the border dales.[2] The basic rural economy of the dales and surrounding moorlands in the early modern period was almost entirely pastoral in emphasis, with the density of rural settlement and of population being much lower than that of the border dales.

In Durham, as in Northumberland, there appears to have been a region whose physiographic characteristics and agrarian practice were intermediate between those of the highland west and lowland south and east. This is the region comprising the sandstone plateau south of the Tyne (the southern counterpart of the transitional low plateau and scarplands to the north). Surveys of Ravensworth, Farnacres, Kibblesworth and Byker, four townships in the northeast of the plateau, give some idea of the form of their open fields in the early eighteenth century.[3] The map of Ravensworth in 1712[4] shows a large area of open arable to the east of the village divided into strips of varying sizes and shapes. To the east of this 'field' and the River Tame was a large area of closes, whose names suggest that this was an area of former open arable ('Mar Flatt', 'Rilling Flat'). To the south was an area of open and enclosed pasture. The pattern of open and enclosed fields seems to indicate a two-field system here. The size of the tenants' farms in this and the other townships showed a preponderance of pasture over arable: at Ravensworth in 1712 'in no case did the proportion of arable and meadow to pasture rise

[1] Cited by Tate, *Proc. Soc. Antiqu. Newcastle*, x, 1943, p. 122.
[2] Smailes, *North England*, p. 151.
[3] The contents of these surveys are described by E. Hughes, *North Country Life in the Eighteenth Century. The North East 1700–1750*, 1952, pp. 132–6.
[4] *Ibid.*, between pp. 132 and 133.

above a third', at Farnacres and Whickham 'in every case the amount of arable was fractional or non-existent'.[1] At Byker, the arable comprised *c.* one-third of the holdings. Cuthbertson's map of Farnacres in 1715[2] shows that most of the land was enclosed, but 'every tenant, in addition to his enclosed lands, had a specified number of riggs on the "townfield"': Edward Liddell had 48 riggs, Thomas Lee 64 and Ralph Surties 51.[3] This is obviously a very late arrangement, but the scale of arable cultivation is very much smaller than that of southern and eastern Durham and of lowland Northumberland, and could be representative of a former two-field or intensive one-field system. It is important to remember, however, that these townships had been strongly influenced (being located in the coalfield area) by the progress of coal-mining, which had facilitated enclosure and agricultural improvement and considerably modified the former appearance of these townships.

2. THE ANATOMY OF THE COMMON FIELDS

The smallest unit in the common fields was the 'rigg' or 'land'. Each rigg was separated from its neighbour by a furrow, colloquially known as a 'floor'. The size of the riggs varied widely, though the majority were less than half an acre in area, and the term 'half acres' occurs frequently in the names of furlongs. Length of riggs again varied widely, with a maximum length of *c.* 600 yards. The breadth of most riggs was between 4 and 16 yards, with an average breadth of about 12 yards. Their shape varied enormously, from short and straight to long and sinuous, with a host of intermediate categories. In most cases the rigg was the basic unit of tenancy and of cultivation, though there are a number of instances where the rigg was shared by two tenants, and references to half-riggs appear in estate surveys. Many of them were separated by grass balks: these were a notable feature of the common arable fields and appear on maps and in documents. Clarkson, in 1567, refers to lands in the common fields at Denwick (Nd) which 'lye in everie place of the said feldes boundred with brode balkes wch. were requisite sholde not be made arable but contynewe yn the same order they now be yn'.[4] The survey of Acklington (Nd) in 1616 gives a total area of 2½ acres of balks in the North field, 4 acres in the East field and 8 acres in the South field (though the latter figure included other pieces of waste land other than balks).[5] The balks functioned as boundaries, access ways to lands

[1] *Ibid.*, pp. 134–5.   [2] *Ibid.*, between pp. 154 and 155.   [3] *Ibid.*, p. 135.
[4] Alnwick Castle Ms., A.I, 1(a).
[5] Alnwick Castle Ms., A.IV, 4 (1616).

and furlongs, and as grazing land for animals: right of way and grazing rights were, of course, jealously preserved, and enforced by the manor court. The boundaries of lands were also delimited by furrows and by marker stones.

Riggs were grouped in furlongs, for which the common names in Northumberland and Durham were 'flatts,' furshotts', and 'sheths', though in many cases the names given to these bundles of strips were simply 'acres', 'lands', or 'riggs', usually prefaced with a descriptive or locational adjective. The number of riggs in each furlong varied considerably.

Sizes of furlongs also varied, with the largest furlongs, often comprised of very long and sinuous riggs, having an area of 50 acres or more. The normal size of furlongs was, however, much smaller than this. The ends of the furlongs were frequently marked by a headland, and they could also be bounded by balks, although, as already seen, there could also be balks within furlongs.

In most townships of Northumberland and Durham, the furlongs were grouped together to form 'fields', whose size and number have already been discussed, and the significance of which is discussed in the following sections.

3. THE MANAGEMENT OF THE COMMON FIELDS

Although comparatively little is known in detail, as yet, of variations in land management in Northumberland and Durham in the period 1550–1750, there is sufficient information in the documents to outline the general principles of arable land management. The practice of fallowing arable land to allow soil to recuperate from exhaustive cropping was widespread, as also was the practice of allowing animals to graze on the stubble of the common fields after harvest and also on the fallow land. Tenants at Beanley (Nd), in 1612, were allowed to keep six cattle and twenty sheep on the common, 'with the help and eatedge of their feilds when the corn and hay is off'.[1] A question asked of deponents in an Exchequer Commission of 1580 seeks to discover the truth of the claim, for Elstwick (Nd), that

'the said late prior and his predecessors have enjoyed the pasture or eatedge of all the usual arable grounds...yearly throughout the year at their will and pleasure when the said arable grounds lay fallow, and yearly from and after the first vesture or crop at usual times where taken away until about the day commonly called

[1] Alnwick Castle Ms., A.IV, 1.

St Cuthbert's day in such years as the same arable grounds were to be sown with summer corn, after the season of that country'.[1]

A deponent confirms this fact. The practice of fallowing arable land survived well into the eighteenth century, and in many places continued after enclosure had taken place.[2] It is difficult, however, to establish the exact details of this practice, and of the crop rotation system with which it was associated. In the early seventeenth century, the earl of Northumberland held in Hazon (Nd) eight tenements called 'Thirckeld's Lands', which comprised '264 acres, of which a third part every year lay fallow and two parts in corn'.[3] According to Heslop, the object of the distinct grouping of holdings into fields or 'athers' 'was to arrange for a rotation of crops. Thus the East field being fallow, the West field would be under oats, the North field under wheat, and so on in annual rotation.'[4] There are, however, few direct indications of a rotational system in which one-third of the land lay fallow in any one year. The frequent occurrence of three common arable fields in townships of this region, and the frequency of near-equal distribution of copyhold tenants' arable between them *may* indicate an attempt to balance the cultivation of crops in two of the fields by the fallowing of a third, but it is also likely that the cropping system was highly complex, with furlongs rather than fields being the units of cropping and fallowing in some places.

Management of the common fields was further complicated by the practice of allowing furlongs in the common fields to revert to pasture and waste, and of reclaiming land from pasture or waste by ploughing and distributing the riggs among tenants. Examples of these practices have already been cited, and such references are very common in the estate surveys of the seventeenth century. The two practices are amply illustrated in the survey of Acklington (Nd) for 1616, which describes 'some of this field called Moore lands, being all lately taken of the common and converted to arable, conteyning 98 (acres) 1 (rood), 27 (perches)'.[5] There were also in the North Field, where the Moor lands were located, 'certain small pieces of common within this field left nonplowed conteyning together 7 (acres) 2 (roods) 39 (perches)'.[6] Part of Deane's Flatt, in the East Field, 'before was comon pasture and now lately plowed upp and devided among the tenants themselves, with their own appointment, without privity of the officer'.[7] Clarkson

---

[1] P.R.O., E.134 *23 Eliz.* (1580), Hil. 6, Elstwick.
[2] Hughes, *North Country Life*, p. 138.
[3] *N.C.H.*, v, 1899, p. 465.
[4] R. E. Heslop, *Northumberland Words. A Glossary*, I, 1892.
[5] Alnwick Castle Ms., A.IV, 4 (1616).   [6] *Ibid.*
[7] *Ibid.*

in 1567 states that the tenants at Guysance have 16 riggs in every new rift (intake) 'wch is to be made arable and wch before was lee or pasture ground'.[1] The tenants at Chatton at this time had their land allotted 'rigg by rigg, as is the custom in every husband towne'.[2] The high proportion of 'waste' in many of the townships of Northumberland and Durham at this time undoubtedly facilitated this practice.

Crops most frequently cultivated were oats, barley, rye and wheat, with peas also figuring prominently. The difficulty of interpretation of the use of the terms 'hard corn' (which could mean wheat or rye) makes assessment of regional variations in cropping practices, as reflected in wills and inventories, very difficult indeed. The evidence of sixteenth- and seventeenth-century surveys and wills and inventories indicates, however, that wheat was more commonly sown in the lowland areas of Northumberland and Durham than in the higher upland areas of the west, where oats were more important.

4. MEADOWS

A crop of ubiquitous importance was grass. The existence of relatively large areas of meadow within the common fields of Northumberland and Durham can be readily understood by reference to the great importance of animals in the rural economy of the region. The breeding and fattening of both sheep and cattle was the most important sector of the rural economy of this region, and is reflected in the very large numbers of sheep and cattle recorded in surveys and inventories, both in the upland and lowland areas. It is not surprising, therefore, that alluvial flats were fully utilised as meadows, both within and without the common fields. The meadows were normally protected by a ditch or fence to prevent cattle from straying into them between Candlemas and the time of mowing. The most common method of working the meadows was to divide them into strips or dales, and these were allocated annually by lot or rotation, or on a more permanent basis. At Denwick in 1618, the Gynsen meadow was divided into 40 dales, each dale being 1 acre 1 rood and thirty-one and nine-sixteenths of a perch in area. Each tenant had three dales in this meadow.[3] The meadows in the common fields there were also divided into dales. A different method of utilisation was the allocation to the tenants of a certain number of swathes or cocks of hay after it had been mown: at Buston (Nd) in 1616, Southwell dales and Short Butts in the North

---

[1] Alnwick Castle Ms., A.I, 1f.
[2] Alnwick Castle Ms., A.I, 1g.
[3] Alnwick Castle Ms., I.IV, 8 (1618).

Field 'being common meadow', were 'divided by cocks of hay'. The Broad Meadows of Denwick (Nd) were divided into 444 'swathes',[1] allocated to tenants as groups of two swathes per tenant. Like the common arable, the common meadows after the hay had been led off were used for grazing, usually on the basis of stints, and fenced again before the spring growth.

In addition to the grazing provided by the stubble of the common arable and of the meadows, the ox pasture was also a common type of pasturage. This was usually an area of good quality grassland, often located on the same type of soil as the common fields. The ox pasture was normally located between the common arable fields and the common waste. At Rennington (Nd) the ox pasture (226 acres) lay in two parts, one in the northwestern part of the township, adjacent to the North and West Fields, the other in the eastern part, adjacent to the meadow.[2] At West Thirston (Nd) there were two ox-closes, one (74 acres) west of the West Crofts (a common arable field), the other located between the common waste and the South Field.[3] Scarcity of good quality pasture was frequently noted by surveyors: a 1586 survey of Birling (Nd) states that 'they be forced to jeyst (agist) their cattle in the summer quarter in Shilbottle Wood because their ox pasture be little in quantity'. The same survey states that 'the ox pasture of Bilton is now but little, they are forced in summertime to agist their oxen in Cawledge Park or elsewhere to their great charge'.[4] The importance of the ox pasture was reflected in rigorous stinting. At Denwick (Nd) in 1567 'the stint of each husbandland in their own several pasture is 6 oxen'.[5] An account of 1539 records that the tenants of the townships of Middle Chirton, Preston, Monkseaton, Backworth and Eastwick, in southeast Northumberland, were each allowed to depasture six oxen in their ox pastures.[6] The term frequently used in seventeenth-century surveys to describe the stinting of pastures was 'gait': Most of the earl of Northumberland's townships recorded in the 1612–24 surveys had 'gaited' pastures.[7] The ox pasture, like the common arable, was sometimes supplemented by land improved from the common waste.

5. CLOSES

Not all of the improved land in the townships of this region was open and common. Enclosure of common arable, meadow and pasture

[1] *Ibid.*   [2] Alnwick Castle Ms., A.IV, 8 (1618).
[3] Alnwick Castle Ms., A.IV, 15 (1620).
[4] Alnwick Castle Ms., A.II, 1.   [5] Alnwick Castle Ms., A.I, 1(a).
[6] W. S. Gibson, *A History of the Priory of Tynemouth*, I, 1846, p. 217.
[7] Alnwick Castle Ms., A.V, 8 (1624).

had begun in the early medieval period, and the amount of land in each township enclosed during or prior to the sixteenth, seventeenth and eighteenth centuries varied widely. Depopulating enclosure took place in the late sixteenth century, notably in southeastern Northumberland, where Robert Delaval, who had been an agent to the earl of Northumberland, had evicted tenants in Hartley and Seaton Delaval, and converted the arable land to pasture.[1] Similar action was taken at Seghill by Robert Mitforth.[2] By the mid-seventeenth century, substantial areas of demesne and freehold land had been enclosed, notably in the townships of the lowland region. The demesne lands at Hedley Woodside (Nd) comprised a number of closes which 'being woodish ground, are occupied among his lordship's tenants and freeholders by stint known to themselves'.[3] At Harlow by 1624, all the land had been enclosed, and each close was shared and farmed by two of the tenants.[4] Instances of partial enclosure of part of the common arable, pasture and meadow by copyhold tenants are rare, for such a process was normally prohibited. The great majority of closes referred to in sixteenth-, seventeenth- and eighteenth-century surveys and documents in townships which had not been totally enclosed, were enclosed demesne land which had been leased to the copyhold tenants. During the course of the seventeenth and early eighteenth century, enclosure by agreement proceeded at a very rapid pace in both Northumberland and Durham, and succeeded in removing the old systems of cultivation and landholding in a very short period of time.

6. 'INFIELDS' AND 'INGROUNDS'

A term frequently used in connection with the common arable, meadow and improved pasture of the townships of Northumberland and Durham is 'infields', or more frequently 'ingrounds', as contrasted with the 'outfields' or 'outgrounds'. A document describing the division of part of Acklington (Nd) in 1686 stated that 'Robert Smart and William Clay shall have the furlong, the Dande flatt, two acres and a half of Smales. . .and the five riggs in the croft for their ingrounds, and for their outpasture the parcell called High Cheveby.'[5] Another document contains the stipulation that 'all neighbours shall separate their infield cattle on the 1st March 1687, and raise their inground division dykes before the 1st May next'. The outpasture dykes were to be raised before 1688.[6] A petition for the enclosure of Inghoe (Nd) in 1696 asked that the Duke of Somerset 'would please to consent to

[1] N.C.H., x, 1914, p. 24.   [2] N.C.H., ix, 1922, p. 69.
[3] Alnwick Castle Ms., A.v (1624).   [4] Alnwick Castle Ms., A.v, 8 (1624).
[5] Alnwick Castle Ms., J.xi, 6 (3).   [6] Alnwick Castle Ms., J.xi, 6 (7).

a division, as well of ye Inngrounds as (ye) Moore of Ingo'.[1] In the enclosure award of 1717 for Heddon on the Wall (Nd) the arbitrators state that they 'have caused all the said ingrounds, viz. arable, meadows and pasture grounds' to be surveyed and measured.[2] It is clear, from consideration of the contexts in which the terms 'ingrounds' and 'infields' are used, that they are not necessarily indicative of that system of agriculture, which has been called the infield–outfield system,[3] for the evidence cited above, which includes references to 'infields' and 'ingrounds' in townships where three common fields are known to have existed, suggests that the terms were used to contrast the 'improved' land near the village with the largely un-improved waste or common. Thus only in a very broad way are they indicative of land management systems.

7. WASTES

Unimproved common pasture, or 'waste', formed an integral part of the land management system of every community in Northumberland and Durham at this time. The high moors of the western uplands were, as has already been indicated, extensively used as sheilings during the summer for the communities of the border dales. The proportion of waste was, however, also high in the townships of the scarplands, coastlands and river valleys, varying in most cases between *c.* 30 and 60 per cent of the total area of the township. The prime function of the common waste was that of providing pasture for animals. The practice of intercommoning was widespread. The tenants of Alnmouth (Nd) had common of pasture 'for all manner of cattle without stint together with the tenants of Lord Houghton in a long common lying between the fields of Lesbury and Houghton'.[4] The inhabitants of Chatton (Nd) had 'a large common for their cattell to depasture upon, in which divers townes adjoining to the said common have by sufference of the inhabitants and bailiff there, pasture for their cattell, and divers townships in Bamburghshire licence to take turf and hather'.[5] Shildon Moor (Nd) was intercommoned in the sixteenth and seventeenth centuries by the townships of Acomb, Beal, Bywell, Newton Hall, Stelling, Clarewood, Halton Shields, East Matfen, Naftenton, Ovington and Welton, for which they paid 'moor silver' to the bailiff of Bywell.[6] Another large intercommoned

---

[1] Alnwick Castle Ms., J.iv, 6 (4).   [2] Northumberland R.O., ZMD. 86.
[3] See: R. A. Butlin, 'The Runrig System', *Area*, no. 3, 1969, pp. 44–7.
[4] Alnwick Castle Ms., A.iv. 3 (1614).
[5] Alnwick Castle Ms., A.iv, 5 (1616).
[6] Alnwick Castle Ms., A.i, 1(q).

moor was the Shire moor north of Newcastle. Complaints about overstocking of common wastes with cattle were frequent, and in some townships stinting applied: at Denwick in 1567 the stint of each husbandland was 6 old beasts above two years old, 37 sheep above one year old besides lambs and other young cattle, four pigs above one year old, two geese and one gander and one horse or mare.[1] In addition to the pasturage, the wastes were also important sources of turf for fuel, and were used as sources of supplementary arable.

8. LAND TENURE

By far the largest class of farmers were the customary tenants, whose holdings or farms made up the greater part of the township. In the lowland townships the number of tenants with husbandlands or farms ranged between c. 10 and 30, with the farms ranging in size from c. 26 to 80 acres. The farms comprised the riggs or lands in the common arable fields, widely scattered and intermixed, and dales in the meadows, with attendant rights of commonage over the common fields, pastures and wastes. Each customary tenant normally had one farm or husbandland, but sometimes two or three or sometimes half. The farm or 'husbandland' was a common unit of tenure, which appears to have derived from the bondage holdings into which many medieval vills and their lands were divided.[2] The important features of these landholdings were almost exact original equality in their size, exact equality of attendant rights of commonage, and of customary services. In time, this equality became less exact, through both differential expansion and contraction, even within the same township. Nevertheless, the husbandlands in the seventeenth century still exhibited a high degree of equality of size. At Rennington (Nd) in 1618 there were ten husbandlands, each farmed by one tenant:[3] nine of these were between 71 and 75 acres in size, the other being 67 acres. They comprised land in the common arable fields, meadows and ox pasture, houses and garths, and the proportions of each of them in each of the fields were virtually the same. At Long Houghton (Nd), South end, there were thirteen husbandlands, farmed by twelve tenants, one of whom had two husbandlands. The size varied little: from 47 to 52 acres. This equality is highly characteristic of the Northumberland townships and occurs also in Durham. The attendant right of commonage was proportionate to the number of husbandlands held, and new intakes of arable were

[1] Alnwick Castle Ms., A.I, 1(a).
[2] F. W. Dendy, 'The Ancient Farms of Northumberland', *Arch. Ael.*, XVI, 1894, pp. 121-56.
[3] Alnwick Castle Ms., A.IV, 8 (1618).

allocated in strict rotation among the tenants according to the number of farms held. It appears from nineteenth-century lawsuits that the fundamental principle behind the husbandland was the notion of entitlement of tenants to a fixed share of the land of a township, a share originally deemed a sufficient basis to provide a living for one family.[1] Labour and other customary services were still performed by these customary tenants in the sixteenth and seventeenth centuries, though they were gradually being commuted for payment. The cottagers, of whom there were usually between 8, 9, or 10 in each lowland township, had a few acres in the common fields, often paid rental in poultry or eggs, and contributed a share of labour (other than ploughing). One service common to the whole region until the seventeenth century was the keeping of arms ready to serve in defence against attacks of the Scots. This service was a condition of the customary tenures of the borders, and gave to some a degree of security of tenure which they would not normally have enjoyed, for in theory they could not be evicted from their tenancies if they were furnished with horse and armour. The border tenures, as they are sometimes called, 'really form a special and a very perplexing subject'.[2] and their relevance to a consideration of agrarian conditions derives essentially from their influence in retarding agrarian change. With the abolition of border tenure, however, in the early seventeenth century, its influence declined and agrarian change followed rapidly.

Freeholders were much less numerous than customary tenants in this region. In most cases their arable lands were interspersed with those of the customary tenants and they had similar rights of common. The demesne lands of the region had largely been demised to freeholders and customary tenants, and great difficulty was experienced by the early seventeenth century in establishing their exact size and location.

After the termination of border warfare in 1603, agrarian change proceeded rapidly. Landlords gradually substituted leases for the traditional customary tenures, and a general dissatisfaction with the old unprofitable agrarian methods resulted in the division of townships into halves and quarters, for more rational concentration of holdings, and ultimately in enclosure, usually by 'agreement'. The growing urban markets, particularly of Newcastle, stimulated more intensive cereal cultivation and the production of better quality cattle and sheep. The rise of the coal industry in this region during the seventeenth and eighteenth centuries speeded the disappearance of common rights over various types of land and was thus a potent influence on agrarian progress. By c. 1750, therefore, the number of townships in the

[1] Dendy, *Arch. Ael.*, XVI, 1894, p. 148.
[2] D. L. W. Tough, *The Last Years of a Frontier*, 1928, p. 57.

region operating under a communal system of management had substantially declined, and in many instances the open and common fields had been replaced by a pattern of enclosed and several fields.

F. MEDIEVAL FIELD SYSTEMS

The antecedents of the field systems of the early modern period are not easily traced, but an attempt can be made on the basis of medieval material to discern the basic features of agrarian practices.[1]

The pattern of distribution of settlements and associated arable land, as evidenced by the medieval land surveys and fiscal documents of Northumberland and Durham, shows remarkable similarity with the pattern of distribution in the sixteenth and seventeenth centuries. The largest and wealthiest vills recorded in the 1296 lay subsidy roll for Northumberland were those in Wansbeck and Coquet Wards, located on the fertile plain and lower scarplands north of the River Wansbeck. The next richest ward was Glendale, including the valleys of the upper and lower Till, followed by East Tynedale Ward, bounded to the south by the Tyne, on the west by Watling Street, on the east by an imaginary line running north from Prudhoe and on the north by the Wansbeck. The latter ward was densely populated, with a high density of vills in the southeast. The coastal plain north of Alnwick had 13 vills. East and West Coquet, and West Tynedale had low vill densities and were the least wealthy districts. The liberty of Tynemouth appears from the subsidy to have been one of the least wealthy divisions of the county, but this is probably the result of the inclusion of outlying members and the fact that not all the population contributed.[2] A truer picture is given by the tallage record for 1294, which shows that the average landholding included 36 acres of arable. Estimates of arable land and population density for Durham in 1183, 1380 and 1418 indicate relatively high densities in the southern and eastern parts of the county.[3] The sandstone plateau and lower Pennine spurs, particularly in the fourteenth century, appear to have had as relatively high densities of population and arable land. The high moors of the west were largely devoid of settlement, as were the upper reaches of the river valleys, but the valleys of the coalfield district were settled,

---

[1] P. Dickenson and W. B. Fisher, *The Medieval Land Surveys of County Durham*, University of Durham, Department of Geography, Research Papers series no. 2, 1959; F. Bradshaw, 'The Lay Subsidy Roll of 1296 – Northumberland at the End of the Thirteenth Century', *Arch. Ael.*, XIII, 3rd Ser., 1916, pp. 186–303.

[2] Bradshaw, *Arch. Ael.*, XII, 1916, p. 216.

[3] Fisher and Dickenson, *Medieval Land Surveys of Durham*, 1959, pp. 7–9.

and colonisation of the wastes above them had begun. The settlement units in the west were small, contrasting with the larger villages of the lowlands and plateaux. The strong pastoral emphasis in many of the vills of Durham at this time is reflected in the large number that paid cornage dues, although the vills in the Tees vale in Darlington ward did not render this due: a reflection of the greater emphasis on corn-growing.[1]

Although broad regional variations in population density and in agrarian emphasis can be distinguished, it is virtually impossible to give a clear picture of the form of cultivation. The basic unit of cultivation referred to in documents appears to have been the furlong. In 1334, for example, the castle demesne lands, held by the men of Bamburgh (Nd), comprised: '11 acres at Netheredlange, $11\frac{1}{2}$ acres in a cultivated piece called Querredlanges, 4 acres in Rankestane flat, $4\frac{1}{2}$ acres in Horselawes, $4\frac{1}{2}$ acres 1 rood in Katacre, $28\frac{1}{2}$ acres in Estcrosflat, 27 acres in Westcrosflat, 6 acres in Sewleyes, $6\frac{1}{2}$ acres 1 rood in Baserflat, 9 acres 1 rood in Swanlawflat, 33 acres in Northfield, 10 acres 1 rood in Querelflat, $5\frac{1}{2}$ acres in Blyndewell flat, 12 acres 1 rood in Shelrygge, 9 acres in Stokflat, $4\frac{1}{2}$ acres 1 rood in Grenwell-flat'.[2] Of the existence of small intermixed riggs in the furlongs of many of the medieval villages there is no doubt, but the evidence for the concentration of furlongs into definite fields is very scanty. Gray cites evidence which hints at the existence of three fields at Billingworth (Nd), and of two fields at Whittonstall (Nd), Cramlington (Nd) and Leighton (Nd) in the thirteenth century, but the evidence is not conclusive.[3] The account of medieval Durham in the Victoria County History assumes that the model three-field system operated in Durham, although 'this ideal system had ceased to correspond to the actual even before the Black Death'.[4] Before attempting any conclusive assessment of the form of the common arable fields in the medieval period, two other factors should be considered: the intaking of land for arable, and the rotations practised.

There is much evidence to suggest that from the twelfth century onwards, the conversion of pasture and waste to arable land was a common activity. A perambulation of Shoreston (Nd) in 1250 makes reference to a series of lands newly broken up out of the common pasture of the township.[5] The Black Book of Hexham Priory (1379) records that if the lord of Fenwick and Matfen (Nd) wish to plough up part of the common, the Prior and convent 'shall receive their share for their portion in such ploughland by lot; as they did before

[1] Smailes, North England, p. 92.   [2] N.C.H., I, 1893, p. 126.
[3] Gray, English Field Systems, pp. 218–20.
[4] V.C.H. Durham, II, 1907, p. 196.   [5] N.C.H., I, 1893, p. 310.

in the other arable land, namely by the old intakes, in each place a third'.[1] This practice was also experienced in Durham.[2]

The second notable feature was the existence of a three-course rotation over the arable acres. Gray cites a three-course rotation at Hextold (Nd) in 1232 of wheat and rye, oats, and fallow, and a one-third fallow at Hepscott (Nd).[3] The 30 acres of a serf at Billingham (D) were cultivated as follows: 10 acres fallow, 5 acres wheat, 5 acres barley, and 10 acres of peas and oats. The prior of Tynemouth (Nd), according to a custumal dated 1200, was entitled to enclose a portion of the land lying fallow in the township, and depasture his cattle there.[4] Intensification of cultivation could, however, result in the sowing of part or whole of the fallow field.[5] Communal grazing rights over the common fields at certain times of the year were also an integral part of the farming system.

The form and management of the common arable lands of this region in the medieval period is a subject which requires much more detailed investigation before any definitive assessments can be made. It is possible, however, to postulate the existence, in the more favoured areas, of an embryonic field system. This comprised a number of furlongs, loosely grouped for the purposes of crop rotation and in some cases more permanently grouped into larger common fields. In time, with the continued expansion of the arable area in regions of increasing population, the grouping of furlongs into two, three or more common fields became a more widespread occurrence, and explains the large number of multiple-field townships which existed in the sixteenth, seventeenth and early eighteenth centuries. In practice, of course, the genesis of medieval fields and field systems was much more complex than this, and a more complete explanation must take into account not only the periodic contraction of arable land, produced for example in the fourteenth century by plague and by the widespread devastation of Scots raids in the border region, but also the question of changes in land tenure and in the form and fortune of demesne land.[6] When such a task has been accomplished, it may then be possible to take a further step back into the past, and discover the antecedents of the medieval system, about which virtually nothing is known at present.

[1] N.C.H., XII, 1926, p. 366.
[2] V.C.H. Durham, II, 1907, p. 194.
[3] Gray, English Field Systems, p. 221.
[4] N.C.H., VIII, 1907, p. 250.
[5] V.C.H. Durham, II, 1907, p. 216.
[6] E. M. Halcrow, 'The Decline of Demesne Farming on the Estates of Durham Cathedral Priory', Econ. Hist. Rev., VII, 1955, pp. 345–56.

G. CONCLUSION

Perhaps the most significant fact which emerges from a study of the evolution of the field systems of Northumberland and Durham is the marked regional contrast in field form and management which appeared in early medieval times and continued into the early modern period. The basic contrast was between, on the one hand, the moorland and fell areas of the west, where arable cultivation associated with hamlets and isolated farms was always limited in scale by the limited quantities of lowland and thus always a relatively minor item in the agrarian economy, and, on the other hand, the more favoured valleys, plains and scarplands to the east, where even in medieval times relatively large areas of arable were recorded for the many large nucleated villages and where increases in the arable areas took place down to the end of the seventeenth century. This basic contrast in the scale of arable farming is also reflected in the number of fields on which cultivation appears to have been based on what might be termed a one-field system. The evidence for this is largely inferential, though there appear to have been single arable fields at Nunwick (Nd) in the North Tyne valley,[1] Eals (Nd) in Knaresdale,[2] Slaggyford (Nd) in the South Tyne valley,[3] and Catton in Allendale,[4] in the early seventeenth and eighteenth centuries, with many instances of small arable fields farmed by family groups recorded in the border dales in the border survey of the early seventeenth century.[5] In contrast to this single-field system was what might be termed the multiple-field system of the physiographically more favoured areas, which reached full development in the late sixteenth and early seventeenth centuries, after which its character was changed by division and subsequently by total enclosure. Very little is known of the crop rotations of the multiple common field townships, but their relative size and the relatively equal distribution of tenant holdings between fields suggests that they were in fact more than merely loosely grouped furlongs (at least in the early modern period). Their long-term evolution is a matter for conjecture, but the general absence of references to fields (as opposed to furlongs) in medieval documents, together with the considerable amount of assarting which took place, might suggest a gradual evolution from

[1] N.C.H., xv, 1940, p. 198.
[2] J. C. Hodgson, A History of Northumberland, Part III, vol. II, 1828, p. 404.
[3] Northumberland R.O., Hedley Ms., ZHE 17/5.
[4] Northumberland R.O., Q.R.A. no. 31.
[5] Sanderson (ed.), Survey of Debateable Lands in 1603.

a system based on groups of furlongs to one based on one, two, three or more common fields. The sixteenth and seventeenth centuries provide much evidence of a 'classic' common field system (including a highly regular distribution of holdings among fields) and of re-distribution and reorganisation of fields and holdings. This raises the interesting hypothesis that such a system may be of relatively recent origin, at least in Northumberland and Durham and possibly in other parts of Britain.

The detailed character of these systems was, of course, influenced by factors other than physiography, including the prevalence of a bond system giving rise to the unit of tenure known as the husbandland, the existence of partible inheritance in the border dales, the influence of border tenure and of the secular and ecclesiastical autocracy, the effects of border warfare and the economic impact of growing population and of coal mining.

Finally, it is perhaps worth noting the difficulty of applying currently accepted terminological labels to the field systems described above. The terms 'infield' and 'outfield', 'ingrounds' and 'outgrounds' are used in documents relating to agrarian practice, but it is not possible to assume that this is indicative of an 'infield-outfield', or 'runrig' system (whatever it may have been) – which is assumed by some to have been prevalent over much of Northern England – except in the sense of a form of agrarian organisation in which a fundamental distinction is made between the better quality land near the main settlement and the poorer quality land beyond. The terms 'three-field system' or 'Midland system' are in some respects equally unhelpful, except as the description of a 'model' system against which regionally experienced forms of field systems may be measured.

4

Field Systems of Yorkshire

BY JUNE A. SHEPPARD

The county of Yorkshire lies athwart H. L. Gray's Midland zone, and evidence collected since 1915 has confirmed Gray's picture of the centre and east of the county as an area where common arable fields cultivated on a fixed rotation once prevailed. Research during the past twenty years however has shown that the contrast between this zone and the western parts of the county, which Gray included in his Celtic zone, was not so great as he suggested; it has also revealed that even in the centre and east there were considerable variations both from one township to another and from one period to another in the details of the field system. While some variations defy easy explanation, others show a relationship to such factors as topography, soil, population numbers and economic influences. This chapter therefore contains three major sections: first a description of field arrangements in the seventeenth and eighteenth centuries, the period for which information is most abundant and regional differences can be demonstrated fairly readily; second, a less detailed account of medieval arrangements and some of the ways in which these differed from those that prevailed later; and third, a discussion of the possible origins of some of the features present by medieval times.

A. SEVENTEENTH- AND EIGHTEENTH-CENTURY ARRANGEMENTS

Although traditional field systems were being obliterated by enclosure from medieval times onward, common land survived until about 1760 in a considerable proportion of Yorkshire townships. The pace of enclosure then increased, and by about 1820 less than 50 townships, mostly in the West Riding, still retained common arable fields.[1] Extant surveys, estate maps, field books and other manuscript records relating to landholdings are more numerous after about 1600. It is the combination of these two sets of circumstances that provides

---

[1] Olga Wilkinson, *The Agricultural Revolution in the East Riding of Yorkshire*, East Yorkshire Local History Series, v, 1956; B. A. English (ed.), *Handlist of West Riding Enclosure Awards*, 1965.

approximate time limits to the description of the field systems of the county in their fully evolved forms. The areas where post-1600 arrangements have been most fully studied are the East Riding, by A. Harris,[1] and the Pickering district of the North Riding by Pamela Allerston,[2] while J. Harvey is currently working on the West Riding.[3] Seventeenth-century or earlier enclosure was particularly common in the northern parts of the county,[4] consequently less is known about the traditional field systems of these areas.

I. ELEMENTS

Four elements were combined in the traditional field systems: village enclosures, common arable fields, common meadowland and common pasture or waste. These occupied all or most of the area of many eastern townships, especially in the Wolds and Holderness, but in other townships, especially in the centre and west of the county, a considerable proportion of the area was under closes. These closes may be regarded as an alien element, the result of medieval and Tudor enclosure, and not requiring further description.

(a) Village enclosures

The nucleus of each township was a cluster of enclosed plots associated with the village or hamlet, in common terminology known as garths, in legal terminology as tofts when they included a dwelling site, and crofts when there was no dwelling included. A few townships, especially in the western parts of the county, contained two or more such clusters; for instance, Brodsworth township near Doncaster contained both the village of Brodsworth and the hamlet of Pigburn.[5] The enclosures varied in size but rarely exceeded three acres, and each was surrounded by a hedge or a fence; crofts were used for a wide range of purposes, from keeping hens to growing hemp. In a number of eastern townships the village enclosures were the only land held in severalty (Fig. 4.1 B).

[1] A. Harris, 'Pre-Enclosure Agricultural Systems in the East Riding of Yorkshire', M.A. thesis, University of London, 1951; *The Open Fields of East Yorkshire*, E. Yorks. Local Hist. Ser., IX, 1959; 'The Agriculture of the East Riding of Yorkshire before Parliamentary Enclosures', *Yorkshire Archaeological Journal*, XL, 1959–62, pp. 119–28; *The Rural Landscape of the East Riding of Yorkshire 1700–1850*, 1961.

[2] Pamela Allerston, 'Field and Village in the Pickering District of North Yorkshire', M.Sc. thesis, University of London, 1966.

[3] In preparation for a Liverpool University Ph.D. thesis.

[4] M. Beresford, 'Glebe Terriers and Open Field, Yorkshire', *Yorks. Arch. Jnl.*, XXXVII, 1948–51, p. 349.

[5] Enclosure Plan 1830, West Riding Registry of Deeds, Wakefield, 1/19.

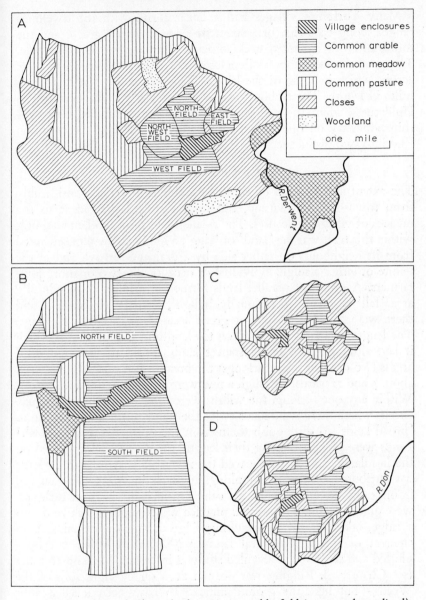

Fig. 4.1 Pre-enclosure land use (each common arable field is separately outlined).
A. Wheldrake (East Riding), a reconstruction. B. Beeford (East Riding) in 1766.
C. Ulley (West Riding) in 1798. D. Cadeby (West Riding) in 1809.
Sources. A, East Riding R.O., Beverley, DDFA 45/5, 7 & 9, and the 1772 enclosure
award, East Riding Registry of Deeds, Beverley. B, A. Harris, 'Pre-Enclosure
Agricultural Systems in the East Riding of Yorkshire', M.A. thesis, University of
London, 1951. C, Enclosure map, West Riding Registry of Deeds, Wakefield.
D, Enclosure map, West Riding Registry of Deeds, Wakefield.

Many Yorkshire villages had a linear form, with the dwellings ranged along each side of a street or a long narrow green, and the tofts and crofts extended back some 200 yards or so on either side. This gave rise to a ribbon of enclosed plots about a quarter of a mile across, which in some of the larger villages extended for up to two miles in length. The ribbon form was particularly well developed in Holderness, where the enclosures in some instances reached the township boundary on one or both sides, thereby splitting the common land into two distinct sections (Fig. 4.1 B).

(b) Common arable fields

The extent and location of common arable land varied considerably from township to township, but it frequently lay adjacent to the nucleus of village enclosures. The smallest and most fundamental unit within this tract was the 'land' or 'rigg', a long narrow plot separated from its neighbours on either side by a drainage furrow, and in the tenure of either a single individual or occasionally two or more joint farmers. A group of parallel lands formed a furlong, known locally as a 'fall' or 'flatt' (occasionally 'faugh', 'bydale' or 'shutt'), and there were frequently balks or green access lanes between furlongs. The length of a land depended on the length of the furlong in which it lay, although in a few instances lands appear to have extended across two or even three furlongs; the breadth was normally between about 5 and 12 yards, although a few were as much as 18 yards across. Within any one furlong, the widths were often approximately equal, except where there were lands twice the standard measure, known as 'broad lands' to distinguish them from the normal 'narrow lands'.[1] Lands were ploughed along their length, the plough being turned on the headlands, and many showed the reverse-S curve that S. R. Eyre has attributed to traditional ploughing techniques.[2] Others curved in only one direction, while yet others, principally in short furlongs, were quite straight. The normal practice was to plough each land into a ridge, and some of the resulting ridge-and-furrow remains as an element of the present rural landscape, although it has not been plotted and subjected to detailed study as in certain Midland counties (see Chapter 5). Ridging was normal even on the light soils of the Wolds,[3] but here the ground appears to have been levelled after

[1] A. Harris, '"Land" and Oxgang in the East Riding of Yorkshire', *Yorks. Arch. Jnl.*, XXXVIII, 1952–5, pp. 529–35; 'A Note on the Ridge and Furrow Controversy', *Amat. Histn.*, VII, no. 3, 1966, pp. 95–8.

[2] S. R. Eyre, 'The Curving Plough-strip and its Historical Implications', *Agric. Hist. Rev.*, III, 1955, pp. 80–94.

[3] W. Marshall, *The Rural Economy of Gloucestershire*, 1789, I, 78, quoted by Harris, M.A. thesis, 1951, p. 64.

enclosure and ridge-and-furrow features are rarely seen today except around the sites of deserted villages. The furrows between lands had two functions: they invariably ran down slope, and therefore acted as minor drainage channels; in addition, they often marked property boundaries. To prevent encroachment, boundary posts, stones, holes or clods of earth known as 'hutts' were located on the balks at the ends of the furrows.[1]

Furlongs were of varying size and shape. Some were roughly square or rectangular and often between 7 and 20 acres in extent. Others were smaller plots of irregular shape known as 'butts' or 'gores'. Both of these types have parallels in the Laxton fields illustrated by the Orwins,[2] but there was also a third type that had no counterpart in Laxton. This was characterised by lands at least 500 yards and in some cases over a mile in length (Fig. 4.2); many such furlongs were also wide, so that their area frequently exceeded 50 acres. Long furlongs were most common in Holderness, where there were also instances of lands crossing furlong boundaries to form long but subdivided units. Such arrangements are characteristic of every Holderness township for which there are surviving plans showing furlongs and lands, as well as of the townships of Burton Agnes and Kilnwick at the junction of the Holderness lowlands with the chalk Wolds;[3] occasional references suggest that similar arrangements may have prevailed round the margins of the Vale of Pickering.[4] Kilham is the only Wolds township with an extant plan showing the layout of furlongs, which were there all of a uniform rectangular shape.[5] It is not known whether Kilham was typical of the region and therefore whether long furlongs were absent from the Wolds. In the central and western districts of the county, many arable tracts were made up entirely of the smaller rectangular or irregularly shaped furlongs (Fig. 4.3B), although some townships had a single large furlong (or several parallel furlongs) with long strips surrounded by smaller units (Fig. 4.3A).

Many furlongs had distinctive names describing the character of the soil (e.g. Stone Fall in Southorpe, Sandy Lands in Wheldrake, Upper Caukhill in Kilham), the location (e.g. Town End in Skirpenbeck, Bottoms in Kilham, Upper East Bank in Wilton) or the shape of the plot (Longlands in Skirpenbeck, Wings in Flaxby). Other

[1] Harris, *The Open Fields of East Yorkshire*, p. 21.
[2] C. S. and C. S. Orwin, *The Open Fields*, 1938.
[3] Maps of Kelk, 1789, DX 125, Kilnsea, 1818, DX 127, and Skeffling, 1721, DDCC (2), G. 2, all in East Riding R.O.; Tithe award maps for Burton Agnes, 1840, and Mappleton and Rowlston, 1839; map of Kilnwick, *c.* 1750, in the possession of E. Ingram.
[4] Allerston, M.Sc. thesis, 1966, p. 153.
[5] East Riding R.O., DDDU/12/54.

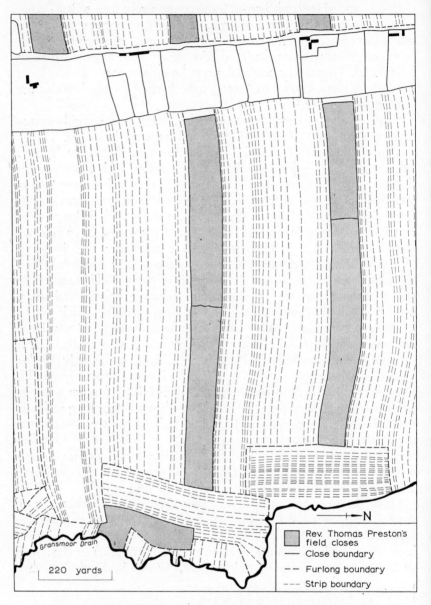

Fig. 4.2 Part of the East Field of Great Kelk (East Riding) in 1789.
Source. Plan surveyed by Robert King, East Riding R.O., DX 125.

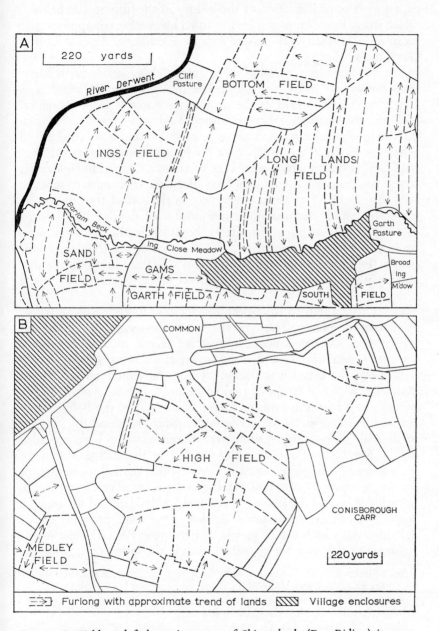

Fig. 4.3 A, Fields and furlongs in a part of Skirpenbeck (East Riding) in 1740. B, Fields and furlongs in a part of Conisborough (West Riding) in 1840.

Sources. A, East Riding R.O., DDDA MP 86. B, Tithe Maps, Borthwick Institute of Historical Research, York.

names gave some indication of the history of the furlong (see below), whilst many long furlongs were identified by numbers or approximate location (e.g. First and Second Fall in Southburn, Against Dalton Garth in Skeffling).

In most townships, furlongs were grouped together to form larger units known as 'fields' or 'sides'. The grouping was in some cases clearly related to breaks in the continuity of arable land. In central and western districts, where common land and closes were often intermingled, each separate tract of open arable land was called a field whatever its size (Fig. 4.1 C). As a result, there might be as many as ten fields[1] and their names were very varied in character. In Holderness it was common for the long ribbons of village enclosures to separate two large fields (Fig. 4.1 B). Elsewhere in the east of the county the arable frequently formed one continuous tract divided into two or three fields by seemingly arbitrary boundaries, the resulting units having simple directional (East, West) or locational (Nether, High) names (Fig. 4.4). In general, therefore, fields were fewer in number and simpler in nomenclature in the east of the county than in the west.

Fields are known to have been the rotation units at this period in a number of places. Thus, in the many townships of Holderness where there were two fields, a crop and fallow rotation frequently operated, both winter- and spring-sown crops being grown in one field while the other was fallow.[2] Three (or sometimes six) fields, associated with a rotation of two crops and a fallow, were found in a number of townships on the lower Wolds slopes, the boulder-clay covered tracts of the Vale of York[3] and probably round the margins of the Vale of Pickering;[4] similar conditions may also have prevailed on the Magnesian Limestone hills. Each year the village officials of such townships fixed the dates between which the fallow or stubble was to be open to common grazing and the number of stock each householder could depasture.[5] Individual landholders had to conform with the broad agrarian regime laid down, but could probably decide for themselves such details as whether to grow rye or wheat in the winter corn field and barley, oats or peas in the spring corn field.

[1] W. S. Rodgers, 'The Distribution of Parliamentary Enclosures in the West Riding of Yorkshire, 1729–1895', M.Comm. thesis, University of Leeds, 1952.
[2] Survey of Sir J. Constabl Estate in Holder, 1575, East Riding R.O., DDCC/App. C (transcript); Harris, M.A. thesis, chs. 9 and 10.
[3] Harris, M.A. thesis, pp. 41, 57, 103.
[4] Evidence of three fields, Allerston, M.Sc. thesis, p. 147; of three-course rotation, W. Marshall, The Rural Economy of Yorkshire, 1788, I, p. 290.
[5] M. W. Barley, 'East Yorkshire Manorial By-Laws', Yorks. Arch. Jnl., xxxv, 1943, pp. 35–60.

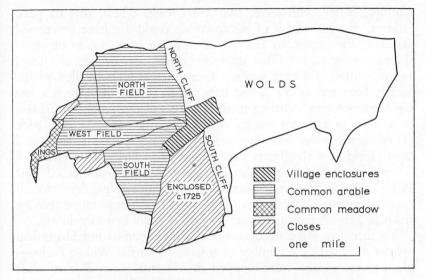

Fig. 4.4 Land use in Bishop Wilton (East Riding) in 1772.
Source. A. Harris, 'Pre-Enclosure Agricultural Systems in the East Riding of Yorkshire', M.A. thesis, University of London, 1951.

A minor but widespread variant on this simple arrangement involved
the devotion of parts of each field to grass leys lasting several years,
whilst adjacent land was being cropped on a two- or three-shift
rotation. There are many references to meadowland within the fields,[1]
and the 1721 plan of Skeffling (Holderness) shows a part of almost
every strip holding under grass.[2]

In contrast with the townships where fields were the rotation units,
there were others in which the role was performed by furlongs or
small groups of furlongs. In Kilham on the Wolds, the village bylaw-
men decided each year which furlongs of Northside and Southside
should be cultivated and what crop should be sown in each.[3] In this
case the arrangement may be linked with the large size of the township
(over 7,000 acres), but elsewhere it may have developed either because
piecemeal enclosure had disrupted traditional field units, or because
new crops and rotations were adopted during the second half of the
eighteenth century.[4] For instance, after Isaac Leatham had persuaded
the farmers of Hunmanby to follow a new seven-course rotation

[1] Beresford, *Yorks. Arch. Jnl.*, xxxvii, 1948–51, p. 334.
[2] East Riding R.O., DX 125.
[3] Harris, *The Open Fields of East Yorkshire*, p. 7.
[4] Harris, *The Rural Landscape of the East Riding of Yorkshire*, p. 61.

(turnips, barley with seeds, two years seeds, wheat, oats or peas, fallow),[1] the four fields of the township could not have functioned as the rotation units. In Sewerby near Bridlington, a plan of 1802[2] shows, instead of the three arable fields and four or five additional furlongs listed in a 1773 survey,[3] four different units labelled wheat, barley, bean and fallow fields; here too there may have been a late eighteenth-century rearrangement. Changes of this type may explain some cases of apparent confusion of field names, as at Withernwick (Holderness), where the Enclosure Act of 1805 speaks of North and South Fields, but the Bylaw Book records East Field, West Field and 'the North end and South end fields of Withernwick called East Fields'.[4] In view of our present limited knowledge, however, it cannot be assumed that all cases of rotation by furlongs rather than by fields originated during the period of the Agricultural Revolution.

Another distinctive arrangement was the modified infield–outfield system operated by a number of townships on the Wolds. Furlongs close to the village were cropped in a normal two- or three-shift rotation, but more distant furlongs with thin soils that received little manure were ploughed only one year in three or even less frequently.[5] Details of the system are known for a few townships only, but there is little doubt that outfields existed in most high Wolds townships.[6] In Bishop Wilton, for instance, the fields lying below the chalk scarp were valued at 10d. per acre in 1611, but the arable on the Wolds 'never sowne above once in tenn or twelve yeres' was worth only 3d. per acre.[7] The infield–outfield system was apparently associated with thin chalk or limestone soils, for it was found only on the high Wolds and possibly in some townships on the Tabular Hills.

Since details of rotations are known for only a small number of Yorkshire townships, it is impossible to give any precise indication of the relative frequency of different agrarian regimes. What is clear is that arrangements varied from a strict adherence to two or three shifts within the same number of fields, through a more flexible system of rotation by furlongs or groups of furlongs, to the apparently rare cases of almost complete freedom of cropping on individual

[1] I. Leatham, *General View of the Agriculture of the East Riding of Yorkshire*, 1794, pp. 45–6.
[2] East Riding R.O., DDLG, not yet calendared.
[3] Survey of the Fields and Tetherings in the Township of Sewerby, Oct. and Nov. 1773, East Riding R.O., DDLG, not yet calendared.
[4] Barley, *Yorks. Arch. Jnl.*, xxxv, 1943, p. 52; see also Harris, M.A. thesis, p. 20.
[5] Harris, *The Open Fields of East Yorkshire*, p. 7.
[6] Harris, *The Rural Landscape of the East Riding of Yorkshire*, pp. 24–5.
[7] Harris, *The Open Fields of East Yorkshire*, p. 7.

lands.[1] Thus the agrarian regime cannot be deduced from the number of fields recorded.

The average small farmer had up to 60 acres of arable land.[2] This was often measured in oxgangs, the traditional tenurial unit that varied in size from township to township between about 6 and 24 acres,[3] often including meadow as well as arable land. An oxgang normally comprised a large number of parcels scattered throughout the fields, each parcel consisting of one or two lands. The parcels were distributed in a very orderly fashion in some townships. Occasionally this orderliness revealed itself in holdings of equal acreage in each field, for instance the glebe in Etton in 1685 consisted of 15 acres in each of South, Middle and North Fields.[4] More frequently it took the form of symmetry of layout within the furlongs, with parcels of different oxgangs occurring in the same position and same sequence in each furlong. Thus the six glebe oxgangs in Langtoft in 1743 were described as 'the 11th, 12th, 26th, 27th, 30th and 31st from the bank on the south side of the flat through out the Fields',[5] and a holding of half an oxgang in Burstwick was described in 1610 as lying 'in every Bydell throughout the fields of Burstwick and Skeckling between the lands of Thomas Mountaine and William Stevenson... and is the utmost land in every Bydell'.[6] In contrast there were other townships where the parcels were distributed in a more haphazard fashion; lands belonging to one occupier had varying neighbours and positions from furlong to furlong.[7] In at least some cases this latter arrangement resulted from a dismemberment of traditional oxgang units by sale or exchange.[8] Symmetrical arrangements were more common in the east of the county than in the centre and west.

Some townships experienced a rearrangement of holdings during the seventeenth and eighteenth centuries known as 'flatting'. An exchange of lands gave each tenant fewer but larger parcels ('flatts') than in the traditional layout. Examples are steadily coming to light of this type of layout,[9] which may have been more widespread in the county than was once realised.

[1] Warmsworth Tithe Book, 1674, Leeds City Library Archives Department, Battie-Wrightson Coll. R. 103; I am indebted to J. Harvey for this reference.
[2] Harris, *The Open Fields of East Yorkshire*, p. 9.
[3] Harris, M.A. thesis, App. I.
[4] Beresford, *Yorks. Arch. Jnl.*, xxxvi, 1948–51, p. 334.
[5] *Ibid.*, p. 337.   [6] East Riding R.O., DDCC/14/79.
[7] Wheldrake Field Plans, East Riding R.O., DDFA 45/5, 7, 9.
[8] E.g. Barmby Moor, 1690, Borthwick Institute of Historical Research, York, R. vii, H. 4582. I am indebted to A. Harris for this reference.
[9] June A. Sheppard, 'Pre-Enclosure Field and Settlement Patterns in an English Township: Wheldrake, near York', *Geogr. Annlr.*, xlviii, Ser. B, 1966, p. 64;

(c) Meadow

Grassland was frequently enclosed earlier than arable fields, so that a number of townships in the centre and west of the county had no remaining common meadowland in the seventeenth and eighteenth centuries. In some other townships, especially on the Wolds, the only common land cut for hay was balks and grass leys within the arable fields;[1] many places, however, retained separate tracts of meadowland known as 'ings'. Ings invariably occupied low-lying ground where a high water-table was experienced for much of the year though flooding was restricted to short periods during winter. Such tracts were limited in extent even in the lowland districts of the county, and since hay was a precious commodity when few fodder crops were grown, it is not surprising that meadowland was highly valued. In Settrington, for instance, the value per acre was more than twice that of the best arable land.[2] The ings were protected from occasional summer floods by means of carefully maintained river banks.[3]

The ings were usually divided into small strip parcels, comparable with the arable lands. Each parcel or 'dole' was normally attached permanently to one holding, but some cases are known where meadows were allocated every few years.[4] In early August, after individual farmers had cut and carried their hay, the ings were thrown open to common grazing.

(d) Pasture or waste

Common waste land was valued principally as pasture, but it sometimes also provided turves, firewood and litter. It was in summer, when livestock were excluded from the fields and meadows, that the pasture was most extensively used.

Most common waste occupied land that was unsuitable for other uses on account of poor soils, steep slopes or persistent waterlogging. On the Wolds, pasture was principally located on the sides of dry

1802 map of Sewerby, East Riding R.O., DDLG, not yet calendared; 1737 map of Adwick-upon-Dearne, J. Harvey, 'Early Maps as a Source for the Study of Field Systems with Special Reference to the West Riding of Yorkshire', read to a conference at the Royal Geographical Society, September 1967 on 'Early Maps as Historical Evidence'.

[1] Harris, The Open Fields of East Yorkshire, p. 11.
[2] H. King and A. Harris (eds.), A Survey of the Manor of Settrington, Yorks. Arch. Soc. Rec. Ser., cxxvi, 1962, p. xiii.
[3] A. G. Ruston and D. Witney, Hooton Pagnell: The Agricultural Evolution of a Yorkshire Village, 1934, p. 148.
[4] E.g. Arram in the Hull valley, see Harris, The Open Fields of East Yorkshire, p. 12; Patrington, Keyingham and Roos in Holderness, see Harris, M.A. thesis, p. 93; Skellow, near Doncaster, quoted by J. Harvey, 'Early Maps as a Source for the Study of Field Systems'.

valleys or on the scarp face. In Holderness, the Vale of Pickering and parts of the Vale of York, most waste consisted of peaty carrland subject to frequent flooding, whilst in the zone of glacial outwash materials in the Vale of York there were extensive commons on the poorest sandy soils. In the Pennines and the North York Moors there were continuous tracts of moorland pasture on the upper valley slopes and intervening plateau surfaces. Such moorlands, as well as some of the larger lowland wastes, were often used by several townships; an extreme example of this arrangement occurred in Wallingfen, in the Vale of York just north of the Humber, where forty-eight villages and hamlets intercommoned.

All long-established households had the right to use the resources of the waste belonging to their township. There were regulations to control the number of turves and the amount of litter that could be taken, as at Grimston near York, where 'the Ancient stynt for a messuage is ffower loodes of turffes and towe loode of whines, and for a cottage tow loode of turffes and one loode of whynnes yearly'.[1] Grazing was also often regulated by means of a stint, with pasture rights or 'gates' attached to both oxgangs and dwellings, so that farmers were able to graze more stock than cottagers.[2] There were sometimes several separate pastures in one township, for instance in Huggate on the Wolds, the Tongue, Cow Pasture and Ox Pasture each had different stocking regulations.[3] The generosity of stints naturally varied with the extent and quality of the pasture, and there were some townships where the small farmer with no alternative pasture resources was able to keep very few cattle or horses. In other places, a considerable number of animals could be kept, and there were some townships (especially those bordering the moorlands) where at least part of the pasture was not stinted. Here the owners of common rights could legally depasture only those animals that could be supported in winter by the fodder produced on the farm, but this limitation was frequently ignored.[4] Then the pasture became overgrazed and of little value, as in Brandesburton Moor in Holderness.[5]

[1] Survey of Grimston Cross, 1606, Leeds City Library Archives Department, Fox-Lane Coll. LXXX 111/1, p. 32. For similar regulations in Barwick-in-Elmet, see F. S. Colman, A History of Barwick in Elmet, 1908, p. 127.
[2] A good example of such regulations is given in J. S. Purvis, Bridlington Charters, Court Rolls and Papers, 1926, p. 110.
[3] Harris, M.A. thesis, p. 34.
[4] J. Tuke, General View of the Agriculture of the North Riding of Yorkshire, 2nd edn, 1800, pp. 198–9.
[5] Harris, The Rural Landscape of the East Riding of Yorkshire, p. 43.

2. REGIONAL VARIATIONS

Differences from one part of the county to another are revealed principally in the proportion of the total township occupied by common land, in the ratios of arable, meadow and pasture within this common land, and in the layout and mode of exploitation of the arable. When more townships have been studied in detail it may be possible to map such regional differences on the basis of criteria drawn from the field systems themselves, but in the meantime, the only practicable framework is one based on soils and topography (Fig. 4.5). Much more is known about some of these regions than about others.

The first regions to be considered, the Wolds, the Tabular Hills and Holderness, had several features in common. At least some townships had no enclosures outside the villages until the late eighteenth century; the arable was normally divided into a small number of fields or sides, often named after the points of the compass; furlongs were either long or rectangular in shape; and there were traces of a regular layout of arable holdings in the furlongs. The associated agrarian regime was frequently fairly rigid.

(a) The Wolds

Studies by Harris have made this the region in which arrangements are best known. Glacial drift covers the lower slopes of the Chalk as it dips towards Holderness, and there is therefore a distinction between townships on the high Wolds, with thin chalky soils throughout, and those on the lower slopes with some tracts of more fertile soils developed on boulder clay. In high Wolds townships, the village was often located in a valley, with the regularly cropped land on adjacent slopes.[1] This infield was usually divided between two fields or sides, and in Duggleby these were the rotation units,[2] but it is not clear whether this arrangement or the Kilham system of furlong rotation (p. 153) was more common. It is also not known whether most furlongs were of uniform rectangular shape as in Kilham. Both two- and three-course rotations were followed, with barley and oats as the principal crops.[3] Beyond the regularly cultivated land lay the outfield, which provided both pasture and occasional crops, whilst permanent pasture usually occupied the remote corners of the township and any steep-sided dry valleys. Very few high Wolds townships had any closes outside the village nucleus, but there were a few places where common rights

---

[1] A good example is Kirby Grindalythe, illustrated in Harris, *ibid.*, p. 23.
[2] Harris, M.A. thesis, p. 16.
[3] *Ibid.*, pp. 19, 28.

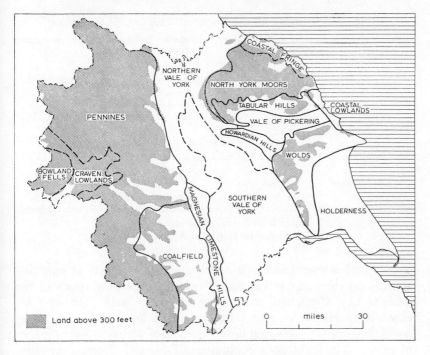

Fig. 4.5 Yorkshire: physical regions.

had been extinguished in the fifteenth and sixteenth centuries and all the land devoted to pastures and rabbit warrens that although unenclosed were held in severalty.[1]

In many townships of this region the distinction between permanent pasture and outfield was an imprecise one, for the frequency of outfield cultivation varied from time to time and seems to have been declining during the seventeenth and eighteenth centuries.[2] Pastures and outfield together probably formed at least two-fifths of the total area of many townships and the short downland grasses that colonised this land were ideal for sheep, which were kept in considerable numbers.[3] It was a common practice to allow the flocks to graze the pastures by day, but to fold them on the fallow sections of the infield by night,[4] thus helping to maintain the contrast in fertility between infield and outfield arable. In contrast with the sheep, cattle and horses were poorly provided for; there was a shortage of both summer

[1] Harris, *The Rural Landscape of the East Riding of Yorkshire*, p. 29.
[2] *Ibid.*, p. 31.
[3] Harris, *Yorks. Arch. Jnl.*, XL, 1959–62, p. 127.
[4] Leatham, *General View of the Agriculture of the East Riding of Yorkshire*, p. 42.

Table 4.1. Pasturing arrangements in Huggate (East Riding)

Pasture	Dates	Rights pertaining to one dwelling	Rights pertaining to one oxgang
Stubble ⎱ arable	9 Oct. – 5 Apr.	none	1 horse, 1 ⅔ oxen, ½ calf
Fallow ⎰ fields	5 Apr. – 9 Oct.	10 sheep	40 sheep*
Oxpasture	14 May – 9 Oct.	1 calf and 1 horse	⅔ ox, ½ calf, 1 horse
Cow pasture	14 May – 9 Oct.	2 oxen	1 ox
Tongue	5 Apr. – 9 Oct.	none	3 sheep

* Varied from holding to holding.
Table based on Harris, M.A. thesis, p. 34.

pasture and winter fodder, in spite of such expedients as tethering animals on the balks in the arable fields and devoting parts of the fields to hay. Cattle and horse stints were extremely restrictive; for example, in Fimber in 1727 a farmer with a house and one oxgang could depasture 13 sheep, but only one-third of a horse and one-quarter of an ox.[1] The regulations in Huggate (Table 4.1) illustrate the complexity as well as the restrictiveness of stints. The impression is of a strictly regulated field system, in which arable and pastoral elements were closely integrated, but which nevertheless contained sufficient flexibility in its outfield land to ensure survival until the late eighteenth century.

Many of the low Wolds townships were linear in form, extending from the relatively low and well-watered Holderness margins across gently undulating drift-covered slopes to a tract of drift-free Chalk at the upper end. These different types of terrain were suitable respectively for meadow, arable and pasture, with the village usually located towards the lower end of the arable zone. Somewhat similar linear layouts prevailed on the northern and western fringes of the Wolds, where there was invariably a zone of arable fields on the relatively fertile soils at the foot of the Chalk scarp and some low-lying meadows farther from the Chalk, whilst the scarp itself was usually given over to pasture. In addition, a fourth zone was often present in these scarp townships, comprising a tract of drift-free Chalk plateau used as outfield arable and sheep-walk.[2] Perhaps as a result of the

[1] Harris, M.A. thesis, p. 33.
[2] B. Loughborough, 'An Account of a Yorkshire Enclosure – Staxton 1803', *Agric. Hist. Rev.*, XIII, 1965, pp. 106–7.

variety of land types available, the field systems of these townships showed a closer approximation to the classical Midland system than those elsewhere in the county. The main arable tract (known as the 'Low' fields in scarp townships) was divided into fields that in at least some cases functioned as the rotation units;[1] there were frequently three fields, but a few townships had two (e.g. Kirby Underdale[2]) or four (e.g. South Cave[3]). The relative abundance of meadowland, and in some cases the presence of well-watered lowland pastures, made it possible to maintain a reasonable number of cattle and horses, while sheep were also numerous. In Bishop Wilton, for instance, a man with a house and one oxgang could keep three horses, three oxen and forty sheep,[4] and Staxton even had an unstinted carr pasture.[5] A broadly based mixed farming economy was possible within the framework of the field system, and perhaps this is why many of these townships remained unaffected by enclosure until the late eighteenth century. Where there was some early enclosure, it was principally the lowland tracts farthest from the Chalk that were affected.

(b) The Tabular Hills

In certain respects this region resembled the Wolds, for the soils were inclined to be thin and stony and the higher parts were bleak and unfavourable for cultivation. As in the Wolds, there were some townships that lay entirely on the upper slopes, but others stretched from the floor of the Vale of Pickering across relatively fertile soils around the junction of the Vale clays and the Corallian limestones and sandstones to the middle or upper slopes. In the linear townships the traditional layout comprised meadows and carr pastures in the Vale, arable fields and village enclosures where the land began to rise towards the hills, and pasture on the upper slopes.[6] The higher townships had only small tracts of meadow in the narrow valleys cutting through the Corallian outcrop, but in compensation often had very large moorland pastures that extended from the Tabular Hills on to the Estuarine sandstones of the North York Moors. Allerston has studied the field systems of part of this region, where she found evidence that prior to enclosure many townships had three open arable fields, which she believes were the rotation units.[7] An interesting variant occurred in several of the linear townships (Brompton, Hutton

[1] Harris, M.A. thesis, pp. 41, 46, 57.
[2] W. R. Shepherd, *The History of Kirby Underdale*, 1928, ch. VI.
[3] Harris, M.A. thesis, p. 46.   [4] *Ibid.*, p. 41.   [5] *Ibid.*, p. 37.
[6] J. H. Rushton, 'Landscape History at Brompton by Sawdon', *Transactions of the Scarborough & District Archaeological Society*, I (no. 6), 1963, pp. 24–5.
[7] Allerston, M.Sc. thesis, pp. 147, 156, 168–9 and App. VII.

Buscel, Middleton and Pickering) in the form of two sets of three fields. In some of the higher townships there are hints that units akin to the outfields of the Wolds may once have existed: a 1598 plan of Old Byland shows two plots on the margins of the township labelled 'somtyme in tillage...but now lying common',[1] whilst in Pockley and Gillamoor there were arable plots outside the main fields.[2] One other higher township, Fadmoor, had three fields in 1609, but fourteen were named in 1763;[3] this may indicate a seventeenth- or eighteenth-century modification of the original system, perhaps by using furlongs as rotation units. A pre-enclosure plan of the northern part of Wilton in 1724 reveals that subdivided long furlongs existed alongside others of more rectangular shape.[4] There is little information about livestock stints, but the relative abundance of pasture suggests that they may have been fairly generous. An interesting contrast with the Wolds was that the majority of townships, including both types discussed above, experienced at least partial enclosure during the seventeenth and eighteenth centuries, which affected particularly the lowland pastures and meadows together with some arable fields.[5]

(c) Holderness

This hummocky drift district, lying east of the Wolds, is another region with relatively well-documented field arrangements. About a quarter of the townships here were enclosed during the sixteenth and seventeenth centuries,[6] but a common field system survived in the remainder until the late eighteenth century. The higher ground provided the sites for villages and arable fields, and in some cases for tracts of pasture, while the valleys of the Hull and its tributary streams were occupied by ings and carrs. Pasture and hay resources were often abundant, so enabling a village farmer to keep more livestock than his counterpart in regions already discussed. In Sutton the stints were so generous that a farmer with a house and one oxgang could depasture 130 sheep and 24 cattle,[7] but this was probably an extreme case. Most townships had two arable fields, one each side of the village, worked as the units in a two-course rotation. The predominance of very long lands and furlongs has already been noted (p. 149).

The second group of regions, consisting of the southern Vale of

[1] M. W. Beresford, ch. 5 in *The North York Moors*, National Park Guide No. 4, 1966, ed. A. Raistrick, p. 53.
[2] Allerston, M.Sc. thesis, pp. 148 and 152.
[3] *Ibid.*, pp. 148 and 165.
[4] East Riding R.O., DDHO/16/52.
[5] Allerston, M.Sc. thesis, App. VI.
[6] Harris, *The Rural Landscape of the East Riding of Yorkshire*, p. 44.
[7] T. Blashill, *Sutton-in-Holderness*, 1896, p. 193.

York, the Magnesian Limestone hills and the Coalfield, had features that contrast with those of the first group. In the majority of townships the common land lay intermingled with closes; the arable was frequently divided by these into numerous small fields with non-directional names; furlongs were of a variety of sizes and shapes; and there is little evidence to suggest a regular layout of arable holdings. The varied framework was generally associated with a flexible agrarian regime.

(d) The southern Vale of York

This is a plain developed on lacustrine sands and clays,[1] with occasional low hills and extensive poorly drained tracts around the Humber estuary. Some townships, especially those like Gribthorpe with heavy clay soils, were fully enclosed by the seventeenth century,[2] but more characteristic were townships with a mixture of closes, open arable fields and common pastures. The villages and the arable fields sought the best-drained sites, and where there was one especially favourable zone in a township, as in Wheldrake, the arable was often in a compact block divided into three or four large fields (Fig. 4.1 A). An equally common arrangement, however, was half-a-dozen or more scattered fields of variable size, separated by closes, as in North Duffield.[3] Holdings in Wheldrake were both irregularly apportioned among the fields and irregularly located within the furlongs,[4] an arrangement that may well have been typical of the whole region. Nothing is known for certain about rotations, but strict regularity seems unlikely within so haphazard a framework. Some of the closes which bordered arable fields had names and shapes that suggest strongly that they were former open field parcels,[5] and in other townships there is documentary evidence of piecemeal enclosure.[6] This has led to the suggestion that the multiplicity of open arable fields in many places by the eighteenth century was a result of the disintegration of an earlier, more regular field system.[7] Other closes originated by the assarting of woodland and waste, whilst many of those in eighteenth-century Wheldrake were the result of subdivision of former stinted pastures.[8] The closes were used for both crops and grass, and must have compensated for

[1] J. Palmer, 'Landforms, Drainage and Settlement in the Vale of York', ch. IV in S. R. Eyre and G. R. J. Jones (eds.), Geography as Human Ecology, 1966, p. 93.
[2] Harris, The Rural Landscape of the East Riding of Yorkshire, p. 54.
[3] Ibid., pp. 53-4.
[4] Plans of Well (or Northwest), Dovecote (or North) and Mill (or West) Fields, c. 1720, East Riding R.O., DDFA 45/5, 7, 9.
[5] E.g. Egbrough Enclosure Plan, 1802, West Riding Registry of Deeds, Wakefield, 2/16.
[6] E.g. in Huntington, Leeds City Library Archives Dept., Newby Hall Coll., 2107.
[7] Harris, M.A. thesis, p. 103.   [8] Sheppard, Geogr. Annlr. B, 1966 (2), p. 64.

any deficiencies resulting from an unequal distribution of open field parcels between the rotation units.

Common meadows were of restricted extent in this region, but extensive common pastures survived especially in poorly drained tracts and where there were infertile sandy soils. A number of commons, including those at Holme-on-Spalding Moor[1] and Elvington,[2] were unstinted, and in Wallingfen stints were first imposed in 1636;[3] the abundance of common pasture and the availability of other pasture in closes probably meant that restrictions on grazing were less necessary than farther east. This feature thus further contributes to the impression of a relatively flexible field system.

(e) The Coalfield

Although the scarp and vale terrain of this region (as defined by D. L. Linton[4]) is very different from that of the Vale of York, field arrangements in many townships were similar. Closes normally occupied at least half the area, surrounding and separating several arable fields of varying size and shape (Fig. 4.1 C). Common pasture often occupied the scarp slopes of sandstone cuestas, as in the case of Ulley Cliff Common, while other commons formed irregularly shaped village greens as at Masbrough (Rotherham). Little is known about how holdings were divided between the fields (except at Adwick-on-Dearne where arable holdings consisted of a few large parcels concentrated in certain parts of the fields[5]), how the fields were cropped, or even whether the fallows and stubble were grazed in common. The impression however is of an even more loosely organised system than in the southern Vale of York. Some commons were probably unstinted, and in the only two cases where stints are known, these were generous: one gate to five acres in Wath-on-Dearne common, first stinted in 1725,[6] and one gate to three acres in Shitlington near Dewsbury in 1542.[7]

(f) The Magnesian Limestone Hills

The Limestone outcrop provides a zone about five miles wide of well-drained and easily cultivable soils, shared by many townships

[1] Harris, M.A. thesis, p. 105.
[2] 1624 survey, Leeds City Library Archives Dept., TM/SH, B4/1.
[3] June A. Sheppard, The Draining of the Marshlands of South Holderness and the Vale of York, E. Yorks. Local Hist. Ser., xx, 1966, p. 20.
[4] D. L. Linton (ed.), Sheffield and its Region, 1956, Fig. 6, p. 25.
[5] Harvey, 'Early Maps as a Source for the Study of Field Systems'.
[6] Sheffield City Library, Dept. of Local History and Archives, Wentworth Wood-house Muniments C2/257.
[7] Yorkshire Star Chamber Proceedings I, Yorks. Arch. Soc. Rec. Ser., xli, 1910, p. 81.

that extend either west on to the Coal Measures or east on to the clays and sands of the Vale of York. Much of the low ground of such townships was in closes by the seventeenth and eighteenth centuries, as in Hooton Pagnell,[1] but except where there was one of the numerous parks a considerable proportion of the limestone plateau itself was occupied by open arable fields and common pastures. The arable sometimes formed a virtually continuous tract, but in other places its continuity was broken by groups of closes that were evidently the result of piecemeal enclosure. Thus, while some townships like Sutton in Campsall and East Keswick had three or four approximately equal-sized fields, others such as Brodsworth and Cadeby had six or seven fields of varying size (Fig. 4.1D). Nevertheless, it is easier in the case of these townships than in those with many scattered fields in the Vale of York and the Coalfield to visualise a former layout in a few large units. Many holdings showed little regularity in the distribution of their parcels,[2] and in some places a considerable amount of consolidation had taken place.[3] The only evidence relating to cropping suggests that the rotation was not a simple one shifting by fields.[4] Common pastures occupied either the steeper slopes as in Cadeby (Fig. 4.1D), or land on the margins of the township as in Brodsworth.[5] Some, like Hooton Pagnell common (on the Coal Measures),[6] and the Firth and the More in Ledston, were stinted, but there were others like Peckfield (327 acres), also in Ledston, that were unstinted.[7] Thus, although there was greater regularity of layout in the Magnesian Limestone hills than was characteristic in the Coalfield region, several features suggest a relatively flexible agricultural organisation within this framework.

Little is known about arrangements in the remaining regions, since most of their lowland tracts were already enclosed by 1650. It is therefore difficult to generalise about their characteristics.

(g) The northern Vale of York

This region consists of two undulating drift zones on either side of the sand and clay plain of the southern Vale, which merge to form

[1] Ruston and Whitney, Hooton Pagnell, pp. 13 and 59.
[2] Ibid., p. 123; Colman, A History of Barwick in Elmet, p. 283; plan of a holding in Darrington, 1783, Leeds City Library Archives Dept., Temple Hirst Coll., 48.
[3] E.g. Campsall and Skellow; Harvey, 'Early Maps as a Source for the Study of Field Systems'.
[4] Information relating to Warmsworth from J. Harvey.
[5] Brodsworth Enclosure Plan, 1830, West Riding Registry of Deeds, Wakefield, 1/19.
[6] Ruston and Whitney, Hooton Pagnell, p. 143.
[7] A Survey of the Lordship of Ledston, 1616, Leeds City Library Archives Dept., L.D. 170. I am indebted to J. Harvey for this reference.

a continuous drift-covered lowland north of Thirsk. The majority of townships in the northern part were fully enclosed before 1650.[1] Some townships in the two southern areas retained common fields until the eighteenth century, but few even of these have been studied in detail. Most of those whose layout is known had three or four arable fields and smaller tracts of common meadow and pasture, but also a considerable area of closes.[2] In this respect there are resemblances with the Wheldrake type of township farther south in the Vale (except that common pasture was probably less extensive), but whether there was the same irregular layout of holdings and flexibility of agricultural organisation is not known. Similarly, although some common arable fields and pastures survived into the seventeenth and eighteenth centuries in the Howardian Hills, nothing is known about the details of the arrangements.

(h) The Pennines, Bowland Fells and Craven Lowlands

Most Pennine townships contained some relatively low and gently sloping land on the fringes of the upland or in one of the dales, as well as some higher and often steeply sloping ground. The low ground was largely in closes by the eighteenth century, although a few places, especially in the Craven lowlands, had fragments of former open fields.[3] The borough of Richmond, situated on the eastern margins of the Pennines, was exceptional in retaining a considerable extent of open arable land until 1810;[4] there were two fair-sized fields, Gallow (144 acres) and West (147 acres) and two smaller ones, High East (29 acres) and Low East (23 acres), but it is not known how these fields were worked. The high ground of Pennine townships was invariably common land, divided into several large stinted pastures and having a total area which usually exceeded that of the lowland arable and meadow. In Thornton Rust (Wensleydale), for instance, there were 707 acres of enclosed land in 1795 and nearly 800 acres of common pasture.[5] In addition, extensive moorlands on the plateau top were shared by all adjoining townships without stint.

[1] Beresford, Yorks. Arch. Jnl., xxxvii, 1948–51, p. 349.
[2] K. J. Allison, 'Enclosure by Agreement at Healaugh (W.R.)', Yorks. Arch. Jnl., xl, 1961, pp. 382–91; enclosure plans of Copmanthorpe, Minskip and Roecliff, West Riding Registry of Deeds, Wakefield, 1/26, 3/9 and 3/19; plan of the manor of Allerton Mauleverer, Hopperton, Flaxby and Clareton, 1734, Leeds City Library Archives Dept.
[3] A. Raistrick, Malham and Malham Moor, 1947, p. 43; Enclosure plans of Burnsall, Cracoe and Linton, West Riding Registry of Deeds, Wakefield, 4/6, 2/6 and 230.
[4] 1802 plan of Richmond, Richmond Grammar School.
[5] Tuke, General View of the Agriculture of the North Riding of Yorkshire, 2nd edn, 1800, pp. 198–9.

Gates in the stinted pastures were not attached to holdings and dwellings as was usual in the lowland parts of the county, but since at least the sixteenth century they had been bought and sold as separate entities.[1] Similar conditions prevailed in the North York Moors, where the lower ground of the dales was enclosed, whilst the moorlands provided vast tracts of unstinted pasture common to several townships and grazed principally by sheep.[2] Vale of Pickering townships and those in the boulder-clay covered Coastal Fringe and Coastal Lowland regions were almost entirely enclosed before the eighteenth century.

A field system integrates the land use of different types of soil and terrain lying within the boundaries of one township, and it is therefore not surprising to find that seventeenth- and eighteenth-century field systems varied to some extent from one physical region of the county to another. It is more difficult to explain the broad contrast that emerges between the orderly and closely regulated systems of the east of the county and the more variable and loosely organised systems of the southwest. There is no doubt that arrangements in the southwest were becoming increasingly flexible during the sixteenth and subsequent centuries; large arable fields were being divided into two or more smaller ones,[3] holdings were being consolidated by sale and exchange, pasture rights were becoming separated from holdings of arable and meadow, and above all piecemeal enclosure was taking place everywhere. It is not immediately obvious, however, why these changes should have affected the southwest so much more than the east, unless there was an initial difference between the field systems of the two regions that gave an impetus to change in the west.

B. THIRTEENTH- AND FOURTEENTH-CENTURY ARRANGEMENTS

Land used in common was much more widespread in late medieval times than in the seventeenth and eighteenth centuries. Almost all Yorkshire townships had some common arable fields and meadows during this period, the exceptions being chiefly a few places where there were monastic estates[4] and some remote dales like Littondale

[1] Raistrick, *Malham and Malham Moor*, pp. 44–6.
[2] Tuke, *General View of the Agriculture of the North Riding of Yorkshire*, 1st edn, 1794, p. 107.
[3] E.g. Halton and Minskip; J. Harvey, 'Early Maps as a Source for the Study of Field Systems'.
[4] T. A. M. Bishop, 'Monastic Granges in Yorkshire', *Engl. Hist. Rev.*, CCII, 1936, pp. 193–214.

and Upper Nidderdale in the Pennines,[1] and Farndale in the North York Moors.[2] There is little direct evidence, however, relating to the ways in which the common land was organised, and few attempts have been made so far to reconstruct field arrangements from contemporary deeds, charters and rentals. The account that follows therefore inevitably has the nature of a reconnaissance survey, its main purpose being to seek comparisons with the arrangements of the seventeenth and eighteenth centuries.

The main arable tracts were divided into the same types of units as those described for the seventeenth and eighteenth centuries: lands or 'selions', furlongs or 'culturas' and fields. Thirteenth-century lands were described as between six and twenty yards wide,[3] which makes them comparable with those of later date, while furlongs often had similar names in the thirteenth and eighteenth centuries.[4] Since there must have been every incentive to continue ploughing within a framework of ridges, headlands and balks once these had been established, it seems legitimate to assume that the trends of lands as well as their breadths, and the boundaries of furlongs as well as their names, altered little over the same period. On the other hand, there is some evidence for two simple types of changes which were accommodated within unaltered frameworks. First, a number of long furlongs may have been subdivided at some date between the thirteenth and seventeenth centuries to form two or more relatively rectangular units, although the trend of lands continued unchanged. Harris and Matzat have found evidence for alterations of this kind in several townships,[5] and the repetition of furlong names in certain eighteenth-century plans (e.g. North Bardales, Bardale Dale and Town Bardales; North, Hanging and Town Wandales in Kilham[6]) could also be explained in this way. It is feasible that this is how many of the later rectangular furlongs originated, and that therefore long furlongs were even more numerous in the east of the county in the thirteenth century than they were later. The second minor change involved the layout of lands

[1] W. T. Lancaster (ed.), *Chartulary of the Cistercian Abbey of Fountains*, 1915, pp. 203–18; *Chartulary of Bridlington Priory*, 1912, pp. 243–7.
[2] W. R. Wightman, 'Some Aspects of the Historical Geography of the Vale of Pickering Area, 1086–1350 A.D.', Ph.D. thesis, University of Durham, 1964.
[3] J. T. Fowler (ed.), *Coucher Book of Selby Abbey* II, Yorks. Arch. Soc. Rec. Ser., XIII, 1893, p. 120; *Guisborough Chartulary* I, Surtees Soc., LXXXVI, 1889, p. 147.
[4] Sheppard, *Geogr. Annlr.*, B, 1966 (2), p. 69.
[5] A. Harris and W. Matzat, unpublished materials.
[6] Plan of Kilham 1729, East Riding R.O., DDDU/12/54.

within certain furlongs. The long boundaries of these furlongs were of reverse S-bend shape, which suggests that the lands were originally parallel with them, but by the eighteenth century they were laid out fairly straight and transverse to the long sides. The few known cases of such a pattern are all in the western part of the county, e.g. Turpitt Field in Flaxby,[1] Garth End Field in Halton,[2] and all three fields in Sutton in Campsall.[3] Eyre suggests a pre-1600 date for this type of change;[4] on the other hand it seems unlikely to have taken place before 1200, since it was only about this time that the new layout was adopted for assarts in Warwickshire.[5] Both types of change therefore indicate that shorter lands came into favour during the late medieval or Tudor periods; no reason can at present be given, although the substitution of the horse for the ox in drawing the plough is a factor worthy of further investigation.

Fields were relatively infrequently mentioned in the medieval records, nevertheless there are enough references to suggest differences in their character between the north and east of the county on the one hand and the southwest on the other. In northern and eastern townships, there was a clear three-tier organisation of units: lands were located by furlongs, and the furlongs were then described as lying within a particular field. Fields were two or three in number[6] and the majority had names of a simple directional type. In southwestern townships, in contrast, there appears to have been a good deal of confusion between furlongs and fields, and in at least some cases a two-tier organisation existed; for instance, West Field in North Duffield was evidently regarded as the equivalent of other plots not called fields, and lands were described as lying in West Field without any indication of intermediate units.[7] In addition, many fields had non-directional names, like Bondfield in Selby,[8] Oldfield in Parlington,[9] and Bromfield in Great Houghton.[10] A field in this part of the county thus seems to have been a tract of open arable land which consisted

[1] Plan of the Manor of Allerton Mauleverer, 1734, Leeds City Library Archives Dept.
[2] Plan of Halton 1731, Leeds City Library Archives Dept., TE/B4.
[3] 1858 Plan of Sutton in Campsall, Northamptonshire R.O., Map 2596.
[4] Eyre, *Agric. Hist. Rev.*, III, 1955, p. 91.
[5] D. J. Pannett, 'Midland Ridge-and-Furrow: the Meso-Study', paper read to the Annual Conference of the Institute of British Geographers, January 1965.
[6] T. A. M. Bishop, 'Assarting and the Growth of Open Fields', *Econ. Hist. Rev.*, VI, 1935–6, p. 14.
[7] *Yorkshire Deeds* V, Yorks. Arch. Soc. Rec. Ser., LIX, p. 31.
[8] J. T. Fowler (ed.), *Coucher Book of Selby Abbey* I, Yorks. Arch. Soc. Rec. Ser., X, 1891, p. 175.
[9] *Chartulary of St John of Pontefract* I, Yorks. Arch. Soc. Rec. Ser., XXV, 1899, p. 148.
[10] A. S. Ellis (ed.), 'Yorkshire Deeds', *Yorks. Arch. Jnl.*, XII, 1894, p. 260.

of either one furlong or several, and which was not necessarily matched by other comparable units. The contrast with the orderly northeastern fields may thus have been even more marked than in the seventeenth and eighteenth centuries.

The regular directionally named fields of the north and east were almost certainly cropping and rotation units. In the fourteenth century one of the two fields of Brandesburton was described as lying idle each year,[1] and in Marton, east of Ripon, various persons were chosen 'to cast the field into three parts, so that one part every year be fallow'.[2] That similar arrangements prevailed in other townships for which there is no direct evidence is suggested by the frequency of approximately equal division of holdings between fields,[3] and by records indicating that several adjacent furlongs were fallowed at the same time.[4] There is no known evidence about cropping in the irregular fields of the southwest, and it seems most likely that each was worked independently.

2. FORELAND AND ASSARTS

Many townships in the thirteenth and fourteenth centuries contained tracts of arable land that were outside and somewhat different in character from the common fields. This land was called 'foreland', 'forbyland' or *afnam* (O.N. 'land detached from an estate') in the north and east of the county, and 'assarts' in the southwest.

Foreland usually lay beyond the common fields and towards the margins of the township, where it was divided into compact blocks comparable with furlongs[5] which were subdivided into lands; in some cases, however, it appears to have consisted of scattered odd plots among the fields.[6] In contrast with field land, where holdings were measured in oxgangs ('bovates'), foreland was measured in acres. Its total area was relatively small in such regions as Holderness, the Tabular Hills and the northern Vale of York,[7] possibly somewhat

[1] D. J. Siddle, 'The Rural Economy of Medieval Holderness', *Agric. Hist. Rev.*, XV, 1967, p. 42.

[2] G. C. Homans, *English Villagers in the Thirteenth Century*, New York, 1941, p. 56.

[3] E.g. *Guisborough Chartulary* II, Surtees Soc., LXXXIX, 1891, p. 9; *Bridlington Chartulary*, p. 96; Wightman, Ph.D. thesis, p. 121.

[4] C. V. Collier (ed.), 'Documents at Scampston', *E. Riding Antiqu. Soc. Trans.*, XXI, 1914, p. 27.

[5] Sheppard, *Geogr. Annlr.*, B, 1966 (2), p. 65; *Yorkshire Inquisitions* II, Yorks. Arch. Soc. Rec. Ser., XXIII, 1898, p. 140.

[6] *Fountains Chartulary*, p. 465; 1589 Survey of Hutton-upon-Derwent, Leeds City Library Archives Dept., Fox-Lane Coll., LXXX, III/I.

[7] *Yorkshire Inquisitions* I, Yorks. Arch. Soc. Rec. Ser., XII, 1892, p. 222; *Yorkshire Inquisitions* II, Yorks. Arch. Soc. Rec. Ser., XXIII, 1898, p. 37.

greater on the Wolds, and of considerable extent in parts of the southern Vale of York. Around 1400, for instance, Wheldrake fore-land covered about twice the area of field land,[1] and in the manor of Escrick in 1291 there were 451½ acres of foreland.[2] At least some of the plots of foreland were enclosed with a hedge or wall,[3] but it is not clear whether it was usual to graze the stubbles and fallows in common. Wightman has suggested that foreland was the medieval equivalent of outfield land,[4] but this is doubtful. The essential feature is more likely to have been freedom from the strait-jacket rotation of the field land; thus, while some tracts on poor soils were probably cropped only intermittently, as in Great Ayton,[5] others may have been used more intensively than the field land.

Foreland was probably transformed into some other type of land between the fourteenth and seventeenth centuries, for it was rarely mentioned in later records. In Wheldrake there is evidence for two stages of transformation; during the fifteenth and sixteenth centuries, most foreland ceased to be cropped and the various plots became instead stinted pastures; by the early eighteenth century, these had been subdivided to form closes farmed in severalty.[6] A similar evolution seems likely elsewhere in the southern Vale of York, thus accounting for some (perhaps most) of the tracts of closes that separated open fields in the eighteenth century. The afnams of the Wolds seem in many cases to have been located where later there was outfield land, but the stages of evolution from the one to the other are not known. Where townships had only small pieces of foreland, the distinction from field land seems to have been lost at some stage, perhaps because it was not economic to maintain an independent cropping regime, and therefore fences, on small plots surrounded by open fields. Thus foreland was described as lying within the fields of Lissett in 1690.[7]

In the southwest of the county, the term 'foreland' was rarely used even in medieval times; instead there were considerable tracts of cultivated land in assarts. Thirteenth-century records indicate that much of this land had been comparatively recently reclaimed from woodland and waste, and that the process continued during the century.[8] The plots ranged from one or two acres to over 50 acres

[1] Sheppard, *Geogr. Annlr.*, B, 1966 (2), p. 66.
[2] *Yorkshire Inquisitions* II, Yorks. Arch. Soc. Rec. Ser., XXIII, 1898, p. 133.
[3] *Bridlington Chartulary*, p. 49.   [4] Wightman, Ph.D. thesis, p. 117.
[5] *Yorkshire Inquisitions* I, Yorks. Arch. Soc. Rec. Ser., XII, 1892, pp. 238–9.
[6] Sheppard, *Geogr. Annlr.*, B, 1966 (2), p. 64.
[7] Information from A. Harris.
[8] 'Yorkshire Deeds', *Yorks. Arch. Jnl.*, XVI, 1901, p. 92; *Yorkshire Inquisitions* II, Yorks. Arch. Soc. Rec. Ser., XXIII, 1898, pp. 37 and 61; *Fountains Chartulary*, p. 522.

in size, and each was probably surrounded by a hedge, wall or ditch.[1] While some were in the tenure of one individual,[2] many were shared among several persons.[3] There is no evidence relating to crop rotations, which were probably decided by the individuals concerned. Grazing rights in assarts were sometimes limited to those who cultivated the land,[4] although in other cases common grazing of the fallows and stubble seems to have been the practice.[5]

It seems legitimate to regard foreland and assarts as the same type of land but with different names. The term 'foreland', or one of its synonyms, appears to have been used where a nucleus of arable land was organised into rotation-unit fields, and the emphasis was evidently on the contrast between the strictly controlled agrarian regime of the fields and the greater flexibility of land use outside their bounds. The term 'assarts' was used, where, in the absence of regular rotation units, there was no such contrast in agrarian organisation, and instead the main distinctive feature of these plots was their recent reclamation. Confirmation of the identity of assarts and foreland comes from Wheldrake, where land described as assarts in the thirteenth century, when there does not seem to have been any grouping of furlongs into fields, was called foreland in the early fifteenth century, by which time fields had come into being.[6]

3. COMMON MEADOW AND PASTURE

Meadowland arrangements and the broad pattern of common pasture usage in the thirteenth and fourteenth centuries were very similar to those described for the later period. The Pennines, the Moors, the Coalfield and the southern Vale of York were already the areas with the greatest abundance of common pasture, and this was even more extensive than in the seventeenth and eighteenth centuries, by which time it had been depleted by Tudor and later enclosures.[7] Such

[1] *Fountains Chartulary*, p. 557; *Coucher Book of Selby Abbey* I, Yorks. Arch. Soc. Rec. Ser., x, 1891, p. 297.

[2] *Yorkshire Inquisitions* II, Yorks. Arch. Soc. Rec. Ser., XXIII, 1898, p. 121; *Coucher Book of Selby Abbey* I, Yorks. Arch. Soc. Rec. Ser., x, 1891, p. 104.

[3] *Coucher Book of Selby Abbey* I, Yorks. Arch. Soc. Rec. Ser., x, 1891, pp. 115, 150; Bishop, *Econ. Hist. Rev.*, VI, p. 20.

[4] *Coucher Book of Selby Abbey* I, Yorks. Arch. Soc. Rec. Ser., x, 1891, pp. 168, 172, 293; *Fountains Chartulary*, pp. 753, 814, 832.

[5] *Coucher Book of Selby Abbey* I, Yorks. Arch. Soc. Rec. Ser., x, 1891, p. 270; *Fountains Chartulary*, p. 833.

[6] Sheppard, *Geogr. Annlr.*, B, 1966 (2), pp. 66–8.

[7] G. G. Gamble, 'A History of Hunslet in the later Middle Ages', *Thoresby Soc. Trans.*, XLI, 1943–51, p. 251; Harris, *The Rural Landscape of the East Riding of Yorkshire*, p. 52; *Yorkshire Surveys*, Yorks. Arch. Soc. Rec. Ser., CIV, 1941, p. xxii;

abundance was reflected in an absence of limitations on the grazing of some commons,[1] and in very generous stints on others; in Malham, the pasture rights per oxgang were fixed in 1264 at six oxen, six cows with their young of three years, four mares with their young of three years, 200 sheep, five she-goats, one sow with the young of one year and five geese.[2] Another feature was the greater frequency than later of intercommoning arrangements.[3] A considerable proportion of the pasture available in the southern Vale of York and in the Coalfield was open woodland (a characteristic largely lost by the eighteenth century) and pasture rights in these tracts were usually available for cattle, horses and pigs, but rarely for sheep. Attached to 22 acres of arable and meadow in Acaster, for instance, were rights for six oxen, two cows, two horses and ten pigs.[4] Pasture was less abundant farther east and north, where the fallows and stubbles of the arable fields played an important role; pigs were rare. The limited pasture resources of Holderness and the northern Vale of York were used primarily for the beasts of the plough, together with a few sheep; e.g. in Newsham near Northallerton, the stint per oxgang was one horse, one ox, one cow and 24 sheep.[5] On the Wolds and the Tabular Hills, pasture suitable for sheep was abundant, and in many townships extensive pasture rights 'in the fields' were granted to monastic houses.[6]

4. TENEMENTS

Tenements were measured in oxgangs (bovates) and ploughgates (carucates) with their appurtenances. Oxgangs were of standard size in any one township but ranged from place to place between about six and thirty customary acres, the average villein or small freeholder tenement comprising one or two oxgangs. The oxgang itself consisted of arable land and sometimes meadow, although at this period it was more usual for meadow to be included among the appurtenances,

---

J. Chapman, 'Changing Agriculture and the Moorland Edge in the North York Moors 1750 to 1960', M.A. thesis, University of London, 1961, pp. 38–64.

[1] *Yorkshire Inquisitions* I, Yorks. Arch. Soc. Rec. Ser., XII, 1892, p. 29; C. V. Collier, 'A Transcript of an Old Malton Document', *Yorks. Arch. Jnl.*, XXVI, 1922, p. 326; *Bridlington Chartulary*, p. 243.

[2] *Fountains Chartulary*, p. 483.

[3] Wightman, Ph.D. thesis, p. 68; *Fountains Chartulary*, p. 546; *Yorkshire Inquisitions* I, Yorks. Arch. Soc. Rec. Ser., XII, 1892, p. 40.

[4] *Coucher Book of Selby Abbey* I, Yorks. Arch. Soc. Rec. Ser., X, 1891, p. 326.

[5] *Fountains Chartulary*, p. 778.

[6] B. Waites, *Moorland and Vale-Land Farming in North-East Yorkshire: the Monastic Contribution in the Thirteenth and Fourteenth Centuries*, Borthwick Papers No. 32, 1967, p. 18.

together with rights in the common waste. In many cases, acres of foreland or assarts were attached to oxgang holdings,[1] although some of this land was held in large demesne plots, especially by monastic houses.

There is every indication that both acres and oxgangs were carefully surveyed units; for instance, when 12 acres at Aldfield were sold to Fountains Abbey, they were 'measured by trustworthy men'.[2] The basic unit of measurement was the perch, which ranged in length from $17\frac{1}{2}$ feet in Cottingham to 24 feet in Balne, with 18 and 20 feet as the most common magnitudes. Both breadth and length measurements were often given for village enclosures, but most other land was measured across one dimension only. In Snaith, Rawcliffe, Hook and Cowick (all near the junction of the River Aire with the Humber), strips in the waste each a few perches wide were said to extend as far as the moor and marsh itself extended.[3] Arable land likewise was evidently measured across the lands, which were sometimes designated 'acres' or 'half-acres' according to their breadths; in one case, it was stated that an acre was 40 feet wide (probably two 20-foot perches).[4] A land one perch in width may thus have been regarded as a half-acre unit. In the several cases where land grants used the formula 'x oxgangs each of y acres by the perch of z feet', the most likely interpretation is therefore that the standard oxgang for the township was made up of the requisite number of acre or half-acre lands, each measured by the specified perch. In several townships, two different lengths of perch were recorded,[5] and it seems feasible that the diversity of land widths in medieval times and later was a result of the use of different perches in varying multiples.

Most of the examples of carefully measured oxgangs come from the north and east of the county, where the function of this unit appears to have been to maintain parity of holdings within each township between tenants of similar status. By the thirteenth century, oxgangs were virtually immutable units, apparently inherited from some earlier period. The oxgangs of the southwest of the county were more subject to change; new ones were being created out of the waste

[1] E.g. *Chartulary of Rievaulx Abbey*, Surtees Soc., LXXXIII, 1887, p. 239; *Bridlington Chartulary*, p. 275; *Fountains Chartulary*, p. 519; *Coucher Book of Selby Abbey* I, Yorks. Arch. Soc. Rec. Ser., x, 1891, p. 230; *Yorks. Arch. Jnl.*, XVII, 1903, p. 103.
[2] *Fountains Chartulary*, p. 28.
[3] *Coucher Book of Selby Abbey* I, Yorks. Arch. Soc. Rec. Ser., x, 1891, p. 3; II, Yorks. Arch. Soc. Rec. Ser., XIII, 1893, pp. 69, 91, 100, 112, 145.
[4] *Guisborough Chartulary* I, Surtees Soc., LXXXVI, 1889, p. 63.
[5] E.g. *Fountains Chartulary*, pp. 223, 250; *Coucher Book of Selby Abbey* I, Yorks. Arch. Soc. Rec. Ser., x, 1891, pp. 235, 240.

during medieval times,[1] while some of the older units were sub-divided[2] and others modified by the absorption of new land.[3] It would have been difficult to maintain exact parity in these circumstances, and the oxgang here was probably an approximate measure only.[4] Associated with these differences between stable and flexible units was a contrast in the layout of oxgangs. In northern and eastern districts, a regular disposition throughout the fields was even more common than in the seventeenth and eighteenth centuries. This was indicated in medieval records by various formulae, including 'an oxgang lying between the oxgangs of X and Y', 'an oxgang lying everywhere throughout the field next to the land of X towards the south', and 'an oxgang lying nearest to the sun in the half carucate of X'. S. Göransson has called this arrangement 'sun-division', and his map showing the distribution of the feature in the whole of England and Wales reveals the contrast in frequency of occurrence between the two sections of Yorkshire.[5] In the upland and southwestern districts of the county where there were few examples of 'sun-division', some oxgangs were in one plot,[6] some were in a large number of plots of varying size and irregular distribution,[7] and some consisted of a plot near the dwelling together with one or two other parcels.[8] There is little doubt that the irregular layout was linked with the frequency of change in the composition of oxgangs in this part of the county.

The medieval evidence cited supports two general conclusions. First, there are sufficient similarities between thirteenth- and eighteenth-century field arrangements to indicate that intermediate changes were evolutionary rather than revolutionary, with a general trend towards increased flexibility and greater freedom for individual decision. Once this evolutionary link is accepted, it becomes possible to use the information available for the later period to illuminate brief and stereotyped references to field arrangements in medieval records, and so build up a reasonably full picture of medieval field systems. Second,

[1] *Wakefield Court Rolls* I, Yorks. Arch. Soc. Rec. Ser., XXIX, 1901, pp. 179, 245, 273; *Bridlington Chartulary*, p. 270.
[2] A. S. Ellis (ed.), 'Yorkshire Deeds', *Yorks. Arch. Jnl.*, XIII, 1895, p. 66; *Wakefield Court Rolls* I, Yorks. Arch. Soc. Rec. Ser., XXIX, 1901, p. 255.
[3] *Fountains Chartulary*, p. 679.
[4] *Chartulary of St John of Pontefract* I, Yorks. Arch. Soc. Rec. Ser., XXV, 1899, p. 222.
[5] S. Göransson, 'Regular Open-Field Pattern in England and Scandinavian Solskifte', *Geogr. Annlr.*, XLIII, 1961, p. 100.
[6] *Guisborough Chartulary* II, Surtees Soc., LXXXIX, 1891, p. 167.
[7] *Yorks. Arch. Jnl.*, XVII, 1903, p. 103.
[8] Ellis, *Yorks. Arch. Jnl.*, XIII, 1895, p. 55.

the major regional contrast in the seventeenth and eighteenth centuries, between relatively rigid systems in eastern lowland districts and more flexible systems in the southwest, appears to have been even more striking in the thirteenth century. In the late medieval period, most lowland townships of the north as well as the east had a high proportion of their area under open arable land, in which furlongs were grouped to form two or three fields functioning as rotation units; oxgangs consisted of lands regularly disposed among the furlongs, and common grazing was closely regulated. Most southwestern townships had in contrast a much smaller proportion of their land under arable, and this was divided among many units of variable size, each probably cropped and fallowed independently; oxgangs were in one plot or irregularly disposed, and there was abundant and often unregulated common grazing. Closer study will certainly reveal variations within each division, and a key region in this respect is the Magnesian Limestone hills, where at least some townships displayed features characteristic of the northeastern zone. The affinities of the Craven lowlands are also difficult to decide. Nevertheless, there is little doubt that a major boundary between two field systems ran through medieval Yorkshire, its approximate course through the lowlands being from near Tadcaster on the Wharfe through York to Brough on the Humber.

C. PRE-THIRTEENTH-CENTURY ARRANGEMENTS

The field arrangements described above pose certain questions of origin. How and when did the complex and closely regulated field system of north and east Yorkshire come into being? Did it evolve gradually within the region, some features being present much earlier than others, or was it imported and imposed in its developed form? If the evidence points to evolution, is it possible to regard the arrangements in southwestern districts as representing a stage in the process, which for some reason was never superseded in that part of the county? Or were there always two distinctive field systems represented, each evolving along its own lines? Categorical answers cannot be given to these questions, but an attempt will be made to assess probabilities.

The simplest starting point is with pre-thirteenth-century arrangements in the southwest of the county, exemplified by the township of Wheldrake in the southern Vale of York. Most of the thirteenth-century assarts in this township were cleared after two significant changes in land administration: in 1234, the Royal Forest Between Ouse and Derwent which surrounded Wheldrake was deforested; and in 1236 the Statute of Merton was passed allowing chief tenants to assart land for their own or their villeins' exclusive use, provided that 'sufficient' common land was left for the needs of the village community. The inner boundary of the assarts thus approximately delimits the cultivated land about 1235 (Fig. 4.6).

Within the bounds so established, a number of later furlongs and closes bore names compounded with the element *rydding* (O.E. 'a clearing'), and other names of this kind are included in medieval charters. These evidently represent pre-1235 assarting. The 'rydding' element was often combined with a personal name, which suggests that these plots were cleared by (or for) individuals. Prior to the Statute of Merton, however, there is little doubt that clearings were subject to common grazing when not being cropped,[1] and this probably led to the rapid disappearance of any original hedges or boundary strips of uncleared woodland. In this respect, 'ryddings' contrasted with many of the later assarts, where restricted grazing rights made the maintenance of hedges imperative.

Surviving 'rydding' names in Wheldrake lie within a zone between the assarts on the outer side and a former turf dyke on the inner side.[2] Within the same zone were other plots with names that contain no element indicating assarting, but which on account of their location can be presumed to have originated in the same way. The Forest Between Ouse and Derwent was established early in the reign of Henry I (1154–89) and the turf dyke may well have been constructed at the same time by the villagers in order to protect their crops from the depredations of the deer. The earliest 'ryddings' outside the dyke were thus probably created some time between 1154 and 1200, the latter being the date of the first recorded clearing.[3]

Within the turf dyke lay the longest cultivated land. It occupied about 350 acres of easily worked sandy loams on the slopes of the Escrick moraine, contrasting with the less well-drained clays and sands that were the sites of most of the 'ryddings' and thirteenth-century assarts. The limits of this old cultivated tract were probably similar in the mid-twelfth century and in 1066, when population numbers are likely to have been comparable. Between these two dates, however, Wheldrake must have experienced a fall in population and a decrease in the cultivated area as a result of William I's systematic devastation of the county in 1069–70; the demesne farm and six tenant holdings recorded by Domesday Book in 1086 are unlikely to have occupied the whole of the 350 acres. Nevertheless, the formerly cultivated land probably remained distinct from the surrounding

[1] *Fountains Chartulary*, p. 557.
[2] Sheppard, *Geogr. Annlr.*, B, 1966 (2), p. 69.
[3] J. C. Holt, *The Northerners*, 1961, p. 163.

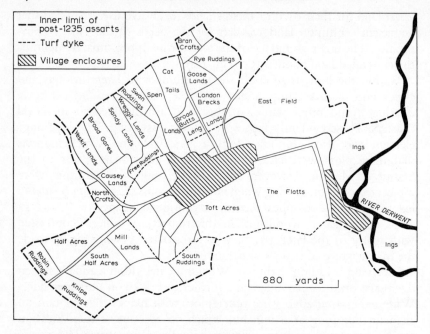

Fig. 4.6 Wheldrake (East Riding): old arable land within the turf dyke together
with the 'ryddings' reclaimed between *c.* 1154 and 1235.

woodland throughout the period of recession, thus representing an
element of stability in the land use pattern.

The picture of Wheldrake that emerges is of a hamlet with an
associated small arable field set in an extensive woodland tract; some
time during the second half of the twelfth century the woodland
began to be cleared, and by 1235 the arable enclave had expanded to
more than double its eleventh-century size.

Field names suggest that a similar process may have occurred in
a number of other townships in the southwest of the county. There
were many medieval plots with names compounded with 'rydding',
or the equivalent elements 'rod' or 'stubbing'. Some of these names
refer to post-1235 assarts, but many clearly belong to the earlier
period.[1] A guide to distribution is provided by the English Place-Name
Society volumes for the West Riding. 'Rydding' and 'rod' elements
were common in most parts of the county south of the River Wharfe,
except in the marshland area around the lower Aire and Don (Fig.
4.7). Since these elements signified forest clearing, it is not surprising

[1] A. H. Smith, *The Place-Names of the West Riding of Yorkshire,* Part 7, 1962, English
Place-Name Society, xxxvi, p. 305.

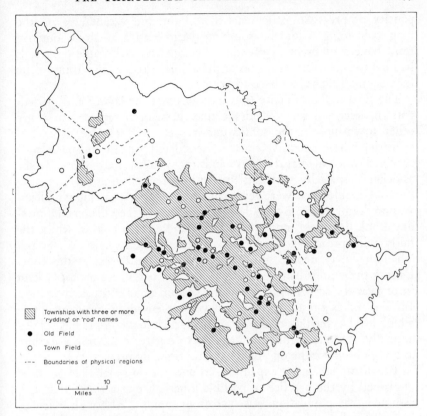

Fig. 4.7 West Riding: names indicative of early medieval field arrangements.
Sources. English Place-Name Society, volumes XXV–XXXVI.

that they were lacking in the latter district, where Domesday Book recorded little or no woodland in 1086.[1] In their place, *croft* (O.E. 'small enclosure'), *thwaite* (O.N. 'clearing, meadow') and *thing* (O.E. or O.N. 'possession, property') were quite numerous and may indicate that a comparable process of marshland reclamation was under way in the district. North of the Wharfe, however, reclamation elements of any kind are relatively less frequent.

The existence of nuclei of old arable land comparable with that in Wheldrake is suggested by the names 'Old Field' and 'Town Field'. In the West Riding, such names are recorded quite frequently in the areas where 'rydding' and 'rod' elements were common (Fig. 4.7). Their absence from the marshland district can be linked with the

[1] H. C. Darby and I. S. Maxwell (eds.), *The Domesday Geography of Northern England*, 1962, p. 53.

paucity of pre-1086 settlements there,[1] but the vacant area on the map coinciding with the southern Magnesian Limestone outcrop must have a different explanation. Perhaps the favourable light soils had led to an earlier expansion of the arable area, and the limits of the former small fields had been forgotten.

The field name evidence thus indicates that the layout and growth pattern described for Wheldrake may have been repeated in many other townships in the southwestern part of Yorkshire. This was a district where extensive tracts of woodland (and some marshland) survived into medieval times, and the pattern may therefore be associated especially with settlements in forest clearings. When only the 'old' arable tracts were being cultivated, the surrounding woodland was no doubt grazed by the domestic animals of the villagers. Domesday Book described most of the woodland as *silva pastilis*, whilst the fairly widespread field and place-name element *skali* (O.W. Scand. 'shieling') may denote summer grazing grounds used at this time. During the winter half-year, however, the cattle were probably kept in or near the settlement, as was the custom at later times in western Britain, and as a result there may have been enough dung to maintain a high level of fertility in the arable field, such that it could be cropped annually. It seems legitimate therefore to regard southwest Yorkshire as a region where the one-field system originally prevailed.

The form taken by expansion around the original field may be explained by the practice of partible inheritance at a time when it is assumed that population was increasing rapidly. Although evidence is available for only a few townships, for instance Holne where two oxgangs were shared between two sons,[2] Alverthorpe where half an oxgang was divided equally among four daughters,[3] and Thorpe Arches and Walton where parceners are mentioned,[4] it seems likely that the practice prevailed in many western parts of the county in medieval times; in a few places it survived into later centuries.[5] T. A. M. Bishop has suggested that where a holding was divided between two or more heirs, each new tenant needed to reclaim some additional land in order to bring his property up to a reasonable size.[6] Subdivision would have started earliest and had most effect on

[1] *Ibid.*, p. 14.
[2] *Wakefield Court Rolls* I, Yorks. Arch. Soc. Rec. Ser., XXIX, 1901, p. 118.
[3] *Ibid.*, p. 255.
[4] *Yorkshire Inquisitions* III, Yorks. Arch. Soc. Rec. Ser., XXXI, 1902, pp. 169–79.
[5] E. Cooper, *Muker, the Story of a Yorkshire Parish*, 1948, p. 115; J. Thirsk, *The Agrarian History of England and Wales, IV: 1500–1640*, 1967, p. 31; W. Consett Boulter, 'The Book of Remarks of William Storr of Scalm Park, 1678–1731', *Yorks. Arch. Jnl.*, VII, 1881–2, p. 52.
[6] Bishop, *Econ. Hist. Rev.*, VI, 1936, pp. 13–29.

the 'Old Field', which thus became shared between many persons; it operated for a shorter period in the early 'ryddings', which were therefore divided into fewer and larger parcels; it had often not affected the later assarts by the time their existence was recorded in thirteenth-century charters. Partible inheritance thus explains the evolution and coexistence of the various types and sizes of plot found in southwest Yorkshire in medieval times.

It seems reasonable to assume that before partitioning led to the creation of 'ryddings', holdings within the original arable field were each one or two oxgangs in size; in at least some instances these may have been relatively compact units. In eighteenth-century Wheldrake, a 70-acre furlong known as Toft Acres, with north–south trending lands, lay between the turf dyke and the garths on the south side of the village street (Fig. 4.6). 'Toft Acres' is synonymous with 'Tofte-agre', a name known to have been used in parts of eastern Denmark for strips held in severalty and continuous with the tofts to which they belonged.[1] A comparable original arrangement seems feasible in this part of Wheldrake, and hints of a similar pattern are also to be found in medieval records relating to certain other townships in the region. In North Studley (near Ripon), for instance, in a grant of two tofts and one and a half oxgangs, seven acres of the oxgangs were said to 'abut on the said tofts'.[2] It is impossible to say, however, whether this arrangement was characteristic of all or even most eleventh-century arable tracts in this region.

If arrangements similar to those outlined for southwest Yorkshire also prevailed in the north and east, this fact is likely to be revealed by field names. Unfortunately little space is given to such names in the English Place-Name Society volumes for the North and East Ridings.[3] The two volumes record only one unlocated 'Old' field (in the East Riding and therefore possibly outside this region[4]) and no 'Town' fields. That other examples exist is shown by Allerston's work on the Pickering district; she found thirteenth-century references to two 'Old' fields, in Spaunton and Appleton-le-Moors.[5] Chapman records a 'Town' field in Westerdale in the North York Moors.[6] On the other hand, no further such names have been met in a variety of medieval records examined, and none is recorded in that part of the

[1] F. Hastrup, *Danske Landsbytyper*, Århus 1964, pp. 67–8, 106, 261, 266.

[2] Ellis, *Yorks. Arch. Jnl.*, XIII, 1895, p. 55.

[3] A. H. Smith, *The Place-Names of the North Riding of Yorkshire*, 1928, English Place-Name Society, vol. V; *The Place-Names of the East Riding of Yorkshire and York*, 1937, English Place-Name Society, vol. XIV.

[4] Smith, *Place-Names of the East Riding*, p. 322.

[5] Allerston, M.Sc. thesis, p. 250.

[6] Chapman, M.A. thesis, p. 70.

northeast region lying within the West Riding (Fig. 4.7). It seems reasonable to assume therefore that names of this type are much less common in the north and east of the county than in the south-west.

Of the various reclamation elements, 'rydding', 'rod' and 'stubbing' are not very common in the northeast. 'Croft' was more widely used; for instance there were five furlongs with 'croft' names in Skirpenbeck, although in no case was the other element a personal name.[1] In many townships, however, even 'croft' names were rare, and the impression is therefore that reclamation by individuals was not extensive. It would appear likely from field name evidence as a whole that early medieval arrangements in north and east Yorkshire were different from those in the southwest, except possibly in districts where woodland survived into medieval times; Spaunton and Appleton-le-Moors with their 'Old' fields lay within the Royal Forest of Pickering.[2] Bishop has argued that the process of individual assarting with subsequent subdivision of the plots and their absorption into the common arable fields was found throughout 'the Yorkshire plain', but since he drew his twenty or so examples almost exclusively from the Vale of York and districts to the west, it is reasonable to assume that he was mistaken about the extent of the practice.[3]

Two sets of circumstances could account for the scarcity of 'Old' fields and of names suggesting individual reclamation. First, a small nucleus of arable land may have existed in each township, but as in Wheldrake it was either never called 'Old Field' or the name did not survive; surrounding this, communal reclamation may have produced open field furlongs that were given names different in type from those of individually reclaimed plots. Second, arable land may have already been extensive at an early date, leaving little to be reclaimed in medieval times, while in the absence of 'new' arable land, the term 'Old Field' would have been inappropriate.

Communal reclamation of open field furlongs in medieval times has often been postulated.[4] Beresford has suggested that in Yorkshire the repetitive layout that Göransson calls sun-division may be a result of this process: 'A newly won piece of land was divided among those who had put their energies to the plough, and within the bundle a rough order was preserved, one settler having always (say) the eleventh strip from the end.'[5] A difficulty inherent in this interpretation,

[1] 1740 plan of Skirpenbeck, East Riding R.O., DDDA/MP36.
[2] Holt, *The Northerners*, map 2.
[3] Bishop, *Econ. Hist. Rev.*, VI, 1936, pp. 13–29.
[4] C. S. and C. S. Orwin, *The Open Fields*, pp. 41–2.
[5] Beresford, *Yorks. Arch. Jnl.*, XXXVII, 1948–51, p. 337.

recognised by Beresford himself, is that if the population grew at a rate that made reclamation necessary, successive plots would have been divided between successively greater numbers of tenants, and a fixed pattern of allocation could not have been maintained. Sundivision cannot therefore be used as evidence for communal reclamation; equally it is not evidence against it, for there could have been a reallocation of holdings after the phase of reclamation.

On the other hand, Domesday Book provides support for the alternative theory that extensive tracts were already under cultivation by the eleventh century. There was little woodland in the region in 1086 outside the districts later to become the Royal Forests of Pickering and Galtres, and apart from marshland in the Vale of Pickering and the Hull valley most of the land can be presumed to have been productive. The proportion that arable formed of this productive land would have been determined primarily by the size of the population. The recorded population in 1086 was small and densities per square mile low in comparison with counties farther south, but there is little doubt that numbers were greater prior to the Conqueror's devastation of 1069–70 and the Scandinavian and Scottish raids of the same period. In the two royal manors of Falsgrave and Northallerton, the only places in the county for which 1066 population numbers are given, there were 290 recorded inhabitants in 1066 compared with 36 in 1086.[1] A similar or even greater percentage decline probably characterised other manors, especially on the Wolds and in the northern Vale of York where many townships were still devoid of inhabitants in 1086. It is easy to believe that in 1066 these regions had population densities little different from those of East Anglia, and that a large part of the productive land was devoted to arable uses. This therefore seems to be a very likely explanation of the paucity of 'Old Field' and individual reclamation names.

If large tracts were arable by the early eleventh century, it is possible that the field system for which there is evidence in the thirteenth century was already in existence. On the other hand, a number of features point to the probability of a later, planned origin. First, some village plans show traces of an original very regular layout, with one or more rows of rectangular garths abutting on to a village street or green oriented approximately north–south or east–west. Allerston suggests that in the Pickering district some of these plans resulted from an organised amalgamation of two former hamlets during the twelfth or early thirteenth centuries.[2] One regular village, Old Byland, is known to have been created in the 1140s by Cistercian monks when

[1] Darby and Maxwell, *The Domesday Geography of Northern England*, p. 120.
[2] Allerston, M.Sc. thesis, pp. 250–2.

they established a community on the former village site.[1] The villages of Wharram Percy[2] and Wawne[3] appear to have been laid out anew in the fourteenth century, but other evidence, not yet fully analysed, seems to suggest a late eleventh- or early twelfth-century date for many regular plans. Second, both sun-division and the uniform shapes of furlongs in certain townships are most readily explained as the result of planning, and there is an interesting similarity between the layout of townships like Kilham[4] and Southburn[5] and that of German settlements east of the River Elbe associated with planned colonisation in the twelfth and thirteenth centuries.[6] Although there is no evidence relating to the dates of origin of either sun-division or regular furlongs, it seems most likely that these came into being about the same time as the orderly rows of village garths, and that all three were the result of a planned reorganisation.

The occasion for such a reorganisation that immediately suggests itself is the phase of recovery from the devastations of 1069–70. In most places there was probably an interval of several years between wasting and recolonisation, and in a considerable number of townships this lasted until at least 1086. Such an interval would allow the former layout of holdings to be largely forgotten, thus providing an ideal opportunity for a new start. Bishop has argued convincingly that lords who owned widely dispersed estates repopulated their devastated manors by moving tenants from other manors that had escaped William I's ravages owing to remoteness and poverty; in particular he postulated large-scale movement from the Pennines to districts farther east.[7] These tenants would have had little knowledge or understanding of former arrangements in their new abodes, and no reason for preferring these to a reorganised layout. Other lords, all of whose manors were devastated, must have relied on alternative methods of procuring colonists, such as the two for which F. W. Brooks finds evidence in Domesday Book: either an agent, like the east German *locator*, sought and established colonists for his lord in return for an estate of his own; or a group of colonists made a communal

---

[1] R. A. Donkin, 'Settlement and Depopulation on Cistercian Estates during the Twelfth and Thirteenth Centuries, especially in Yorkshire', *Bull. Inst. Hist. Res.*, XXXIII, 1960, p. 145.

[2] *Medieval Archaeology*, II, 1958, p. 206.

[3] *Med. Arch.*, VI–VII, 1962–3, pp. 343–5.

[4] 1729 Plan, East Riding R.O., DDDU/12/54.

[5] Plan c. 1790, East Riding R.O., DDBV/43/1.

[6] A. Krenzlin, *Dorf, Feld und Wirtschaft im Gebiet der grossen Täler und Platten östlich der Elbe*, Forschungen zur Deutschen Landeskunde, LXX, 1952.

[7] T. A. M. Bishop, 'The Norman Settlement of Yorkshire', in R. W. Hunt, W. A. Pantin and F. W. Southern (eds.), *Studies in Medieval History presented to Frederick Maurice Powicke*, 1948, pp. 1–14.

agreement to restore the land to cultivation.[1] Where sufficient tenants were procured, all the former arable land may have been cropped again within a few years, whilst most settlements were probably flourishing by the mid-twelfth century.[2]

The hypothesis of a post-Conquest origin for the regular field system of northeast Yorkshire is therefore very attractive. If however it is assumed that each settlement took some years to acquire the number of colonists needed, sun-division creates a problem: an apportionment that represented fair shares for all who finally joined the community must have been made at the end rather than at the beginning of colonisation. Regular reapportionment during the early years of recolonisation seems a possible solution to the problem, and one furlong name, 'Wandales', may be a remnant of such early arrangements. The name occurs once in a large proportion of Wolds townships and in some elsewhere, suggesting that the furlong may have had a special significance. In twelve of the fifteen townships where the location is known, 'Wandales' abuts on the village garths. Smith gives the derivation as O.N. vǫndr meaning 'a wand, a shoot, a measure' and O.N. deill meaning 'a share of land'.[3] Could it be that 'Wandales' was the furlong where agreed shares were measured out, which then formed the model for the subdivision of other furlongs? Reallocation could then have been achieved simply by measuring out 'Wandales' anew. The principle of sun-division could thus have been an inherent part of the new layout, even though the precise distribution of holdings that appears in thirteenth-century records may not have been established until the twelfth century. Division into roughly equal-sized rotation units may also date from the time when the whole arable tract of a township had been brought back into cultivation.

An alternative view of the origins of the regular common-field system has been suggested by Allerston.[4] She postulated that in the Pickering district long furlongs indicate the former existence of fields comparable with the *langstreifenfluren* of northwest Germany, and that therefore a one-field system originally prevailed. Subsequent reclamation expanded the arable area until it reached its full extent in the late twelfth or early thirteenth centuries, when furlongs were regrouped into two or three rotation units and in some cases the village was also laid out anew. The process thus resembles that

[1] F. W. Brooks, *Domesday Book and the East Riding*, E. Yorks. Local Hist. Ser., 21, 1966, p. 25.   [2] *Ibid.*, p. 46.
[3] A. H. Smith, *English Place-Name Elements*, Part 2, English Place-Name Society, XXVI, 1956, p. 245.
[4] Allerston, M.Sc. thesis, ch. 10.

postulated for the southwest of the county, and it may well be that there were a number of townships even in the north and east which developed later than others, and which only adopted the new layout in the late twelfth or early thirteenth centuries. In most of the region, however, the probable large extent of arable in the early eleventh century suggests that any one-field stage would by then have been long outmoded, whilst circumstantial evidence points to revolution in layout rather than evolution.

It is difficult to do more than speculate on what preceded the apparently reorganised layout. It could have been a one-field system or a variant with outfield additions to the original nucleus; G. R. J. Jones has suggested that such an arrangement together with associated hamlet settlements originally prevailed throughout the whole of northern England.[1] In this case, most of the original layout would have been erased when the regular furlongs and linear villages were established. Another possibility, suggested by the combination in Holderness of long street villages and long furlongs perpendicular to the streets is that the original layout was in strip farms like those of the German *Waldhufendörfer*. This arrangement is known to have existed in areas of forest clearing in France and Germany by at least the ninth century,[2] so that its presence in what was probably a well-wooded district in early Anglo-Saxon times[3] would not be surprising. Holderness had few uninhabited vills in 1086, and continuity of occupation through the 1070s and inheritance of the village form from pre-Conquest times therefore seem feasible. If the soil had already been ploughed into high ridges, this could explain the retention of the major lineaments when common field furlongs replaced the strip farms. It remains to be investigated whether there are traces of strip farms elsewhere, and whether this system could have operated side-by-side with a one-field system.

There is similarly little positive evidence about the source of the planned layout and the associated field system. The nearest parallels were in medieval southern Sweden,[4] eastern Denmark[5] and Germany east of the Elbe.[6] An eleventh-century origin for the Yorkshire

[1] G. R. J. Jones, 'Basic Patterns of Settlement Distribution in Northern England', *Advmt. Sci.*, XVIII, 1961, pp. 192–200.

[2] M. M. Postan (ed.), *The Agrarian Life of the Middle Ages*, 2nd edn, 1966, *The Cambridge Economic History of Europe* I, 46.

[3] Smith, *The Place-Names of the East Riding*, pp. xiii–xiv.

[4] S. Göransson, 'Field and Village on the Island of Öland', *Geogr. Annlr.*, XL, 1958, p. 133; S. Helmfrid, 'Östergötland "Västanstång"', *Geogr. Annlr.*, XLIV, 1962, pp. 189–213.

[5] Hastrup, *Danske Landsbytyper*, p. 261.

[6] Postan (ed.), *The Agrarian Life of the Middle Ages*, pp. 461–6.

arrangements would however indicate that sun-division was approximately contemporary with Danish *bolskifte* and Swedish *solskifte*[1] and that the regular linear villages were apparently earlier than their counterparts in northern and eastern Europe. These regions are therefore unlikely to have provided the model on which the Yorkshire field and village layout was based, and the possibility of a local origin must be admitted. It may be that the particular mixture of peoples of Anglo-Saxon, Danish, Irish–Norse and Norman–French extraction in north and east Yorkshire during the eleventh century brought together various traditions of field and settlement arrangement, whilst the devastation that left large tracts of arable land vacant provided an environment in which the resultant hybrid was able to take root and flourish.

D. CONCLUSION

The broad outlines of the picture that emerges from this retrogressive analysis can now be summarised. Two contrasting field systems were present in early medieval Yorkshire. In the Coalfield region, the southern Vale of York, and possibly the Magnesian Limestone hills, there was a one-field system associated with hamlet settlement which shows every sign of having evolved out of the arrangements of Anglo-Saxon or earlier times. A more complex and carefully organised system with many classic *Midland* features, and often associated with regularly laid-out villages, occurred in the northern Vale of York, the Wolds, Holderness and round the Vale of Pickering; this system appears to have been the result of a planned reorganisation in the late eleventh and early twelfth centuries in which relatively few elements of earlier arrangements were retained. The contrast between the two parts of the county may have been at its peak in the twelfth century, although even then some townships may not have conformed to the local pattern. The differences become blurred during late medieval and Tudor times, as southwestern townships adopted certain northeastern features, and as both systems were modified in response to social, economic and technological changes. Thus by the eighteenth century the distinction between the two regions was superficially inconspicuous, although quickly revealed by fuller investigation.

This thesis rests in places on a relatively tenuous chain of assumptions, and modification will doubtless be needed in the light of later findings and work in other regions. In the meantime, it provides feasible explanations for some otherwise puzzling features of Yorkshire field systems.

[1] Göransson, *Geogr. Annlr.*, XLIII, 1961, p. 101.

5

Field Systems of the West Midlands

BY B. K. ROBERTS

A. INTRODUCTION

The term 'Midland field system' was adopted in 1915 by H. L. Gray
to describe the routine of open field husbandry which characterised
a large irregular area lying chiefly within the clay vales and limestone
scarplands of Lowland England, a routine by which the village fields
were regularly divided into two or three parts for the purposes of
cropping, and to each of which one-half or one-third of every tenant's
parcels were assigned. These regular systems constituted a model,
against which all other modifications and divergencies were measured
and assessed. Gray demonstrated that the study of any field system
involves a consideration of four interrelated problems: the form which
the system takes, the character of the husbandry and the rotations
practised, the development of the system through time, and, finally,
its territorial extent.

The first of these problems – that of form – is concerned with the
shape of the system within the landscape, its overall plan and relationship to terrain, the disposition of individual holdings, the constituent
structural elements, and relationship to settlement. Since Gray wrote in
1915 much work has been done by economic historians, archaeologists
and geographers in the identification and examination of the relict
features of former field systems, and these studies, linking together
document and landscape, have added much to our understanding of
the structure of the systems described by such scholars as Gray and
Seebohm. Secondly, there is the problem of the system's functional
aspect, the course of husbandry followed within the formal framework
to grow crops and raise beasts and provide subsistence for man. This
must lead to a consideration of the place of the individual farm unit
within the whole, for a 'system' embraces a number of individual
farms, and through the medium of a manorial court or village meeting,
establishes a general pattern of management. Clearly, both form and
function are intimately interlocked, and while it is dangerous to attach
uncritically a rotational significance to a formal layout, in practice a link
did occur frequently, and much of the work done since Gray wrote
consists of an examination of the variations in this relationship which
occur under a variety of physical, economic and social circumstances.

A field system is never static, for neither form nor rotational practice are immutably fixed; both can change comparatively rapidly under the influence of lordship, and changing technology and economic pressures, and the origin and development of field systems presents a distinct and fascinating problem which has in this country received, since Gray wrote, less attention than it deserves. Finally, a given field system will prevail over a definable territory, and to understand any system it is essential to appraise its distribution, and to consider its external relationships in terms of affinities and parallels. Local variations in physical terrain and settlement history have, within England, resulted in a multitude of local peculiarities as well as in larger-scale regional differences, and much post-1915 work has been directed to a critical appraisal of the regional characteristics defined by Gray.

The evidence available for reconstructing field systems varies very much, both in time and space, and quality and quantity, but tends, in general, to become increasingly unsatisfactory as one retrogresses to more remote periods. As the landscape evidence becomes more difficult to recognise, and as documentation becomes more attenuated and more inadequate, the correct interpretation of what does survive becomes increasingly difficult, until a stage is finally reached when it is impossible to document conclusively even the basic skeleton of form and of cropping systems. In these circumstances there is the danger of a deceptive and uncritical projection of the conditions prevailing in a well-documented age into periods with poorer evidence; without doubt the problem of Anglo-Saxon and early medieval field systems falls into this category. Nevertheless, much of the early evidence can only assume significance when viewed critically in the light of later sources and patterns, and for this reason it has been decided to adopt a retrogressive approach, and, while using a geographical framework to bind together the complex dichotomy of form and function, to work backwards from the well-documented period after 1600 towards the problems of earlier developments and origins.

The area termed the West Midlands in this study embraces the three counties of Warwickshire, Worcestershire and Staffordshire. In justification for this rather limited interpretation, it was considered that the borderland character of Shropshire and Herefordshire introduced complications which could not be properly treated within the present essay. Furthermore, this difficulty was magnified by the few studies available relating to field systems in those two counties in the half-century since Gray wrote, although work is at present in progress.[1] The boundaries of the region are arbitrary in the sense that county boundaries have been adopted, but this has the advantage that

[1] D. Sylvester, *The Formation of the Rural Landscape of the Welsh Borderland*, 1969.

the three shires, while focussing on early developed valley lands, included within their orbit substantial upland tracts, particularly the South Staffordshire plateau, together with associated high land in northern Worcestershire and northern Warwickshire. The region as a whole may be seen as a transition zone between the scarp and vale country of Lowland Britain, whose Jurassic outliers fall just within the southern boundary, and the bleak, windswept Palaeozoic uplands of the Highland Zone to be seen in north Staffordshire. Nevertheless, the core of the area is to be found on the drift-veneered clays, marls and sandstones of the Lias, Keuper and Bunter series, through which the Trent, Severn and Warwickshire Avon carve distinctive valleys. This pattern of physical diversity is reflected in the cutural landscapes of the region, and, as will be shown, while the three counties lie securely within the territory of the 'Midland field systems', they straddle a critical transition zone between two very distinctive types of open field arrangement, which may, following Gray, be broadly termed 'regular' and 'irregular'.

B. COMMON FIELDS AND ENCLOSURE

There is a well-established link between communal agriculture and open arable land, fields in which the individual holdings lie open to one another, and any discussion of field systems must devolve initially around those extensive areas of open fields enclosed by act of Parliament between 1720 and 1880. Figs. 5.1 and 5.2 have been prepared using figures derived from the work of Tate, Thomas, Yelling and Pannett. One source of inaccuracy arises from the fact that Tate lists the area estimated in the act, rather than the actual amount involved in the award, and in some instances this figure includes a proportion of non-open field land. Nevertheless, Tate's figures for Worcestershire have been checked against the award data cited by Yelling, and the margin of error is insufficient to alter the essential character of the distribution at the scale which it is mapped. As far as possible the location of non-Parliamentary enclosures from 1600 onwards have been noted, and, in Staffordshire in particular, such enclosures constitute a significant proportion of the total. Fig. 5.1 is demonstrably imperfect in detail, but it does serve to indicate, in general terms, the distribution of open field land during the period 1600 to 1880 within the three west Midland counties included in this study.[1]

[1] W. E. Tate, 'Enclosure Acts and Awards Relating to Warwickshire', *Transactions of the Birmingham Archaeological Society*, LXV, 1943–4 (1949), p. 45; 'Worcestershire Field Systems', *Transactions of the Worcestershire Historical Society*, XX, 1943, p. 226;

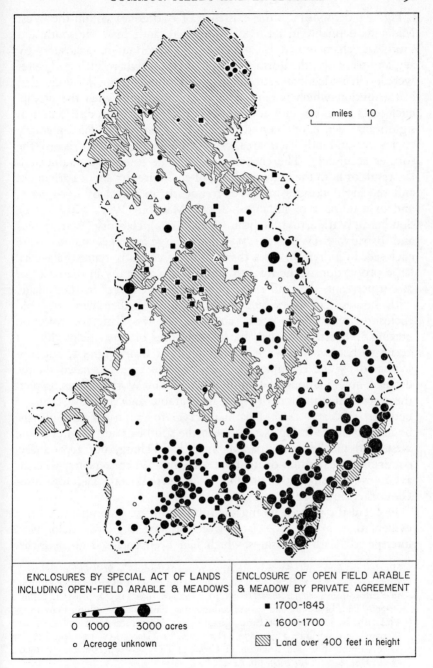

Fig. 5.1 Open field land in the West Midlands enclosed between
c. 1720 and 1880.
Sources. See fn. 1, p. 190.

Fig. 5.1 demonstrates the existence of two zones within the West Midlands definable in terms of open field land; first, the south and southeast, characterised by a dense concentration of enclosures by act, and secondly, the north and west, a region where such enclosures were less in evidence and smaller in extent, often forming loose clusters, a distribution which is reinforced and emphasised when the private enclosures are taken into account. It is evident that this distribution is significant even if one considers only the *occurrence* of Parliamentary enclosures and not their area, for Tate's lists generally record the former accurately. The concentration in the south and southeast is the result of both the high incidence of enclosures by act of Parliament and the high acreages involved, frequently in excess of 1,000 acres, and in a number of instances, Prior's Marston (War., 3,368 acres), Southam (War., 2,165), Napton (War., 3,672), Harbury (War., 3,180) and Broadway (Worcs., 1,713), very large acreages indeed were enclosed. In individual cases these figures frequently represent a very large proportion of the total township area, generally in the order of 70–80 per cent, the land remaining being given over to the village, with houses, curtilages and home closes, together with any old enclosures which may occur, and areas of woodland, or common grazing. Nevertheless, such block enclosures of open fields did not occur within every township, a fact evident from Fig. 5.1, but substantiated by the example of Warwickshire. Fig. 5.2, based on the detailed investigations of D. J. Pannett within Warwickshire, depicts the overall distribution of open field arable and meadow enclosed between 1720 and 1880. This map serves to emphasise strongly the boundary visible in Fig. 5.1 between the southeast and the north and west, and indeed a comparable map by Yelling, not reproduced, confirms the extension of the boundary into Worcestershire, whence, as Gray's work suggests, it possibly continues to skirt the Herefordshire–Gloucestershire border.

In detail the pattern within the south and east is complex and it is evident that, in say 1700, large tracts of surviving open fields were interspersed with townships which had been enclosed at an earlier

'Enclosure Acts and Awards Relating to Staffordshire', *Staffordshire Historical Collections*, 1942, p. 3; H. R. Thomas, 'The Enclosure of Open Fields and Commons in Staffordshire', *Staffordshire Historical Collections*, 1931 (1933), p. 61; J. Yelling, 'Open-Field, Enclosure and Farm Production in East Worcestershire, 1540–1870', Ph.D. thesis, University of Birmingham, 1966; 'Common Land and Enclosure in East Worcestershire, 1540–1870,' *Trans. Inst. Br. Geogr.*, XLV, 1968, pp. 157–68; 'The Combination and Rotation of Crops in East Worcestershire, 1540–1660', *Agric. Hist. Rev.*, XVII, 1969, pp. 24–43.

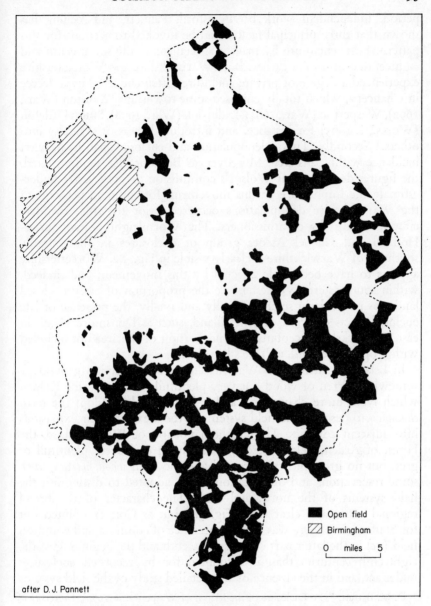

Fig. 5.2 Warwickshire open field land enclosed between 1720 and 1880.
Sources. Warwickshire Enclosure Awards in the C.R.O. at Warwick and in the City Reference Library, Birmingham. Compiled by D. J. Pannett.

period. Independent work by Beresford, Pannett, and Yelling has shown that three principal factors can be invoked to account for this pattern. First, enclosure by private agreement in the seventeenth and eighteenth centuries or earlier. Both Warwickshire and Worcestershire experienced a degree of private enclosure, often endorsed by a decree in Chancery, which totally enclosed some townships, Wolston (War., 1692), Wasperton (War., 1664), Ladbrook (War., 1998), South Littleton (Worcs., c. 1605) for instance, and introduced areas of severalty into others.[1] Secondly, Tudor depopulation and enclosure had its heaviest incidence within this area. Moreover, as Beresford has demonstrated, the figures derived from Wolsey's commission of 1517 vastly under-estimate the importance of this movement, for some 72 per cent of the Warwickshire depopulations occurred prior to 1485, the date circumscribing the commissioners. The Wormleighton–Radbourne–Hodnell and Chapel Ascote group of enclosures in the extreme southeast of Warwickshire is clearly visible in Fig. 5.2. Worcestershire appears to have been little affected by this movement, and, indeed, within southeastern Worcestershire the proportion of early enclosed land was particularly small.[2] Thirdly and finally, the presence of late enclosed tracts of waste and heathland, such as Dunsmore Heath in east Warwickshire, accounts for a proportion of the area not included within open field land, as Tate's lists show.

In Leland's words south Warwickshire was 'champion ground... somewhat barren of wood but very plentifull of corne...the Fielden which lyeth more champion', and it is proposed to adopt the term *champion* to describe the field systems of the area and their extensions into adjacent counties. The northern portion of Warwickshire, the Forest of Arden, Leland described as 'much enclosyed, plentifull of gres, but no great plenty of corne' and the term *woodland* has, with some reservations and qualifications, been adopted to distinguish the field systems of the north and west. The character of the broad regional contrast is clear from Fig. 5.1, but as Gonner pointed out for Staffordshire there was more appearance of common and common field (*sic*) in the latter part of the seventeenth and the beginning of the eighteenth centuries than is accounted for by recorded enclosures under act, and in the absence of any detailed study of the field systems

[1] D. M. Barratt, 'The Enclosure of the Manor of Wasperton in 1664', *University of Birmingham Historical Journal*, III, no. 2, 1952, p. 138; Wolston, Warwick R.O., CR 222/1-2 and CR 611, DR 85/4; Yelling, 'Open-Field, Enclosure and Farm Production in East Worcestershire', pp. 37-9.

[2] M. W. Beresford, *The Lost Villages of England*, 2nd edn, 1965, *passim*; 'The Deserted Villages of Warwickshire', *Trans. Birm. Arch. Soc.*, LXVI, 1945-6 (1950), p. 49; H. Thorpe, 'The Lord and the Landscape', *Volume Jubilaire M. A. Lefèvre*, Paris, 1964, p. 71; Yelling, 'Open-Field in East Worcs.', p. 65.

of this county it is difficult to assess the significance of the data mapped in Fig. 5.1, a problem to be considered later. In the account below, following Gray, the field systems of the champion areas will be treated as a model against which variations can be described and assessed.[1]

C. THE CHAMPION FIELD SYSTEMS

At the level of the individual township the methods adopted to sub-divide and work the open field lands were far from uniform, and, as Fig. 5.3 shows, in detail, the pattern was exceedingly complex. Nevertheless, it is possible to recognise a number of distinct sub-regions within the champion country, made partially on the basis of variations in form and layout, the distribution of the major elements within the system, arable, meadow and grassland, and partially on variations in the routine of husbandry practised within the formal framework. The discussion focusses on the period after 1600, stressing the regional contrasts, but also incorporating some appraisal of the changes in rotational practice and structure within each sub-region during the seventeenth and eighteenth centuries.

I. THE FOUR-FIELD SYSTEMS OF SOUTH WARWICKSHIRE AND WORCESTERSHIRE

During the eighteenth century the four-field system was pre-eminent within south Warwickshire and Worcestershire. Physically this sub-region exhibits great contrasts. Within Warwickshire is an area of almost drift-free scarp and vale topography, with two limestone escarpments separated by the broad Vale of the Red Horse, developed in the intractable Lower Lias clays; within Worcestershire the basin of the Lower Avon, overlooked by the limestone escarpments and outliers of the Cotswold fringe, possesses great individuality, with heterogeneous drift and alluvial deposits overlying the Lower Lias clays. To the north, east, and west, the boundaries are indistinct, and it is possible to recognise transition zones. Nevertheless, the characteristic features of field layout within this zone are exemplified by the detailed reconstruction by Pannett of the Warwickshire township of Crimscote in the mid-nineteenth century (Fig. 5.3). Crimscote is an excellent

---

[1] L. Toulmin Smith (ed.), *The Itinerary of John Leland*, 1906–10, II, 47–51; V, 155–6; E. C. K. Gonner, *Common Land and Inclosure*, 2nd edn, 1966, p. 261; J. Thirsk, in *The Agrarian History of England and Wales, IV: 1500–1640*, 1967, pp. 1–112, establishes the fundamental distinctions between champion and wood-land country.

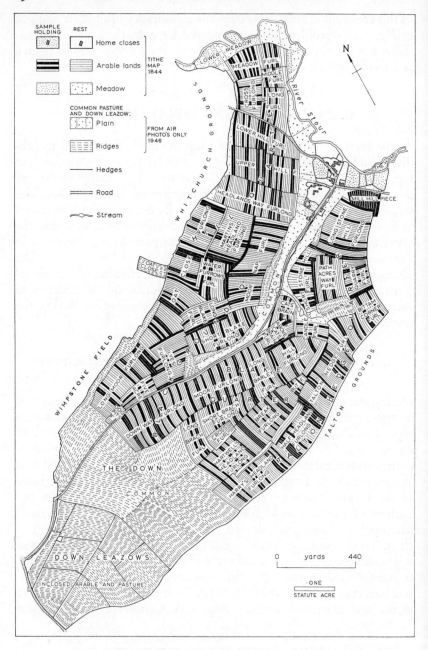

Fig. 5.3 The township of Crimscote (Warwickshire) in 1844.
Sources. See fn. 1, p. 197.

example of a four-field system, with the four fields or 'quarters' being clearly named. In the absence of superimposed field names, however, the dominant impression would, without doubt, be one of a *two-field* complex, because of the 'slade' or drainage line visible down the middle of the system, but without this slade the furlong units would not be readily divisible by the eye into sections. Significantly there was a clear tendency in south Warwickshire for contemporary writers to talk merely of 'The field', a term used for instance in the Armscote enclosure award. Each furlong block is, in detail, composed of a group of strips, and these groupings are worth closer examination.[1]

Individual strips or lands tend to average 220 yards in length by 26.5 feet in width (200 metres by 8 metres) and in area vary between one-quarter and one-third of an acre. The lands are grouped into furlongs so that the furrows drain down the slope in the best possible way, within the limitations of a sub-rectangular shape, for there was an understandable tendency to avoid 'gores' or 'piked lands' (triangular furlongs), which, although they could follow the slope more closely, would be less satisfactory for ploughing. The result is a pattern of furlongs, each built up of strips about 200 yards in length, but extending laterally along the slope to form a series of parallel bands reflecting the underlying relief. Only on ridge crests and occasionally in valley floors are 'cross' furlongs discovered. The majority of the strips shown in Fig. 5.3 are derived from the Tithe Map of 1844, for Crimscote was not enclosed until 1870, and fortuitously the actual ploughlands of the late nineteenth century survived the ploughing campaigns of 1914–18 and 1939–45 to be visible on post-war aerial photographs. These show that the strip and furlong structures of the arable portion of the township in 1844 were continued, without perceptible interruption, beneath Down Pasture (the cow-pasture in 1844) and the enclosed farm of Down Leasows. This leads inescapably to the conclusion that at some stage almost the entire township was under the plough though not necessarily concurrently, and the possible economic implications of this fact will be raised below.

The relationship between the ploughed 'land' and the tenurial strip has been the subject of much debate. Each land, whether a property

[1] This analysis of Crimscote is based on D. J. Pannett, 'The Cartographic Analysis of some English Open-Fields', an unpublished paper presented at Symposium S4*a* of the International Geographical Congress, London, 1964. Fig. 5.3 is based upon the Whitchurch Tithe Apportionment and Map, 1844, Warwick R.O., CR 569/261, vertical aerial photographs in the possession of the Ministry of Housing and Local Government, and field work undertaken by Mr Pannett. See also B.M. Add. Ms. 36586, Sheldon papers, vol. 3, fo. 168; Stratford upon Avon, Shakespeare's Birthplace Library, Bloom Coll., vol. 26, p. 68; B.M., Add. Ms. 34740, West Papers, F. 449; Warwick R.O., QS 75.

unit or not, was separated from the next by a strip of grass, some three or four feet wide, often called a 'baulk'. This practice seems to have been normal throughout the whole of the south Warwickshire four-field region and these 'grass furrows' were carefully maintained, along with the lands, by the rules of the field; thus at Brailes in 1672 the pains and orders enacted that 'every furrow that lyes between two lands shall be one yard in breadth', and at Little Wolford in 1750 that 'all the greensward furrows in the common field that are now above three feet wide shall remain'; the existing field structure was carefully preserved. Within this framework the strips of the individual farms were scattered and intermixed, but at Crimscote the three largest farms all held parcels containing two or three contiguous lands. Nevertheless, it is field evidence for at least two further farmsteads which points to a reduction in the size of the settlement, and the amalgamation of holdings, an observation which may be linked with the former extent of tillage.[1]

The arable lands were the dominating feature of the landscape within mid-nineteenth-century Crimscote and of the champion country as a whole prior to the enclosure movement, but reference must be made to other vital elements of the total pattern. Meadowland resources were limited, and confined to the low-lying lands adjacent to the river and the slades in the fields. Such 'ancient sward' was subject to careful rules concerning usage and management. In addition, characteristic of the four-field zone in both Warwickshire and Worcestershire was a tract of grazing land termed the 'beast-pasture' or 'cow-pasture', for example the Down Pasture of Crimscote, which could constitute up to 20 per cent of the township area, and was permanent pasture. In terriers, usage rights in this land were normally expressed in terms of 'leys', i.e. 'lands' of pasture, suggesting, as does the Crimscote map, that such land was former arable which had been allowed to revert to grass. At Tidmington, Warwickshire, in 1616 the glebe contained '9 lands in the Lower Furson, in the beaste pasture, (with) the thornes and furzon on them'; the brushwood invading such land may well have been a useful source of temporary fencing material and fuel. Finally, within the arable fields themselves were substantial areas of grass in the form of 'slades', 'green furrows' and 'hades'. Hades were the unploughed ends of strips, where an individual might turn his plough on his own land, which also provided access ways. At Brailes in 1672 it was ordered that 'every hade that butteth upon a hadland

[1] M. J. Harrison, W. R. Mead and D. J. Pannett, 'A Midland Ridge-and-Furrow Map', *Geogrl. Jnl.*, CXXXI, pt. 3, 1965, p. 366 (which contains a bibliography on the subject of ridge-and-furrow); Birmingham Ref. Lib., Ms. 167908, Warwick CR 450.

shall be seven yards in length and that every hade where two furlongs butt upon another, five yards apeece, in the whole tenne yards'. Such grass was a valuable addition to the grazing resources of the township, and formed a substantial proportion of the total area. It was grazed either with the fallow or by tethered beasts.[1]

The quotations from various township bylaws given above and elsewhere in this essay emphasise the degree to which within such a field system agricultural practice was directed and controlled by an assembly of cultivators, the manorial court, who coordinated and regulated the season-by-season activities of the whole community. Arable and meadowland were normally thrown open for common pasturing by the stock of all the commoners after harvest and in fallow times, and this necessitated some rules about cropping, fencing and grazing beasts. Similarly, all the cultivators of the intermixed strips enjoyed common pasturage in the waste, and in addition, the rights to gather timber, peat and other commodities were essential concomitants of the possession of arable and meadow shares. Thirsk has pointed out that a close association of four elements – strips, common rights over the arable and meadow, common rights over the pasture and waste, and disciplinary assemblies – is necessary to make a fully fledged common field system and it is too frequently assumed that these always existed together. While they might not always have so existed in the remote past, there seems little doubt about the presence of a close relationship between these four elements in the centuries after 1600.[2]

The physical structure of this one champion township, Crimscote, has been examined in some detail, partially because it exhibits the characteristic features of a south Warwickshire and southeastern Worcestershire field system, and partially because, with minor modifications, it is characteristic of the whole champion zone and provides a valuable norm against which all divergencies can be measured. Within Worcestershire, Yelling's analysis of maps and terriers reveals a situation comparable to Crimscote. An estate map of Cleeve Prior in 1772 indicates similar field structures, and the glebe, traditionally a conservative holding, revealed a high degree of fragmentation, comprising 45½ acres, made up of 123 parcels, of which 85 per cent were single-land strips, although the detail is insufficient to allow an analysis of furlong structures. Yelling concluded that within southeastern Worcestershire, where the percentage of enclosed land within a township could be as low as 5 per cent, the four-field system was dominant during the seventeenth and eighteenth centuries, and indeed

[1] Warwick R.O., CR 450, DR 72/115; Birm. Ref. Lib., Ms. 167908.
[2] J. Thirsk, 'The Common Fields', *Past and Present*, XX, 1964, pp. 3–25.

was prominent from 1540 onwards; thus at Flyford Flavell in 1585 a holding was said to lie in the four fields, 'by eight or ten acres in every field'. There were undoubtedly fluctuations in rotational practice and possibly the extent of arable, but the studies at present available suggest that there are reasonable grounds for arguing that the field structure found at Crimscote in 1844 can be used as a generalisation, and projected back to 1600 or earlier, within the whole southern portion of the champion zone of the West Midlands.[1]

Field divisions are not always a faithful indication of rotational practice, but nevertheless, within the southern champion zone there is ample evidence for two grain crops, a legume, and a fallow being rotated in a regular four-course shift, using the quarters as units. Pitt, writing in south Worcestershire in 1813, stated that the most general practice was (1) fallow, (2) barley, (3) beans, peas, vetches or red-clover, and (4) wheat, and in his 1807 itinerary he cites examples of this rotation in the open fields of Sedgeberrow and Aldington. This course was traditional on the heavy clays of south Warwickshire, and the bare fallow, an essential part of this rotation, remained important even after enclosure, partially because of the force of tradition, and partially because of the necessity of cleansing the strong clay loams or the heavy clays. The shift was without doubt followed in the seventeenth century. At Dorsington (War.) in 1679 there is a reference to the 'Field lying East', the 'Stirring Field', the 'Fallow Field' and the 'Pease Field', while the glebe terriers of Binton (War.) in both 1635 and 1714 list fallow, pease, barley and wheat fields. A glebe terrier of 1585 for Norton Beauchamp (Worcs.) mentions 24 acres of arable in North Field (46 lands) and South Field (41 lands) and continues, 'which said two fields are divided into four parts according to the course of husbandry for three crops of corn to be had and taken thereof, and the fourth to lie yearly fallow', indicating both the presence of a fourfold rotation and the development of this within the physical framework of a two-field system. Yelling is of the opinion, with some qualification, that there was a general conversion from two- to four-field systems within south Worcestershire at a date prior to 1540. Thus in his detailed analyses of probate inventories for southeast Worcestershire between 1540 and the mid-eighteenth century he comments on the fact that while in most townships the respective crop acreages for wheat, barley and pulses, together with vetches, were accordant, implying a very regular rotation, in some the acreage given in the pulse field frequently failed to approach that of the other two, and commonly it lay at half the value. He concludes that this

[1] Yelling, 'Open-Field in East Worcs.', pp. 70–1, 383–5, 328–50, citing Worcester R.O., 1691/7 and 1691/32.

'missing' land was in fact part of the fallow, and that this practice emphasises the close link between the four- and two-field systems and rotations; indeed it seems that certain land in four-field parishes had not been fully converted to the more intensive routine, even as late as the eighteenth century, and obviously in this case the boundary between four-field and two-field practice becomes quite thin. Within Warwickshire, although the pre-1700 situation has yet to be closely studied, there is some evidence for a two-field system developing into a four-field; Avon Dasset in 1693–1701 possessed East and West fields, but by 1720 fields divided into quarters appear and the two-field systems shown in Fig. 5.4 are derived from late seventeenth and early eighteenth-century sources, suggesting that the swing to a four-course shift was later on the heavier clay lands.[1]

While the fourfold shift may be regarded as the norm from the late seventeenth century onwards, southeastern Worcestershire and possibly south Warwickshire saw other improvements in the form of the development of somewhat more flexible multiple field complexes, i.e. field systems in which terriers distinguish between five, six or more field units. Such a pattern could be the result of either piecemeal enclosure, or, more particularly, the addition of a specialised field unit or the alteration of the basic four-course rotation. The addition of an 'every year's' field to a four-field system is well attested in both counties; for instance at Harvington (Worcs.) in 1714 the glebe included 15 lands of 'every years arable', besides land in four standard fields. Every year's land was kept in heart by heavy manuring and by using 'traces or vetches' instead of fallow, or clover sown *with* the crop preceding the fallow. Similarly a 'crop and fallow' field was sometimes developed on poor land which lay 'a great way from the fold yeard so as to get no other assistance except sheep penning'. After 1750 clover was introduced into south Worcestershire as a fourth choice in a pulse shift (third shift), and turnips at least partially replaced fallow. It is likely that prior to this date certain fields in some townships were divided into distinct parts, particularly for the cropping of the pulse shift, and during the eighteenth century such divisions may well have crystallised into 'fields' and must have taken on a new significance

---

[1] W. Pitt, *General View of the Agriculture of the County of Worcestershire*, 1813, pp. 67, 327–8; A. Murray, *General View... Warwickshire*, 1813, map; A. Young, 'Vale of Evesham Husbandry', *Annals of Agriculture*, xxxvII, 1801, p. 484; Gloucester City Lib., 107 T2, Warwick R.O., 72/27; D. M. Barratt (ed.), 'Ecclesiastical Terriers of Warwickshire Parishes', I, *Dugdale Soc.*, 1955, xxII, pp. 47–56; and Yelling, 'Open-Field in East Worcs.', pp. 335–42, Warwick R.O., DR 72. A very full description of rotations found on the Midland plain between the sixteenth and nineteenth centuries is to be found in E. Kerridge, *The Agricultural Revolution*, 1967, pp. 91–115.

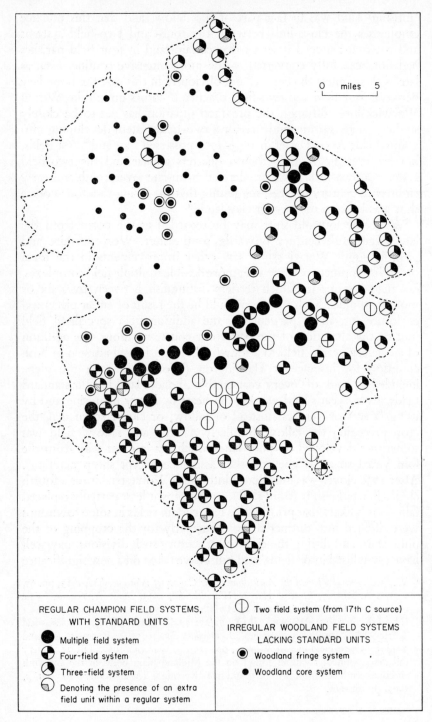

REGULAR CHAMPION FIELD SYSTEMS,
WITH STANDARD UNITS

⬤ Multiple field system

◕ Four-field system

◔ Three-field system

◓ Denoting the presence of an extra
field unit within a regular system

① Two field system (from 17th C source)

IRREGULAR WOODLAND FIELD SYSTEMS
LACKING STANDARD UNITS

◉ Woodland fringe system

● Woodland core system

Fig. 5.4 Warwickshire field systems, 1720–1880.
Sources. See Fig. 5.2.

with the introduction of clover and turnips. Multiple fields were frequently grouped for the purposes of crop rotation; at Cropthorne in 1714 there were three yardlands in the glebe, 'that is to say, in the field or fields this present year sown with barley, in that called Stevens are 12 lands, in that called Southern Heath are 19 lands, in the furlong behind the town are three butts or lands, in all 34; secondly, in the field or fields sowed with pease 25 lands...' The basic course was, according to Yelling, rarely prolonged beyond four shifts, and it is unlikely that the multiple fields of south Worcestershire, in this county found intermixed with the four-field systems, are to be assigned a rotational significance.[1]

The cow-pasture represented another innovation. Hoskins and Thirsk have linked the appearance of such grassland from the seventeenth century onwards with a movement towards convertible husbandry, but within Worcestershire Yelling is of the opinion that this did not occur, and that cow-pasture and ley lands were really large commonable closes, made on behalf of the whole farming community of the township, and the pasture leys within them were allotted at a fixed rate per yardland, although in practice grazing may well have been controlled by stinting. Appearing in Worcestershire from the late seventeenth century onwards, cow-pastures frequently had their origin in open field arable, a point admirably confirmed by the Crimscote evidence cited above.[2]

In terms of field arrangements close parallels existed between south-eastern Worcestershire and southern Warwickshire, and in both areas a substratum of two-field systems occurred. However, in Worcester-shire, inventory evidence suggests that the change from the two- to the four-field system had occurred prior to 1540, and significantly of the glebe terriers for 1584–5 examined by Yelling only one, Peopleton, involved two fields. The glebe-terrier evidence for southern Warwick-shire, on the other hand, suggests the persistence of a two-field system into the late seventeenth and early eighteenth century in many parishes (Fig. 5.4) and this differing chronology may well be the product of both a strong tradition and the intractable nature of the heavy clay lands of this region. By the mid-eighteenth century four-fields were dominant throughout the whole zone, but the appearance of 'extra' fields (Fig. 5.4) suggests that experiments with improved rotations

[1] Yelling, 'Open-Field in East Worcs.', pp. 350–65.
[2] W. G. Hoskins, *Essays in Leicestershire History*, 1950, pp. 123–83; J. Thirsk, 'Agrarian History, 1540–1950', pp. 248 ff.; *V.C.H. Leics.*, ii, 199–264; Yelling, 'Open-field in East Worcs.', pp. 242–54. In practice it can be difficult to distinguish clearly, particularly in published studies, between ley lands which formed a compact block and ley lands scattered throughout the fields; the distinction would seem to be an important one.

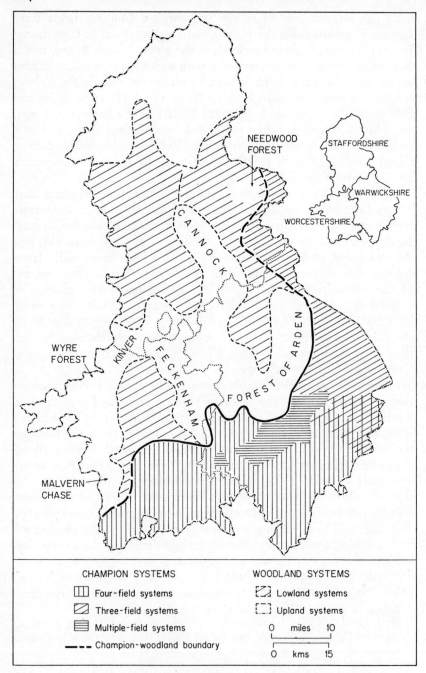

Fig. 5.5 West Midland field systems.

Sources. A generalisation, based upon Figs. 5.1, 5.2, and 5.4, using the sources cited there.

were occurring. By the late eighteenth century, as a result of the introduction of clover and turnips, which could replace the pulses on the lighter land, systems within individual townships were probably finely adjusted to local soil factors and economic and social conditions. When enclosure came in force, from the mid-eighteenth century onwards, it took the form of block enclosures made by private act of Parliament.

2. THE MULTIPLE-FIELD SYSTEMS OF THE MIDDLE AVON VALLEY

Within southeastern Worcestershire Yelling noted an occasional example of a multiple-field system,[1] but a separate sub-region may be recognised within the middle Avon valley in Warwickshire, a sub-region characterised by the predominance of systems (Fig. 5.5) with between five and as many as fifteen fields per township. The soils of the Avon valley, based partially on Lower Lias clays, Keuper Marl, valley gravels and drift deposits, are very variable in character, but may in general be described as light and warm. In outward form these multiple systems were very similar to Crimscote, but with the furlong units grouped into smaller fields, and it is evident that a sub-stratum of two- and four-field systems underlies them. For instance, at Whitnash (War.) in 1765 articles of agreement were drawn up for 'separating and dividing four of the Common Fields of Whitnash... into Eight several parts, or fields, and for the Quicking, Ditching, Fencing and Mounding of the same', and four additional fields were to be 'taken from the old Cow-pasture, which will make twelve fields'.[2] Two structural points are worthy of note. First, in south Warwickshire wide balks or green-furrows were normal, but within the Avon multiple-field area these were removed, except where a narrow one foot boundary-balk was preserved, and in this area the hades were tilled. Secondly, the permanent cow-pastures were frequently absent. This reduction of permanent pasture was compensated for by improved rotations based on a five or six years shift, and incorporating wheat, barley, legumes, turnips, and two years of ley grass. At Whitnash in 1765, for instance, it was agreed that 'six of the fields were to be used and employed in grazing grass ground, the other six... to be used and employed in tillage', and no more than three crops of grain were to be taken before the fields were to be laid down to grass, using clover and rye-grass seed. Turnips were certainly used in open field rotations by the mid-eighteenth century;

[1] Yelling, 'Open-Field in East Worcs.', pp. 347–65.
[2] Warwick R.O., CR 770, Box 14.

at Snitterfield in 1741 it was ordered 'that the left hand Grissel Way in Brook Field shall be sowed with turnips the next summer...the seed to be provided by the overseers'.[1] Within many townships the advent of such improved rotations during the eighteenth century made a former permanent cow-pasture redundant, so that it was either incorporated within the rotation, as at Whitnash, or allowed to revert to scrub and woodland; Snitterfield Bushes and Bearley Bushes survive in the present landscape as visible evidence for this decay.[2] Multiple-fields, and by implication the improved rotations, appear in different townships at different times during the seventeenth and eighteenth centuries, developing from two-, three-, and four-field systems, but some rotations adopted are peculiarly distinctive in that the cow-pasture was specifically incorporated within the rotation, and at Snitterfield in 1741 it was ordered that the 'cow-pasture next summer shall be Pale Lane End Quarter, the Further Brook Field, and the little Hard Hill'.

3. THE THREE-FIELD SYSTEMS OF NORTHEAST WARWICKSHIRE

Northeastern Warwickshire is a region characterised by broken terrain, drift-covered, with patches of glacial sands and gravels giving rise to light heathy soils, particularly on the ridge tops, while the lower slopes carry medium and heavy loams. During the eighteenth century this area was dominated by three-field systems, structurally comparable to the remainder of the champion zone, with the arable fields and associated meadowland occupying a large proportion of the township, but in practice this proportion could vary very much, depending upon the amount of heathland present. The three-field structure tended to be emphasised by boundary hedges between the individual fields, often extending radially from the village. In detail, the furlong units, although basically similar to those described at Crimscote, tended to be smaller and more irregular because of the more broken terrain, but, nevertheless, the same banding of 220 yard furlongs was present. A distinctive feature is again to be found in the frequent occurrence of an 'extra' field, smaller than the rest. In many cases the origin and purpose of this is not clear, but at Clifton upon Dunsmore it was possibly former demesne lands, and the reference to 'Hall Field' at Stivichall may point in the same direction. Cow-pastures consisting of grass leys, as in south Warwickshire, were less evident,

[1] Str. on A., Shakespeare's Bp. Lib., Trevelyan Mss., Snitterfield.
[2] *Ibid.*, C.S. War., Alverston/13, Warwick R.O., CR 611 and QS 75/1. See also Gloucester R.O., D 1447 Manorial.

although common pastures did exist, such as Nuneaton Gorse, Attleborough Gorse and Pailton Pasture, each of about 200 acres in extent. Other townships relied, however, on the dry heathlands of Dunsmore and Wolvey, or the Outwoods of Atherstone. As a result of these conditions grass balks in the fields were narrower and served more as boundaries than important reserves of pasture.[1]

During the eighteenth century, rotations within this sub-region were based upon a threefold shift, two crops and a fallow, normally comprising wheat, legumes and fallow, but barley was sometimes incorporated within the first shift, and oats within the second. A survey of the manor of Chilvers Coton in 1684 gives a particularly detailed picture of the rotation practised there, and provides an illustration of one way in which an 'extra' unit could be incorporated within an otherwise standard three-field system; 'our three home common fields are fallowed by turns (as for example) Windmill Field bore winter corn and some barley now in this present year 1684 and will bare beans, pease and oats in 1685, and be fallow in 1686'. Warmebrook Field and Greenmore Field follow suit, and the survey continues 'Synefield (detached) wee doe never keep all fallow in one year, but we sowe most of it every year and keep it in for that pupose tho' in some part or other fallows every year are made in Synefield. And after the corn and grass is taken away everyone puts in cattle according to his holding.' The extra field in this case corresponds to the 'every year's land' of the south.[2]

Within northeast Warwickshire the glebe terriers of the seventeenth century consistently reveal the presence of three fields, but the southern boundary of this sub-region is indistinct, and a broad transition zone can be recognised in the east of the county, where the post-1600 period was characterised by innovation and experiment. Grandborough is an illustration of this: in 1612 a glebe terrier mentions two fields, North and South Field, but in 1685 the glebe was 12 lands in Sawbridge (Wheat Field), 7 lands in Barley Field, 6 lands in Fallow Field, 15 lands in Pease Field and 6 lands in Ley Ground. By the mid-eighteenth century the holding was 15 lands and 5 leys in North Field, 6 lands and 3 leys in Middle Field, and 19 lands and 1 ley in South Field. While one can see a numerical relationship between this last terrier and that of 1685, a distinction must surely be made between terriers which list field

[1] See Warwick R.O., Enclosure Awards, Shuttington, Bubbenhall, and Ryton-upon-Dunsmore for characteristic layouts, QS/75, Stivichall, 18th-cent. estate map in the possession of Mr Gregory Hood, Loxley Hall; Clifton on Dunsmore, ex. inf. A. and E. A. Gooder; Warwick R.O., L289.

[2] W. Marshall, *Rural Economy of the Midland Counties*, 1790, II, 225–6; Warwick R.O., CR 136, v. 109, p. 73.

units, and those which list rotational units. A further note of caution must be entered concerning taking glebe terriers at their face value, for within them anachronistic terminology must have often been preserved as a result of conservatism, and the apparent long survival of the two-field system in south Warwickshire, when Worcestershire sources suggest that changes were possible, may be no more than a fiction of documentation. Nevertheless, it is striking that in one particular portion of Warwickshire terriers and surveys should suggest an overall pattern of variation. Napton, possessing two fields in 1652, was described as having three in 1752, with one, possibly a smaller, 'extra' unit, being termed the 'Inn Field', and in 1779 four fields and a cow-pasture were enclosed. Within this transition zone generalisation becomes virtually impossible, and the final pattern, represented in Fig. 5.5, is misleading in its apparent simplicity.[1]

The pattern of field systems which had emerged within Warwick-shire immediately prior to the main period of Parliamentary enclosures is shown in Fig. 5.4, but inevitably this map incorporates some chrono-logical fictions; in particular it telescopes evidence falling between 1720 and 1880 into one map, and even incorporates some seventeenth-century sources in the form of the two-field systems shown on the basis of glebe terriers. The chronology of change within the champion zone was in practice complex, and a distinction must be made between Worcestershire and Warwickshire; in the former the four-field system was dominant by 1600, if not by 1540, and multiple systems appear from the late seventeenth century onwards; in Warwickshire, in about 1600, the two-field system may well have dominated within southern Warwickshire and the Avon valley, and as far north as the Leam, with the northeast being under the three-field system. The change to the four-field system began in the seventeenth century, possibly in the Avon valley, and spread gradually across the heavy clay lands, but its presence in many townships is not conclusively documented until the mid-eighteenth century. On the light and warm Avon valley soils multiple-field systems appear from the mid-eighteenth century, and at the same period the townships between the Avon, Leam and Itchen in east Warwickshire show a tendency to fluctuate widely between three, four and multiple systems. This is not the context for examining the processes of change in detail, but there are grounds for suggesting that an essential preliminary was to be seen in the isolation of an 'extra' unit from the standard fields of

[1] Warwick R.O., DR 72a; see also Stockton, DR 72a, QS 75/104, Birdingbury, QS 75, DR 43a/208, Napton, N1/1, DR 72a Box 6, QS 75, Priors Marston, Spencer Mss., documents in chancery case, cupboard K in outer muniment room, shelf 1, bundle 7.

the system; this permitted the introduction of more complex rotational practices, which in turn probably stimulated more structural changes.

D. THE WOODLAND FIELD SYSTEMS

The remainder of the three west Midland counties area are, with one major reservation, grouped under the heading *woodland* for reasons which Fig. 5.1 makes clear; to the north and west of the champion lands the enclosure of open field arable by act of Parliament was less usual, the acreages involved were smaller, so that the total area involved formed only a relatively small proportion of the whole, while within the individual township the percentage of open field land was often well below the 70–80 per cent normal throughout the champion zone. This distinction has been admirably demonstrated by the maps of Gonner, but, nevertheless, it would be a mistake to underestimate the importance of open field land in the north and west. Thomas estimated that within Staffordshire during the eighteenth century nearly 50,000 acres of such land were enclosed, a figure which may be compared with totals of 125,000 acres for Warwickshire, and 50,000 acres for Worcestershire. Staffordshire, however, presents a particular problem in that no really definitive statement at present exists concerning the extent of open field land and field systems, and the figure cited above certainly includes a substantial amount of extra-Parliamentary enclosure, not included within the figures for Warwickshire and Worcestershire. The Orwins went as far as stating that within Staffordshire evidence from medieval records and from sixteenth- and seventeenth-century sources shows that open field farming was the rule, except in the north. This is at variance with Tate's statement 'there was always relatively little open field' within the county, a conclusion which appears to be substantiated by the ample, often voluminous, evidence for direct enclosure from the waste between the twelfth and eighteenth centuries. Fig. 5.1 shows that in the period after 1600 substantial tracts of open field existed within the county, but, nevertheless, Gonner's maps are correct in grouping Staffordshire with north Warwickshire and northeast Worcestershire in the woodland zone.[1]

Physically the woodland zone lacks the relative homogeneity of

[1] Gonner, *Common Land and Inclosure*, maps A, C, and D; Thomas, *Staffs. Hist. Coll.*, 1931 (1933), p. 79; G. Slater, *The English Peasantry and the Enclosure of Common Fields*, 1907, p. 143; C. S. and C. S. Orwin, *The Open Fields*, 1938, p. 62; Tate, *Staffs. Hist. Coll.*, 1942, p. 12.

the champion areas, the principal contrasts being between the lowlands, generally below four hundred feet, and the upland watershed areas above this height. The lowlands vary from relatively featureless alluvial floodplains and gravel terraces, to rolling plains developed on Triassic marls and sandstones, about 200 to 300 feet in height, moulded by ice, and overlain by glacial sands and gravels. Where such country has been dissected by stream action, a broken terrain with sharp small-scale local contrasts is the result, with flat marshy valleys alternating with well-drained heath-capped ridges, and medium and heavy soils appearing along the valley sides where the drift has been stripped away. The upland areas are mostly associated with the highly significant Palaeozoic inliers of south Staffordshire and north Warwickshire, rising to 600 or even 900 feet, surrounded by drift-covered surfaces at about 400–500 feet developed on Triassic rocks, while the high, bleak uplands of north Staffordshire may properly be regarded as part of the Pennines and a portion of the Highland Zone. Fig. 5.5 emphasises that it was these well-wooded interfluves which formed the core areas for the ancient forest lands of the Midlands, Kinver, Cannock, Feckenham, Needwood and Arden, all but Arden being Royal Forest at some stage of their history. This physical dichotomy provides the fundamental framework within which to view the field systems of the woodland zone, but before attempting to outline the regional contrasts within the area a number of general points must be established.

The evidence for the history of settlement within this zone presents a picture of a general expansion from primary settlements along the river valleys into the forested uplands, and detailed research, to be discussed below, suggests that most old-established settlement nuclei usually lay within the lowlands, below 400 feet, and possessed at least some open field land, so much so that it is possible to regard old-established nucleated settlements virtually as a diagnostic feature of the presence of such land. Secondly, as a corollary of these facts, the uplands during the Middle Ages possessed substantial reserves of waste, woodland and heath, and although from the twelfth century onwards direct enclosure was occurring, this abundance of common grazing land had inevitable repercussions, as under these circumstances, there was less need to safeguard grazing facilities within such open field areas as existed. A characteristic feature of the whole woodland zone is that individual, and frequently adjacent, townships exhibit great variations in the amount of open field present, and a township with over 70 per cent of its total area given over to open fields may be found adjacent to one with barely 10 per cent under this usage. In such conditions generalisation becomes difficult, and this situation is the result of a complex and variable balance between the factors tending to produce a communal field system, and those tending to encourage individualism and severalty. At one end of the scale is the township dominated by open field land, at the other the township dominated by severalty, and individual examples can fall at any point on the scale between these two extremes.[1]

When enclosure came to the field systems of the champion zone it took the form of relatively cataclysmic block enclosure brought about by the dominant landed interests; within any one township it was a comparatively rapid process whether it occurred in the sixteenth, seventeenth, or eighteenth century. The progress of enclosure within the woodland township tended, in contrast, to be more attenuated, more variable in effect, and more dependent upon an initial landscape which presented greater heterogeneity than did the champion country. From 1250 onwards as will be shown, the piecemeal enclosure of open field land was taking place, and this process frequently resulted in the fragmentation of the fields to create the appearance of multiple-field complexes. In 1614, when the open fields of Tunstall, Staffordshire, were enclosed, six fields were mentioned by name; the largest of these did not exceed 25 acres, and the whole complex totalled about one hundred acres. This may well represent the final enclosure of fields which had already suffered substantial attrition, and the susceptibility of open township fields to this process must be regarded as a function of the strength of the communal tradition. This will depend in turn upon the period of initial colonisation and settlement, the character of seignorial control, the extent of early enclosure and severalty, and the availability of reserves of common pasture, for the pasture arrangements were not merely an adjunct to a champion system, they were a vital and wholly integral part, and the presence of substantial reserves of common waste within a township was a powerful solvent, tending to promote change, just as the absence of such a reserve tended to encourage rigid adherence to the established routine.[2]

Once again the evidence of post-1600 conditions only will be discussed at this stage but in the case of the woodland certain imbalances of treatment arise inevitably from the variable character of the studies available, and Staffordshire in particular is poorly documented.

[1] H. Thorpe, 'The Growth of Settlement before the Norman Conquest', *Birmingham and its Regional Setting*, British Association, 1950, pp. 87–112.
[2] Thomas, *Staffs. Hist. Coll.*, 1931 (1933), p. 70.

I. THE LOWLANDS

Three lowland zones can be distinguished (Fig. 5.5), all of which, while exhibiting broad similarities of field structure and rotational practice, are distinct enough to warrant separate mention, although a finer subdivision is excluded by the absence of evidence. First, the vale of the mid-Trent in southeastern Staffordshire may be linked with the Tame and Blythe valleys of northern Warwickshire; secondly, the Severn, Stour and Salwarpe lowlands of northern Worcestershire form a distinctive area, and thirdly, the Sowe and Penk valleys of west Staffordshire appear to possess some features in common.

(a) The field systems of the Trent–Blythe–Tame lowlands

This sub-region has been grouped with the woodland zone only with strong reservations, for as Fig. 5.2 demonstrates, north Warwickshire was characterised by extensive areas of open field during the eighteenth century, and within many townships a regular three-field system was found. In practice a gradual transition may be recognised, from the true champion lands of northernmost Warwickshire and southeastern Staffordshire, to true woodland-type systems further up each valley, and considerable variations occur in the forms of field systems between one township and the next. The contrasts are best illustrated by some examples. The township of Elford (Staffs.) lay at one extreme, and in 1765 there were enclosed some 1,500 acres of open arable and meadow, 75 per cent of the total area, the remainder being given over to the settlement, enclosed land of the demesne, common grazing, and a small block of woodland. The township, co-terminous with the parish, was essentially champion in character, with furlong and strip structures comparable to Crimscote, and regular meadow doles occupying the low-lying land along the River Tame. Four fields were present, and bore separate names, but a close examination of a map of 1719 suggests the existence of three standard fields and one extra unit, Down Field, somewhat smaller, which seems to have been created partially from meadowland, and partially from common waste. Thomas took the view that this field was a later addition, and this may be accepted, but his postulation that the system originally comprised a two-field system cannot be substantiated. The system possesses one further peculiarity: no less than six small blocks of common grazing were scattered throughout the township fields, adjacent to drainage lines and roadways.[1]

This champion pattern seems to have been normal in those portions of the Trent and Tame valleys where settlement was old-established.

[1] Ibid., map.

Warton in Polesworth (War.) possessed three open fields at enclosure in 1772, covering 80 per cent of the township area, and in 1779 the fields of Comberford and Wiggington (Staffs.) were enclosed, in all some 2,261 acres, involving six fields, three for each settlement. The landscape patterns on the modern map suggest in fact that true champion country occupied the whole of the lower Tame valley to its junction with the Trent. Champion systems must also have at some stage been present in the villages in and flanking the Trent valley; Alrewas and Orgreave possessed only some 450 acres of open land in 1740, divided between fifteen units ranging in size between one and one hundred acres, but this particular discrete pattern was evidently the result of piecemeal enclosure, for within one field, Spellow Field, some 91 acres of open land and 5 acres of 'new enclosures' were mentioned. In 1771 some open field lands were enclosed at Stretton, near Burton-upon-Trent, and an eighteenth-century estate plan shows that while this then represented only about 15–20 per cent of the township, the sinuous hedgerows and distinctive field names of the remainder reveal that the two fields shown were but a remnant of a system which at an earlier date must have embraced at least 70–80 per cent of the whole township.[1]

Further up the main valleys, however, and along the tributaries and on the lowland interfluves more typical woodland field systems of a type which may broadly be termed 'irregular' were to be found, i.e. field systems which deviated markedly from the normal champion pattern or were based on no observable pattern of standard field units, even though the rotation practised within them may have been based upon a regular shift. Fig. 5.6 illustrates two such systems from the Tame–Blythe valley of Warwickshire, Coleshill and Sheldon. Coleshill parish, some 6,500 acres in extent, possessed two field systems immediately prior to enclosure in 1780, one associated with Coleshill, the other with the adjacent hamlet of Gilson, comprising in all about 900 acres of open field land, and 16 per cent of the parish area. Both Coleshill and Gilson had three fields, although a regular rotation based upon this is to be doubted, but a distinctive peculiarity is to be found in the number of small blocks of open field land, interdigitated with closes in severalty. The origin and significance of these will be discussed in a later context but this particular pattern is *not* the product of piecemeal enclosure of more extensive fields. The remainder of Coleshill comprised the settlements, closes in severalty, woodland blocks, and over 1,000 acres of common pasture, Coleshill Heath. One small detached area of open field, which may have persisted into

[1] Warwick R.O., QS 75; Tate, *Staffs. Hist. Coll.*, 1942, p. 14; Thomas, *Staffs. Hist. Coll.*, 1931 (1933), p. 79; Stafford R.O., D 1841/1, D 1734/2/3/138.

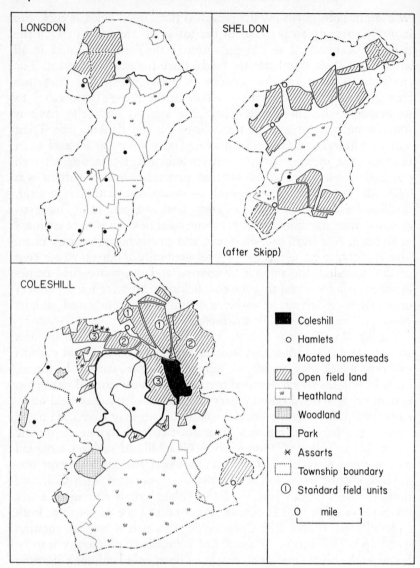

Fig. 5.6 Woodland field systems in Warwickshire.

Sources. B. K. Roberts, 'Settlement, Land Use and Population in the Western Portion of the Forest of Arden, Warwickshire, between 1086 and 1350', Ph.D. thesis, University of Birmingham, 1965, Figures 19 and 43; Tate, *Trans. Birm. Arch. Soc.* 1943–4 (1949), p. 83; V. H. T. Skipp, *Discovering Sheldon* (Dept. of Extra-Mural Studies, Birm. Univ.), 1963, pp. 15–18.

the eighteenth century, is also shown. Although Coleshill itself possessed three standard fields, the overall pattern shown in Fig. 5.6
contrasts markedly with the characteristic champion township. It falls
between this and the highly irregular system mapped for Sheldon,
where Skipp reconstructed not one block of open fields, but two
irregular groups of small fields comprising 25 per cent of the township
area. The origins of this pattern, before 1600, will be considered
later, but it is evident that while a three-course shift, wheat, pulse, and
fallow, with local variations, may be postulated for the whole of the
Trent–Tame–Blythe sub-region, it is inadvisable to apply the generalisations concerning the course of husbandry and grazing rights based
on very regular champion systems to a discrete pattern such as
Sheldon.[1]

It is fortunate that for Sheldon there exists a set of extracts from
court rolls dating from the mid-seventeenth century, which, while
not constituting a complete set of pains and orders (bylaws), do
throw light on the workings of such a complex pattern. The most
significant entry dated 1639 runs as follows:

'Item, whereas there are divers anciente standinge paynes in force for
the well moundinge of the Common and severall Corne feilds in
Sheldon and all persons are thereby injoyned to doe the same within
a certaine space after the firste Corne sowed, now wee of the jury
doe injoyne all persons that have any moundes or fences make in
any of the Common or severall Corne feildes in Sheldon that they
shall sufficiently make the same in all such feilds as shall hereafter
bee sowed with winter Corne at or before the ffeaste of St Michaell
Tharchangell and in all such feildes as shall hereafter be sowed with
lente Corne before the Annunciation of St Marye the Virgin under
such penaltyes as are expressed in the said former paynes.' Furthermore, the jury find that 'all and every such person and persons who
have or at any time hereafter shall have any mounds or fences
adjoyning or belonginge to any of the Common feildes within
this Mannor shall according to the usuall Custome of the said
feildes sufficiently make their said mounds and fences before the
feaste day of St Matthewe yearely for ever hereafter when the said
feildes are sowed or to be sowed with winter Corne and before

[1] B. K. Roberts, 'Settlement, Land Use and Population in the Western Portion of
the Forest of Arden, Warwickshire, between 1086 and 1350', Ph.D. thesis,
University of Birmingham, 1965, Figs. 19 and 43; Tate, *Trans. Birm. Arch. Soc.*,
1943–4 (1949), p. 83; V. H. T. Skipp, *Discovering Sheldon* (Dept. of Extra-Mural
Studies, Birm. Univ.), 1963, pp. 15–18; Kerridge, *The Agricultural Revolution*,
p. 108.

the feaste daye of St Mathias yearely for ever herafter when any of the said feildes are sowed or to bee sowed with lent Corne and soe shall keep and maintaine the same at all tymes untill the said feildes shall or may be Ridd of Corne.'

These entries, in association with others, show that within Sheldon a court existed, part of whose duty was to regulate and control the working of the field system and the grazing arrangements of the manor, and they strongly suggest that 'common' and 'several' lands were in some way combined and integrated within a system of rotation, and that a three-course shift may well have been practised, although these last two points are open to question. These instructions refer to the discrete blocks shown in Fig. 5.6, as a closer examination reveals, thus Elder Field, enclosed in or after 1766, and then comprising open field strips, was described in 1657 as a 'severall' field. Nevertheless, in 1657 it was certainly subdivided between a number of tenants, the grazing and the cropping were controlled by the court, and the tenants each contributed to the support of a 'common gate'; without doubt this was one of the 'severall' fields of 1639, but to anticipate the argument of a later section, as early as the thirteenth century this field was an open field subdivided into strip holdings. In 1657 two further blocks, Great and Little Hatchford, were described as 'common' fields, and possessed identical fencing, stinting and cropping arrangements as Elder Field, but it is specifically stated that these were to 'bee kept severall for the space of tenne days next after such time as all the Corne bee Ridd and Carryed away'. While problems undoubtedly still exist, these extracts point to two significant conclusions: first, that irregular as the Sheldon fields were, they possessed in the seventeenth century all the characteristics of true common fields defined by Thirsk; and secondly, that it was possible for such discrete blocks of open arable to be incorporated within a rotation, which may have been regular, enforced by the decision of a manorial court.[1]

The Trent–Tame–Blythe sub-region may be regarded as a transition zone between champion and very irregular woodland core systems of the uplands described below. Hence in Fig. 5.4 a category of 'Woodland fringe system' has been used to distinguish field structures falling between that of Coleshill, and that at Sheldon, and as can be seen these were not confined to the Tame–Blythe valley, but also appear along the woodland–champion boundary throughout Warwickshire.

[1] Birm. Ref. Lib., Ms. 377545; J. Thirsk, 'The Common Fields', *Past and Present*, XXIX, 1964, p. 1.

(b) The field systems of the Severn, Stour and Salwarpe lowlands

The field systems of north and east Worcestershire present many formal comparisons with the woodland systems already described, for instance Bredicote in 1776 had three fields occupying approximately 50 per cent of the township, while Himbleton in 1771 had ten fields, occupying about 50 per cent of the manor, and divided between three hamlets, patterns comparable to those at Coleshill (War.) and Alrewas (Staffs.). Yelling commented on the tendency for open field in this area to be concentrated near the major nucleations, the dominant villages around which the parish system was organised. These fields were often broken into a series of discrete blocks; at Tibberton in 1776 some 42 acres were divided between eight fields, ranging in size from seven to one hundred and seventy-six acres, with individual holdings scattered between six or seven of these, so that the whole pattern was exceedingly irregular, although in detail the two main fields (176 and 140 acres) contained some land of all but one of the fifteen open field estates, and it is possible that these dictated the use of the remainder, the smaller fields being grouped to make a third sector for rotation. Within individual townships the proportion of open land could vary from 70 to 80 per cent to as little as 7–8 per cent. An example of the former is found at Ombersley, where in 1605 all the important hamlets possessed open fields, while at Claines in 1750 as little as 8 per cent of the township was open field. It is a general rule that the further south a township lay, the greater the extent of open field, but as in Warwickshire (Fig. 5.2), the break between champion and woodland country was comparatively sharp. Where standard units can be identified three fields were common, as at Ombersley, Suddington and Bredicote, but four fields are found, as at Uphampton and Pirton, five, as at Severn Stoke and Belbroughton; nevertheless the three-course rotation was generally followed, but with a number of local variations in cropping depending on physical diversity. On the clay plain of Worcestershire the three-course shift traditionally involved some combination of wheat, barley, pulses (together with oats and vetches) and fallow, while in the Severn valley rye, barley and fallow combinations were followed. During the eighteenth century the boundary between the three- and four-course rotations became blurred, and the appearance of clover and turnips introduced more diversification on the lighter soils, where a course of wheat, turnips, barley, pulses or clover became common, even in the surviving open field lands. In detail the pattern was one of great complexity, and the concentration of attention on the open field structures tends to obscure the true position, for irregular as these were in themselves, the pattern of land use was related not only to field structure and the demands of communal agriculture, but to the needs of the individual farm unit. At any period between 1650 and 1850 it was possible to discover townships containing a range of farms, varying from crop-oriented units lying within the 'core' area, and retaining a large sector of open arable, to entirely enclosed and often entirely pastoral farms in the outer parts, so that the possible range of land use permutations was enormous. Yelling concludes that within the woodland zone of north and east Worcestershire a decided economic advantage was derived from the fact that in the late sixteenth century, unlike the champion south, it was not committed to any particular type of economy, and immense flexibility existed, a fact reflected in the complex variations in cropping and in the balance between crops and livestock. It is likely that these conclusions are broadly applicable to the three lowland territories included within the woodland zone. The Sheldon material cited above is in accord with this situation, and although the evidence is variable, in both quality and incidence, the field structures and basic rotations were essentially the same in each sub-region. In Fig. 5.5 the east-central portion of Worcestershire has also tentatively been included within this area of lowland woodland systems.[1]

(c) The field systems of the Sowe and Penk lowlands

The whole of eastern Staffordshire, including the upper Tame valley as well as the Sowe and Penk lowlands may conveniently be regarded as a third sub-region, although at best this is a generalisation based upon insufficient material. The evidence discussed by Thomas suggests that a basic three-field system was elaborated during the seventeenth and early eighteenth centuries, to result in a scatter of three-, four- and multiple-field complexes by the late eighteenth century, but a fundamental problem is to be found in the degree to which the multiple systems were purely the result of elaboration and piecemeal enclosure, or the result of fragmentation *ab initio* as at Sheldon. Thomas was clearly of the opinion that the multiple systems enclosed in the upper Tame valley between 1700 and 1800, such as Walsall, Wednesfield, Wednesbury and Wolverhampton, were the product of the former, and the appearance of a three-field system at Bilston would appear to afford some degree of confirmation, but this concentration may well not be purely accidental, and the multiple systems may have been of a type comparable to Sheldon. Enclosures of the same period in the Sowe and Penk drainage areas, however, usually involve three

[1] Yelling, 'Open-Field in East Worcs.', pp. 369–447, 515–41; Worcester R.O., 1691/2, 1691/4 and 1691/32.

fields as at Hatherton, Codsall, Trysull and Siesdon, although the latter fields comprised at enclosure three non-adjacent units, each containing many parcels, involving in all 101 acres (52½, 28 and 20½ acres) and this pattern is best interpreted as the end product of piecemeal enclosure. The nearby manor of Perton contained two hamlets, Perton and Trescott, each possessing a regular three-field system, which together occupied about 40 per cent of the total area, comprising respectively 263 acres (105, 94 and 64 acres) and 259 (102, 79 and 78 acres). These figures place the systems firmly within the woodland zone, and a map of the two hamlets in 1663, printed by Thomas, shows that some piecemeal enclosure had taken place at the edges of the surviving fields, although its extent is difficult to assess.

P. and M. Spufford, writing on Eccleshall, further north, concluded that many of the hamlets surrounding the town possessed one or more 'town fields', and that in some of these open field strips, survivals of once-extensive systems, persisted into the nineteenth century, although the bulk of enclosure had been achieved by 1700. For Eccleshall itself Thomas documents two fields, but in the absence of further evidence this fact cannot be evaluated. On balance one can conclude that although persistent piecemeal enclosure during the seventeenth and eighteenth centuries had a tremendous impact on the open fields of the area, they were never of champion proportions, and the three-field system was basic. Concerning rotations nothing can be stated, but in common with north and east Worcestershire, from the seventeenth century onwards Staffordshire was noted for cattle breeding, feeding, and later dairying, and a threefold rotation was probably usual.[1]

2. THE UPLANDS

In this final section it is proposed to do no more than outline the nature of the field system characteristic of the uplands – what will be termed woodland core systems – for within the various sub-regions included within this term open field cultivation was never extensive, and frequently disappeared silently before the advent of the seventeenth century. Agriculturally the uplands exhibit great variety, ranging from potentially first class arable land on drift-covered Triassic surfaces, to elevated grit, shale and limestone moorlands, bleak, rainswept and inhospitable, gashed by the upper courses of the Dove and Manifold. All, however, share one characteristic: all are environments which, by-passed by the main waves of pre-eleventh-century settlement,

[1] Thomas, *Staffs Hist. Coll.*, 1931 (1933), *passim*; P. and M. Spufford, *History of Eccleshall* (Dept. of Extra-Mural Studies, Keele Univ.), 1964, pp. 30–5; J. Thirsk (ed.), *Agrarian History of England and Wales, IV: 1500–1640*, 1967, pp. 102–3.

experienced a vigorous colonising movement during the period between the twelfth and mid-fourteenth century, and hence open fields usually form only a small proportion of the township area. Fig. 5.6 illustrates the manor of Longdon, in the parish of Solihull (War.) and is based on an enclosure survey of 1820. At this date there existed about 200 acres of open field, some 15 per cent of the township area, comprising four main units, Berry Field, Seed Furlong, Wheatcroft, and Hain Field; the remainder of the township was given over to closes in severalty, associated with moated farmsteads and extensive tracts of surviving common waste in the form of heathland. The field structure was compact in comparison with Sheldon, and there are grounds for believing that this type of compact core was characteristic of the Forest of Arden, although discrete units were found, particularly along the edges. The traces of these systems which appear on eighteenth- and nineteenth-century maps often survive where intermixed glebe or charity land hindered normal piecemeal enclosure, as at Claverdon or Lapworth. In the latter example, a few selions in a close were, in 1844, the sole remains of a block of some 200 acres of open field, whose presence is well attested by medieval land charters.[1]

The extent and early history of these woodland core systems are often difficult to reconstruct as a result of frequent early enclosure, but it is probable that all of the ancient settlement nuclei, both the primary nucleations associated with parish centres, and early secondary nuclei, possessed an open field core, an area of strip fields, with intermixed ownership, and subject to some degree of communal control over cropping and grazing. At Feckenham (Worcs.), Hilton and Yelling have described an open field system very similar to that of Sheldon, with the field units forming discrete blocks, while for Shenstone (Staffs.), c. 1700, Hebden has reconstructed a series of small open fields associated with the various hamlets of the parish, none of which exceeded 200 acres. With regard to Shenstone itself he argues that the permanent fields were added to in the form of temporary brecks, such as are described by Plot, but he was unable to describe the system in detail. He postulates, however, that the irregular blocks of open field land associated with individual hamlets were sometimes grouped for the purposes of rotation, and cites one example which involved three years cropping, followed by one or two years fallow, with sheep grazing; in other cases three or four fields are documented.[2]

[1] Roberts, 'The Forest of Arden', pp. 526–56; Birm. Ref. Lib., Ms. 184962.
[2] R. H. Hilton, 'Old Enclosure in the West Midlands', *Annales de l'Est*, XXI, 1959, pp. 279–80, and map opposite p. 282; Yelling, 'Open-Field in East Worcs.', pp. 411–12; R. Hebden, 'The Development of the Settlement Pattern

Plot described temporary 'brecks' in Staffordshire during the seventeenth century, temporary enclosures on the heathy lands of the county, which were cropped under a five year course, rye, barley, pulse and oats (×2), after which the land was permitted to revert to grass. In north Warwickshire, at Sutton Coldfield, Beresford described a very similar system, in this case followed on the sandy soils of the Bunter, by which fields were taken from the waste by householders in lots of one acre, cropped for five years, and then thrown open again. This particular system would seem to be of sixteenth-century origin, made possible by the large reserves of waste, but encouraged by the character of the political and legal controls over the chase. Nevertheless, it is probable that the arrangements formalised by the Crown Commissioners who established the Sutton system in 1581 reflect the traditional arrangements applied to intakes or brecks within Staffordshire and north Warwickshire.[1]

Small areas of irregular open fields, in some cases associated with temporary intakes, must have been characteristic of most of the upland areas within the West Midlands in the seventeenth century, for instance comparable patterns seem to have existed in the Manifold valley within northeast Staffordshire, associated with such settlements as Alstonfield, Carlton, and Wetton, and there are hints of similar arrangements from Malvern Chase in Worcestershire. In the centuries after 1600 these systems were very much subsidiary to the closes in severalty, which predominated in the uplands because of the generally late colonisation. As has been shown, there is some evidence in Worcestershire for the emergence of complex relationships between open field lands and closes in respect of rotational practices by the seventeenth century, a situation which must have stimulated further piecemeal enclosure within a system where the bonds of communal control had been seriously weakened before 1600.[2]

E. THE EARLY HISTORY OF THE WEST MIDLAND FIELD SYSTEMS

The evidence from post-1600 sources within the West Midlands reveals on the one hand a sharply defined division between champion and

and Farming in the Shenstone Area', *Lichfield and Staffordshire Archaeological and Historical Society*, III, 1961–2, pp. 27–39.

[1] R. Plot, *Natural History of Staffordshire*, 1686, pp. 107, 109, 340, 343, 345; M. W. Beresford, 'Lot Acres', *Econ. Hist. Rev.*, XIII, 1941–3, pp. 74–9; see also Kerridge, *The Agricultural Revolution*, p. 106.

[2] Stafford R.O., negatives and slides of surveys for the earl of Newcastle by William Senior in 1631; B. S. Smith, *A History of Malvern*, 1964, pp. 86–9, 142.

woodland systems, and on the other a complex pattern of local and temporal variations. An explanation of the regional differences clearly lies in the centuries before 1600, and in this final section it is intended to trace from Warwickshire evidence what is known of the antecedents of the post-seventeenth-century patterns. In 1960 J. B. Harley produced for Warwickshire an interim map showing the distribution of medieval field systems, a map which has not been reproduced here because the salient conclusions derived from it are readily intelligible in terms of Fig. 5.4. The most clear-cut conclusion, already hinted at in Fig. 5.4 by the evidence of seventeenth-century glebe terriers, is that in the Middle Ages the two-field system was widespread, indeed dominant, in the middle Avon, the Stour and upper Itchen valleys and over the inter-vening clay plains and limestone escarpments below Edge Hill. As many of the townships for which information was available, Hampton Lucy, Old Stratford, and Tredington for example, were manors of the Bishops of Worcester, townships forming part of a singly ad-ministered estate, this uniformity is perhaps not surprising, and may have been imposed by the bishop's administration. A comparable example appears in the northeast of the county, where the available evidence is more restricted, but a three-field system was found on the manors of Coventry Cathedral Priory, as at Southam, Whitmore and Sowe. Nevertheless, in the south two-field systems were so common, appearing for instance at Harbury, Ladbroke, Brailes and Tysoe, that their distribution cannot be attributed to estate patterns. The conclusion is inescapable that regional contrasts observable in south and northeast Warwickshire after 1600 were already well established by the thirteenth century, with two-field systems in the south and three-field systems in the northeast, and possibly four- and multiple-field complexes in the middle Avon valley. To the north and west of the Avon, Harley mapped a variety of three-field, multiple and irregular systems, but the bulk of the evidence for the woodland manors of Arden pointed to a prevalence of holdings in severalty and of enclosure, and even where a communal organisation existed there was often no organised grouping of the strips into two or three main field areas.[1]

What are the implications of these conclusions? First, with regard to the champion country, it is deceptively easy to assume that the plans and structures of the medieval field systems resembled those at Crimscote, but concrete evidence for this is elusive. For the presence of two fields thirteenth-century evidence is often quite explicit; at

[1] J. B. Harley, 'Population and Land Utilisation in the Warwickshire Hundreds of Stoneleigh and Kineton, 1086–1300', Ph.D. thesis, University of Birmingham, 1960, Fig. 41 and pp. 210–13.

Hampton Lucy for example the Bishop of Worcester was holding
288½ acres of demesne land in 1299 lying divided in two fields called
'Overfelde' and 'Netherfelde', but three problems are raised by
such evidence; first, were the complex furlong and strip patterns
of the type shown in Fig. 5.3 present by the thirteenth century, and
what was the disposition of individual holdings; second, what proportion of the total township area did the medieval systems occupy,
and finally, what rotational practices were followed?

Contemporary documents provide some clues to these: a land
charter concerning property in Avon Dasset, for example, dated 3rd
October 1310, granted 7 acres of arable land lying in the fields of
'Avenederset', 3½ in West Field and 3½ in East Field. Each portion was
further subdivided into units ranging in size between 1½ acres and
¼ acre, the norm being the ½ acre selion, and the grant includes half
a virgate of meadowland lying in the common meadow. Harley
regarded this fragmentation of strips as a reflection of the impact of
centuries of farming upon the field system and of population pressures
upon the available land resources, and cites the example of a holding
at Farnborough in 1260 comprising 27 acres divided into 58 parcels,
the majority of which were half-acre units. Comparable evidence is
available from charters relating to manors scattered throughout
southern Warwickshire, Warmington, Priors Hardwick, Southam,
Long Itchington, Willoughby and Snitterfield for instance, and the
half-acre strip or selion seems to have been normal in the thirteenth
and fourteenth centuries. It is reasonable to conclude that by the late
thirteenth century patterns of furlongs and strips comparable to those
at Crimscote had emerged within the champion zone. The alienation
of small numbers of acres, portions of holdings, may be viewed as
part of the process of parcellation, as was the grant of a moiety of
a messuage at Gaydon in 1324, and it is clear from the charters that
not only were individual properties scattered through the open fields,
but that a regular distribution obtained. Thus, the seven acres at
Avon Dasset were consistently bounded by the lands of Roger de
Mossenden and John Ennoc, neither of whom appear as grantor or
grantee, implying that in this particular example strips were not being
split. There are no reasons for believing that this general conclusion
concerning the presence of complex field structures by the late thirteenth
century cannot be extended to embrace the whole of the champion
zone in the West Midlands, although it is possible that population
pressure, and hence morcellation of holdings was less marked in northeast Warwickshire where reserves of waste must have been present.[1]

[1] M. Hollings, 'The Red Book of Worcester', *Worcestershire Hist. Soc.*, 1934,
p. 263; Str. on A., Shakespeare's Bp. Lib., Archer Coll., Charters, Avon Dasset,

This raises the problem of the proportion of the township given over to open fields in the Middle Ages; Harley, using data from Domesday Book and the Hundred Rolls of 1279, cautiously concluded that in 1279, and indeed in 1086, the townships of south Warwickshire already had relatively high proportions of their total area under arable cultivation, frequently as much as 60 per cent, and usually over 40 per cent, while this proportion in Arden was usually well below 40 per cent. This observation may be paralleled by population trends, for while the north, an area of late colonisation, was a zone of rapid population growth after 1086, the south, an area of primary Anglo-Saxon settlement, revealed essentially similar density patterns in 1086 and 1279, and Harley concluded that by 1086 the south had already reached near-saturation level relative to the technical organisation of agrarian resources. These conclusions may be open to question, but, if they are correct, their implications are interesting. As there is sound evidence for two-field systems within the south in the late thirteenth century, and as there were apparently no marked improvements in agrarian technique between 1086 and 1279, an obvious inference would seem to be that the technical organisation of 1086, the ploughlands and plough-teams of Domesday Book, were based on a form of two-field system. This conclusion, based ultimately on documents and methods of analysis which contain many possible sources of error, does not exclude the possibility of some degree of regularisation, but the conclusion that there were no major developments in agrarian technique between 1086 and 1279 certainly seems tenable in view of the apparent stability of population levels. If, as Harley's preliminary examination of the evidence would seem to imply, the two-field system was widespread in south Warwickshire by the late thirteenth century, and if by this date a fairly strict crop rotation was adhered to (by which half the land was fallowed every year, and valuations on the Bishop of Worcester's manors do suggest this), then we have an explanation for the relatively high proportions of the townships under arable in 1279, and the same argument could well apply in 1086. It is tempting to wonder if the tillage of an entire township, for which there is field evidence at Crimscote, was a product of local population pressure during the High Middle Ages: the topic would repay investigation. A long history of occupation was certainly reflected in the extent of the systems by the late thirteenth century, in the complexity of internal structures, and possibly also in the regular disposition of holdings, and the grouping of individual holdings into field units. The impact of seigneurial control, systems of inheritance, technological

3 October 1310, Gaydon, 14 September 1324; Harley, Ph.D. thesis, p. 220, n. 77; Magdalen College, Oxford, *Cal. of Deeds*, Willoughby Deeds, 19A.

innovations and the action of the land market on the genesis of champion field systems and the parallel emergence of common field practices are topics which await further research. Gray established that the two-field system was of greater antiquity than the three-field system, and the appearance of three-field systems in northeast Warwickshire should be in accordance with his conclusion; certainly they were present by the late thirteenth century, but significantly there is for Willoughby a charter of 1280–90 which records a two-field system, while Gray himself cites evidence which suggests a comparable change at Long Lawford.[1]

Accessible information concerning the actual rotational systems within the champion zone during the Middle Ages is so scanty as to be virtually non-existent, and it must be presumed that throughout the south a two-course rotation was used to maintain arable production; this must be viewed partially as a reflection of an agrarian tradition whose origins are at the moment obscure, and partially it may reflect a well-tried and proven method of maintaining fertility on lands which have been continuously farmed since the Anglo-Saxon period. Nevertheless, this association of field systems with rotational practice may be challenged by an example cited by Harley; at Little Wolford in 1325, a township securely within the two-field zone, 36 per cent of the sown acreage was devoted to wheat, 28 per cent to dredge and mixtilium (mixtures of basic grains), and 28 per cent to leguminous crops, perhaps implying that not only had the medieval farmer begun to take advantage of the nitrifying properties of leguminous crops in order to reduce the proportions of fallow, but had adopted the four-course shift (more general in this region later) and possibly a four-field system was already present, although as these statistics relate to demesne lands they do not form a secure basis for wider generalisation. In the northeast of the county thirteenth-century evidence from the estate of Coventry Cathedral Priory suggests a clear-cut relationship between a three-field system and a three-course rotation; 'and there are three carucates of arable land in (Southam, Whitmore or Sowe, for instance) where two parts are worth by the year to sow 60s., and the third part lies every year fallow and is common'. Nevertheless, the multiple-field systems of the middle Avon valley must surely point to the early emergence of more complex rotations.[2]

[1] Harley, Ph.D. thesis, pp. 88, 160, 168; 'Population Trends and Agricultural Developments from the Warwickshire Hundred Rolls of 1279', Econ. Hist. Rev., XI, 1958, pp. 8–18; 'The Settlement Geography of Early Medieval Warwickshire', Trans. Inst. Br. Geogr., XXXIV, 1964, pp. 115–30; Magdalen College, Oxford, Cal. of Deeds, 14A (1280–90); Gray, English Field Systems, p. 500.
[2] Harley, Ph.D. thesis, pp. 203, 220.

To the north and west of the Avon valley Harley's map revealed the predominance of irregular systems within the Forest of Arden, but significantly the data he was able to map suggested that within the drainage areas of the Arrow and the Alne, on the southern fringe of the woodland, a variety of traditional, multiple and irregular field systems seem to have been intermixed. At Aston Cantlow in 1273 a two-field system existed, but by 1348 this had been modified to a three-field system, while later four, then five fields evolved. Within Arden, the work of Hilton, Skipp and Roberts strongly suggests that, as Yelling postulated for north Worcestershire, the old established nucleations were associated with open field land, and Stedman, when discussing the pattern at Feckenham, and describing the pattern of fragmented open fields surrounding the village and encased in later enclosures in severalty, concluded

> 'a possible explanation of this pattern is that the open-fields developed and spread around the earliest settlement...and...by the time the forest further from the original centre began to be cleared open-field cultivation had gone out of fashion, at least to the extent that no new open-fields were being formed...It seems reasonably certain that the inner area occupied by open-fields...represents the end of one stage in the expansion of settlement into the surrounding forest.'[1]

One of the principal problems raised by such a conclusion is that the process of expansion described can rarely be documented with any great degree of certainty, so that the conclusion must remain largely hypothetical. However, the evidence for the woodland core parish of Tanworth, in the heart of Arden, is particularly strong; in about 1500 there were about 100 acres of open field surviving, but by using a detailed survey of this period it proved possible, on the basis of land charters, to reconstruct the fields in 1250, when there were about 200 acres, in two major blocks, Pirihull on one hand, and Hemfeld or Karsewellefelde on the other, but there is no evidence at all to suggest that these can be regarded as 'two fields' in the usual sense of the term. This situation may be projected back to 1200, and this land, representing barely 2 per cent of the total parish area, must

---

[1] R. H. Hilton, *The Social Structure of Rural Warwickshire in the Middle Ages* (Dugdale Soc. Occasional Papers, IX), 1950, pp. 22–5; Skipp, *Discovering Sheldon*, pp. 15–18; V. H. T. Skipp and R. P. Hastings, *Discovering Bickenhill* (Dept. of Extra-Mural Studies, Birmingham Univ.), 1963, pp. 15–33; Roberts, 'The Forest of Arden', pp. 450–76, 526–56; Hilton, 'Old Enclosure in the West Midlands', *passim*; M. B. Stedman, 'The Forest and Manor of Feckenham in 1591', unpublished study; see also R. H. Hilton (ed.), *The Stoneleigh Leger Book* (Dugdale Soc.), 1960, Introduction.

be regarded as an extremely ancient feature of settlement for not only is this core adjacent to the nucleated settlement of Tanworth, but in 1200 the colonising movement which opened up the parish, and is closely documented by charters, had scarcely begun; in 1200 such developments as were taking place were occurring at the edge of the open field land. Similarly, the area of open field mapped at Longdon (Fig. 5.6) can be projected back to the mid-thirteenth century with reasonable certainty, and was thus already present at a time when the creation of closes in severalty was actively occurring. Skipp postulated the presence of about 200 acres of such land in the north of Sheldon by 1200, and took the logical step by arguing that Rye Eddish field may have been the original nucleus of clearing, present by 1086, taking the form of what was essentially one furlong unit, divided into strips, and probably delimited by an enclosing bank; the presence of the furlong name 'Whete-eddish' as a core unit in Tanworth field must surely be significant in this context? Comparable small areas of open field have been identified in many Arden parishes, and there are sound grounds for accepting Stedman's conclusion that these open field cores represent the earliest clearings.[1]

This conclusion poses three allied questions; first, to what extent may these early irregular open field cores be regarded as true common fields in the sense defined by Thirsk? Secondly, it is clear that some of these fields survived into the eighteenth century while others disappeared centuries before this, and is it therefore possible to examine the processes involved in survival and disappearance, expansion and contraction? Finally, what conclusions can be reached concerning the cropping arrangements within the woodland areas in the Middle Ages? The evidence of the Sheldon document cited above shows that by the seventeenth century the open field blocks of that parish were arranged in a form of common field system, and that all the concomitants, strip holdings, common pasturing over stubble, common pasturage of the waste, and the ordering of these by an assembly, were present, and there are hints of such arrangements in the sixteenth century from Tanworth. Earlier sources, however, while demonstrating beyond doubt the presence of strip fields, throw no clear light on their working. Within Arden, indeed, the term 'open field' may not be strictly applicable, as a reference to 'a certain furlong (cultura)... as it is surrounded with a quick hedge' shows, and yet this, and

---

[1] Roberts, 'The Forest of Arden', Figs. 19, 44, 45 and 48; Skipp, *Discovering Bickenhill*, p. 10. For the term 'eddish' see F. Seebohm, *The English Village Community*, 1883, pp. 377-80; it is possible that some link exists between 'eddish' and the German 'Esch': see H. Uhlig, 'Old Hamlets with Infield and Outfield Systems in Western and Central Europe', *Geogr. Annlr.*, XLIII, nos. 1-2, 1961, pp. 285-7.

references to 'selions within a croft' do accurately describe the situation in which small open field units must, as at Sheldon, have been individually hedged. At Stoneleigh, however, Hilton noted the presence of irregular open fields during the thirteenth century, apparently forming a series of discrete blocks, but concluded that, while there was no evidence of the way in which cropping was arranged, references to common rights in the arable and to certain open furlongs shows that a fallow, subject to common pasture, was a feature of the agrarian practices followed within such irregular systems, and they may reasonably be classed as a form of common fields.[1]

There appears to have been no general expansion of open field land within Arden during the thirteenth century, indeed contraction was probably more usual, and clearing within this period produced enclosure and severalty. Nevertheless, in Sheldon and Bickenhill, Skipp argued for the appearance of open fields during this period, although this may reflect better documentation rather than colonisation, for within Tanworth, infinitely better documented, all clearing after 1220 certainly saw the creation of enclosed severalties. Two instructive examples of the expansion of open field land can, however, be documented in detail: it will be noted that within Coleshill (Fig. 5.6) certain areas of open field are detached from the main units, and are shown as assarts. One such, lying to the west of the park, originated in the mid-thirteenth century as a piece of assart land granted to Simon March by Sir Thomas de Clinton, and in the latter half of the century this was progressively subdivided, until by 1300 eleven separate tenants were holding selions within Marchesfeld. As at Sheldon, the control of grazing over this commonable close could well have brought it within the orbit of the manor court, and have been instrumental in drawing it into the routine associated within the more ancient field land, so that it was preserved to be enclosed with this in the eighteenth century. A somewhat different process can be documented at Baddesley Clinton in the early decades of the thirteenth century; small pieces of waste land were granted to various individuals, pieces ranging in size from $\frac{1}{2}$ acre to $2\frac{1}{2}$ acres; all abut on to comparable pieces, without any references to hedges, ditches, or banks, a noteworthy point in an Arden context, and in all at least fifteen tenants are known to have held land there. The descriptions seem to refer to strips, and several documents refer to the Whitemarlpit, so that in 1408–9 it comes as

[1] J. Thirsk, 'The Common Fields', *Past and Present*, XXIX, 1964, p. 3; Str. on A., Bp. Lib., Archer Coll.; Tanworth Charters, John Archer to William Herbert, c. 1290; Roberts, 'The Forest of Arden', p. 542; Hilton, 'Old Enclosure in the West Midlands', pp. 274–7.

no surprise to read of 'six selions in a field called Wyth Marlputfeld'. This may again represent the sub-granting of an assart made by the lord, but the end product was a form of open field. While these two examples are probably fairly typical of the origin of closes divided into selions within which at least some degree of communal organisation must have been essential, such explanations are not necessarily applicable to the larger areas of open field which may have been the product of communal activity, indeed the distribution of such closes in Coleshill shows that they were the exception rather than the rule. The fact that even within closely studied parts of Arden it has not generally been possible to prove the expansion of open field land after 1250, even where ample documentation is available, suggests that the extent of open field land within woodland core townships is a reflection of the clearing achieved by 1250, if not by 1200; it is this land which is adjacent to the oldest nucleation, often bearing an Anglo-Saxon place-name. Open field land can therefore be viewed as a reflection of the extent and intensity of early settlement, and however it was worked, and whatever degree of communal control was present, it remained throughout the Middle Ages sharply distinct from the newer enclosures in severalty. Throughout the whole of the woodland zone the rise of the doctrine of the lord's ownership of the waste during the twelfth and thirteenth centuries, and the provision of a defence against actions of *Novel Disseisin* by the Statute of Merton in 1235, are key factors in explaining the swing to individual colonisation and emphasis on personal rather than communal rights.[1]

The history of the woodland core systems in the Middle Ages is one of contraction and enclosure rather than expansion and if such systems persisted into the eighteenth century it is as much a reflection of apathy and conservatism as of any inherent inertia arising from communal strength, although this factor became increasingly important in those townships fringing the woodland core, where open fields were relatively extensive and firmly established by the late twelfth century, and persisted to be enclosed piecemeal in the post-medieval period. The dissolution of the Arden systems began at an early date, particularly in those townships where enclosure and severalty were predominant, and their concomitants, freehold tenure, a vigorous land market, and cash relationships, were strongly developed. In Tanworth open field land was appearing on the market as early as 1250, and by 1300 certain individuals were engrossing selions, so that some enclosure took place by the end of the fourteenth century. Skipp has

[1] Skipp, *Discovering Sheldon*, pp. 16–17; *Discovering Bickenhill*, pp. 15–16; Birm. Ref. Lib., Wingfield Digby Coll., A19, A20, A23, A34, A37, A83; Str. on A., Bp. Lib., Ferrars Coll., Charters 16–19, 29, 36 and 165.

documented the same process in Sheldon, but not significantly within Bickenhill, and there is evidence to suggest that the process was most vigorous in the smaller, more irregular open field cores, deep within the woodland and surrounded by enclosures in severalty, for under such circumstances there can have been little incentive to maintain communal cultivation. A tendency for open field holdings to be alienated once farms in severalty were viable, i.e. by about 1250, was noted by Roberts. Even within townships on the fringes of the wood-land core, as at Hatton and Coleshill, this process was occurring; in Coleshill of fifty-four charters dating between 1200 and 1350 referring to any of the three fields by name, only three mention more than one field and these reveal a disproportionate allotment of selions, and engrossing was certainly taking place in the fields of Hatton by the late thirteenth century.[1]

This irregular distribution of strips within Arden field systems was noted by Hilton, who concluded that it was not possible to envisage the even grouping of winter crops, spring crops and fallow over such irregular fields. He cites the evidence for Knowle, where in 1408–9 although three fields were mentioned, one field alone was sown with 13 acres of wheat, 3 acres of rye, 5 acres of peas, and 2 acres of dredge, and the disproportionate allotments of strips at Coleshill suggests that even within a township where open fields were extensive and apparently regular no rotations based on the three fields were likely to have been followed. Be this as it may, the basic rotation of the whole woodland zone was probably two crops and a fallow, winter corn, spring corn and fallow, but with many local peculiarities adopted to suit particular requirements and soil conditions. In view of the conclusions reached by both Harley and Roberts concerning the possible importance of sheep within Arden in the Middle Ages, it is tempting to wonder if the practice of folding these on the arable was followed. A hint of this is perhaps found in an entry in a sixteenth-century court roll from Tanworth which states that 'none shall keep sheep in the common feelde but according to the quantity of his tenure' and a sheepfold certainly lay adjacent to the open field in the early thirteenth century. Hilton has pointed out that the proximity of the Coventry market may have been affecting agrarian practice within Arden, and that as a result of this factor the woodland cultivators in the Middle Ages may be regarded as more advanced socially and economically than their fellows in the big, old-established open field villages of the champion lands in the valleys.[2]

---

[1] Skipp, *Discovering Sheldon*, p. 18; Roberts, 'The Forest of Arden', 391–5, 431, 540, 543–50.

[2] Hilton, *Social Structure of Rural Warwickshire*, p. 22; Harley, Ph.D. thesis, pp. 205–6;

F. CONCLUSIONS

The imbalances of treatment within this essay, reflecting the availability of post-1915 studies, need no emphasis; much new ground still remains to be broken. The Welsh border counties of Shropshire and Hereford-shire were excluded for this very reason; in the absence of any large-scale studies scant justice could have been done to this area. Within the three counties considered, Gray's broad conclusions are vindicated, but, as could have been predicted, the post-1915 work demonstrates the presence of more complex local variations than Gray was able to consider. Two major trends emerge, however; first, within the frame-work of the basic two- and three-field systems the eighteenth, seven-teenth and, in some areas, the sixteenth centuries, saw many develop-ments, adaptations to take advantage of variations in location and soil, for even after 1750 open field farming was far from moribund and showed clear signs of vitality. Secondly, the evidence available suggests a remarkable overall stability of patterns within the West Midlands; in particular the fundamental contrast between champion and woodland was firmly established by the late thirteenth century and there are good reasons for arguing that the outlines of the sub-regional divisions shown in Fig. 5.5 were then already present. The early history of open field agriculture has yet to be written, but in view of the strong association between the two-field system in the West Midlands and the middle and lower Avon valley, the heart of the principality of the Hwicce, it is worth concluding with Finberg's observation that more than one element of the two-field system may have been known in Roman Britain, and there is indeed not a single feature of the system which has yet been proved to have originated after the coming of the Saxons.[1]

Roberts, 'The Forest of Arden', pp. 567–71; Hilton, 'Old Enclosure in the West Midlands', p. 283.

[1] H. P. R. Finberg, *Roman and Saxon Withington*, Occasional Papers, Dept. Engl. Local Hist., Univ. of Leicester, VIII, 1959, pp. 24–5.

6

Field Systems of the East Midlands

BY JOAN THIRSK

A. INTRODUCTION

A field system was essentially a product of communal effort. Not all land, therefore, necessarily formed part of a field system. A farmer dwelling away from his neighbours could easily get his living from the soil and have no part in a field system. And so long as this land was kept in undivided possession from generation to generation, this state of affairs could continue indefinitely. But wherever people lived in villages or hamlets, that is, in close proximity to one another, they were liable to create a field system. In short, field systems could be, and usually were, as numerous as nucleated settlements. But whence originated the plan and the orderly arrangements by which it was maintained? We lack records going back to the beginning of settlement and can only base our conclusions upon a balance of probabilities. The earliest documents recording communal farming regulations in manor court rolls begin in the later thirteenth century (c. 1270); the earliest record of a village meeting dates from the fourteenth century. From these dates the evidence points unequivocally to the autonomy of village communities in determining the form of, and the rules governing, their field systems. They made their decisions in the light of their own circumstances and their own requirements. In villages which possessed no more than one manor, matters were agreed in the manorial court, and the decisions sometimes, but not always, recorded on the court roll. Decisions affecting villages which shared the use of commons were taken at the court of the chief lord, at which all the vills were represented. In villages where more than one manor existed, agreement might be reached at a village meeting at which all tenants and lords were present or represented. Field systems were man-made, and were intended to fulfil the purposes of those who owned and occupied the land.[1]

Yet there are strong similarities between the field systems of individual villages. How do we explain them? No one has ever suggested the

---

[1] P.R.O., E.134, 10 Chas. I, Mich. 66; below, p. 250; W. O. Ault, 'Open-Field Husbandry and the Village Community', *Trans. Amer. Phil. Soc.*, LV, part 7, 1965, pp. 12, 51, 54; Joan Wake, 'Communitas Villae', *Engl. Hist. Rev.*, XXXVII, 1922, pp. 406–7.

existence of a guiding hand directing matters from outside the village, and enforcing the rules of a national, or local tribal authority. But another explanation has found some favour among historians, namely, that certain rules of farming were implanted in men's minds before they arrived in England as settlers in a new land. It is held that these preconceived notions, based upon experience in their original homeland, governed the conduct of the first colonists and set a pattern which was followed in its essentials by their descendants for the next thousand years. This hypothesis greatly simplifies matters, for it enables us to view the field patterns and customs of many villages, as they are portrayed in the maps and bylaws of the eighteenth century, as a faithful image of a field system that was brought into existence some thousand years earlier. But it strains credibility too far. Such documents portray a field system at one moment in time after centuries of increasing and often complex changes in the ownership and occupation of land, after long experience of cultivation, and many adaptations to meet changing circumstances. There are enough well-documented illustrations from English history showing how field divisions and farming customs could be transformed in a comparatively short space of time to warn us against the assumption that farming is essentially timeless.

This, however, does not dispose of the argument that the original settlers in English villages brought certain fixed ideas of land allotment and land cultivation with them. We know from our own experience that migrants from one country to another carry pride and prejudice with them. But it is doubtful if these even outlast the first generation if they do not effectively meet the challenge of the new environment. One has only to consider the experience of seventeenth-century Englishmen migrating to the New World. When the first colonists settled in New England they divided the arable land into strips on the model familiar to them at home. But this system was soon abandoned for one better adjusted to the circumstances.[1] It did not meet with the approval of visitors from England in the later seventeenth century. They judged it to be deplorably bad husbandry. Their fellow countrymen, migrating from a kingdom where land was in short supply and all natural resources were carefully conserved, to one where land was limitless, seemed to them to have changed into ruthless despoilers. 'When the strength of their ground is worn out', wrote an English traveller in Virginia, 'they never manure it to bring it in heart, but let it lie for pasture for all men's cattle to graze upon, and clear more ground out of the woods to plant it.' They did not make hay. They did not understand how to drain land. Their richest meadows

[1] Ault, 'Open-Field Husbandry', pp. 10-11.

were left in the condition of bogs and swamps, in which their cattle were frequently lost, while farmers were obliged to engross vast tracts of land, 1,000 to 3,000 acres apiece, in order to ensure enough corn land and grass for their animals. English visitors were indignantly critical: population became scattered; 'their living solitary and unsociable, trading confused and dispersed, besides other inconveniences. Whereas they might improve 200 or 300 acres to more advantage, and would make the country much more healthy.'[1] Where in seventeenth-century England, it may be asked, did the colonists learn to farm on the prairie principle? Why did they so quickly abandon the practice of haymaking and draining land? Whence did they get a taste for the lonely life on farms miles from their neighbours and miles from their markets? The lesson of all this, surely, is that farmers farm empirically, making their rules as they go along. Whatever customs the first settlers bring to virgin territory, in whatever numbers they group themselves, and by whatever methods they appropriate land, experience is a school in which all lessons can be quickly unlearned and the most deeply entrenched ideas easily overthrown.

If we set aside the proposition that the common-field systems of villages in the East Midlands were preserved unchanged for a thousand years out of loyalty to a set of rules imported by the early settlers, we still have to account for the many resemblances among them. The precise nature of these resemblances will be explored later. But a general explanation may be offered here in anticipation of the more detailed argument that follows: the likenesses result from the similar social and economic pressures to which all villages were exposed in the course of centuries. Field systems in their beginnings were almost certainly as varied as villages were numerous. But similar influences tended to iron out diversity and to bring them gradually into closer conformity with one another. Thus, some settlements may have originated as servile communities under the watchful eye of an ever-present lord; others were free associations of men acknowledging none but the loosest ties of dependence. Yet all settlements which developed into villages, and did not dwindle into single farms or disappear from the map altogether, came eventually to consist of all classes of men, holding intermingled lands. Many economic and social trends exerted pressure on them all. All, for example, had to accept the partitioning of land and encroachment on the waste as numbers rose; all could consolidate parcels, or abandon land as demand fell.

---

[1] Thomas Glover, 'The Account of Virginia', *Phil. Trans. R. Soc.*, no. 136, reprinted in John Lowthorp, *The Philosophical Transactions and Collections to the End of the Year 1700...abridg'd*, 1716, III, 569, 585, 588; C. Bridenbaugh, *The Colonial Craftsman*, 1950, p. 5.

All were driven to rationalise their use of land as the markets for agricultural produce expanded. And, as each community discussed and changed its bylaws, all were inevitably influenced by the example and experience of their neighbours. The likenesses of many field systems do not prove their origin in a single plan but denote rather the unifying influences which shaped their later development.

Yet not all diversity was ironed out. Some persisted because of the differing size of village communities. Nor could the landscape of the East Midlands be tamed into uniformity. But since all field systems were designed to exploit the natural resources to the best advantage of the community, villages experiencing the same geographical conditions tended to divide their land in similar proportions between different uses and to govern it by similar bylaws. It is therefore possible to reduce the multitudinous field systems of East Midland villages into three main groups, each coinciding with a physical region. Hill and vale, forest, and fen preserved their separate identity throughout the life of field systems. These types, however, are not peculiar to the East Midlands alone. The system found in hill and vale country in the sixteenth to eighteenth centuries bears a strong resemblance to that found in parts of Durham, Yorkshire, Wiltshire, and Buckinghamshire – to take widely separated counties with very different histories of early settlement. The reason is not far to seek: in all these counties, and others besides, the geographical conditions, the farming objectives, and the social organisation of village communities were sufficiently alike to produce similar solutions to the practical problems of land management and the fair distribution of natural resources.

What, then, are the most influential common factors giving rise to the rough conformity of many field systems? This is the fundamental question to be explored in this essay. It is one which may be fruitfully investigated in any region however small or large. Here the area comprises the five counties of Nottinghamshire, Leicestershire, Rutland, Lincolnshire and Northamptonshire. They are only a unity in the proximity of the counties to one another. In all other respects they represent a considerable diversity of geographical conditions and historical experience. But this makes them an ideal subject for study, for it is in the exploration of the differences and the similarities of their agricultural and social situation that one may expect to uncover the principal factors which shaped their field systems. The three major predisposing conditions which must be examined are the physical structure of the East Midlands, the farming objectives and the social structure of the farming communities.

B. THE PHYSICAL SETTING

To describe the east Midland landscape before the Norman Conquest would be a mainly imaginative exercise, and no such attempt will be made here. But it is not impossible to reconstruct from documents the main agricultural regions and patterns of settlement in these counties in the early Middle Ages and to follow the changes thereafter. This is a necessary prelude to the discussion of field systems, for both vegetation and forms of settlement influenced them directly.

The East Midland region, as defined here, begins effectively in the northwest with Sherwood Forest (Fig. 6.1). Sherwood Forest lies on Bunter Sandstone which produces a porous, dry, sandy soil which was not very fertile and could only serve the plough if assiduously folded with sheep. Large grants of land were being made in the forest in the thirteenth and fourteenth centuries to hopeful farmers and monastic lords intent upon clearance and cultivation.[1] But at this late date many new settlements were yet to be established, while others already in existence consisted of little more than a farmstead or two in a clearing. In Domesday Book few settlements were recorded and it is likely that even some of these included people living in scattered clearings in the forest who were only assembled under the umbrella of a village name for administrative convenience. The area defined as royal forest fluctuated during the Middle Ages: in the first half of the thirteenth century it stretched from Nottingham northward as far as Warsop and Cunigsworth Ford (north of Wellow). But in the tenth century it stretched for at least another seven miles northward, since a charter defining boundaries in Sutton, four miles northwest of Retford, described them touching Sherwood.[2]

Sherwood, however, was only one of several forests in the East Midlands. Another was Charnwood Forest, a pre-Cambrian outcrop of rocks and hills in northwest Leicestershire which rise to over 400 feet and in some places to over 900 feet. The only place of habitation recorded within the forest in Domesday Book was Charley and here four carucates lay waste in 1086. Thus it was almost entirely a grazing ground for surrounding village settlements, which were thinly

[1] D. Gray and V. W. Walker (eds.), *Newstead Priory Cartulary 1344 and other Archives*, Thoroton Soc. Rec. Series, VIII, 1940, pp. 42, 45, 177–8.
[2] H. C. Darby and I. S. Maxwell (eds.), *The Domesday Geography of Northern England*, 1962, p. 239; Helen E. Boulton (ed.), *The Sherwood Forest Book*, Thoroton Soc. Rec. Ser., XXIII, 1965, pp. 35–6; F. M. Stenton, *Anglo-Saxon England*, 1950 edn, p. 281.

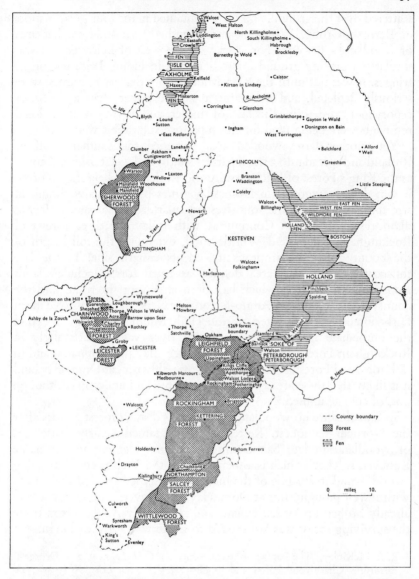

Fig. 6.1 The East Midlands. A location map showing forests, fens and places mentioned in the text. The Sherwood Forest boundary is that of 1218, represented in Helen E. Boulton (ed.), *The Sherwood Forest Book*, Thoroton Soc. Rec. Ser., XXIII, 1965. The boundaries of the Northamptonshire forests are those of the thirteenth century, represented in M. L. Bazeley, 'The Extent of the English Forest in the Thirteenth Century', *Trans. Roy. Hist. Soc.*, IV, 1921. The Leighfield Forest (Rutland) boundary is that of 1269 described in J. C. Cox, *The Royal Forests of England*, 1905, p. 235. The Charnwood Forest boundaries are only approximate, based on G. F. Farnham, 'Charnwood Forest and its Historians', *Trans. Leics. Arch. Soc.*, XV, 1927–8. The Leicester Forest boundary is conjectural for 1628, based on Levi Fox and Percy Russell, *Leicester Forest*, 1948.

scattered over the ground, and were contained in the four great manors of Barrow, Groby, Whitwick and Shepshed.[1] Another smaller area of woodland – Leicester Forest – lay to the west of Leicester and was similarly a grazing ground for settlements, including Leicester, on its fringes. It was not until the later Middle Ages that its resources were seriously depleted, and it became a pasture rather than a forest. A report in 1523 described its lack of timber, and in 1605 its unenclosed remnants were being used for sheep pasture and rabbit warrens.[2]

Yet another large wooded area occupied the southern half of Rutland and spread into a small part of southeast Leicestershire. Known as the King's Forest of Leicestershire and Rutland, or Leighfield Forest, it was densely wooded in Domesday times but gradually shrank in size until it occupied the southwestern quarter of the county. It was disafforested in 1630.[3] Continuous with it lay the three forests of Rockingham, Salcey and Whittlewood, extending the full length of the county of Northamptonshire on its eastern side. In the late thirteenth century the area defined as royal forest included lands along the River Nene which had been an important route into the county for the earliest Anglo-Saxon invaders and must have been fairly intensively cultivated by the High Middle Ages. But beyond the immediate neighbourhood of this river valley, particularly in Rockingham Forest, where heavy Boulder Clay predominates, and in Whittlewood Forest, settlement was noticeably thin at Domesday, and it is likely that these areas were still uncleared and unoccupied, though not, of course, unused.[4]

In Lincolnshire no woodlands survived as distinct forest entities after the Norman Conquest. Kesteven had contained a fairly dense area of woodland in late Saxon times – the first element in the name Kesteven is 'chet' which is associated with the Welsh 'coed' meaning 'wood' – and it was one of the more thinly settled areas of the county with fewest ploughteams at Domesday.[5] However, it was a woodland already broken up by settlements and from early Anglo-Saxon times the surviving forest was fast eroded to make way for the plough.

[1] R. A. McKinley, 'The Forests of Leicestershire', *V.C.H. Leics.*, II, 268; George F. Farnham, 'Charnwood Forest and its Historians', *Trans. Leics. Arch. Soc.*, XV, 1927–8, p. 4; H. C. Darby and I. B. Terrett (eds.), *The Domesday Geography of Midland England*, 1954, p. 317.
[2] *V.C.H. Leics.*, II, 267.
[3] *V.C.H. Rutland*, I, 251, 224.
[4] J. E. B. Gover, A. Mawer and F. M. Stenton, *The Place-Names of Northamptonshire*, English Place-Name Society (hereafter E.P.N.S.), X, 1933, pp. xv–xxiii; Darby and Terrett, *Domesday Geography of Midland England*, p. 385.
[5] Darby and Terrett, *Domesday Geography of Midland England*, p. 59 and maps, pp. 53, 57.

Another kind of landscape which imposed limitations on the early settlers were the ill-drained fenlands of south Lincolnshire around the Wash (encroaching into a small district of northeast Northamptonshire in the soke of Peterborough), and of northwest Lincolnshire, in the Isle of Axholme and northeast Nottinghamshire. In the Romano-British period the fens around the Wash were dotted with settlements, many of which were later flooded and abandoned. Nevertheless, some survived into Anglo-Saxon times,[1] although by this date sluggish meandering rivers, criss-crossing this flat land, constricted the choice of settlement sites and made arable cultivation difficult. The villages that are deemed of Anglo-Saxon and Danish origin thus lay in a long string on the higher ground, and dispersed settlements, which had been a remarkable feature of the map in Roman times, did not again proliferate until the mid-thirteenth century when drainage had improved the condition of the outlying fen. Although the amount of arable land that could be created in this countryside was limited, it was rich in grassland and lakes. Natural conditions thus gave the economy a strong pastoral bias which was only slightly weakened in the second half of the twelfth century, when settlements began to increase in size and number and ambitious programmes of dyking and draining were put into effect.[2]

In considering the form of East Midland field systems and the nature and date of their origins, therefore, differences in landscape and the pace of clearance in the different regions are significant variables from the outset. The forests and fens were thinly settled, and their natural resources exploited mainly by communities living outside them, until at least the late twelfth century. The districts, which were most intensively settled and cultivated in the Anglo-Saxon period and even earlier (for the possibility of continuous settlement from earlier times cannot everywhere be discounted) were first the main river valleys of the Trent, the Nene, the Witham, and the Welland, and subsequently all the hill and vale country of these five counties.[3]

Scarps, hills and vales span the East Midlands in five successive belts running mainly north to south. The Trent valley is the broadest vale, whose fertile soils invited the earliest Anglo-Saxon invaders to settle alongside the river by which they had entered the Midlands. This vale country of Keuper Marls, some Keuper Sandstones and

[1] One such site is described in W. G. Hoskins, *Field Work in Local History*, 1967, pp. 170–8. See also below, p. 278.

[2] H. E. Hallam, *Settlement and Society*, 1965, pp. 35–9 *et passim*.

[3] J. E. B. Gover, A. Mawer and F. M. Stenton, *The Place-Names of Nottinghamshire*, E.P.N.S., XVII, 1940, p. xiv; *Place-Names of Northamptonshire*, E.P.N.S., X, pp. xv–xvii.

river gravels in east Nottinghamshire and west Leicestershire, continues on to the Liassic Clays – some cold and heavy, some lightened by Northampton Sands – of east Leicestershire, west Lincolnshire, Rutland, and west Northamptonshire. Here the plain is interrupted by limestone hills which terminate the belt of Oolite running diagonally across England from the Cotswolds. North of Lincoln they consist of an escarpment called the Lincoln cliff, but further south they broaden into a heathy upland of limestone rock, overlain in Kesteven by sandy loam and clay, and in east and south Northamptonshire by soils that include the hungriest and lightest Brashes, a deeper Cornbrash that makes good sheep and barley land, and heavy cold clays. Beyond the cliff and heath lies another flat plain of Oxford and Kimmeridge Clays – the Ancholme valley – which merges south into the fens. In the north, it is brought to a gentle halt by the rising, rolling hills of the chalk wolds. These then fall away into another flat countryside of fertile clay and marsh on the edge of the North Sea.

Hill and vale country do not make one homogeneous agricultural region for all purposes. But in the study of field systems they belong together, and are distinct from the forest and fens. Both hill and vale were extensively settled in the Anglo-Saxon period and except in minor details the farming practices which shaped their field systems were much the same. They were all based upon the regulation of cropping over considerable areas of arable land and the control of grazing over diminishing areas of pasture. Their field system suited the needs of village settlements whose inhabitants lived at close quarters, and pursued an economy directed mainly towards corn growing. In practice, moreover, hill and vale land were frequently combined on individual farms, and certainly in many parishes. This is most clearly illustrated by parish shapes in Lincolnshire. Many parishes consisted of long, narrow rectangles of land which ran from the hill down into the vale, thus giving to each a share of upland pasture, arable on the lower slopes, and meadow in the vale.

C. THE AGRICULTURAL NEEDS OF VILLAGE COMMUNITIES

The three distinctive landscapes of the East Midlands yielded different natural resources, and gave rise to important differences in the chronology of settlement. At the same time it must be emphasised that the basic requirements of all agricultural communities, whatever the countryside they inhabit, are substantially the same. Lords and tenants require arable ground for their corn, grazing for their animals in summer and hay for winter fodder. They also require a few closes near their houses, either for cultivating special crops which, for one reason or another, it is inconvenient to include in the rotation of crops in the arable fields, for example, hemp, flax, and vegetables, or for the occasional pasturing of animals needing special attention, such as cows in calf or sick beasts, or animals needing pasturage close at hand, such as working oxen.

Wherever possible meadows were laid out near the river, though some communities had to make do with upland meadows which lacked the benefits of river-flooding in winter. The arable land ideally lay as near the farmhouses as possible. Hence most villages were more or less tightly encircled by the oldest of their arable fields – the land that was originally considered to be the best for cultivation. The remainder of the village territory, which was unsuitable as meadow and was not yet needed for cornland, remained a waste, to be freely used as common pasture by the inhabitants until such time as it was needed to increase the supply of corn or hay. These minimum requirements were common to all agricultural communities whose members expected to get their principal living from the land. When the documents become more abundant in the later Middle Ages, we find additional amenities such as fishponds, dovecotes, and rabbit warrens. These were frequently privately owned and often were the prerogative of the lord alone. Fishponds might be constructed to exploit a natural depression in a field or an old marl or lime pit. Rabbit warrens were laid out from the mid-thirteenth century onwards on sandy, barren heath or thin, chalky upland soils with little herbage. They made the best of a poor tract of worthless land, and were profitable to the owner, though they quickly became a nuisance to all other inhabitants except the skilled poachers.[1]

Since the basic necessities of agricultural life were the same in all regions, they gave rise to a certain uniformity in the layout of land of east Midland villages, which is conspicuous in all seventeenth- and eighteenth-century maps. It may be illustrated by two maps of characteristic settlements in the hill and vale country of the East Midlands in 1758. The first shows Breedon on the Hill (Leics.) – a nucleated village of houses backed by crofts and closes (Fig. 6.2). Four arable fields – Great Field, Dam Field, Nether Field and Wood Field – almost encircled the village. The bulk of the meadows were ranged along the river. Remnants of waste and common pasture in the north of the township indicated the places where it once lay in

[1] E. M. Veale, 'The Rabbit in England', *Agric. Hist. Rev.*, v, 1957, pp. 85–90; 'Sir George Heneage's Estate Book, 1625', *Lincolnshire Archit. and Arch. Soc. Reports and Papers* (hereafter *L.A.A.S.*), I, 1938, p. 58.

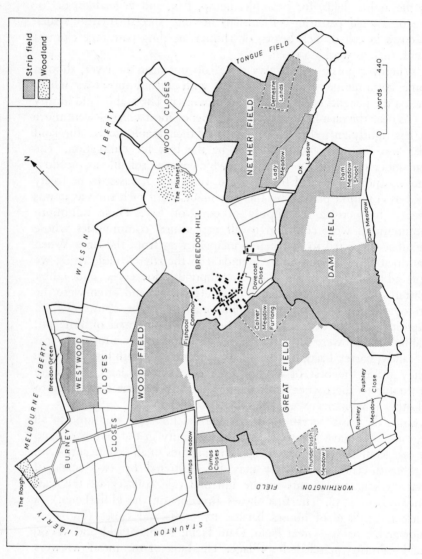

Fig. 6.2 Breedon on the Hill (Leics.) in 1758.
Source. Leicestershire R.O, Grey Mss. DG 20/MA.

greater abundance: it can be safely assumed that the whole of Breedon Hill was once a common grazing ground; the scrubby woodland, called Plashets, and the closes to the northeast of the hill were probably originally carved out of woodland, as was Wood Field in the north-west; some of the land beyond this on the northwestern boundary was still rough pasture in 1758. The last moves in the long process of colonising and improving the land of Breedon almost certainly ended here in its northern sector.

An additional asset to the township was a piece of common near the centre of the village called Fish Pool Common. It evidently had fish ponds at some time, and the presence of a brick kiln suggests that brickearth may once have been dug here by the community, thus creating pits which were subsequently adapted as fish ponds.

Somewhere on this map of Breedon we have to locate the manorial demesne. A field on the northeast boundary is called Demesne Lands; this must at some time have been demesne though it later passed into other hands and was divided into parcels. Dovecoat Close at the village centre possibly belonged to the demesne also, since the keeping of doves was usually a privilege of the lord. The rest of the demesne could have lain anywhere amid the scattered strips or in the closes; a consolidated demesne, or a demesne consisting of scattered strips, were equally usual.

The map of Tonge, a hamlet in the parish of Breedon, illustrates the form of a township which has grown up as a daughter settlement on the fringes of land belonging to a mother settlement (Fig. 6.3). Its boundary suggests that it gradually established a claim over its own territory, in the interstices of the land of its neighbours, though in its early days it probably shared all the land with its parent vill. There are documented examples of vills sharing common rights of pasture over each other's fields (as at Gayton le Wold and Grimble-thorpe (Lincs.), c. 1162) which almost certainly originated in the same situation.[1] In most cases the arable fields and meadows (though not necessarily the common pastures) of two vills associated in this way eventually became separated. The division may have taken place by formal agreement; more probably it evolved naturally with the growth of administrative practices separating the two vills, and was facilitated by voluntary exchanges and sales of land to suit the practical convenience of the inhabitants. However it came about, the lands of Tonge in 1758 were entirely separate from those of Breedon. The village community was small, the manor house occupied a prominent place, and the demesne, or some of it (e.g. Hall Close and the closes

[1] F. M. Stenton, *Documents illustrative of the Social and Economic History of the Danelaw*, 1920, p. xliv and n. 3.

around it), afforded the lord a consolidated home farm. The tenants' lands lay almost entirely in strips in common fields. The names, and hence, the number of fields is not made clear by the map, but the common arable fields, the common meadow (one of which is called significantly Rainswallow Lott Meadow)[1] occupied most of the village lands except at the southern end where there was pasture and woodland. Whether this pasture and woodland was grazed in common cannot be deduced from the map, but if not, then some of the community must have been acutely short of summer grazing.

These maps of places in the hill country of northwest Leicestershire illustrate land use in a typical village where arable crops were the main object of farming and the ploughed fields occupied at least half the available land. In the sixteenth century the proportion of meadow in such villages was usually between 8 and 15 per cent: the average holding had roughly one acre of meadow to every nine or ten acres of arable.[2] But the varied landscape of the East Midlands did not always afford arable, meadow and pasture in the same balanced proportions. Some Lincolnshire heath villages had no low meadows at all and were driven to buy in hay from elsewhere. Not all grasslands in hill and vale country were equally suitable for sheep and cattle: villages in the vale usually kept larger herds than the hill farmers; hill farmers suffered from a lack of water on the higher ground, and kept more sheep. Villages in the forests had a superabundance of grazing pasture, and in the fens of meadow, but neither were generously endowed with corn land.

The proportion of land devoted to different uses was also influenced by the social composition of the community. The presence of a lord farming his own demesne in the interests of a sizeable household might call for more cornland (both to feed the lord and to feed the families of the tenants he required to perform labour services on the demesne) than a village composed of independent freeholders. In other cases the edict of the lord led to the preservation of large commons for the pleasures of the hunt long after they had been eroded in other places. Forest law, for example, inhibited the clearance of land for arable in all royal forests before the sixteenth century.

In short, every village displayed a broad similarity in the layout of the essential land needed to satisfy all cultivators. But within this broad framework, every village was in some way unique in its assets of land and in the agricultural needs of its inhabitants. Moreover, as land was used, its potential altered; and in the course of generations

---

[1] See below, p. 248.
[2] J. Thirsk, 'The Content and Sources of English Agrarian History after 1500', *Agric. Hist. Rev.*, III, 1955, p. 70.

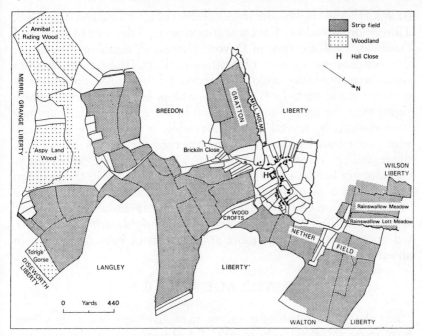

Fig. 6.3 Tonge (Leics.) *c.* 1758.
Source. Leicestershire R.O., Grey Mss. DG 20/MA.

so did the needs of the community. Throughout the thousand years of its existence, therefore, land use and the agrarian bylaws of every village had continuously to be adapted to changing circumstances.

From the earliest documents of the thirteenth century onwards it is clear that in most villages of the East Midlands much land was minutely subdivided: the bulk of the arable and the meadow lay in strips or blocks of varying sizes. The lord occasionally possessed a ring-fence farm, or at least one composed of a few large parcels, and other cultivators might have some arable, meadow, and pasture in closes, but the great bulk of tenants' land lay in scattered parcels distributed haphazardly through the township. They all shared rights in common pastures and waste.

The sharing of rights in common pasture and waste is one common factor in the customs of all village communities throughout England, no matter what the other idiosyncrasies of their field systems. Nor was it peculiar to England; it was a convention throughout the British Isles, and throughout Europe; and it can be found in other continents as well. In England these practices seem to go back to a period well before the Anglo-Saxon invasions, when the inhabitants of whole

---

counties claimed rights over large expanses of moorland and woodland. Thus Andredsweald in Kent was common to all the men of Kent, and Dartmoor to all the men of Devon; Sherwood, meaning Shirewood, was common to the men of Nottinghamshire. These more spacious rights were gradually whittled down as the land filled up with new settlements and more lords claimed lordship. In Lincolnshire common rights over the fens of south Holland in the early thirteenth century were claimed by several wapentakes while in more congested areas, many commons by this time were reserved for the inhabitants of a single vill. Nevertheless, examples are cited in this essay of inter-commoning between two or more vills, particularly in the fens and forests, which continued until the date of Parliamentary enclosure in the eighteenth century. And more than one dispute about commons, whose boundaries were demarcated between neighbouring settlements, fed upon the memory of more ample rights of intercommoning in an earlier age.[1]

D. VILLAGE BYLAWS

Since almost no inhabitants except manorial lords had a ring-fence farm in east Midland villages, but all had parcels of arable, meadow, and pasture rights in dispersed places, some rules were essential to protect the rights and interests of all. Rules of cultivation and land conservation are known to us through village bylaws. These come down to us in a few documents of the twelfth century, gradually increasing in number in the thirteenth, fourteenth and fifteenth centuries, but the most informative and complete examples date from the sixteenth to eighteenth centuries. Our knowledge of field systems, therefore, largely derives from these bylaws, and some analysis of their content is essential. Unfortunately, it is rarely possible to find a set of bylaws for a village that is complete for any one period or year. Bylaws were regularly reviewed at the court baron, in the light of changing circumstances, but the central corpus of custom was not restated or codified.[2] It was merely agreed that the old bylaws should continue in force so long as they were not repugnant to the new. Thus a document which contains the bylaws of the village of Medbourne (Leics.), beginning with an entry for 1623 and ending in 1736, nowhere contains any clear statement of all the rules governing the cultivation and grazing of the arable fields, meadows and common

[1] L. D. Stamp and W. G. Hoskins, *The Common Lands of England and Wales*, 1963, pp. 5–13; Hallam, *Settlement and Society*, p. 31.
[2] One notable exception is the Barrow-on-Humber town book. See M. W. Barley (ed.), 'The Barrow-on-Humber Town Book', *L.A.A.S.*, II, 1938, pp. 13–33.

pastures. It merely elaborates upon this theme without codifying the basic essentials. It must be assumed that the dates when fields and meadows were closed and opened again, and the stints and kinds of stock allowed into each place were so rarely changed that no reminder was necessary. Other adjustments, forced upon the inhabitants by unseasonably bad or good weather, were agreed upon at short notice, were recognised as temporary, and were not written down as permanent bylaws. We catch a glimpse of such ephemeral decisions in the later pages of the Medbourne document. A bylaw was recorded in October 1716, but a note written into the margin states that it was discontinued in October 1717. Another agreed in October 1714 bears the comment that it was discontinued in October 1717.[1] The following examples of agrarian bylaws are taken from different regions of the East Midlands and are designed to illustrate the main preoccupations of each region and the variety of detail within each village.

1. BYLAWS IN HILL AND VALE REGIONS

Medbourne lies in the southeast corner of Leicestershire on the border of Rutland and Northamptonshire. It was the last village in the county to be enclosed in 1844. At that time half its land was under the plough and half under grass. Some of the grass was grazed in common, as were the three corn fields after harvest and in fallow seasons. The bylaws regulated the dates when stock were to be allowed into the common fields and other grazing grounds, and when they were to be kept out. They insisted on the erection of fences and on proper tethering arrangements. They defined places where the stock were allowed to graze singly, and other places where all cattle had to be in the charge of the village herdsman and all sheep folded with the village flock. The stint of animals allowed to each tenant with land and common rights was specified. Pigs had to be ringed to prevent them rooting up the land or the grass. No geese were allowed into the common fields. Watering places and rivers had to be scoured and the water kept pure; no hemp or flax might be soaked in them. The cutting of hedges and trees was restricted. The carrying of fire was prohibited except in a closed dish, as was the smoking of tobacco in barns and stables.[2]

We do not have a complete picture of the farming routine of this community, but we see enough to recognise the characteristic economy of the Midland plain. It is no different in its essentials from that

---

[1] Leics. R.O., Medbourne Court Orders; *Lincs. Notes and Queries*, XXII, p. 71.
[2] Leics. R.O., Medbourne Court Orders; *V.C.H. Leics.*, v, 229, 235.

portrayed in the better-known bylaws of Laxton (Notts.).[1] Farmers observed certain crop sequences in the arable fields. Almost certainly since there were three clearly named fields, Medbourne farmers observed a three-course rotation of legumes or fallow, spring corn, and winter corn, and grazed their beasts and sheep in common on the fallows and common pastures.[2] At fixed dates in the year common meadows were laid up for hay and thrown open for common grazing again.

In all villages it was customary to fix dates when the common meadows were shut up in the spring and opened again after hay harvest. The kinds and numbers of stock to be pastured in the meadows were also specified. Sometimes the bylaws included the practice of reallocating the strips of meadow annually by lot. It appears to have been the practice at Coleby (Lincs.), and at Glentham (Lincs.), where, in the words of a Parliamentary survey of 1649, the common meadows were set forth yearly by a meadow book. The procedure was somewhat confusingly described, but it seems that every tenant changed at least one parcel every year and all parcels were reallocated in the course of eight years. At Warkworth (Northants.), in the early eighteenth century lot meadows were still being allocated once a year with great ceremony, accompanied by feasting that lasted a whole weekend.[3]

Stints of stock on the common grazings were not set down in the bylaws of Medbourne, but in other villages in the Midland plain we can observe wide variations in the allowance, based on many different principles. In some an allowance was made in respect of each messuage and another in respect of each virgate, in others the allowance was determined by tenurial or residential status. Frequently there were different stints for different pieces of common pasture within the same township. At Coleby on the Kesteven Heath, for example, landholders were allowed 2 beasts, 1 follower, and 5 sheep in respect of their messuages, while in respect of their oxgangs they had the right to graze two oxen or horses in *Oxpasture* and 2 kine, 2 young beasts, and 30 sheep in *Cowpasture*. Lambs could be put in both places from Lammas till Martinmas; calves could be put in *Oxpasture* from May Day till the stubble fields were broken. At Donnington on Bain (Lincs.) in 1609, each occupier of an oxgang of 20 acres was allowed to graze 40 sheep in the two common fields. But the community only had one common pasture called *Cowpasture* of 20 acres (even this represented an enlargement by the addition of former

---

[1] C. S. and C. S. Orwin, *The Open Fields*, 3rd edn, 1967, pp. 147ff.
[2] For a fuller discussion of crop rotations, see pp. 256 ff.
[3] P.R.O., C.2 Jas. I, A6/52; Lincs. R.O., D and CL, CC 10, 152794; J. Bridges, *The History and Antiquities of Northamptonshire*, ed. P. Whalley, 1791, I, 219; Orwin, *Open Fields*, pp. 59–60, 144–5.

copyhold and freehold land), and here the tenants of oxgangs were allowed to graze three beasts. At Belchford (Lincs.) in 1609 the only common pasture was an acre of land on the highway. For every oxgang occupiers had a stint in the two fields of 40 sheep, 6 beasts, and 2 horses. At Waddington at the same date the stint per oxgang of 14–15 acres was 5 beasts and 25 sheep except in the Toft and Mearefield, where the allowance was 4 beasts and 20 sheep. In practice, however, the grazings here would not bear more than two-thirds of the permitted number of animals.[1]

All stints were at some time calculated in accordance with the stocking capacity of the common grazings and the number of commoners, and revisions were carried out from time to time. But conventions hardened for long periods, and in many places sixteenth-century documents indicate that the concordance between the supply of grass and the permitted number of animals had broken down. Freeholders occasionally eased the problem by contributing pieces of land from their own holdings, but a more general curb on overgrazing was effected by the convention, commonly accepted from at least the fourteenth century, that no one should keep more animals in summer in the township than he could winter.[2]

Not all common grazing rights were shared equally among all commoners. Apart from differences in the stints of lords, holders of virgates (or oxgangs or fractions thereof) and cottagers, some lands were grazed in common by freeholders only or by copyholders only, and some were shared only between owners of particular tenements.[3] At Greetham on the Lincolnshire wolds, for example, the only common pasture in 1609 consisted of two sheepwalks, one of which belonged to the lord's demesne, the other to the tenants. In one of the arable fields common pasture rights were accorded to the cattle and sheep of the lord and to tenants' cattle, but not to tenants' sheep.[4]

It is noticeable that common rights in hill and vale country in the East Midlands consisted by the sixteenth century almost entirely of grazing rights. Bylaws sometimes governed the taking of timber and underwood but many vills had none to share. Thus, whereas common rights in forests and fens covered an impressive list of natural resources, they meant little more than grass in hill and vale, and even the grass was inadequate and jealously stinted.

---

[1] P.R.O., E.134, 15 Jas. I, Hilary 17; DL 42/119, fos. 69ff., 37ff., 9ff.; Lincs. R.O., Solly 22.
[2] P.R.O., E.134, 14 Chas. I, Mich. 11; E.178, 1334; W. O. Ault, 'Village By-laws by Common Consent', *Speculum*, XXIX, 1954, p. 379.
[3] Lincs. R.O., Crowle Manor 8/10, fo. 189; Wake, *Econ. Hist. Rev.*, XXXVII, p. 408.
[4] P.R.O., DL 42/119, fos. 57ff.

2. BYLAWS IN FEN-EDGE VILLAGES

Villages of the Midland plain which lay on the fringe of other regions, however, often enjoyed the advantage of more generous common rights outside their township boundaries, in a more distant place where several townships intercommoned. Parishes at the southern end of the Lincolnshire wolds, for example, had very little meadow, and no common pastures within their boundaries; their draught cattle were tethered on odd patches of grass in the corn fields and in closes, while their sheep and common herds grazed only the stubble of the fallow fields. For at least fifteen such townships their safety valve was their rights of common grazing in Wildmore Fen. Other Lincolnshire townships such as Steeping Parva in the vicinity, had rights of grazing in Earles Fen, East and West Fens.[1]

3. BYLAWS IN THE FENS

The bylaws of two Lincolnshire fenland villages serve to illustrate customs of farming cooperation under a different economy, in a countryside offering abundant grassland, particularly in the summer, generous opportunities for taking fish, fowl, and plants in the fen and marshes, but poorly endowed with cornland. In the example given here the bylaws represent a joint agreement of two neighbouring vills, Spalding and Pinchbeck, which intercommoned over the same pastures. Spalding, Pinchbeck, and Deeping Fens were one undivided common grazing ground for both communities. Four fen reeves enforced the rules in each township, of whom two were elected by the lesser lords and commoners of the vill, the other two by the prior of Spalding, who was the chief lord of both villages. Had it not been for the large landed interest of the prior in both villages it is possible that the customs of intercommoning would eventually have given way to a partition of the pastures between the two townships. This occurred frequently in other kinds of countryside in the sixteenth century, as pressure grew on the available grazing grounds.

Six sets of bylaws have survived for Spalding and Pinchbeck, dated 1422, 1545, 1590, 1591, 1620, and 1734. As at Medbourne, none is a complete list in itself; most are a selection of those bylaws which needed emphasis at the time because they were most neglected. They differed in one important respect from those of Medbourne. They were all exclusively concerned with the common pastures and meadow

[1] P.R.O., E.134, 11 Chas. I, Mich. 39; DL 42/119, fos. 184ff. For a vale township near the Trent with fen-like perquisites, see E. Peacock, 'Notes from the Court Rolls of the Manor of Scotter', *Archaelogia*, XLVI, 1881, pp. 377ff.

land, and contained no rules governing the cultivation of the arable. This in itself tells us much about the economy. The fen extended over thousands of acres, but since it was liable to flooding in winter, its use was predetermined: except in specially favoured places it could not grow corn, but it could yield plentiful grass.

The bylaws of Pinchbeck and Spalding show very clearly the wide variety of natural resources that were at the disposal of the fenlanders – far in excess of those enjoyed by the commoners of Medbourne. The great size of the fens created special difficulties in ensuring that all commoners had their fair share and none attempted to take more than the rest; so a special restriction applied here: everyone had a fixed place in the fen where he exercised his rights of common. When he died his place (or 'labour' as it was called) passed to his wife, if she claimed it, or if not, to the first man who 'manured' it, i.e. expended his labour upon it. No one could sell his 'labour' to another, but exchanges were permitted so long as public notice was given.[1]

The bylaws laid down the time of year, and in some cases the days of the week when commoners were permitted to fish for eels, hunt with dogs in the marshes, gather down, firing, sallow (willow), rushes for ropes, reeds and peat turves. No one was allowed to appropriate more than six fishings (wearesteads), no one might light a fire without licence in the fen, dig a dyke, watch or search crane's nests, catch fowl in breeding time with nets or engines, snare swans, or cut bushes without the sanction of the reeve.

No one was allowed to steep hemp in the dykes or lakes, but only in 'haff' holes (holes made with a special dyking tool), and these had to be blocked up when the steeping was finished. No one might dry hemp or flax in his dwelling house. No one was allowed to keep his pigs unringed on the common, to build a common dunghill near a common sewer or highway, or wash sheep except in certain specified places. No one might mow hay before sunrise or after sunset.

Strangers coming into the town but having no land could enjoy free common for their cattle for one year. After that they had to abide by the rules governing all other inhabitants. These were generous provisions that reflected the abundance of grazing. Single men without freehold or copyhold land could have common of pasture for their cattle, but no other common rights. None but the inhabitants of the township could have common rights of any kind; and none could take other men's animals into the fen claiming them as their own.

No one was allowed to sell any peat, reed, or firing from the

[1] This and the following paragraphs are based on H. E. Hallam, 'The Fen Bylaws of Spalding and Pinchbeck', *L.A.A.S.*, x, 1963, pp. 40–56.

common except to fellow inhabitants, and anyone who dug more peat turves than he could carry away between May Day and Martinmas surrendered the excess to other commoners. Those who had fishing rights were ordered to cut back bushes and weeds from the dykes at regular times, and all had to share responsibility for scouring the dykes. Those who wanted to lie in the fen all night had to take up their positions by 8 p.m. in the evening and remain until 2 a.m. Those sleeping at home but wishing to go into the fen in the early morning were not allowed to stir abroad until 2 a.m. In this way marauders prowling at irregular hours of the night could be easily recognised.

The absence of bylaws governing the cropping of the arable fields calls for explanation. All fenland villages had cornland and some at least consisted of bundles of strips of anything from one rood in size upwards. Why did these communities not adopt common rules of cultivation? It is true that if the fenlanders of Pinchbeck and Spalding had deemed it desirable to regulate the cultivation of their arable in common, they would have done so on a village rather than an inter-village basis, and the bylaws of Pinchbeck *and* Spalding would not necessarily record them. But some clues would assuredly appear elsewhere in manorial court rolls. Yet no such laws for the villages of the Holland fenland have been found, and so, for the present, it must be assumed that there were none. There are several possible reasons, arising out of the special natural conditions of the Holland fenland. The arable was relatively small in area, and much of it confined to a narrow silt ridge on which the villages were situated. The rest lay in scattered parcels amid the fen pastures, raised above the level of winter flooding, but not too far from the villages. These fields were usually separated from neighbours by dykes and therefore could be conveniently cultivated in severalty. The arable which was clustered around the villages and was more consistently parcelled into strips may have been subject to agreements about cultivation between neighbours, which are unrecorded in documents. But it is more likely that rules were considered neither practicable nor desirable. The amount of arable in the occupation of individual peasants was small. The average husbandman in the sixteenth century had about eight acres under crop in any one year. Some land was customarily cropped almost continuously; some was used alternately for pasture, meadow, and arable. Common rules of cropping would have imposed severe restrictions on the choice of crops and the benefits would have been small. They would have permitted only very short periods of common grazing between the end of harvest and the beginning of ploughing, and there can have been no urgent necessity to graze the stubble when the fens afforded such luxuriant pasture. Freedom of cropping was perhaps the most sensible solution.[1]

This rationalisation of practices in the Holland fenland does not, however, apply to the fenland villages of Kesteven, and there is doubt as to how far it applies in the Isle of Axholme. In the Kesteven fen common field regulations catered for a conventional three-course rotation on the arable and common grazing after harvest. But the layout of land in these vills closely resembled that of many hill and vale settlements: the parishes are long, narrow rectangles which were divided more or less clearly between the three types of land use. The fenland grazings and meadows lay at one end of the parishes, arable in the middle and heath common at the other.[2] This clear-cut separation of land use, comparable with that found in hill and vale villages facilitated, and probably explains the utility of, common field bylaws. In Axholme, the evidence is less clear. Crowle agreed to divide its arable into four fields in the fourteenth century, which means that some agreed crop rotation must have been in operation. But in the seventeenth century the ploughland in some parts of the island, at least, was cropped continuously. In such circumstances, convenient rules of cropping must have been difficult to devise.[3]

4. BYLAWS IN THE FORESTS

Forest villages, like those in the fens, possessed a limited amount of arable land and abundant common pastures. The arable was restricted in area by poor soils, and, in royal forests during the Middle Ages, by forest law, which discouraged ploughing. Such assarts as were permitted seem to have been held at the outset in severalty. That many remained enclosed was probably due to the absence of any very pressing demand for arable land. The economy was pastoral and the arable did not occupy a dominant position. Hence, less subdivision of parcels took place, and assarts did not regularly become fragmented into bundles of strips. Nevertheless, some arable land lay in strips immediately around the nucleated setttlements, and posed the same problems of regulation as in hill and vale country. Court orders of Brigstock in Rockingham Forest (Northants.) in 1741 show their

[1] Hallam, *Settlement and Society*, pp. 137-8, 141; J. Thirsk, *English Peasant Farming*, 1957, pp. 22-3, 14.
[2] See, for example, the plan of Potter Hanworth in Kate Norgate and Maurice H. Footman, 'Notes for a History of Potter Hanworth', *Assoc. Soc. Rep. and Papers*, XXVI, 1901-2, p. 384.
[3] J. Thirsk, 'The Isle of Axholme before Vermuyden', *Agric. Hist. Rev.*, I, 1953, p. 19; P.R.O., E.134, 13 Eliz., Easter 5; Misc. Books, Augmentations Office, 390, fos. 23, 36-7.

resemblance to the bylaws of hill and vale country. The dates for grazing cattle, horses and sheep, and the stints allowed in the three fields were prescribed. No outsiders' animals could be agisted in the fields. No one might glean until the fields were clear; no one might gather peas in any selions except an owner and his family; no balks were to be ploughed up unless equivalent land was laid down in another place; all broken hedges were to be mended by the field keeper. The fields were folded with sheep, and cottagers who put sheep into a larger farmer's flock, had to allow them to be folded with his in summer.[1]

On their own the field orders of Brigstock might give the impression that cornland occupied the same place in the forest economy as in hill and vale townships. The balance is put right in the orders governing common rights in the forest, listed at the swanimote court at King's Cliffe in 1575. From these it is clear that in the grazing and pannage seasons all commoners had unlimited pasture in the forest for all their cattle, horses and pigs. The restrictions were of a minor kind. Verderers inspected the forest each year in the middle of September to decide the period when swine were to be allowed to eat pannage in the forest. Strangers' animals and store cattle above four years old were excluded from the forest. Sheep were excluded in theory, but the law was not strictly enforced; a convention grew up in Rockingham Forest by which commoners were allowed to shelter their sheep there on wet nights so long as they drove them out again the following morning. The commoners were not allowed to gather acorns, or take wood to mend hedges without the consent of the woodward.[2]

The relative importance of arable and pasture in forest areas is also illustrated in a document describing Garendon manor, on the edge of Charnwood Forest, in 1652. On the demesne little land was under the plough, and much of that was almost certainly under some form of convertible husbandry, being described as 'meadow and arable', 'pasture and arable', in two cases as 'pasture now converted into tillage', and in one case as 'meadow converted into tillage'. Part of the manor lay in Thorpe Acre, where there were three common fields, but the generous stint of animals in the fields (a holding of 45 acres including 28 acres in the common fields had three cowpastures for nine cows and common for six horses and sixty sheep) suggests that a large portion of the arable was under temporary grass, and that more bountiful grazing resources were assured elsewhere.[3]

---

[1] Northants. R.O., ML 146, fos. 104–5. See also below, p. 262.
[2] Northants. R.O., Brud. E. xxiii, 6; Westmorland Apethorpe Collection, 4, XVI, 5. See also P. A. J. Pettit, *The Royal Forests of Northamptonshire*, Northants. Rec. Soc., XXIII, 1968, pp. 152–3.   [3] P.R.O., C 54/3673, no. 11.

Although the examples of village bylaws given above contain many similar orders relating to stock and fields which insured against common dangers and punished common misdemeanours, the same problems often produced different solutions. Some of these differences can be explained by the uneven distribution of population in relation to the amount, type and quality of the land. The hill and vale lands which were the most intensively cultivated lands of the East Midlands in the seventeenth and eighteenth centuries were also among the earliest to be settled by the Anglo-Saxons and were the most populous in the Middle Ages. In many of them assarting had ceased by the thirteenth century because the community had reached the limits of its village territory.[1] The common grazings were sacrificed to the plough, and the rights of pasture that still had to be met were necessarily carefully delimited. In the fens and the forests, on the other hand, early settlement had been inhibited by adverse natural conditions. In the forests it was later inhibited by royal forest law, and when virtually unrestrained immigration was under way in the seventeenth century, it still did not give any serious cause for alarm.[2] In short, the chronology of settlement in different parts of the East Midlands varied greatly, and as population increased or diminished, changes in field systems and farming regulations were carried through to allow for changing circumstances.

E. CHANGES IN BYLAWS AND FIELD SYSTEMS

The numbers and kinds of stock customarily grazed on common pastures and in the fallow fields underwent frequent alteration as pressure of numbers increased. Killingholme (Lincs.) had a common saltmarsh of 200 acres which was stinted in 1582 but had not always been so.[3] In Holland Fen a dispute developed in the 1570s because local people had started taking in large numbers of strangers' cattle, sheep, and horses with their own. The practice had started about 1548 and had spread to such an extent that the grass was insufficient for everyone. A stint was suggested but was not adopted. Instead the manorial lord who had brovage rights – an acknowledged right appertaining to lords of manors of taking in strangers' animals – and who was probably among the worst offenders in overcharging the common, agreed to surrender his rights in return for an enclosure of 480 acres of fenland. Similar complaints of overgrazing were heard

[1] See below, p. 259; W. G. Hoskins, The Midland Peasant, 1957, p. 63.
[2] Thirsk, English Peasant Farming, p. 11.
[3] Lincs. R.O., Nelthorpe V/13/9.

in other parts of the Lincolnshire fens in the 1620s and 1630s; some were pacified by an agreement to extinguish the lord's rights in return for an enclosure of land; one township agreed upon an enclosure of the whole fen. In some places a stint was imposed or an old one reduced: in Swaton (Lincs.) a stint was in force and was regularly reviewed in the late eighteenth century. In Leighfield Forest (Rut.) urgent representations were made in 1609 for a reduction in the customary allowances of firewood, thorns, hedging and deer browse, since the quantities removed each year threatened to destroy the forest. In this case the problem was solved by disafforestation.[1]

It would be wrong to give the impression that all alterations in common rights were carried through by amicable agreements between all tenants of the vill and their lord. Some practices crept in by stealth, and if the community failed to oppose them at the outset and disputes reached the courts, they were liable to be claimed as custom and the claimant's case upheld. The tenants of Eastcroft (Isle of Axholme) in the early seventeenth century had no right to claim common in Luddington High Pasture, but Alexander Thornton's aged father-in-law used to tell him that their cattle were allowed to rake thither, and if he got up early in the morning and no one from Luddington saw him, he could even drive his cattle there and they would be allowed to remain. The people of Misterton in Elizabeth's reign had uncertain and ill-defined rights of grazing in Haxey Carr. They were separated from it by Bickersdike and could only reach it by a roundabout route. But after a bridge was built across the dyke they began to put increasing numbers of animals into the carr and a dispute developed. One labourer admitted in evidence that Misterton people had long been in the habit of putting animals into the carr but they did it secretly for fear of being espied. In both these examples we see encroachments which, if not contested, would have developed into established rights.[2]

Regulations governing the cornlands of village communities likewise show substantial changes over time. In the hill and vale country the most common rotations of crops observed in the common fields were either a two-course, a three-course, or a four-course. In Leicestershire between 1500 and 1800 four-fifths of the villages had three fields, which implies a three-course rotation. In the vale lands of Northamptonshire, most villages in the north of the country had three fields, but in the south most had two fields. A late eighteenth-century report on Rutland agriculture suggests that at that time most

[1] Thirsk, *English Peasant Farming*, pp. 37–8, 112–17; Lincs. R.O., Smith 5 (Swaton) 3, 7; *V.C.H. Rutland*, I, 224.
[2] P.R.O., E.134, 13 Jas. I, Trin. 3; E.134, 39 Eliz., Easter 14.

vills followed a three-course rotation. A study of Lindsey, Lincolnshire, on the eve of Parliamentary enclosure suggests that two fields were most usual: 71 villages had two fields, 24 had three fields, 11 had four fields, and 12 had one or five or other irregular numbers. Professor Stenton, examining medieval charters of Lincolnshire also thought that a two-field system was most usual in the county in the twelfth and thirteenth centuries, and assumed that this remained the dominant rotation until enclosure. Yet a more strictly localised study of seventeen villages around Corringham in northeast Lincolnshire in the mid-seventeenth century showed that 9 villages had three fields, 6 had two fields, and 2 had four fields. In the marshland of Lincolnshire the majority of townships continued with two fields and a two-course rotation until Parliamentary enclosure.[1]

These varied conclusions concerning the most usual crop rotation in the county of Lincoln, together with the variations in the number of fields in north and south Northamptonshire, suggest that a more refined topographical and agricultural analysis of field rotations is needed. In the vales and on the hills, where farmers strove continually to increase the productivity of their arable land, it is generally true that the most fertile land in the sixteenth to eighteenth centuries was subject to a four-course, while average land carried a three-course and only the most barren land was reserved for a two-course. But soil considerations within a single parish sometimes compelled men to adopt different rotations in different fields. Thus at Barton on Humber in the mid-seventeenth century, some arable was fallowed every fourth year, some every second year. At Kirton in Lindsey in 1776 the low fields were fallowed every third year, while the high fields, because of their lighter and shallower soil, and more especially because of the lack of manure, were fallowed every second year.[2] But this does not explain everything. The two-field rotation was most practised by communities in the early Middle Ages when land could not be, or did not have to be, cropped intensively. It often gave way gradually to the three-course and sometimes to the four-course. But the two-course continued to be observed on fertile land in populous marshland townships in Lincolnshire until the eighteenth and nineteenth centuries.

[1] Hoskins, *Midland Peasant*, p. 153; W. E. Tate, 'Inclosure Movements in North-amptonshire', *Northants, Past and Present*, I, 1949, p. 19; John Crutchley, *General View of the Agriculture in the County of Rutland*, 1794, p. 8; T. H. Swales, 'The Parliamentary Enclosures of Lindsey II', *L.A.A.S.*, I, 1938, p. 120; Stenton, *Danelaw Documents*, pp. xxxi–xxxii; Ian Beckwith, 'The Remodelling of a Common-field System', *Agric. Hist. Rev.*, xv, 1967, p. 111; Thirsk, *English Peasant Farming*, pp. 60–1.

[2] P.R.O., E.317/Lincs. 5; Duchy of Cornwall, Particular and Valuation of Kirton in Lindsey Manor, 1776.

9

It is therefore clear that rotations reflect a mixture of influences: they must suit the whole economy, and this in its turn is a complex system which must accommodate the needs of men and animals in relation to the available land. In the marshland the persistence of the two-course rotation may best be explained in terms of its highly individual, mixed corn and stock system. Corn and stock were not integrated enterprises as they were in the hill and vale country. The grain was grown on the fields of the middle marsh and the stock grazed on the coastal pastures. It therefore seems likely either that the farmers did not have enough manure to keep their fields under a more intensive rotation, or that they valued the stubble and grazing on the fallow above the value of another arable crop.

A variety of crop rotations persisted in the common fields of east Midland villages until enclosure. But this variety is also found in the history of individual villages, for every rotation was liable to periodic alteration. H. L. Gray noted that the three townships of Holdenby, Drayton and Evenley (Northants.) changed their fields from two to three between the thirteenth and the sixteenth centuries. At Kislingbury (Northants.) the same change occurred somewhere between the thirteenth and mid-fourteenth centuries. At Culworth (Northants.) the date of the same change could be narrowed down to a year in Edward II's reign, somewhere between 1307 and 1327. At Harleston (Northants.) a change from two fields to three fields took place somewhere between 1310 and 1410. In the court rolls of Crowle manor (Isle of Axholme) the clerk recorded a decision of the lord and his tenants in 1381 to divide their fields into four parts and fallow one quarter each year. Unfortunately the document does not state the rotation in force before this.[1]

Clearly, it was not unusual to change the crop rotation in the common fields. In Great Corringham (Lincs.), indeed, it was done more than once. In 1200 the holdings of tenants were divided between two halves of the village: some strips lay in the West Field and some in the East Field. At an unknown date between 1200 and 1600 the fields were redivided into four. Later documents suggest that this was done by dividing each field (not necessarily equally) into two. In 1601 a new agreement was reached ('to the prejudice of some of the inhabitants', it was alleged in the courts in 1610–11) to reduce the four fields of Corringham to three: all were to observe the new arrangements the following season. This reorganisation was achieved by leaving East and West Fields as before, but counting the third and fourth fields as one field, even though they were physically separated

[1] H. L. Gray, *English Field Systems*, 1959 edn, pp. 78–80; Wake, *Econ. Hist. Rev.*, XXXVII, 1932, p. 406; Lincs. R.O., Crowle manor 1/34/4.

from each other by East (now called Middle) Field. By 1758, however, yet another arrangement was in operation: part of the third field was now united with West Field, its nearest neighbour, while the rest of the third field survived in truncated form.[1]

Why and how were these changes in rotations achieved? The reorganisation might take place after new land had been assarted, which added a new field to those already in use, and thus made easy the change to a new rotation. In some cases, the layout and names of the fields (for example, Wood Field in Breedon) suggest that this is a reasonable explanation.[2] But it is not always the satisfactory answer. In Corringham, it is clear that when the changes of rotation occurred, recent assarting was not the pretext. Already by the beginning of the thirteenth century the arable fields had reached the extreme edges of the parish; in 1758 there was no more arable than there had been in 1200.[3] Thus all rearrangements after 1200 must have taken place within the same territory, or, indeed, a smaller one, for piecemeal enclosure which diminished the size of the common fields must have precipitated a change in the field divisions as often as did the addition of newly colonised land. Other circumstances in which more intensive rotations became necessary and practicable arose when the population and the stock available to manure the fields increased. Conversely, a shortage of animals, following a fall of population, or a sudden mortality among the herds and flocks, might lead to the introduction of a less intensive rotation.

The weight of evidence from the East Midlands points to the conclusion that more intensive rotations were often adopted in the thirteenth and early fourteenth centuries in response to the rising pressure of population on the land. This pressure was relieved by the Black Death, only to return again in the sixteenth century when rotations and field divisions were again changed. But by this time, men were exploiting more varied ways of increasing the productivity of their land: changes in rotations included such innovations as the alternation of arable crops with temporary grass.

How were changes in field divisions and rotations achieved? It used to be thought that every peasant had an almost equal number of acres in each field and that a change of field course necessitated a redistribution of the arable strips between tenants – a major task of great complexity which could not have been undertaken lightly. In practice, however, it seems to have been carried out by the stroke of a pen, by

[1] Beckwith, *Agric. Hist. Rev.*, xv, 1967, pp. 108–12; P.R.O., E.134, 8 Jas. I, Easter 23.
[2] See above, p. 243.
[3] Beckwith, *Agric. Hist. Rev.*, xv, 1967, p. 110.

redrawing the boundaries between the fields, without too meticulous an investigation into the physical distribution of tenants' parcels between different crops in the rotation. Not that the detailed consequences were ignored. The change could only be carried through if the majority of landholders concurred. But the rearrangement did not need to preserve absolute equality in the acreages which all tenants held in each field. Individuals made up awkward deficiencies by adapting their rotations on their enclosed land or by renting additional acres. Every change inevitably worked 'to the prejudice of some of the inhabitants' as the complaint from Great Corringham reminds us.[1]

Changes in the detailed regulations governing common lands and common interests were a flexible response to the vicissitudes of the whole village community. Some necessarily imposed on the individual peasant the need to change the layout of his holding. But individual family needs were also constantly changing, and the composition of peasant holdings had to be reshaped to suit them.

Various solutions were open to the farmer faced with this predicament. He could lease additional land from his lord as it fell vacant, become the sub-tenant of another peasant with too much land on his hands, or arrange an exchange. None of these solutions altered the landscape or affected the scope of village bylaws. But other solutions were possible which modified both. The land-hungry peasant could take in a piece of land from the waste and hold it in severalty. Alternatively, he could consolidate a few strips in the common fields, and enclose them. Either way he achieved freedom of cropping, but the amount of common grazing available to the community was thereby reduced.

Before the fifteenth century, and sometimes later still, some east Midland lords and village communities maintained a permissive attitude to assarts in severalty and the consolidation of strips.[2] It may be that they were aware of the temporary nature of many such enclosures for until the mid-fourteenth century all closes, whether they lay at the heart of the village or were assarts from the waste, were liable to become subdivided into strips in course of time, and then were assimilated into the common fields.[3] In the later Middle Ages, mainly, no doubt, because of the reduced population, fragmentation was resisted, but enclosure continued. Thus the boundaries of common fields and the extent of common rights fluctuated like the sea shore.

[1] See above, p. 258.
[2] Lincs. N. & Q., III, 1890–1, pp. 174ff.; D. M. Stenton, The Earliest Northamptonshire Assize Roll, A.D. 1202 and 1203, Northants. Rec. Soc., V, 1930, p. xxxii.
[3] R. H. Hilton, 'Medieval Agrarian History', V.C.H. Leics., II, 158.

Alterations in the grouping of the common fields, which inaugurated new rotations, were a major change in common-field husbandry that was intended to last for some decades, if not for several generations. But short-term changes were constantly being tried out by individuals, groups of neighbours, or the whole village community without disturbing the fundamental framework. A not unusual expedient in the thirteenth century and later was to take land in 'inham', i.e. to cultivate for a season land which, under normal routine, would have lain fallow and been subject to common grazing. A dispute at Billinghay (Lincs.) in 1260–2 describes an 'inham' (also known as an 'inlik' or 'inhoc') which was agreed upon by the Prior of Catley and certain other tenants, with the permission of their neighbours, and which resulted in a piece of land (*cultura*) that should have lain fallow being cropped four times in the twenty years up to 1260. Similar agreements were concluded between all the commoners of Alford and Well (Lincs.) in 1281, and of West Torrington (Lincs.) in 1348.[1] Even the communally agreed rotation, however, left room for considerable individual choice for many common fields were an amalgam of smaller units of land, called furlongs or shotts, and the furlongs could be treated as cropping units to separate wheat from rye, and spring grains from legumes;[2] and if neighbours with contiguous strips could be persuaded to agree upon a common policy, even the furlong was not the smallest cropping unit.

Traditional rotations were further modified by the growing of peas, beans, and vetches in increasing quantities from the mid-fourteenth century onwards. Sometimes these replaced spring corn in the rotation, sometimes they replaced the fallow. The inhabitants of Caistor (Lincs.), for example, agreed in 1623 to sow peas in the fallow field, which they explained was 'a manner especially used in places where the strength and nature of the land will bear it and where the inhabitants have great store of manure and compost to lay upon it, whereby the land is fed and nourished'. In this case the landholders admitted having a large supply of manure, but a stronger incentive to sow the fallow field was the fact that the occupiers were many and their fields small.[3]

A further measure which preserved the common fields intact but modified the sometimes irksome consequences of common rotations

[1] Hallam, *Settlement and Society*, p. 172; *Lincs. N. & Q.*, XII, 1912–13, pp. 150ff. Original Ms. now in Lincs. R.O., Cragg 4/3. I owe the West Torrington reference to Mrs Joan Varley, formerly archivist of the Lincs. R.O. and Mrs Enid Ballard of Holton Beckering. The original charter is B.M. Harleian charter 45 H 34.
[2] Hoskins, *Midland Peasant*, pp. 154–7; R. H. Hilton, *The Economic Development of some Leicestershire Estates in the Fourteenth and Fifteenth Centuries*, 1947, p. 152.
[3] Hilton, *V.C.H. Leics.*, II, 160–1; *Lincs. N. & Q.*, III, 1890–1, pp. 174ff.

was the practice of putting some arable parcels under temporary grass. These leys, as they were called, increased the productivity of the land in the long run and temporarily alleviated the shortage of grazing. The value of leys in the common fields may have been borne in upon cultivators by the presence of many untilled acres in the overworked common fields in the later fourteenth and fifteenth centuries. People could observe the recuperative effects of leaving land to lie for years under grass. Alternatively, the system may have been copied from districts in the Highland Zone where it was standard practice. When once the lesson was taken to heart, it was not difficult to devise a way to exploit these benefits in common fields as well as in closes. Early evidence of the use of leys in the common fields has been found at Wymeswold (Leics.) in 1425. By the sixteenth century common fields in all regions of the East Midlands generally consisted of a mixture of strips under the plough and strips in ley.[1]

F. SUMMARY CLASSIFICATION OF FIELD SYSTEMS

This account of the common field systems and bylaws of east Midland villages has underlined the variety of local customs and regulations; they differed between villages and changed over time. But within this variety, some unity can be discerned. The nature of the farming economy in each agricultural region gave a certain bias to its bylaws; communities inhabiting the same kinds of countryside upheld some regulations with great fidelity, while others did not. In hill and vale country cropping rotations were a consistent feature of village bylaws; in the fens they were not. More hill villages had sheepfolding customs than did the vales; forest villages folded their arable but the fens did not.[2] Hill and vale villages stinted their pastures, forest and fen communities did not. Many of the changes in rotations and common rights, however, reveal general, if temporary, economic factors at work in all regions, urging people to use their ploughland more intensively in the thirteenth and early fourteenth centuries, for example, to turn some ploughland over to temporary ley between the fifteenth and eighteenth centuries, and to introduce stints or reduce long-standing ones whenever men came near to ruining the commons by

[1] HMC Report LXIX, Middleton Mss. 1911, pp. 106–9; P.R.O., E.317/Lincs. 6; E.134, 18 and 19 Eliz., Mich. 13; 13 Eliz., Easter 8; 10 and 11 Chas. I, Hil. 8; C54/3725, no. 18; Gray, *English Field Systems*, p. 35.

[2] For an emphatic statement that the inhabitants of Luddington (Isle of Axholme) never folded their sheep on the land, see P.R.O., E. 134, 14 Chas. I, Mich. 11.

overgrazing. The range of alternative solutions available to farmers working in similar environments was not infinitely variable.

Beyond and behind these signs of partial conformity can be seen certain basic principles of procedure which all villages accepted in their farming routine. They were all agreed that the natural wealth of the community in the waste and common lands must be conserved in the long run and fairly shared in the short run. They were agreed that every individual householder must take his share of responsibility for the upkeep of hedges, banks, dykes, streams, etc. They were agreed that no one should be allowed to damage or encroach upon the interests of others. These rules, however, are not peculiar to the East Midlands but are embedded in the field systems of the whole of the British Isles and throughout Europe. They are basic to any community where the majority get their living from the land, and where land is so intermingled that the responsibilities and rights of each individual have to be defined.

In short, we may recognise three sources for the similarities in bylaws of common field farming in the East Midlands: first, a pattern of intermingled parcels of land involving all classes of tenants and lords; second, some commonly accepted principles governing social life, which may fairly be regarded as the necessary outcome of the first proposition; third, a similar physical environment which influenced the choice of farming objectives; and last, similar economic pressures arising from the basic human need for food, and developing along similar lines, as the market in agricultural produce expanded, and communities were driven to pursue change in the same general direction.

If the similar principles which underlie the manifold variety of village bylaws are reduced to their *simplest* terms we could maintain the notion of a single field system in the East Midlands. But this would be so general in its terms that it would embrace all other regions of Britain and, indeed, most of Europe as well, for it would emphasise two elements only: the communal regulation of arable rotations, and the communal regulation of grazing – over the arable after harvest and in fallow seasons, over common meadows after hay harvest, and over common pasture and waste. By taking account of technical differences in agrarian practice (the social differences in village communities are discussed below and do not seem to account for any significant differences in customs and bylaws) we can observe three field systems in the East Midlands, based on the three types of agricultural region. This, however, does not mean that they differed from the systems found in other parts of England. The system in hill and vale country, in particular, is found without significant variation in many other districts of lowland England.

G. THE TENURIAL DIVISION OF LAND

The agrarian customs and bylaws of the East Midland region illustrate and explain the influence of physical environment and market forces. There remains the question why landholders in east Midland villages came to hold their land in intermingled parcels and to share common rights. The answer to this question calls for a study of the composition and changes in the structure of village society, which will lead us finally to the basic question of all – who were the makers of the English village? But we should not attempt at the outset to go back to a period before documents. Between the time of Domesday and the thirteenth century we can observe settlements coming into existence for the first time, and others undergoing transformation. What light does this shed on the pattern of land occupation?

Village society was composed of lords, bond tenants who owed their lord labour services in return for their holdings, and free tenants who owed rents and certain non-servile services but were generally free to dispose of their land as they pleased. At Domesday these three classes were not always represented in all villages of the East Midlands. Some had a lord occupying a demesne, and bond tenants, but no sokemen. Other villages had free tenants but no lord: Lincolnshire possessed thirty such vills; the Soke of Newark (Notts.) included over 16 vills, inhabited by 174 sokemen and 14 bordars, without demesne.[1] In the light of our knowledge of the different rights of free and unfree tenants over their land at a later date, it is not impossible that the holdings of these two classes of men stem from different origins, that is, that they were originally appropriated or granted on a different basis with different rights and duties attached to them. This possibility is discussed below.[2] But in the course of the Middle Ages lordless villages acquired lords and land was appropriated to make demesne.[3] Some vills, indeed, acquired several lords. Bond communities were joined by freemen who received privileged grants from their lord, free communities were joined by bondmen, labouring for the free tenants or their lords.[4] The tendency over time was for villages to move towards closer social conformity with one another. Thus some of the distinctive class characteristics of village populations which are

[1] Stenton, *Danelaw Documents*, p. lvi; Darby and Maxwell, *Domesday Geography of Northern England*, p. 248.
[2] See below, p. 275.
[3] Stenton, *Danelaw Documents*, p. cviii.
[4] Stenton, *Northern Danelaw*, p. 19.

apparent in Domesday Book, and which doubtless yield important clues to their past, were lost. They became communities representing all classes, though the proportions of each class, of course, continued to vary.[1]

In the same way we can observe changes in the distribution of land between tenants and lord which brought villages into closer physical conformity with one another. One vill may have begun life as a modest family farm with only one household to maintain; another may have started as a more lordly establishment supporting servants with their own family holdings, who formed the kernel of an incipient village community. Whatever the original layout, the land came to be redistributed in new combinations as numbers increased: some parcels were consolidated, some parcels were divided. But fragmentation was a stronger influence than amalgamation at least until the mid-fourteenth century. Thus the conglomeration of parcels multiplied until in some places they engulfed the whole village territory except that portion which of necessity had to be reserved as common grazing. This process can be illustrated in the land transactions of different classes on the manor.

I. LORD'S DEMESNE

The land over which the lord exercised greatest authority was his demesne and the land of his bond tenants. In the Lincolnshire Domesday, demesne and bondland are occasionally grouped together under one heading as 'inland', in contrast with the 'sokeland' of the freemen. Even this sheds no clear light on the location of 'inland' but the term is suggestive; we should bear in mind the possibility that in some places at least the lord's land was physically separated from the sokeland; it was a consolidated estate out of which the lord carved a demesne for himself and a portion for the villein tenants whom he needed to work his land.[2]

In the twelfth and thirteenth centuries charters generally indicate that the demesne consisted of one block of land, or at worst, a group of furlongs or fields of reasonable size, scattered through the village territory. It did not usually consist of scattered strips. But demesne lay open to fragmenting influences like all other land in the vill, though these influences were slower in working their effects. The lord was occasionally moved to grant a piece of land to the church or to

[1] See, for example, R. H. Hilton, 'Kibworth Harcourt. A Merton College Manor in the Thirteeenth and Fourtenth Centuries', *Studies in Leicestershire Agrarian History*, ed. W. G. Hoskins, 1949, p. 20.
[2] Stenton, *Northern Danelaw*, pp. 5–8.

a favoured individual, and did so by surrendering a portion of his demesne.[1] More disruptive were the claims of the lord's own family. At some time or another, he was bound to have to find land for more than one son, for whom he might provide by granting a portion of demesne;[2] or his only heirs were daughters, and his executors had to divide the land equally between them. An example of the partition of a manor is given in an *inquisition post mortem* of 1425 relating to Allerton in Sherwood Forest. The estate was originally granted by Edward III to his uncle, Edmund, earl of Kent. Two of his sons inherited it in turn but neither had heirs, and it passed to his daughter Joan. Joan's son, Thomas, inherited it but again it passed to two of his sons in turn, neither of whom had heirs. In the third generation it devolved upon Thomas's five daughters who divided it among them, and in the next generation one of the five portions was again divided among three sisters. It is not clear that a physical division of the estate took place on both the last occasions but it was evidently divided on the first round since one of the three sisters, who had received *a third of a fifth part*, was receiving in 1425 *one third* of a rent of 35s. 8d. A similar partition threatened Kibworth Harcourt manor (Leics.) when the estate of Walter de Merton was divided at his death in 1278 between six relations (sisters or their children) and Merton College. In this case the estate was put together again by college purchases during the decade after 1278.[3]

Many demesne lands in the East Midlands were preserved as more or less consolidated farms or achieved this state by dint of judicious exchanges, amalgamations and enclosures. But in other places the action of lords who granted away pieces of demesne here and there inexorably led in the end to the demesne, or a segment of it, becoming a welter of small pieces of land intermingled with tenants' scattered holdings.[4] The process was accelerated when the demesne ceased to be farmed by the lord, and was divided among tenants, as happened in many places in the second half of the fourteenth century.[5] Sometimes the intermingling was such that it became impossible to

---

[1] Stenton, *Danelaw Documents*, p. xxvii; T. H. Aston, 'The Origins of the Manor in England', *Trans. R. Hist. Soc.*, VIII, 1958, pp. 79–81.

[2] For a possible illustration of this at Wilsford (Lincs.), in Domesday, see Stenton, *Northern Danelaw*, p. 29.

[3] K. S. S. Train (ed.), *Abstracts of the Inquisitions post mortem relating to Nottinghamshire, IV, 1350–1436*, Thoroton Soc. Rec. Ser., XII, 1952, p. 183; Hilton, *Essays in Leics. Agrarian History*, pp. 22–6.

[4] Hilton, *Essays in Leics. Agrarian History*, p. 29.

[5] C. N. L. Brooke and M. M. Postan, *Carte Nativorum*, Northants Rec. Soc., XX, 1960, p. l.

define the boundaries between demesne and tenant land, and all was swallowed up in the routine of cultivation observed by the village as a whole.[1]

2. PEASANT HOLDINGS

Throughout the East Midlands the standard peasant tenement of freemen and villeins was the virgate, of approximately 20 to 30 acres of arable and meadow, or the half-virgate, bovate, or oxgang, with appurtenant common rights. Charters which record conveyances of land among peasants are a relatively late innovation, and particularly late in the fenland where the religious houses of Bardney, Crowland, and Spalding, which were in existence in the first years of the twelfth century, did not regularly record grants of land until the reign of Stephen. Before the twelfth century conveyances of land were satisfactorily accomplished by an act of seisin before witnesses, so that we catch our first glimpse of peasant dealings in land only after many generations of oral land transactions.[2] At this late stage in the history of settlement, then, the standard peasant tenement usually consisted of strips of land scattered about the village fields and meadows.

In places where colonisation took place at a comparatively late date in the Middle Ages, however, consolidated bovates were not unusual. A charter from the early years of Henry II's reign described a bovate in Kelfield by the Trent (Isle of Axholme), which consisted of a block of arable land stretching westward from the river with nine acres of marsh alongside. At Habrough (Lincs.) a bovate (c. 1190) consisted of arable, meadow, and marsh in one *cultura* or furlong. Sometimes the lord exerted his authority to create a consolidated estate out of a pre-existing conglomeration of parcels in divided ownership. At Barnetby le Wold an estate of four bovates was created c. 1160 by putting together some demesne land and contiguous pieces of other men's land.[3] But none but a lord could ride roughshod over others and impose his will in this way. In short, while it is likely that all holders of land would have preferred a consolidated holding, property rights were usually dispersed by the twelfth century.

(a) Freeholders' lands

Among all classes fragmenting influences on land were very strong. Free peasants had no constraints on their liberty to alienate or sell their land as they pleased. The earliest charters conveying these lesser

---

[1] This process is well illustrated in A. C. Chibnall, *Sherington. Fiefs and Fields of a Buckinghamshire Village*, 1965, pp. 107–8.

[2] Stenton, *Danelaw Documents*, p. xlix.

[3] *Ibid.*, pp. xxxiii–xxxiv, 140; Hilton, *Leics. Estates*, 1947, p. 59; Hallam, *Settlement and Society*, p. 5.

estates begin in the twelfth century and from the outset show a flourishing market in land and a willingness to carve up holdings in all manner of ways in order to convey portions as gifts, exchanges, or sales.[1] And the charters only show the tip of the iceberg, since a host of transactions continued to take place by livery of seisin without written record. All these had the effect of dividing some holdings and consolidating others. Both purposes were promoted by the market in small parcels of land.

A more uniformly disruptive effect was exerted in certain districts of the East Midlands by the custom of partible inheritance. Much work remains to be done in estimating the prevalence of this custom among all classes of peasants. But it was a common custom in the fenland of Holland among freemen – variously called bond sokemen, molemen, and freemen – who were the largest class in the community, and Professor Hallam has demonstrated the profound consequences it had for the social structure of fenland villages in the second half of the thirteenth century. Small holdings proliferated in this period as population increased, and men who had small hopes of acquiring land in the open market clung more fiercely than ever to their rights by inheritance. The effect of this custom on land units was to divide fields and closes into smaller fractions, producing the 'selions in closes' which occur in many surveys of manors at a later period, and extending the pattern of strips in some places to the very frontiers of village territory.[2]

Outside the fenland of Holland the influence of partible inheritance has not yet been properly assessed. But it was the custom among sokemen in the soke of Rothley, a district embracing thirteen villages between Loughborough and Melton Mowbray (Leics.), and in Oswaldbeck soke, a district of north Nottinghamshire between the rivers Idle and Trent. It was also the custom of the manor in other villages in high Lincolnshire, at Askham, Laneham, and Sutton cum Lound (Notts.), and at Ilpen (Northants.), though here its affects may have been stronger among customary tenants than among freemen. It may be suspected as an early influence in the Northamptonshire forests, for at a later date Borough English, or descent to the youngest son, prevailed among copyholders, and it has been persuasively argued that this custom is the vestige of a former custom of partible inheritance.[3]

Further fragmentation of land resulted from the methods by which

[1] Stenton, *Danelaw Documents*, *passim*; Hilton, *Essays in Leics. Agrarian History*, pp. 34–5, 37; Hilton, *Leics. Estates*, pp. 96–8.
[2] Hallam, *Settlement and Society*, pp. 217ff.; H. E. Hallam, 'Some Thirteenth-Century Censuses', *Econ. Hist. Rev.*, x, 1958, pp. 344–61.
[3] G. T. Clark, 'The Custumary of the Manor and Soke of Rothley' *Archaeologia*, XLVII, pp. 89–130. The soke had rights over a much wider area, covering 22 vills,

fenland was colonised in the Middle Ages. The reclamation of fenland meant something more than clearing an acre or two of timber and scrub, and ploughing it up. Large-scale work in dyking and draining was a necessary preliminary to improvement and cultivation, and cooperation between neighbours and between villages was indispensable for success. Thus the reclamation of the fen south of Asgardike between 1229 and 1241 involved an agreement of all interested parties in seven Hundreds of South Holland. They began with a partition of the fen between the seven Hundreds, followed by a partition of land between villages, and then finally between individuals. Each holding of a carucate received an equal share in the reclaimed fen. Such an allocation of land created a new landscape. A wide uninterrupted expanse of common waste gave place to a multitude of parcels in divided ownership. Though each was held in severalty, we see in this example the process of fragmentation at its inception.[1]

(b) Bondland

Freemen did not everywhere hold as much land as they did in the fen. Elsewhere, and particularly in the hill and vale country of the East Midlands, bondmen constituted a large class, whose dealings in land were more closely supervised by the lord. Villeins were the core of the lord's labour force, and labour services had to be assured despite all changes in the personnel occupying the land. The lord therefore had a legal right to dispossess his villeins at will even in the midst of their tenancies. His commanding authority is evident in charters by which he redistributed the land of his bond tenants in order to grant a piece of land to a monastery in a place that satisfied the recipient's desires for peace and solitude.[2] The lord's interests were also protected by the manor court at which all transactions involving villein land were supposed to be witnessed and recorded, at any rate from the twelfth century onwards. These interests were further protected by the customs of the manor governing the transfer of holdings after death. Primogeniture was, therefore, the strongest custom outside the fens and the forests of the East Midlands. Yet in spite of all this it is evident from the earliest court rolls that villein tenements consisted for the most part of fragmented strips of land, which a flourishing land market only maintained and multiplied. The

in Domesday: G. Farnham, 'The History of Rothley. The Descent of the Manor', *Leics. Arch. Soc. Trans.*, XII, 1921–2, p. 36; Hallam, *Econ. Hist. Rev.*, X, 1958, p. 341; R. J. Faith, 'Peasant Families and Inheritance Customs in Medieval England', *Agric. Hist. Rev.*, XIV, 1966, pp. 93–5, 84; Northants. R.O., Montague (Boughton) Mss., Box X 356.
[1] Hallam, *Settlement and Society*, pp. 31–5.
[2] Stenton, *Danelaw Documents*, pp. xxxiv, 140.

pace of fragmentatoin was almost certainly slower on bond than on free land, because of the lord's supervision, but it proceeded nevertheless.[1]

At the height of the period of land shortage from the mid-thirteenth to the mid-fourteenth centuries a remarkable document was compiled by a comparatively efficient landlord – the abbot of Peterborough – recording all the land transactions of his bond tenants on estates in all five counties of the East Midlands. Despite all that the law had to say about the arbitrary power of lords over their villeins, their liberty to buy and sell land on this estate was evidently unimpeded. Bond land was conveyed by charter to free men and free land conveyed by charter to bondmen. If this could happen on an estate that was probably more carefully supervised than most, what was the situation on the estates of lesser landlords? The question is impossible to answer. But it does not seem likely that the Dean and Chapter were exceptional landlords in permitting this traffic in land. Indeed, Professor Hilton's study of changes of tenancy at Kibworth Harcourt (Leics.), on an estate owned by Merton College in the first half of the fourteenth century, clearly shows that they were not.[2]

Evidence of the flourishing market in free and villein land dates from the second half of the thirteenth century, but the sudden appearance of such documents should not lead us to think that tenants were now engaged in a novel activity. It is far more likely that the administrative efficiency of landlords had improved. As Professor Postan has argued, 'The needs and resources of individual families are too unequal in use and size'; it must be assumed on grounds 'of mere common sense and of comparable experience in other peasant cultures' that all tenants have always had to have means of remedying the inadequacies of their holdings or their labour resources. Sub-letting was one method; so was the purchase and sale of labour. The land market supplied another remedy. Its records take us back by implication to the beginning of the thirteenth century and even to the later decades of the twelfth century.[3] It is almost certainly much older.

The holdings of all classes of tenants on the manor were subject at one and the same time to divisive and and consolidating influences. The consolidating tendencies were continually at work because of

---

[1] V. W. Walker (ed.), 'An Extent of Upton, 1431', A Second Miscellany of Nottinghamshire Records, Thoroton Soc. Rec. Ser., XIV, 1951, p. 31; Hilton, Leics. Estates, pp. 96, 98; Hilton, Essays in Leics. Agrarian History, pp. 37–8.
[2] Brooke and Postan, Carte Nativorum, introd. by M. M. Postan et passim; Hilton, Essays in Leics. Agrarian History, p. 36.
[3] Brooke and Postan, Carte Nativorum, pp. xxxi–xxxvii.

the obvious practical convenience of owning and farming one large plot of land rather than several small ones.[1] They were probably most influential in periods of falling population and slackening pressure on land, particularly in the years immediately after the Black Death. The divisive influences were in the long term much stronger for the land of the East Midlands had to support a much larger population at the end of the Middle Ages than it did in A.D. 800. While the demand for additional land could often be met by assarts, this was not always the answer in practice, and it must have been increasingly difficult during periods of rapid population growth such as the twelfth and thirteenth centuries. Proof of this proposition is contained in studies of medieval estates in the thirteenth to fourteenth centuries, which indicate a rise in the number of individual parcels of land and a decline in their average size. This evidence may give an exaggerated idea of the pace at which land was subdivided in earlier periods, but it indicates the general trend which must have been continuous from the beginning of settlement.

H. THE EARLIEST HOLDINGS

One of the explanations for the strip pattern in arable fields and meadows of east Midland villages then lies in the divisive influences upon land exerted by all classes on the manor. But what was the shape of the original peasant tenement? Such a question takes us back long before the period of documentary evidence, and there can be no certain answer to it. But there survived into the period of manorial documentation a terminology and certain notions of what a standard holding should be which offer certain clues. Moreover, the question can be put in better perspective as a result of recent progress in the study of pre-Saxon settlement.

In Norman times and throughout the Middle Ages peasant land in the East Midlands was reckoned in virgates, or half-virgates or bovates. In Lincolnshire the bovate was roughly twenty acres and it can be equated with the Old English word 'manslot'.[2] In the twelfth century it was a notional holding, from which pieces were freely taken out and put in as it suited its holder or his lord;[3] it did not comprise the same land throughout its existence. In consequence bovates were frequently of unequal size, but they conformed in a rough and ready way to a notion of what a man's fair share of land should be. At Brocklesby (Lincs.) a grant of three bovates, described

[1] See, for example, Stenton, *Northern Danelaw*, p. 63; above, p. 266.
[2] Stenton, *Danelaw Documents*, pp. xx–xxi, xx, n. 9.
[3] *Ibid.*, pp. xxxiv, xl, lxx, lxxi, 180–2, 342–3.

in a late thirteenth-century charter, seems to contain the underlying notion that when a holding was conveyed as a nominal bovate or group of bovates, it should, if possible, be made up to the standard size. The charter in question recorded the grant by Eudo of Alford to Newhouse Abbey of three arable bovates, each comprising equal quantities of land on both sides of the village. One bovate contained four separate pieces of demesne land in one half of the village, and 5 pieces of demesne in the other. The arable of the other two bovates consisted of peasant land (*terra rusticorum*), but in one half of the village the total fell short of the standard allotment by 5 acres; hence 5 acres in three pieces were added from the demesne to complete it. On the other side of the vill the arable of the two bovates, again made up of peasant land, also fell short of the correct total by three acres. This amount was therefore added from elsewhere, presumably out of the demesne, though the charter does not say this but merely describes its location.[1]

By the twelfth century then the bovate was a notion of a fair-sized peasant holding. Although it generally comprised scattered bits of land, perhaps the ideal bovate was still a consolidated estate. At any rate, where it was possible to create by assarting a compact holding with adequate land of all kinds this was done.[2] Moreover, the terms of some grants of assarts which emphasised the rights of grantees to cultivate them continuously and in whatever way they pleased, imply that this freedom of cultivation was a desirable state of affairs.[3] But after the earliest settlers had bespoken the best sites in the East Midlands it cannot have been easy except in the fens, marshes, and forests to find room for a self-sufficient peasant holding, which was compact and yet afforded adequate land of various kinds. Thus charters exemplifying the creation of a new holding frequently reveal it as a group of parcels rather than a ring-fence farm.[4]

But what of the first virgates? The suspicion still lingers among some historians that at the dawn of settlement they started life as bundles of scattered selions allotted to peasants by some orderly system of allocation. The notion draws its strength from documents of the thirteenth and fourteenth centuries which show scattered selions with

---

[1] *Ibid.*, pp. 186–7.
[2] See above, p. 267.
[3] D. Gray and V. W. Walker (eds.), *Newstead Priory Cartulary 1344 and other Archives*, Thoroton Soc. Rec. Ser., VIII, 1940, pp. 42, 177; Stenton, *Danelaw Documents*, pp. xli–xlii.
[4] Stenton, *Danelaw Documents*, p. xxvii, shows a bovate created from demesne at Normanton on the Wolds (Notts.) which was deliberately made up of pieces that gave a share of best, middling, and poor land.

the same neighbours in many cases.[1] But in the light of our knowledge of the land market it is impossible to believe that such order can have survived from several centuries before. These examples can be explained more plausibly by changes of more recent date: by an arbitrary redistribution of land by the lord for his own convenience; by the partition of one holding between heirs or other claimants which involved the division of every parcel;[2] or by assarting by cooperative effort, which caused a block of new land to be allocated in portions in some prescribed order among a limited group of shareholders. Nevertheless, this evidence does suggest at least three ways by which subdivided fields might come into existence. And in attempting to reach back to a period before documents, when we have small hopes of establishing anything with certainty, and when our archaeological skills are not yet adequate to identify the shape of early peasant holdings, these three possibilities are significant clues. For analogous studies of other economic and social institutions have shown that they are usually more diverse in origin than in their more developed forms. The study of social classes, for example, has revealed how the be-wildering variety of privileges and obligations of individuals in local communities was classified and rationalised in the course of the Middle Ages until they could be grouped into a comparatively small number of manorial classes. In this case the lawyers hastened the process of rationalisation. Similarly, we have seen how economic rationality led in neighbouring villages to the creation of rules of cultivation which sufficiently resembled one another for us to classify them as a system. Thus it seems that the original forms of social and economic institutions are frequently more varied than those which we are able to examine in documents, for when once documents begin to accumulate the process of rationalisation has already begun.

When we debate the form of the earliest peasant tenements, we cannot fix upon any one period of time for this exercise. As the estates of lords and peasants varied in their degree of consolidation and fragmentation throughout the period when documents exist, so they must have varied at all previous periods. Some villages were new in A.D. 900, some were already old in A.D. 600. Those that were old in A.D. 600 must already have succumbed in some degree to the process of fragmentation; some of those that were new at the same date may have had arable fields that were divided into strips from the

[1] *Ibid.*, p. xlviii, n. 4; G. C. Homans, 'Terroirs Ordonnés et Champs Orientés: une Hypothèse sur le Village Anglais', *Annales d'Histoire Economique et Sociale*, VIII, 1936, pp. 438–9; F. Seebohm, *The English Village Community*, 1926 edn, p. 27.

[2] Cf. M. Spufford, 'A Cambridgeshire Community. Chippenham from Settlement to Enclosure, *Occasional Papers, Dept. of Engl. Local History, Univ. of Leicester*, XX, 1965, p. 22.

outset. If so, we may perhaps reasonably see in them the compelling and immediate authority of a lord or leader at work. At least, historians have generally been inclined to argue that the advantages of a consolidated holding were less likely to be enjoyed by bondmen than free men.[1] Other holdings, on the other hand, that were new in A.D. 900 and had started life as consolidated units of land, could not continue so for long. Thus the notion of an empty countryside, newly peopled at one moment in time eludes us, together with the notion of one single explanation for the origins of subdivided fields. It is much more lifelike to suppose that every village had its own beginning in time, that its allocation of land was designed to suit its own peculiar needs, but was brought into increasing conformity with other villages as men's social and administrative experience broadened.

In explaining the origin of English villages, historians have found a convenient starting point in the arrival of the Anglo-Saxon settlers in the sixth century A.D. It is clear that their culture can be invoked to explain some distinctive characteristics of social organisation and the terminology of administrative and fiscal institutions, which survived to a much later date in the East Midlands. But a careful regional classification on the basis of social institutions, language, or geographical settlement by the Anglo-Saxons and later by the Danes, does not coincide with any lines of demarcation between field systems inside or outside the East Midlands.[2] In any case, while no one would deny the influences that can be exerted by foreign immigrants on social structure and land distribution, in practice such influences have proved extremely difficult to identify. Whereas it used to be argued with confidence that the large numbers of free peasants in the East Midlands, and in eastern England generally at Domesday, were the heirs of the Danes, this explanation is now treated with great scepticism.[3]

No evidence has emerged to suggest that the proportion of free to unfree peasants in the village community had any significant effect on the *course of development* of common field systems. Indeed, all the facts adduced in this essay suggest otherwise. But there remains some doubt whether a high proportion of unfree tenants could act as an early forcing-house for the initial growth of common rules of land

[1] This seems to be the drift of P. Vinogradoff's argument in *English Society in the Eleventh Century*, 1908, p. 277.

[2] For the geographical complexities of Anglo-Saxon and Danish influence, see Stenton, *Northern Danelaw*, pp. 2–3; *Place-Names of Northants.*, pp. xxi, xxviii–xxix; *Place-Names of Notts.*, p. xvi.

[3] F. M. Stenton, *Anglo-Saxon England*, 2nd edn, 1947, pp. 507–10; R. H. C. Davis, 'East Anglia and the Danelaw', *Trans. R. Hist. Soc.*, V, 1955, pp. 23–39; P. H. Sawyer, 'The Density of the Danish Settlement in England', *Univ. of Birmingham Hist. Jnl.*, VI, 1958, pp. 1–17.

management. This is only plausible if it be argued that in such villages a lord, establishing an estate and supporting a household by the labour of serfs, allocated to them scattered strips in a well-defined arable field and meadow, supervised this allotment closely, and even re-allocated it periodically in order to maintain equality among his labour force. Some charters establish the existence of a well-defined area of arable field and meadow belonging to peasant cultivators. At Thorpe Satchville (Leics.) a thirteenth-century charter, phrased in terms that go back to the Conquest, refers to land lying between the lord's meadow and the 'tunmanne medwe', i.e. the villagers' meadow.[1] This does not, of course, prove that an allocation of *parcels* took place under lordly direction; it is only guesswork which rationalises two pieces of later evidence: the prevalence of intermingled parcels in the fields and meadows, and the concept of a virgate as a holding of a standard size. It also draws upon examples from a later and different set of circumstances when parcels of arable and meadow were allocated by lot. Nevertheless, the possibility of such lordly direction is real, and it follows reasonably from the argument advanced earlier that an institution appearing at one period in a single guise could have originated in several entirely different ways.

If the early growth of common field regulations be associated with strong lordship in early village society, can we grope our way towards a clearer notion of the strength of lordly authority in the East Midlands by following its footprints in place-names and in the archaeological record? Many Anglo-Saxon place-names consist of the elements 'tun' and 'ham', preceded by a personal name. 'Ham' is the more ancient suffix with a more lordly connotation: examples in the East Midlands are Syresham (Northants.) – Sigehere's Ham – and Ingham (Lincs.) – Inga's Ham – but they are relatively uncommon.[2] 'Tun' signifies a more humble settlement, originally a farmstead, later a hamlet or village, and these are more numerous in the East Midlands: e.g. Chadstone (Northants.) – Ceadd[i]'s t un; Darlton (Notts.) – Deorlufa's tun. Some of these place-names are known to date from the early period of Anglo-Saxon settlement and seem to signify the settlements of men, accompanied by their families or other followers, carving out farms and creating larger settlements under their leadership or authority. But the exact nature of their leadership eludes us. Some, or indeed all the elders may have been free men, subject only to the requirement of acknowledging lordship; but what in turn was their relationship to their followers and how did that relationship survive

[1] Stenton, *Danelaw Documents*, p. xli. See also T. H. Aston, *Trans. R. Hist. Soc.*, VIII, 1955, p. 71.
[2] A. H. Smith, *English Place-Name Elements*, I, 1956, p. 229.

in the next generation? Men who freely attached themselves to a kinsman or leader in one generation could have no assurance that all their heirs, generations later, would continue freemen; similarly the serfs of one generation could by various means escape their bonds in another. It is true that by 1086 there was a higher than average number of *liberi homines* in the East Midlands, but it is impossible to tell whether this situation was a survival, or a change, from the situation at the beginning of Anglo-Saxon settlement. The free men of 1086 may have been descended from those who managed to preserve their free status from the sixth to the eleventh centuries; or they may equally well have achieved this status in course of time, profiting most of all perhaps from the disturbance caused by the Scandinavian incursions.[1]

Not all the Anglo-Saxon 'tuns' are equally reticent about their origins, however. Many east Midland villages bear the name Charlton or Carlton. The 'ceorl' in Old English charters was at one time considered to be a synonym for a 'free peasant'. But the geographical and tenurial circumstances of many Carltons and Charltons (= ceorls' tuns) do not suggest free status. They are mostly settlements, appendant to other manors which were royal or had at some time been carved out of royal demesne as gifts to favoured subjects. Moreover, the Charltons lie so near the lord's demesne as to suggest that they bore this distinctive name because they contributed to its upkeep, i.e. they were populated by husbandmen doing labour services on a royal estate.[2]

Clues to the structure of early Anglo-Saxon society are meagre indeed. Perhaps they hint more at serfdom than freedom among the earliest Anglo-Saxon settlers, and so introduce us to a society of lords and dependents that was already feudal.[3] But it is no more than a convention to start the history of English society with the Anglo-Saxons. It may well be true that many villages which have Anglo-Saxon or Danish place-names were founded by these people. But we cannot wipe the whole East Midland slate clean at the end of the Roman occupation, and start afresh with a new set of colonists moving into England from the late fifth century and occupying virgin territory. Some villages with Danish names are known to have borne earlier Anglo-Saxon names; some so-called Anglo-Saxon settlements are known to have borne an earlier Celtic name. Some Celtic names survived more or less unscathed. Some settlements – Breedon among them – lie on or near prehistoric hill forts, a fact which hints at, though

[1] Smith, *Place-Name Elements*, II, 1956, pp. 188ff.; H. P. R. Finberg, *Lucerna. Studies of some Problems in the Early History of England*, 1964, pp. 148–9.
[2] Finberg, *Lucerna*, pp. 144–60.
[3] T. H. Aston, *Trans. R. Hist. Soc.*, VIII, 1955, pp. 60–2, 74.

it does not, of course, prove, some continuity from the Iron Age.[1] Even Anglo-Saxon place-names speak of the presence of communities of British or Welsh surviving from an earlier age in the midst of a predominantly Anglo-Saxon countryside. Walton means 'the tun of the Britons or British serfs'; Walcot means 'the cottage of the Welsh or serfs'. There is a Walton on the Wolds and a Walcott in Leicestershire; in Lincolnshire there is a Walcot near Billinghay, a Walcot near Folkingham, and a Walcot near West Halton; Northamptonshire has a Walcot near Barnack, and Walcot Lodge in Fotheringhay.[2] Other traces of the survival of Celtic settlements into a later period have been found in the tenurial structure of manors which in Domesday times embraced many small hamlets, some of which included a Walcot or Walton. Their lords, it is suggested, were supported by communities of bondmen, living together in these small hamlets, occupying and cultivating small family plots in return for labour services and dues to their lord. They were a survival from the Celtic 'maenor' which was a discrete estate comprising a focal settlement with a court and a number of appendant bond hamlets. The focal settlement or 'mansio' of Walcot near Folkingham was Folkingham itself, that of Walcote near Billinghay was probably Branston. West Halton (Lincs.) was another centre of a discrete estate, while other possible examples which require further investigation were Breedon (Leics.), Oakham (Rut.), King's Sutton (Northants.) and Mansfield (Notts.).[3] In labelling these estates Celtic, however, their ethnic origins are not clearly defined, nor is their date of origin finally established. The evidence associates many of them with the building of the hill forts in the Iron Age, and takes us back to between 200 and 100 B.C. Even then there is nothing to disprove a still earlier origin for this kind of territorial organisation.[4]

If we begin to contemplate the structure of communities inhabiting the East Midlands in the Iron Age, it is unrealistic to suppose that they had no influence upon the later shape of the fields and the pattern of land occupation. Glanville Jones who has done so much to uncover traces of these Celtic estates from later documents sees the influence of the Anglo-Saxons and Danes in their adaptation of the existing framework rather than in a complete remodelling of estates and landscape. They did not occupy virgin or depopulated land, but

[1] Sawyer, *Univ. of Birmingham Hist. Jnl.*, VI, 1958, p. 10; G. R. J. Jones, 'Early Territorial Organization in England and Wales', *Geogr. Annlr.*, XLIII, 1961, pp. 180, 176–8.
[2] A map showing the distribution of these place-names in England and Wales is in G. R. J. Jones, *Geogr. Annlr.*, XLIII, 1961, p. 179.
[3] G. R. J. Jones in a personal letter to the author.
[4] Jones, *Geogr. Annlr.*, XLIII, 1961, *passim*.

rather 'adapted a pre-existing and in large measure surviving territorial organization'. Even the 'soke' which has often been regarded as a Danish innovation was simply a Danish name for the discrete Celtic estate.[1]

To sum up, then, in the Celtic period there already existed in the hill and vale country of the East Midlands, and particularly in Lincolnshire, some single farmsteads, of the kind usually associated with Celtic settlement, as well as estates composed of a central 'mansio' with bond hamlets. In Roman times new additions to the landscape took the same varied physical form: some were small isolated farms, some more substantial villas, and some closely knit hamlets. In the fenland of Holland, the first settlements of which we have any archaeological record date from the Iron Age. These were supplemented, and in some cases displaced, by others in the early Roman period (c. A.D. 50–80). Two generations later, probably under the direct encouragement of Hadrian, larger hamlets appeared and roads and canals were built. However, later flooding reduced the number of these settlements, as people were forced to remove on to the higher silt ridges. In the forests, settlement started last of all, in the later Anglo-Saxon period, but there are notable exceptions to this general statement which remind us of the neglected state of studies on the English forests, and warn us to be cautious in passing sweeping judgements in our present state of knowledge: an elaborate villa at Mansfield Woodhouse proves the existence of civilised life in Sherwood Forest in Roman-British times, while the name Clumber indicates the continued presence there of Britons into the Anglo-Saxon period.[2]

By pushing our enquiry into the origins of settlement in the East Midlands back to the Iron Age, if no further, we find ourselves groping for the beginnings of field systems in almost unrelieved darkness. But we place the question of their origin in better perspective. Small communities of settled peasants go back into prehistory. The Anglo-Saxon and Danish invasions introduced additional numbers, but the problems of agricultural cooperation were already present. Even if the pressure of lordly authority upon the peasantry was less harsh in some places than in others, nevertheless everywhere some accepted code of neighbourly behaviour in agricultural routine was

---

[1] G. R. J. Jones, 'Early Territorial Organization in Northern England and its Bearing on the Scandinavian Settlement', *The Fourth Viking Congress*, 1965, pp. 71–2.

[2] S. Frere, *Britannia. A History of Roman Britain*, 1967, pp. 264–7, 276; Peter Salway, 'New Light on Fens under the Romans', *The Times*, 1 Feb. 1963; C. Thomas (ed.), *Rural Settlement in Roman Britain*, C.B.A. Research Report no. 7, 1966, pp. 15–18, 21, 24, 27, 99–100; Gover, Mawer, and Stenton, *Place-Names of Nottinghamshire*, p. xv.

imperative from the moment that the first head of a household, dwelling in a community, divided land among his children and set each on the path to independence. In many circumstances, of course, even in the thirteenth century, neighbourly agreements were adequate to protect everyone's interests. The lawbooks of this period generally discuss common rights of grazing in terms of rights agreed between neighbours. The notion survived in charters of the twelfth and thirteenth centuries which appealed to 'the custom of neighbours', 'the laws of neighbouring men'. Even when Englishmen went to America in the early seventeenth century, they managed their affairs on the same basis: proprietors of parcels in each individual field devised their own rules.[1] How long these casual and friendly agreements continued no doubt depended on the size of the community, the degree of land fragmentation, the authoritarian inclinations of lords and peasants, and the problems posed by the local agricultural routine. If all cultivators followed a simple two-course rotation of barley and fallow, or oats and fallow, then cropping and grazing on individual strips might perhaps proceed without much risk of conflict between neighbours. But when winter- and spring-sown grains were incorporated in a rotation and the number of tenants and animals increased, cropping seasons were diversified and it became more difficult to protect the harvest of each man. And it is the risk to the harvest which prompts the earliest bylaws that were inscribed in court rolls.

By the later twelfth century some holdings in Lincolnshire had land that was more or less evenly divided between two halves of the village.[2] This implies that a substantial group of tenants in these villages had agreed upon a field course and had divided their arable accordingly. Common grazing of the stubble – a commonsense solution to the problem of controlling animals which were grazing narrow strips of land – was being practised, in some cases by neighbours, in others by the whole community, from the late twelfth century.[3] By the later thirteenth century villages were beginning to record in court rolls some rules as well as the pains and penalties imposed on those who broke them. Casual and temporary expedients became systematised. It was all part and parcel of the drive for greater

---

[1] Thirsk, *Past and Present*, XXIX, pp. 16–17; Stenton, *Danelaw Documents*, p. lxi, n. 1; Ault, *Trans. Amer. Phil. Soc.*, LV, 1965, p. 10. See also the Statute of Westminster, 1285, legislating 'when two or more do hold wood, turfland or fishing, or other such thing in common': *Statutes of the Realm*, I, 83.

[2] F. M. Stenton (ed.), *Transcripts of Charters relating to the Gilbertine Houses of Sixle, Ormsby, Catley, Bullington, and Alvingham*, Lincs. Rec. Soc., XVIII, 1920, pp. 94, 97, *et passim*; Stenton, *Danelaw Documents*, pp. xxix, xxx–xxxii.

[3] Stenton, *Danelaw Documents*, pp. 332–3; C. W. Foster (ed.), *Registrum Antiquissimum of the Cathedral Church of Lincoln*, IV, Lincs. Rec. Soc., XXXII, 1937, p. 169.

administrative efficiency that was carried out by manorial lords in many parts of England. It was closely linked with the rise of population which magnified all administrative problems and made it impossible for men to continue satisfactorily with more casual arrangements. After the Black Death, when the numbers of cultivators fell drastically and many holdings went out of cultivation, the stringency with which some rules were enforced was probably relaxed. In some places the manorial court seems to have lost effective authority, and to have been supplanted by the village meeting; this, no doubt, reflected the changing balance of power between lord and tenants.[1] But as numbers rose again in the sixteenth century the documents recording village bylaws multiplied again and the authority of the manorial court was reasserted. Continuing pressure on the land accelerated the search for ways of relieving it, and among these enclosure made headway and finally killed the common field system. But because of the strength of corn-growing economies in the East Midlands, many common field systems survived relatively unscathed throughout the sixteenth and seventeenth centuries. It is in these villages that we find the most consistent and informative records on East Midland common field systems.

[1] W. O. Ault, 'Some Early Village By-laws', *Econ. Hist. Rev.*, XLV, 1930, pp. 208ff.

7

Field Systems of East Anglia

BY M. R. POSTGATE

A. INTRODUCTION

In his survey of the English agrarian landscape H. L. Gray outlined the main features of the open field system commonly found in East Anglia before enclosure, a system which he recognised as different and distinctive from the two- and three-field systems that were common in Midland England.[1] His interpretation of the visual pattern and terminology employed remains valid but subsequent investigation has modified to some extent his conclusions about the method of tillage. Also, although his largely ethnic explanations of the origins of this field system have withstood the test of time, increasing recognition has been given to the influence of the physical environment on the development of local variations within the region as a whole. Furthermore, geographical boundaries are seldom precise and later studies have also shown that many of the features of the Midland field system are known to have been practised outside the area in which Gray found them typical and many of the features which he ascribes to the East Anglian system were found in neighbouring areas of his Midland region. Southern or upland Cambridgeshire in particular was a transitional zone between two major regions and it is worthwhile, therefore, taking an occasional glance at this area when examining the main features of the East Anglian field system as evidenced in Norfolk and Suffolk in order to see the deformations from normal practice that were caused by the impingement of one field system upon the other.

Since the differential development of the local field system within East Anglia was affected by the physical environment, a brief summary of the major physical features of the region follows. The basic geology of East Anglia is relatively simple. The greater part of Norfolk and Suffolk is underlain by the Upper Chalk whose eastward dip exposes the upper horizons of the Lower Chalk along the eastern margin of Fenland in the low-lying cuesta of the East Anglian Heights. This ridge, an extension of the Chilterns, forms the watershed between the drainage systems of the Wash and the London Basin; it is well developed in southeast Cambridgeshire but becomes increasingly lower and more

[1] H. L. Gray, *English Field Systems*, Cambridge, Mass., 1915, pp. 305–54.

dissected towards the northeast. In the 25-mile stretch between Newmarket (Suff.) and Swaffham (Norf.) that is occupied by Breckland this ridge is hardly apparent and hardly more so when it reaches the Norfolk coast between Hunstanton and Sheringham. West of this ridge the Gault and Greensand outcrops in southern Cambridgeshire give way to Jurassic Clays and Limestone in the western part of that county but all are obscured further north by the marine deposits of the Fenland Basin. Above the Chalk in Norfolk and Suffolk there is a wide gap in the geological succession, the remaining Cretaceous and all the Tertiary deposits being absent except for scattered gravels of the latter series east of a line from Norwich to Bury St Edmunds.

Obscuring this comparatively simple basic geology, however, is a complex series of glacial tills which cover most of East Anglia. The principal deposit, Boulder Clay, varies in texture from a brown, calcareous clay, less than 25 feet deep in Breckland, to the heavy blue–grey clay that reaches depths of over 250 feet in the central parts of Norfolk and Suffolk. Associated with this Boulder Clay, especially in the coastal areas, are beds of glacial sand, gravel and brickearth, while estuarine deposits further complicate the drift geology of East Anglia.

Soils derived from this diverse parent material vary considerably in agricultural potential and are the basis of the subdivision of the region that is shown on Fig. 7.1. In northwest Norfolk the Boulder Clay is masked by warm, easily worked sands in Arthur Young's 'Good Sand' region[1] which give a natural sterility to the soil and rendered them relatively infertile before the introduction in the eighteenth century of systematic 'marling' or claying techniques and crop rotations involving leguminous plants. Similar soils are found in the coastal parts of Suffolk between the River Orwell and Yarmouth, an area still known as The Sandlings. To the south of the 'Good Sand' region the soil deteriorates into shallow wind-blown sands directly overlying the basal chalk which make Breckland, even today, an area that is regarded as sub-marginal for cultivation. To the east, in the hinterland of the Norfolk coast from Sheringham to Yarmouth, the soil is enriched by light loams similar to those found on the central plateau and eastern parts of southern Cambridgeshire. Between these areas of relatively light soils lie the heavier and inherently more fertile Boulder Clay soils of central Norfolk and Suffolk which cover one-third of the former county and two-thirds of the latter, and are similar in quality to the soils developed on the clays of western Cambridgeshire.

[1] A. Young, *A General View of the Agriculture of the County of Norfolk*, 1804, pp. 10–12.

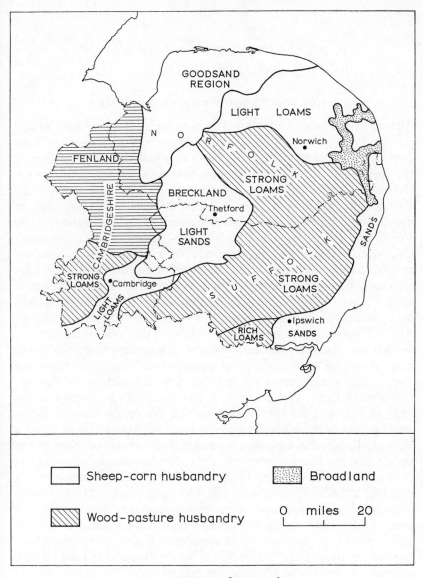

Fig. 7.1 Regions of East Anglia

B. FIELD SYSTEMS IN THE EARLY MODERN PERIOD

I. GROWING REGIONAL SPECIALISATION

Against a background of general fertility with local variations in soil potential can be set the agricultural history of East Anglia, with its development of regional specialisations that had a significant effect on the formation of local field systems. Owing to its proximity to the continent and its ability to support a relatively dense population, East Anglia has always been a region of increment, not only of population but also of new ideas and techniques of cultivation, while its position astride the main trade routes from London to the Low Countries facilitated the growth of a trade in agricultural produce that formed the basis of the regional economy from the Middle Ages onwards. In the fourteenth century the fame of the region rested on the export of wool and a developing local cloth industry, which, by providing prosperous employment to town dwellers, increased the demand for corn and meat and stimulated the local market trade. By the late sixteenth and early seventeenth centuries local industries were absorbing most of the wool produced and the export trade was sustained by grain from north and west Suffolk which passed through the ports of Lynn, Wells, Burnham and Yarmouth in Norfolk to the industrial areas of the Low Countries, and also up the Fenland waterways to the increasingly demanding London market. Local markets flourished and the cash nexus which had influenced agricultural production in many townships since the late fourteenth century, became more pronounced. Traditional methods of cultivation which acted as a brake upon innovation and agricultural efficiency were abandoned over large areas. New crops, crop rotations, methods of stock feeding and conditions of land tenure were introduced from the continent and their systematic application in the eighteenth century formed the basis of the 'Norfolk' husbandry that was to revolutionise agricultural practice as a whole and make famous the names of great Norfolk landowners such as Townshend, Coke, L'Estrange and Walpole.

One effect which the development of commercialised agriculture had was the increasing specialisation of local production, a phenomenon which had been evident even in the thirteenth century. The Suffolk Hundred of Blackbourne covers an area stretching from the infertile sandy soils of Breckland to the clay soils of the central part of the county and subsidy-returns for this area in 1283 reveal marked variation in agricultural produce between these two areas.[1] Thus, while barley was the main crop in both areas its predominance was most marked in the former and frequently amounted to over half of the total crop production. Wheat, absent altogether in central Breckland parishes, was the second most important crop in central Suffolk while the reverse was true for rye. Oats, of considerable importance in the former area, ranked only third in the latter, while the growth of peas and beans was noticeably concentrated in the central clay districts. Examination of stock-returns shows a similar situation. Flock totals in Breckland averaged over 800 per township and were four times the size of those in the central Suffolk area. Sheep represented nearly 50 per cent of the total wealth in the former area, as much as the remainder of the stock and all the crops together, but accounted for only 10 per cent of the total wealth of townships in the latter area and ran a poor second to the income derived from cattle.

Already the main lines of regional production were evident and with the rise of a market economy and the declining demands of a quasi-subsistence agriculture they became even more apparent. The main distinction lay between the unshaded and shaded portions of Fig. 7.1. For sixteenth- and seventeenth-century Norfolk, K. J. Allison termed these areas the Sheep–Corn Region, characterised by open arable fields and equally extensive heaths, and the Wood–Pasture Region where open fields and heathland were less extensive, there was more wood and enclosure had progressed more rapidly.[2] In the former region large flocks of sheep dunged or 'tathed' the light soils and made the area famous for its barley production. In the latter region conditions were more favourable for the development of good grassland, and cattle formed the basis of the economy. This distinction was equally applicable to Suffolk at that time and contemporary topographers were in no doubt that it provided one of the most obvious and enduring features of the East Anglian landscape. One writer noted that Norfolk was 'compounded and sorted of soyles apt for grayne and sheep and of soyles apt for the wood and pasture'[3] while R. Reyce, writing in 1618, noted that in Suffolk, 'the soyle receveth not in every place once certain kind but in some places, as among the enclosures, it is heavy with clay and sometime intermixed with Chalks, in other places, as neare the Champion, it is lighter and

[1] E. Powell, *A Suffolk Hundred in 1283*, 1910.
[2] K. J. Allison, 'The Sheep–Corn Husbandry of Norfolk in the Sixteenth and Seventeenth Centuries', *Agric. Hist. Rev.*, V, 1957, pp. 12–14.
[3] Norwich Public Library (hereafter Norwich P.L.) Ms. 2641 (undated, 17th cent.).

with a variable and sandy earth'.[1] In the former area he noticed that 'the woodland and pasture is sustayned chiefly by graseinge, by Deyries and rearinge of Cattell' while 'the Champion parte is of another nature, consistinge wholly in effect of Corne and Sheepe'.

The successful integration of sheep and corn production in the western parts of Norfolk and Suffolk was praised by one observer who noted that 'the barren heaths...by the compasture of sheep (which we call Tathe) are made so rich with Corne that when they fall to be sowne, they commonly match the fruitfullest grounds in other counties'.[2] Barley remained the dominant crop in this region, so much so that a complaint was registered in 1642 that its cultivation had caused a scarcity of bread corn 'the husbandmen choosinge rather to sow barlye than wheate or rye, by reason of his readie vent thereof'.[3] Nevertheless, the region as a whole produced more corn of all sorts than was required by its population and the surplus was sent to neighbouring counties and London or was exported through the ports of the east coast. In 1662 Justices of the Peace for Suffolk noted that 'we are continually relieved with corn out of Norfolk and Cambridge...for our County consists of the Champion...which doth not only serve itself with corn but is forced continually to supply the woodland, especially in cold wet years'.[4]

Analysis of contemporary estate records confirms these observers' impressions of the appearance and productivity of the land. In 1698 the manor of West Harling, Middle Harling, Hockford and Bridgham in west Norfolk contained 1,000 acres of open arable land, 400 acres of heath land and virtually no meadow or improved pasture[5] while the nearby manors of Eriswell cum Chamberlains and Elveden in Suffolk contained 3,500 acres of arable, 10,500 acres of heathland and only 530 acres of meadow and pasture.[6] In the 'Good Sand' region to the northeast the manor of Wymondham possessed 820 acres of arable, 400 acres of improved pasture and 620 acres of mixed arable and pasture lands.[7] Further east, on the rich loams and alluvial soils of

[1] R. Reyce, *A Breviary of Suffolk*, 1618, transcript in B.M., Harleian (Harl.) Ms. 873, also edited by W. Hervey (1902).

[2] Sir Henry Spelman, information on Norfolk contributed to Speed's *The Theatre of the Empire of Great Britaine*, 1611.

[3] Ms. printed by W. Rye (ed.), *State Papers relating to Musters, Beacons, Shipmoney etc. in Norfolk, from 1625 to 1642*, 1907, p. 180.

[4] P.R.O., State Papers (SP) 14/128, no. 65.

[5] Norwich P.L., Ms. 6495.

[6] Mss. in the possession of the earl of Iveagh of Elveden Hall, Suffolk (Elveden Mss.), 22. H. II.

[7] P.R.O., Augmentations Office (Aug. Office), Miscellaneous Books (Misc. Books), 360, quoted by J. Spratt, 'Agrarian Conditions in Norfolk and Suffolk, 1600–1650', unpublished M.A. thesis, University of London, 1935, pp. 199–200.

Broadland and in the northeast corner of Suffolk, where dairy produce provided the mainstay of the economy, little reference is made to the produce from arable land in seventeenth-century tithe custumals. From this area, between Easter and Michaelmas 1601, 1,200 barrels of butter and 1,195 cheeses were shipped to London from Walberswick and Southwold alone while surveys of Stockton (Suff.) and Stradbrooke (Suff.) in 1608 shows that 60 to 70 per cent of their land lay under pasture.[1]

2. THE SPREAD OF ENCLOSURES

The main effect which the increasing specialisation and commerciali-sation of agriculture in the late sixteenth and seventeenth centuries had on the development of East Anglian field systems was to encourage the spread of enclosure, particularly in the central and eastern districts. Informal piecemeal enclosure had long been apparent throughout East Anglia, however, and references to 'terras inclusas', to single open field strips enclosed as 'pightles', or to 'crofts' or strips that were 'partly enclosed' are commonplace in land charters from the thirteenth century onwards. Usually such entries referred to small parcels of 5 acres or less but at Thetford (Norf.) in 1549 'duas pec. de terra in campis' amounted to 120 acres[2] while the demesne at Ixworth (Suff.) in 1627 contained 123 acres 'inclosed in ye feeld' and 221 acres 'lying open in ye feeld'.[3] The preliminary processes of piecemeal enclosure, the consolidation of sufficient strips of land in the open fields to justify such action and the eradication of intervening grass balks marking former property limits, can be seen in references to 'two or three strips now plowed together' or to parcels of land 'sometimes dyvers pieces', as at Kennett, Kentford and Eriswell (Suff.) in 1563.[4]

Not that the consolidation of ownership was a necessary preliminary to such enclosure. Five persons held strips within an arable close at Tostock (Suff.) in 1561 and there were fourteen 'pieces' in another close called Fulwell Field in the same parish.[5] This agreement to enclose contiguous parcels under different ownership undoubtedly facilitated informal enclosure and can be recognised in such references as 'tres pecie divise in Lyckemillecroft' as early as the thirteenth

[1] P.R.O., Aug. Office, Misc. Books 413; P.R.O., Lands and Revenues (LR.), 2/203, quoted by Spratt, M.A. thesis, p. 204; P.R.O., Port Books of Yarmouth 482/4.
[2] Elveden Ms., unpublished collection for a history of Elveden by the Rev. George Burton (EHC) (1740).
[3] P.R.O., Ms. Duchy of Lancaster (DL) 43/7/29, 15 Eliz; B.M. Harl Ms. 368, fo. 171.
[4] West Suffolk Record Office (West Suffolk R.O.), Ms. 1563; Elveden Ms. 32/K. 120.
[5] West Suffolk R.O., Ms. 553/39.

century.[1] However, the substitution of scattered holdings by compact ones, either by purchase or formal agreement between landlord and tenant, was the usual prelude to enclosure. In 1523 Fitzherbert noticed this process in Suffolk: 'every tenant is to change with his neighbour and to laye their (strips) together and to make him one several close in every field'.[2] Kent noted a similar process in Norfolk at the end of the eighteenth century, one that had long been familiar in that county; 'whenever a person can get four or five acres together, he plants a white thorn hedge round it and sets an oak at every rod distance, which is consented to by a kind of general courtesy from one neighbour to another.'[3] One impediment to such enclosure was noted by Marshall who saw that it was common for the final consolidation of holdings to be delayed by strips of glebe land,[4] a natural enough phenomenon as the receipt of tithes hardly encouraged incumbents to take an interest in the management of their lands. Glebe lands, therefore, figure prominently in exchanges of land prior to final enclosure. At Wilton (Norf.) in 1635 Mr Dersyngham exchanged twenty-nine acres in Great West Field, thirty-two acres in East Field and twenty-two acres in North Field for equivalent amounts of glebe land,[5] while the lord of the manor of Elveden (Suff.) in 1706 gave the parson two contiguous blocks, each of forty-four acres, in exchange for eighty-eight acres of glebe land 'in above six score pieces' which alone fragmented his demesne land.[6] In both cases the parties concerned were given licence to enclose as they saw fit. Similarly at Walton in east Suffolk in 1613 a close 'latelie taken out of Langland Field, late of divers persons' belonged to one person except for two strips, each of less than half an acre, of which one belonged to the vicar.[7]

This process of piecemeal enclosure had progressed to a considerable extent in the central and eastern districts of Norfolk and Suffolk by the end of the seventeenth century. Gray, when examining the Norwich Hospitals' Estates in nineteen townships in the vicinity of the city, found that 80 per cent of the total land was enclosed by 1714, but as much of this had been recently reclaimed from the waste, he inferred that not more than half of the open fields in this area

[1] P.R.O., Ancient Charter A. 3138, temp. Edw. I, quoted by Gray, *English Field Systems*, p. 310.
[2] A. Fitzherbert, *Book of Surveying and Improvements*, 1523, fo. 53.
[3] N. Kent, *A General View of the Agriculture of Norfolk*, 1796, p. 22.
[4] W. Marshall, *The Rural Economy of Norfolk*, I, 1787, p. 8.
[5] Norwich P.L., Ms. 18262.
[6] Elveden Mss. 24/J. 16 and 29/M. 30; Elveden Ms. EHC (1740).
[7] East Suffolk Record Office, Ms. 50/1/74 quoted by E. D. R. Burrell, 'An Historical Geography of the Suffolk Sandlings', M.Sc thesis, University of London, 1959, p. 42.

had been enclosed by this time.[1] Further evidence suggests, however, that this is a conservative estimate and that only a small amount of open field land still survived in the central and eastern districts of East Anglia by the end of the seventeenth century. At Glemsford (Suff.) in 1621 there were at least eight open 'fields' but less than 5 per cent of its total land is recorded in strips lying within them.[2] At Aylsham (Norf.) in the same year only 24 out of the 2,171 acres surveyed were recorded as 'field land',[3] as were 253 out of the 2,424 acres that were surveyed at Stockton (Suff.).[4] In east Suffolk all the open arable land of Trimley and Falkenham was enclosed by 1613 while that at Walton, fragmented into numerous irregular open fields of widely varying size that were interspersed among extensive areas of enclosed land, reflected the widespread decay of the open field system in this area.[5] Even some townships in northwest Norfolk and on the borders of Breckland, such as Little Ryborough, Wolferton and Hargham, had over 50 per cent of their land enclosed by the end of the seventeenth century.[6]

In the face of such uniform evidence it is not surprising to find that contemporary observers and later writers bore witness to the extent to which the open land of Norfolk and Suffolk had been enclosed by this time. As early as 1573 Tusser had referred to Suffolk as a 'typical enclosed county'[7] while Norden remarked in 1608 that the county was notable for its furze hedges.[8] Scrutton said of Suffolk that enclosure seemed to have been completed by the sixteenth century, if not earlier,[9] while Gray noticed that enclosure awards for both Norfolk and Suffolk parishes after 1750 showed little surviving open arable land.[10]

Such evidence is somewhat deceptive, however, for large areas of open field survived right up until Parliamentary enclosure, particularly in northwest Suffolk and west and north Norfolk. Marshall writing in 1787, although he called east Norfolk 'a very old-inclosed country',

---

[1] Gray, *English Field Systems*, p. 308.
[2] P.R.O., LR. 2/203, quoted by Spratt, M.A. thesis, p. 39.
[3] P.R.O., Aug. Office, Misc. Books 360, quoted by Spratt, M.A. thesis, p. 41.
[4] P.R.O., LR. 2/201, quoted by Spratt, M.A. thesis, p. 41.
[5] East Suffolk R.O., Ms. 50/1/74.
[6] B.M., Stowe Ms. 765; Harl. Ms. 247; Additional (Add.) Mss. 36536, 39248, quoted by Spratt, M.A. thesis, p. 43.
[7] T. Tusser, 'Comparison between Champion County and Several', from *Five Hundred Points of Good Husbandrie*, ed. J. H. Parker, 1848.
[8] J. Norden, *Surveyor's Dialogue*, 1607, quoted by W. E. Tate, 'A Handlist of Suffolk Enclosure Acts and Awards', *Proc. Suffolk Institute of Archaeology*, xxv, 1951, p. 242.
[9] J. Scrutton, *Commons and Common Fields*, 1907, p. 144.
[10] Gray, *English Field Systems*, p. 305.

also noted extensive common fields towards the north coast and in the southern Hundreds of the county.[1] Similarly Young remarked that Suffolk must be one of the earliest enclosed of all counties but that there existed large tracts in the western districts 'which still awaited the benefits of this first and greatest of all improvements'.[2] Tate confirmed this regional distinction in his analysis of Suffolk enclosure awards which showed that out of 30 awards for east Suffolk only six concerned themselves with open arable land, which was dealt with in 43 out of 54 awards relating to west Suffolk parishes.[3]

It is to these western districts, therefore, that we must look for the clearest evidence of the former open field system in East Anglia as that of the central and eastern districts was rapidly disappearing when the first adequate cartographic record and systematic township surveys made their appearance in the late sixteenth and seventeenth centuries. These surveys illustrate not only the pattern of subdivision of the land and the method by which it was tilled but also those elements of the regional field system which afforded the seeds of its own eventual destruction. Using this unequivocal evidence as a datum it is possible to trace the origins of this field system back through a plethora of earlier charters to pre-Conquest times and to show that the patterns which were still commonplace in western Norfolk and Suffolk and eastern Cambridgeshire in 1650 were once typical of the whole of East Anglia.

3. FIELD ARRANGEMENTS

A cursory glance at these surveys shows a tripartite division of the open arable land into units of descending order of magnitude similar to that commonly found in Midland townships.[4] The only difference appears to be one of terminology; instead of 'fields', 'furlongs' and 'selions', enumeration of the parcels of individual owners commonly proceeds by 'precincts', 'stadia' or 'quarentinae' and 'pecia'. It soon becomes clear, however, that the first and second order subdivision of the land were not used in the same technical sense as they were in the Midlands. Precincts, for example, were often of widely different sizes within the same township and could not be equated with particular courses in the cropping rotation. They were, in fact, arbitrary divisions of the township's cultivated land, both arable and pasture, open and

---

[1] Marshall, *Rural Economy of Norfolk*, pp. 4, 8.
[2] A. Young, *A General View of the Agriculture of Suffolk*, 1797, p. 30.
[3] Tate, *Proc. Suffolk Inst. Arch.*, xxv, 1951, p. 240.
[4] W. J. Corbett, 'Elizabethan Village Surveys', *Trans. R. Hist. Soc.*, xi, 1897, pp. 67–87.

enclosed, which were delineated by highways or other salient topographical features. They were used solely as a guide to the location of
landholdings and were not universally employed in all surveys, even
in those of the same township that were drawn up at different dates.
Gray noted that, in the sixteenth century, East Carleton (Norf.) and
Hethilde (Norf.) were each divided into five precincts while Burnham
Sutton (Norf.) had three and Weasenham (Norf.) had two.[1] Such
subdivision into between three and nine precincts was typical of
East Anglian custom but occasionally a surveyor's enthusiasm for
accurate reference is reflected in further subdivision. A field book for
Great Barton (Suff.) in 1612 records no less than 37 precincts, all of
which are carefully numbered and delineated.[2] Thus the fourteenth
precinct was bounded by Millhillpathwaye to the west, Millhillwaye
to the south, Westhallwaye to the east and Westhallane to the north.
In the first precinct of this township there were 16 pasture closes,
totalling 250 acres in extent and designated 'meadowes', 'pitells' or
'yardes', while the second precinct contained but two 'pitells' of
three and four acres respectively. In contrast precinct number 27
contained 15 'stadia', each with between three and 15 parcels of
individual owners.

That precincts were employed entirely for purposes of reference
at Great Barton is evident by comparing this survey with another
that was made in 1566 in which no mention is made of them.[3]
Enumeration of the land in this case proceeded in the first instance
by stadia, but just as precincts could not be equated with Midland
fields neither could stadia with Midland furlongs. They were far
more variable in size and, like precincts, referred equally to meadow
and pasture land to as open arable. The sixth stadia in the fourth
precinct at Great Barton in 1612, for example, contained 35 acres of
meadow known as St Edmund's Watering, while the quarentinae at
Narford (Norf.) in 1473 and Great Hockham (Norf.) in 1599 varied
between one and a half and over 100 acres in extent.[4]

Only when examining the third order subdivision of cultivated land
in surveys of East Anglian townships do we find the nearest equivalent
to Midland custom. This is not surprising as pecia and the Midland
selion served the same function as the basic unit of ploughland. As in
the Midlands, the need for ploughteams to take periodic rests dictated
that the majority of pecia were approximately one furlong in length

[1] B.M., Stowe Ms. 870; Rawlinson Ms. B. 390; Holkham Ms., quoted by Gray,
   English Field Systems, p. 314.
[2] West Suffolk R.O., Ms. 645/1.
[3] West Suffolk R.O., Ms. 643/2.
[4] Norwich P.L., Ms. 11353; Norwich P.L., Ms. 18713.

and half an acre in area. The widespread occurrence of half-acre strips as the basic unit of tenure in East Anglian surveys shows that they were usually coincident with pecia. The variety of soils and the ease with which they could be ploughed, however, is evident in the variation of the area of pecia from a little over one rood at Methwold (Norf.) in 1545[1] to three roods at Merton (Norf.) in the late fourteenth century.[2] As in the Midlands, 'butts', 'gores' and 'shortlonds' were commonly used to define the division of stadia attenuated by topography or the pattern of neighbouring strips.

While precincts, stadia and pecia were terms that were widely employed throughout East Anglia and serve as distinguishing features of the regional field system, they were not used as ubiquitously or uniformly as were field, furlongs and selions in the Midlands. Precincts appear to have been restricted to Norfolk and Suffolk but stadia were also recorded in surveys of several townships in upland Cambridgeshire. In all three counties the term stadia was often employed in association with the Midland terms furlong and quarentinae, even within the same township. At Carbrooke (Norf.), for example, a sixteenth-century lease of two strips of land records that both lay in the same field, one in a 'quarentina vocat Lyttle Thorne', the other in a 'stadio vocat Longe Furlonge'.[3] Other terms employed to describe units of similar size to furlongs were 'shotts', 'wents' and 'wongs'.

Perhaps the most confusing of all terms that appear in surveys of East Anglian townships, however, is 'field' which was used indiscriminately for either the first or second order subdivision of the land. Narford (Norf.) in 1473 contained a 'Westfeyld' and an 'Estfeyld', comprising 47 and 42 quarentinae respectively,[4] while Walsingham (Norf.) in 1485 possessed North, West and East Fields, each approximately equal in area.[5] Here field patterns resembled those of typical Midland townships. More commonly, however, fields were as inconsequent as precincts, being determined by topography, the relative position of highways or points of the compass. In the sixteenth century Marham (Norf.),[6] Tostock (Suff.)[7] and Brandon Ferry (Suff.)[8] had 5, 9 and 12 fields respectively, all of widely differing sizes. At Sporle with Palgrave (Norf.) in 1646[9] an East and a West field had been added to the North and South fields which had existed there in 1566[10] and

[1] Norwich P.L., Ms. 4071; P.R.O., Ms. DL. 43/7/29 (15 Eliz.).
[2] Mss. in the possession of Lord Walsingham at Merton Hall, Norfolk (Merton Mss.) (undated, 14th cent.).
[3] Norwich P.L., NRS. 21195.   [4] Norwich P.L., Ms. 11353.
[5] Norwich P.L., Ms. 135.   [6] Norwich P.L., Ms. 3335.
[7] West Suffolk R.O., Ms. 645/Z.
[8] Norwich P.L., Ms. D.S. 74; Norwich P.L., Ms. 3993.
[9] Norwich P.L., Ms. 20877.   [10] Norwich P.L., Ms. 20876.

comparison of furlong names at both dates shows that Estfeyld had been formed out of North and South Fields while Westfeyld was formed entirely from North Field. Lest it be thought that such re-organisation reflected a change in agricultural practice and not just a more refined survey for reference purposes it is worth noting that Northfeyld in the later survey contained 100 acres of woodland, 26 acres of pasture and numerous enclosed meadows but no arable land. Here the term field is equatable with precinct but elsewhere it was used with less discrimination. At Norton (Suff.) in 1561 Thurston and Church Fields were both divided into 'dyvers furlonges' many of which bore the title field;[1] Wangford (Suff.) in 1542 contained 18 stadia, two of which were known as Townfield and Eastfield,[2] while Mildenhall (Suff.) in 1618 contained over 40 fields, two of which bore the further appellation of furlong.[3]

Given that the basic unit of cultivated land in East Anglia and the Midlands, the pecia or the selion, were similar in appearance and function but that in the former region they were grouped into units of varying size whose main purpose was to assist in the location of tenurial strips rather than as units of cultivation, as in the Midlands, it is pertinent to ask how and when the distinction arose. The answer can best be given by a brief consideration of the processes involved in the development of mature open field patterns and an examination of how they affected certain townships in the transitional zone of southern Cambridgeshire, some of which developed along the lines of the Midland field system while others followed the East Anglian pattern.

C. MEDIEVAL FIELD SYSTEMS

The conversion of primitive shifting agriculture to permanent arable cultivation probably resulted in the transformation of transitional field plots into a pattern of strips that was farmed in common in order to benefit from co-aration and a greater facility for defence and ease of management in a largely self-sufficient community. This nucleus was expanded by the creation of assarts, either by individuals or small groups, a process which connected the growth of communal agriculture with the natural increase in the population. Although these intakes may have been farmed separately at first, they were eventually brought within the purlieu of the common field in order to gain the advantages of communal agriculture. The names of many, however, retained the

[1] Norwich P.L., Ms. 3681.
[2] Norwich P.L., Ms. 4071.
[3] P.R.O., Ms. DL. 43/9/6 (17 Jas. I).

patronymic prefix of their founders together with the suffix 'toft' or 'croft' as an indication of their initial enclosure from the waste. Sometimes these assarts were absorbed into existing common fields and sometimes they formed the basis of new ones. In either case the uniformity in cropping practice that was essential for the management of communal husbandry and the provision of grazing facilities for the township's stock on unsown arable land was achieved by the superimposition of regular cropping shifts, or areas reserved for the cultivation of particular crops, on to this haphazard agglomeration of embryonic fields. The consolidation of these shifts into two or three large open fields, each coincident with a course in the annual rotation of crops, represented the final development of a mature open field system, after which reclamation was undertaken communally and the resultant intakes were incorporated into existing fields as new furlongs.

This development from initial settlement to mature field system reached its fullest expression in Midland townships but in East Anglia it was usually interrupted at the penultimate stage, the superimposition of regular cropping shifts on to an irregular field pattern.[1] This distinction was already well established by the thirteenth century and earlier evidence is insufficient to identify the processes involved in the development of field systems. Fortunately, however, the settlement and reclamation of large areas of woodland on the Boulder Clays of west and southeast Cambridgeshire was delayed until the thirteenth century, when it was assiduously undertaken by the ecclesiastic landlords whose records provide an insight into the initial stages of the creation of field systems.

In western Cambridgeshire field systems developed according to the Midland pattern. Thus at Hardwick in 1215 the demesne arable land of the bishop of Ely still showed signs of recent assarting, two large parcels totalling 46¼ acres being located in two 'doles' or shares of assarted land while 74½ acres lay 'in diversis partices' in two embryonic fields.[2] Similarly at Little Gransden the demesne land of the bishop in 1251 lay in 22 parcels bearing such assart names as 'Stockinge', 'Dreyhirst' and 'Forestcruch'.[3] Assimilation of these assarts into the common field was evident in an earlier survey made in 1222 in which 11 out of these parcels were assigned to 'Northendestfeld

[1] For a detailed example, see M. Spufford, 'A Cambridgeshire Community. Chippenham from Settlement to Enclosure', *Occasional Papers, Dept. of Engl. Local Hist., Univ. of Leicester*, xx, 1965.
[2] Ely Diocesan Registry (hereafter Ely D.R.), J. 1. (these records are lodged in the Cambridge University Library).
[3] B.M., Cotton Mss. (Cott.) Claudius (Claud.), C. xi, fo. 145.

cum pertinenciis'.[1] Like Hardwick this township supported a regular three-field system by 1615.[2]

In central Cambridgeshire, where the majority of field patterns had reached maturity by the thirteenth century, it is possible to infer a similar sequence of events to that in Hardwick and Little Gransden by comparing field and furlong names extant at that period with those found in later surveys. Thus the demesne arable at Melbourne and Meldreth in 1318 lay in numerous strips, many of them in crofts such as 'Schyuerescroft', 'Wynardscroft' and 'Sinekenescrofte', whose names recall their founders.[3] Among these assarts were Caluendenfeld and Foxoles Fields which doubtless formed the nuclei of the Cawdon and Foxholes Fields which survived in these parishes until Parliamentary enclosure. Commonly, many of the 'campi' recorded in townships of western Cambridgeshire in the thirteenth century can be identified with furlongs of later open fields. Thus 'Segenesfendenbrede', 'Ridunesbrede' and 'Milnebrede' (whose suffix records the allocation of land for reclamation) were recorded at Fen Ditton in 1251[4] and are identifiable with the Sedgefen, Royden and Mill Furlongs that were located in the three regular open fields of this parish at the time of its final enclosure.

Turning from central and western Cambridgeshire to the southeast of that county it is clear that the development of field systems occurred, not according to Midland custom, but according to that common in East Anglia. Thus the bishop of Ely possessed 21 'campi' at Balsham in 1251[5] and the dean and chapter of Ely a further 43 at West Wratting in 1318,[6] many of which bore assart names and were held in severalty, sometimes being described as 'clausae semper seperabilis et circumfossatis'. Some amalgamation into embryonic open fields was apparent at Balsham where the largest parcel of land, called 'Ayssele', contained 176¾ acres and was nearly three times the size of the next largest. At the time of its final enclosure, however, Balsham still contained 13 open fields of widely varying sizes. As in western Cambridgeshire assart names provide a lasting record of the expansion of the open fields but instead of being found among the furlong names of the sixteenth century and later, many assarts became fields in their own right. The names of five out of the eight 'campi' recorded amongst details of assarts at Ashley cum Silverley[7] in the thirteenth

[1] B.M. Cott. Tiberius (Tib.) B.ii, fo. 172.   [2] Ely D.R., I.8.
[3] Mss. in possession of the Dean and Chapter of Ely Cathedral (hereafter Ely D.C.), Extenta Maneriorum (1318).
[4] B.M., Cott. Claud. C.XI, fo. 115.
[5] B.M., Cott. Claud. C.XI, fo. 121.
[6] Ely D.C., Extenta Maneriorum (1318).
[7] B.M., Cott. Nero C.IX, fos. 49–133.

century and of four out of five at West Wratting in 1318[1] appear among the names of open fields in these parishes on their final enclosure in 1794 and 1809. Similarly the etymology of Stocking, Portway, Garth Row and Cotlow Fields at Balsham in 1811[2] can be traced back to 'campi' called 'Stockinge', 'Pytelowe', 'Garebrede' and 'Callowgrove' in 1251.[3]

The development of irregular field patterns out of the amalgamation of original assarts which is typical of the East Anglian field system raises the question of how they were organised for cropping purposes. Again a comparison of the practices carried out in townships of western and central Cambridgeshire with those in the southeast of that county illustrate the essential differences between the Midland and the East Anglian field system.

D. CROPPING PRACTICES

I. FIELDS AND COURSES

In western and central Cambridgeshire the main factor in the amalgamation of numerous irregular fields into two or three fields of approximately equal area was a superimposition of a pattern of cropping shifts corresponding to the common rotational practice of either one or two crops to one fallow. Assarts at Newton and Hauxton and at Melbourne and Meldreth were all allotted in approximately equal proportions to three 'culturae' in 1318 which probably coincided with cropping shifts.[4]

Although reference to the proportion of fallow land cannot be regarded *per se* as evidence of the field organisation, since the rotation which this signifies could be practised over an irregular field pattern, there is ample collateral for the symbiosis between field and cropping shifts in western and central Cambridgeshire. Thus, while 80 out of the 160 acres of demesne arable at Boxworth in 1338[5] were sown and the remainder 'nichil valent quia iacet in communi campo', the equal distribution of strips recorded in contemporary conveyances between the North and the South Fields of the township indicate the presence of a two-field system.[6] A more usual field system was the three-field under which the arable land was equally divided among fallow, winter

---

[1] Ely D.C., Extenta Maneriorum (1318).
[2] Cambridgeshire R.O., R. 50.7.6(12b); B.M., Cott. Claud. C.XI, fo. 121.
[3] B.M., Cott. Claud. C.XI, fo. 145.
[4] Ely D.C., Extenta Maneriorum (1318).
[5] P.R.O., Calendar Inquisitiones Post Mortem (Cal. I.P.M.), fo. 51 (ii) (2 Edw. III).
[6] B.M., Harl. Ms. 2697.

sown and spring sown shifts. Thus, while several terriers record the presence of West, More and North Fields at Madingley in the fourteenth century,[1] one of 1338 records that 'due partes possunt seminari quolibet anno...et tertia pars nihil valet quia iacet quolibet anno ad warectam et in communi'.[2] By the sixteenth century reference is commonly made to the 'wheat', 'barley' and 'fallow' (or to the 'Tilth', 'Breach' and 'Fallow') Fields in three-field townships of upland Cambridgeshire and the lasting effect which this rotation had on field patterns can be seen in the 22 townships of this region which practised this course over three equally sized fields in 1794.[3]

The close correlation between fields and courses which characterised regular field systems of the Midland type is evident in those townships of Cambridgeshire which adopted more complex patterns as a result of the adoption of more intensive crop rotations. Two-field patterns can be identified in several townships in southwest Cambridgeshire during the thirteenth and fourteenth centuries and since they all supported three-field systems by the sixteenth century it is a reasonable assumption that the creation of an additional field was inspired by the substitution of a two-course by a three-course rotation of crops. The introduction of pulse crops in the fourteenth century, as at Cottenham in 1322[4] where parts of the fallow land were sown with peas and beans, was often the reason behind the adoption of a four-field system for, when such 'inhoc' land obtained parity in the area with other sown shifts, field boundaries were usually redrawn to incorporate a new field. As early as 1300 the arable land at Shingay was fallowed only once in every four years[5] while one of the four fields of Melbourne in 1318 was devoted to winter corn, another to spring corn and the other two either lay fallow or else were sown with peas and beans.[6] Several fenland townships at this time possessed three-field systems but by the end of the fourteenth century, Witcham and Sutton at least followed rotations of three courses to one fallow[7] and the correlation between four fields and four-course rotations was evident in the neighbouring townships of Wicken, Isleham and Rampton in the eighteenth century, each of which followed a rotation of wheat, barley, peas, beans and oats, and fallow.[8] The logical

[1] St John's College, Cambridge, Ms. XXVII.1, XXV.2.100.
[2] P.R.O., Cal. I.P.M., fo. 46 (33) (10 Edw. III).
[3] C. Vancouver, *A General View of the Agriculture in the County of Cambridge*, 1794.
[4] Queens' College, Cambridge, Ad. 34. m. 17r.; F. M. Page, *The Estates of Crowland Abbey*, 1934, App. II.
[5] P.R.O., De Banco Roll. Hil. (28 Edw. I), m. 77d; B.M. Add. 21570, fo. 174.
[6] B.M., Add. 25866.   [7] Ely D.C., Liber 'G', fos. 11, 25.
[8] Cambridge U.L., bb.53(1).01; Cambridge R.O., R.50.7.27 and R.60.24.2.42; Pembroke College, Cambridge, A.13; Cambridge U.L., bb.53(1).01 and Ms.

development of this correlation was evident at Ely where only one-fifth of the arable demesne lay fallow in 1422[1] and a five-field system was practised by the end of the eighteenth century in which one field was devoted to wheat, two to barley, one to peas and beans while the last lay fallow.[2]

Even where the numbers of fields exceeded the number of cropping shifts in townships of western and central Cambridgeshire, a relatively simple field system was achieved by the combination of two or more fields for cropping purposes. In the East Fields of Cambridge in 1155, the prior and canons of Barnwell possessed 260 acres in Bradmerefeld and Meledich, 288 acres in Middelfeld and 240 acres in Fordefeld and Estenhale, the last two being considered 'pro uno campo' for cropping purposes.[3] The same arrangement was evident in 1632 when Sturbridge and Ford Fields were comprised the 'tilth' shift, Bradmore Field the 'breach' and Middle Field lay fallow.[4] At Teversham in 1636 it was recorded that 'Mylleditchfeld and Holmefeld make but one shift'[5] and similar linkages of two fields for cropping purposes can be found for most places in Cambridgeshire which contain four-field patterns that were cropped under three-course rotations.

In southeast Cambridgeshire, however, townships contained between 7 and 16 open fields of widely varying size by the sixteenth century and it was not so easy to combine any of them for cropping purposes if an equal ratio of sown to fallow land was to be maintained. The solution to this problem was found by superimposing a pattern of shifts asymmetrically on to the field pattern. Since a three-course husbandry was general throughout the area in the sixteenth and seventeenth centuries frequent reference is made to three 'common field shifts' or to the 'forecrop', 'after crop' and 'fallow' shifts. A similar non-correlation of field and shift pattern was to be found further west in the East Fields of Cambridge. Here, in 1474,[6] the fields were divided into 'the three severall seasons or times of plowinge', one of which in 1608 contained 'all Grethow Fild and the first furlong of Middilfelde', the second 'part of Middilfelde' while the third lay in two parts 'ye one a mile at least from ye other, ye one pte...is

Plans 177(R); Cambridge R.O., R.50.7.27 and R.60.24.2.42; Pembroke College, Cambridge, A.13; Vancouver, General View Cambridge, pp. 33, 134.
[1] Ely D.C., Liber 'G', fo. 6.
[2] P.R.O., H.O. 67/9; Cambridge U.L., Ms. Plans 122; Cambridge R.O., 2.50.7.11 (75B).
[3] B.M., Harl. Ms. 3601, fo. 35b.; J. W. Clark (ed.), 'Wayside Crosses in Cambridge', Cambridge Arch. Soc., 20, LXVIII, 1917, p. 98.
[4] Corpus Christi College, Cambridge, XIV.148.
[5] Gonville and Caius College, Cambridge, XIV.32.
[6] St John's College, Cambridge, Ms. XXXI.29.

called ye Colledge fild, it doe contayne Carmefelde, Lytilfelde and pte of Middilfelde'.[1]

The lack of correlation between field and shift that was evident in southeast Cambridgeshire was commonplace throughout Norfolk and Suffolk and, where no recognisable fields or precincts existed, groups of furlongs or strips were allocated to individual shifts. Gray produced evidence for a three-course cultivation in references to one-third of the demesne land lying fallow in townships in both eastern and western Norfolk and Suffolk,[2] thus fixing the custom on the region as a whole. That these courses were organised under a shift system of cultivation is evident from the numerous references made to this practice, as for example at Rushford, Ixworth and Elveden in Suffolk and at Stanford, Harling Methwold and Mundford in Norfolk during the period 1550–1670.[3]

Where a three-course rotation was found in conjunction with a pattern of three equally sized fields in East Anglia, a regular three-field system might emerge, as at Kennett (Suff.) where East, North and South Fields, each containing 12 furlongs, were alternatively known as Meadow, Bury Way and Willow Shifts in 1670.[4] Such symmetry was rare in East Anglia, however, as it was usual for shift boundaries to be flexible, frequently transgressing the boundaries of fields and stadia. Notes appended to a seventeenth-century terrier of Wangford (Suff.) recorded that 'Brakie fields were sown in A.D. 1643, which doth containe parts of Thankles furlongs, Middlebank furlonge, Downbanckes, Tanfield furlonge and Grangemere furlonge, 419 acres; Whitefields were sown in A.D. 1644 which doth contayne other part of Thankles furlonge, part of Middleweysty, Cowpit, Downdale and Garling furlonges, 407 acres; Sandys Shifts sowne in A.D. 1645, which doth conteyne Sleane furlonge, Garling furlonge, Wronglond, Long-wrongland, and Middleweysty.'[5]

A system such as that at Wangford, where cropping patterns were not restricted by field or furlong boundaries, was capable of adaptation to changing economic conditions by adjusting the proportion of land in fallow and sown shifts. The flexibility of this system was increased where there were more than the three shifts required by a three-course rotation of crops and it is significant that, where precincts did exist in Norfolk townships, they were commonly enumerated in multiples

[1] Corpus Christi College, Cambridge, Ms. XIV.143.
[2] Gray, *English Field Systems*, p. 332.
[3] Norwich P.L., Ms. 121 and 9995; B.M., Harl. Ms. 368, fo. 171; Townshend Ms. Garsett House, Norwich; Historical Mss. Commission Report, Gawdy Ms. 1221; P.R.O., DL. Ms. 43/7/29; Elveden Ms. EHC (1740).
[4] West Suffolk R.O., Ms. 647/2.
[5] Norwich P.L., Ms. 4071.

of three. In the 'Good Sand' region it was usual for one-third of any township's shifts to be left fallow each year but on the poorer soils to the south the proportion of fallow land was generally increased. Thus only one-third of the land recorded at Wangford (Suff.) between 1643 and 1645 was cropped in any year and details of Elveden (Suff.) in 1616 also reveal a high proportion of fallow land.[1]

> 'The six shiftes and feldes of Elden...are used to be tylled and eared as follows, vid; every year one of the said Feldes newly broken up and sowne with wynter corn and is called one year land, and the same felde the next year shall be sowne with somer corn and is then called two year land and the next year shall be broken up one other felde for wynter corne and pte of the said two year land shall also be sowne a third year and is then called three year land, and then it shall lye lay until all the feldes have been sowne in the like fashion and so every year one feld is newly broken up and beene always in tylthe the two feldes and part of the third feld and there are always three feldes in laye londe and part of the fourthe, upon which laye feldes the Foldcourse have their contynuall feed and have been anciently accustomed.'

Details of the crop rotation practised at Elveden in 1750[2] show little change from those recorded 150 years earlier while farms at nearby Merton (Norf.) and Tottington (Norf.)[3] at the end of the eighteenth century, even after consolidation of ownership and partial enclosure, were still divided into five shifts of which not more than two were to be sown in any year.

2. INFIELDS, OUTFIELDS AND BRECKS

The logical development of a flexible shift system of cultivation was its adaptation to the potential of different land within the same township. This resulted in the practice of dual crop rotations, the basis of the infield–outfield system that has been recognised as a common adaptation to the cultivation of unrewarding soils where the area of potentially cultivable land greatly exceeded that needed for the support of the population. Evidence for such a practice is abundant in Breckland. In 1327 Croxton (Suff.) contained quarentinae that were alternatively designated 'Infeldlond' or 'Utfeldlond'[4] while Stanford (Norf.) in 1560 supported six 'Outfield Shifts', cropped in rotation with not more than two successive crops of each, and four

---

[1] Elveden Ms., EHC (1740).
[2] Elveden Ms., EHC (1740).   [3] Merton Ms.
[4] B.M., Add. Ms. 34560, fos. 35ff.

'Infield Shifts', only one of which was left fallow each year.[1] That the boundary between infield and outfield land was arbitrary and subject to fluctuation was evident at Icklingham (Suff.) where the same land parcels were placed in different categories at different dates.[2] Nor was the infield land necessarily that which lay closest to the village since in 1702 and 1813 land so described was located over half a mile from Icklingham (Suff.) while outfield land appeared immediately west of the village street.[3] The infields did not necessarily form a central core or nucleus, and the outfields were not necessarily peripheral lands within a township. It was not in practice an infield–outfield system strictly in terms of the location of fields, but it was in principle, in terms of the rotation of crops.

The cultivation of infield and outfield land under rotations of different intensity persisted in Breckland until the era of Parliamentary enclosure and in some cases afterwards. At the end of the eighteenth century infield land at West Tofts,[4] Barnham[5] and Roudham[6] in Norfolk was cropped on a five-course and the outfield land on a six-course rotation while as late as 1854 a four-course rotation was practised over the demised land of Icklingham (Suff.) but only one-sixth of the 'outshift' land was cropped annually.[7] Across the county border in southeast Cambridgeshire outfield land was recorded at Burrough Green,[8] Brinkley,[9] Weston Colville[10] and Chippenham[11] at various times between the fifteenth and eighteenth centuries. At West Wratting (Cambs.) in 1757 the outfield land was let for 2s. 6d. per acre, in comparison with 6s. per acre for infield land, not however because of differences in soil quality but because the tenants of Jesus College, Cambridge 'had much land for little money and can easily make their Rents without it they do not chose to be at the expense and trouble of cultivating lands which lye remote'.[12]

Besides a differentially cropped infield and outfield Breckland also contained a third element in its field system, to which it owes its name. According to A. Simpson the cultivation of heathland intakes

[1] Townshend Ms., quoted by A. Simpson, 'The East Anglian Foldcourse: Some Queries', *Agric. Hist. Rev.*, VI, 1958, p. 94.
[2] West Suffolk R.O., Ms. E. 3/10/G.4 and G.2; Elveden Ms., Icklingham/F. 340 and G.10.
[3] Elveden Ms., Icklingham/C.28, G.10, G.77.
[4] West Suffolk R.O., Ms. E. 7/10/29.
[5] West Suffolk R.O., Ms. 654/2.
[6] Norwich P.L., Ms. 6722.
[7] Elveden Ms., Icklingham/J. 83.
[8] St Catharine's College, Cambridge, 13.14.   [9] Ely D.R., J.1.
[10] Cambridge R.O., L.89.15; St John's College, Cambridge, xxx.26.
[11] Cambridge R.O., R.55.7.1.
[12] Jesus College, Cambridge, Caryl. T.27.

beyond the open field probably occurred in this region 'as long as there had been flocks to make periodic cropping possible'[1] and reference to such 'brecks' are occasionally made in fourteenth- and fifteenth-century documents. By the sixteenth century these become more frequent and evidence such as that given at Kilverstone (Norf.) in 1592 was not uncommon; here it was said that one tenant 'some fifty years ago did plough up and sow with corne xii acres of heth groune adjoyning a fyld called Smythfyld'.[2] Presentments for 'sowing the lords heath', however, illustrate the opposition that existed towards this practice and it is unlikely that such brecks involved more than the appropriation of a few acres. For this reason the 800 acres recorded in nineteen brecks at East Wretham (Norf.) in the seventeenth century[3] and the 400 acres in the seven 'Brakes' of West Wretham (Norf.) at this time[4] must be regarded as outfield shifts in the common field.

During the eighteenth and early nineteenth centuries, however, the economic conditions which prevailed, particularly during the Napoleonic Wars, placed a premium upon corn production that was reflected in the reclamation of over one-fifth of existing Breckland. Heathland brecks developed from being mere appendages to the open fields until, in some cases, they exceeded it in area. East Hall Farm in Mundford (Norf.) in 1771 contained 73 acres of enclosed infield land, 136 acres of dispersed outfield land and 315 acres of 'brake' land[5] while another farm at Kentford (Suff.) in 1767 had 55 acres of enclosed arable, 403 acres in 'divers shifts' and 336 acres of heath land of which all but 16 acres were described as 'heath broke up' or 'newly enclosed'.[6] Such brecks, however, merely represented the expansion of land over which transient cultivation was practised and it is unlikely that they came under the plough more than once in ten years. It is significant that the Tithe Surveyors of 1840, at a time of relative agricultural prosperity in Breckland, recorded the utilisation of sixteen brecks at Elveden (Suff.) as 'heathland'.

The various elements that were recognisable in the field system of Breckland have been dealt with at some length because they throw light on the development of field systems on all the light soils of East Anglia and indeed on the origins of field systems in general. Some duality in cropping practice probably occurred as the natural result of the change from shifting to permanent agriculture, since the

[1] Simpson, *Agric. Hist. Rev.*, VI, 1958, p. 94.
[2] P.R.O., Ms. E.134 (35. Eliz.), 24 East.
[3] Norwich P.L., Ms. 10701.
[4] Norwich P.L., Ms. 10687; H. C. Darby and J. Saltmarsh, 'The Infield–Outfield System on a Norfolk Manor', *Econ. Hist.*, III, 1935, pp. 30–44.
[5] Norwich P.L., Ms. 18262.
[6] West Suffolk R.O., Ms. 339/6.

best land became a permanently cultivated and manured infield while the remaining arable land became a periodically tilled outfield. Beyond lay the open heath, interrupted in some places by scattered and only occasionally tilled brecks. More intensive cultivation, in response to increasing population or the profitability of corn production, would be reflected in the first instance, not in the expansion of the arable area, but in the spread of infield rotations into the outfield and the increasing permanence of temporary brecks. Eventually the original nucleus of the infield land, most likely cultivated under a three-course rotation, expanded until it absorbed the outfield which was then represented by the outlying brecks, until they in turn were absorbed into a uniformly tilled arable area.

Following the expansion of the intensively cultivated area came the tide of enclosure which had overtaken all but a few scattered remnants of the open fields in the central districts of Norfolk and Suffolk by the seventeenth century. In the 'Good Sand' region of northwest Norfolk, the process of expansion of the intensively cultivated area of the open fields was interrupted in the seventeenth century by the enclosure of the existing arable land as infield, while the heaths and commons were divided into enclosed brecks and became the outfield[1]. Only in Breckland could the regional field system still be recognised in various stages of development on the eve of Parliamentary enclosure. At Elveden (Suff.) some intensification of cultivation in the permanently tilled area was evident in the reorganisation, between 1616 and 1723,[2] of the six shifts of arable land occupying 1,980 acres into five shifts containing 2,307 acres, with a coincident increase in the proportion of sown to fallow land from $2\frac{1}{2}:3\frac{1}{2}$ to $3:2$. Beyond the open fields of this parish sixteen new brecks were formed in the eighteenth century. The dynamic process of enclosing the infield land, the expansion of infield into outfield areas and of outfields into brecks and heathland, is illustrated by the Enclosure Award for Hilborough (Norf.) which details 237 acres of 'Whole Year Closes', 186 acres of 'Half Year Closes' in the penultimate stage of enclosure, 581 acres of 'Infield' arable land, 628 acres of 'Outfield' arable land, 940 acres of 'Breck or Old Warren' and 420 acres of heath and sheep walk.[3]

3. THE FLEXIBILITY OF ROTATIONS

One of the advantages of a flexible shift system of cultivation was that it could easily be adapted to permit variations in the proportion of land devoted to particular crops and also enabled new crops to be

---

[1] Allison, *Agric. Hist. Rev.*, v, 1957, p. 29.   [2] Elveden Ms., EHC (1740).
[3] Enclosure Award with the Clerk of the Peace, Norwich.

introduced into traditional rotations with the minimum of disturbance. It is not surprising, therefore, once the necessity of producing a balanced ratio of the major grain crops had been obviated to some extent by the rise of a local market economy, that cropping patterns of East Anglian field systems began to show more variety than their Midland counterpart. The introduction of pulse crops into the fallow shift and the spring sown shift increased from the fourteenth century onwards and there were signs that the division between winter and spring sown crops was being disregarded by leaving part of the wheat or rye shift fallow until it could be sown with barley, oats, peas or beans in the spring. As the evidence from Blackbourne Hundred shows, barley was already the dominant crop in Breckland by 1283.[1] It was more difficult to augment the area of winter sown crops at the expense of barley and oats without violating grazing rights on the autumn stubble but it is clear that wheat was sown in the spring as well as autumn by the eighteenth century and the dominance of the area devoted to wheat in details of crops grown at Stapleford in southern Cambridgeshire in 1422[2] suggests that this practice may have had a long history.

As well as the system of moveable cropping shifts, flexibility of East Anglian cropping practice was enhanced by the custom of leaving certain strips fallow within sown shifts which could, if the occasion demanded, act as a reserve from which to supplement the allotment of a particular crop. Such 'leys' or 'ollands' appear frequently in descriptions of open field land in this region from the thirteenth century onwards and they commonly occupied a considerable proportion of the cultivated land. In 1588 38 out of 199 strips of open field arable that were recorded at Weasenham (Norf.)[3] were described as 'ollands' and a similar situation prevailed at Narford (Norf.) in 1473.[4]

In the eighteenth century the increasing amount of open field that was put down to sown grass was one of the bases of the new and improved rotations which made 'Norfolk' husbandry famous. The other was the introduction of root crops. Turnips were grown as a garden crop near Norwich by Dutch immigrants as early as the 1570s and the first reference to their cultivation as a field crop dates from a century later.[5] In 1674 tithes were taken on turnips at Theberton in Suffolk and by 1681 they were being grown in the fields of Shropham in northeast Norfolk.[6] Similarly carrots were grown in the fields

[1] E. Powell, Suffolk Hundred, pp. xxx–xxxi.   [2] Ely D.C., Liber 'G', fo. 18.
[3] Holkham Ms., quoted by Gray, English Field Systems, p. 320.
[4] Norwich P.L., Ms. 11353.
[5] P.R.O., SP 12.20.49 (1775); J. Woolidge, Systema Agricultura, 1669, p. 42.
[6] J. Thirsk and J. Imray (eds.), 'Suffolk Farming in the Nineteenth Century',

around Framlingham (Suff.) since the early seventeenth century and were a routine part of the husbandry of that region of east Suffolk by the eighteenth century, while the practice of feeding dairy cattle on cabbages in the fields of the central clay districts was developed after 1770.[1] These new crops were introduced mainly in the enclosures of central and eastern Norfolk and Suffolk but they also helped to give variety to the cropping pattern of many open field parishes in the sheep–corn region. At Linton in southeast Cambridgeshire in 1695, for example, nearly 24 acres of 'carrott roots, pease, turneps and parseneps' occupied 40 strips in 14 furlongs distributed in seven of the nine open fields of this parish.[2]

The shift system of cultivation as commonly practised over East Anglian open fields fostered a flexible cropping practice which in turn encouraged experimentation and the assimilation of new farming methods. These ensured that the farmers of Norfolk and Suffolk had already attained a higher standard of productivity than their Midland counterpart by the sixteenth century. This system was not, however, a *sine qua non* of agricultural progress. 'Leys' as the basis of convertible husbandry were to be found in Midland parishes as early as they were in East Anglia, while details of the estates of Crowland Abbey in the typically 'Midland' three-field townships of Cottenham, Oakington and Dry Drayton[3] in western Cambridgeshire show that, by the fourteenth century, considerable areas of barley and 'dredge' (barley and oats) appeared in the wheat and 'maslin' (wheat and rye) fields while mixed corn crops were sometimes used as cleansing crops on the fallow field. All the sown fields of these townships contained a variety of crops between 1383 and 1391 with sometimes as many as four in each and a similar situation was evident at Teversham (Cambs.) in 1724 where one tenant sowed adjoining strips in Mill Field with wheat, barley and clover and in Causeway Field with barley, oats, peas, lentils and tares.[4] If such individualistic practice could be introduced within the framework of conventional three-field systems, and indeed helped to preserve them by reducing the incentive for change, then some further explanation is required to explain why a shift system of cultivation was commonly employed over the open fields of East Anglia. The answer would seem to lie in the peculiar tenurial and pastoral customs of this region.

Suffolk Records Society, I, 1958, p. 20; W. Rye, *Norwich Court Books*, 1905, p. 164; H. W. Saunders, 'Estate Management at Raynham in the years 1661 to 1686 and 1706', *Norfolk Archaeology*, XIX, p. 44; E. Kerridge, 'Turnip Husbandry in High Suffolk', *Econ. Hist. Rev.*, VIII, 1956, pp. 390–2.

[1] Thirsk and Imray, *Suffolk Rec. Soc.*, I, 1958, p. 19.
[2] Pembroke College, Cambridge, T.5.   [3] Page, *Crowland Abbey*, App. II.
[4] Gonville and Caius College, Cambridge, XIV.35.

E. TENURIAL PRACTICES

Tenurial customs which affected the conduct of agricultural practice in East Anglia were the size and distribution of individual estates and the pattern of the typical tenant holding. Manors in Norfolk and Suffolk during the Middle Ages were generally small and rarely coincided with individual townships, most places containing more than one manor and some as many as four or five. This feature of land ownership was also evident in upland Cambridgeshire, where half of the townships in 1086 contained more than two manors. Little reduction in the number of independent lordships in East Anglia occurred before the seventeenth century but efforts to rationalise the confused pattern of landholding then began to take effect. At Cornard Parva (Suff.) it was suggested that the lord of Capon's manor should purchase Peacock's Hall in order to avoid controversy over their respective holdings[1] while the disappearance of eight independent manors in the Hundred of South Erpingham (Norf.) between 1600 and 1650 reflected the progress of the amalgamation of estates.[2] By 1650 nearly 71 per cent of the townships of Norfolk and Suffolk contained only one manor.[3] This development was most marked in the central and eastern districts where it was generally accompanied by the engrossment of tenant strips. On five manors of central Suffolk at this time, for example, copyhold land amounted to only 500 acres in comparison with the 3,000 acres in demesne.[4] The compact demesne thus achieved was then enclosed and divided into tenant farms. To the west, however, in the sheep–corn region, although some amalgamation was apparent, the intermingling of the land of various manors remained an impediment to the progress of enclosure.

A further aspect of the tenurial structure of East Anglia which affected agricultural progress was that the region as a whole was less rigidly feudalised than the Midlands throughout the Middle Ages.[5] The proportion of freemen to villein tenants was considerably higher, commonly amounting to over half of the inhabitants of individual townships. The creation of this large body of freemen, and of the large number of petty manors in East Anglia, has been ascribed to the Danish occupation

[1] B.M., Davy Ms. Add. 19077.
[2] F. Blomefield, *An Essay towards a Topographical History of Norfolk*, 1739, v, 305.
[3] Spratt, M.A. thesis, p. 20.
[4] At Hawstede, Whepstede, Brockley, Hopes Reed and Chedber, B.M. Add. Ms. 19107.
[5] D. C. Douglas, 'The Social Structure of Medieval East Anglia', *Oxford Studies in Social and Legal History*, IX, 1927, pp. 64ff.

and the body of 'sokemen' it created who held their land by commendation and were free to transfer it at will from one lord to another in return for protection.[1] Most of this class were reduced to the level of servile tenants after the Norman Conquest (of the 900 'sokemen' in Cambridgeshire in 1066 only 213 survived in 1086)[2] but the services expected of them and the large body of freemen were mainly personal in nature and not burdensome. Similarly the services required of the villein tenants were less onerous than those performed by the Midland peasant and were rapidly eroded by the rising tide of commutation which reached a climax in the early fourteenth century. The comparative freedom of the tenure that was typical of East Anglia is summed up in the entries for Chilford Hundred in southeast Cambridgeshire in the Hundred Rolls of 1279 which show that only 15 per cent of the total land recorded lay in villein holdings while 37 per cent was freehold and 48 per cent lay in demesne.[3]

The freeholders of thirteenth-century East Anglia survived and even prospered during the sixteenth and early seventeenth centuries when the steep rise in the prices of agricultural produce was reflected generally in the intensification of commercial agriculture and the engrossment of estates by capitalist farmers. It is not surprising, therefore, to find that these yeomen farmers, heirs to a tradition of freehold tenure untrammelled by customary labour services, were precocious in the assimilation of new farming methods, including experimentation with new crops and crop rotations and, particularly in the central and eastern districts of Norfolk and Suffolk, the enclosure and conversion of arable land to pastoral pursuits.

The aspect of tenurial custom which most distinguishes the East Anglian field system from that of the Midlands, however, was not the higher proportion of land held by freeholders but the pattern of the typical tenant holding. Among the haphazard agglomeration of precincts and stadia which characterised East Anglian field patterns we should hardly expect to find an equal distribution of the parcels of individual holdings but we might expect to find that the allocation of land of varying quality and the need to hold land in the various cropping shifts would ensure, as in the Midlands, that individual holdings were distributed throughout the open field area. Even a cursory glance at the earliest extant estate maps of East Anglian townships, however, shows that holdings, while not completely

[1] Gray, *English Field Systems*, pp. 352-3.
[2] F. W. Maitland, *Domesday Book and Beyond*, 1897, pp. 62-3.
[3] E. A. Kosminsky, *Studies in the Agrarian History of England in the Thirteenth Century*, 1956, p. 90 and 'The Hundred Rolls of 1278-9 as a Source for English Agrarian History', *Econ. Hist. Rev.*, III, 1931, pp. 16-44.

consolidated, possessed a marked tendency towards concentration in one part of the township's land (Figs. 7.2 and 7.3).

Gray recognised this distinctive feature of East Anglian tenemental patterns at Castle Acre and West Lexham[1] in Norfolk but it was equally typical of Suffolk and southeast Cambridgeshire. The 1612 field book of Barton Magna (Suff.)[2] that has already been quoted shows that the majority of the parcels of individual landholdings were concentrated in adjoining or nearby precincts. Thus Moses Baxter held land in those precincts numbered 13 to 19 and 26 to 37 and Joseph Cooke held land in those numbered 22 to 37. A similar pattern was evident at Walsingham (Norf.) in 1485 where the land of Edward Bullock lay in 19 out of 27 stadia in East Field and in 6 out of the 16 stadia in North Field but he possessed no land at all in any one of the 48 stadia of West Field.[3] To the south one tenant of Carbrooke Manor (Norf.) in 1549 held 24 strips of land in 'Myll-feild', 7 in 'Wetherinfeld', 7 in 'Westfeilde' and only one in 'Brom-hillfeild'.[4] A similar pattern was evident at Aldeburgh and Hazelwood in east Suffolk in the sixteenth century where twenty-one tenants of the manor of Snape held land in 8 open fields, of whom ten held strips in only one of those fields while only two held strips in as many as 6.[5] Parcels thus concentrated were not normally completely consolidated, however, even where exchange with one other land-owner would have made this a relatively simple achievement. Robert Bright and Joseph Spalding, for instance, held alternately 13 out of the 15 strips in the eighth stadia of the third precinct at Barton Magna in 1612.[6] Although exchanges of land did take place as a preliminary to piecemeal enclosure this was a slow and cumbersome process and it seems unlikely that a pattern of near-consolidated holdings was a result solely of this process. The weight of evidence tells against a wide distribution of an individual's parcels even in earlier periods. Widespread alienation and sub-tenancies of parcels and holdings in the late thirteenth and fourteenth centuries hinder the identification of the size and distribution of original tenemental units but Gray found that tenant holdings at Martham (Norf.) in 1291[7] displayed similar characteristics to those at Wymondham (Norf.) in the late

[1] Holkham Deeds 57; Holkham Maps no. 18; Gray, *English Field Systems*, p. 314.
[2] West Suffolk R.O., Ms. 645/1.
[3] Norwich P.L., Ms. 135.
[4] Norwich P.L., Ms. NRS 20381.
[5] East Suffolk R.O., Ms. 406/67.16, quoted by Burrell, M.Sc. thesis, 1959, p. 33.
[6] West Suffolk R.O., Ms. 645/1.
[7] B.M., Stowe Ms. 936, fos. 37–115, quoted by Gray, *English Field Systems*, p. 335.

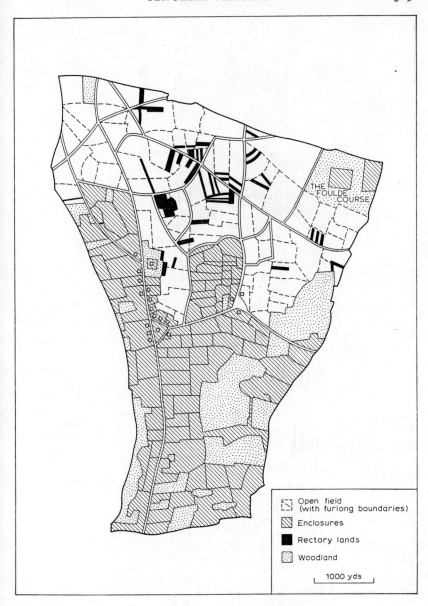

Fig. 7.2 The open fields of Barrow (Suff.) in 1597.
Source. West Suffolk R.O., Maps and Plans 862.

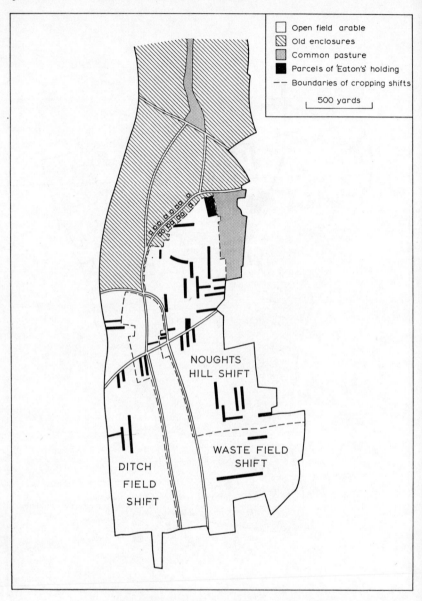

Fig. 7.3 The open fields of Stetchworth (Cambs.) in 1770.
Source. Cambridge University Library, Ms. Plan 237.

fifteenth century[1] with a tendency towards concentration in one area of the township's field land.

Gray ascribed this distinctive pattern of landholding to the unique unit of villein tenure that was found in East Anglia, known as the 'tenementum' in the fourteenth century, before that as a 'plena terra' and before that by the Anglo-Saxon term 'eriung'. The area of this unit was relatively constant throughout the region and commonly amounted to 12 or 24 acres in the thirteenth century. Thus at Martham (Norf.) in 1291 it was recorded that Thomas Knight held 'xii acras terre de villenagio que vocatur i eriung...est de tenementa de Thome Knight...et habentur in Martham xxii eriung et iii acre de villenagio'. That the tenementum was the local and distinctive unit of villein tenure of East Anglia is shown by the frequent reference that is made to it in charters of land belonging to Sibton Abbey in forty-seven places in Norfolk and Suffolk between 1325 and 1509.[2] No mention at all is made of virgates, the unit of peasant landholding most commonly employed throughout the Midlands and this unit is also absent from the Domesday record of Norfolk and Suffolk. That these tenemental units were the original unit of landholding in East Anglia is clear from those thirteenth-century conveyances which ascribe land parcels to the tenementa to which they originally belonged irrespective of their current occupance. Gray supposed that they originally formed compact blocks of land similar to the Kentish 'iuga' but that sale, exchange and division amongst co-heirs under the system of partible inheritance which prevailed in East Anglia led to their partial disintegration some time before the Norman Conquest. A similar process is revealed by the fragmentation of compact blocks of land in the Isle of Ely that were granted by the bishop of Ely in the thirteenth century to individuals or partners in cooperative reclamation ventures. However, since evidence from the thirteenth century shows that the typical East Anglian tenant holding was relatively if not absolutely compact in comparison with its Midland counterpart, Gray argued that the decay of original tenemental patterns was interrupted at some stage. According to Gray it was the Danish influx which fossilised existing patterns of semi-dispersed landholdings for rating purposes, thus creating the typical East Anglian unit, the 'eriung'. The large number of petty manors that were created by the Danes accentuated the concentration of individual holdings in one part of a township's land as each lord allocated new tenant holdings from his own demesne

[1] P.R.O., LR. MB. 206, fos. 188, 215, quoted by Gray, *English Field Systems*, pp. 339–40.
[2] A. H. Denny (ed.), 'The Sibton Abbey Estates, Select Documents 1325–1509', *Suffolk Records Society*, 1960, p. 13.

and attempted to prevent the wide dispersal of lands within his protection. The Normans feudalised the existing territorial unit but did not alter its main characteristics. More recently, B. Dodwell has shown that the decay of tenemental units in Norfolk and Suffolk between 1066 and 1400 was associated with inheritance practices and with a market in land.[1]

The contrast between the landholding patterns of East Anglia and the Midlands is evident in the transitional zone of upland Cambridgeshire. At Weston Colville in the southeast of the county the 35 acres of one holding that was donated to St John's College, Cambridge in 1566 were concentrated in only two of the six open fields on this township,[2] a pattern typical of East Anglia. In the western districts, however, the greater degree of coincidence between manor and township than commonly found in Norfolk and Suffolk, the dominance of villein over free tenure in the Middle Ages, the employment of the virgate as the basic unit of tenure and the practice of primogeniture are all redolent of Midland practice and it is not surprising to find that the constituent parts of individual holdings were widely scattered. Thus the 36 strips that were given by Morris Ruffus to the Hospital of St John in Cambridge in the early thirteenth century were scattered throughout all the open fields of the town[3] and evidence that they represented an original widespread distribution can be seen in the fact that 19 of them abutted the land of Adam, son of Eustace. The dead hand of corporate ownership helped to stultify the land market in Cambridgeshire and preserved the pattern of tenemental units from their acquisition until final enclosure. That they remained virtually unchanged during this period can be seen by analysis of representative college and church estates over 20 acres in extent in 32 parishes in western and central Cambridgeshire in the late eighteenth and early nineteenth centuries.[4] All comprised strips averaging less than one acre in extent, all were located in each of the open fields of their respective townships and all were located in over half of the furlongs in each of these fields.

In East Anglian townships, the concentration of an individual's land in one part of a township's cultivated area, coupled with the lack of demarcation of this area into fields of uniform size, led Gray to believe that there could have been no regular tillage plan. In order that everyone

---

[1] B. Dodwell, 'Holdings and Inheritance in Medieval East Anglia', *Econ. Hist. Rev.*, XX, 1967, pp. 53–67.

[2] St John's College, Cambridge, Ms. xxx. 29.

[3] F. W. Maitland, *Township and Borough*, 1898, App. 89c, p. 172.

[4] M. R. Postgate, 'The Open Fields of Cambridgeshire', Ph.D. thesis, University of Cambridge, 1964, p. 175.

should attain a fair proportion of sown and fallow land he postulated
that the strip was the main unit of agricultural production and everyone
sowed as he pleased so that strips of winter and spring corn and fallow
land were indiscriminately intermingled. Since such a system would
not permit the concentration of fallow and harvested land for the
benefit of the township's stock, one of the major attributes of the
Midland field system, he thought that all sown strips must have been
fenced off by wattle hurdles while the sheep and cattle grazed on the
adjacent land. This theory of unlimited individualism, attractive in
view of the high proportion of freeholders which characterised East
Anglian society in the Middle Ages, has been shown above to be
untenable. Not only would the management of open fields within
such a system be exceedingly difficult and lead to constant abuse
unless proprietors were assiduous in protecting their fallow strips
from grazing animals, but there is ample evidence, as has been shown,
that a definite tillage plan did exist in the form of cropping shifts.
The system of multiple, flexible shifts could be adapted more easily
than could a rigid field pattern of the Midland type to a tenemental
pattern of semi-concentrated holdings in order that each proprietor
should receive a reasonable proportion of fallow and sown land in
any one year. Nevertheless, it was likely that in some years most of
the strips of certain proprietors would fall within a fallow shift, a
situation that would be unacceptable in a semi-subsistence or a market
economy unless there was an overriding reason for accepting it. The
reason why the shift system survived in the open fields of western
Norfolk and Suffolk, despite the increasing opposition of independently
minded freeholders in the sixteenth and seventeenth centuries, and
why strips were not cropped as their occupiers wished, or consolidated,
enclosed and converted to pasture as they were in the central and
eastern districts of East Anglia, lay in the necessity of providing
adequate grazing facilities for the flocks of sheep whose integration
with arable husbandry provided the basis of the economy of the
sheep-corn region.

F. PASTORAL PRACTICES

The importance of sheep in the local economy of western and northern
Norfolk and Suffolk was apparent even in 1086 when the 17,000 sheep
that were kept in the demesne flocks of Breckland represented the
largest concentration in East Anglia. By 1341 demesne flocks in these
areas, such as that of the bishop of Ely at Eriswell,[1] often included

[1] B.M., Ms. 25340.

over 1,000 sheep and their management had become a commercialised industry involving the supply of breeding lambs as replacements for the ewe flocks while three-year-olds were imported from as far away as Ipswich (Suff.) and fattened for market on fenland pastures. Despite these large demesne flocks, the 1283 subsidy-returns for Blackbourne Hundred in Suffolk show that sheep farming at this time was still concentrated mainly in the hands of tenant farmers or small freeholders, each with one or two dozen sheep.[1] By the sixteenth century, however, the dominance of capitalist flock masters was complete, most of those in west Norfolk at this time owning over 5,000 sheep in several flocks. Sir Henry Fermor of East Barsham (Norf.) and Sir Richard Southwell of Wood Rising (Norf.) both kept over 15,000 sheep in flocks averaging 800 to 900 head apiece and were concerned not only with the production of wool and store lambs but also mutton for the expanding local and London markets.[2] Further east few sheep were to be found in the central clay districts of Norfolk and Suffolk, where dairying and mixed farming dominated the economy, but sizeable flocks grazed such heaths as Kelling, Edgefield, Roughton and Mousehold in east Norfolk and the coastal marshes of the Norfolk coast and Suffolk Sandlings.

The successful management of these flocks depended on the provision of abundant pastures at all seasons and in this respect the main flock owners benefited from the East Anglian custom whereby the entire grazing of a township's lands was usually the prerogative of the manorial lord or his lessee, irrespective of the occupance of the land. This practice was in contrast to Midland townships where pasturage rights inhered in the community as a whole and were jointly exercised by all its landholding members. Since, however, there was rarely only one manor in East Anglian townships, there was commonly more than one demesne flock competing for the available grazing. Each flock was restricted, therefore, to its own foldcourse or sheepwalk, a clearly defined area which provided essential grazing at various seasons. Open field arable, for grazing after harvest ('shack' land) or when it lay fallow, and heath or common land for grazing throughout the year, but especially in the summer months when unsown arable land was scarce, were the essential elements of a foldcourse if the flocks were to have adequate support. Some foldcourses also contained areas of meadow, fen or saltmarsh and arable or pasture closes, to which their owners were obliged to afford entry for the demesne

[1] Powell, *Suffolk Hundred*, tables following p. 121.
[2] Norwich P.L., Ms. NRS. 19437, 11310, 12396; B.M., Stowe Ms. 775, quoted in K. J. Allison, 'Flock Management in the Sixteenth and Seventeenth Centuries', *Econ. Hist. Rev.*, XI, 1958, p. 100.

flocks at certain times of the year. In some townships, as at Holkham (Norf.) (see Fig. 7.4)[1] the entire area was occupied by a number of foldcourses, but in others part of the open fields was reserved for the grazing of commoners' cattle at certain seasons. Only in east Suffolk, in the Sandlings, was this typical pattern difficult to recognise by the seventeenth century. Here heath and marsh were divided into demesne and common sheepwalks but there is no evidence of similar rights over the scattered remnants of the open fields. The extensive areas of closes in the majority of townships in this region had abrogated the necessity for open arable grazing.

In a few places, in west and north Norfolk and Suffolk as at Downham (Norf.) in 1550, foldcourses even transgressed township boundaries. In almost all cases, owing to the irregular subdivision of the cultivated land, foldcourses took little regard of precincts, field or quarentinae limits and consequently had to be carefully demarcated by other means. Details of such a system were given in a court case at Elveden (Suff.) in 1539 which also showed that the exact number and type of sheep which flock owners were supposed to depasture on their fold-courses were carefully stipulated.[2] The plaintiff in this case complained that the townspeople had encroached upon his foldcourse by moving 'certain Hills erected and made for Metes and Bounds and Dools for the partition of the Foldcourse of the said late Priory of Chanons and the Feedinges and furlonges of the Inhabitents'. The demesne prerogative was upheld when the inhabitants were ordered to replace these boundary marks, and lest they forgot to whom the shackage of the foldcourse belonged, they were reminded that it was customary for them to 'tie up their Horses with Cordes in their mouths in time of Harvest...to the Intent it might appear they had no liberty of feeding within the same pcell of Fouldcourse but only the tilling of their lands and the crop when it was sown'. Since there were eleven such foldcourses in Elveden (Suff.), covering over 5,000 acres of arable and heathland and depasturing 3,200 sheep, divided into hog, ewe and young sheep flocks, the problem of maintaining their boundaries and preserving their grazing must have been considerable, as it must at nearby Weeting (Norf.) where twelve flocks containing 4,700 sheep were depastured in 1542.[3]

The benefits of the foldcourse system were not entirely one-sided, however, for in return for providing grazing facilities for the lord's flocks, tenants' lands were 'tathed' or dunged and this helped to restore fertility to the relatively infertile soils of western Norfolk and

[1] Holkham Ms., Map 1 (1590).
[2] Elveden Ms. EHC (1740).
[3] Norwich P.L., Ms. 13489.

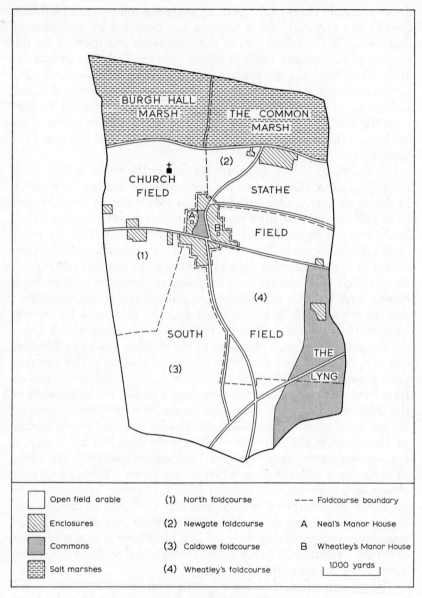

Fig. 7.4 The open fields of Holkham (Norf.) in 1590.
Source. Holkham Ms. Map 1.

Suffolk. To avoid dissipating the effects of the tathe it was necessary to confine the flocks within a fold and it was this attribute of a fold-course which distinguished it from a sheepwalk. According to Spelman,

'a fouldcourse is a liberty to erect a fold within a certain precinct of grounde for ordering ye shepe of ye fould and tathing ye land therein, and also to feede ye shepe...at (all) seasons of the yeer...some shep's courses there be wch properly may not be fouldcourses, namely such as lye upon waste, heath or commons, where never any plough or fould for tashing doth com.'[1]

Once concentrated, dung from the fold was distributed over the arable land according to a predetermined plan. Thus 9 out of 22 acres at Fornham (Suff.) in the early fourteenth century were 'composte cum faldi' and 30 acres were 'composte cum carecta'.[2]

In order to prevent indiscriminate use of the fold and to ensure that the demesne lands received its benefits it was customarily reserved as a seignorial prerogative. Tenants were 'tyed to laye their shepe in the lord's fold for tashing his lands' and fines were exacted from tenants who 'would not let their sheep be in the lord's fold but will fold them on their own grounds'.[3] The demesne privilege of the fold was of long standing in East Anglia, both Tate and Douglas considering that it was known before 1086.[4] References to 'fold-soke' in the Domesday survey of East Anglia show that some tenants chose to pay for the privilege of using their sheep on their own land rather than in the lord's fold while Gray noted a few instances in east Suffolk of 'falda libera'[5] by which tenants were free to erect their own fold, a practice reflected in references to tenants who 'habet suam falda' or whose sheep 'non iacabunt in falda domini' which occasionally occur in cartularies of Ramsey Abbey that related to East Anglian townships.[6]

In general, however, the lord's privilege of foldage was jealously preserved, as evidenced by frequent presentments before manorial courts for transgression of this right. In 1426 for example, John Skyroop was presented at Merton (Norf.)[7] for erecting a 'fald' while William

---

[1] B.M., Add. Ms. 27403 (undated 17th cent.).
[2] Feudal Aids (1889–1921), vol. III.
[3] B.M., Add. Ms. 27403.
[4] B.M., Add. Ms. 27403; Tate, Proc. Suffolk Inst. Arch., xxv, 1951, p. 239; Douglas, Social Structure of Medieval East Anglia, p. 25.
[5] At Glemsford, 'Herthirst', Rattlesden, Hitcham, Barking, Wetheringsett, Brandon; B.M., Cott. Ms. Claud C.xi, fos. 259b, 265, 272, 279b, 288b, 296b, quoted by Gray, English Field Systems, p. 342.
[6] W. H. Hart (ed.), Cartularium Monasterii de Rameseia, Rolls Series, 3 vols, 1884–93, I, 423; III, 261, 262, 264.
[7] Merton Ms.

Hert was similarly indicted at Freckenham (Suff.) in 1550 for 'setting up a fouldage where he ought not to'.[1] By this time, however, there had been a change in emphasis in the management of foldcourses. No longer were folds stocked by communal effort so that the lord's land would receive the benefits of the tathe; the fold was now dominated by manorial flocks, much of the demesne had been leased and landlords were concerned to reserve the grazing rights of their tenants' lands for their own use in return for farming out the benefits of the fold. Tenant flocks were now limited to those few sheep that were allowed to run with the lord's flocks. In 1559, for example, such 'cullet' or 'parr' rights accounted for 150 out of the 875 sheep in Caldowe flock at Holkham.[2]

Since foldcourses and the associated seignorial prerogative of the fold were one of the distinguishing features of the East Anglian field system it is interesting to note that they were to be found throughout upland Cambridgeshire in the thirteenth and fourteenth centuries at such places as Fulbourne, Wood Ditton, Burrough Green, Sawston and Oakington.[3] The beneficence of the abbot of Crowland in relaxing his monopoly at Dry Drayton in 1322,[4] so that his tenants could benefit from the tathe in times of dearth, only serves to underline the common practice on his estates. In the sixteenth century the four exclusive sheepwalks at Sawston and the six at Snailwell in southeast Cambridgeshire were as jealously preserved as those in western Norfolk and Suffolk.[5] The transitional nature of Cambridgeshire was evident, however, in the deformations to this system that were apparent from an early date in the western regions of the county. The decline of the custom of exclusive landlord grazing which was evident in Norfolk and Suffolk by the late sixteenth century in grants of common folds, as at Kilverstone (Norf.),[6] was an early and persistent feature of Cambridgeshire pasturage arrangements. At Cottenham in 1580[7] tenants of the manor of Lyles and Crowland were given leave to 'organise the town flock and erect as many sheep folds as they shall think good', and references to the 'stint' of sheep allowed in common flocks can be found in verdicts of medieval Courts Leet for manors

[1] West Suffolk R.O., Ms. 613/687, 1–12.
[2] Holkham Deeds 10318, quoted by Allison, *Agric. Hist. Rev.*, v, 1957, p. 21.
[3] P.R.O., Court Rolls 358 and Rentals and Surveys, Portf. 6 no. 7; W. M. Palmer, 'A History of the Parish of Borough Green', *Cambridgeshire Arch. Soc.*, LIV, 1939, p. 14; T. F. Teversham, *A History of Sawston, Cambridgeshire*, 1947, p. 26.
[4] Queens' College, Cambridge, Ad. 23. m. 9r; Page, *Crowland Abbey*, App. II.
[5] Teversham, *History of Sawston*, p. 64; Pembroke College, Cambridge, 5.17.
[6] West Suffolk R.O., Ms. (undated 16th cent.).
[7] Cambridge R.O., Cot. C.39; W. Cunningham, *Royal Hist. Soc.*, Camden Ser., X, 1910, p. 202.

throughout Cambridgeshire, especially those in the west. Typical of the impact of Midland and East Anglian custom in this transitional zone was the abolition of five exclusive sheepwalks in favour of a common flock at Stow cum Quy[1] and Waterbeach[2] at the end of the eighteenth century, the juxtaposition of five exclusive sheepwalks with four common sheepwalks at Haddenham in 1834[3] and of three demesne flocks with a town flock at Landbeach in 1650.[4]

The foldcourse system that was typical of East Anglian pasturage arrangements was the main reason for the adoption and maintenance of the shift system of cultivation which provided the necessary compact areas of fallow and stubble for its efficient management. It required, however, the closest cooperation between landlord and tenant. It was essential that occupiers of open field strips complied with the common system of cropping shifts in order to preserve the uniformity of winter shackage and summer fallows. In compensation for their potential losses in any year when most of their strips lay fallow it was customary for foldcourse owners to give 'allowance for ye (somer pasture) either in rent or exchange or shepegate'.[5] At Sedgeford (Norf.) in the sixteenth century, whenever the copyhold or freehold lands were shacked by the lord's flocks he allowed the tenants 'in exchang recompense for the same a like quantity of his Demesne arable land'.[6]

By the late sixteenth and early seventeenth centuries it is clear that the inherent dichotomy of interest between sheep farming landlords and corn growing tenants was causing customary agreements to be increasingly abused by both parties. Landlords extended their fold-courses and overstocked the common, refused to give an allowance for the use of unsown arable land, lengthened the period of shack, fed their flocks on tenants' winter corn and denied tenants their cullet rights which enabled them to keep a few sheep in with the lord's flocks. By such means rentier landlords were enabled to increase the size of their flocks to and beyond their legitimate limits without having recourse to enclosure and conversion to pasture. Between 1537 and 1628 the flocks on the Monkshall Ewe Ground at Elveden (Suff.)[7] and on a neighbouring foldcourse at Kilverstone (Norf.) were both increased from under 400 to over 700 head.[8] Such abuses, particularly

[1] Corpus Christi College, Cambridge, XXII.25.
[2] Cambridge R.O., R. 56.22.3.
[3] Gonville and Caius College, Cambridge, XIX.58.
[4] Corpus Christi College, Cambridge, XXXV.176.
[5] B.M., Add. Ms. 27403.
[6] L'Estrange Ms. Box 1C (18th cent.).
[7] Elveden Ms. EHC (1740).
[8] Merton Ms.; Norwich P.L., NRS. 15151.

the attenuation of common rights, sometimes caused the depopulation of whole villages. At Merton (Norf.) in 1517 it was recorded that 'tota villa amisit le Shakke'[1] while an enquiry into the desertion of the nearby village of Sturston (Norf.) revealed that the lord, who owned three 'sheeps courses' for 1,900 sheep in the village, had converted all the commons and waste ground 'to his own privat grounds' and the five remaining village houses into outhouses of the demesne farm.[2] Similar infringements of tenant rights by landlords determined to create an economic entity within which to manage their sheep farming activities occurred at Kilverstone, Alethorpe, Narford, Hargham, and West Wretham in west Norfolk at the end of the sixteenth century.[3]

On the tenants' side practices which tended to disrupt the proper management of foldcourses were reflected in the directives issued from the manorial court at Ingham (Suff.) in the fifteenth century which stated that 'all tenants ought to forbere the werkynge of there londe eny yere the lord's course or fould shall chance to be' and that 'no man ought to enclose any gronde in purlui of the lord's sheps course'.[4] Similarly, at Icklingham (Suff.) in 1702 one tenant was ordered not to 'cross or hinder the walkes of any of the other flocks by plowinge or sowinge contrary to the accustomed manner sheifts of the fields'.[5] Increasingly, however, such directives were ignored. At Anmer (Norf.) in 1627 it was found that the sowing of strips within the 'shacks and winter feeding' of the foldcourse and 'the refusal of a few wilful persons to lett ye owners of ffoldcourses have their quilletts of land (lying intermixt in the places where ye sheep pasture is layd) upon indifferent exchange or other recompense' were 'things very mischeevous and will tend to ye overthrow of very manye foldcourses'.[6] One tenant at Anmer had converted his strips to pasture and threatened to prosecute the foldcourse owner for trespass as his rights related only to land that was sown or fallow while certain tenants at West Rudham and Docking in Norfolk in the sixteenth century had disregarded the shift system by sowing spring and winter corn on adjacent strips and sowing land set aside for summer fallowing.[7]

[1] Merton Ms.
[2] P.R.O., E.134/38, 39 (Eliz./Mich. 9).
[3] Ms. printed in Norfolk Archaeology, x, 1888, pp. 150–1; P.R.O., E.134: 21–22 (Eliz./Mich. 31); P.R.O., E.134: 42, 43 (Eliz./Mich. 28); Blomefield, Essay towards a History of Norfolk, I, 471; P.R.O., E.134: (35 Eliz./24 East.).
[4] B.M., Add. Ms. 34689; B.M., Add. Ms. 31970, fo. 91.
[5] Elveden Ms., Icklingham/F. 5.
[6] Rye, State Papers relating to Norfolk, Privy Council Orders 1627, pp. 70–1.
[7] P.R.O., C2.R6.61 (temp. Eliz. I), and C2.H.11.45.

Piecemeal enclosure of open field strips, which denied their feeding to the lord's flocks and could prevent their access to other parts of the open field, was even more inimical to the efficient management of foldcourse. Spelman noted in the seventeenth century that 'enclosures have gen^rlly and little by little interrupted and abridged ye Shacks'[1] while an enquiry at Foxley (Norf.) in 1592 found nineteen tenants had enclosed 21 open field strips totalling 70¼ acres which prevented the flocks from reaching a further 14½ acres.[2]

At first tenants were obliged to remove these obstructions but as the practice became more widespread many landlords, as at Swaffham (Norf.) in 1630, were persuaded to tolerate them provided gaps were left in these closes for their sheep to enter when the land lay unsown.[3] The conversion of these 'half-year' closes to 'whole-year' closes from which demesne flocks were totally excluded gained momentum in the late sixteenth and seventeenth centuries, especially after the introduction of turnips into crop rotation as this meant that the land never lay unsown and therefore subject to shackage rights. Faced with this situation many landlords abandoned their rights over their tenants' lands and references such as that at Merton (Norf.) in 1630, where Sir William de Grey gave licence to a tenant to 'enclose another little pightle from the shack of my sheep',[4] became increasingly frequent. Similarly, at Kenninghall (Norf.) in 1616, the tenants of one manor were allowed to purchase their lands in order to make them whole-year lands and enclosure doubtless followed.[5] The decay of the foldcourse system was so marked by this time that a jury at Harthill (Norf.) claimed in 1634 that it was the common custom for the tenants to 'enclose their lands and to sow their winter corn at their will and pleasure'.[6]

In the 'Good Sand' region of north and northwest Norfolk progressive landlords, faced with the complete breakdown of their foldcourses, reorganised their estates into enclosed leasehold farms on which flocks were folded and fattened on turnips, while the heaths and commons were divided as brecks and leased out as a new type of foldcourse. Elsewhere, more reactionary proprietors strove to maintain their traditional foldcourses by inserting penalty clauses in covenanted leases against abuses of customary cropping practices or enclosure of open field strips. At Foxley (Norf.) in 1755 one owner came to terms with his tenants' desire to benefit from turnip husbandry by accepting

[1] B.M., Add. Ms. 27403.
[2] Holkham Ms. Billingford and Bintree Deeds 12:846.
[3] Norwich P.L., Ms. 24072.   [4] Merton Ms.
[5] Blomefield, *Essay towards a History of Norfolk*, I, 220.
[6] Norwich P.L., Ms. NRS. 16473, 32, D.2.

2s. per acre for the shackage lost from land thus sown, provided that it comprised contiguous strips that were hurdled from his flocks.[1] By such means foldcourses survived, often in an attenuated form, up until Parliamentary enclosure. This was the case in Breckland where the influence which they had on the maintenance of the open fields and prevention of improved crop rotations called down the opprobrium of contemporary observers. At both Barrow and Troston in north-west Suffolk the open fields were subject to the exclusive grazing of the flock of one person which Young considered to be 'a disgrace to a more enlightened age and prevents him and all others from following an improved course...nothing could be considered more beggarly than the husbandry and crops on these lands'.[2] Here the foldcourse system, once mutually beneficial to both landlord and tenant, was an anachronism of little use to either as the grazing provided by a course of one crop to fallow at Troston was so meagre that some at least of the hundreds of starving sheep that were noted by Young in the area north of Bury St Edmunds (Suff.) were doubtless located here.[3]

G. CONCLUSION

It is clear that the East Anglian open field system was both more complex and more advanced than that which prevailed in the majority of Midland parishes and it is this complexity, as well as the apparent lack of uniformity in its terminology, that has created difficulties in the interpretation of the available evidence. Gray's ethnic explanations of the main characteristic of the East Anglian field system, the peculiar tenemental pattern and the privileged position of the lord of the manor with regard to pasturage arrangements, would seem to be still essentially correct but subsequent investigation has clarified the links between them and the patterns into which the open field areas were subdivided for purposes of reference and for tillage. These studies have also shown, not surprisingly, that many of the features of the system that was common to Norfolk and Suffolk were found in adjacent parts of Cambridgeshire and Essex. Increasing recognition has also been given to the influence of physical environment on the development and final decay of this system for it determined whether the local economy was based on arable cultivation or pastoralism. The inherent suitability of the Boulder Clay soils of the central and eastern districts of Norfolk and Suffolk to the development of good

[1] Holkham Ms. Billingford and Bintree Deeds 15:1003-4.
[2] Young, *General View of the Agriculture of Suffolk*, 1797, p. 32.
[3] A. Young, 'A Week in Norfolk', *Annals of Agriculture*, XIX, 1792, p. 95.

grassland and an economy based on dairy and mixed arable farming was largely responsible for the enclosure and conversion of most of the open fields formerly located there by the mid-seventeenth century. To the northwest, however, the inherently more infertile soils were best suited to extensive arable farming which relied to a great extent on the folding of sheep to maintain soil fertility before the introduction of improved crop rotations and fertilisers.

Explanations of why the open field system survived in parts of the sheep–corn region up until Parliamentary enclosure and why it developed its distinctive characteristics depend on the correlation between the unique tenurial structure of East Anglia and the pastoral arrangements by which sheep and arable farming were integrated. Partible inheritance practised in East Anglia meant that some inter-mixture of the parcels of tenants' holdings appeared naturally but the evidence is clear that individual tenements retained a certain degree of compactness within the open fields of individual townships, a pattern that was accentuated by the number of independent manors commonly located there. This characteristic tenemental structure militated against the development of a rigid field pattern for there could be no equal division of an individual's strips between two or three regular open fields. It was also associated with a relatively pronounced freedom of tenure which encouraged individualism in agricultural practice that undoubtedly facilitated enclosure. The progress of enclosure, however, was intimately connected to the peculiar pasturage arrangements that arose from the presence of a number of petty manors each with its privilege of independent foldage. Throughout the sheep–corn district, traditional open field cultivation was fostered by the foldcourse system while the central wood–pasture region, freed from such restrictions because of its greater reliance on cattle, yielded readily to enclosure. Foldcourses were also a main determinant of the cropping pattern in East Anglia. A pattern of semi-consolidated holdings in a cultivated area in which there was no connection between cropping course and field pattern, as there was in the Midlands, was conducive to individualistic cropping practices in order to ensure a balanced ratio of the major grain crops and also encouraged experimentation with new crops and rotations and the consolidation and enclosure of individual estates. Only the foldcourse system discouraged such action.

To meet the demands of several demesne flocks a series of shifts was imposed on the open fields in order to provide compact areas of fallow and harvested land which, together with co-aration, were the traditional benefits of communal open field husbandry as practised in the Midlands. The flexibility of the shift system, however, represented a considerable advance on Midland practice, as within the limitations imposed by the foldcourse system, it facilitated the introduction of new crops and rotations. It also enabled land to be cropped to its optimum capacity under given economic circumstances, an aspect of the East Anglian field system which was particularly evident in the infield–outfield system that was once common on all the light soils of the region and which survived in Breckland up until, and even after, Parliamentary enclosure. Flexible cropping shifts were one of the main characteristics of the East Anglian field system throughout the period of open field agriculture. At West Rudham (Norf.) in the sixteenth century it was stated that 'the custom and usage therein and time out of mind of man has been that the lands...have been divided into several shifts or parts of which some have been used yearly and every year in course have been sown with corn and some yearly left fallow'.[1] The origins of these shifts predate adequate documentation but at least eight shifts were recorded at Thetford (Norf.) in 1338,[2] while evidence from the assarted land of southeast Cambridgeshire in the thirteenth century shows that their superimposition on to a haphazard pattern of irregular field plots was the most important step in the development of a mature open field system. However, by the sixteenth century the main beneficiaries of the regular tillage plan which these shifts imposed over the irregular field patterns of East Anglia were the foldcourse owners and it was the final breakdown of the necessary cooperation between them and their corn-growing tenants which caused the decay of open field farming in this region.

[1] P.R.O., C2.R6.61 (temp. Eliz. I).
[2] Norwich P.L., Ms. 121, unpublished account of the Thetford district by W. G. Clarke.

8

Field Systems of the Chiltern Hills and their Environs

BY DAVID RODEN

H. L. Gray considered the chalk hills which extend across southeastern England from the Thames to East Anglia to be one of the fundamental divides of English field systems, separating the two- and three-field townships of the Midland region from the country to the south where a very different physical and social environment had produced less regular field arrangements. The Chiltern Hills were an important part of this boundary zone, and as such, according to Gray, experienced both Midland and Kentish influences. Development of agrarian systems had, however, been so affected by topography that the original affiliations were difficult to discern.[1]

The aim of this chapter is to describe these distinctive Chiltern systems before they began to disintegrate in the sixteenth century, viewing them in the context of neighbouring districts, for which purpose the arbitrary limit of the five counties of Oxfordshire, Buckinghamshire, Bedfordshire, Hertfordshire and Essex has been chosen. Consideration of Chiltern arrangements in their regional setting may also help to illuminate the early functioning of field systems in the two very different regions separated by the Hills.

A. MEDIEVAL FIELD SYSTEMS

I. THE CHILTERN HILLS

The Chiltern Hills is that part of the Middle Chalk outcrop between the Thames at Goring (Oxon.) and the Hitchin Gap 50 miles to the northeast (Fig. 8.1). From a crest rising 300–400 feet above the clay vales of Oxford and Aylesbury, the Chiltern plateau slopes gently southeastwards for about ten miles down to the gravel terraces of the Thames and the glacial sands and gravels of the Vale of St Albans. The plateau surface is broken by five troughs, now occupied by the principal streams, and between these it is further scored by a network of deep, steep-sided and mostly dry valleys. Dissection is deepest in the southwestern and central Chilterns, where plateau remnants rarely

---

[1] H. L. Gray, *English Field Systems*, 1915, Cambridge, Mass., pp. 63, 401, 417–18.

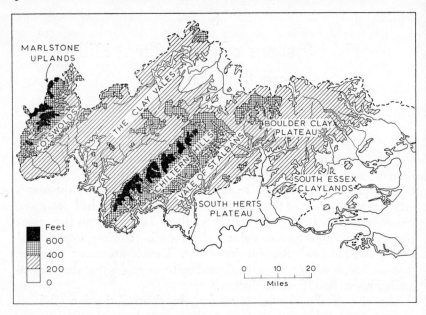

Fig. 8.1 Relief of Oxfordshire, Buckinghamshire, Hertfordshire, Bedfordshire, and Essex.

exceed two miles in width, but towards the northeast slopes become gentler and plateau surfaces more extensive. Chalk is exposed only on the scarp-face and valley slopes, for everywhere the plateau is thickly mantled by superficial deposits (mainly Clay-with-flints, with brickearths in the northeast), and by scattered outliers of Eocene sands and gravels. There is thus considerable variety of soils, and although all are well-drained and essentially dry, the soils of the lower, eastern Chilterns are on the whole more loamy and less stony than those of the more dissected west. Throughout the Hills some of the most easily worked soils are along the lower valley slopes.

During the thirteenth century, the rising value of private woodland and growing pressure to conserve dwindling areas of common waste brought an end to the large-scale clearing of forest and heath that had continued in this region throughout the early Middle Ages.[1] The pattern of land use, fields and settlement that had been evolving over several centuries was thus stabilised, and was to remain basically

[1] D. Roden, 'Changing Settlement in the Chiltern Hills Before 1850', Folk Life, VIII, 1970, p. 60; D. Roden, 'Woodland and its Management in the Medieval Chilterns', Forestry, XLI, 1968, pp. 59–71.

unchanged for 300 years. Much wood and common waste survived, especially in the southwest and centre of the Hills where the pace of colonisation had been slower than on the loams of the northeast. Private timber was generally regarded as a valuable source of capital, to be exploited on a large scale only under special circumstances.[1] Common woods and, on the sandier soils, heaths ranged from tiny wayside plots to the 700 acres of Berkhamsted Frith (Herts.), and were prized by peasants with smaller holdings as major sources of fuel and building materials. Together with open downs on parts of the chalk crest, 'moors' on marshy sections of the river flood-plains, and the numerous greens, they also provided large areas of grazing and pannage.[2]

Rearing and breeding were not as important as these abundant pastures might suggest. First, the quality of common grazing was generally poor, particularly as the larger wastes were intercommoned by many townships, both Vale and Chiltern, as well as by individuals and institutions who had received special grants: the two vills of Stoke and Woodcote and the monks of Caversham shared rights in Exlade Wood (Oxon.), while men from Wyfold, Rotherfield Peppard and Harpsden commoned together in the woods of Wyfold (Oxon.).[3] Secondly, private woodland was not normally used for grazing other than swine pannage, partly because herbage was limited by the shade, and partly because flocks and herds would have damaged valuable timber resources.[4] Grassland in general was in short supply. Sufficient meadow to meet local hay requirements existed only in common meadows and closes along the flood-plains of the main streams. The greatest areas of grassland were in the parks, already very numerous in the Hills. These were often devoted to beasts of the chase, and only occasionally entered the local farm economy. Meadow aftermath, patches of poorer forage along the flood-plains, and pasture closes on the upper dip-slope all provided grazing, yet on many manors permanent pasture was limited to small closes and orchards near to the farmsteads, and to hedgerows, greenways and roadside verges. Scarcity of grassland was reflected in the high values that it commanded. There was some increase in pasturage after the epidemic of 1349 as ploughland tumbled to grass, but this was mostly a temporary trend –

[1] Roden, *Forestry*, XLI, 1968, pp. 64–5.
[2] D. Roden, 'Studies in Chiltern Field Systems', Ph.D. thesis, University of London, 1965, pp. 358–63.
[3] H. E. Salter (ed.), *The Cartulary of the Abbey of Eynsham*, Oxford Historical Society, LI, 1908, p. 127; H. E. Salter (ed.), *The Feet of Fines for Oxfordshire, 1195–1291*, Oxfordshire Record Series, XII, 1930, p. 192; H. E. Salter (ed.), *The Thame Cartulary*, Oxfordshire Rec. Ser., XXV–VI, 1947–8, p. 124, no. 177.
[4] Roden, *Forestry*, XLI, 1968, pp. 66–7.

within a few years as much land was being cultivated as in the decade before 1350.[1]

Most farms consisted almost entirely of arable fields and over these a form of mixed husbandry was practised. Grain and wool were the main products of commercial value on the larger holdings, and London was the most important market. Demesne yields were, with the possible exception of wheat, comparable with those elsewhere in England, while variations of soil and slope within the region itself were reflected in differing emphases on the various crops rather than in changing levels of production. The little evidence there is concerning the smaller peasant tenements also suggests a rudimentary sheep–corn husbandry. Fourteenth-century tenant flocks were often large, 100 sheep or more on a single farm being quite common. Pig keeping may have been important for the numerous small holders who had built cottages along the edges of common woods and heaths, and who found additional employment on the larger farms, in the woods, and at the brick and tile kilns established on many commons.[2]

The pattern of settlement contained elements of both nucleation and dispersal, with small towns and villages along the valleys, and hamlets and isolated farmsteads more usually up on the ridge tops and plateau surface. In the northeast, hamlets were often grouped around greens or patches of common wood that later degenerated to open spaces, while towards the southwest great common wastes were major foci for settlement agglomerations.[3]

Although common arable land existed throughout the region, it steadily increased in extent from the southwest, where some townships were entirely in severalty, towards the northeast, where as much as half the farmland of many manors lay as strips in intermixed ownership. The strips, generally one acre or less, were the basic tenurial units within the common arable, and comprised one or a number of plough ridges (selions). They were grouped into open furlongs and hedged fields, but the distinction between fields and furlongs, and even between separate fields, was often blurred. Terminology was vague: *quarentena* and *cultura*, for example, were applied variously to common field furlongs, common fields themselves, and closes of several land. The common fields differed considerably in size, there being a marked distinction between the larger units around the main settlements on the better soils of the lower valley slopes, and small groups of strips, often with names suggestive of late assarting, that were scattered

---

[1] D. Roden, 'Demesne Farming in the Chiltern Hills', *Agric. Hist. Rev.*, XVII, 1969, pp. 9–23; Roden, Ph.D. thesis, pp. 306–11.

[2] Roden, *Agric. Hist. Rev.*, XVII, 1969, p. 23.

[3] Roden, *Folk Life*, VIII, 1970, pp. 57–64.

amongst woods and closes on higher land (Fig. 8.2).[1] Towards the southwest, common arable in the valleys was often severely limited by steepness of slope and constriction of the valley bottoms, producing, as at High Wycombe, a series of elongated fields extending up-slope and penetrating along tributary dry valleys.[2]

The largest Chiltern common fields were small compared with the great open units typical of Midland districts, and tenants of a particular field rarely included more than a small proportion of the cultivators in a manor. The number of common fields in a parish ranged from a single field in parts of the southwest to ten, twenty or thirty in such Hertfordshire townships as Berkhamsted, Great Gaddesden and King's Walden.[3] Even the small parish of Bramfield (Herts.) contained at least fourteen common fields early in the fourteenth century.[4] Such multiplicity reflected, in part, the existence of separate systems within one parish. At King's Walden, for example, the village and the hamlets of Wandon and Flexmore, all well established by 1086, had their own sets of strip-divided fields in the thirteenth century (Fig. 8.3).[5] Analysis of Tudor and Jacobean surveys also shows distinct groupings of common fields in manors and parishes, the holdings of individual tenants generally being confined to fields of one group. These groups probably represented earlier hamlet areas.[6] Within the field systems of one settlement there was still often a large number of common fields: the hamlet of Three Houses had eight fields which were quite distinct from the three of the parent village of Knebworth (Herts.).[7]

Strips were added to some fields as a result of twelfth- and early thirteenth-century assarting, and a few completely new common fields may have been created in the higher and more remote areas where most clearing was then concentrated.[8] Once established, however, the pattern of common arable was only slightly modified before the sixteenth century. Two or three small *culturae* were occasionally amalgamated with a larger field, perhaps, as at King's Walden, in response to some modification of cropping and grazing practices.[9] A few common fields were also enclosed by manorial lords, incorporated into their demesnes, and continued in tillage. But, except in the southwest where common arable was limited, the disappearance of

[1] Roden, Ph.D. thesis, pp. 136–8, 188–9, 316–22; D. Roden, 'Enclosure in the Chiltern Hills', *Geogr. Annlr.*, Ser. B, LII, 1969, pp. 115–26.
[2] West Sussex R.O., Chichester Chapter Archives, Cap. 1/29/7, fos. 2–60.
[3] Roden, Ph.D. thesis, pp. 132–3, 221–2, 320–1.
[4] Hertfordshire R.O., 40702–3.
[5] Roden, Ph.D. thesis, pp. 133–5.   [6] *Ibid.*, pp. 43–4.
[7] Hertfordshire R.O., 21840–2, 21871, 21877, 21893.
[8] Roden, *Geogr. Annlr.*, Ser. B, LII, 1969, pp. 116–17.
[9] Roden, Ph.D. thesis, pp. 138–9, 189, 325–6.

330

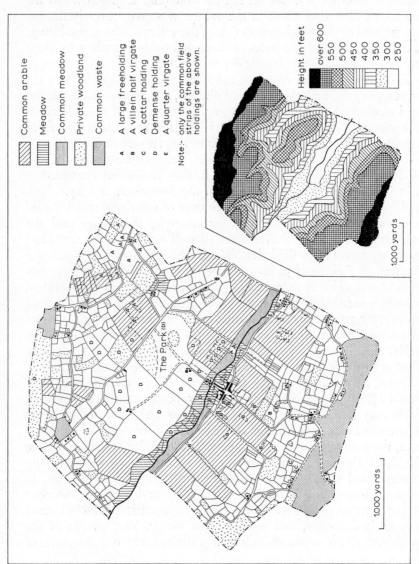

Common arable

Meadow

Common meadow

Private woodland

Common waste

A   A large freeholding
B   A villein half virgate
C   A cottar holding
D   Demense holding
E   A quarter virgate

Note:- only the common field
strips of the above
holdings are shown.

Height in feet

over 600
550
500
450
400
350
300
250

1000 yards

The Park (D)

1000 yards

Fig. 8.2 Generalised diagram of medieval field arrangements in a typical Chiltern parish.

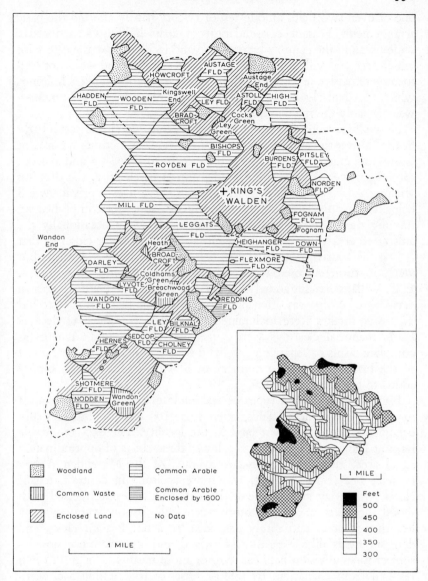

Fig. 8.3 A reconstruction of fields and land use in King's Walden (Herts.)
c. 1600.

Sources. B.M., Add. Ch. 35839–40, 35853, 35996,3 5998; Hertfordshire R.O., 54521, 67083.

one or even two fields among ten or twenty hardly affected the basic arrangement. Peasant consolidation of strip holdings – particularly widespread in the century before 1350 and facilitated by the ease with which free and villein tenants alike could transfer land – did not lead to any extensive enclosure. More efficient distribution of holdings which, particularly in the northeast, were often highly fragmented, was probably the main aim.[1]

New closes were also being improved from wood and scrub early in the thirteenth century in a variety of ways. Sometimes an area of waste was marked out, to be subsequently grubbed-up and fenced; sometimes woodland was enclosed prior to its clearing, the decision whether to fell all or part of it, or to preserve it as a private wood being taken only later; some enclosure was simply accomplished by moving the boundaries of an existing field; while occasionally the cultivated area was extended beyond a nucleus of older closes so that at first the assarts formed an open belt between arable and waste, but were, in turn, enclosed to prevent livestock straying on to crops. E. C. Vollans has suggested that, in the Missenden (Bucks.) area, a network of crofts was often produced when the fences made around successive intakes were maintained rather than being left to decay.[2] Large manorial clearings were sometimes rented out to tenants as complete farms or separate closes, and sometimes, like the great assart of the Flamstead (Herts.) nunnery of St Giles-in-the-Wood, simply added to the demesne farm.[3]

By 1300 two distinct types of arable closes had appeared on most manors. Huge demesne fields, often 50 to 100 acres or more, usually occupied some of the best land in the locality. The 840-acre arable farm at Flamstead (Herts.), 1264, lay as three closes of approximately equal area, although the 50-acre average of the Missenden Abbey farm at Lee (Bucks.), 1335, was more typical.[4] In contrast, tenant closes, which lay around the settlements and were interspersed with wood and heath in areas of more recent colonisation, were generally less than 5 acres and rarely exceeded 10 acres. Peasant closes and demesne fields alike were usually hedged, and both were occasionally subject to subdivision between two or more tenants. This most often resulted from alienation, by sale or lease, of land within a close to more than occupier, or from partial alienation by one tenant to

---

[1] Roden, *Geogr. Annlr.*, LII, 1969, p. 118.

[2] E. C. Vollans, 'The Evolution of Farmlands in the Central Chilterns in the Twelfth and Thirteenth Centuries', *Trans. Inst. Br. Geogr.*, XXVI, 1959, pp. 210, 222.

[3] P.R.O., SC6/863/2; Hertfordshire R.O., 17465.

[4] Roden, *Agric. Hist. Rev.*, XVII, 1969, p. 15; P.R.O., C132/31/3; B.M., Harleian Ms. 3688.

another. Very occasionally divided succession to property had the same effect. Although reproducing the strip pattern and scattered holdings of the common fields on a small scale, fractionated closes were in fact quite distinct from them. The subdivisions had neither the regular size nor the systematic organisation into furlongs character-istic of common arable strips; the closes were divided into five to ten parcels at the most; and the separate pieces of land were generally reconsolidated or fenced off into new closes after a few years.[1] Crawley Croft, in Codicote (Herts.), passed through a complete cycle of fragmentation and compaction over a fifty-four year period, and ended up as two closes.[2]

The basis of most tenant farms, free and villein alike, was a half virgate of 25 to 30 acres or its fractions, the ferlingate and the cotland. By 1300, however, many customary tenements had been considerably modified by the operation of a peasant land market. Some family farms had become dispersed, while some men were able to accumulate sub-stantial properties over the years by buying and leasing small plots of land. On most manors there was also a large class of very small peasant holdings, actual numbers varying according to local opportunities for employment.[3] Demesne farms were quite large: 382 acres was the average cultivated area of fourteen demesnes in the thirteenth and fourteenth centuries, that is twice the Leicestershire average in 1300.[4] The economic difficulties of the fourteenth century saw growing engrossment of peasant tenements – especially after the epidemic of 1349 in which 50 to 60 per cent of the population of some manors died – and a gradual leasing-out of manorial demesnes.[5]

The typical Chiltern farm combined common and several arable in varying proportions, although the degree of fragmentation differed considerably within the Hills. Many properties were wholly enclosed, especially in the southwest – at Ibstone (Bucks.) some complete half virgates comprised no more than two or three closes and two quarter virgates were each a single field; some manorial demesnes lay together as single blocks in a few giant closes; while in the northeast tenant farms often consisted almost entirely of small and scattered strips.[6]

[1] D. Roden, 'Fragmentation of Farms and Fields in the Chiltern Hills in the Thirteenth Century and Later', Mediaeval Studies, XXXI, 1969, pp. 225–38.
[2] B.M., Stowe Mss. 849, fos. 16d, 32, 37, 38d, 46d, 48, 48d, 49d, 60, 61d.
[3] D. Roden, 'Inheritance Customs and Succession to Land in the Chiltern Hills in the Thirteenth and Early Fourteenth Centuries', Jnl. Brit. Stud., VII, 1967, pp. 1–11.
[4] Roden, Agric. Hist. Rev., XVII, 1969, p. 10; R. H. Hilton, 'Medieval Agrarian History', V.C.H. Leics., II, 1954, p. 173.
[5] Roden, Folk Life, VIII, 1970, p. 66; Roden, Agric. Hist. Rev., XVII, 1969, p. 10.
[6] D. Roden, 'Field Systems in Ibstone, a Township of the Southwest Chilterns, During the Later Middle Ages', Records of Buckinghamshire, XVIII (part 1), 1966,

Common arable holdings were dispersed amongst only some of the common fields of a township, where these exceeded two or three in number, and usually lay in the fields nearest to the farmstead. At Knebworth (Herts.), for example, strips held by families living in the three hamlets in the west of the parish were confined to the group of eight common fields there – no one had land in the fields around the village.[1] There was no attempt at any regularity in the distribution of common arable tenements either between the individual common fields or between groups of fields. Thus the strips of the St Albans Abbey farm at Codicote (Herts.) were confined to five of the twenty common fields in the manor in the proportions of 55, 40, 35, 18 and 9 acres, while peasant holdings showed an equally uneven scatter between up to eight fields.[2]

Pasturing on the arable fallow and stubble was an integral part of field systems throughout the Hills, important as a means of manuring the land and valuable as a source of fodder. In the twelfth and early thirteenth centuries enclosed demesne tillage, as well as common field land, woods and wastes, was often subject to rights of common grazing. Twelfth-century Flamstead tenants were free to forage over the entire demesne; a mid-century grant in Missenden (Bucks.) to the new abbey there was accompanied by the right to pasture all the grantor's land; and closes and woods owned by the monks of Thame at Wyfold (Oxon.) were grazed in common by more than thirty farmers until 1230.[3] There is no unambiguous evidence concerning practice on peasant property at this early date. Free pasturage on demesne land was later limited, and by 1300 more orthodox techniques were followed on a majority of holdings. Common arable was thrown open to the stock of the parceners or of the entire township, practice apparently varying. Thus the 204 acres of the St Ledger demesne scattered amongst the open strips of Offley (Herts.) – another 96 acres lay in severalty – were said to be without value when unsown because they were in common, and Pinnocks Field in Whitchurch (Oxon.) (still a common field in the eighteenth century) was specifically mentioned as subject to rights of common grazing.[4] Stints rationing the number of

p. 51; D. Roden and A. R. H. Baker, 'Field Systems of the Chiltern Hills and of Parts of Kent from the Late Thirteenth to the Early Seventeenth Century', *Trans. Inst. Brit. Geogr.*, XXXVIII, 1966, Fig. 3.

[1] Hertfordshire R.O., 21860, 21866, 21869, 21871, 21890, 21920, 21941.
[2] B.M., Add. Ms. 40734, fos. 1–1d.
[3] Hertfordshire R.O., 17465; J. G. Jenkins (ed.), *The Cartulary of Missenden Abbey, Part 1*, Records Branch of Buckinghamshire Arch. Soc., II, 1939, p. 66 no. 65; W. H. Turner and H. O. Coxe (eds.), *Calendar of Charters and Rolls Preserved in the Bodleian Library*, 1878, p. 315 no. 53.
[4] P.R.O., C134/101/10, C135/42/18.

animals allowed on the common arable had been introduced in the north-east, and no doubt reflected a growing shortage of fodder.[1] Subdivided closes were also sometimes pastured in common by the co-tenants,[2] while, conversely, grazing in closes in a single holding was generally restricted to the flocks and herds of the farm, unless this was under-stocked, in which case fallow and stubble might be leased out on an annual basis.[3] Sheep were often folded on limited areas within the larger demesne closes.[4]

As far as cropping practices are concerned, it is particularly important in this region of varied field types to distinguish between the rotations followed on individual holdings, and communal crop sequences enforced over all or a substantial part of the township. Cropping on the farm was usually organised so as to leave a regular and frequent fallow. This was as much a part of the system of husbandry on totally enclosed holdings as on those in which a substantial proportion of the arable lay in common fields. Careful preparation of the fallow (at least on the demesnes) was combined with widespread marling and manuring – dung from stables and cowsheds, litter collected from the streets of towns and villages, and dead leaves and deer droppings gathered from parkland were all spread over the arable from time to time. Usual practice on the demesne farms was to leave between one-third and one-half of the holding fallow each year, although the exact proportions varied seasonally according to changing demand and weather conditions.[5] Three-course arrangements had appeared by the twelfth century. Eighty acres of the Kensworth (Beds.) demesne lay fallow in 1152 and the two sown courses each contained 70 acres, while twelfth- and thirteenth-century Missenden charters imply the existence of similar methods in the central Chilterns.[6] By the early fourteenth century, triennial fallowing was common throughout the region on tenant as well as demesne farms, but a biennial fallow was sometimes applied on poorer soils or at times of economic difficulty (such as the years immediately after 1349).[7] Peasants occasionally attempted, unsuccessfully, to cultivate the fallow course.[8]

Although rotations were straightforward, the ways in which the

[1] B.M., Add. Ch. 35694, Stowe Ms. 849, fo. 55d.
[2] Hertfordshire R.O., 40703.
[3] Roden, *Agric. Hist. Rev.*, XVII, 1969, p. 17.
[4] P.R.O., *Register of Edward the Black Prince*, 1933, IV, 82; B.M., Add. Ch. 35684.
[5] Roden, *Agric. Hist. Rev.*, XVII, 1969, pp. 16–19.
[6] W. Hale (ed.), *The Domesday of St. Paul's of the Year M.CC.XXII*, Camden Soc., LXIX, 1859, pp. 230–1.
[7] Roden, *Agric. Hist. Rev.*, XVII, 1969, pp. 18–19, 23.
[8] Merton College Muniments, 5219; B.M., Stowe Ms. 849, fo. 94d.

arable was organised into coherent cropping systems – designed to ensure a regular sequence of cultivation over the plots comprising a tenement – became increasingly complex. During the twelfth and thirteenth centuries three-course rotations were often translated into simple three-field arrangements on both common and several arable – field and cropping course were one. The furlongs of the manor of Gynaunt's Fee in High Wycombe (Bucks.) were, for example, grouped into east, middle and west fields (only a few of the many common fields along the Wye valley in the parish), and a 3-acre grant was taken in equal proportions from each.[1] Arable of the Missenden Abbey farm at Honor (Bucks.) about 1170 was, on the other hand, probably confined to three closes, one of which lay fallow each year, whereas the eight closes of the West Wycombe (Bucks.) demesne were apportioned between three shifts c. 1260 with the same combination of fields recurring year after year.[2]

By the end of the century larger tenant and demesne closes were often sown with a variety of grains in any one year, and during the next few decades increasingly complex patterns of cropping developed while the range of crops widened. There was now rarely any clear grouping of fields on the demesnes but instead a confusing variety of combinations, with separate courses appearing at the same time in one enclosed field, with one course of the farm rotation comprising different units in a single close and arable in a number of closes and common fields, and with the same shift being followed in one enclosure for many successive seasons, presumably on separate pieces of land. Cropping was rotated within individual closes as well as between closes, and hurdles were used to control grazing on the subdivisions. At Ibstone and West Wycombe it was customary for a few demesne fields, normally left under pasture, to be brought into cultivation occasionally – thus supplementing the large core of continuously farmed land – somewhat in the manner of the convertible husbandry that obtained in parts of Kent and Sussex. This system was expanded after 1350 to absorb the greater area then being left unsown.[3]

A variety of grains might be grown in each common field, but they were always of the same season, sown and harvested at about

[1] J. G. Jenkins (ed.), *The Cartulary of Missenden Abbey, Part 3*, H.M.C., J.P. I, being Buckinghamshire Record Society, XII, 1962, pp. 114–16 nos. 710–12, pp. 118–19 nos. 715–16.

[2] Jenkins, *The Cartulary of Missenden Abbey, Part 1*, p. 178 no. 192; Hampshire R.O., Eccl. 2/159294ff.

[3] Roden, *Agric. Hist. Rev.*, XVII, 1969, pp. 20–1; Roden, *Records of Bucks.*, XVIII (part 1), 1966, pp. 50–1; T. A. M. Bishop, 'The Rotation of Crops at Westerham', *Econ. Hist. Rev.*, IX, 1938–9, pp. 38–44.

the same time.[1] Separate fields, and not individual furlongs, were thus the normal units of common arable cultivation, the large number of relatively small fields in many Hill manors apparently being sufficiently flexible for practical purposes. Sixteenth- and seventeenth-century evidence suggests that multiple common fields of such Hertfordshire townships as Little Gaddesden and Offley were loosely organised, for greater convenience, into three divisions, the fields in each group being subject to the same cultivation sequence and lying fallow every third year.[2] In effect, these combinations were the Chiltern equivalent of the large units of the typical two- or three-field township, the role of the constituent fields being closer to that of the Midland furlongs. But whereas the common fields of Midland districts were usually simple geographical units, each Chiltern 'season' comprised fields lying throughout the common arable and not necessarily adjacent to each other.

Common grazing in the fields precluded any variation from the customary routine, and as a result cropping on individual farms had to be organised in such a way that cultivation of their common arable holdings conformed with practice in the fields in which this land lay – strips in a fallow common field, for example, had to be in the uncropped course of the farm rotation. This was achieved on demesne ploughland by balancing several and common arable within the rotation. One shift of Codicote manor farm in 1332 contained 82 acres in three common fields and 53½ acres in two closes, another course comprised common arable alone (in two fields), and the third was entirely enclosed.[3] Although there is no information relating to practice on peasant farms at this time, it is difficult to see how it could have been very different. Through combinations of enclosed and common field land, or, failing this, through permutations of arable in a variety of common fields, the tenants must have been able to adjust cropping on their own holdings to suit the communal systems. For the same reason, equitable division of a common arable holding between individual common fields, or even between communal 'seasons' comprising groups of fields, was unnecessary. If enough of a farm was in severalty very varying amounts of common arable could, as on the Codicote demesne, be left fallow each year. Such flexibility meant, in turn, that there was no practical obstacle to the concentration of individual tenements in one part of a township, especially as the broad common arable cropping courses, where these

[1] Westminster Abbey Muniments, 8807ff.; B.M., Add. Ms. 40734, fos. 1–1d; Harl. Ms. 3688.
[2] Roden, Ph.D. thesis, pp. 66–8, 380–2.
[3] B.M., Add. Ms. 40734, fos. 1–1d.

existed, were not confined geographically but extended to all sectors of the township's strips. A holding in one part of the manor could, if necessary, still be represented in all three common arable shifts.

2. DISTRICTS TO THE SOUTH AND EAST OF THE CHILTERNS

Medieval field systems in the districts immediately to the south and the east of the Chilterns, although extremely varied, were basically of the same pattern as that which obtained in the Hills. Settlement mosaics combining elements of both nucleation and dispersal were associated with multiple strip-divided fields, while enclosed land was always present in significant amounts. The main variant was, as within the Chilterns, the ratio of several to common arable: relatively light, free-working soils were areas of predominantly common field farming, while colder clays and sterile sands were largely enclosed and retained extensive woods and heaths. Thus the territories of villages on the river terraces – along the Thames immediately south of the Chilterns and in southwest Essex, along the Colne in Buckinghamshire, and the Lea in Hertfordshire and Essex – usually included common fields on the loams around the main settlements, common meadows (often subject to annual redistribution) and marshland pastures on the flood-plains, and a mixture of timber, waste and closes on the plateau lands above. Occasional small common fields were also scattered in these last areas: the Oxfordshire parish of Mapledurham, for example, included a set of irregular common fields on the Chiltern dip-slope which were quite distinct from the larger areas of common arable on Thames-side gravels below.[1]

The Hitchin Gap along the eastern edge of the Chilterns marked no radical change in either physical or agrarian conditions. The Middle Chalk outcrop is continued in the slightly lower hills of east Hertfordshire and northwest Essex, and is mantled by boulder clays which weather to produce soils similar to the brickearth-enriched loams of the northeastern Chilterns. On the upper part of the plateau (and also in the Hitchin Gap itself) numerous common fields were combined

---

[1] M. H. Long, 'A History of the Manors of Mapledurham Gurney and Mapledurham Chazey', B.Litt. thesis, University of Oxford, 1953, pp. 69–127; R. Allison, 'The Changing Geographical Landscape of South-west Essex from Saxon Times to 1600', M.A. thesis, University of London, 1958; *V.C.H. Essex*, 1966, v, 105–7, 127–30, 144–5, 162–8, 214–17, 281–3; E. J. Erith, 'The Strip System of Cultivation in Buckhurst Hill in the Thirteenth Century', *Essex Review*, LVII, 1948, pp. 96–9; P. E. Rooke, 'Medieval Cheshunt', *East Hertfordshire Arch. Soc. Trans.*, XIII, 1950–4, pp. 172–203; W. H. Ward and K. S. Block, *A History of the Manor and Parish of Iver*, 1933, pp. 46–7, 77–81, 154; Gray, *English Field Systems*, pp. 375–6, 380, 385–6.

with substantial areas of enclosed arable and woodland, and were associated with village and hamlet settlement. Meadowland was generally confined to the flood-plains of the main streams, and there was a consequent emphasis on mixed sheep–corn husbandry.[1] Conditions such as these mirrored, almost exactly, arrangements west of the Gap. Medieval field systems in, for example, Saffron Walden (northwest Essex) and King's Walden (northeast Chilterns) included many features in common: hamlets had their own sets of subdivided fields; furlongs were sometimes treated as independent units; while there was the same distinction between the continuous common arable and larger common fields of the lighter valley-side soils, and small groups of strips, often with names suggestive of a late assart origin, that were scattered amongst woods and closes on the clays above. Nothing approaching a two- or three-field layout existed, and no tenant had land in every common field.[2]

Heavier soils increase in extent down the dip-slope of the boulder clay plateau, as chalk exposures become more restricted and the clay component more prominent. This change was reflected in a gradual reduction of common arable land, until, along the lower edge of the plateau, townships such as Terling (Essex) were completely enclosed; and it resembled the northeast to southwest transition in Chiltern patterns. Agrarian arrangements in Harlow (Essex) were typical of the lower part of the dip-slope. Most of the market tenants of High Street held strips in Mollond and Chipping Fields, but the larger virgate and half virgate holdings usually consisted of crofts and closes grouped around isolated farmsteads and with a little meadow by the Stort. One farm, for example, comprised a messuage and 30 acres lying together in seven crofts.[3] Conditions on the glacial gravels of the Vale of St Albans, immediately south of the Hertfordshire Chilterns, were somewhat similar. Villages and hamlets on the better soils of

[1] D. Monteith, 'Saffron Walden and its Environs: a Study in the Development of a Landscape', M.A. thesis, University of London, 1957, pp. 81–129; D. Cromarty, *The Fields of Saffron Walden in 1400*, Essex R.O., XLIII, 1966; K. C. Newton, *Thaxted in the Fourteenth Century*, Essex R.O., XXXIII, 1960; G. Eland (ed.), *At the Courts of Great Canfield, Essex*, 1949, pp. 33–4; F. Hull, 'Agriculture and Rural Society in Essex, 1560–1640', Ph.D. thesis, University of London, 1950, pp. 2–20; F. B. Stitt, 'The Manors of Great and Little Wymondley in the Later Middle Ages', B.Litt. thesis, University of Oxford, 1951, pp. 1, 17–34; Gray, *English Field Systems*, pp. 370, 374–5, 389–91.

[2] Cromarty, *The Fields of Saffron Walden in 1400*; Roden, Ph.D. thesis, pp. 114–58.

[3] J. L. Fisher, 'Harlow in the Middle Ages', *Essex Rev.*, XLVI, 1937, pp. 138–44, 209–13; J. L. Fisher, 'The Harlow Cartulary', *Essex Arch. Soc. Trans.*, XXII,. 1936–40 (pub. 1940), pp. 239–71; C. A. Barton, *Historical Notes and Records of the Parish of Terling, Essex*, 1954, pp. 20–4; J. French, 'On Some Ancient Surveys of Felsted', *Essex Rev.*, XXVIII, 1919, pp. 62–76; Hull, Ph.D. thesis, pp. 20–8.

the east had their own groups of small common fields and riverside meadows, while woodland, waste and arable enclosures increased both up the slopes of the Vale and westwards as coarse sands and gravels become more extensive.[1] Hedged closes, scattered amongst great woods and heaths, were characteristic, too, of the gravel plateau south of Beaconsfield (Bucks.), although common fields were located along its southern edge where glacial deposits give way to the Thames terraces.[2]

The area of London Clays and Bagshot and glacial sands which stretch over most of the southern and eastern half of Essex, around the edge of the boulder clay plateau, was also, in the thirteenth century, an enclosed region, as was its western extension across the Lea, the clay plateau of south Hertfordshire and north Middlesex. There were areas of subdivided arable: phrases in thirteenth-century fines for townships such as Rawreth, Rocheford and Havering in southern Essex suggest the existence of small common fields; common arable at Lawling between the Crouch and Blackwater estuaries is referred to about 1309; while a group of townships on the lighter loams around Colchester contained fairly extensive common fields akin to those on the boulder clay plateau to the west. But there is no indication that communal cultivation was ever widespread, and most of the thirteenth-century common fields had been enclosed by c. 1600.[3] Descriptions of land in feet of fines, charters of such religious bodies as Hornchurch Priory and Beeleigh Abbey, and rentals and extents like the Ingatestone survey of c. 1275 suggest that this was above all a country of hedged crofts, private woods, heaths and open forest.[4]

[1] Workers' Educational Association (Hatfield Branch), *Hatfield and its People*, parts I and II, 1959–60; A. E. Levett, *Studies in Manorial History*, 1938, p. 388.

[2] M. W. Hughes (ed.), *A Calendar of the Feet of Fines for the County of Buckingham – 7 Richard I to 44 Henry III*, Buckinghamshire Arch. Soc. Records Branch, IV, 1940 (pub. 1942), p. 13 no. 53, p. 39 no. 1; J. G. Jenkins (ed.), *The Missenden Cartulary*, Part 2, Buckinghamshire Rec. Soc., X, 1946 (pub. 1955), p. 92 no. 410, p. 94 nos. 413–14.

[3] R. G. Kirk (ed.), *Feet of Fines for Essex*, 1899–1910, I, p. 145 no. 767, p. 171 no. 960; H. F. Westlake (ed.), *Hornchurch Priory. A Kalendar of Documents in the Possession of the Warden and Fellows of New College Oxford*, 1923; J. F. Nichols, 'The Extent of Lawling, A.D. 1310', *Essex Arch. Soc. Trans.*, XX, 1930–1, pp. 176, 182; J. L. Fisher (ed.), 'The Leger Book of St. John's Abbey, Colchester', *Essex Arch. Soc. Trans.*, XXIV, 1951, pp. 99–100; S. A. Moore (ed.), *Cartularium Monasterii Sancti Johannis Baptiste de Colecestria*, 1897, I, 266, 276, 286; II, 321, 329–30, 344, 649, 653, 656; G. Martin, *The Story of Colchester from Roman Times to the Present Day*, 1959, pp. 26–7; Hull, Ph.D. thesis, pp. 29, 34, 37–41.

[4] Westlake, *Hornchurch Priory*; R. C. Fowler and A. W. Clapham, *Beeleigh Abbey Essex*, 1922, pp. 37–40; G. Rickwood, 'A Rent-Roll of Sir Harvey Marney of Layer Marney', *Essex Arch. Soc. Trans.*, XIII, 1913–14, pp. 92–106; Gray, *English Field Systems*, pp. 391–4; Hull, Ph.D. thesis, pp. 42–3; Essex R.O., D/DP M150.

Settlement was dispersed in small villages, hamlets, waste-side agglomerations and isolated farmsteads. Later maps show that the pattern of closes was often surprisingly rectilinear.

Pre-eminence of enclosed land did not mean that the economy was based primarily on pastoral or woodland activities. Extensive wastes, surviving in particular on the sands and gravels, provided rough grazing together with fuel and building materials for surrounding townships; marshes and saltings which fringed much of the Essex coast and Thames estuary were important sheep rearing districts, often held by interior townships as well as coastal parishes; while private timber was also sometimes a valuable source of supplementary income, especially in areas accessible to tidewater.[1] Yet meadow was limited in inland districts, possibly because the numerous streams which cross the London Clay do not have well-developed flood-plains, and details of demesne cropping suggest that most closes were in tillage about 1300.[2] Herding and woodland crafts may have been rather more important on tenant holdings, but it was not until the second half of the fourteenth century that the larger farmers on the London Clay began to adopt the pastoral bias for which they were later famous. Mid-century pestilence – which affected some manors severely – combined with the general economic decline to encourage widespread amalgamation of holdings and a permanent reduction in the cropped area on heavier soils. The sown acreage of the Hutton (Essex) demesne was more than halved between 1342 and 1389, no complete villein holding was leased out, and sheep and cattle farming became increasingly important. Arable was still being converted to pasture early in the sixteenth century.[3]

[1] Allison, M.A. thesis, pp. 81–222; W. R. Fisher, *The Forest of Essex*, 1888, pp. 230–80; J. L. Fisher (ed.), *Cartularium Prioratus de Colne*, Essex Arch. Soc. Occas. Publns. I, 1946, p. 66 no. 20, p. 73 no. 40, p. 80 no. 68; Fisher, *Essex Arch. Soc. Trans.*, XXIV, 1951, pp. 103–4; *V.C.H. Essex*, I, 1903, pp. 369–78; V, 1966, pp. 127–30, 144–5, 162–3, 167, 214–16, 238, 282, 289–92; B. E. Cracknell, 'Canvey Island: the History of a Marshland Community', *Occasional Papers, Dept. Engl. Local Hist. Univ. of Leicester*, XII, 1959, pp. 10–16; A. Clark, 'Feering Manor, Essex, 1289', *Essex Rev.*, XXI, 1911, p. 211; A. E. Bland, P. A. Brown and R. H. Tawney, *English Economic History. Select Documents*, 1914, pp. 56–8; J. F. Nichols, 'Custodia Essexae: a Study of the Conventual Property Held by the Priory of Christ Church Canterbury in the Counties of Essex, Suffolk and Norfolk', Ph.D. thesis, University of London, 1930, pp. 213–30; W. M. Sturman, 'Barking Abbey. A Study in its External and Internal Administration from the Conquest to the Dissolution', Ph.D. thesis, University of London, 1961, pp. 68–100.

[2] H. C. Darby (ed.), *The Domesday Geography of Eastern England*, 1952, pp. 239–40, 261–2; Nichols, Ph.D. thesis, pp. 232–3.

[3] K. G. Feiling, 'An Essex Manor in the Fourteenth Century', *Engl. Hist. Rev.*, XXVI, 1911, pp. 336–7; J. L. Fisher, 'The Black Death in Essex', *Essex Rev.*, LII,

Essex closes were apparently rather larger than those in the Chilterns. Areas of 10 to 20 acres are quite frequent in fines and charters, while the larger fields of 70 to 80 acres or more that are sometimes recorded were probably, as in the Hills, demesne property. Enclosed land was being extended in a number of ways. Common fields were occasionally taken into severalty: the strip system at Chigwell (Essex) fell into disuse early in the thirteenth century after Waltham Abbey had obtained possession of the whole estate, and at Colchester, about 100 years later, the abbot of St John's and others were enclosing fields which had once been common to the burgesses.[1] Scattered subdivided fields on the London Clay may also have been fenced in by the sixteenth century, for F. Hull found almost no evidence of common arable land there after 1560.[2] Consolidation was taking place, especially on seigneurial holdings. The average size of demesne strips in the common fields of Thaxted (Essex), 1393, was 18 acres, and the largest single open unit contained over 77 acres.[3]

But most enclosed farmland in Essex and Hertfordshire had probably, as Gray suggested, been improved from the wastes directly into severalty.[4] Creation of new closes in this way was still occurring on a large scale during the twelfth and thirteen centuries, especially on the lower part of the boulder clay plateau and on the clays and sands south and east of it. Thirty-five acres were reclaimed and added to the Chingford (Essex) demesne between 1181 and 1222, a further 40 acres was incorporated during the thirteenth century, and about 20 per cent of tenant property in 1222 was described as assart. Essex manors of Christ Church, Canterbury, also received rents for freshly cleared land: almost 200 acres of their Lawling fee was assart c. 1309 and more than 500 acres of wood still survived there.[5] Assarts generally appear in the charters as individual holdings – tenant intakes at Ardley (Essex) ranged from tiny plots to complete half virgates – and often as surrounded by a ditch or a fence.[6] The character of the enclosed

1943, pp. 13–20; K. C. Newton, *Medieval Essex from the Conquest to the Eve of the Reformation*, Essex R.O., XXXVI, 1962, item 26; Sturman, Ph.D. thesis, pp. 252, 259–60; *V.C.H. Essex*, v, 1966, p. 127.

[1] E. J. Erith (ed.), *Essex Parish Records, 1240–1894*, Essex R.O., VII, 1950, pp. 96–9; I. H. Jeayes (ed.), *Court Rolls of the Borough of Colchester*, 1921, I, 168, 177; 1938, II, 2, 143.

[2] Hull, Ph.D. thesis, Map 2.

[3] Newton, *Thaxted in the Fourteenth Century*, pp. 34–7.

[4] Gray, *English Field Systems*, p. 391.

[5] Hale, *The Domesday of St. Paul's*, pp. 90–2, 144; Nichols, Ph.D thesis, p. 227; Nichols, *Essex Arch. Soc. Trans.*, XX, 1930–1, pp. 176–7, 181, 194.

[6] Hale, *The Domesday of St. Paul's*, pp. 23–6; Kirk, *Feet of Fines for Essex*, 1899–1910, I, p. 16 no. 62, p. 94 no. 323, p. 109 no. 433, p. 127 no. 659, p. 128 no. 662, p. 265 no. 1577.

landscape reflected the nature of its colonisation. Two sub-manors in Saffron Walden were given virgin land which was then grubbed-up and worked as large enclosures, whereas small crofts were typical of the clearings around peasant farmsteads and settlements of cottagers on small intakes.[1] Both assarts and established closes were occasionally subdivided by grants or sale of land within them.[2]

Large areas of timber were fenced off for preservation as private woodland, and were often taken to form new parks or extend existing ones so that by the sixteenth century few Essex parishes were without a park.[3] Inning of coastal marshes was usually for improved pasture – only small areas were under the plough c. 1300 – and although some of the Thames-side marshes were common land, the majority of holdings were marked out by banks and ditches and held in severalty.[4] Enclosure of wood and heath for cultivation had generally ended by 1300 (there are few fourteenth-century references to new assarts), while repeated inundations along the coast discouraged further attempts to extend the reclaimed area, and focussed efforts on the preservation of what had already been won from the sea.[5]

The system of land holding throughout the country south and east of the Chilterns was fundamentally the same as that in the Hills. The virgate and, more usually, the half virgate were the basic units of customary tenure, but by the mid-fourteenth century they had often been modified considerably through sale and lease.[6] A large number of small holdings had appeared on some manors, especially in townships with extensive common wastes or a market centre to attract landless men from neighbouring districts.[7] Conversely, some tenants acquired substantial farms by engrossing villein tenements and leasing of demesne arable. Holdings in common field townships usually combined several and common arable in varying proportions – a 6-acre Mundon (Herts.) tenement mentioned by Gray comprised a mixture of closes, assarts and open strips – while customary tenures in enclosed districts consisted of closes alone.[8] Chiltern patterns of common-field

[1] Cromarty, *The Fields of Saffron Walden in 1400*, pp. 11–13.
[2] Westlake, *Hornchurch Priory*, p. 9 no. 1, p. 87 no. 370, p. 125 no. 524.
[3] Allison, M.A. thesis, pp. 201–2.
[4] *Ibid.*, pp. 81–104, 127–32; Sturman, Ph.D. thesis, pp. 70–7; H. Grieve, *The Great Tide*, 1959, pp. 4–11.
[5] Grieve, *The Great Tide*, pp. 12–16; Allison, M.A. thesis, pp. 104–27.
[6] Newton, *Thaxted in the Fourteenth Century*, pp. 10–29; Fieling, *Engl. Hist. Rev.*, XXVI, 1911, p. 337; Levett, *Studies in Manorial History*, pp. 185–8, 191–2.
[7] Newton, *Thaxted in the Fourteenth Century*, p. 31; *V.C.H. Essex*, v, 1966, p. 127.
[8] Hughes, *A Calendar of the Feet of Fines for the County of Buckingham*, p. 39 no. 1; Levett, *Studies in Manorial History*, p. 187; Gray, *English Field Systems*, pp. 374–5, 380, 391–2.

holding were also repeated. The limited medieval evidence suggests, and sixteenth- and seventeenth-century surveys and terriers confirm, that the strips of a farm usually lay in one part of the common arable, in the fields nearest to the dwelling, and with no apparent regularity in their distribution between these fields.[1]

Cropping and grazing arrangements were characterised both by their variety and, again, by the similarity to Chiltern conditions. Common fields were open to pasturing by livestock of all kinds – early fourteenth-century extents of Lawling, Borley and Milton in southeastern Essex speak of the easements of the common fields after harvest and in the fallow season[2] – and the strong demand for arable grazing, especially in townships such as Saffron Walden (Essex) without access to large wastes, was reflected in the early enforcement of stints.[3] Several demesne fallow was also subject to pasturing by tenant stock, sometimes as a common right at a nominal rent,[4] but usually in return for more substantial payment and only when the demesne farm itself was understocked. Some tenant closes at Colchester, too, may have been grazed by the burgesses, while pasturage in Saffron Walden was regulated by a system of folds which included enclosed as well as common arable (although the precise nature of its operation is not clear).[5]

Three-course rotations were widely adopted by 1300 on totally enclosed holdings and farms in common-field townships alike. Both demesne and peasant tenements were apportioned among three shifts in roughly equal amounts,[6] but there is no evidence that a substantial part of any township was ever divided into two or three areas for communal rotations. Custom as to cropping within the common arable varied. At Saffron Walden, c. 1400, the furlong was the basic

[1] Gray, English Field Systems, p. 380; Cromarty, The Fields of Saffron Walden in 1400, p. 9; Fisher, Essex Arch. Soc. Trans., XXII, 1936–40 (pub. 1940), pp. 245, 254–9; Levett, Studies in Manorial History, p. 388.

[2] Nichols, Essex Arch. Soc. Trans., XX, 1930–1, pp. 176, 182; G. Beaumont, 'The Manor of Borley, A.D. 1308', Essex Arch. Soc. Trans., XVIII, 1925–7, p. 263; J. F. Nichols, 'Milton Hall. The Extent of 1309 and an Inventory of 1278', Southend-on-Sea and District Antiqu. and Hist. Soc. Trans., I, 1923, p. 14.

[3] Cromarty, The Fields of Saffron Walden in 1400, pp. 13, 14.

[4] Sturman, Ph.D. thesis, p. 53; J. L. Fisher, Harlow New Town. A Short History of the Area that it will Embrace, 1951, p. 26.

[5] Jeayes, Court Rolls of the Borough of Colchester, 1941, III, 176; Cromarty, The Fields of Saffron Walden in 1400, pp. 14–16.

[6] Cromarty, The Fields of Saffron Walden in 1400, pp. 5, 7, 9–10; Hale, The Domesday of St. Paul's, p. cxviii; Nichols, Ph.D. thesis, p. 187; Sturman, Ph.D. thesis, p. 54; Gray, English Field Systems, pp. 396–8; A. Clark, 'Church Hall Manor, Kelvedon, in 1294', Essex Rev., XIX, 1910, p. 140; Clark, Essex Rev., XXI, 1911, p. 211; Levett, Studies in Manorial History, pp. 183–4.

unit whereas only a few miles away, at Thaxted, each common field contained no more than one component of the three demesne shifts.[1] Regular allotment of a common arable holding between the farm courses was apparently unnecessary, although cropping at Saffron Walden 'was so arranged that within the fixed limits of the sheepfolds there was some land under each of the rotational elements' so that grazing was available in every fold throughout the year.[2] As in the Chilterns, such flexibility was made possible by the combination, within one cropping system, of enclosed and common arable or of strips lying in a number of fields or furlongs (depending on whichever was the main unit of tillage). Two of the Thaxted demesne seasons, for example, each contained land in two common fields, the third being confined to a single field.[3] Farm cultivation was not tied to the fixed routine of the open strips. For the same reason the existence of common fields did not imply a nucleation of settlement: land within them was worked from isolated farmsteads as well as from dwellings in hamlets, villages and small towns.

3. DISTRICTS TO THE NORTH OF THE CHALK ESCARPMENT

North of the Middle Chalk escarpment lies an area of mixed soils and varied relief. A narrow belt of easily worked loams immediately below the scarp (the Icknield zone) widens towards the northeast, and overlooks a broad clay vale. The Oxford, Kimmeridge and Gault Clays exposed in the Vale of Oxford are generally mantled in Buckinghamshire and Bedfordshire by boulder clays of varying consistency, while isolated limestone hills and an extensive out-crop of Lower Greensand rocks break the surface of the vale in Oxfordshire and Bedfordshire respectively. The lowlands con-tinue beyond the northern borders of three of the counties, but in Oxfordshire they give way to the Oolitic Limestone plateau of the Cotswolds and, beyond these, the Liassic Marlstone hills of north Oxfordshire.

The most distinctive feature of medieval field systems throughout this region, on light and heavy soils alike, was the existence of a myriad of open strips, usually half an acre or one rood in size and grouped, on the basis of communal routines enforced over them, into two or three great fields (Fig. 8.4). This was Gray's 'Midland system' at its fullest development. Of the five counties, Essex alone contained no

[1] Cromarty, *The Fields of Saffron Walden in 1400*, p. 9; Newton, *Thaxted in the Fourteenth Century*, pp. 34–5.
[2] Cromarty, *The Fields of Saffron Walden in 1400*, p. 9.
[3] Newton, *Thaxted in the Fourteenth Century*, pp. 34–5.

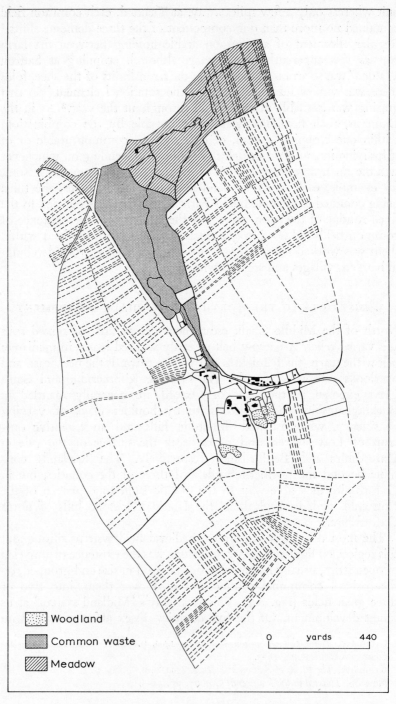

Woodland

Common waste

Meadow

0   yards   440

Fig. 8.4 The three-field township of Cuxham (Oxon.) in 1767.
Source. J. L. G. Mowat, *Sixteen Old Maps of Properties in Oxfordshire*, 1888, no. 8.

Midland country and Hertfordshire was represented only by a narrow belt immediately below the Middle Chalk.

Meadow, while generally scarce in manors on the Oolite plateau and the Bedfordshire greensands, was relatively abundant along the many streams of the clay lowlands and the marlstone uplands, and especially extensive along the Thames, the main Cotswold valleys and the Ivel and Ouse.[1] Subdivided meadows were numerous, and were often subject to annual reallotment according to complicated procedures. The hay aftermath was generally open to common grazing.[2] Some townships also had access to substantial common wastes. The marshes of Otmoor, downs and woods on the Chiltern plateau, the Cotswold sheepwalks, nine or ten royal forests in the clay lowlands and on the Oolite south of the Cherwell, and the woods and heaths of the greensand hills were all open, in varying degrees, to neighbouring manors.[3] Many parishes, however, contained no more than a few acres of common cow pasture or 'moor' on patches of poorly drained ground, and in these the shortage of forage was so acute that, as at Sherington (Bucks.), roadside verges were prized.[4] Considerable areas under private timber survived, especially where preserved as parkland or royal forest. Other townships were virtually treeless by the thirteenth century.[5]

Five or six or more common fields existed in many parishes, usually because the original village and its later hamlets each had independent agricultural systems. The territory of Beckley (Oxon), for example, included four hamlets, in addition to the village, and at least three of these were associated with their own groups of subdivided fields. Occasionally the reverse had occurred: in Marsh Baldon (Oxon.) four hamlets shared two fields.[6] The two-field division of common arable

[1] H. C. Darby and E. M. J. Campbell (eds.), *The Domesday Geography of South-East England*, 1962, pp. 35, 171, 216.

[2] J. G. Jenkins (ed.), *The Cartulary of Snelshall Priory*, Buckinghamshire Rec. Soc., IX, 1945 (pub. 1952), p. 47 no. 129; G. H. Fowler (ed.), 'Tractatus de Dunstaple et de Houcton', *Bedfordshire Hist. Rec. Soc.*, XIX, 1937, pp. 71, 90; E. Chambers, *Eynsham Under the Monks*, Oxfordshire Rec. Ser., XVIII, 1936, pp. 91–2.

[3] M. G. Hobson and K. L. H. Price, *Otmoor and its Seven Towns*, 1961, pp. 9–13; *V.C.H. Oxon.*, V, 1957, pp. 21, 69–70, 83, 111, 119, 128, 163, 181, 197, 216, 250, 275–8, 293–5; F. W. Bateson, *Brill. A Short History*, 1966, pp. 4–6; G. H. Fowler (ed.), 'Some Saxon Charters', *Bedfordshire Hist. Rec. Soc.*, V, 1920, p. 45 no. vi.

[4] A. C. Chibnall, *Sherington. Fiefs and Fields of a Buckinghamshire Village*, 1965, p. 109; G. H. Fowler (ed.), *Calendar of the Roll of the Justices on Eyre, 1247*, Bedfordshire Hist. Rec. Soc., XXI, 1939, p. 69 no. 176.

[5] P. D. A. Harvey, *A Medieval Oxfordshire Village. Cuxham 1240 to 1400*, 1965, pp. 96–7.

[6] *V.C.H. Oxon.*, V, 1957, pp. 38, 67–8; G. R. Elvey, 'Buckinghamshire in 1086', *Records of Bucks.*, XVI, 1953–60, pp. 342–62.

was by far the most usual arrangement before 1300 on lowlands and uplands alike. Of 148 villages and hamlets for which suitable thirteenth-century information has been examined, 118 were probably worked as two fields, while only 28 had three fields or more. A few hamlets contained a single field which may have been cultivated continuously or which may, for practical purposes, have been subdivided into two or three parts.[1] Tenant holdings – customarily based on a virgate of 24 to 35 acres or on the half virgate – were highly fragmented, but were usually apportioned evenly between the fields, and often had one or two acres of meadow attached as well. A Beachampton (Bucks.) virgate with 12 acres in one field and 12 acres in the other c. 1200, and a 12-acre half virgate divided regularly between the three fields of Cuxham (Oxon.) are only two of many examples.[2] Manorial demesnes were also frequently distributed in equal amounts between the main fields, even where the farm included a large enclosed area.[3] Development of peasant sale and leasing during the thirteenth century brought disintegration of customary tenements to many manors, with a growing inequality in holding sizes and a less even dispersal within the common arable.[4] The tenurial strip might consist of one or more plough ridges, and half an acre was the usual equivalent of a single selion.[5] Furlongs were marked by merestones, paths and stakes; ridges may simply have been delimited by intervening furrows;[6] and the fields themselves were hedged.[7] Closes as well as the common arable were laid in selions.[8] Ridge and furrow still survives on the clays where, in order to facilitate drainage, 'lands' were thrown up to a greater height than on the lighter soils and hill slopes.[9]

[1] V.C.H. Oxon., v, 1957, p. 67; vi, 1959, p. 272.
[2] Jenkins, The Cartulary of Snelshall Priory, p. 40 no. 108; Harvey, A Medieval Oxfordshire Village, p. 130.
[3] P. Hyde, 'The Winchester Manors at Witney and Adderbury, Oxfordshire, in the Later Middle Ages', B.Litt. thesis, University of Oxford, 1955, p. 131; V.C.H. Oxon., v, 1957, p. 313; vi, 1959, p. 109.
[4] M. K. Dale (ed.), Court Roll of Chalgrave Manor 1278–1313, Bedfordshire Hist. Rec. Soc., xxviii, 1948 (pub. 1950), p. xxiv; V.C.H. Oxon., v, 1957, pp. 38, 200; vii, 1962, p. 153; viii, 1964, p. 188; Harvey, A Medieval Oxfordshire Village, pp. 114–19.
[5] V.C.H. Oxon., vi, 1959, p. 156; G. Fowler (ed.), The Records of Harrold Priory, Bedfordshire Hist. Rec. Soc., xvii, 1935, p. 194.
[6] V.C.H. Oxon., vii, 1962, p. 131; G. B. Grundy (ed.), Saxon Oxfordshire. Charters and Ancient Highways, Oxfordshire Rec. Ser., xv, 1933, pp. 63–73; Harvey, A Medieval Oxfordshire Village, p. 23.
[7] G. C. Homans, English Villagers of the Thirteenth Century, 1942, p. 65.
[8] Jenkins, The Missenden Cartulary, Part 2, p. 114 no. 443, p. 115 no. 445, p. 120 no. 435, p. 134 no. 475, p. 148 no. 499; J. Godber (ed.), The Cartulary of Newnham Priory, Bedfordshire Hist. Rec. Soc., xliii, 1963–4, p. 243 no. 531, p. 306 no. 689.
[9] W. R. Mead, 'Ridge and Furrow in Buckinghamshire', Geogrl. Jnl., cxx, 1954,

Disputes over intercommoning and attempted enclosures, together with grants of special grazing privileges to religious bodies and lay lords, leave little doubt but that the common arable stubble and fallow was open to grazing by the flocks and herds of entire townships. A Buckinghamshire fine of 1226 speaks of 'common of pasture in the common field of Westleg...in every year in which the field lies fallow or uncultivated', while a Bedfordshire dispute concerning intercommoning by two villages in 1240 states that 'according to the custom of the vills of Stantbrig' and Tulleswirth when a field of Tulleswirth lies out of tillage and in fallow so that they ought to common horn under horn'.[1] Such was the demand for forage that stints were sometimes applied before the end of the thirteenth century.[2] Existence of common pasturage rights over the fields did not necessarily preclude temporary enclosure for foldage on fallow plots, such as occurred on the Cuxham (Oxon.) demesne and at Dorchester (Oxon.). Folding allowed more efficient use of grazing and more concentrated manuring – Dorchester cottagers were even obliged to keep five sheep in the lord's fold for part of each year.[3]

In most townships the fields were clearly the basic units for regulating common farming routines, and, with some exceptions, cultivation in the individual fields was uniform in that all strips were apparently subject to the same sequence of cropping. Manorial accounts for Adderbury, Cuxham and Cottisford (Oxon.) show that the whole of one field lay fallow each year, and that demesne holdings were no exception to this rule even when they lay as consolidated blocks within the arable.[4] But deviations from the communal systems were also quite frequent, and were often apparently prompted by a need to increase the amount of forage available. Fallow field hitchings had appeared before 1200 at Upper Heyford (Oxon.); while it was agreed that the thirteenth-century lords of Waterperry (Oxon.) could put

pp. 34–42; J. E. G. Sutton, 'Ridge and Furrow in Berkshire and Oxfordshire', *Oxoniensia*, XXIX–XXX, 1964–5, pp. 99–115; M. J. Harrison, W. R. Mead, D. J. Pannett, 'A Midland Ridge-and-Furrow Map', *Geogrl. Jnl.*, CXXXI, 1965, pp. 366–9.

[1] Hughes, *A Calendar of the Feet of Fines for the County of Buckingham*, p. 53 no. 131; G. H. Fowler (ed.), 'Roll of the Justices in Eyre, 1240', *Bedfordshire Hist. Rec. Soc.*, IX, 1925, p. 83 no. 31.

[2] Chibnall, *Sherington*, p. 110; *V.C.H. Oxon.*, VI, 1959, p. 211; G. H. Fowler (ed.), *A Calendar of the Feet of Fines for Bedfordshire, Preserved in the Public Record Office, of the Reigns of Richard I, John, and Henry III*, Bedfordshire Hist. Rec. Soc., VI, 1919, p. 130 no. 467; G. H. Fowler (ed.), *Cartulary of the Abbey of Old Wardon*, Bedfordshire Hist. Rec. Soc., XIII, 1930, p. 169. no. 218.

[3] Harvey, *A Medieval Oxfordshire Village*, p. 119; *V.C.H. Oxon.*, VII, 1962, pp. 45–6; W. Potts, *A History of Banbury*, 1958, p. 73.

[4] Harvey, *A Medieval Oxfordshire Village*, pp. 20–2, 41, 52; *V.C.H. Oxon.*, VI, 1959, p. 109.

temporary fences around that part of their open demesne which, for lack of pasture, they did not leave fallow. For Cowley (Oxon.), too, there is evidence both of three- and four-course cultivation in the common fields, and of the temporary enclosure of fallow plots.[1] Arable headlands were also sometimes left as mowing ground.[2]

Traditional cropping systems were disrupted on a much larger scale by the change from two- to three-field arrangements that took place along the scarp-foot loams and in the clay vales during the later Middle Ages, and that was virtually complete by 1550. Already, in the thirteenth century, triennial fallowing was practised in some common field manors, and by c. 1250 a significant number of townships had become organised on a three-field basis. At South Stoke (Oxon.), for example, the switch from a double to a triple division of the common arable was probably in progress in 1240, while details of the reorganisation at Mursley and Dinton (Bucks.) survive in an agreement of 1345.[3] The fact that around some villages the strips of one farm were usually adjacent to the same neighbours throughout the fields may have reflected such recent rearrangement.[4] Two-field systems survived on the poorer and lighter stonebrash soils of the Cotswolds which were incapable of supporting two grain crops in three years.[5]

Additional common fields were also appearing in quite a different way in the twelfth and thirteenth centuries. Strips newly improved from the waste were often simply added to existing fields, as the frequent occurrence of *ruding, brache, stocking* and *inning* as furlong names testifies.[6] But where reclaimed land was isolated from the main body of common arable it might form a fairly small common field more typical of the chalk hills to the south. Sart Field, which lay across the Cherwell from Islip (Oxon.) village and its adjacent ploughland, was probably part of 200 acres cleared in the township between 1086 and 1300; a single large field in the Beckley (Oxon.) hamlet of Horton became divided into three or four units as the arable was extended by intakes from Otmoor and Bernwood; and early thirteenth-century reclamation by the Templars from Shotover

[1] *V.C.H. Oxon.*, v, 1957, pp. 85, 255, 301; vi, 1959, pp. 26, 198.

[2] *V.C.H. Oxon.*, vi, 1959, p. 349.

[3] Gray, *English Field Systems*, p. 80; F. K. Gurney, 'An Agricultural Agreement of the Year 1345 at Mursley and Dinton', *Records of Bucks.*, xiv, 1941–6, pp. 245–64.

[4] F. Seebohm, *The English Village Community*, 2nd edn, 1883, pp. 24–6.

[5] Gray, *English Field Systems*, pp. 135–6; M. A. Havinden, 'The Rural Economy of Oxfordshire, 1580–1730,' B.Litt. thesis, University of Oxford, 1961, pp. iv, 17, 56.

[6] Jenkins, *The Missenden Cartulary, Part 2*, p. 111 no. 440, p. 148 no. 499; Godber, *The Cartulary of Newnham Priory*, p. 241 no. 190, p. 142 nos 239–40, p. 143 no. 244, p. 156 nos 285–6, p. 169 no. 326.

Forest may have resulted in the addition of two fields to the common arable of Cowley.[1]

Much assart land was, however, taken directly into severalty, and as a result many two- and three-field manors contained, by 1300, fairly substantial areas of enclosed arable quite apart from crofts immediately around the settlements. Closes were often in an outlying part of the township, where they were generally intermixed with woodland and waste, and associated with dispersed farmsteads and hamlets. Such was the pattern produced by the extensive felling still taking place in Bedfordshire in the twelfth and thirteenth centuries, especially in the northwest of the county which, with north Buckinghamshire, formed part of the heavily wooded country around the Forests of Whittlewood and Salcey. Between Bedford and Biggleswade, too, Cistercian monks from Rievaulx had established their house of St Mary-of-the-Assarts in Wardon in 1135 and were clearing on a large scale.[2] The majority of Bedfordshire intakes were individual holdings – some were just extensions of existing crofts – and might include, as at Odell and Cranfield, complete virgate and half virgate tenements.[3] Townships such as Harrold, Wooton, Stagsden and Colmworth thus came to comprise considerable enclosed areas in addition to their two or three great common fields.[4] Hedged closes and private woods were also being marked-out around the forests of Buckinghamshire and Oxfordshire,[5] while the strip parishes of the chalk edge often included hill hamlets with their own woods and closes.

Late assarting was sufficiently widespread in a few districts to produce distinctive field systems in which numerous relatively small common fields were combined with large areas of enclosed arable

[1] V.C.H. Oxon., v, 1957, pp. 67, 83; vi, 1959, pp. 216–11.
[2] Fowler, Cartulary of the Abbey of Old Wardon, p. 7, p. 76 no. 101, p. 78 no. 104, p. 81 no. 108, p. 188 no. 241, p. 218 nos. 282–3, p. 224 no. 292, p. 244 no. 325, p. 286 no. 344.
[3] Fowler, The Records of Harrold Priory, p. 111 nos. 169–70, p. 115 no. 178; J. A. Raftis, The Estates of Ramsey Abbey, Pontifical Institute of Medieval Studies, Studies and Texts III, 1957, pp. 70, 72–3, 83–4.
[4] Fowler, A Calendar of the Feet of Fines for Bedfordshire, p. 129 no. 466; Fowler, The Records of Harrold Priory, p. 19 no. 7, p. 20 no. 10, p. 26 no. 15, p. 35 no. 33, p. 123 no. 185; Godber, The Cartulary of Newnham Priory, pp. 221–3; G. H. Fowler (ed.), 'Roll of the Justices in Eyre at Bedford, 1202', Bedfordshire Hist. Rec. Soc., I, 1913, p. 163 no. 70; G. H. Fowler (ed.), 'Early Records of Turvey and its Neighbourhood, Part I', Bedfordshire Hist. Rec. Soc., XI, 1927, p. 49 no. 1; F. G. Emmison, Types of Open-Field Parishes in the Midlands, Historical Association Pamphlet, CVIII, 1937, pp. 6, 8, 12–14.
[5] S. Hilton, The Story of Haversham and its Historical Associations, 1937, pp. 61, 94, 110; Fowler, Beds. Hist. Rec. Soc., XI, 1927, p. 65 no. 19, p. 67 no. 21; Jenkins, The Cartulary of Snelshall Priory, p. 46 no. 127a; V.C.H. Oxon., v, 1957, pp. 123, 254, 279, 300.

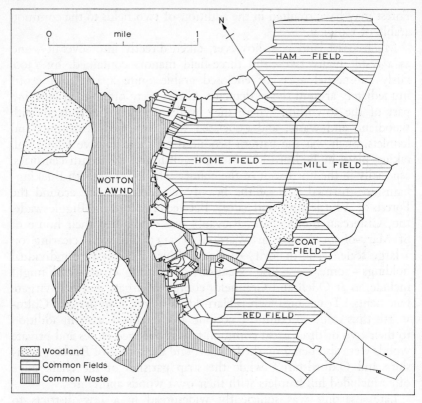

Fig. 8.5 Wotton Underwood (Bucks.) in 1649: a five-field manor in an area of late-surviving waste on heavy clays in the Vale of Aylesbury. The five fields were, in 1657, worked as three.

Sources. Buckinghamshire County Museum, 95/47; 'Wotton Underwood in 1657', *Records of Buckinghamshire*, XIV, 1941-6, p. 142.

and wood, and which resembled the arrangements of the chalk hills rather than surrounding two- and three-field villages (Fig. 8.5). The forest hamlets of Wychwood and Woodstock contained, in the sixteenth century, many features reminiscent of the Chilterns, with holdings distributed unevenly between common fields of varying sizes and amongst arable closes. The seventeenth-century field pattern in Long Combe (Oxon.) was similar to that of Great Hampden (Fig. 8.8), while in Ramsden (Oxon.) there was the same confusion of field and furlong to be found in Hertfordshire or northwest Essex.[1] In parts of central Bedfordshire, too, an irregular field system may have developed by *c.* 1300 as a result of prolonged clearing. Charters for

[1] Gray, *English Field Systems*, pp. 84-6.

Wilden and Colmworth suggest the existence of a multiplicity of common fields (some of them described as 'croft'), assarts, hedged closes, woodland and hamlets.[1]

A single close sometimes comprised a complete customary tenure in districts of substantial thirteenth-century reclamation – an Eversholt (Beds.) half virgate was one field[2] – again as in the Chilterns. Both assarts and established closes were occasionally subdivided by gift, sale or lease of parcels from them, and fractionation of a compact demesne holding at Sherington (Bucks.) actually led to the creation of what were later regarded as common fields.[3] Arable closes might follow the same cropping sequence as one or other of the common fields – 'fields' at Wolverton and Tattenho (Bucks.) included crofts[4] – but were sometimes cultivated independently.[5] Enclosed land was often also, during the twelfth and early thirteenth centuries, subject to common grazing. An agreement of 1240 arranged for the grange field at Putnoe (Beds.) to be opened at fixed places 'so that when the crops have been carried those who want may common there'.[6] Many of the covenants to mutual common made between manorial lords and special grants of common pasture in demesne ploughland to religious bodies probably included at least some several arable, although the nature of the land is rarely specified.[7] Small groups of peasants were also occasionally entitled to forage over demesne fields in return for the performance of minor labour services, while pasturage rights pertaining to common waste sometimes persisted over intakes from it.[8] Grazing over enclosed land was gradually restricted, with lords deciding to forgo pasture over one another's property and tenants quitclaiming rights in demesne fallow for common elsewhere, in woods and strip fields.[9]

---

[1] G. H. Fowler and J. Godber (eds.), *The Cartulary of Bushmead Priory*, Bedfordshire Hist. Rec. Soc., XXII, 1940 (pub. 1945), pp. 136–57; Fowler, *A Calendar of the Feet of Fines for Bedfordshire*, p. 38 no. 166.

[2] G. H. Fowler (ed.), *A Digest of the Charters Preserved in the Cartulary of the Priory of Dunstable*, Bedfordshire Hist. Rec. Soc., X, 1926, p. 138 no. 429.

[3] Chibnall, *Sherington*, pp. 108–10, 170; Fowler, *The Cartulary of Bushmead Priory*, p. 80 no. 71; Fowler, *Cartulary of the Abbey of Old Wardon*, p. 222 no. 288; Godber, *The Cartulary of Newnham Priory*, p. 294 no. 665, p. 297 no. 671.

[4] Jenkins, *The Cartulary of Snelshall Priory*, p. 9 no. 18, p. 47 no. 129.

[5] Chibnall, *Sherington*, p. 109.

[6] Fowler, *Cartulary of the Abbey of Old Wardon*, p. 184 no. 240.

[7] Fowler, *A Calendar of the Feet of Fines for Bedfordshire*, p. 129 no. 466; Fowler, *Calendar of the Roll of the Justices on Eyre, 1247*, p. 55 no. 123.

[8] Fowler, *A Calendar of the Feet of Fines for Bedfordshire*, p. 129 no. 466; Fowler, *A Calendar of the Roll of the Justices on Eyre, 1247*, p. 104 no. 309; *V.C.H. Oxon.*, V, 1957, p. 162; VI, 1959, p. 10.

[9] Fowler, *A Calendar of the Feet of Fines for Bedfordshire*, p. 139 no. 501; Fowler, *Calendar of the Roll of the Justices on Eyre, 1247*, p. 104 no. 309.

The area in severalty was further increased, in the thirteenth century and later, by fencing from the common arable. Some considerable consolidation of open holdings was accomplished by peasant farmers, using the usual methods of exchange and purchase, but the land concerned generally remained in communal tillage, and the main effect was a growing irregularity in strip sizes.[1] Manorial lords, too, were rationalising their common field properties, ecclesiastical land-owners such as Newnham Priory and Thame Abbey being particularly active in this respect.[2] Often their purpose was simply to create larger demesne cropping units within the open arable so that, for example, more intensive techniques such as folding might easily be adopted. Ralph de Cheinduit brought his Cuxham (Oxon.) demesne together into large furlong blocks which remained subject to the village routine, although sheep folds were moved over them at time of fallow – these large units were still distinctive 500 years later (Fig. 8.4).[3] Quite frequently, however, seigneurial consolidation was a prelude to en-closure. In Goldington (Beds.), Newnham Priory gradually acquired a complete furlong, obtained the consent of commoners to extinguish grazing rights, and then incorporated it with the priory garden. Thame Abbey likewise built up a compact holding of 83 acres by exchange in Sydenham (Oxon.) before separating it from the rest of the common arable.[4] Even in this Midland country some demesnes were already completely enclosed by the eleventh century, and subsequent con-solidations, such as that carried out at Thame (Oxon.) itself, simply extended them.[5]

But twelfth- and thirteenth-century enclosure was insignificant when compared with the growing conversion for sheep grazing that was to turn much subdivided arable into large fenced pastures. Beginning in some townships before 1300,[6] the trend to pastoral farming gathered pace during the fourteenth century as direct demesne cultivation ended on many manors, and especially after the depopulating epidemics of 1349 and 1361, which saw considerable areas leaving arable production and encouraged extensive farm engrossment.[7] Enclosure for con-

[1] *V.C.H. Oxon.*, VI, 1959, p. 28.
[2] Godber, *The Cartulary of Newnham Priory*, p. xii; *V.C.H. Oxon.*, VII, 1962, p. 188; VIII, 1964, pp. 119, 203.
[3] Harvey, *A Medieval Oxfordshire Village*, pp. 20–2, 119; *V.C.H. Oxon.*, VI, 1959, p. 156; Seebohm, *The English Village Community*, p. 23.
[4] Godber, *The Cartulary of Newnham Priory*, p. xii, p. 149 no. 266, p. 156 no. 285; *V.C.H. Oxon.*, VIII, 1964, p. 119.
[5] *V.C.H. Oxon.*, VII, 1962, pp. 153, 188.
[6] *V.C.H. Oxon.*, VI, 1959, p. 255; F. E. Hyde and S. F. Markham, *A History of Stony Stratford and the Immediate Vicinity*, 1948, p. 23.
[7] Hyde and Markham, *A History of Stony Stratford*, pp. 24–6; T. H. Lloyd, 'Some

version was further stimulated by rising wool prices, reached a peak between 1450 and 1550, occurred on intractable clays and light stone-brash alike, and continued on a diminishing scale well into the seventeenth century. There were occasional agreements between lords and tenants for partial enclosure, but often landowners simply refrained from filling vacant tenements which had reverted to them, or, failing this, evicted. Desertion of settlement thus frequently accompanied the change to pasture. Small parishes with only a few tenants and hamlets more marginal for tillage were especially susceptible, but parts of many other townships were also turned to grass.[1]

B. FACTORS IN THE EARLY DEVELOPMENT OF FIELD SYSTEMS

The Chiltern scarp and its lower and less well-defined continuation in east Hertfordshire and northwest Essex were clearly a major divide in field system types. The contrast between the multitude of open strips immediately below the escarpment – even in some townships extending up to the very crest of the chalk itself – and the country of closes, woods and wastes which, in Oxfordshire and Buckingham-shire, lay over much of the plateau above, could hardly have been sharper. Although the distinction between the two regions became less marked towards the northeast, as the chalk hills become lower and the area of common arable within them became more extensive, there were still major differences in the nature of the common fields and the ways that these were organised. It is now necessary to examine the possible reasons for these differences.

I. SOCIAL AND ECONOMIC FACTORS

Social and economic conditions did not, by the thirteenth century, reflect variations in agricultural arrangements. There is no evidence of the supposed relationship between, on the one hand, persistence of great areas of common arable with village settlements, and a tightly

Documentary Sidelights on the Deserted Oxfordshire Village of Brookend', *Oxoniensia*, XXIX–XXX, 1964–5, pp. 121–8; *V.C.H. Oxon.*, VI, 1959, pp. 27–8.
[1] M. D. Lobel, *The History of Dean and Chalford*, Oxfordshire Record Series, XVII, 1935, pp. 6–7, 12, 17, 21, 70; K. J. Allison, M. W. Beresford and J. G. Hurst, 'The Deserted Villages| of Oxfordshire', *Occasional Papers, Dept. of Engl. Local Hist. Univ. of Leicester*, XVII, 1965, pp. 5–8, 30–47; Chibnall, *Sherington*, pp. 171–5, 199–200; W. E. Tate, *A Hand-List of Buckinghamshire Enclosure Acts and Awards*, 1946, pp. 17–21.

controlled manorial organisation vigorously maintaining customary tenements; and, on the other hand, largely enclosed districts with scattered farmsteads where a more permissive manorial lord had allowed the disintegration of traditional tenures and the consequent consolidation of land into severalty.[1] Social structure in the Chilterns resembled that of many two- and three-field townships on the loam belt below the escarpment. Both districts were strongly manorialised in that a majority of tenements owed services and rents to a lord, and villeins could not transfer property without reference to the manorial courts; but permission to alienate was usually freely given in return for a payment; services demanded from the average villein holding were not particularly heavy and were in varying stages of commutation by 1300; and there was a substantial proportion of freeholders on most manors. In both areas, too, active peasant land markets saw the break-up of some family holdings and the growth of new ones, frequently from very humble beginnings.[2] In contrast, customary obligations appear to have been heavier and to have persisted longer in Essex. Week work and heavy carrying services were still being demanded on many manors c. 1300,[3] yet field systems there were much the same as in other districts south of the chalk scarp. Often the greatest social dissimilarity was between neighbouring manors: rigid control at Cuxham contrasted sharply with the lax conditions of Shirburn (Oxon.) two miles away and also a three-field township in the thirteenth century.[4]

Inheritance customs are another aspect of social organisation that may have been influential in producing different field patterns, but by the time that there is sufficient information to reconstruct them, they showed no particular correlation with agrarian conditions in the five counties. In particular, there is no evidence of the large-scale fragmentation following partible inheritance that was elsewhere still

[1] Homans, *English Villagers of the Thirteenth Century*, pp. 200–4; Levett, *Studies in Manorial History*, pp. 184–5; J. Thirsk, 'The Farming Regions of England', in J. Thirsk (ed.), *The Agrarian History of England and Wales: IV*, 1967, p. 8.

[2] See above, p. 333; Dale, *Court Roll of Chalgrave Manor 1278–1313*, pp. xxii–v; A. T. Gaydon (ed.), *The Taxation of 1297*, Bedfordshire Hist. Rec. Soc., XXXIX, 1959, p. xxvi; Lobel, *The History of Dean and Chalford*, p. 15; H. M. Colvin, *A History of Deddington*, Oxfordshire, 1963, pp. 15, 83; *V.C.H. Oxon.*, V, 1957, pp. 38, 144, 199–200, 226; VI, 1959, pp. 108, 140, 164, 177, 187, 226.

[3] Nichols, Ph.D. thesis, pp. 244–59; Fisher, *Essex Arch. Soc. Trans.*, XXII, 1936–40 (pub. 1940), p. 248; Newton, *Thaxted in the Fourteenth Century*, pp. 10–17; Clark, *Essex Rev.*, XIX, 1910, pp. 141, 146; XXI, 1911, pp. 212, 217; Hale, *The Domesday of St Paul's*, pp. 13–92; W. C. Waller, *Loughton in Essex*, 1899–1900, p. 14; E. P. Dickin, *A History of Brightlingsea*, 1939, pp. 24, 30.

[4] Harvey, *A Medieval Oxfordshire Village*, pp. 113–35; *V.C.H. Oxon.*, VIII, 1964, pp. 187–8.

leading to the formation of subdivided fields in intermixed ownership. Primogeniture was widely followed throughout the region, although often modified in operation by the relative ease of villein alienation, and by the adoption of such devices as joint tenure and conditional surrender to facilitate transfers between parents and children.[1] Borough English, which has been described as akin, in practice, to the Kentish custom of gavelkind, was quite common in Essex and east Hertfordshire, but it has yet to be shown that ultimogeniture ever encouraged the actual dismemberment of either holdings or individual fields in these areas.[2] Apart from occasional fractionation arising from the widow's dower rights and partible descent to daughters in the absence of male heirs[3] – both features characteristic of primogeniture – there are three or four cases which suggest that transfer to a number of male successors had perhaps taken place.[4] Some form of partibility may, for example, have led to the disintegration of Tetsworth (Oxon.) virgates by 1300;[5] but probably more important was the simple fact of rapid population growth coupled with a permissive manorial organisation which allowed the dispersal of villein holdings. Thirteenth-century population pressures resulted in the division and redivision of tenements in the fields of Adderbury (Oxon.), whereas the Halton (Bucks.) manor insisted on maintaining family farms, yet both remained typical two-field townships. There was also less tenurial fragmentation in areas of extensive assarting like the Witney (Oxon.) district, because reclamation helped to relieve local land hunger.[6]

[1] Homans, *English Villagers of the Thirteenth Century*, pp. 116, 127–32, 144–6, 152–3, 179, 196–9, 204; Dale, *Court Roll of Chalgrave Manor 1278–1314*, pp. 9–10, 14; *V.C.H. Oxon.*, VI, 1959, p. 236; Roden, *Jnl. Brit. Stud.*, VII, 1967, pp. 1–111; R.J. Faith, 'Peasant Families and Inheritance Customs in Medieval England', *Agric. Hist. Rev.*, XIV, 1966, pp. 87–9.

[2] *V.C.H. Essex*, V, 1966, p. 144; A. Hills, 'Essex Manor Customs', *Essex Rev.*, LI, 1942, p. 100; L. L. Rickman, 'Brief Studies in the Manorial and Economic History of Much Hadham', *East Herts. Arch. Soc. Trans.*, VIII, 1928–33, p. 303; J. Thirsk, 'Industries in the Countryside', in F.J. Fisher (ed.), *Essays in the Economic and Social History of Tudor and Stuart England*, 1961, p. 77; Homans, *English Villagers of the Thirteenth Century*, p. 127; Faith, *Agric. Hist. Rev.*, XIV, 1966, pp. 83–4.

[3] Kirk, *Feet of Fines for Essex*, 1899–1910, I, p. 47 no. 261; Hills, *Essex Rev.*, LI, 1942, p. 97; Fieling, *Engl. Hist. Rev.*, XXVI, 1911, p. 337; Westlake, *Hornchurch Priory*, p. 63 no. 274; Fowler, *Beds. Hist. Rec. Soc.*, I, 1913, p. 167 no. 74; Fowler, *A Calendar of the Feet of Fines for Bedfordshire*, p. 11 no. 19, p. 14 no. 34; Fowler, *A Digest of the Charters Preserved in the Cartulary of the Priory of Dunstable*, p. 138 no. 434; Fowler, *Beds. Hist. Rec. Soc.*, XIX, 1937, p. 33 no. 53.

[4] Fowler, *A Calendar of the Feet of Fines for Bedfordshire*, p. 84 no. 321; Fowler, *Beds. Hist. Rec. Soc.*, IX, 1925, p. 97 no. 81; Chambers, *Eynsham Under the Monks*, p. 9.   [5] *V.C.H. Oxon.*, VII, 1962, p. 153.

[6] Hyde, B.Litt. thesis, p. 125; Homans, *English Villagers of the Thirteenth Century*, pp. 196, 204.

A supposed preponderance of woodland and pastoral pursuits, and the presence of strong commercial influences have been variously forwarded to explain the absence of any simple field layout and the occurrence of large enclosed areas such as existed in the Chilterns, Hertfordshire and Essex. Gray argued, at one point, that in 'a territory where woodland was relatively extensive, where it was somewhat difficult to transform waste into arable, tenants can have had no concern about a compact fallow field to supplement the pasture', while M. W. Beresford considers the Buckinghamshire Chilterns to have been a district in which 'villagers were able to maintain themselves...by exploiting the resources of a forest economy', and that consequently cultivation was of secondary importance.[1] J. Thirsk, too, has suggested that whereas two- or three-field arrangements were typical of regions of mixed farming, villages with more or fewer common fields were mainly pastoral communities in which arable grazing was unimportant and where, as a result, early enclosure was easily achieved through agreement between individuals to extinguish common rights. Pastoralism was, in turn, said to typify areas being reclaimed from woodland, a phase through which Hertfordshire was supposed to be passing during the later Middle Ages.[2]

In the five counties none of these theories bears close examination. Both two- and three-field townships and the districts with less regular field systems were characterised by mixed farming in the Middle Ages. Except on the Essex marshes, along the Thames and in parts of northern Oxfordshire, forage, although often extensive, was not usually of a sufficiently high quality to support rearing and breeding to the detriment of tillage, while meadow might be in particularly short supply. Many two-field manors had access to greater areas of pasture, in marsh or in forest, than such townships up on the chalk as King's Walden and Saffron Walden. Moreover, grazing on fallow and stubble was not only important as a source of pasturage: it was also a vital means of maintaining soil fertility, especially where three-course rotations had been introduced at an early date. Numerous references to foldage indicate its significance for manuring. Nor was forest clearing associated with a grazing economy – twelfth- and thirteenth-century assarts were normally under crops and some were said to have been made specifically for tillage[3] – while the suggestion that early fencing of open strips occurred on a significant scale in

[1] Gray, *English Field Systems*, p. 401; M. W. Beresford, 'Glebe Terriers and Open-Field Buckinghamshire', *Records of Bucks.*, XVI, 1953–60, p. 6.

[2] J. Thirsk, 'The Common Fields', *Past and Present*, XXIX, 1964, pp. 23–4; Thirsk, *The Agrarian History of England and Wales: IV*, 1967, p. 52.

[3] Hale, *The Domesday of St Paul's*, pp. 69, 85, 144; P.R.O., SC 6/866/27.

districts of irregular common fields is not borne out by the available evidence. There was far more medieval enclosure from common arable north of the chalk, and when pastoral farming did become prominent it was in response to the economic changes of the later Middle Ages and was most marked in the Midland country.

2. ETHNIC FACTORS

Gray concluded that the character of the Anglo-Saxon settlement and the degree to which earlier features survived were responsible for the main variations in English field systems. More particularly, he saw the Chilterns and Essex as regions where 'Kentish' and 'Midland' (i.e. Anglo-Saxon) influences met, leaving their marks on agrarian organisation in different ways. Yet apart from vaguely relating the consolidated Essex virgate to the Kentish *iugum* and noting the presence of the daywork in Essex as in Kent, he never specified the nature of the Kentish link north of the Thames.[1] In fact, there were compact virgates and half virgates in enclosed areas on both sides of the chalk scarp; they were still being created in the thirteenth century by direct reclamation into severalty; and they were no more than tenurial units of a roughly standard size in each manor, quite different from the *iuga* which varied considerably in area within one township.[2] The Essex daywork was simply a unit of measurement representing one-tenth of an acre, and usually referring to a house plot.[3]

R. C. Coles favoured the continuation of Celtic and Roman arrangements in parts of Essex. Arguing that Saxon agriculture was only partially absorbed – East Saxons moving in from the coast and West Saxons coming from the northwest introduced common arable cultivation to the northeast, southwest and northwest of the county – he has suggested that the southeast retained the hamlet settlement and unified holdings of Romano-British farmers due to peaceful Saxon penetration there.[4] The degree of Germanic superimposition was probably greatest, according to F. Hull, on the good soils and light forests of the chalk hills and weakest on the belt of heavy clays.[5] Again it is difficult to find any logic in these conjectures, which are, in any

[1] Gray, *English Field Systems*, pp. 389, 394, 401, 417–18.
[2] A. R. H. Baker, 'The Kentish *iugum*: its Relationship to Soils at Gillingham', *Engl. Hist. Rev.*, LXXXI, 1966, pp. 74–9.
[3] J. L. Fisher (ed.), 'The Petre Documents', *Essex Arch. Soc. Trans.*, XXIII, 1942–5, pp. 92–6.
[4] R. C. Coles, 'Enclosures: Essex Agriculture, 1500–1900', *Essex Naturalist*, XXVI, 1937–8, pp. 6–8.
[5] Hull, Ph.D. thesis, p. 43.

case, contradicted by evidence from elsewhere in the region. Areas of densest Romano-British settlement, such as the Icknield zone, the river terraces and the larger valleys of the chalk and Oolite hills, were generally those of earliest Germanic occupance and later of extensive common arable.[1] The medieval pattern of common fields at Wymondley (Herts.) in the Hitchin Gap may even have existed since Roman times or at least developed from the surviving Roman fields.[2] Conversely, the main districts of consolidated medieval holdings and hamlets were, like many two-field townships on the clays, very sparsely settled by Romans and early Saxons alike, and were brought into cultivation only during the later stages of the Anglo-Saxon colonisation. Haverfield's suggestion that traces of centuriation survive in central Essex has recently been strongly criticised.[3]

3. THE PACE AND PROGRESS OF COLONISATION

Whatever the origins of the German settlers, and whatever the character of their settlement one thing is clear: with the possible exception of southeast Essex, those parts of the five counties where colonisation had been completed at a relatively early date were, in the thirteenth century, areas of nucleated settlement and common arable farming, while districts in which, largely for reasons of topography, the process of secondary occupance was much more prolonged, were later characterised by less regular field systems. Thus by the eleventh century relatively little woodland survived on the loams below the chalk scarp, over large areas of the clay lowlands to the north and on the marlstone hills of north Oxfordshire.[4] Common field cultivation around villages was already firmly established, and extended in many cases to the boundaries of the later parishes, which even now trace the

[1] M. V. Taylor, 'The Roman Period', and J. N. L. Myers, 'The Anglo-Saxon Period', in A. F. Martin and R. W. Steel (eds.), *The Oxford Region*, 1954, pp. 85–102; J. F. Head, 'Buckinghamshire, A.D. 450–700', *Records of Bucks.*, XIV, 1941–6, pp. 301–40; J. F. Head, *Early Man in South Buckinghamshire*, 1955, pp. 80–100; K. Branigan, 'The Distribution and Development of Romano-British Occupation in the Chess Valley', *Records of Bucks.*, XVIII (part 2), 1967, pp. 146–7; K. Branigan, 'Romano-British Rural Settlement in the Western Chilterns', *Archaeological Journal*, CXXIV, 1967 (pub. 1968), pp. 129–60; *V.C.H. Beds.*, I, 1904, pp. 144–5; *V.C.H. Herts.*, I, 1902, p. 251; IV, 1914, p. 119; A. C. Edwards, *A History of Essex*, 1958, pp. 6–10.

[2] Seebohm, *The English Village Community*, pp. 431–2; S. Applebaum, 'Agriculture in Roman Britain', *Agric. Hist. Rev.*, VI, 1958, pp. 73, 79.

[3] F. Haverfield, 'Centuriation in Roman Britain', *Engl. Hist. Rev.*, XXXIII, 1918, p. 294; *V.C.H. Essex*, III, 1963, p. 16.

[4] Darby and Campbell, *The Domesday Geography of South-East England*, pp. 32, 168, 215.

irregular outline of the original furlong pattern.[1] Probably, too, the simple division into two great fields that was so characteristic of these areas in the thirteenth century had already appeared,[2] although the common arable of smaller and rather later hamlets was sometimes worked as a single field. Perhaps the two-field system had developed from a more primitive form such as this.

In the hilly and heavily wooded country south of the Middle Chalk scarp early Anglo-Saxon colonisation, only slightly later in origin, was restricted to the main valleys where the better soils are and where water was readily available, and to peripheral areas like the river terraces. As in the lowlands to the north, early farmsteads were probably clustered in small nucleations – later the dominant forms along the valleys – which may have reflected the social structure of the English immigrants or may have survived from Romano-British times. Each settlement was associated with its own area of subdivided arable along the valley slopes, and simple field arrangements occurred in some hamlets and manors – Gynaunts Fee in High Wycombe (Bucks.) had east, west and middle fields which, in the thirteenth century, were the basis of a three-course rotation.[3] Usually, however, the broken relief inhibited formation of unified cropping areas, producing instead a complex of small common fields and furlongs as scattered areas were cleared piecemeal. Primary occupance and its accompanying common arable were most widespread where conditions of soil and slope were more favourable to early agriculture, as on the Hertfordshire chalk plateaux east of the Gade and in northwest Essex.

The reclamation of townships north of the chalk was generally associated with extension of the common arable, and hence with the simple expansion of village and hamlet centres. In contrast, the much more prolonged secondary colonisation occurring to the south saw the foundation of a mosaic of hamlets – many of them linear and loosely knit – and dispersed farmhouses on the drift-covered ridges and plateaux surfaces of the chalk hills and on the London Clay. Although settlement of these districts often began relatively early – isolated farmsteads and hamlets had appeared in one of the most inaccessible parts of the southwestern Chilterns by the tenth century, perhaps even by the eighth century – it was still taking place on a large scale during the 200 years prior to 1250, with the creation of new hamlets and compact holdings carved out of virgin territory, and

[1] Grundy, *Saxon Oxfordshire. Charters and Ancient Highways*, pp. 1–4, 5–8, 15–17, 18–22, 22–4, 28–33, 43–55, 63–73; *V.C.H. Oxon.*, VI, 1959, pp. 14, 134, 205, 338; VII, 1962, p. 147.
[2] Chibnall, *Sherington*, pp. 12, 89, 105; Elvey, *Records of Bucks.*, XVI, 1953–60, p. 343.
[3] See above, p. 336.

the extension of established farms.[1] New common fields were formed and existing fields occasionally enlarged, but lengthy secondary occupance was mainly associated with direct enclosure of waste into severalty, both for cultivation and the preservation of timber in private woods.[2]

The medieval pattern of landholding evolved from this slow and fragmentary settlement. Expansion of the ploughed area from a large number of relatively small nuclei and from isolated homesteads meant that individual tenements were concentrated around these in one part of the township, rather than being held from a central village and dispersed throughout its territory. The survival of such a pattern c. 1300, although much modified by the growth of a peasant land market, is most evident where hamlets were distinguished as units of some importance in their own right. At the same time, the division of a holding between enclosed and common arable or between a number of common fields, which also reflected the nature of colonisation, made possible the utilisation of cropping systems that were sufficiently pliable to accommodate any irregularity.

There was a similar response in those parts of the two-field country where, for one reason or another, extensive wastes had escaped pre-Domesday clearing. Around the more substantial forests, irregular common field systems and settlement mosaics had developed; elsewhere, closes and woods simply fringed the great fields, and a new small common field was occasionally created.[3]

The actual process of common arable formation in the five counties remains a matter of surmise. Some common fields may have been a product of communal clearing, or may have developed from co-operative ploughing in a closely knit tribal community during the earlier stages of post-Roman settlement. Labour services often later involved joint ploughing of the arable demesne, and co-aration must also have been practised on tenantry lands: but this would be necessary on enclosed and common tillage alike.[4] Although partitioning of compact farms through partible inheritance or partible succession to property may have produced some subdivided arable, no unambiguous examples have been found. E. C. Vollans' suggestion – based on charters for the Missenden area – that unenclosed parcels were sometimes created during the twelfth and thirteenth centuries by a lord allocating freshly cleared land to his tenants, is supported by evidence

[1] Roden, Folk Life, VIII, 1970, p. 59; Cromarty, The Fields of Saffron Walden in 1400, p. 12; Allison, M.A. thesis, pp. 45–53; P. H. Reaney, 'The Face of Essex. A Study in Place-Names', Essex Rev., LVIII, 1949, pp. 10–21.
[2] See above, pp. 327, 332.   [3] See above, pp. 350–3.
[4] Newton, Thaxted in the Fourteenth Century, p. 17.

from elsewhere in the Chilterns: a few small common fields in areas only recently improved from the waste had the same names as prominent local freeholders.[1] The Sherington example of late common arable formation through fractionation of demesne property, and the subsequent piecemeal granting of pasture rights over it, was exceptional. Subdivision of closes and assarts by partial or diverse alienation generally produced temporary features quite distinct from the common arable. The only thing that is clear is that common field forming processes had usually ceased to operate by the mid-thirteenth century, and that already, in some Midland districts, open arable had begun to disappear.

C. DISINTEGRATION OF THE MEDIEVAL FIELD SYSTEMS

Disintegration of medieval field systems north of the chalk was well under way by 1400 with enclosure and conversion to pasture, accompanied by depopulation and some abandonment of settlement during the fifteenth and early sixteenth centuries. In contrast, in the areas of irregular field systems to the south there was no radical change of either field or settlement patterns, in spite of declining population, because the flexibility of arrangements there facilitated adaptation to changing circumstances. Existing villages shrank but there was very little actual desertion; some arable tumbled temporarily to grass after 1349, but permanent conversion occurred only on the intractable clays of southern Essex, already largely a district of hedged closes. Elsewhere, strip consolidation continued, but it was very much reduced in scale, and enclosure was confined to imparking from farmland and waste.[2]

I. SPECIALISATION AND RENEWED CLEARING AFTER c. 1550

The end of late medieval stagnation was heralded by a rapid rise in population between 1550 and 1600, and particularly by the expansion of London, the main market for much of the region.[3] Growing agricultural specialisation, extension of the cultivated area, and intensification of existing mixed arable husbandries all followed. Merchants

[1] Vollans, Trans. Inst. Brit. Geogr., xxvi, 1959, p. 233; Roden, Ph.D. thesis, pp. 135–6, 300.
[2] Roden, Folk Life, viii, 1970, pp. 66–9; Roden, Geogr. Annlr., lii, 1969, pp. 115–18.
[3] L. Munby, Hertfordshire Population Statistics, 1563–1801, 1964, pp. 21–2; F. J. Fisher, 'The Development of the London Food Market, 1540–1640', Econ. Hist. Rev., v, 1934-5, pp. 46–64; Havinden, B.Litt. thesis, pp. v–vii, ix.

and professional men, buying property accessible to London, often took over the former demesne farms, and no doubt introduced greater commercialism to agriculture.[1] Heavy and elaborate manuring was practised by the more enterprising farmers; market gardening spread out from London, particularly along the Thames-side loams, but also appearing, a little later, on the sandy soils around Colchester and in the common arable of Sandy (Beds.); wheat and barley for London millers and Hertfordshire maltsters became major cash crops in much of the five counties; while growing demand for meat, tallow and wool encouraged greater emphasis on livestock production in the Midland country, and further pastoral specialisation in districts nearer the capital, particularly on the Essex clays and marshes.[2]

There was renewed clearing for cultivation in most areas. Marshland reclamation, together with consolidation of scattered marsh holdings, around the coast, was mainly for improved pasture; and seventeenth-century development of under-drainage brought a gradual amelioration of the heavier Essex boulder clays.[3] Many private woods were grubbed-up and turned to grass or tillage.[4] Disparking also released land for agriculture, producing distinctively large fields and a number of completely new farms, but counterbalanced somewhat by continued imparking from arable and waste.[5] Intakes from open woods and heaths ranged from the many piecemeal encroachments around the edges of most commons to complete farms such as the 300-acre holding

[1] Havinden, B.Litt. thesis, p. 49; Rickman, *East Herts. Arch. Soc. Trans.*, VIII, 1928–33, p. 288; *V.C.H. Herts.*, 1914, IV, p. 216; F. G. Emmison and F. Hull, 'Survey of the Manor of Woodham Ferrers, 1582', *Essex Arch. Soc. Trans.*, XXIV, 1951, p. 6; Roden, *Agric. Hist. Rev.*, XVII, 1969, p. 22.

[2] Thirsk, *The Agrarian History of England and Wales: IV*, 1967, pp. 49–55, 64–7, 167, 186, 192, 195–7; A. Everitt, 'The Marketing of Agricultural Produce', in J. Thirsk (ed.), *The Agrarian History of England and Wales: IV*, 1967, pp. 507–9; Allison, Ph.D. thesis, pp. 295–301, 304–7; Hull, Ph.D. thesis, pp. 66, 84, 89, 93, 100–5, 109; M. A. Havinden, 'Agricultural Progress in Open-Field Oxfordshire', *Agric. Hist. Rev.*, IX, 1961, pp. 73–4; F. Beavington, 'Early Market Gardening in Bedfordshire', *Trans. Inst. Brit. Geogr.*, XXXVII, 1965, pp. 91–100.

[3] Cracknell, *Canvey Island*, pp. 15–37; Grieve, *The Great Tide*, p. 32; Allison, Ph.D. thesis, pp. 69–71, 307, 326; K. H. Burley, 'The Economic Development of Essex in the Later Seventeenth and Early Eighteenth Centuries', Ph.D. thesis, University of London, 1957, pp. 50, 53.

[4] A. J. Mansfield, 'The Historical Geography of the Woodlands of the Southern Chilterns, 1600–1947', M.Sc. thesis, University of London, 1952, p. 22; Roden, *Geogr. Annlr.*, LII, 1969, pp. 120–2.

[5] Newton, *Thaxted in the Fourteenth Century*, p. 10; Emmison and Hull, *Essex Arch. Soc. Trans.*, XXIV, 1951, p. 13; H. Smith, *A History of the Parish of Havering-atte-Bower*, 1925, p. 61; H. C. Schulz, 'An Elizabethan Map of Wotton Underwood, Buckinghamshire', *The Huntingdon Library Quarterly*, III, 1939–40, p. 45; *V.C.H. Oxon.*, V, 1957, pp. 66, 234; VI, 1959, p. 64.

enclosed out of Berkhamsted Frith. Waste was now always taken into severalty, although common grazing was occasionally enforced for a while over new closes.[1] Denser tracts of standing timber were often preserved and patches of scrub and heath allowed to revert to woodland, as growing demand for fuel encouraged afforestation in areas more marginal to cultivation.[2] Large-scale enclosures, which were being attempted by agreement or unilateral action, often met with considerable opposition.[3] Larger wastes were intercommoned on a substantial scale – the Essex heath of Tiptree by sixteen villages, Berkhamsted Frith in the central Chilterns by men from eleven villages and hamlets, and Otmoor by seven Oxfordshire parishes[4] – while a rapidly growing class of smallholders and squatters around most woods and heaths depended for an important part of its livelihood on the grazing, fuel and raw materials available from the commons.[5] Such variety of claims was a major obstacle to any enclosure agreements. By the seventeenth century many former common woods and royal forests had been reduced by overgrazing and uncontrolled felling to heath-like formations. The forests of Oxfordshire, Buckinghamshire and Essex, for example, were seriously depleted during the Civil War and by the demands of the navy. Stowood, Shotover Forest and Bernwood were disafforested and converted to farmland and private timber before the century was out.[6]

2. ARABLE ENCLOSURES AND READJUSTMENTS

Enclosed arable holdings were rationalised in the move to more efficient farming. Big fields, especially the giant closes of former arable demesnes and pastures created during the fifteenth-century conversion, were divided into smaller and more manageable units, while excessively enclosed landscapes were opened up by the removal of hedges to allow more light into crops and to increase the cultivated area.[7] As far as common arable farming was concerned, the need to intensify

[1] P.R.O., E 317/Herts., nos. 9, 11.
[2] Mansfield, M.Sc. thesis, pp. 27, 29–31; Roden, *Forestry*, XLI, 1968, pp. 68–9; *V.C.H. Oxon.*, v, 1957, p. 280; Allison, Ph.D. thesis, pp. 146–7.
[3] Hull, Ph.D. thesis, pp. 60–2; Roden, Ph.D. thesis, pp. 102–3.
[4] W. A. Gimson, *Great Braxted 1086–1957*, 1958, p. 47; *V.C.H. Herts.*, II, 1908, p. 162; Hobson and Price, *Otmoor and its Seven Towns*, p. 9.
[5] Havinden, B.Litt. thesis, pp. 48, 180–1; Bateson, *Brill*, p. 7; Chibnall, *Sherington*, p. 201; Thirsk, *The Agrarian History of England and Wales: IV*, 1967, pp. 423, 426–8.
[6] *V.C.H. Oxon.*, v, 1957, pp. 216, 280, 288, 294; Bateson, *Brill*, p. 6; Allison, Ph.D. thesis, pp. 85–109, 128, 133–4.
[7] W. Ellis, *Chiltern and Vale Farming Explained*, 1744, p. 197; *V.C.H. Oxon.*, v, 1957, pp. 68, 289, 302; VI, 1959, pp. 157, 288, 319–20; VII, 1962, p. 13.

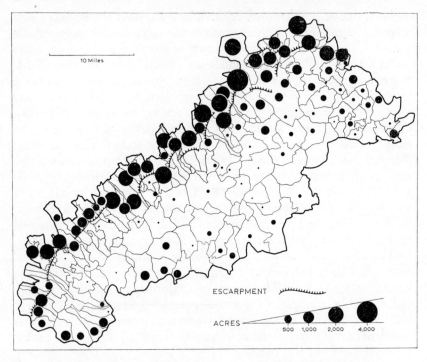

Fig. 8.6 Common arable land within and around the Chilterns *c.* 1800.
Sources. Enclosure maps and awards, estate maps and surveys, tithe maps etc.

agriculture produced very different responses on either side of the chalk scarp. Irregular common field systems had all but disappeared in many parishes by 1800, whereas common arable farming in two- and three-field townships was often strengthened and survived until the early nineteenth century, albeit in a modified form (Fig. 8.6).

Improvement of the traditional mixed husbandries of the chalk plateaux meant primarily the elimination of common grazing rights over the arable and consolidation of dispersed holdings. The enlarged flocks and herds necessary for higher grain yields were supported by crop-feeding rather than by any substantial extension of pasture.[1] Common fields were gradually reduced through piecemeal enclosure, effected by individual strip amalgamations and by private arrangements between a few men. Thus at least twenty-two exchanges of copyhold land are recorded in the Great Gaddesden (Herts.) court rolls between 1556 and 1583, half of them involving land in only two fields, and by 1600 a substantial part of the open arable had already been fenced

[1] Thirsk, *The Agrarian History of England and Wales: IV*, 1967, pp. 51, 211.

off.[1] The change from common arable to closes held in severalty was rarely a direct and immediate transformation. Most frequently single strips or consolidated blocks were fenced in while the rest of the field remained open, although larger units often remained in inter-mixed ownership for a while before being brought into severalty completely.[2] Enclosure in these ways was a slow process (Fig. 8.7). Almost half the former common arable of Saffron Walden (Essex) had been fenced off by 1608, but the common fields were not entirely eliminated until 1823 and then only by act of Parliament.[3] Even the actual process of fencing might take place in several stages: strips were sometimes hedged on three sides while remaining open on the fourth.

Enclosure was encouraged by the adaptability of field systems in these districts. Subtraction of strips from the individual common fields necessitated neither radical readjustments throughout the parish nor wide agreement, because where common arable was extensive it was divided into a large number of relatively small fields with only a minority of tenants holding in any one, while townships with few common fields were already largely in severalty. For similar reasons, secondary dispersal of settlement, such as followed the fencing and reallotment of a few great fields, was virtually unknown south of the chalk scarp, even where substantial areas had been taken into severalty; only a small part of the total arable area was affected at any one time; the common arable holdings of individuals were near to their farm-steads; and settlement was, in any case, widely dispersed before enclosure began.

The routine of centuries often continued over the open strips that survived, although inevitably distorted by creeping enclosure. Com-mon grazing, regulated by the manorial courts, was still practised, but periodic reductions of the stints that were by now universal indicated an ever-increasing pressure on the open pastures.[4] Three-course rotations were maintained well into the eighteenth century, and on many smaller farms until after 1800. Remnants of the Offley (Herts.) common fields were organised into three broad cropping seasons less than fifty years before final enclosure, while triennial fallowing was followed in parts of northwest Essex as late as 1840.[5] Quite often,

---

[1] Hertfordshire R.O., 28–49, 59; Roden, Ph.D. thesis, pp. 52–5.
[2] V.C.H. Herts., IV, 1914, p. 221; W. J. Hardy (ed.), Notes and Extracts rom the Session Rolls 1581 to 1698, I, 1905, pp. 1, 7; Hull, Ph.D. thesis, pp. 16–20, 32–4; Monteith, M.A. thesis, pp. 166, 170, 207–9.
[3] Monteith, M.A. thesis, pp. 165, 214.
[4] Roden, Ph.D. thesis, pp. 46–51; Allison, Ph.D. thesis, p. 356; Hull, Ph.D. thesis, p. 24; Eland, At the Courts of Great Canfield, Essex, pp. 33–4.
[5] Hertfordshire R.O., 57594–5; E. A. Cox, 'An Agricultural Geography of Essex, c. 1840', M.A. thesis, University of London, 1963, p. 183.

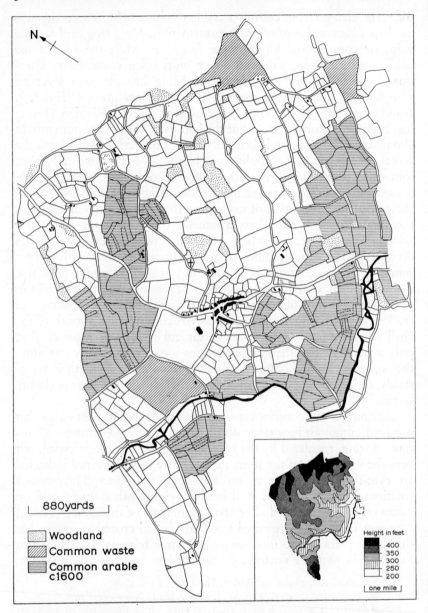

Fig. 8.7 Late eighteenth-century field patterns in Codicote (Herts.) (northeast Chilterns), and the area of common arable there *c.* 1600.

Sources. Hertfordshire R.O., AR 178/63743; B.M., Add. Mss. 40735; P.R.O., C 142/236/97.

however, common arable cropping had been modified. Cultivation of the saffron crocus on temporary enclosures made any regular sequence of tillage impossible in at least part of the common arable of Saffron Walden by 1550; while on the Thames terraces south of the Chilterns, strip occupiers in a number of townships were free to crop their land as they wished by the late eighteenth century, and a four-course rotation was followed in some of the common fields of Medmenham (Bucks.).[1]

Many farms now contained a greater proportion of arable in severalty, and the irregular distribution of holdings between local common fields became even more marked. Where not immediately followed by enclosure, continuing consolidation was also reflected in a growing irregularity of strip sizes, some of which had already been enlarged as a result of medieval peasant amalgamation. Single strips at Great Hampden (Bucks.), for example, ranged from one quarter of an acre to $13\frac{1}{2}$ acres in 1741 (Fig. 8.8). The number of common fields in a parish often stayed constant or even increased, in spite of the complete enclosure of some, because the remaining common fields were broken up into smaller units that were also called 'fields'. The eighteen common fields of King's Walden, 1805, were only six fewer than c. 1600 although the area of subdivided arable had been reduced by half. Some of the new units were no more than recent closes that had not been completely consolidated prior to enclosure, whereas others had been separated from the parent field by a few hedged strips. Division of some common fields had, however, preceded fencing within them – occasionally by a century of more – perhaps to allow for greater flexibility in cropping and grazing, in which case subdivision itself would have facilitated enclosure. The two procedures frequently took place contemporaneously and were complementary symptoms of the gradual disintegration of earlier common field systems.[2]

Enclosure for conversion to sheep pasture continued in the Midland districts during the late sixteenth and early seventeenth centuries, especially in north Buckinghamshire and, fifty years later, on the Oolitic uplands.[3] Piecemeal fencing, often for meadow and pasture, together with enclosure by private agreement, also occurred in the vales throughout this period, and especially in small parishes with

[1] Monteith, M.A. thesis, pp. 164–70; W. James and J. Malcolm, *General View of the Agriculture of the County of Buckingham*, 1794, p. 27; Buckinghamshire R.O., ST 114; Buckinghamshire County Museum, M/1 1376/79.

[2] B.M., Add. R. 35853x; Hertfordshire R.O., 51479, 51489–528, C2/S.4, E/67; Roden, *Geogr. Annlr.*, LII, 1969, p. 120.

[3] Chibnall, *Sherington*, pp. 169, 170–5, 199–200; Hyde and Markham, *A History of Stony Stratford*, pp. 38, 40–1; Beresford, *Records of Bucks.*, XVI, 1953–60, p. 12.

Fig. 8.8 Eighteenth-century field patterns on the central Chiltern plateau: the manor of Great Hampden (Bucks.) in 1741. Late medieval imparking may have eradicated some common arable.

Source. Map in the Hampden Estate Office (Great Hampden, Bucks.).

low populations and few landowners.[1] But many attempts failed because of tenant opposition, the small freeholder class on the thickly populated Icknield loams and the marlstone uplands, in particular,

[1] Gray, *English Field Systems*, pp. 114–18; A. Ballard, 'Three Surveys of Bladon', *Oxfordshire Archaeological Society Report for 1910*, 1911, p. 24; G. N. Clark, 'Enclosure by Agreement at Marston near Oxford', *Engl. Hist. Rev.*, XLII, 1927, pp. 87–94; J. H. Brown and W. Guest, *A History of Thame*, 1935, p. 44; *V.C.H. Oxon.*, V, 1957, pp. 22, 39–40, 103, 129–30, 217; VI, 1959, pp. 28, 120, 149, 248, 272, 306; VII, 1962, pp. 190, 224; VIII, 1964, pp. 11–12, 29, 49, 70, 86, 162; Hyde and Markham, *A History of Stony Stratford*, p. 73; Beresford, *Records of Bucks.*, XVI, 1953–60, pp. 5, 8–12; Buckinghamshire R.O., D/LE/1, no. 307; Buckinghamshire County Museum, 55/51; G. H. Fowler, *Four Pre-Enclosure Village Maps*, Bedfordshire Hist. Rec. Soc. Quarto Memoirs, II, 1928–36, pp. 18, 34, 41.

strongly resisting efforts to fence off large areas of common arable. An agreement between the parishoners of Pirton (Herts.) to defend each other if prosecuted for putting beasts on land enclosed by Thomas Dowcara from the common fields, is typical of continued support for communal farming in these districts.[1]

The alternative to enclosure was to improve common arable production itself by reducing the shortage of pasture which had long limited livestock and thus kept yields at a low level. Increased profitability of both animal products and the better grains now demanded that flocks and herds be enlarged, and by the early seventeenth century common field leys were widespread. A Sherington (Bucks.) agreement to set out grass strips specifically mentions the scarcity of manure arising from a lack of sheep grazing. Most leys were introduced by all farmers deciding to put part of their land to grass, and in some townships they took the form of balks, a foot or two wide, laid down between individual strips.[2] Paradoxically, earlier conversions to pasture may have strengthened the surviving common arable by raising local stock-carrying capacities. Common field hitchings, which had appeared in some townships by the thirteenth century, were also extended. Although cropping within the open arable thus became more varied, the field generally remained as its basic unit. One Wendlebury (Oxon.) field was, for example, sown with both wheat and barley every year, while at Sherington these two crops may also have been grown on separate sectors of the same field partitioned off by moveable fences.[3]

With the introduction of improved legumes and grasses in the mid-seventeenth century to meet continued demand for better winter fodder, it became possible to expand livestock numbers even further, especially on the lighter soils. Complete furlongs were sown, by agreement, with sainfoin, vetch or clover, and enclosed temporarily. Turnip cultivation was later adopted in many common fields on sands and limestones, and, as at Great Tew (Oxon.), was folded by

[1] Hertfordshire R.O., 72036; *V.C.H. Oxon.*, VI, 1959, p. 141; Havinden, B.Litt. thesis, pp. 69–70, 85, 116–17, 178–9, 186, 220, 263.

[2] Chibnall, *Sherington*, pp. 235–6; F. Page-Turner, 'Ancient Bedfordshire Deeds III', *Bedfordshire Hist. Rec. Soc.*, VIII, 1924, p. 57 no. ix; G. D. Gilmore (ed.), 'The Black Book of Bedford', *Bedfordshire Hist. Rec. Soc.*, XXXVI, 1955 (pub. 1956), pp. 35, 37; R. W. Jeffery (ed.), *The Manors and Advowson of Great Rollright*, Oxfordshire Rec. Ser., IX, 1927, pp. 27, 117–84; W. O. Hassal (ed.), *Wheatley Records 956–1956*, Oxfordshire Rec. Ser., XXXVII, 1956, pp. 70–1; Havinden, *Agric. Hist. Rev.*, IX, 1961, pp. 74–5; *V.C.H. Oxon.*, V, 1957, p. 127; VI, 1959, pp. 171, 200, 212, 236, 247, 256, 265, 281; VII, 1962, pp. 76, 190; VIII, 1964, p. 162.

[3] *V.C.H. Oxon.*, VI, 1959, pp. 225, 342; VII, 1962, pp. 47, 192; VIII, 1964, p. 49; Chibnall, *Sherington*, pp. 224–7; Colvin, *A History of Deddington*, p. 89; Havinden, *Agric. Hist. Rev.*, IX, 1961, p. 78.

the tenants' own sheep.[1] Partial elimination of the fallow followed. Increased flocks and herds meant more manure, while the use of nitrogen-fixing legumes meant that fallow could be cropped without loss of fertility. Rotations became more complex, and the old fields were often redivided to accommodate these advances. Traditional sheep–corn husbandries on the stonebrash of northern Oxfordshire were intensified, and two-field arrangements there – unaffected by the medieval change to three-field farming – were now subdivided, at first into four quarters and subsequently into a multiplicity of units. The two fields of Kirtlington were eventually broken up into five and seven 'quarters' respectively, although many holdings retained an approximately equal distribution between the original two.[2]

Common fields on the loams at the base of the Middle Chalk scarp and along the Thames in Oxfordshire had also often become highly fragmented by the eighteenth century, but not on any apparent systematic basis. The three fields of medieval Pitstone (Bucks.) had increased to eight by 1653, and Monks Risborough (Bucks.) contained sixteen small common fields at enclosure in 1839. Subdivision here was probably associated with the extensive piecemeal enclosure that was also occurring, and thus resembled the break-up of common arable units on the chalk above rather than the redivision of the Oolite dip-slope.[3] Fields continued to be grouped into three 'seasons' for cropping and grazing, but, as in the Chilterns, the fields in each season could be widely separated.[4] Simple three-field arrangements

[1] Havinden, *Agric. Hist. Rev.*, IX, 1961, pp. 75–7; *V.C.H. Oxon.*, V, 1957, p. 185; VI, 1959, p. 225; VII, 1962, pp. 76, 196; VIII, 1964, pp. 45, 105, 258; E. J. Lainchbury, *Kingham the Beloved Place*, 1957, p. 90; P. Vinogradoff, 'An Illustration of the Continuity of the Openfield System', *Quarterly Journal of Economics*, XXII, 1908, pp. 70–82; Jeffery, *The Manors and Advowson of Great Rollright*, pp. 27–8; T. Stone, *General View of the Agriculture of the County of Bedford*, 1794, p. 18; *V.C.H. Herts.*, IV, 1914, p. 223.

[2] *V.C.H. Oxon.*, VI, 1959, pp. 65, 141, 177, 201, 295, 329; VII, 1962, p. 47; Gray, *English Field Systems*, pp. 125–37; Havinden, *Agric. Hist. Rev.*, IX, 1961, pp. 78–9; A. M. Lambert, 'Oxfordshire about 1800 A.D.: A Study in Human Geography', Ph.D. thesis, University of London, 1953, pp. 65, 75–6, 79–92; Jeffery, *The Manors and Advowson of Great Rollright*, p. 23; Potts, *A History of Banbury*, p. 72; Colvin, *A History of Deddington*, p. 87; A. Ballard, 'The Open Fields of Fritwell', *Oxfordshire Archaeological Society Report for 1907*, 1908, p. 17; W. W. Fowler, *Kingham Old and New*, 1913, p. 16; L. E. Rose, *The History of Churchill (Oxfordshire)*, 1934, pp. 52–5.

[3] Buckinghamshire County Museum, P30/1, P30/2–3; Buckinghamshire R.O., 187/50, IR/94; Beresford, *Records of Bucks.*, XVI, 1953–60, pp. 13–24; Lambert, Ph.D. thesis, pp. 76, 93; *V.C.H. Oxon.*, VIII, 1964, p. 29.

[4] *V.C.H. Oxon.*, VIII, 1964, p. 189; Buckinghamshire County Museum, I/3, 6/12–17, 128–143/49; Hertfordshire R.O., 47390; Seebohm, *The English Village Community*, pp. 9–11; Fowler, *Four Pre-Enclosure Village Maps*, pp. 51–2.

remained longest on the heavier clays of the Vale of Oxford and north Buckinghamshire.[1]

3. THE PARLIAMENTARY ENCLOSURES AND AFTER

During the eighteenth century the number of common field parishes on the Cotswold plateaux was gradually reduced, largely by Parliamentary enclosure, and sheepwalks were turned over to farmland following the introduction of sheep–turnip husbandry.[2] Elsewhere, common arable cultivation survived in strength until the turn of the century, although in many parishes there was extensive strip consolidation and concentration of land ownership in a few hands. The high prices of the war years then brought a spate of legislation: most of Bedfordshire was taken into severalty (although not necessarily enclosed) between 1794 and 1807, with fifty-two acts passed, while one-third of all private bills for Buckinghamshire were enacted in the same period.[3] Along the chalk edge, good soils and favourable market conditions enabled small freeholders to remain independent at a time when this class was disappearing in other districts. They usually had to be bought out before enclosure could proceed, and as a result common arable farming lingered on in townships such as Crowell and Chinnor (Oxon.) until mid-nineteenth century.[4] Parliamentary enclosure did not always lead to an immediate improvement of cultivation – triennial fallowing sometimes continued[5] – nor did it necessarily produce a radical change in the landscape – the Lower Chalk bench in Hertfordshire and Bedfordshire is still largely open countryside although the old multiplicity of strips has gone. Usually, however, hedges were planted and, on the Oolitic Limestone, walls built, and new large farmhouses were erected away from the old villages.

In districts south of the chalk scarp, legislation was used primarily for the allotment and fencing of common wastes, and by 1850 many of the larger commons and surviving forests had been divided into a network of regular fields. Others were to remain as open spaces, but often only after protracted legal process such as saved Berkhamsted Frith and the Essex forests of Epping and Hainault.[6] New settlement

---

[1] Gray, *English Field Systems*, pp. 124–5; James and Malcolm, *General View of the Agriculture of the County of Buckingham*, p. 21.

[2] Havinden, B.Litt. thesis, pp. 297–301; Lambert, Ph.D. thesis, pp. 65, 71.

[3] L. M. Marshall (ed.), *The Rural Population of Bedfordshire, 1671 to 1921*, Bedfordshire Hist. Rec. Soc., XVI, 1934, p. 24; Tate, *A Hand-List of Buckinghamshire Enclosure Acts and Awards*, pp. 33–9.

[4] M.A. Havinden, review, *Agric. Hist. Rev.*, XIII, 1965, pp. 62–3.

[5] *V.C.H. Oxon.*, VI, 1959, p. 343.

[6] G. H. Whybrow, *The History of Berkhamsted Common*, 1934; C. S. Bayes, 'A

on small plots laid out by the Enclosure Commissioners supplemented the old waste-side hamlets and formed loosely knit agglomerations. Extensive marshland reclamation in Essex was largely undertaken privately, often by companies.[1] Some common arable enclosure was also effected by act of Parliament in these regions of irregular common fields, especially in Essex and Hertfordshire where strips in at least thirty-three and fifty parishes respectively were fenced off.[2] Usually it was only to eliminate the remnants of three centuries of piecemeal private enclosure, and the common fields of many townships disappeared completely without planned redistribution of any kind.

Removal of hedges, fences and walls to create the larger areas required by steady mechanisation of farming has been one of the more significant changes in field patterns since the mid-nineteenth century. Conversely, rapid urban expansion has seen the widespread fragmentation of agricultural land into building lots.

D. CONCLUSION

Differences in field systems on either side of the crest of the chalk hills did not reflect major changes in farming economies, nor, by the thirteenth century, variations in social organisation and inheritance customs. But there was a striking correlation between the pace of permanent colonisation – which was influenced to some extent by relief – and the medieval pattern of field systems. The distinctiveness of Chiltern arrangements, as of the country to the south and east, was linked with a history of gradual and piecemeal settlement, in turn reflecting very varied conditions of soil and slope.

Whatever their racial origins, it is clear that throughout the five counties the majority of early settlers preferred, for some reason which is not immediately apparent, to cultivate their land in intermixed strips which, at a later date at least, were open to common grazing. Conversely, the more prolonged the process of occupance the greater the likelihood that new farmland was enclosed straight into individual ownership. Most of the region north of the Chalk had been settled by the eleventh century, and arable land there lay as a multitude of

Historical Sketch of Epping Forest', *London Naturalist*, 1944 (for 1943), pp. 40–1; *V.C.H. Essex*, v, 1966, pp. 107, 290.

[1] D. W. Gramholt, 'The Coastal Marshland of East Essex Between the Seventeenth and Mid-Ninteteenth Centuries', M.A. thesis, University of London, 1960, pp. 146–7; Cox, M.A. thesis, pp. 94–6.

[2] F. G. Emmison, *Catalogue of Maps in the Essex Record Office, 1566–1855*, Essex R.O., III, 1947, pp. 47–50; W. E. Tate, 'A Handlist of Hertfordshire Enclosure Acts and Awards', *East Herts. Arch. Soc. Trans.*, XII, 1945–9, pp. 18–31.

strips held from nucleated settlements. Village growth had been accompanied by extension of the existing ploughland. Post-Domesday clearing on the fringes of many townships added an outlying area of closes and private woods, although in a few districts of late-surviving woodland, reclamation was sufficiently extensive to produce irregular field mosaics resembling those south of the chalk scarp.

To the south, early colonisation was greatest on the river terraces and the upper parts of the chalk and boulder clay plateaux of Hertford-shire and northwest Essex – by the thirteenth century areas of pre-dominantly common arable farming – but decreased southwestwards along the Chilterns as the Hills become higher and more deeply dissected, and southeastwards down the boulder clay plateau as soils become heavier. The southwestern Chilterns and the clays of southern Essex had probably been cleared directly into severalty, apart from a few and scattered areas of subdivided arable.

Whereas common ploughland in the Midland districts was, by the thirteenth century, generally organised as two great fields between which cropping alternated and within which farms were dispersed in roughly equal proportions, strips on the chalk hills and their southern environs lay as a large number of relatively small fields, some of the smallest and least regular having been improved from the waste in the twelfth and early thirteenth centuries. Such multiplicity indicated the difficulty of creating large, unified common-field areas in hilly districts where colonisation had emanated from numerous small settlements. There is no evidence that common arable here was, in the Middle Ages, arranged into simple cropping systems, although a triple grouping of common fields was apparent in some Chiltern townships during the sixteenth century and later. Nor were holdings apportioned evenly between the common arable units, but usually lay near to their respective farmsteads, again probably a product of gradual and piecemeal assarting. The three-course rotations that were followed on most farms by 1300 were very flexible because they combined enclosed arable with land in a variety of common fields.

The two-field systems down in the clay vales and on the uplands of north Oxfordshire also allowed some variation from the communal routines, with strip consolidation, cultivation of forage crops on fallow plots, and folding on large seigneural holdings in the common arable. Between the thirteenth and mid-sixteenth centuries the cropped area was increased by a general change to three-field farming on all but the impoverished stonebrash soils.

The first major enclosures from common arable in the five counties were made in the Midland country, and were coupled with late medieval conversion to pasture and considerable depopulation. In the districts with less regular common fields the end of communal farming began in earnest only in the sixteenth century, with a gradual and piecemeal fencing of individual strips or small consolidated areas, and finally rounded off in the nineteenth century with Parliamentary enclosure of common fields wherever these survived on a substantial scale. Enclosure here had been prompted by the rapid expansion of sixteenth-century markets – particularly London's – and it was neither associated with a widespread change to grassland, nor, initially, with the introduction of new crops. Intensification of established husbandries was the main aim, and to this end private woods, parkland and waste were also turned over to tillage, while enclosed fields were rationalised.

North of the Chalk, many of the smaller townships more amenable to consolidation had, by mid-sixteenth century, already been converted to pasture; and the need for widespread agreement limited major reallocations in the majority of surviving common field parishes. In the absence of enclosure the quality of farmland could only be raised – to meet the demands of growing population and markets – by improving communal farming itself, especially to raise local stock-carrying capacities. There thus developed what has been described as a 'spiral of progress',[1] which culminated in the introduction of complex rotations and extensive field redivision. Change was most marked on the Cotswolds where the old two-field system had survived, and where the light stonebrash soils were particularly favourable for the new husbandry.

Parliamentary enclosure has since redrawn much of the Midland landscape, while up on the Chalk and to the south and east of it there has been a growing uniformity of field patterns as enclosed landscapes have been opened up by the removal of hedges.

[1] Havinden, *Agric. Hist. Rev.*, IX, 1961, p. 83.

9

Field Systems of Southeast England

BY ALAN R. H. BAKER

A. CONTEXT

'It will be convenient to begin our examination of the field arrangements of the southeast of England with a study of Kent.'[1] Thus
H. L. Gray opened his essay on the Kentish field system and his
approach will be followed in this present chapter. Gray devoted an
entire chapter, some thirty-two pages of his book, to a consideration
of the field system of Kent, that of Surrey he discussed in fourteen
pages within the chapter on field systems of the Lower Thames Basin
and that of Sussex he did not treat separately at all, only mentioning
it briefly as the southeastern extremity of the area of the Midland
(two- and three-field) system.[2] Gray's pioneer study focussed attention
on the anomalies and enigmas of field systems in Kent and numerous
studies have subsequently investigated one or more of them.[3]
Much research has endeavoured to answer a few central questions
about the development of Kentish society, economy and landscape:
these questions have been about the extent of open as opposed to
enclosed field systems within the county, about the nature of common
pasturing (especially over the fallow arable), about the characteristics
of cropping practices (especially during the medieval period), about
the impact of gavelkind tenure upon patterns of fields and rural

[1] H. L. Gray, *English Field Systems*, Cambridge, Mass., 1915, p. 272.
[2] *Ibid.*, pp. 272–304, 255–69, 63 and 33–4.
[3] Among the most important are: J. E. A. Jolliffe, *Pre-Feudal England: The Jutes*,
1933; R. A. L. Smith, *Canterbury Cathedral Priory*, 1943; D. C. Coleman, 'The
Economy of Kent under the Later Stuarts', Ph.D. thesis, University of London,
1951; M. Nightingale, 'Some Evidence of Open Field Agriculture in Kent',
B.Litt. thesis, University of Oxford, 1952; J. L. M. Gulley, 'The Wealden Land-
scape in the Early Seventeenth Century and its Antecedents', Ph.D. thesis,
University of London, 1960; A. Smith, 'A Geographical Study of Agriculture
on the Kentish Manors of Canterbury Cathedral Priory, 1272–1379', M.A. thesis,
University of Liverpool, 1961; A. R. H. Baker, 'The Field Systems of Kent',
Ph.D. thesis, University of London, 1963; C. W. Chalklin, *Seventeenth-Century
Kent. A Social and Economic History*, 1965; F. R. H. Du Boulay, *The Lordship of
Canterbury. An Essay on Medieval Society*, 1966; M. N. Carlin, 'Christ Church,
Canterbury, and its Lands, from the Beginning of the Priorate of Thomas
Chillenden to the Dissolution (1391–1540)', D.Phil. thesis, University of Oxford,
1970.

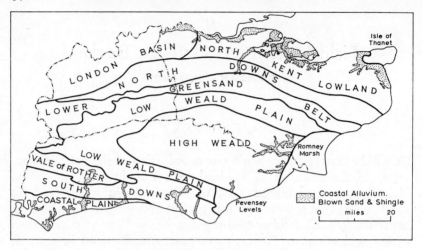

Fig. 9.1 Regions of Southeast England.

settlements, about the origin and role of the *iugum*, about the relative influences of ethnic customs and of physical environmental conditions upon field systems, and about the existence of the characteristics of the Kentish system within the neighbouring counties of Sussex and Surrey. Complete answers to these questions are still not available – and the nature of the surviving evidence inevitably means that complete and unequivocal answers are unobtainable. Nonetheless, our picture of the field systems of Kent in particular and of Southeast England in general has become increasingly clear and this chapter endeavours to summarise the present state of our knowledge.

As a region, the counties of Kent, Surrey and Sussex have shared some fundamentally important influences on the development of their patterns of fields and farmsteads. Among these influences, those attributable to geographical location are not readily encountered in the historical record and are therefore perhaps easily overlooked. But proximity both to the continent and to the capital must have greatly stimulated movements of peoples, goods, ideas and money, while the considerable length of the coastline in the region (and particularly in Kent) must have greatly facilitated these flows (Fig. 9.1). It is, then, in some measure to locational factors that the complexity and diversity of the historical geography of settlement and agriculture in Southeast England must be ascribed. Some role was also clearly played by the physical differences of soils and terrain within the region,[1] although

[1] There was certainly a close relationship between soils and agricultural productivity by the early fourteenth century: E. M. Yates, 'The Nonae Rolls and Soil Fertility', *Sussex Notes and Queries*, xv, 1962, pp. 325–8.

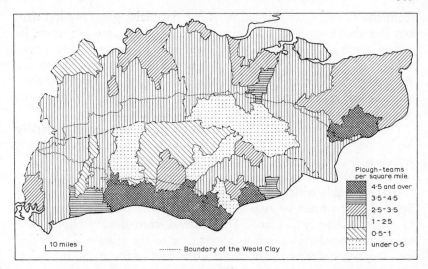

Plough-teams
per square mile.
4·5 and over
3·5 - 4·5
2·5 - 3·5
1 - 2·5
0·5 - 1
under 0·5

10 miles

·········· Boundary of the Weald Clay

Fig. 9.2 Domesday plough-teams in 1086 in Southeast England.
Source. Based upon Figure 170 of H. C. Darby and E. M. J. Campbell (eds.), *The Domesday Geography of Southeast England,* 1962, p. 589.

it is as difficult precisely to assess this role as it is that of geographical location. But both undoubtedly find themselves expressed in the developing patterns of economic prosperity which can be identified during the early Middle Ages.

The distribution of Domesday plough-teams in Kent, Surrey and Sussex in 1086 illustrates some early contrasts in their degree of agricultural development (Fig. 9.2). The major contrast was undoubtedly between Wealden and extra-Wealden areas.[1] Much of the High Weald rises to over 400 feet above sea-level, an upland region formed of Hastings Beds which comprises three groups of strata (Ashdown Sand, Wadhurst Clay and Tunbridge Wells Sand). The interior of the High Weald is composed largely of the two sandstone formations that yield light soils and over much of the area there was less than one plough-team per square mile recorded in 1086. Only in the eastern High Weald – where it meets the coast, is of lower elevation, and the Wadhurst Clay gives rise to heavier soils – were there quite high densities of Domesday plough-teams and population (up to five and up to nine per square mile respectively). The Low Weald Plain, which encircles the High Weald on the north, west and south, derives

[1] The following description of aspects of the Domesday geography of Southeast England is drawn from H. C. Darby and E. M. J. Campbell (eds.), *The Domesday Geography of Southeast England,* 1962, pp. 364–610.

from the Weald Clay formation. It is a flat plain, generally less than 100 feet above sea-level but rising in places to 200 feet and more. Its soil is a stiff, ill-drained clay or loam which becomes very heavy when wet, and hard and cracked when dry. The evidence of Domesday Book suggests that we should envisage it in 1086 as a wooded area, with woods and swine pastures attached to settlements outside the Weald, and with only occasional centres of cultivation.

Densities of population and plough-teams in 1086 were generally higher outside the Weald than within it. On the Sussex Coastal Plain, which is occupied by soils derived from Valley Gravels and Brick-earths, densities of Domesday plough-teams and of population compared favourably with those of the greater part of England. The adjacent South Downs must be regarded as among the most fertile districts in eleventh-century England. They extend from Beachy Head to the Hampshire border in a belt of about four to six miles wide, divided into separate tracts by the north–south valleys of the Arun, the Adur, the Ouse and the Cuckmere. The higher levels of the Downs are covered with thin soils but the lower slopes and valley floors provided much more rewarding soils. Villages were numerous, especially in the valleys and along the scarp-foot zone of the Downs' northern edge. To the west of Steyning the Lower Greensand formation is broad enough to form a distinctive tract between the Downs and Weald. Here, the Lower Greensand is composed of Sandgate Clays which yield easily worked and rewarding loam soils. Here, too, is the alluvium of the western Rother. Not surprisingly, this was in 1086 an area of frequent and sizeable villages, not only near the Rother itself but also to the south in a line along the scarp-foot zone below the Downs. Despite the difficulties involved in interpreting the evidence of Domesday Book, there is no doubt that the Rother valley was a fairly prosperous and developed area in 1086.

To the north of the Weald is the Lower Greensand Belt, rising westwards from Kent into Surrey, its generally light, hungry, soils standing in great contrast with the heavy Weald Clay. It, too, formed an underdeveloped countryside in 1086. The dip-slope of the Lower Greensand descends northwards into a narrow belt of Lower Chalk, Upper Greensand and Gault, known as the Vale of Holmesdale. This Vale is wide and significant in Kent, narrower but still important in Surrey until to the west of Dorking it all but disappears as a separate feature. The Vale of Holmesdale is overlooked by the Chalk escarpment of the North Downs. Low and broad in the east, higher and narrower in the west, the Downs themselves are largely covered with superficial deposits of Clay-with-flints providing soils of only moderate fertility. The Chalk slopes northward to dip beneath various Tertiary deposits, comprising deposits of sand and clay with some fertile loams. The arrangement of parish and hundred boundaries, across the grain of relief and soils, makes it difficult to arrive at density figures for Domesday plough-teams and population. There were some districts with relatively few villages – on the London Clay to the north of Canterbury, and on the Isle of Sheppey. But in general settlements were frequent and widely scattered throughout the area, with preferred locations along the valleys such as those of the Darent, the Medway and the Stour, along the Vale of Holmesdale, and on the loamy surface of the Chalk in eastern Kent.

Further west, there were marked contrasts to be observed in the London Basin. There were relatively few settlements on the Black-heath beds of northwest Kent while the infertile sands of the Bagshot plateau in Surrey supported few plough-teams in 1086. Between these two relatively poor areas lay a much more prosperous region. To the south of the Thames stretches a belt of London Clay the surface of which is varied by patches of sand and gravel and by the gravel terraces of the Wey, the Mole and the Wandle that flow northwards across the clay surface to join the Thames. Here, in the region of greatest prosperity in eleventh-century Surrey, there were recorded population densities of about seven to eleven per square mile and plough-team densities of about three. How much of this was due to the moderate fertility of the region and how much to the proximity to London, it is hard to say.

Finally, reference should be made to the areas of estuarine and coastal marshland – the North Kent Marshes, the East Kent Marshes, Romney Marsh and the Pevensey Levels. Densities of plough-teams and of population were not high in 1086, but they are sufficient to indicate that life in these areas was far from being entirely dependent on salt and sheep, and fish and fowl.

The period between the late eleventh century and the early four-teenth century saw many dramatic changes in the social and economic geography of Southeast England and the 1334 Lay Subsidy provides a useful general guide to the variations in wealth from place to place which these changes had brought about. A map of the 1334 assessment in Kent, Surrey and Sussex (Fig. 9.3) has to be treated with caution, for it excludes urban and ecclesiastical wealth, but it does provide part of the context within which to consider regional differences in the field systems of Southeast England.[1] The poorest areas in 1334 were the Bagshot region of Surrey and much of the central and western Weald. In his reconstruction of the geography of the Weald in the

[1] R. E. Glasscock, 'The Distribution of Lay Wealth in Kent, Surrey and Sussex, in the Early Fourteenth Century', *Archaeologia Cantiana*, LXXX, 1965, pp. 61-8.

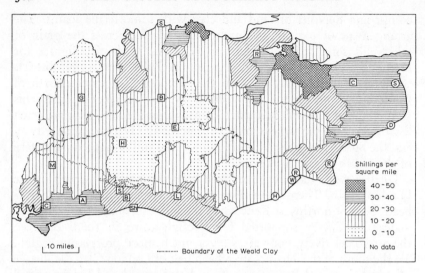

Fig. 9.3 The 1334 Lay Subsidy assessment in Southeast England. The quotas of all cities and boroughs denoted by initial letters are excluded from the calculations. They are: in Kent – Canterbury and Rochester; in Surrey – Bletchingley, Guildford and Southwark; in Sussex – Chichester, Arundel, Bramber, East Grinstead, Horsham, Lewes, Midhurst, Shoreham and Steyning. The Cinque Ports, for which there is no 1334 data, are also marked by initial letters, from north to south, Sandwich, Dover, Hythe, New Romney, Rye, Winchelsea and Hastings. There is no information for the Lowey of Pevensey.

Source. Based upon Figure 2 of R. E. Glasscock, 'The Distribution of Lay Wealth in Kent, Surrey and Sussex, in the Early Fourteenth Century', *Archaeologia Cantiana*, LXXX, 1965.

early fourteenth century, J. L. M. Gulley has shown that while much woodland remained, the Weald was already an area of mixed farming with an emphasis on animal husbandry. Cattle and swine were reared and grazed on both enclosed and open pastures. While oats was the commonest grain crop, wheat was cultivated on the heavier soils, especially on the Weald Clay. Much heathland must have remained in the western Wealden districts. The most prosperous part of the Weald was its eastern, maritime, section between Pevensey and Rye.[1] Nearby, in Romney Marsh, the 1334 assessments were higher than in the Weald as a whole and even higher than in some extra-Wealden areas. While Romney Marsh was an important centre of pastoral farming and especially of cheese-making, it was also important for the cultivation of oats and beans, crops particularly suited to heavy

[1] Gulley, Ph.D. thesis, pp. 294–387.

soils. The work of marshland reclamation during the thirteenth and early fourteenth century must have added considerably to the prosperity of this area.[1]

The richest area of Southeast England, according to the 1334 assessment, was the North Kent Lowland, between the Medway and the Isle of Thanet. Indeed, as R. E. Glasscock has emphasised, the lay wealth of northeast Kent was the highest in England southeast of a line from Great Yarmouth to Southampton. Only parts of the Sussex coastal plain and the Thames Valley carried comparable wealth.[2] The prosperity of northeast Kent must be due in part to its particularly fertile soils and in part to the specialised and efficient grain (wheat and barley) and sheep farming which had been developed there by the early fourteenth century. More than anywhere else in Kent this area was concerned with producing surpluses of corn and wool for market.[3] Similarly, the production of corn and wool was a major contributor to the wealth of southern Sussex.[4] Glasscock explains that the prosperity of the coastal fringe of Southeast England, outside the Weald, was due not only to its fertility but also to its nearness to markets at home and on the continent and to the sea-borne nature of much medieval trade. Together these advantages made northeast Kent one of the richest parts of early fourteenth-century England.[5]

Already by this time marked contrasts in degrees of prosperity and in types of rural economy had been superimposed on the strong differences in physical geography among the regions of Southeast England. Medieval field systems, in consequence, could vary markedly over only short distances in their form, functioning and formation. It is not, however, until the sixteenth and seventeenth centuries that

---

[1] R. A. L. Smith, 'Marsh Embankment and Sea Defence in Medieval Kent', *Econ. Hist. Rev.*, X, 1939–40, pp. 29–37; Smith, *Canterbury Cathedral Priory*, pp. 146–89; A. Smith, 'Regional Differences in Crop Production in Medieval Kent', *Arch. Cant.*, LXXVIII, 1963, pp. 147–60.

[2] Glasscock, *Arch. Cant.*, LXXX, 1965, p.66.

[3] R. A. Pelham, 'Some Aspects of the East Kent Wool Trade in the Thirteenth Century', *Arch. Cant.*, XLIV, 1932, pp. 218–28; R. A. Pelham, 'The Relations of Soils to Grain-Growing in Kent in the Thirteenth Century', *Empire Journal of Experimental Agriculture*, I, 1933, pp. 82–4; Smith, *Arch. Cant.*, LXXVIII, 1963, pp. 149–53; Smith, *Canterbury Cathedral Priory*, pp. 129–31 and 151–6; Du Boulay, *Lordship of Canterbury*, pp. 209–12.

[4] R. A. Pelham, 'Studies in the Historical Geography of Medieval Sussex', *Sussex Archaeological Collections*, LXXII, 1931, pp. 157–84; R. A. Pelham, 'Some Medieval Sources for the Study of Historical Geography', *Geography*, XVII, 1932, pp. 32–8; R. A. Pelham, 'The Agricultural Geography of the Chichester Estates in 1388', *Sussex Arch. Coll.*, LXXVIII, 1937, pp. 195–210. Glasscock, *Arch. Cant.*, LXXX, 1965, p. 68.

sufficiently graphical evidence becomes available, in the form of estate maps, to enable us confidently to reconstruct the significant regional variations in field and rural settlement patterns.

B. FIELD PATTERNS AND FARMING PRACTICES IN KENT c. 1550 – c. 1650

I. FIELD PATTERNS

(a) Field forms

Almost 200 Kentish estate maps of the sixteenth and seventeenth centuries provide a clear picture of field patterns.[1] Detailed analysis of some of these maps demonstrated marked regional variations in the sizes of fields. The largest fields, with a mean size of over eleven acres, were found in East Kent and in Romney Marsh. The smallest fields, with a mean size of under four acres, were found on the Low Weald Plain. Fields in Holmesdale and the High Weald were somewhat larger than those in the Low Weald but they were still only about half the size of those in East Kent and in Romney Marsh.[2] There were regional variations, too, in the shapes of fields and the nature of their enclosures. The most striking contrast was again between the small, irregularly shaped fields of the Weald and the large, more rectangular fields of East Kent.[3] Some field shapes probably reflect ploughing patterns. Long, narrow fields with smoothly flexing boundaries seem to produce aratral curves; but with the Kentish turn-wrest plough it was just as possible to plough squarish plots as rectangular strips.[4] The curving plough-strip in Kent does not necessarily have the historical implications which have been suggested for it elsewhere.[5] Very commonly Wealden fields were bordered not by a single row of bushes as a hedge but by narrow strips of scrub and trees, called 'shaws' or 'rews'. Shaws occupied 11 per cent of 680 acres of an estate in Little Chart and Pluckley in 1626.[6] On many maps, the acreage of a field is given in two parts: first, the part that

---

[1] A. R. H. Baker, 'Some Early Kentish Estate Maps and a Note on their Portrayal of Field Boundaries', *Arch. Cant.*, LXXVII, 1962, pp. 177–84.

[2] A. R. H. Baker, 'Field Patterns in Seventeenth Century Kent', *Geography*, L, 1965, pp. 18–30.

[3] *Ibid.*, Fig. 4, p. 27.

[4] M. D. Nightingale, 'Ploughing and Field Shape', *Antiquity*, XXVII, 1953, pp. 20–6.

[5] S. R. Eyre, 'The Curving Plough-Strip and its Historical Implications', *Agric. Hist. Rev.*, III, 1955, pp. 80–94.

[6] Kent R.O., U275 P1. Cited in Gulley, Ph.D. thesis, pp. 82–3.

could be ploughed or mown, and secondly the part that was rough scrub around the edges of the field.[1] Shaws provided shade for beasts in pasture fields and served as small access ways to fields which had no frontage on a road.[2] The combination of shaws surrounding small fields gave the Wealden landscape a densely wooded appearance.[3] By contrast, use of ditches and post-and-rail fences around large fields gave the landscape of Romney Marsh – and other marshland areas – an extremely open appearance.[4]

The estate maps demonstrate that totally enclosed farms were to be found throughout the entire county but they also indicate the existence in some locations of fields subdivided into unenclosed parcels in intermixed ownership and/or occupation – that is to say, open fields.[5] These were certainly not found throughout the county. Open arable fields were largely confined to the North Kent Lowlands (being most numerous in East Kent), and the Vale of Holmesdale, while subdivided meadows were found on low-lying alluvial lands bordering the rivers and the marshes. Topographers often commented upon the unenclosed landscape of East Kent and surveys, rentals and maps testify to the existence here of open fields in the seventeenth century and indeed to their persistence into the eighteenth and nineteenth centuries. Open fields in seventeenth-century Kent were often small, no more than fifteen or twenty acres. Along the North Kent Lowland and the Vale of Holmesdale small open fields lay scattered among the more numerous closes.[6]

[1] Kent R.O., U86 P2, U49 P4, TRP 431/5, U24 P26 and U47 P7.

[2] Kent R.O., U31 P3 and U86 P2. Cited in Gulley, Ph.D. thesis, p. 83.

[3] C. Morris (ed.), *The Journeys of Celia Fiennes*, 1949, pp. 135–6. For a discussion of the comments of many topographers upon the wooded nature of the Weald, see Coleman, Ph.D. thesis, pp. 18–21.

[4] Kent R.O., U86 P24; All Souls College, Oxford Hovenden Maps, Portfolio 2, no. 10; P.R.O., LR2/197, fo. 78; Kent R.O., S/Rm P1/3 and P1/4; Lambeth Palace Library CC 8908; J. Boys, *General View of the Agriculture of the County of Kent*, 2nd edn, 1813, pp. 12–13.

[5] The terms 'open fields' and 'common fields' are used in this chapter to refer respectively to fields composed of unenclosed parcels which are not definitely known to have been cultivated or grazed in common and to fields composed of unenclosed parcels over which common rules of cultivation and grazing are known to have operated. See Joan Thirsk, 'Preface to the Third Edition' in C. S. and C. S. Orwin, *The Open Fields*, 3rd edn, 1967, pp. v–xv; A. R. H. Baker, 'Some Terminological Problems in Studies of British Field Systems', *Agric. Hist. Rev.*, XVII, 1969, pp. 136–40.

[6] For a discussion of the comments of topographers on the unenclosed landscape of East Kent, see Coleman, Ph.D. thesis, pp. 18–21 and Nightingale, B.Litt. thesis, pp. 4–6; for other evidence, see Baker, *Geography*, L, 1965, pp. 21–2; Chalklin, *Seventeenth-Century Kent*, pp. 15–16; Nightingale, B.Litt. thesis, chap. VI, pp. 50–2.

(b) Field functions

Enclosed fields, then, dominated the Kentish rural landscape in the early seventeenth century but the open fields have aroused as much if not more interest. Were they not only open but also common fields? It has sometimes been suggested that field names with the suffix 'furlong' or 'shot' imply the existence of a common field system.[1] Many arable fields in seventeenth-century Kent had such names but their significance is not at all clear. A field named 'Stony-furlong' at Wrotham in 1620 was part of the former demesne and had been since at least the end of the thirteenth century: it was not associated with a common field system.[2] The terms 'virgate' and 'furlong' occur widely in the Weald and 'layne', another name often associated with a common field system, was there applied to land, held in severalty, which had no surrounding enclosure.[3] It is clearly impossible to rely solely on field names as evidence of common arable fields. Specific references in surveys to 'common fields' – such as those of Northborne, Otford, Tymberwood (in the parish of Chalk), Islingham (near Cliffe) and Northfleet in 1608 and Lydden in 1616 – are equally difficult to interpret.[4] M. Nightingale's assertion that such references provide 'conclusive evidence that the farmers of this period treated these parcels as common fields and not merely as unfenced land' is unacceptable and it seems preferable to refer, as has E. Melling, to such fields as 'so-called common arable fields'.[5] A field specifically named 'Common Field' at Wrotham was part of the demesne, leased out in unenclosed parcels to a number of tenants. It was not called 'Common Field' until at least the middle of the sixteenth century and was not part of a common field system.[6] A survey of the manor of Lydden in 1616 and others of the nearby manors at the same date suggest that surveyors in the early seventeenth century seem to have described fields containing intermixed, unenclosed parcels as 'common fields', without intending any reference to their functioning. The surveyors themselves were often strangers to the manors being surveyed

[1] For example, J. C. Jackson, 'Open Field Cultivation in Derbyshire', Derbyshire Arch. Jnl., LXXXII, pp. 54–72 and 'Fossil Field Boundaries', Amat. Histn., IV, 1958–9, pp. 73–7.
[2] A. R. H. Baker, 'Field Systems in the Vale of Holmesdale', Agric. Hist. Rev., XIV, 1966, pp. 1–24.
[3] Gulley, Ph.D. thesis, p. 87.
[4] P.R.O., LR2/196, fos. 266–70 and 117–19; P.R.O., LR2/197, fos. 39–43, 72–3 and 149–52; Lambeth Palace Library V/T/3/2, fos. 32–3.
[5] Nightingale, B.Litt. thesis, pp. 50–2; E. Melling (ed.), 'Aspects of Agriculture and Industry', Kentish Sources, III, 1961, p. 5.
[6] Baker, Agric. Hist. Rev., XIV, 1966, pp. 7–9.

and may have applied terms acquired elsewhere to what they thought were comparable conditions in Kent.[1] There is no evidence for the Parliamentary enclosure of any common arable fields in Kent, nor of any enclosures of such fields by Chancery Decree.[2] In the eighteenth century, there are clear statements by agricultural writers that open fields in Kent were not used communally. William Marshall, commenting on the unenclosed fields of Thanet in 1798, noted the advanced farming methods in the island and their superiority 'over the whole common field practice' and John Boys, a farmer at Betteshanger in East Kent and author of the Board of Agriculture's report on agriculture in the county, wrote in 1796 'there is no portion of Kent that is occupied by a community of persons, as in many other counties'.[3] The open arable fields of Kent in the seventeenth and eighteenth centuries were not common fields. Furthermore, the number of such fields in a parish was not of agrarian importance, because there is no evidence of communally fixed crop rotations.[4] Open arable fields were not, it seems, either cultivated or grazed in common.

Open meadows lay beside the rivers Medway and Stour and in the marshlands of the Thames estuary.[5] Within the Weald, meadows were prized for their good lush grass, often in contrast with surrounding pastures which tended to be thin and coarse on sandy soils or rank on the ill-drained clays. Water meadows were regarded as an important source of hay for fattening.[6] The extent of common usage of these meadows is difficult to ascertain except in a few cases. In 1608, Thomas Ellis, lessee of the manor of Kennington, adjoining the River Stour below Ashford, had common pasturing for 12 cows and 1 bull from 14 August until 24 March in a meadow called 'Broadmeade', and he had the right to the first crop of hay from a number of the open meadow parcels.[7] This is the only clear example of the regulation of common meadows that has come to light for the seventeenth century, but others exist for the following two centuries.[8] Common meadows certainly existed in Kent.

[1] Lambeth Palace Library, V/T/3/2, fo. 33.
[2] F. Hull, 'Kent from the Dissolution to the Civil War', unpublished notes (1955), p. 6; W. E. Tate, 'A Hand-list of English Enclosure Acts and Awards; Part 17. Open Fields, Commons and Enclosures in Kent', *Arch. Cant.*, LVI, 1943, pp. 54–65.
[3] W. Marshall, *Rural Economy of the Southern Counties*, vol. 2, 1798, pp. 6 and 13; J. Boys, *General View of the Agriculture of the County of Kent*, 1796, p. 53.
[4] Chalklin, *Seventeenth-Century Kent*, p. 16.
[5] Baker, *Geography*, L, 1965, pp. 28–9.
[6] Gulley, Ph.D. thesis, p. 95.
[7] P.R.O., LR2/197, fo. 138*v*.
[8] For example, at Edenbridge in 1714: Kent R.O., uncatalogued map among the Streatfield Mss.; at Shorne in 1754: Kent R.O., U86 M16 and Q/R Dc 16; at Cliffe in 1811: Nightingale, B.Litt. thesis, pp. 50–2 and Kent R.O., Q/R Dc 15.

So, too, did common pastures. Patches of common were to be found in most parts of the county, located principally on the less fertile soils. They were usually small but sometimes large, and they tended to be pastured by the stock of only half a dozen or so tenants and landowners rather than by the stock of an entire agrarian community. There were numerous small heaths in the Weald and many commons, some of them quite large, on the Lower Greensand ridge.[1] In a dispute in 1635 concerning Langley heath, most of the parties agreed that the right of common pasturing was limited to only four or five of the manor's tenants. Estimates of the size of the heath varied from 25 to 70 acres.[2] In the nearby manor of Wall, in Ashford, it was agreed in 1584 that seven of the manor's tenants had pasturing rights on a common called 'Chart Lekyn'. One of them, Vincent Engham, on paying his yearly rent of 9d. for the lands which he held of the manor, was allowed to keep on the common 'four great beasts or for every one of them two twelve monthlings either budds or colts, or for every great bullock four sheep, lambs or swyne'.[3] One of the largest commons, Ightham, three miles east of Sevenoaks, was probably about 500 acres and was carefully stinted, tenants of the manor not being allowed to pasture livestock there after the end of April.[4] Other large commons were located on the gravelly plateaux formed either by the Blackheath Pebble Beds or by tracts of high-level gravels in the northwest of the county. The common at Blackheath covered 250 acres, Sydenham Common on the Surrey border about 500 acres.[5] Many small, some large, commons lay on the higher parts of the North Downs. In 1632, thirty-seven people had the right of pasturing their stock on the 500 or so acres of Swingfield Minnis, in the east, and an additional eleven people paid for the privilege; the common was to be pastured by sheep, horses and cattle, but not by pigs or geese.[6] On 5 July 1664, however, twenty-nine tenants had on the common 867 sheep, 31 cattle and 37 horses; eleven people who paid for the pasturing had 204 sheep, 20 cattle and 11 pigs; and three people with no right of common at all had 24 sheep and 1 horse. In addition, there were illegally on the common 126 pigs and 109

[1] Kent R.O., U31 P3, U86 P2, U55 P22; C. W. Chalklin, 'The Rural Economy of a Kentish Wealden Parish, 1650–1750', Agric. Hist. Rev., x, 1962, pp. 29–45; P.R.O., E164/17/Jas I/Michaelmas 23.
[2] P.R.O., E164/11 Chas I/Easter 28.
[3] Kent R.O., U455 M33.
[4] E. Harrison, 'The Court Rolls and other Records of the Manor of Ightham', Arch. Cant., XLVIII, 1936, pp. 169–218; E. Harrison, 'Some Records of Ightham Parish', Arch. Cant., LIII, 1940, pp. 17–23.
[5] Chalklin, Seventeenth-Century Kent, pp. 19–20.
[6] Kent R.O., U270 E37.

geese.[1] The complaints of local people when common rights were infringed – in some cases by attempts of landowners to enclose the commons, in others by encroachments by squatters or by illegally grazing livestock – suggest that livestock-feeding on the heaths was greatly valued, especially for the poorer classes and despite the poor quality pasturage they afforded. But as C. W. Chalklin has commented, 'perhaps the greatest limitation of the commons in the agrarian economy of the county was the restricted areas which they served: in much of north Kent, especially towards the east, there was little or no waste, and in the Weald and even on the sandstone ridge there were many parishes where the commons were too small to be of much value to more than a handful of the poorer inhabitants.'[2]

2. FARMING PRACTICES

(a) *Patterns of production*

Any precise picture of regional variations in farming in Kent in this period must await a detailed and systematic statistical analysis of the numerous probate inventories that are extant – there are an estimated 40,000 inventories for the diocese of Canterbury alone.[3] But the general outlines are discernible and it is clear that variations in soils and in accessibility to markets underlay spatial variations in Kentish agriculture. While a mixed husbandry was practised throughout the county, the particular mix of crops and livestock varied from one part of the county to another. Varied physical conditions, combined with the fact that farms comprised for the most part enclosed fields, permitted a wide variety of crops and cropping systems. Enclosed fields could also be fallowed irregularly and manured when it was thought necessary.

In the Weald, the emphasis was on the rearing and fattening of cattle. The ploughland acreage on the average farm was small – usually not more than 10 acres – and the greater part of it given over to the cultivation of fodder crops (oats, peas and tares) to supplement the grass and hay supplies. To the north, on the light soils of the Lower Greensand and of Holmesdale, farming was more truly mixed and based essentially on sheep and barley. To the south, in Romney Marsh, fattening beef and mutton and producing wool were the main concerns and many of the larger farmers in other parts of the county rented or bought pastures in the Marsh. Again, while most resident farmers grew a little corn, nearly all were chiefly graziers. Farming was more

[1] Kent R.O., U270 E39.
[2] Baker, Ph.D. thesis, pp. 243–5; Chalklin, *Seventeenth-Century Kent*, pp. 20–2.
[3] Melling, *Kentish Sources*, III, 1961, p. 8.

genuinely mixed in the marshland areas around the Isles of Thanet
and Sheppey and along the Thames' shore. On the rich loams of the
north Kent lowlands and on the easily tilled, though less fertile, chalk-
lands farming had an arable bias, although sheep, in demand for their
manure as much as for their wool or meat, were an integral part of
this arable husbandry. On farms here, the main crops were wheat
and barley while peas and beans were usually more important than
oats as the major livestock fodder. Few cattle were kept, but many
farms had small sheep flocks, some had large ones.[1]

Spatial variation in farming practice was paralleled by a temporal
specialisation and commercialisation. The growth of the London food
market was an important agent of agricultural change in Kent. During
the late sixteenth century, Kent in normal years supplied nearly
75 per cent of London's corn imports and in the period 1625–49
London was taking two-thirds of the cereal exports from Sandwich
and over nine-tenths of those from Milton and Faversham. Much of
the cereal trade went along the coast.[2] The stimulation provided by
the London food market led to cash-cropping and to efforts to increase
crop yields. Gradually during the seventeenth century convertible
husbandry became more widely practised and in the later half of the
century new crops, cultivated grass crops and root crops, began to
be introduced. The spread of specialised cash crops, such as fruit,
vegetables and hops, began early but spread slowly at first.[3] By the
late sixteenth century, the area between Rainham and the Blean was
becoming 'The Cherrie gardein and Apple orcharde of Kent', and
at Teynham in 1608 orchards were valued at 30s. an acre, arable at
only 8–10s., and the estate of Thomas Palmer, of 197 acres, included
105 acres of orchards and gardens.[4] Market gardening was also
developing here, as well as nearer to London and around Sandwich.
By 1650 hop gardens were scattered throughout the Weald, with a concentration on the borders of the Weald and the Lower Greensand belt.[5]

[1] Gulley, Ph.D. thesis, pp. 115–28; Chalklin, *Agric. Hist. Rev.*, x, 1962, pp. 29–45;
Chalklin, *Seventeenth-Century Kent*, pp. 73–109; E. C. Lodge, 'The Account Book
of a Kentish Estate, 1616–1704', *Records of Social and Economic History*, vi, 1927,
pp. xv–xlviii; Coleman, Ph.D. thesis, pp. 57–137; J. Thirsk, 'The Farming Regions
of England. F. South-Eastern England: Kent and Sussex' in J. Thirsk (ed.), *The
Agrarian History of England and Wales: IV, 1500–1640*, 1967, pp. 55–64.
[2] F. J. Fisher, 'The Development of the London Food Market, 1540–1640', *Econ.
Hist. Rev.*, v, 1934–5, pp. 46–64; T. S. Willan, *The English Coasting Trade, 1600–
1750*, 1938, p. 138.
[3] Coleman, Ph.D. thesis, p. 63; Melling, *Kentish Sources*, iii, 1961, p. 10; Chalklin,
Seventeenth-Century Kent, p. 75.
[4] W. Lambarde, *A Perambulation of Kent*, 1576, edn 1826, p. 222; P.R.O., LR2/197,
fos. 11–12.
[5] Gulley, Ph.D. thesis, pp. 131–2.

(b) Patterns of farms and estates

By 1600 Kent was a county of largely enclosed, often compact, individually cultivated farms and small holdings. Most farms seem to have been between 5 and 25 acres, although some were much larger larger than this. Farms in the Weald were generally smaller and more compact than those in north and east Kent, and husbandry was more usually combined with by-employment in the iron and cloth industries. The majority of farmers were tenants. Although Kent was a county of mostly small landowners, the majority of them probably possessing no more than one or two small farms or cottage holdings, it was not a county of owner-occupiers. The pattern of land ownership was complex. There were the extensive estates of the three great ecclesiastical landlords, the Archbishop and the Deans and Chapters of Rochester and Canterbury. There were the properties of perhaps a dozen wealthy noblemen and gentry, more compact but almost as large in acreage. Below them were the properties of several hundred gentry and scores of wealthy yeomen with scattered lands in from four or five to perhaps a dozen parishes. Finally, there were many thousands of freeholders, mostly with land in just one parish. Apart from demesnes and the wastes, nearly all land in Kent was freehold. A freeholder's indefinite ownership of his land was dependent only upon the payment of a nominal annual quit-rent and of a fixed fine, and perhaps a heriot, at the time of purchase or inheritance. A freeholder could freely dispose of his land if he so wished. Copyhold tenures were few and most in fact were as secure as copyholds. An active market in land was thus facilitated.[1]

The pattern of land ownership changed, sometimes through marriages and by inheritance, but more often through purchases. Smaller estates changed hands more frequently than did larger ones and the land market seems to have been especially active in northwest Kent, where properties within easy reach of London were profitable investments for wealthy merchants, tradesmen and professional men from the City of Westminster.[2] The smaller estates were more unstable than larger ones not only because all or parts of them came on to the market more often, but also because of the predominant customs of inheritance among the middle classes. According to the prevailing custom of gavelkind, which affected even the estates of the gentry except where they were held by knight service, lands were divided

---

[1] Chalklin, *Seventeenth-Century Kent*, pp. 45–72.
[2] A. M. Everitt, 'The County Committee of Kent in the Civil War', *Occasional Papers, Department of Engl. Local Hist., Univ. of Leicester*, IX, 1957, p. 8; W. K. Jordan, 'Social Institutions in Kent, 1480-1660', *Arch. Cant.*, LXXV, 1961, pp.132–8.

among the sons equally on a father's death. By 1600, nearly all the
gentle families made sure that most if not all property descended to
the eldest son, while money or rent charges, or perhaps one or two
small outlying estates, were given to younger sons and daughters.
On the other hand, among farmers and tradespeople division of an
estate consisting of several holdings among the sons was a normal
practice. Where single holdings were left to two or more co-heirs
it was usual either to settle the property on one of themselves or to
sell it to another person.

Only rarely were individual holdings physically divided among
co-heirs during the seventeenth century.[1] At Tonbridge in 1573 John
and Edmund Latter, as sons and co-heirs, partitioned a holding near
Southborough Common: Edmund quitclaimed to John, *inter alia*
a parcel of 'Parkfield', a parcel of 'Hyckemans' and part of a field
called 'Le Gretegretfyld', which adjoined to the residue of these three
fields already assigned to Edmund. Single fields could be subdivided.
Further evidence of this is seen in the marriage settlement of Edmund,
son of the Edmund just mentioned, in 1602, in which reference is
made to 'the further part of the further part of greater greatfield, and
the hither part of the greater greatfield'.[2] At Chevening in 1603 three
brothers partitioned their father's estate: two of them jointly received
four fields and 'a piece of grounde taken out of the close there from
the barne to the said staule', and the third received two fields and
'the residue of the sayd close'.[3] Field subdivision did occur in Kent
in the seventeenth century but only exceptionally.

If the partitioning of holdings was of little importance in seventeenth-
century Kent, there are hints that it had once been more so. The dis-
gavelling statutes of the sixteenth and seventeenth centuries specifically
aimed at destroying partible inheritance, 'by reason whereof many
and great inconveniences to severall persons have beene found by the
experience of latter times to grow and arise'.[4] The period between
1538 and 1624 was one when many Kentish estates were disgavelled
and the relevant acts altered no characteristic of gavelkind tenure
except that of partible descent.[5]

While the general features of Kentish agrarian history during the
late sixteenth and early seventeenth century can be sketched, the
specific lines will only become clear once the massive task of analysing

[1] Baker, Ph.D. thesis, pp. 259–63: Chalklin, *Seventeenth-Century Kent*, pp. 55–7.
[2] Kent R.O., U55 T468.
[3] Kent R.O., U55 T96.
[4] Kent R.O., U274 E7: a copy, *c.* 1670, of an act for altering the custom of gavelkind
on the estates of Sir Thomas Twysden and Sir John Knatchbull.
[5] C. I. Elton, *The Tenures of Kent*, 1867, pp. 365 and 382–402.

the thousands of inventories, wills, deeds and other agricultural records
has been attempted. Nonetheless, it is obvious that the rural landscape
and society of seventeenth-century Kent already had many of its
modern characteristics and that their origins have to be sought in the
Middle Ages and perhaps beyond.

C. FIELD SYSTEMS IN MEDIEVAL KENT

I. ON ONE MANOR IN PARTICULAR

The manor of Gillingham, in north Kent on the southeastern side of
the mouth of the River Medway, is of particular interest: Gray based
a number of his conclusions about the Kentish field system on a
mid-fifteenth-century survey of the manor and considerable additional
sources relating to the manor have come to light since 1915.[1] A study
of its field system has been published and its principal conclusions will
be recapitulated and extended as a specific case study before any
attempt is made to examine the open field systems of the county as
a whole.[2]

There is some evidence of a few unenclosed parcels of arable land
in Gillingham surviving into the eighteenth century and rentals of
1608 and *c.* 1575 suggest that open fields were then a not unusual
feature in the parish, for they refer to many parcels of land as lying
within named fields.[3] Unfortunately the information provided by
these two rentals is not consistently detailed to permit a reconstruction
of anything like the complete field system. Such a reconstruction has
been possible from a survey dated 1447 which describes lands of the
manor as yokes (*iuga*), *logi, ferthings* or *ferlings, campi* and other names.[4]
For each of these divisions the survey states the total area and describes
their boundaries to the north, south, east and west in terms of adjacent
divisions as well as in terms of landscape features such as roads and
messuages. It was because of this detailed description of bounds that
Gray claimed the yokes were 'clearly rectangular'.[5] Assuming that
the yokes and other divisions were rectangular, and assuming that the
Kentish acre was equal in area to the modern statute acre, it has
been possible diagrammatically to reconstruct the relative positions and

[1] Gray, *English Field Systems*, pp. 284–5 and 303.
[2] A. R. H. Baker, 'Open Fields and Partible Inheritance on a Kent Manor', *Econ. Hist. Rev.*, XVII, 1964, pp. 1–23.
[3] Kent R.O., U103 P4; Gillingham Public Library: copy of map of York Farm, 1763; P.R.O., E17/26, fos. 28–35; Gillingham Corporation Ms. M2.
[4] Kent R.O., U398 M1A.
[5] Gray, *English Field Systems*, p. 284.

absolute areas of most of the yokes and the other fiscal divisions in Gillingham in 1447 (Fig. 9.4).[1]

These divisions themselves comprised arable, meadow, marsh and wood, and fields and crofts existed within them. Some of the crofts and fields were subdivided into unenclosed parcels marked by boundary stones. The yokes and other divisions were not topographical features in 1447. The fact that a field could lie in two adjacent yokes shows that the boundaries of yokes were not physical features except when they happened to coincide with field boundaries. Yokes were fiscal rather than agrarian units. A yoke comprised fields and crofts, some of them subdivided into open parcels, and they were held by varying numbers of tenants. What united these pieces of land and their tenants were the quit-rents and services due from them, which is why the survey records land according to yokes rather than according to tenants.[2] But by 1447 services had been commuted which meant that in practice a tenant paid a single money rent. By 1447, therefore, the yokes and other divisions were not even important fiscally. The commutation of services must, consequently, be seen as a critical act in the history of the yokes of Gillingham. There is evidence that services were still being exacted in 1442 and the 1447 survey includes a *novum rentale* which might indicate that commutation of services took place that year.[3]

When the services had been performed, there had existed a fundamental distinction between the yoke and the *logus*: the services associated with each were distinctive. Tenants of other fiscal divisions mentioned in the survey had been obliged to pay some, not all, of the payments, and perform some, not all, of the services associated with yokes and *logi*: the fact that these various divisions were usually much smaller than the yokes could explain their more limited obligations. Some fiscal divisions had no services at all due from them and these nearly all belonged to that group of irregular, usually small, divisions designated by a name with the suffix -'feld', -'land', -'acre', -'dane', -'reede', etc., which suggests that they were probably brought into cultivation after the *iuga* and *logi*. These assarts were shared by a number of tenants just as were the yokes and *logi*.

The lands of individual holdings tended to be concentrated in one part of the township rather than dispersed throughout it (Fig. 9.4).

[1] In fact, the Kentish rod was usually of 16 feet in contrast to the statute rod of 16½ feet: Elton, *Tenures of Kent*, p. 219. As the reconstruction has been made on the scale of six inches to one mile, the error involved in this difference is negligible and is further minimised by the scale at which the diagram is reproduced here.

[2] For convenience, the term 'tenants' is used because quit-rents were payable but it needs to be remembered that they were in fact freeholders.

[3] Lambeth Palace Library, CR 461; Kent R.O., U398 M1A, fos. 97–121.

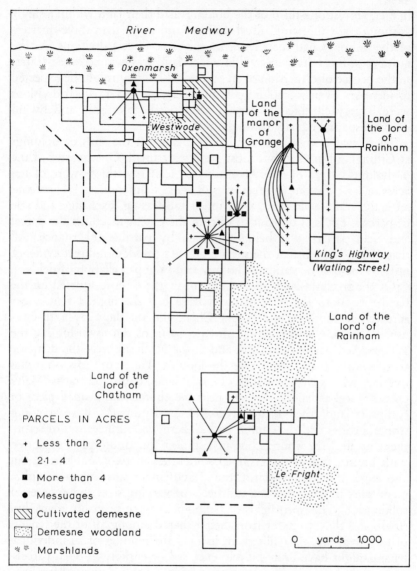

Fig. 9.4 Approximate locations of five messuages and their parcels of land in Gillingham (Kent) in 1447. Parcels of an individual holding are connected by continuous
lines to its messuage. The pecked lines indicate an uncertainty in the locational
relationships of those fiscal units on either side.

Source. Reconstructed from a manorial survey: Kent Records Office, U398 M1A.

In fact, almost one-third of the holdings had their land within a single (although not the same) fiscal division and more than three-quarters of the holdings had their lands in only five or less divisions. As the number of fiscal divisions within which land was held became greater, so the degree of dispersion of an individual holding might be expected to increase. Even so, holdings lying in 25, 31 and 43 fiscal divisions were largely clustered in certain areas of the township and by no means dispersed equally throughout it.

There was a very considerable inequality in the sizes of holdings at Gillingham in 1447 but most were very small. One quarter of the 98 holdings were of only two acres or less; two-thirds were of ten acres or less; but one in seven was of more than 50 acres.[1] There was an active market in land, with much sub-leasing, exchange and sale of parcels, but it is difficult to discern the extent to which the parcel and field pattern was being modified by partible inheritance. All that may be said is that the survey of 1447 provides indirect evidence of both the fragmentation of holdings and the parcellation of fields.

Of the freehold lands in Gillingham in 1447, those situated on the fertile loams to the west of the village had the highest rentals per acre, while those on the Upper Chalk and on the Clay-with-flints usually had the lowest rentals. In the north of the township lay the salt marshes, partly reclaimed, and in the southeast were the demesne woodlands. To the south rose the Downs. The entire township was overlain with a close network of roads, lanes, paths and tracks. Many crosses stood as landmarks, and near the church was a small piece of common land, the village green. Other landmarks were standing stones, hedges and the church itself. There was a nucleation of settlement around the church but in addition the landscape was dotted with houses and barns, grouped sometimes in twos and threes, but also existing as isolated farmsteads.[2] Settlement was dispersed within a complex mosaic of crofts and fields of varying sizes and degrees of subdivision. The open fields of Gillingham were probably many but small, and they were far from being shared among all of the tenants of the township. At Gillingham in 1447 the holding of an individual tenant might have been entirely enclosed or entirely in open parcels, or it might have been a combination of both; and it would have been located in one part of the township rather than distributed throughout it.

---

[1] The picture of holding sizes given by this survey is not entirely accurate, because a freeholder of this manor may have held additional lands of other manors. Nevertheless, the picture would probably only be modified in detail, not in broad outlines, were the information more complete.

[2] See Fig. 2 of Baker, *Econ. Hist. Rev.*, XVII, 1964, p. 11.

The situation in the late thirteenth century was not so very different, as a rental for the manor in 1285 indicates.[1] The parcels of an individual holding were almost certainly even less dispersed throughout the township in 1285 than they were to be by 1447: almost three-quarters of the holdings in 1285 were located within a single (although not the same) fiscal division compared with one-third at the later date. And it seems that there were proportionately more small holdings in the late thirteenth than in the mid-fifteenth century. There was greater equality of holding size in 1285 than in 1447. The rental of 1285 makes clear the family relationships of many tenants and equally makes it clear that, in those cases where brothers held land in two or more fiscal divisions, usually each brother claimed his share in each of the fiscal divisions in which his father's holding lay. The rental suggests that partitioning of holdings involved the subdivision of individual parcels of land. Both the fragmentation of land among a number of tenants and the division of a single holding into scattered strips or parcels was accentuated. One alternative to partitioning, of course, was joint-holding, but it is difficult to decide from the rental how far this was practised. Tenants referred to as *heredes* are numerous but it is uncertain whether they actually worked holdings jointly. That some form of co-aration was practised is proved by the statement that on the demesne *omnes carucae junctae infra precinctum manerii arabit* (*sic*) *dimidiam acram*: this could have been a cooperation in tillage between neighbours and not necessarily between inheriting kindred groups.[2] Partitioning of holdings was also counteracted by the operation of the land market. The importance of the selling, leasing and exchanging of parcels of land in Gillingham is seen in deeds of the later medieval period.[3] In many, descriptions of the lands being purchased or exchanged show that much piecemeal enlarging and consolidation of holdings was going on during this period. In Gillingham the land pattern and its fluidity was certainly a product of gavelkind tenure, but it has to be remembered that this meant not only the partitioning of holdings but also the free alienation of land.

The 1285 rental shows that the yokes and other divisions were units for the assessment of rents and services: their areas and numbers of tenants varied but the rents and services due from them followed a detectable pattern. Services were still being exacted in 1285, which meant that the fiscal division had some validity: the services expected of different tenants varied according to the division in which they held land. The services performed in 1285 show that demesne fields

[1] Canterbury Cathedral Library, E24, fos. 29v–33v.
[2] *Ibid.*, fo. 33.
[3] Gillingham Corporation Ms. T1/1–19 and 68–111.

at least were sometimes surrounded with fences and that growing corn was temporarily enclosed. Services included the making of folds and on occasions additional wattles were purchased for folding, which suggests a careful control of grazing on the demesne, to ensure the efficient utilisation of dung and to provide an elasticity in the system of crop rotations.[1] Some of the tenants also folded sheep on their own lands.[2]

Services due from yokes were distinct from those due from *logi*. But even in 1285 there were some fiscal divisions from which few services were due. These were small areas of recently cleared land. The names of the yokes and *logi* contain a high proportion of personal elements and it seems probable that at the time of its introduction the fiscal assessment was applied to compact family farms. Certainly at times the rental of 1285 suggests that yokes had previously had fewer tenants: for example, *Pieresyok* in 1285 had eight tenants but it is described as the yoke formerly of Peter. The stability of the names of the yokes and *logi* between 1285 and 1447 is remarkable and this also suggests, retrodictively, that the 1285 name may have been that given to the compact holding at the time of the original fiscal assessment. What is certain is that this assessment was of land potential, not of land area. Variations in the total rental values (from commuted services and customs as well as from rents) of yokes and *logi* were related not to the sizes but to the soil qualities of the assessed areas. It is therefore not surprising that attempts to discover the approximate size of the Kentish yoke have arrived at considerably varying figures: the area of a yoke has been variously stated to have been between 25 and 250 acres. Such variation is to be expected if, in the county as a whole, fiscal assessments were related to soil qualities as they were at Gillingham.[3]

The system of 'jugation' was possibly introduced into the area by the Romans;[4] certainly there is considerable evidence of Roman settlement in Gillingham and neighbouring districts and it has been suggested that the parallel nature of the road pattern is evidence of the centuriation of the district.[5] The 1447 survey suggests that the

[1] B.M., Add. Ms. 29794, m3: in 1273–4 36 wattles were purchased for folds.
[2] F. R. H. Du Boulay, 'Gavelkind and Knight's Fee in Medieval Kent', *Engl. Hist. Rev.*, LXXVII, 1962, pp. 504–11.
[3] A. R. H. Baker, 'The Kentish *iugum*: its relationship to soils at Gillingham', *Engl. Hist. Rev.*, LXXXI, 1966, pp. 74–9.
[4] F. Seebohm, *The English Village Community*, 4th edn, 1890, pp. 288–93; F. Lot, 'Le Jugum, le Manse et les Exploitations Agricoles de la France Moderne' in *Mélanges d'Histoire Offerts à Henri Pirenne*, I, 1926, pp. 307–26.
[5] *V.C.H.* (*Kent*), III, 1932, pp. 154–5; G. Ward, *The Belgic Britons, Men of Kent in B.C. 55*, 1960, pp. 121–4.

fiscal divisions were more or less rectangular and their rectangularity may have been connected with centuriation.[1] The origin of the *logus* is even more obscure. N. Neilson has suggested that the *logus* or *loghus* may originally have been a *sumerhas*, which she believed was too small to be a denn but which might have been a house or tenement in a denn.[2] P. H. Reaney has suggested that *logus* may be a Latinisation of the Anglo-Saxon *logge*, meaning a lodge.[3] F. Hull has noted that there was an Anglo-Saxon word *loh*, meaning a place or stead, and that this had a genetive form *loges*, and he wondered whether *logus* might not be a Latinisation of *loh*. *Loggus Cobbe* would thus be Cobbe's farmstead.[4] The problem remains unsolved but might it be that the yoke was a fiscal assessment introduced by the Romans and carried over into the medieval period and that the *logus* was introduced somewhat later, during the post-Roman settlement and applied to those homesteads that had come into existence after the assessment by yokes? If so, then it becomes possible, in conjunction with the lands identified in 1285 as having been only recently cleared and with the few additions to the cultivated area made between 1285 and 1447, to reconstruct the approximate chronology of settlement and of the expansion of the cultivated area (Fig. 9.5).[5] Certainly the area of pre-Conquest settlement and cultivation at Gillingham was considerable: in 1086 (Stage 1) the manor was assessed at six sulungs, and, at four yokes to the sulung, this comes very close to the total of 30 yokes recorded in 1285.[6] Considerable additions to the cultivated area would seem to have been made between 1086 and c. 1225 (Stage 2)[7] and yet further clearances made between c. 1225 and 1285 (Stage 3) by which time the cultivated area had almost reached its maximum extent. Only a few additions, small in total area, were made to the cultivated area between 1285 and 1447 (Stage 4).

Study of the manor of Gillingham by itself has thrown light on some of the enigmatic aspects of Kentish field systems. But it would

---

[1] This seems a more probable explanation than the view that the yokes produced a rectangular pattern 'the land's configuration requires'; Du Boulay, *Engl. Hist. Rev.*, LXXVII, 1962, p. 506. There was no inherent characteristic of the topography that 'required' a rectangular pattern of yokes.

[2] N. Neilson, *The Cartulary and Terrier of the Priory of Bilsington, Kent*, 1920, p. 15.

[3] This information was kindly conveyed by Professor F. R. H. Du Boulay.

[4] F. Hull, 'The Custumal of Kent', *Arch. Cant.*, LXXII, 1958, pp. 148–59.

[5] For details see: Baker, Ph.D. thesis, pp. 382–4.

[6] *V.C.H. (Kent)*, III, 1932, pp. 203–52.

[7] The *logi* may even have been associated with yokes through the enterprise of yokeland tenants in moving out and making fresh clearances and settlements: there was, for example, a Mellesyok and also a Melleslogh, with some tenants common to both in 1285. Du Boulay, *Lordship of Canterbury*, p. 122.

Fig. 9.5 The extension of the cultivated area in Gillingham (Kent). For a discussion of the stages of colonisation, see p. 399.

Source. Reconstructed from manorial records: Kent Records Office, U398 M1A and Canterbury Cathedral Library Ms. E24.

be rash to assume that all of the features observed at Gillingham were typical of the county as a whole. The single township must now be seen in a wider context.

2. IN THE COUNTY IN GENERAL

(a) Patterns of farmsteads and fields

The settlement pattern of the early fourteenth century in the Weald comprised mostly hamlets and isolated farmsteads. It has often been claimed that the hamlet settlements in the Weald and nearby areas reflected an individualistic agriculture, where manorial rights and common obligations were relatively unimportant.[1] But as Gulley has emphasised, common institutions did exist – common land was widely distributed in the Weald. Gulley has convincingly argued that the individualistic nature of Wealden tenure was not the primary cause of dispersed and hamlet settlement in the area; rather it was a reflection of tardy colonisation, of physical restraints on settlement sites and the production of food. During the Middle Ages it is almost certain that the density of agricultural population in the Weald was lower than in southern England as a whole, or than in the common field districts of Midland England. Wealden population density increased somewhat but the limitations were considerable – the sands were very poor in plant food, the clays difficult to till and irregular in yield. Difficulties of tillage made it advisable for the farmer to live near his fields so that he could fully utilise those short periods when the land was neither cracked nor boggy, and the difficulty of transport over clay terrains gave similar encouragement.[2] A pattern of dispersed farmsteads evolved. The early medieval period was the great age of Wealden assarting and secondary colonisation. Although some plough-teams were in operation in 1086, clearing was most widespread on the swine pastures (*denns*) in the two succeeding centuries.[3] Similar patterns of settlement probably developed on the heavily wooded Clay-with-flints capping the Downs and on the London Clay of the Blean.

Elsewhere, and most notably on the lower dip-slope of the Downs and in the Vale of Holmesdale, the earlier development of permanent settlement and greater density of population had produced a pattern of settlement which included villages as well as hamlets and isolated farmsteads.[4] The rural settlement pattern in the township of Gillingham

[1] Jolliffe, *Pre-Feudal England*, pp. 1–10.
[2] Gulley, Ph.D. thesis, pp. 364–6.
[3] *Ibid.*, pp. 396–405.
[4] S. W. Wooldridge and D. L. Linton, 'The Loam-terrains of Southeast England and their Relation to its Early History', *Antiquity*, VII, 1933, pp. 297–310 and

was indeed repeated in much of the county. Settlement on the manors
of Canterbury Cathedral Priory, such as Ickham and Eastry in east
Kent and Hollingbourne and East Peckham further west, was in each
case partly clustered into a village and partly dispersed in a number of
hamlets.[1] The archiepiscopal manor of Wingham was centred on the
village itself, surrounded by its demesne fields, but the whole manorial
area occupied a wedge-shaped territory of some 20 square miles. The
area contained many hamlets and farmsteads, of which some were
in the hands of the archbishop's own demesne tenants, some belonged
to his knights and their tenants, and others where the tenures were
mixed. Although at Wingham the demesne of the archbishop himself
was large in comparison with most of his other demesnes, its 1,200
acres seem few compared with the tenant's lands, amounting to some
8,500 acres scattered through 34 hamlets and farmsteads.[2] A rental
of the manor of Wrotham in 1494 reveals that few farmsteads had
been erected in the heavily wooded Clay-with-flints country above
the escarpment of the North Downs (some tenants who held land
above the escarpment in fact had cottages below it), many dwellings
were nucleated around the church at the foot of the escarpment,
and there were hamlets and numerous isolated farmsteads dispersed
throughout the township. A similar pattern of settlement existed in
1285.[3] At Ightham, immediately to the west of Wrotham, settlement
at the end of the fifteenth century comprised a village, seven hamlets
and numerous dispersed farms.[4] There had been a rapid growth of
population in these and other Kentish townships during the twelfth
and thirteenth centuries[5] – some townships saw a four- or five-fold
expansion of their tenant populations – resulting not only in an increase
in the sizes of the villages and hamlets but also in a dispersal of settlement. A fluid market in parcels of land had as one consequence the
building of dwelling-houses and private barns in the fields and lanes,
in isolation or swelling a small hamlet of kinsmen and neighbours,
rather than in some central village. Some were no doubt ephemeral
shacks like the one knocked down by Henry Herbert in 1291 on his

'Some Aspects of the Saxon Settlement in Southeast England Considered in
Relation to their Geographical Background', *Geography*, xx, 1935, pp. 161–75;
P. H. Reaney, 'Place-names and Early Settlement in Kent', *Arch. Cant.*, LXXVI,
1961, pp. 58–74.
[1] Carlin, D.Phil. thesis, p. 142.
[2] Du Boulay, *Lordship of Canterbury*, pp. 58–9.
[3] Kent R.O., U55 M59 and Canterbury Cathedral Library, E24, fos. 76–84v.
[4] Harrison, *Arch. Cant.*, XLVIII, 1936, pp. 169–218; XLIX, 1937, pp. 1–95; and LIII,
1940, pp. 17–23.
[5] Du Boulay, *Lordship of Canterbury*, pp. 134–5; F. R. H. Du Boulay, *Medieval
Bexley*, 1961, pp. 18–21.

brother's land in Bexley, others substantial structures, like the Cul-
peper's house of Kentish ragstone, built at almost the same time at
Old Soar near Wrotham. Gavelkind tenure probably encouraged
population growth and it certainly encouraged settlement dispersal.
That the partitioning of patrimonial holdings sometimes produced
isolated farmsteads is seen in a custumal of Wingham manor in 1285:
'if an inheritance is divided into two or three portions where there
are heirs, and each makes his messuage upon his portion', then each
will owe a separate hen-rent.[1]

Tenurial conditions also affected field patterns, although these are
even more difficult to discern than settlement patterns. There is good
evidence in many townships for the existence of some, in places
many, open fields intermixed with the numerous enclosed fields and
crofts. About 8 per cent of about one thousand Feet of Fines for the
period 1182–1272 refer to holdings consisting in part of parcels of
land lying within fields.[2] Usually, a Fine was concerned with parcels
of land in a single subdivided or open field and it is impossible to
establish a picture of a typical landholding from them: they often
record the transference of part, rather than the whole, of an individual
holding. Nevertheless, some Fines record parcels lying in many open
fields, the largest number involved being 23 at Barfreston in 1236.
Other Fines record 13 open fields at Ash-next-Sandwich in 1197,
ten at Wye in 1227 and seven at Aylesford in 1208. Certainly the
parcels of a Kentish holding could be scattered in any number of
fields.[3] Open fields were probably mostly small but numerous, and
associated as much with dispersed farmsteads and hamlets as with
villages.

Many of these open fields were products of tenurial conditions, the
effect of partible inheritance and early developed leasing on a pattern
of enclosed fields. For example, at Wye in 1227 individual fields were
halved and halves of fields were halved again to effect subdivision:
the holding of Richard le Brun comprised fields and halves of fields,
and on his death his four sons acknowledged one half of the holding
to a third party and retained the other half themselves. The parcels
thus comprised halves and quarters of fields.[4] Partitioning of land
holdings at times led to *morcellement*, fragmentation of holdings as

[1] Du Boulay, *Lordship of Canterbury*, p. 136; Canterbury Cathedral Library, E24,
fo. 15.
[2] I. J. Churchill, R. Griffin and F. W. Hardman (eds.), 'Calendar of Kent Feet of
Fines to the End of Henry III's Reign', *Kent Records*, xv, 1956.
[3] Baker, Ph.D. thesis, pp. 265–72; Gray, *English Field Systems*, pp. 281–2 and 285.
[4] Churchill *et al.* (eds.), *Kent Records*, xv, 1956, pp. 94–5. See also Fig. 5 of A. R. H.
Baker, 'Some Fields and Farms in Medieval Kent', *Arch. Cant.*, LXXX, 1965,
pp. 152–74.

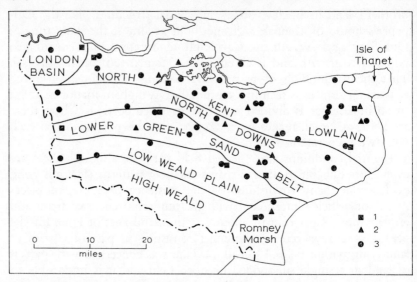

Fig. 9.6 The distribution of some subdivided fields in Kent in the thirteenth century:
1, Subdivided marsh and meadow; 2, Fields which were probably arable and which
were subdivided into only two parcels; 3, Fields which were probably arable and
which were probably subdivided into more than two parcels.
Source. Final Concords 1182–1272. See I. J. Churchill, R. Griffin and F. W. Hardman
(eds.), 'Calendar of Kent Feet of Fines to the end of Henry III's Reign', *Kent
Records*, xv, 1956.

a whole, field by field or parcel by parcel, and at other times it led to
parcellement, the subdivision of individual fields and of individual
parcels. But the evidence of Feet of Fines 1182–1272 suggests that the
form that partitioning took varied regionally (Fig. 9.6). In predominantly arable regions it produced subdivided fields as the more fertile
soils were often claimed equally by co-heirs, whereas in predominantly
pastoral regions, where soils were less conducive to arable cultivation,
fragmentation of holdings caused less disruption of animal husbandry
than would have subdivision of fields and parcels.[1] Most arable open
fields in medieval Kent were located on fertile soils in Holmesdale, in
the valleys of the Darent, Medway and Stour, and on the lower
dip-slopes of the Downs. In contrast, few were located in the Weald, in
the Clay-with-flints country at the crest of the Downs and in the Blean
on London Clay. Another reason for the relative absence of subdivided
fields in these areas was that, being heavily wooded and having
generally poor soils, they were brought into cultivation by secondary

[1] See below, pp. 412–19.

colonisation and had lower densities of population than other parts of the county in the early fourteenth century. In these areas, with only slight pressure of population upon land resources in the early Middle Ages, much land was enclosed direct from the waste and was rarely subdivided into unenclosed parcels.[1] The highest densities of population were in north and east Kent and it is here that most subdivision of fields took place.[2] Pressures of population upon land increased during the thirteenth century, resulting in much partitioning of holdings. By the fifteenth century, with pressure upon land much reduced and with the growing practice of disposing of land by will, the partitioning of holdings and fields was probably exceptional; it was certainly so by the sixteenth century.

(b) Patterns of yokes

Partitioning of holdings, together with the subdivision of rents and services attached to them and the ultimate commutation of the services led to the disintegration of yokes. Most early discussion of the sulung and its quarter fraction, the yoke, was based on the evidence of Domesday Book and was concerned with identifying their function, size and origin. The word 'sulung' seems to have been derived from the Anglo-Saxon *sulh*, a plough, and sulung has therefore been taken as meaning a ploughland.[3] But argument has centred on whether the ploughland was an artificial unit of assessment for taxation purposes or a real unit of husbandry. One school of thought has related the sulung to the area of land that a plough-team could cultivate in a year, another has claimed that sulungs were related to soil qualities, being therefore an assessment of land values. C. I. Elton began the discussion in 1867 by suggesting that the sulung was related to soil qualities because the size of the ploughland varied from one kind of soil to another.[4] F. Seebohm maintained that the assessment was related to land value rather than area and thus he explained the variations in the sizes of yokes.[5] P. Vinogradoff similarly believed the yoke was a fiscal unit and he asserted that it was comparable with the hide of the Midlands and the carucate of East Anglia, having a standard areal value.[6] On the other hand, G. J. Turner claimed that the yoke was the land which

---

[1] Gulley, Ph.D. thesis, pp. 354–5 and 364–5.
[2] H. A. Hanley and C. W. Chalklin, 'The Kent Lay Subsidy of 1334/5', *Kent Records*, XVIII, 1964, pp. 58–172, especially pp. 63–7.
[3] G. Slater, 'Social and Economic History', *V.C.H. (Kent)*, III, 1932, p. 322.
[4] Elton, *Tenures of Kent*, p. 126.
[5] Seebohm, *English Village Community*, pp. 290–1.
[6] P. Vinogradoff, *The Growth of the Manor*, 1905, pp. 57–60 and *English Society in the Eleventh Century*, 1908, pp. 144–5.

belonged to half a plough-team;[1] G. Slater believed that the yoke was the ploughland of a light plough;[2] J. E. A. Jolliffe considered the yoke to have been inseparable from an assessment by ploughlands and he thought the yoke was the ploughland of two oxen, a view with which G. Ward has agreed.[3]

Those who have associated the yoke with an assessment by ploughlands have believed that in consequence the yoke was a reality in the landscape. Seebohm thought that the original assessment may have been related to plough-teams, that the single or double yoke may have been taken as the basis for taxation, but that gradually it became an hypothetical unit of assessment, when no attempt was made to make the assessment accord with the actual number of yokes of oxen employed.[4] Jolliffe considered that each tenement was originally a yoke, and that a yoke of two oxen was 'a normal tenement'.[5] W. E. Tate came to the conclusion that the yoke seemed 'clearly enough' to have been the old Jutish family holding, and Ward claimed that the yoke of Saxon times was a single family farm.[6] On the other hand, those who have considered the yoke as primarily a fiscal unit of assessment have not attempted to equate it with an agricultural holding, at least in the later stages of its development.[7]

Whatever the origin of these units, the 'jugation' which appears in Domesday was already old, had long been applied to cultivated tenements, yet continued to be used and even extended in some places.[8] The iugum was devised at the end of the third century by Roman administrators as a means of assessing rapidly the contribution of taxes from parts of a large land area and attempts have been made to trace the Kentish yoke to this.[9] What is certain is that the medieval evidence shows that 'jugation' at Gillingham was an assessment of land potential and that by the early Middle Ages it had become a system, an adaptable system, of assessing rents and services due from land holdings. The yokes on a given manor were, in some instances,

[1] G. J. Turner (ed.), 'A Calendar of the Feet of Fines Relating to the County of Huntingdon, 1194–1603', *Cambridge Antiquarian Society Publications*, Octavo Ser., XXXVIII, 1913, p. lxxv.

[2] Slater, *V.C.H. (Kent)*, III, 1932, p. 324.

[3] Jolliffe, *Pre-Feudal England*, p. 105; Ward, *Belgic Britons*, p. 127.

[4] Seebohm, *English Village Community*, pp. 290–1.

[5] Jolliffe, *Pre-Feudal England*, pp. 7 and 105.

[6] Tate, *Arch. Cant.*, LVI, 1943, p. 56; Ward, *Belgic Britons*, p. 134.

[7] Gray, *English Field Systems*, pp. 296–8; H. E. Muhlfeld, *A Survey of the Manor of Wye*, Columbia, 1933, p. xxx.

[8] Du Boulay, *Lordship of Canterbury*, pp. 117–18.

[9] Lot, *Mélanges d'Histoire Offerts à Henri Pirenne*, I, 1926, pp. 307–26; G. Ward, 'A Note on the Yokes at Otford', *Arch. Cant.*, XLII, 1930, pp. 147–56. See also: D. Herlihy, 'The Carolingian *Mansus*', *Econ. Hist. Rev.*, XIX, 1960–1, pp. 79–89.

re-formed and sometimes newly cleared land was grouped into new yokes.[1] The woodland area which belonged to the manor of Aldington and which was divided into *denns* had, by 1285, been arranged into half and quarter yokes, burdened with carrying services. Of Haythurst and Finchurst, two Wealden *denns* of the manor of Gillingham, it was said that 'the tenants of these *denns* shall associate together as two yokes when a collection happens to be made for Rochester bridge or for a taxation of the yokes'.[2] The yokes at Bexley also show signs of regrouping at the hands of the lord's agent.[3] Gray realised that by about 1400 yokes were 'primarily financial, not agricultural units', but he attached much more agrarian importance to them during the thirteenth century. Even then, however, the yoke was primarily a system for the assessment of rents and services rather than the 'unit of villein tenure' as he claimed.[4]

Yokes were a notional division of land into fiscal units for the assessment of rents and services and as such they embraced fields and farmsteads. But they themselves were fiscal artificialities rather than topographical realities, at least from the thirteenth century onwards. In only three out of more than 70 deeds for the period 1315–1450 were parcels of land at Gillingham described in terms of the fiscal divisions in which they lay.[5] The field clearly had far greater reality than the yoke for the fourteenth-century freeholder. Many rentals and surveys show that thirteenth-century yokes – and *logi*, virgates and *tenementa*, the other principal fiscal units of assessment – had personal names which perhaps suggests that they had often formerly been in the hands of a single tenant, or at least of a small group of tenants, probably collaterals. Some were held this way at the beginning of the thirteenth century and as late as 1285 John Brutyn was the sole tenant of Jugum Brutyn in Gillingham.[6] In *c.* 1214 the 17 yokes of gavelkind land at Bexley were held by forty-seven persons. Of these 17, 3 were held by only one tenant, 5 more were probably held in a previous generation by only one tenant and 2 more were probably held by single tenants two generations back. Even in the early thirteenth century few of these yokes were held by more than two or three partners, who were often brothers. By 1284, however, these same yokes had at least 150 tenants.[7] *Tenementum Osberti* in West Wickham had five tenants

[1] Du Boulay, *Lordship of Canterbury*, p. 119.

[2] F. R. H. Du Boulay, 'Denns, Droving and Danger', *Arch. Cant.*, LXXVI, 1961, pp. 75–87.

[3] Du Boulay, *Medieval Bexley*, p. 19. [4] Gray, *English Field Systems*, pp. 290–415.

[5] The three deeds were dated 1370, 1402 and 1408: Gillingham Corporation Mss. T2/93, 105 and 78.

[6] Canterbury Cathedral Library, E24, fo. 30v.

[7] Du Boulay, *Medieval Bexley*, pp. 21–2.

in 1310 and *Tenementum Elfryy atte Derefold*, in Lenham had twelve in 1302.[1] The fact that a fiscal unit had at one time been in the hands of a single tenant or small group of tenants, together with the fact that at the end of the thirteenth century the parcels and fields of an individual holding were still concentrated in one part of a township, suggests that the early assessment was concerned with more or less compact family holdings. A yoke was not necessarily a single farm, however, rather single family farms were assessed as yokes or as multiples or fractions of a yoke, according not simply to the size of the farm but to the qualities of its soils. By the end of the thirteenth century – with the growth of population, the partitioning of holdings and the impact of an active land market – a yoke had often lost its character as an agrarian unit, for by then it was often occupied by many tenants. Nevertheless, it retained its importance as a fiscal unit, the services and rents of which were minutely subdivided among these tenants. With the commutation of services, a yoke lost even its fiscal validity and it gradually disappeared from the record. Thus a rental of Wrotham in 1285, by which time most services on the manor had probably been commuted (they certainly had by 1309), refers to only seven full or half yokes and a rental of the manor dated 1494 makes no reference to yokes at all.[2]

(c) Patterns of land holdings

Gavelkind tenure was widespread in Kent and applied not only to the anciently settled arable, but to assarts, marsh, wood and burgages, so that by the thirteenth century the legal presumption was that land in Kent was in gavelkind unless the contrary could be proved.[3] A tenant in gavelkind could freely give or sell or let his land to whom he wished during his lifetime, provided that the old rents and services were properly secured to the lord. After a tenant's death his lands were partible equally among all the male heirs. His widow received during her lifetime as dower one-half of her former husband's holding, instead of one-third as in knight's fee, unless she married again or bore an illegitimate child. A tenant at gavelkind attained his majority at the age of 15 for the purposes of marriage and controlling an inheritance.[4]

Partible inheritance undoubtedly resulted in both the fragmentation

---

[1] Kent R.O., U312 M21 and U55 M210.
[2] Canterbury Cathedral Library, E24, fos. 76–8; Lambeth Palace Library, CR119; Kent R.O., U55 M59.
[3] Du Boulay, *Lordship of Canterbury*, p. 146.
[4] Elton, *Tenures of Kent*, pp. 38–56; N. Neilson, 'Custom and the Common Law in Kent', *Harvard Law Review*, XXXVIII, 1924–5, pp. 482–98; F. Hull, *Arch. Cant.*, LXXII, 1958, pp. 148–59.

of holdings and the subdivision of fields. Many historians, following Elton, have asserted that partitioning was usual and that the large number of tenants and the small size of holdings in Kent were due chiefly to this. The minute sizes of some parcels and the extreme fragmentation and small size of individual holdings in the thirteenth century have been taken as evidence that partitioning did take place.[1] Recently, detailed study of the manors of the archbishop of Canterbury has led F. R. H. Du Boulay to conclude that the physical partitioning of holdings was the normal practice in the thirteenth century, a conclusion which has been confirmed independently in other studies.[2] A charter of 1275-6 makes it plain that it was possible for excessive partitioning over generations to reduce holdings below subsistence size.[3] Holdings were not always partitioned as much in practice as they might have been in theory. There was a variety of ways in which the effect of partitioning could be mitigated. One or more heirs to a holding can be seen waiving their claim to a part of it, in return for a money payment and/or rent upon their portion.[4] Joint tenure of family holdings sometimes prevented their being partitioned, but this seems to have been usually restricted to that short period after a man's death when his estate was awaiting its disposal among his heirs and they (perhaps children) had not yet been able to make up their minds about how the holding was to be divided.[5]

More important as a counterbalance to the divisive effects of partible inheritance was the free alienation of land *inter vivos*. This freedom stimulated the market in land, enabled the more enterprising and more prosperous tenants to augment their holdings by purchase or lease and resulted in a growing inequality in the size of land holdings. The importance of the selling, leasing and exchanging of parcels of land in Gillingham is seen in deeds of the fourteenth and fifteenth centuries which demonstrate that holdings were being consolidated and enlarged.[6] In 1315 and 1317, for example, Arnold Ychdene bought two

[1] Elton, *Tenures of Kent*, pp. 41, 290-1, 369 and 384; Vinogradoff, *English Society in the Eleventh Century*, pp. 93-4 and 274-7 and *Growth of the Manor*, pp. 205-6 and 315-18; Gray, *English Field Systems*, pp. 292, 297 and 303; Muhfeld, *Survey of the Manor of Wye*, p. 1; Neilson, *Harvard Law Review*, XXXVIII, 1924-5, p. 495; M. Campbell, *The English Yeoman under Elizabeth and the Early Stuarts*, 1942, p. 146; G. C. Homans, 'Partible Inheritance of Villagers' Holdings', *Econ. Hist. Rev.*, VIII, 1937-8, pp. 48-56 and 'The Rural Sociology of Medieval England', *Past and Present*, IV, 1953, pp. 32-43.
[2] Du Boulay, *Lordship of Canterbury*, pp. 146-8; Baker, Ph.D. thesis, pp. 272-88; Baker, *Arch. Cant.*, LXXX, 1965, pp. 158-66.
[3] *Cal. Ch. Rolls*, 1257-1300, no. 198.
[4] Baker, Ph.D. thesis, pp. 277-87.
[5] Du Boulay, *Lordship of Canterbury*, pp. 147-8.
[6] Baker, *Econ. Hist. Rev.*, XVII, 1964-5, p. 20.

small parcels of land, both of which lay in the same field, adjacent to parcels already in his possession.[1] Some parcels of land – half-acres and quarter-acres – set within larger fields changed hands often and at high prices in the parish of Preston near Wingham in the late thirteenth and early fourteenth centuries. A series of deeds for the manor of Aldington show enclosed parcels of arable lying within a larger field in the fourteenth century and the whole field enclosed a century later.[2] Such examples could easily be multiplied. Many tenants participated in the land market in a small way, some in a large way. Those like the de la Reyes at Otford and the Peckhams at Wrotham provide good examples of the sort of private enterprise in medieval Kent which came to distinguish the families of yeomen and gentlemen from those of little or no estate who rarely enter the records by name save as malefactors. As the fourteenth and fifteenth centuries progressed, so it was not only local men who accumulated land but outsiders, from London and elsewhere, who brought investment and perhaps their persons into the local communities.[3]

The net effect of both the partitioning of holdings and a free market in land was an accentuation of the gap between large and small holdings. And a consequence of the growing size of some holdings was that their constituent fields and parcels came to be more widely scattered. It will be recalled that at Gillingham in 1285 almost three-quarters of the tenants had land which lay in only one of the manor's fiscal divisions and almost all tenants had their land within five or fewer divisions. By 1447 just under one-third of tenants had their lands in only one fiscal division and three-quarters had their lands in five or fewer divisions. Furthermore, the proportion of small holdings was far higher in 1285 than in 1447. Similar characteristics have been observed on other Kentish manors. By the fifteenth century the stratification of rural society in terms of holding sizes was marked. For example, at Ickham in the early fifteenth century two tenants held about 150 acres each; five others held more than 30 acres and three others between 10 and 30 acres. But all the rest (41) held less than 10 acres and twenty-eight of these held less than 5 acres.[4] There was similarly considerable inequality of holding sizes at Wrotham in 1494 and this had been accentuated further by 1538.[5]

One important contributory factor in this connection was the leasing of manorial demesnes, for these tended to be large-scale mixed farming

---

[1] Gillingham Corporation Mss. T2/67 and 68.
[2] Du Boulay, *Lordship of Canterbury*, pp. 135–6.
[3] *Ibid.*, pp. 148–9, 153–6 and 162–3; Carlin, D.Phil. thesis, p. 142.
[4] Carlin, D.Phil. thesis, pp. 138–9.
[5] Kent R.O., U55 M59 and M60/2.

enterprises. The 'average' lessee of the archbishop at the end of the fourteenth century took on almost 200 acres of arable (inclusive of fallow), about 15 acres of meadow and perhaps 200 acres of pasture for sheep, cattle or both. Leased demesne arables might be as small as 25 acres, as at Petham, or as large as 500 acres, as at Wingham, but by the standards of the time they were mostly large holdings – and they were usually on some of the best soils in their localities.[1] The demesnes of the archbishop began to be permanently leased out between the 1380s and 1420s, and most had been leased by 1422.[2] The leasehold system was established on almost all the estates of Canterbury Cathedral Priory by 1396.[3]

The demesnes of manors in Kent in the thirteenth century did not lie intermingled in strips with those of tenants, as was often the case with demesnes in the Midlands, but were situated in blocks, sometimes within larger fields, and cultivated in severalty even if not always separated off by permanent physical barriers from other men's crops.[4] Demesne fields were large and usually close to each other. Two of the Wingham demesne arable fields were of over a hundred acres each, most of them between 20 and 60 acres, none of them less than seven acres, and they were all concentrated near the township of Wingham itself, not scattered over the vast manorial area.[5] At Wrotham, 1285, the arable lay on either side of the village in large blocks such as the 50 acres in Eastfield and the 32 acres in Stony Furlong as well as in a number of smaller 'shots'. From later account rolls which refer to the demesne fields as Westfield and Eastfield and from a map of the demesne in 1620 it is clear that these arable demesne lands constituted just two blocks of crofts, fields and 'shots'.[6]

While demesne fields were being directly cultivated by manorial lords and their agents, they were frequently sown in sections with more than one kind of crop in any given year.[7] And as the fields had

---

[1] F. R. H. Du Boulay, 'Who Were Farming the Demesnes at the End of the Middle Ages?', *Econ. Hist. Rev.*, XVII, 1964–5, pp. 443–55 and *Lordship of Canterbury*, pp. 207–23.

[2] F. R. H. Du Boulay, 'A Rentier Economy in the later Middle Ages: the Archbishopric of Canterbury', *Econ. Hist. Rev.*, XVI, 1963–4, pp. 427–38.

[3] Smith, *Canterbury Cathedral Priory*, p. 192.

[4] Du Boulay, *Lordship of Canterbury*, pp. 130–3.   [5] *Ibid.*, p. 207.

[6] Canterbury Cathedral Library, E24, fo. 76; Kent R.O., U55 M67 and U681 P31.

[7] This practice has been observed on a number of manors. For example, at Wrotham: Baker, *Agric. Hist. Rev.*, XIV, 1966, p. 15; at Westerham: T. A. M. Bishop, 'The Rotation of Crops at Westerham, 1297–1350', *Econ. Hist. Rev.*, IX, 1938, pp. 38–44; at Otford: F. R. H. Du Boulay, 'Late-continued Demesne Farming at Otford', *Arch. Cant.*, LXXIII, 1959, pp. 116–24; at Bexley: Du Boulay, *Medieval Bexley*, p. 7; at Westwell: Smith, M.A. thesis, p. 47; and at Thurnham: Kent R.O., U512 T2.

often been sown in sections with different crops, so in some places they came to be leased out in parcels to different tenants. At Otford small portions of demesne fields were being leased to tenants by the early fifteenth century.[1] The leasing of small parcels of demesnes acquired increasing importance during the fourteenth century on some of the manors of Canterbury Cathedral Priory, such as Monkton and Ickham in East Kent.[2] At Wrotham, 1399–1400, the lord was cultivating most of his 250 or so acres of arable but about 12 acres were leased to tenants in various of the manor's fields, for a total rent of 11s. 2d. By 1406–7 this practice had been extended, for although most of the demesne was being cultivated by the lord, leased portions produced a rent of £2 16s. 0d. Some of the demesne was still being leased as unenclosed parcels in the sixteenth century in a part of the former Eastfield that had come to be called 'the Common Field'.[3] Some open fields in Kent developed from the cropping and the leasing of demesne fields in sections. This discussion of land holdings has now led on to a consideration of farming practices.

(d) Patterns of farming practices

It has often been suggested that open fields in the Midlands were closely associated with co-aration, that each contributor to a joint plough-team was allotted a strip or strips of each day's ploughing.[4] The extent to which subdivided arable fields in Kent were similarly produced is difficult to decide. Nightingale assumed that open fields in Kent resulted from co-aration.[5] The practice of co-aration in the county can certainly be substantiated. Some tenants in the thirteenth century had full plough-teams, others a beast or two, and others none.[6] At Wingham in 1285 'every tenant who resides in the hundred and who has a fully-yoked plough shall...plough one acre of *gerserth* and he who has less shall plough proportionately, in such a way that if any tenant shall join with a non-tenant or with any-one who does not owe ploughing service, he shall come to the plough with as many beasts as he has at the plough and the bedel shall make up one plough team from the horses of those who do not have a full plough team'.[7] At Grain, every joint-plough on the manor was required to plough half-an-acre of the demesne.[8] Similar references to co-aration come

---

[1] Du Boulay, *Arch. Cant.*, LXXIII, 1959, p. 121.
[2] Smith, *Canterbury Cathedral Priory*, p. 142.
[3] Lambeth Palace Library, CR1142 and 1145; Kent R.O., U55 M73.
[4] C. S. and C. S. Orwin, *The Open Fields*, 2nd edn, 1954, pp. 1–68.
[5] Nightingale, *Antiquity*, XXVII, 1953, pp. 20–6.
[6] Du Boulay, *Lordship of Canterbury*, pp. 133–4.
[7] Canterbury Cathedral Library, E24, fo. 11v.
[8] *Ibid.*, fo. 33.

from Lyminge, Northfleet and Teynham.[1] At Sundridge, *c.* 1258, ploughing services were assessed in proportion to a tenant's ownership of a whole or part of a plough-team: those who possessed only a part must have joined with others to make a full team.[2] Co-aration might have given rise to a pattern of unenclosed parcels in some parts of Kent, although there is no direct evidence that it actually did so. The pattern of farmsteads and of fields, the compactness of holdings, suggest, as does the wording of the Wingham custumal, that co-aration in Kent was a venture in agricultural cooperation by individuals, by friends, neighbours and relations on an *ad hoc* basis, rather than a collective enterprise by a manorial community.

Since cooperative ploughing was practised to some extent, collective grazing might be expected to have featured similarly. Most land in Kent was, of course, held in severalty.[3] And it was specifically pleaded in 1332 that no man in Kent could pasture his livestock in common on gavelkind lands.[4] Control of livestock and protection of crops presented few problems in enclosed fields, although numerous cases of trespassing livestock and of the illegal reaping of crops indicate that the security offered by enclosed fields was relative rather than absolute.[5] There would, however, have been much greater practical difficulties in grazing and cultivating open fields and the evidence suggests that these difficulties were overcome in at least two ways: first, the erection of temporary fences; second, limited agreements about pasturing collectively. It is also possible that shepherds and dogs were used: a cottar at Wrotham was allowed an acre upon which he might keep his dog.[6]

Tenants of many Kentish manors had to provide hurdles for the lord's folds and it may be reasonably assumed that some tenants followed the demesne practice of folding livestock.[7] Folding was practised on the demesne at Deal in the fourteenth century and on the open fields of the tenantry in the seventeenth century, and sheep folding was required by covenant in some leases on land in the nearby

[1] *Ibid.*, fos. 40, 64 and 87*v*.
[2] H. W. Knocker, 'The Evolution of the Holmesdale. No. 3. The Manor of Sundridge', *Arch. Cant.*, XLIV, 1932, pp. 189–210.
[3] Jolliffe, *Pre-Feudal England*, pp. 7 and 14.
[4] A. Fitzherbert, *Grand Abridgement of the Common Law*, II, 1516, pp. xiv–xv, cited in Gulley, Ph.D. thesis, p. 320.
[5] Kent R.O., U55 M13–17; R. Virgoe, 'Some Ancient Indictments in the King's Bench referring to Kent, 1450–2', *Kent Records*, XVIII, 1964, pp. 214–65.
[6] Canterbury Cathedral Library E24, fo. 83*v*.
[7] For Wrotham, Canterbury Library, E24, fo. 84; for Gillingham, Canterbury Cathedral Library, E24, fos. 29*v* and 33, and B.M., Add. Ms. 29794. See also Carlin, D.Phil. thesis, pp. 970–8.

Folkestone area in the eighteenth century.[1] In an exchange of lands at Kennington, near Ashford, in 1268–9, one man was granted in the woods of another 'reasonable estovers for housebote and haybote for burning and fencing and for repairing folds'.[2] It seems that individuals folded their own stock on their own lands, there being no evidence of foldcourses such as were used in East Anglia.[3]

An alternative to folding was the common pasturing of open fields by private agreement. Livestock of lord and of tenants certainly grazed collectively on many demesne arable fields. Some tenants at Wrotham at the end of the thirteenth century, as well as providing the lord with hurdles for folds, were required 'to common over the demesne with all their ewes and...to go to the fold of the lord from Hokeday until the feast of St Martin'. The 1285 rental suggests a curious mixture of tenants' duties and rights, for some were 'able to have five ewes and no more' commoning the demesne, while others could only common their sheep if they had ploughed twelve furrows of the demesne for each ox that they owned.[4] On many of the archbishop's demesnes the lord's crop was fenced, but the enclosures were taken down after the harvest so that the beasts of the lord could graze there collectively with the beast of those tenants who had helped him to plough and of any others who had arranged terms with him by which their animals should feed upon his stubble.[5] Again, it may reasonably be assumed that tenants sometimes followed this practice by mutual agreement in the open fields in which they had parcels. Such agreements would have represented no more than commonsense arrangements which were rarely written down. That this sort of arrangement could be made is seen in an agreement, made in 1246 between two brothers, about grazing of cows belonging to each of them in a pasture which was to belong to only one of them.[6]

Both subdivided arable fields and subdivided meadow fields in Kent were usually shared by only a few tenants. At Snave four people shared three and a half acres of meadow in 1202; at Chatham at least two people shared a meadow in 1214; and at Willesborough a meadow was shared among three people in 1205.[7] Subdivision of meadows

[1] A. R. H. Baker, 'The Field System of an East Kent Parish (Deal)', *Arch. Cant.*, LXXVIII, 1963, pp. 96–117; G. E. Mingay, 'Estate Management in Eighteenth-Century Kent', *Agric. Hist. Rev.*, IV, 1956, pp. 108–13.
[2] Churchill, *Kent Records*, XV, 1956, p. 355.
[3] K. J. Allison, 'The Sheep–Corn Husbandry of Norfolk in the Sixteenth and Seventeenth Centuries', *Agric. Hist. Rev.*, V, 1957, pp. 12–32.
[4] Canterbury Cathedral Library, E24, fo. 84.
[5] Du Boulay, *Lordship of Canterbury*, p. 131; Lambeth Palace Library, CR 119.
[6] Churchill, *Kent Records*, XV, 1956, p. 192.
[7] *Ibid.*, pp. 26, 56 and 271.

reflected their limited acreage and high value: the primary importance of meadows, before the introduction of cultivated grasses, was that they produced at least one large cut of grass yearly as well as providing lush grazing.[1] It seems likely that subdivided meadows were grazed in common during the thirteenth century, as they were in later years. On the other hand, many meadows in medieval Kent were undivided and grazed individually.[2] Common pasturing in woods, wastes and rough pastures was certainly practised in Kent during the thirteenth century. Even then, however, there is evidence that such common grazing was being reduced and common pastures enclosed.[3] The overall impression is that in medieval Kent agricultural cooperation, at least so far as arable and meadow land was concerned, was by the mutual consent of the few rather than a duty or right of the many.

Similarly, cropping courses were not common to a township or manor. Demesnes were cultivated and fallowed in blocks independently of tenants or others.[4] It is, of course, almost impossible to discern the nature of crop rotations and livestock production on the bulk of the lands of the tenantry in medieval Kent. On the other hand, a clear picture has been reconstructed of farming enterprise on the demesnes, especially of those of the archbishop and of Canterbury Cathedral Priory. It has long been realised that in broad terms there was a striking contrast in Kent about 1300 between the area north of the chalk escarpment, where wheat and barley predominated, and the Weald, where oats was the principal crop. This contrast is seen in proportions of wheat, barley and oats supplied from each of the Hundreds for an expedition in Gascony in 1297 and in the nature of crop production on archiepiscopal manors 1273-4.[5] Livestock figures for these manors in the same year show that east Kent was notable for its sheep as well as for its wheat and barley, while on manors peripheral to the Weald cattle and pigs were more important than sheep.[6] Although the need for draught animals and for manure ensured that mixed farming was practised throughout the county, agriculture received a different emphasis in different parts.

[1] At Smeeth, 1246, arable land was valued at 9d. an acre, meadow at 1s. 1d. an acre: one holding included 98 acres of arable but only 16 acres of meadow. *Cal. I.P.M.* (Henry III), no. 59.

[2] Churchill, *Kent Records,* xv, 1956, pp. 51, 259 and 368.

[3] *Ibid.*, pp. 8, 103-4, 147-9 and 359; Gulley, Ph.D. thesis, pp. 398 and 405; Du Boulay, *Arch. Cant.*, LXXVI, 1961, pp. 82-5.

[4] Du Boulay, *Lordship of Canterbury*, pp. 132 and 208.

[5] Pelham, *Empire Journal of Experimental Agriculture*, I, 1933, pp. 82-4; R. A. Pelham, 'Fourteenth Century England', in H. C. Darby (ed.), *An Historical Geography of England Before A.D. 1800*, 1936, pp. 237-8; B.M., Add. Ms. 29794.

[6] B.M., Add. Ms. 29794.

416 FIELD SYSTEMS OF SOUTHEAST ENGLAND

Within the Weald, mixed farming showed a certain bias towards animal husbandry and, of the animals, cattle were more important than sheep. Swine herds were large and grazing rights and pannage in common woods were an integral part of agricultural activity. By the early fourteenth century, however, there were no longer any seasonal migrations of large herds of swine into and out of the Weald, as had taken place earlier, although there was still a limited movement of stock to the eastern marsh pastures in summer.[1] By about 1300, many of the Wealden swine pastures had become divided into farm units and land was being reclaimed for tillage.[2] Oats was the chief grain crop; wheat was second to oats and sown in quantity on the clay lands, especially the Weald Clay. Only small amounts of barley were produced. It is exceedingly difficult to establish cropping systems in the Weald, for few demesnes were located here, but it is clear that cultivated lands frequently lay fallow and that rotations varied within short distances, partly because of the great local soil variations. Most Wealden soils produced indifferent arable crops and some grain was imported via the ports of the eastern Weald.[3]

On the Wealden fringe, in Holmesdale and on the dip-slope of the Lower Greensand, cultivation of crops was as important as tending of livestock. The principal contrast between this locality and the Weald was the greater importance here of sheep and wheat. It is true that the manors of Great Chart, Little Chart and Peckham had no sheep in c. 1322, but there were 200 at Mersham, 600 at Westwell, 300 at Hollingbourne, 100 at Loose, 300 at East Farleigh, and 250 at West Farleigh.[4] Wheat occupied a larger acreage than oats in 1322 at Mersham, Great Chart and Little Chart, but the position was reversed at Hollingbourne, Westwell, East Farleigh, West Farleigh and Peckham, while at Loose wheat and oats occupied equal acreages.[5] Statistics relating to a single year might have been atypical, but more detailed studies of the cropping systems on particular manors over a period of time show that this was not the case. At Westerham, 1297–1350, there was a nucleus of more or less permanent arable amounting to about 120 acres, which T. A. M. Bishop called the infield. This was associated with outfields, expanding in total area from 400 to 600 acres, of which relatively small amounts were sporadically cultivated. On the infield, a three-course rotation was

1 Gulley, Ph.D. thesis, pp. 329–36.
2 *Ibid.*, p. 405; Du Boulay, *Lordship of Canterbury*, pp. 137–8; Du Boulay, *Arch. Cant.*, LXXVI, 1961, pp. 82–7.
3 Gulley, Ph.D. thesis, pp. 337–48.
4 Smith, *Canterbury Cathedral Priory*, p. 152.
5 *Ibid.*, p. 140. See also Smith, *Arch. Cant.*, LXXVIII, 1963, pp. 147–60.

practised; on the outfields, rotations were far more irregular, some of them being continuously cropped for four or five years in succession and then rested, others being sown only at long intervals. Wheat and oats were the most important crops, the former being grown mainly on the infields and the latter as much on the outfields as on the infields. Legumes were grown principally on the infields.[1]

Such a flexible system of husbandry might in part have been a response to the light soils of the Greensand formation, but similar features have been observed on all of the manors of Canterbury Cathedral Priory, except those in Romney Marsh.[2] At Westwell, on chalky marls, six infields, comprising about 180 acres, were cultivated fairly continuously, while other fields were cropped at irregular intervals. These seven fields comprised a smaller area of outfield and included a meadow which occasionally underwent cultivation. On the infield, a three-course rotation was followed and involved at various times wheat, rye, barley, oats, peas, vetches and beans. On the outfield, rotation was irregular and usually involved only oats and barley.[3] The cropping practice adopted on the Priory's manors is perhaps misleadingly called an 'infield–outfield system' because the continuously cultivated lands, the so-called infield, did not form a central core or nucleus but were intermingled with the sporadically cultivated lands.[4] It was an infield–outfield system in principle, in terms of the rotation of crops, but not strictly in practice, in terms of the location of fields.

A similar system of cropping was practised on the Priory's manors in east Kent, on some of the richest soils of the county, such as the manors of Eastry and Adisham. Manors in east Kent, in fact, generally had the largest acreages of cultivated land, most of which was devoted to barley and wheat. At the same time, these manors had the largest sheep flocks. In c. 1322 there were 2,000 sheep at Monkton, 2,000 at Eastry, 600 at Adisham and 400 at Ickham.[5] At an early period, surplus corn was marketed: in 1207 corn from Canterbury Cathedral Priory's estates was being shipped abroad, and in 1230–1 the sale of corn at Monkton realised £74, at Adisham £50. Corn production in east Kent was at an advanced stage of development even in the early thirteenth century and it received an added impetus as prices rose during the

---

[1] Bishop, *Econ. Hist. Rev.*, IX, 1938, pp. 38–44.

[2] Smith, M.A. thesis, p. 46.

[3] *Ibid.*, pp. 46–7.

[4] *Ibid.*, pp. 47–8. See also: A. Smith, 'Medieval Field Systems on Some Kent Manors' in R. W. Steel and R. Lawton (eds.), *Liverpool Essays in Geography. A Jubilee Collection*, 1967, pp. 173–91.

[5] Smith, *Canterbury Cathedral Priory*, pp. 140 and 152; Du Boulay, *Lordship of Canterbury*, p. 209; Smith, *Arch. Cant.*, LXXVIII, 1963, p. 149.

latter part of the century. The years 1306–24 were the 'high farming' period *par excellence*.[1] Livestock marketing developed at a much later date than corn marketing, but R. A. L. Smith concluded that the general upward movement of prices was the determining factor which led the Priory to organise certain manors especially for stock-marketing, as well as to rear stock on a small scale for the market on a number of manors. On the east Kent manors, however, the peculiar richness of the soil and the large downland and marsh pastures, together with locational advantages, made mixed husbandry both desirable and profitable. At Eastry and Monkton, for example, sheep-breeding and cattle-rearing were as much a feature of the husbandry as corn growing. Sales of wool took place in the early thirteenth century but the years 1285–1331 saw a great expansion of sheep production. Most Kentish wool in the late thirteenth century was bought by Italian merchants and the bulk of it was shipped abroad through Sandwich.[2] East Kent was the most advanced part of the county agriculturally and the scene of a profitable sheep–corn husbandry. In a less accentuated form, similar features were to be found westwards, along the lower dip-slope of the North Downs.[3]

Marshland regions of the county showed some distinctive features in their agriculture. Systems of cultivation utilised on Romney Marsh were different from those practised elsewhere, because of the poorly drained soils despite the intensive dissection of the area by drainage channels. The continuously cultivated land was limited in extent. At Ebony, for example, it was only 50 to 60 acres. Most of the arable was irregularly cropped, mainly with oats. A two-course rotation was usually followed, occasionally a three-course.[4] Attempts to increase the acreage under wheat met with little success.[5] Nevertheless, the area of reclaimed and cultivated marshland was extended.[6] The arable acreage in 1300 was almost certainly larger than it was in 1600, by which time the marshlands were primarily pastures. During the early fourteenth century, Canterbury Cathedral Priory increasingly concentrated its sheep flocks in the marshes of Romney and east Kent. Monkton, with large marshland pastures in addition to valuable arable lands, became an important sheep-farming centre, large flocks being drafted there from neighbouring manors. Normally the Romney

[1] Smith, *Canterbury Cathedral Priory*, pp. 130–1 and 142.
[2] *Ibid.*, pp. 147–50; R. A. Pelham, 'Some Aspects of the East Kent Wool Trade in the Thirteenth Century', *Arch. Cant.*, XLIV, 1932, pp. 218–28.
[3] Du Boulay, *Medieval Bexley*, pp. 7–16.
[4] Smith, M.A. thesis, pp. 48 and 68.
[5] Smith, *Canterbury Cathedral Priory*, p. 179.
[6] Smith, *Econ. Hist. Rev.*, X, 1939–40, pp. 29–37; Du Boulay, *Lordship of Canterbury*, pp. 139–40.

pastures were used solely for fattening in the fourteenth century and breeding took place in the rich pasture lands of Thanet and east Kent, but sheep were also bred on a small scale in some manors valued primarily for their arable lands, such as Godmersham and Chartham. On these manors, sheep were valued principally for their manure and the sheep-fold was a familiar device on the Priory's demesnes. The marshland manors were also important centres of dairy farming and sales of dairy products, cheese in particular, increased during the first quarter of the fourteenth century, to decline after the great livestock pestilence of 1327 and the advent of the leasehold system of demesne farming.[1]

Regional variations in farming enterprise were but one of the many facets of the spatial and temporal diversity of the field systems of Kent. The phrase 'the Kentish field system', brought into common usage more than half a century ago by Gray, has outlived its usefulness. It is clearly now necessary to admit to the plurality of Kentish field systems for there were considerable variations in 'the manner in which the inhabitants of a township subdivided and tilled their arable, meadow and pasture land'. In Kent, different periods of colonisation, the differing impact of gavelkind tenure, varied types of farming enterprise, contrasting densities of population and differing degrees of accessibility to markets combined to produce different field systems in physically contrasted parts of the county. It now becomes necessary briefly to examine the extent to which patterns of farmsteads, fields, holdings and agricultural practices observed in Kent have also been discerned in the neighbouring counties of Surrey and Sussex.

D. FIELD SYSTEMS IN MEDIEVAL SURREY AND SUSSEX

I. EXPECTATIONS

Some similarities between field systems in Kent and those further west would not be surprising. The east–west trend of Kent's physical geography means that some of its topographic, edaphic and vegetational characteristics extended in some measure westwards into Surrey and Sussex. Similar physical conditions might have been responded to in not entirely dissimilar ways by widely separated groups of colonists and agriculturalists. Gulley, for example, has argued that the practice of Wealden swine-pasturing was encouraged by the existence of a belt of settled land around a core area largely covered with woodland

[1] Smith, *Canterbury Cathedral Priory*, pp. 135, 150–1 and 159–65.

in A.D. 500, and that woodland was not only very extensive but also thickest on the outer claylands of the Low Weald, near the peripheral agricultural settlements. Gulley considered that in this natural contrast lay the origin of Wealden swine-herding, a consideration encouraged by the absence of identical pasturing arrangements elsewhere in England and by the virtually complete restriction to the Wealden counties of place-names ending in -denn.[1]

On the other hand, some similarities of agricultural practice in medieval southeast England might be expected to stem in part from the process of cultural diffusion, from the spread of particular methods of agricultural organisation. Jolliffe, for example, has argued that it was the fifth-century settlers from the Middle Rhineland who introduced into Kent and subsequently into eastern Surrey and eastern Sussex the economic structure of parent estate and woodland swine pastures. It was not, in his view, the greatness of the Wealden forest which imposed this structure, but a general custom.[2]

More specifically, widely separated agricultural estates in medieval southeast England were in many cases subject to the common management of a single lord and his agents. Thus similarities of field system might in part be a consequence of the disposition of estates and of their administration. The archbishop, for example, in addition to his Kentish properties, had a group of manors in Surrey between Croydon and Mortlake and two groups in Sussex, one on the coastal plain between Pagham and Tangmere and the other in the east of the county, based around South Malling. The carrying services performed by tenants of the archbishop were important in functionally integrating manors widely scattered over Kent, Sussex, Surrey and Middlesex.[3] Some aspects of field systems might be a consequence less of *local* physical and socio-economic circumstances than of the exercise over long distances of seigneurial jurisdiction. This was, for example, certainly the case with the service known as *gerserthe*, which was the ploughing of one acre of demesne from every full plough-team in the tenant's possession. This service was found on most of the archbishop's manors, irrespective of local conditions. An early fourteenth-century regulation laid down that all of the archbishop's manors should marl as much land as possible in summer.[4] Again, the demesnes of the manors of Canterbury Cathedral Priory during the fourteenth century, widely scattered and located on a variety of sites and soils, all, with the exception of the Romney Marsh manors, showed similarities

---

[1] Gulley, Ph.D. thesis, pp. 468–9.
[2] Jolliffe, *Pre-Feudal England*, pp. 82–3.
[3] Du Boulay, *Lordship of Canterbury*, p. 167.
[4] *Ibid.*, pp. 170–1; B.M., Cott. Ms. Galba E iv, fo. 74.

in their cropping systems. Thus for administrative, cultural and physical geographical reasons some of the features characteristic of Kentish field systems are observable outside of the county.

2. EXTRA-WEALDEN SURREY

From his examination of the evidence, Gray was led to conclude that the 'Kentish field system' had once prevailed in Surrey.[1] Rentals, surveys and charters make it clear that during the thirteenth to fifteenth centuries many townships contained both open and enclosed fields. Typical holdings comprised a messuage, a few fields and crofts, and a number of unenclosed parcels of land lying within larger fields. Within any individual township there might be many open fields but there was no evidence to suggest that they were grouped in any systematic fashion. Similarly, where furlongs were recorded they do not seem to have been amalgamated into larger functional units. While many fields were explicitly called 'common fields', it is equally the case that they were frequently relatively small and that their unenclosed parcels were not shared among large numbers of tenants. The parcels and fields of an individual's holding were distributed irregularly among the fields and furlongs, without any of the symmetry and uniformity which might be expected under a regulated field arrangement. There was a tendency for the constituents of a holding to be clustered in one part of a township rather than to be regularly (or even randomly) distributed throughout it.[2]

The similarity of these field arrangements to those in Kent was supported strikingly in one manor, Ewell, where a thirteenth-century extent describes holdings in terms of *iuga* and multiples and fractions of *iuga*, and subdivides the rood into 'day works' as was the case in Kent. By 1406 the pattern of yokes at Ewell had been fragmented among an increased number of tenants and holdings had come to be described as *tenementa*.[3] This break-up of individual yokes into larger numbers of *tenementa* during the later Middle Ages corresponds well with events on some Kent manors.[4]

Similarly, the Surrey manors of the archbishop of Canterbury differed in no significant way from those in Kent, which is something that cannot be said about the archbishop's manors in Sussex.[5] A recent

[1] Gray, *English Field Systems*, pp. 402–17.
[2] *Ibid.*, pp. 356–69.
[3] *Ibid.*, pp. 399–400.
[4] Muhlfeld, *Survey of the Manor of Wye*, p. liii; Gray, *English Field Systems*, p. 300.
[5] Du Boulay, *Lordship of Canterbury*, *passim* but see for specific statements pp. 173 and 207–8.

detailed study of settlement patterns and field systems in a group of ten parishes in west Surrey, around and including Dorking, in the Vale of Holmesdale and the adjacent Chalk lands of the North Downs, demonstrated their close affinities with the situation in Kent. Systems of multiple open and enclosed fields were associated with patterns of hamlets and isolated farmsteads. It seems that many of the open fields were grazed in common by the livestock of at least some tenants, but there were in addition considerable wastes, woods and heaths available for common grazing. E. M. Yates has hypothesised that the primary settlement pattern was a series of farms and hamlets, occupied by agnatic groups, each hamlet having one arable field used continuously. Secondary colonisation extended on to more difficult soils: where population was very scattered, the enforcement of labour services would have been difficult and their early commutation likely. Some hamlets, as population grew, developed into villages and, where there was a shortage of pastures, grazing on the townfield – the arable nucleus – became subject to manorial control. Inheritance practices and the operation of the land market could account for the multiple open fields in extra-Wealden Surrey in the later Middle Ages as they do substantially for those in Kent. Yates made little reference to either, although he did suggest that with the decay of kinship groups and the growth of population the fields associated with the primary settlement were divided into unenclosed strips.[1] A detailed and comprehensive analysis of the field systems of Surrey has not yet been attempted. So far less attention has been paid to those of the London Basin, the North Downs and the Lower Greensand Belt than to those of the Weald.

3. THE WEALDEN DISTRICTS OF SURREY AND SUSSEX

While the Low Weald Plain arcs westwards from Kent through Surrey and then south and southeastwards through Sussex, the central core of the Weald, the High Weald, is restricted almost entirely to Kent and Sussex (Fig. 9.1). P. F. Brandon has recently defined clearly the extent and established accurately the chronology of medieval woodland clearances and colonisation in the east Sussex Weald. On manors he investigated, in the High Weald, there was little cultivated land in 1086. Extensive tracts were then opened up by individual enterprise and partitioned into freehold and customary farms in the twelfth and early thirteenth centuries. The remaining wastes were then flung open to assarters who, although individually responsible for only small clearings, in sum transformed vast areas of wilderness

[1] E. M. Yates, 'A Study of Settlement Patterns', *Field Studies*, I, 1961, pp. 65–84.

into a neat and orderly landscape of which many features have persisted to the present day.

On the manor of Rotherfield, for example, the number of tenants holding land of the manor rose from the 24 recorded in 1086 to 294 individuals listed in a custumal of 1346. This increase was made possible in part by the subdivision of existing holdings – the custumal states that each *ferling* was held originally by a single person but most of them had by 1346 been subdivided into smaller holdings. But more important was the creation of new holdings on the freshly cleared ground. About six square miles of woodland in Rotherfield manor were cleared and partitioned into farms and smallholdings between 1086 and 1346. The zest with which lords, both ecclesiastical and lay, encouraged the clearances in the High Weald is evident both from the steeply rising rents from assarted lands and from the complete lack of legal and other obstacles placed in the way of assarters. Thus the archbishop's reeves in the manor of South Malling were authorised to grant land freely to whomsoever would take it up and holders of customary land were permitted to take up assart land in addition to their bondland.[1] Land was eagerly sought after for purchase and lease. A survey of the Wealden lands of South Malling at the end of the thirteenth century describes the virgates, the original core of cultivated land, as grouped in many small units (often still identifiable as hamlets) and in the once-uncultivated areas between these hamlets assarts had been made, with their cottages. On this manor, the erection of a cottage and smoke issuing from its chimney were the tokens that the encroachment was permanent and thus that rents should regularly be charged. These scattered cottages contrasted with the more clustered hamlets of the virgates. The process of assarting came to be reflected not only in field but also in settlement patterns.[2] In detail, it was also topographically and edaphically selective even within the High Weald itself. In the early stages, assarters sought out the more eligible sites which invariably lay in the wider valley bottoms on the Tunbridge Wells Sands or the Hastings Beds where a greater depth of soil, and adequate shelter, meadow and water-power could be obtained. Settlers avoided at first the deep ravine-like valleys, which retained their woodland; the larger patches of low-lying heavy clay which supported common woods for swine and cattle grazing; and the windswept ridges. By the early thirteenth century, this phase was

---

[1] P. F. Brandon, 'Medieval Clearances in the East Sussex Weald', *Trans. Inst. Br. Geogr.*, XLVIII, 1969, pp. 135–53.

[2] Gulley, Ph.D. thesis, p. 397; Du Boulay, *Lordship of Canterbury*, p. 137; E. M. Yates, 'Dark Age and Medieval Settlement on the Edge of Wastes and Forests', *Field Studies*, II, 1965, pp. 133–53.

ending and small farmers, holding by assart tenure, were directed from the better areas up on to the steeper hillsides and ridges in the remoter parts of the manor and down into the deeper valleys.[1]

This rapid and vigorous assarting of so much hilly and remote land in the High Weald followed upon the colonisation of the much more accessible lands of the Low Weald Plain. This separated the High Weald from the nucleated settlements along the Chalk escarpment and narrow Lower Greensand outcrop which for several generations provided the pioneers for the wooded districts farther north. By the mid-thirteenth century, woodland clearance had virtually ceased throughout the Sussex Low Weald: woodland itself was valuable and by that time a new balance had been struck between the demands for cultivated land and for woodland. In the High Weald, assarting came to an abrupt end on some manors after the Black Death while on others it continued but on a substantially reduced scale, gradually ebbing away in the middle years of the fifteenth century.[2]

The evolution of a mosaic of fields and farmsteads in the Wealden districts of Sussex and Surrey, then, was very similar to that of the Kentish Weald. Just how close were the affinities between a field system in the Low Weald of Sussex and field systems in Kent has been examined by J. S. Moore in a detailed study of Laughton. The main outlines of the agrarian landscape here had been established by about 1325. At the end of the eleventh century there were two nuclei of colonisation, one in the north of the parish and the other in the south, separated by a vast expanse of common waste. The first half of the thirteenth century saw a major effort to expand the cultivated area, while the second half saw mainly an 'in-filling' of the gaps in the general frontier of colonisation already established. Moore argues that the old cores of cultivation were held not only in compact blocks like the later assarts but also as partially dispersed tenements in some sort of open field system. There is evidence that common grazing of the livestock of both lord and tenants was practised on the demesne and that one-third of the demesne lay fallow in 1338 in consequence.

Right of commonage over the demesne was restricted, it seems, to those tenants whose holdings had been cleared before about 1283 and this, together with the survival within the compact demesne of some parcels of tenant land, led Moore to suggest the old field system was largely abolished in the late thirteenth century by a redistribution

[1] Brandon, *Trans. Inst. Br. Geogr.*, XLVIII, 1969, p. 149.
[2] *Ibid.*, pp. 141–2 and 145–6; E. M. Yates, 'History in a Map', *Geogrl. Jnl.*, CXXVI, 1960, pp. 32–51.

and rearrangement of holdings. The normal tenement in the early thirteenth century on the old lands was neither compact nor regularly distributed throughout the cultivated area, but fairly localised and of irregular distribution. Some but not all of this dispersed nature of a holding could be ascribed to the partitioning of former large and compact holdings. Whatever its precise origins, Moore considered the field system at Laughton to be more clearly related to that of Kent or even of East Anglia than to that of the Midlands,[1] which adds considerable interest to the fact that Laughton was only half-a-dozen miles northwest of the Cuckmere Gap through the South Downs which, in Gray's view, was the southeastern extremity of the Midland field system. Townships of the South Downs and of the Sussex Coastal Plain were included by Gray within the ambit of the Midland system.[2]

4. EXTRA-WEALDEN SUSSEX

The most comprehensive and careful studies of medieval field systems on the Sussex South Downs and Coastal Plain have been made by P. F. Brandon and what follows draws substantially upon his published and unpublished work.[3] It was because the parcels of some holdings in two townships of the manor of Alciston in 1433 were distributed equally among three *leynes* that Gray regarded the manor as the eastern outpost of the three-field system. Brandon has investigated the field systems of this scarp-foot manor in east Sussex in detail and has concluded that a description of Alciston as a three-field manor is 'highly inadequate'. For this reason, and because Brandon considers that a farming organisation similar to that observed at Alciston was practised in the scarp-foot zone of Sussex generally, it is worth looking closely at conditions in this manor.[4]

Certainly, in 1433 there were at Alciston three common fields – West, Middle and East *leyne* – subdivided into more than 400 parcels grouped into 32 furlongs. The holdings of twenty-one tenants were dispersed throughout the fields in parcels of usually less than half of an acre. These common fields covered together only about 190

[1] J. S. Moore, 'Laughton: a Study in the Evolution of the Wealden Landscape', *Occasional Papers, Dept. of Engl. Local Hist., Univ. of Leicester*, XIX, 1965.
[2] Gray, *English Field Systems*, pp. 33–4 and 63.
[3] P. F. Brandon, 'Arable Farming in a Sussex Scarp-foot Parish During the Late Middle Ages', *Sussex Arch. Coll.*, C, 1962, pp. 60–72; 'The Common Lands and Wastes of Sussex', Ph.D. thesis, University of London, 1963; 'Demesne Arable Farming in Coastal Sussex During the Later Middle Ages', *Agric. Hist. Rev.*, XIX, 1971, pp. 113–34.
[4] Brandon, *Sussex Arch. Coll.*, C, 1962, p. 69. See also J. A. Brent, 'Alciston Manor in the Later Middle Ages', *Sussex Arch. Coll.*, CVI, 1968, pp. 89–102.

acres, their small size reflecting in part the fact that corn growing was combined with sheep farming. The demesne had some 30 acres dispersed in small parcels among tenant land in the common fields – but these parcels the lord had acquired after the Black Death, when vacant customary tenements for which the lord was unable to find a new lessee were farmed with the demesne. But the main part of the arable demesne – about 170 acres – lay in severalty in unenclosed blocks of land contiguous with the common fields. Cropping arrangements were flexible. The basis of crop rotation was not three fields but the constituent furlongs which were bundled together to make up the acreage prescribed for the sowing in any given year. Each *leyne* was a 'season' of variable acreage, not a field of fixed acreage. In any given year one *leyne* was sown with wheat, the second with barley and oats, and the third partly sown with leguminous crops and partly left fallow. Demesne parcels intermixed with the tenants' were bare fallowed, presumably to allow common pasturing, but the demesne blocks in severalty were sown in part if not entirely with leguminous crops. Besides this core of almost permanently arable fields on the Chalk marl, there was a group of intermittently cultivated fields in the northern part of the parish, on the Upper Greensand and Gault, analogous to the 'outfields' on Westerham and other Canterbury Cathedral Priory manors in Kent. The 'outfields' were occasionally tilled, principally for fodder crops to sustain cattle and horses through the winter. The 'infields' yielded mainly grains for human consumption and were the site of carefully regulated sheep-folding. Unlike the 'infields', the outfields were entirely part of the demesne.[1]

Many of the features of the field system at Alciston were also to be seen elsewhere in extra-Wealden Sussex. Townships in which some at least of the cultivated land lay in three fields or three *leynes*, or in which two-thirds of the land was sown and one-third lay fallow and in common annually, were widely scattered in and around the South Downs (Fig. 9.7). Certainly a three-course rotation seems to have been ubiquitous in extra-Wealden Sussex during the Middle Ages. But the common field system and its associated landscapes in the Chalk scarp-foot zone and Coastal Plain of Sussex differed markedly from that of the Midlands. First, common fields in Sussex were generally much smaller. In parishes on the downland around Lewes the three fields or *leynes* in sum extended over no more than 300 to 500 acres and in the Cuckmere valley and in parts of the Coastal Plain they were a good deal less. Second, it was frequently the case that within a single parish there existed two or more settlements each with its own common arable lands. This was especially so in the

[1] Brandon, *Sussex Arch. Coll.*, c, 1962, pp. 60–72.

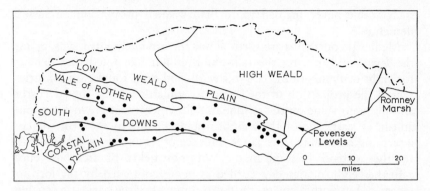

Fig. 9.7 The distribution of places in Sussex for which there is evidence of a three-field system before *c.* 1620.
Source. Based upon Figure 39 of P. F. Brandon, 'The Common Lands and Wastes of Sussex', Ph.D. thesis, University of London, 1963; H. L. Gray, *English Field Systems*, Cambridge, Mass., 1915, pp. 498–9.

Coastal Plain and in the scarp-foot zone of western Sussex, where the common fields were small and hedged. On the Downs themselves and in the scarp-foot zone of eastern Sussex the common fields tended to be larger and unenclosed. Throughout the whole area, common fields were being enlarged by the addition of freshly cleared furlongs right up until the Black Death in response to growing populations. Third, isolated farms with hedged fields lay on the outskirts of the parishes and in the interstices between the hamlet and village settlements and their associated common fields. Despite their ubiquity, common fields were not the basis of agriculture but only one of its elements. At least from the early thirteenth century there is evidence of farming being conducted in severalty alongside the tenants' lands in common fields or else based on some isolated farm reclaimed from waste. Fourth, by 1300 most demesnes in extra-Wealden Sussex lay separate from the lands of tenants, as more or less compact blocks, and they were cultivated in severalty. The intermingling of demesne arable with tenants' lands and its usage in conformity with peasant practice was not general in Sussex. Most demesnes reported to have been 'in common' appear, according to Brandon, to have been either the smaller estates, not held by the greater magnates, or those in townships with few customary tenants. The greater estates in the second half of the fourteenth century incorporated tenements vacated at the Black Death and absorbed into the demesne whenever they could not be let. Such lands constituted dispersed parcels amidst the remaining tenanted lands in each of the three *leynes*, but such arable never formed more than a small proportion of Sussex demesnes.[1]

Medieval court rolls are silent about the arrangements for cropping the *leynes* and grazing the fallows. Brandon has noted that extents for eight demesnes in the late thirteenth and early fourteenth centuries record the proportion of the demesnes which could be sowed yearly and place no value on the residue in fallow because it lay in common, and in at least four of these eight instances some of the demesne lay intermingled with tenants' lands. This seems reasonably good evidence for the existence of some mature common fields. Brandon also cites a further eight demesnes recorded as being cultivated by the lord in severalty but within enclosures taken down after the harvest to enable collective grazing on the fallows. Again, this suggests that in those cases where the demesne and unenclosed tenants' lands were contiguous, they were converted temporarily into common fields.[2]

This practice is remarkably similar to that observed on the manor of Wrotham in Kent. There 'Westfield' of the tenants' seems to have been located between the village itself and 'Westfield' of the demesne. Livestock of some tenants certainly grazed in common over the demesne and they must also have grazed in common over the adjacent lands of the tenants themselves. Few tenants held land within 'Westfield' at the end of the thirteenth century and by then parcels within it were already being consolidated by purchase. But it does make it reasonable to hypothesise that at some period before the thirteenth century most tenants dwelt in Wrotham village and cultivated a single town-field.[3] This is the early field and settlement form postulated for Southeastern England by Jolliffe and, difficult though it is to substantiate this idea, it seems plausible as an explanation of the early stages of development of many settlement and field systems in Kent, Sussex and Surrey.[4]

What is clear is that by the end of the thirteenth century at Wrotham, settlement had become much more widely dispersed and the cleared area more extensive. This, indeed, was the case over much of Southeastern England by this time. But it is equally clear that the later histories of field systems in extra-Wealden Kent and extra-Wealden Sussex became divergent, for by the sixteenth century mature common fields, with regulations enforcing the simultaneous sowing of each of the courses (*leynes* or seasons) and the strict observance of a regular fallow and its collective grazing, had evolved in Sussex but not in

[1] Brandon, Ph.D. thesis, pp. 216–37.
[2] Brandon, *Agric. Hist. Rev.*, XIX, 1971, pp. 119–21.
[3] Baker, *Agric. Hist. Rev.*, XIV, 1966, pp. 19–20.
[4] Jolliffe, *Pre-Feudal England*, pp. 1–19.

Kent.[1] Many of the medieval agricultural practices in Sussex were similar to those in Kent – flexible rotations, subdivision of larger fields by temporary fences for folding and sowing purposes, the early cultivation of legumes on the former fallow, the almost continuous cropping of some fields and the intermittent cropping of others. An important – and perhaps significant – difference is that regulations relating to the folding of sheep were made more explicit in Sussex than was the case in Kent, at least by about 1600.[2] A further important difference seems to have been that piecemeal consolidation and enclosure of open field parcels in extra-Wealden Sussex went on during the later Middle Ages but rather more slowly and tardily than it did in Kent, perhaps in some measure because the greater freedom of tenants and the more developed land market in the latter county.[3] Some open arable fields survived in Sussex until the nineteenth century when they were enclosed by acts of Parliament.[4]

While we now know much more than did Gray about the similarities and the differences existing among field systems in Kent, Sussex and Surrey, there remain many questions to which answers will only be found by further local investigations of the sort undertaken so far on such manors as Alciston, Laughton and Gillingham. Generalised answers need to be based on particular questions.

[1] Brandon, *Agric. Hist. Rev.*, XIX, 1971, pp. 119–20.

[2] A. E. Wilson, 'Farming in Sussex in the Middle Ages', *Sussex Arch. Coll.*, XCVII, 1959, pp. 98–118; A. M. M. Melville, 'The Pastoral Custom and Local Wool Trade of Medieval Sussex, 1085–1485', M.A. thesis, University of London, 1931; J. Cornwall, 'Farming in Sussex 1560–1640', *Sussex Arch. Coll.*, XCII, 1954, pp. 48–92; J. Cornwall, 'Agricultural Improvement, 1560–1640', *Sussex Arch. Coll.*, XCVIII, 1960, pp. 118–32.

[3] Du Boulay, *Lordship of Canterbury*, pp. 173 and 182–4; J. E. Ray, 'Life on a Sussex Manor in the Middle Ages', *The South-Eastern Naturalist and Antiquary*, LI, 1946, pp. 16–23.

[4] W. E. Tate, 'Sussex Inclosure Acts and Awards', *Sussex Arch. Coll.*, LXXXVIII, 1949, pp. 116–56.

10

Field Systems of North Wales

BY GLANVILLE R. J. JONES

In his pioneer work on the growth of the manor, Sir Paul Vinogradoff drew particular attention to early Welsh social and agrarian conditions. He did so because the Welsh evidence is especially suggestive and, as he put it, 'the Welsh facts are more characteristic of Celtic society on English soil' than the Scottish or the Irish.[1] The written evidence to which he alluded consists on the one hand of medieval texts of the Welsh laws and, on the other, of a body of record material – extents, rentals and deeds – ranging in the main from the late thirteenth to the early seventeenth centuries. In the account which follows, pride of place is given to the picture of agrarian organisation, and hence of field systems, afforded by the laws. The more concrete evidence of the records is then deployed in order to refine the idealised picture presented by the lawbooks, and to portray the evolution of the field systems of North Wales.

A. THE EVIDENCE OF THE LAWBOOKS

In any attempt to establish the antiquity of the field systems of Wales, the evidence of the laws is essential. But the whole body of Welsh custom as recorded in the texts could hardly have been in force at any one time for the legal texts were essentially the handbooks of lawyers, each handbook comprising a number of distinct parts, or tractates, arranged by each lawyer to suit his own convenience, so that archaic edicts jostled with later glosses or even entirely new tractates.[2] Our legal picture of the field systems of North Wales is based on a group of manuscripts written in Welsh from the standpoint of Gwynedd, and now designated by the generic title *Llyfr Iorwerth* (the Book of Iorwerth).[3] All these manuscripts, save one, are of the thirteenth

[1] P. Vinogradoff, *The Growth of the Manor*, 1905, p. 7.
[2] J. G. Edwards, 'The Historical Study of the Welsh Law Books', *Trans. R. Hist. Soc.*, XII, 1962, pp. 141–55; R. R. Davies, 'The Twilight of Welsh Law', *History*, LI, 1966, pp. 143–5.
[3] J. G. Evans (ed.), *The Chirk Codex*, 1909; T. Lewis (ed.), 'The Black Book of Chirk', *Zeitschrift für Celtische Philologie*, XX, Halle, 1933, pp. 30–96; A. R. Wiliam (ed.), *Llyfr Iorwerth*, 1960; D. Jenkins (ed.), *Llyfr Colan*, 1963; the other texts have not yet been published.

century and the oldest certainly precede the Edwardian conquest in 1283. Where necessary, their evidence has been supplemented by specific reference to texts of other periods, among them the oldest extant text, Peniarth Ms. 28, written in Latin from a south Wales standpoint in the late twelfth century, but based on an earlier archetype.[1] Despite the relatively late dates of all these manuscripts, and the searching criticism of historians, the traditional connection between Hywel Dda, who died c. 950, and Welsh law has not been altogether eroded.[2] The texts emphasise this connection and also refer to modifications introduced by Bleddyn ap Cynfyn of Powys who died in 1075. There are good reasons therefore for regarding the picture of field systems culled from the earlier tractates of the thirteenth-century lawbooks as representative of an old order.

In the Book of Iorwerth this picture is provided through the medium of an idealised tax assessment. Thus there were four 'acres' (erwau) in – or by – a 'homestead' (tyddyn), four homesteads (tyddynod) in a 'shareland' (rhandir), four sharelands in a 'holding' (gafael), four holdings in a 'township' (tref), four townships in a 'multiple estate' (maenol), and twelve such multiple estates (maenolau) plus two townships in every commote. The two extra townships were for the use of the king, one to be his demesne land (tir maerdref) and the other to be his waste and summer pasture. Since there were two commotes in every hundred (cantref) the latter in theory contained 100 townships or, in all, 25,600 erwau 'neither more nor less'.[3]

Each 'acre' was 30 rods, of 16 Welsh feet (12 statute feet) in length and 3 rods in breadth so that it contained 1,440 square yards in statute measure.[4] There were therefore $4\frac{3}{4}$ statute acres in a shareland, 19 in a holding and 76 in a township. Of the twelve 'multiple estates' in a legal commote, four were assigned to bondmen, one was for the chancellor, and another for the commote reeve, leaving six for free 'notables' (uchelwyr, optimes). From each of the last eight 'multiple estates' the king was to have a food-rent worth a twnc pound (240d.) yearly. Each township of the four in such a 'multiple estate' contributed 60d. and the assessment was further subdivided into quarters in succession until every 'acre' of the 'homestead' was assessed, but leaving a surplus of 4d. in every 'township'. Some authorities regard the areas in the scheme of assessment as being confined to those of the home crofts.[5]

[1] H. D. Emanuel (ed.), The Latin Texts of the Welsh Laws, 1967, pp. 97–171.
[2] J. G. Edwards, Hywel Dda and the Welsh Lawbooks, 1928; Edwards, Trans. R. Hist. Soc., XII, 1962, pp. 141–55; Emanuel, The Latin Texts of the Welsh Laws, p. 85.
[3] Wiliam, Llyfr Iorwerth, p. 60; cf. Jenkins, Llyfr Colan, p. 39.
[4] Wiliam, Llyfr Iorwerth, p. 60; Jenkins, Llyfr Colan, pp. 10, 69.
[5] Jenkins, Llyfr Colan, p. 156; J. E. Lloyd, A History of Wales, I, 1911, p. 297;

The fiscal assessment in practice, however, is likely to have embraced both home crofts and other arable lands. In any case the whole elaborate scheme, with its affectation of numerical exactness, bears the impress of unreality and its provisions probably concern only the taxable area.[1] Nevertheless they must bear some relationship to real conditions at some particular date.

Half the value (120d.) of the pound rendered from each free 'multiple estate' was deemed to be for 'bread', and a further quarter for 'drink'. Thus only a quarter consisted of 'relish' derived principally from pastoral produce. Originally, moreover, the food-rent had comprised a load of the best flour from the land, the carcase of a beast, a vat of mead, sheaves of oats, a three-year-old swine, a salted flitch and a vessel of butter. The food-gift due from each bond 'multiple estate' in winter and summer was likewise made up of the produce of both arable and pastoral farming.[2] In short, the laws provide little warrant for that assumption of an almost all-prevailing pastoralism which continues to distort the interpretation of the field systems of North Wales and to belie the antiquity of the customary tenures recorded in the Book of Iorwerth.[3]

I. *TIR GWELYOG* (HEREDITARY LAND)

The normal tenure, taken for granted in the lawbooks, was *tir gwelyog* (hereditary land).[4] Continued occupation of the land by members of an agnatic lineage over a period of four generations converted bare possession of land into legal proprietorship (*priodolder*) and the 'fourth man' became a proprietor. A hereditary proprietor's share of his patrimony frequently consisted of a personal holding of appropriated land (*tir priod*) and an undivided share of joint land (*cytir*). The appropriated land included a homestead as well as parcels of 'scattered land' (*tir gwasgar*) lying in one or more arable sharelands. The joint land consisted of an expanse of wood, pasture and waste, subject to joint

---

T. Jones Pierce, 'Pastoral and Agricultural Settlements in Early Wales', *Geogr. Annlr.*, XLIII, 1961, p. 187; but cf. A. N. Palmer and E. Owen, *A History of Ancient Tenures of Land in North Wales and the Marches*, 2nd edn, 1910, pp. 57–8.

[1] H. Lewis, *Ancient Laws of Wales*, 1892, p. 95.

[2] G. R. J. Jones, 'The Distribution of Bond Settlements in North-West Wales', *Welsh Hist. Rev.*, II, 1964, p. 28; Wiliam, *Llyfr Iorwerth*, p. 64.

[3] C. Parain, 'The Evolution of Agricultural Technique' in *The Cambridge Economic History of Europe: I, The Agrarian Life of the Middle Ages*, ed. M. M. Postan, 2nd edn, 1966, p. 171; cf. G. R. J. Jones, 'The Tribal System in Wales; a Reassessment in the Light of Settlement Studies', *Welsh Hist. Rev.*, I, 1961–2, pp. 111–32.

[4] D. Jenkins, 'A Lawyer looks at Welsh Land Law', *Trans. Hon. Soc. Cymmrodorion*, 1967, pp. 236–48.

control but within which the proprietor exercised proportional rights calculated in terms of his acreage of appropriated land.[1]

In accordance with partible succession, known in the vernacular as *cyfran* which corresponds to the English *gavelkind*, rights over appropriated land were divided equally *per stirpes* among heirs male. Correspondingly, rights over the still undivided joint land would be reduced in proportion to the diminution of the personal holding of appropriated land. The only favour shown was that to the youngest son who succeeded to his father's homestead while his brothers were expected to remain in the homesteads they had made for themselves on the family land in their father's lifetime.[2] Following this partition, homesteads could be subject to no further redistribution but, after the brothers had died, their sons being first cousins, *if they wished*, could have the rest of the appropriated land reallocated. Likewise the second cousins, *if they wished*, could re-share the lands as distinct from the homesteads. After this 'final partition' (*gorffenran*) there was to be no more re-sharing, or, as one text puts it, no more sharing except for the joint land (*cytir*).[3]

These rules are described in a section of the laws stated specifically to be concerned with *tir gwelyog* (*terra hereditas*, *gwely* land, hereditary land), whose designation appears to be derived from the term *gwely*.[4] According to the most recent interpretation, *gwely* seems to have as its primary meaning a group of relatives of some kind, but not necessarily the same kind in every instance.[5] Most of the examples of *gwely* in the lawbooks occur in connection not with land holding but rather with the payments made by large groups of relatives in lieu of blood-feud. In itself this implies that the *gwely* was old-established, an interpretation supported by the frequent use of the term *gwelygordd* (*gwely* group, lineage, kindred) in verse of the twelfth century.[6] In keeping with the primary meaning of *gwely* as a group of relatives was the basic idea that the land should be divisible on inheritance. Moreover a proprietor's rights were exercised conditionally on behalf of his descendants, and freedom to dispose of land was severely restricted by a complex of customs. These were designed to perpetuate hereditary succession so as to preserve continuity of control by the agnatic

[1] T. Jones Pierce, 'Landlords in Wales' in *The Agrarian History of England and Wales: IV, 1500–1640*, ed. J. Thirsk, 1967, p. 366.
[2] Wiliam, *Llyfr Iorwerth*, pp. 53–4; Emanuel, *The Latin Texts of the Welsh Laws*, p. 132.
[3] Jenkins, *Llyfr Colan*, pp. 36, 149–50.
[4] Wiliam, *Llyfr Iorwerth*, p. 54.
[5] Jenkins, *Trans. Hon. Soc. Cymmrodorion*, 1967, pp. 220–48.
[6] I am particularly indebted to Professor M. Richards and Mr D. Jenkins for discussion on this theme.

lineage over the hereditary land as a whole. Thus the land of the *gwely* came in due course to be known as a 'resting-place', or bed in the sense of a permanent stake in the soil.[1]

But at least as early as the thirteenth century, a proprietor, with the consent of the lord and the kindred, could allow an alienee to take over possession of his land for a term of four years in return for an agreed payment. If this vifgaged land (*tir prid*) were unredeemed at the end of the stipulated term, the transaction became renewable without limitation for further quadrennial periods. When, with successive renewals, four generations had elapsed the vifgaged lands could then pass permanently into the hands of the alienee.[2] In this manner land could be transmitted to persons having no hereditary title.

Non-kinsmen could also become proprietors. Aliens settled on the lord's waste, or occupying land under 'notables', became proprietors 'in the fourth man' and henceforward bound to the soil (*adscripti glebae*). Endowed with homesteads and 'plough-share and coulter land' they were to inherit these according to the same rules as the Welsh.[3]

2. *TIR CYFRIF* (RECKONED LAND)

The most important of the early bond tenures was that associated with geldable land.[4] This was also known as *tir cyfrif* (reckoned land) for it was shared out equally *per capita* among the bondmen of the township by the commote reeve and chancellor. Irrespective of family relationship, every adult male in the bond township received an equal share in terms of area save that the youngest son had to await his father's death.[5] Hereditary land (*tir gwelyog*) could revert to the lord as escheat when the proprietors failed in their obligations, but usually there would be no escheat 'acre' in reckoned land. If however an escheat 'acre' lay within reckoned land then it was to be shared equally 'in common' (*yn gyffredin*) among all.[6] Just as the commote officials shared out the reckoned land of ordinary bond townships, so the lesser reeve shared out the land of the *maerdref* (reeve's township) which adjoined the lord's court.

---

[1] Jones, *Welsh Hist. Rev.*, I, 1961–2, p. 114.
[2] T. Jones Pierce, 'The Laws of Wales – The Last Phase', *Trans. Hon. Soc. Cymmro-dorion*, 1963, pp. 17–18; Jenkins, *Trans. Hon. Soc. Cymmrodorion*, 1967, pp. 239–40.
[3] Wiliam, *Llyfr Iorwerth*, p. 55; Jenkins: *Llyfr Colan*, pp. 38, 158.
[4] Wiliam, *Llyfr Iorwerth*, p. 54; Jenkins, *Llyfr Colan*, p. 36.
[5] A. Owen (ed.), *Ancient Laws and Institutes of Wales*, II, 1841, 64–5.
[6] Wiliam, *Llyfr Iorwerth*, p. 54.

3. *TIR CORDDLAN* (NUCLEAL LAND)

The Book of Iorwerth refers to a third type of land known as *tir corddlan*.[1] This was not to be shared as *tyddynod*, meaning probably home crofts or enclosures; instead it was to be shared as 'gardens' (*gerddi*), a term which here probably means strips or quillets rather than gardens as in modern Welsh.[2] On hereditary land the youngest son was to inherit his father's homesteads; again, on reckoned land the youngest son inherited his father's homestead. If there were buildings on *tir corddlan* however, the youngest son was no more entitled to them than the eldest, but they were to be shared as *ystefyll* (cells or rooms). There is some confusion in the texts between *corddlan* and *corfflan*, meaning a cemetery. This is not surprising since we are told that the measure of a *corfflan* 'is a legal acre in length with its end to the graveyard and that, circling the graveyard, is to be its compass'.[3] Taken together these brief observations in the lawbooks suggest that *tir corddlan* may, for convenience, be translated as nucleal land for it appears to have lain in a nucleus of settlement for a community.[4] Who the occupants were we do not know but they could well have included the voluntary slaves who make a fleeting appearance in the texts and are described as living with a 'notable' and holding his land 'at spade and fork'.[5]

The 'gardens' were to be manured every year. Thus no one was to retain 'gardens' in his possession for more than a year on account of having manured them. In other words nucleal land appears to have been the Welsh equivalent of the continuously manured and cultivated *infield* recorded many centuries later for the Scottish or Irish hamlet. There was also other land in less regular cultivation which resembles Scottish or Irish *outfield*.[6] On this land, advantage from manuring could be derived for a longer period than one year and the individual who applied the manure was allowed to grow crops on this land for the longer period. Fallow (*brynar*), like fresh soil, could be ploughed for two years whereas land manured by the folding thereon of flocks and herds could be ploughed for three years, and land manured with carted dung for four years.

[1] *Ibid.*, p. 58; Jenkins, *Llyfr Colan*, pp. 38, 155–6.
[2] Jenkins, *Llyfr Colan*, pp. 155–6; A. N. Palmer, *A History of Ancient Tenures of Land in the Marches of North Wales*, 1885, p. 8.
[3] Wiliam, *Llyfr Iorwerth*, pp. 44, 54; cf. Jenkins, *Llyfr Colan*, pp. 35, 36, 38.
[4] Owen, *Ancient Laws and Institutes of Wales*, I, 181.
[5] *Ibid.*, II, 82–3.
[6] Wiliam, *Llyfr Iorwerth*, p. 58.

4. AGRARIAN COOPERATION

The laws provide abundant evidence of agrarian cooperation especially where ploughing was concerned.[1] For co-tillage an ideal partnership of twelve men was envisaged; a ploughman and a driver contributed their labour, another his plough, a fourth the irons and the remainder an ox each to make a team of eight. The contract applied to twelve 'acres', namely one for each partner, and care was taken to regulate precisely the order and conditions of ploughing so that, for example, the first 'acre' to be ploughed was that of the ploughman. The laws record that there were sometimes plough teams of six or eight oxen,[2] but the underlying principles of co-tillage were clearly adaptable to all kinds of variations in the number of partners and oxen to a contract. It must be emphasised, however, that the rules were frequently, though probably not invariably, applied to 'acres' already in the occupation of the partners to the contract. Had the 'acres' been distributed to the partners only after the ploughing it would not have been necessary to have the rule that a defaulter who sold his ox should nevertheless 'maintain the yoke'.[3] Further confirmation is provided by the rules for settling disputes, whereby one partner wanted distant lands ploughed in return for the ploughing of nearby lands, or to have fresh soil ploughed in return for land already in cultivation.[4] There is no warrant whatsoever in the laws *proper* for the assumption made by Seebohm, and by later writers, that the 'acres' were allocated only *after* the ploughing.[5] This assumption, often invoked as a general explanation for the scattering of 'lands' in open field, was based on *The Triads of Dyvnwal Moelmud* which were fabricated only in the eighteenth century.[6]

Although the rules for voluntary co-tillage probably applied to freemen, such practices were also likely to have been imposed on at least some bondmen.[7] Thus among the duties of the lesser reeve was that of ordering the ploughing in the reeve's township (*maerdref*) and

---

[1] *Ibid.*, pp. 96–9; Jenkins, *Llyfr Colan*, pp. 10–12, 68–73.

[2] Wiliam, *Llyfr Iorwerth*, p. 63; Owen, *Ancient Laws and Institutes of Wales*, II, 458–9.

[3] Jenkins, *Llyfr Colan*, pp. 10–11, 68.

[4] Wiliam, *Llyfr Iorwerth*, p. 58.

[5] F. Seebohm, *The English Village Community*, 1883, pp. 118–25, 186; and C. S. and C. S. Orwin, *The Open Fields*, 2nd edn, 1954, pp. 5–12; E. Kerridge, *The Agricultural Revolution*, 1967, p. 157.

[6] Seebohm, *The English Village Community*, pp. 191–3; G. J. Williams, *Iolo Morgannwg a Chywyddau'r Ychwanegion*, 1926, pp. 157, 196–8, 214; Lloyd, *A History of Wales*, I, 318–19; Owen, *Ancient Laws and Institutes of Wales*, II, 474–567.

[7] T. P. Ellis, *Welsh Tribal Law and Customs in the Middle Ages*, II, 1926, pp. 57–8.

this was certainly ploughing done by bondmen.[1] The Latin texts make it clear that the renders of a bond township (*villa rusticana*) were a communal obligation whether the tenants were few or many (*vel unus vel plures*).[2] These Latin texts, like the Book of Iorwerth, reveal that the cheese of the summer food-gift of the bondmen was a communal render, made from milk of all of the cows of the township.[3] Significantly, this township (*tref*) or *villa rusticana* is called a shareland (*rhandir*) in some of the Latin texts, and Peniarth Ms. 28 of the late twelfth century refers to a *pastor communis ville*, a neatherd of the common township.[4] The communal organisation for grazing thus implied is confirmed by references in a Welsh text of the early thirteenth century to common grazing in practice.[5] If a man sought sanctuary in a church settlement occupied by members of a church community (*clas*) and their abbots, his cattle were to go with the cattle of the community and abbots to the furthest limits they grazed.

A Latin text of the mid-thirteenth century glosses *communis villa* with *id est trefgord*, which is best translated as hamlet.[6] Occasional references to a hamlet bath-hut used for special ablutions hint that this communal organisation affected many aspects of life. Since the bath-hut, like the hamlet smithy, was tiled and, ideally, was placed at least 7 fathoms away from the nearest *houses*, the *trefgordd* was presumably a nucleated settlement in which fire damage was an ever-present hazard.[7] Such references in thirteenth-century texts suggest that the complement of the hamlet as listed in a fifteenth-century text was not entirely fanciful.[8] This complement was: nine houses, one plough, one kiln, one churn, one cat, one cock, one bull and, appropriately, one herdsman. The unmistakable implication of the texts is that all the occupants of the hamlet formed a cooperative group and, since they possessed only one plough, it is reasonable to infer common field cultivation.

The texts also reveal that the 'acres' of the shareland usually lay in open field where they were interrupted by the occasional headland (*talar*) for turning the plough. These 'acres' were divided from each other only by 'skirts', or by balks which were two furrows (18 in.)

[1] Owen, *Ancient Laws and Institutes of Wales*, I, 62–3.
[2] Emanuel, *The Latin Texts of the Welsh Laws*, pp. 136, 382.
[3] *Ibid.*, pp. 136, 204, 382; Wiliam, *Llyfr Iorwerth*, p. 64; Jenkins, *Llyfr Colan*, p. 41.
[4] Emanuel, *The Latin Texts of the Welsh Laws*, pp. 124, 136, 382.
[5] Lewis, *The Black Book of Chirk*, pp. 59–60.
[6] Emanuel, *The Latin Texts of the Welsh Laws*, p. 266.
[7] *Ibid.*, p. 123; Wiliam, *Llyfr Iorwerth*, p. 81; Owen, *Ancient Laws and Institutes of Wales*, II, 576–7.
[8] Owen, *Ancient Laws and Institutes of Wales*, II, 692–3.

wide.[1] The emphasis in the laws on compensation for corn damage caused by grazing animals confirms that these arable lands lay in open field.[2] When the boundary between two townships lay on cultivable land, a not-infrequent state of affairs given the scarcity of arable land, even the boundary could lie open, hence the severe penalties imposed for ploughing the boundary between two townships.[3]

The compensatory arrangements made for the grazing of winter or spring corn at an early stage of growth in spring differed from those adopted for the standing crop of later months. Such arrangements seem to be old-established, for they were recorded in both the Latin and Welsh texts, and Bleddyn ap Cynfyn is credited with their modification during the eleventh century.[4] No compensation was to be paid for corn left standing after the Kalends of Winter (1 November), for after this date the sharelands could presumably be grazed in common. Some rotational sequence is implied by the provision that where a man had removed his corn from the stubble to the ley he was not to have redress. Such a sequence was probably necessary, for winter wheat and rye as well as spring oats and barley were grown, though the latter were probably the more characteristic since winter tilth was deemed to be worth twice as much as spring tilth.[5] Since individuals could put fences around corn and grass, it would appear that flexible arrangements for temporary fencing were adopted on at least some lands. These are more likely to have been the sharelands of freemen than the normally more extensive open fields of bond hamlet communities.

Meadow, defined as land appropriated for hay only, was enclosed by a fence from the feast of St Patrick (17 March) to the Kalends of Winter because it was mown twice a year. In addition to a meadow, an enclosure (*cae*) was permitted as a reserve of grass. Nevertheless, the prominence of open field husbandry is suggested by the rule that no compensation was to be paid for damage to vegetable gardens, for these were to be so strongly fenced that beasts could not break in.

Thus the general impression created by a study of the laws is of an old-established practice of *mixed farming* organised in the main on an open field basis and with a degree of communal control. A crucial question for the student of common field origins is the antiquity of

[1] Lewis, *The Black Book of Chirk*, p. 47; Wiliam, *Llyfr Iorwerth*, p. 19; Owen, *Ancient Laws and Institutes of Wales*, II, 268–9.
[2] Wiliam, *Llyfr Iorwerth*, pp. 99–103; Jenkins, *Llyfr Colan*, pp. 12–13.
[3] Wiliam, *Llyfr Iorwerth*, p. 63; Jenkins, *Llyfr Colan*, p. 41.
[4] Jenkins, *Llyfr Colan*, p. 12.
[5] Emanuel, *The Latin Texts of the Welsh Laws*, p. 157; Wiliam, *Llyfr Iorwerth*, p. 95.

these practices. To this question the laws themselves provide some answers. If the rules concerning proprietorship were part of the customary law codified by Hywel Dda, then the acquisition of rights in land by the act of settling is likely to have begun at least thirteen generations before c. 950, that is at the latest in the seventh century and probably in the sixth century, if not much earlier. For once proprietorship had been acquired as a result of continued occupation of land over four generations, subsequent abandonment of the land did not extinguish the rights of proprietorship so acquired until nine generations had elapsed. Meanwhile continued occupation of the same land by the descendants of a second settler could in turn have created rights of proprietorship for them. If this happened, the descendants of the first settler could utter 'a cry louder than that of the Underworld' and be allocated a share of the land in question.[1]

Similarly, early cultivation may be inferred from a statement in a Welsh text of the Book of Iorwerth, dating from the early thirteenth century. This is a statement to the effect that a cultivated 'land' (*tir*), said to be of $20\frac{1}{4}$ feet in width, was called in 'new Welsh' a ridge (*grwn*).[2] Yet this word in new Welsh was sufficiently old and traditional in the twelfth century to have been used in verse, so that the cultivated 'land' must be even older.[3]

B. THE EVIDENCE OF OTHER RECORDS

Fuller understanding of the field systems of North Wales can be achieved when the evidence of the laws is tested against that of tenurial records. This approach was effectively demonstrated by the inspired amateur historian A. N. Palmer in his pioneer studies of the eastern border, an area where English and Welsh elements were 'instructively commingled'.[4] The same approach was emulated by Frederic Seebohm who sought to interpret the structure of what he described as 'the tribal system in Wales' by reference to territories further west and thus ethnically less confused.[5] For this purpose Seebohm used, in particular, the superb extents of various parts of North Wales compiled

---

[1] Wiliam, *Llyfr Iorwerth*, pp. 55–6; Jenkins, *Llyfr Colan*, pp. 35, 147.
[2] Evans, *The Chirk Codex*, p. 65; cf. Wiliam, *Llyfr Iorwerth*, p. 59 and Jenkins, *Llyfr Colan*, pp. 39, 160.
[3] F. G. Payne, *Yr Aradr Gymreig*, 1954, p. 49.
[4] A. N. Palmer, *A History of Ancient Tenures of Land in the Marches of North Wales*, 1885, p. ii; see also Palmer, *The Town, Fields, and Folk of Wrexham in the Time o James the First*, 1895.
[5] F. Seebohm, *The Tribal System in Wales*, 1895.

shortly after the Edwardian conquest. At the present day, however, many more records than were available to Seebohm can be used in the study of our field systems.

I. THE EARLIEST RECORDS

The earliest of these records refers to a fourth-century dispute about the kind of conflicting claims to proprietorship that could arise under the nine-generation rule cited above.[1] This particular aspect of customary law, stemming probably from at least the Iron Age,[2] conflicted with Roman principles and raised issues of such importance that recourse was made to the Emperor's court in what seems to have been a test case. Presumably therefore an estate of some substance, belonging to well-to-do freemen, seems to be involved.[3]

Definite testimony to the relatively high status of some early freemen is provided by two records contained in the *marginalia* of the Book of St Chad and attributed to the ninth century.[4] These record the grant of a *tref* by a certain individual named *Ris* and a kindred known as *luith Grethi*. The details of the *census* of this township recall the food-gift of the bondmen and suggest that the territory granted was a bond unit.[5] The *Surexit* memorandum, written into the same book in the eighth century, records a suit concerning the rival claims of two kindreds to the possession of some land and, in so doing, provides a clear pointer to the existence of a social order much more stable than that envisaged by earlier investigators.[6] Correspondingly an impression of a settled agrarian organisation is conveyed by a reference in the verse of Llywarch Hen, *c.* 850, to the ploughing of fallow (*brynar*) on the eastern borders of Powys.[7]

For these reasons it is not surprising that Domesday Book should yield hints of a settled organisation in the limited Welsh territories it surveyed. In Moldsdale (Flint) each of the six men of King Gruffydd appears to have owned a plough team in the years before 1063,[8] and

[1] C. E. Stevens, 'A Possible Conflict of Laws in Roman Britain', *Jnl. Roman Stud.* XXXVII, 1947, pp. 29–33.

[2] Jones, *Welsh Hist. Rev.*, I, 1961–2, p. 130; Jones, 'Settlement Patterns in Anglo-Saxon England', *Antiquity*, XXXV, 1961, pp. 227–32; cf. L. Alcock, *Dinas Powys*, 1963, pp. 196–7.

[3] C. E. Stevens, 'The Social and Economic Aspects of Rural Settlement', in *Rural Settlement in Roman Britain*, C. Thomas (ed.), 1966, p. 109.

[4] J. G. Evans and J. Rhys (eds.), *The Text of the Book of Llan Dav*, 1893, p. xlv.

[5] Jones, *Welsh Hist. Rev.*, I, 1961–2, p. 128.

[6] I. Ll. Foster, 'Summary and Suggestions', *Welsh Hist. Rev.*, Special Number 1963, *The Welsh Laws*, p. 65.

[7] I. Williams, *Canu Llywarch Hen*, 1940, p. 40, cited by Payne, *Yr Aradr Gymreig*, p. 51.

[8] Record Commission, *Domesday Book*, I, 1783, fo. 269.

the same was true of three Welshmen living by Welsh law (*iii Walenses lege Walensi viventes*) in Gwent (Mon.) in 1086.[1] In the same locality where one township was *shared by the sons* of Wasuuic, there were other whole townships held by individuals who may therefore be equated with the 'notables' of the laws. Among these can be numbered the ninety-six men in Archenfield (Heref.) having 73 ploughs 'with their own men',[2] the latter presumably being undertenants. To the manor of Cleeve on the eastern border of Archenfield there belonged in 1086 'so many Welshmen as have 8 ploughs' (*tot Walenses qui habent viii carucas*), a statement which hints at the existence of a number of ploughing communities, each perhaps organised like a hamlet (*trefgordd*). Here also there were two settlements containing *Welsh hides* which still had Welsh 'custom' (*consuetudo*) in 1086.[3] Significantly, in the nearby manor of Ballingham there were four freemen with 4 ploughs who rendered 4 sesters of honey,[4] a characteristic Welsh render, and 16*d*. as 'custom'. This assessment in fours suggests that the schematic arrangement in the Book of Iorwerth may have ante-dated 1066 and, possibly, the English conquest of Cornwall in the tenth century, for there too a system of fours is found in customary measures of area.

2. THE POST-CONQUEST RECORDS

Evidence that the schematic arrangement in the Book of Iorwerth remained in force is provided by the detailed *Survey of the Honour of Denbigh* which was compiled in 1334. In the township of Cegidog, near Dinorben, a 'homestead' which was escheat contained 3½ roods by the measure of the survey,[5] or 5,373 square yards statute measure; this is only slightly less than the 5,760 square yards of the legal 'homestead' of 4 acres. Before 1283, in the interior township of Prys, 1 'acre' rendered ½*d*. for *twnc*, which is in accordance with the increased assessments of 8 or 12 'acres' to the 'homestead' attributed in the laws to Bleddyn ap Cynfyn.[6] In keeping however with the statement that notwithstanding these changes the usual assessment was only ¼*d*. per 'acre', is the assessment for ¼*d*. *twnc* of the one *erw* specified in the coastal township of Hendregyda (Denb.). This 'acre' is stated to be from a *gafael*, one of the many 'holdings' into which each *gwely* in the township was divided.

[1] *Ibid.*, fo. 185b. [2] *Ibid.*, fo. 181.
[3] *Ibid.*, fos. 181a, 181b.
[4] *Ibid.*, fo. 181a; V. H. Galbraith and J. Tait (eds.), *The Herefordshire Domesday, c. 1160–70*, Publications of the Pipe Roll Society, LXIII, 1947–8, p. 19.
[5] P. Vinogradoff and F. W. Morgan (eds.), *Survey of the Honour of Denbigh, 1334*, 1914, p. 226; cf. also pp. lvii–lxiii.
[6] *Ibid.*, p. 102; Jenkins, *Llyfr Colan*, p. 53.

By this date the term *gwely* was certainly being applied to the holding of a group of agnatic relatives as well as, if not instead of, being applied to the relatives who might have rights to this holding. Hence frequent references in the fourteenth century to the '*gwely* of the *gwely*', that is the 'resting-place of the group'.[1] Already by 1334 the term *gwely* meant 'resting-place' in Hendregyda.[2]

(a) Permanent and temporary cultivation

The 'resting-place' of Gurg' Gogh in Hendregyda was divided into four 'holdings', two named after a son of Gurg' Gogh and two separate 'holdings' named after two grandsons of Gurg'. Each of these four 'holdings' was assessed for *twnc* at 15*d*. The remaining resting-place in Hendregyda, that of Ithel ap Griff', was divided into 6 'holdings' held by eight progenies, every progeny save one bearing the name of a son of the apparently fecund Ithel ap Griff'. Thus every progeny held three-quarters of one 'holding' in Gwely Ithel ap Griff' and rendered $7\frac{1}{2}d$. for *twnc*. In other words Gwely Ithel as a whole had been assessed, among other dues, for *twnc* at 60*d*., in this respect resembling Gwely Gurg'.

The three parts of one 'holding' in Gwely Ithel which had been held by the progeny of Eynon ap Ithel were escheat, save that two surviving members of this progeny, in return for *twnc* of $\frac{1}{4}d$. and other dues, held '1 *erw* from three parts of one *gafael*'. On this basis every whole '*holding*' in Gwely Ithel might have contained at one time 40 'acres' and every whole 'holding' in Gwely Gurg' 60 'acres'. The whole township might have contained 480 'acres' (*erwau*) or 112a. 3r. in local measure (143 acres statute measure). In 1334 however the recorded acreage of 'land, wood and waste' in the township of Hendregyda was 1,299 acres (1,649 statute acres) and the areas recorded in the *Survey in Denbigh* appear to be accurate within about ten per cent. By this date no less than 275a. 1r. (349 statute acres) of appropriated land with its appurtenant wood and waste were escheat and, of these, 196 local acres (249 statute acres) were leased out as arable lands at rents ranging from 1*s*. 6*d*. to 2*d*. per local acre. Escheat land was a fractional share of the 'holding', of the resting-place and, here, ultimately of the township. Since over two out of every three acres of escheat were arable, it is likely that a similar proportion of the township area was regarded as potential arable land, though not necessarily cultivated. Some of the arable escheat lands in other townships of the

[1] Record Commission, *The Record of Caernarvon*, 1838, pp. 1, 17–18, 22–3, 48–50, 57–62, 66–7; Jenkins, *Trans. Hon. Soc. Cymmrodorion*, 1967, pp. 241–8.
[2] *Survey of Denbigh*, pp. 233–9.

Honour of Denbigh, which were rented in 1334 at 6d. or less per local acre, were later described in the sixteenth century as lands which could be cultivated only temporarily even after the paring and burning of the sod.[1] It is likely therefore that in Hendregyda township it was mainly lands like those deemed to be worth 1s. per local acre in 1334 which were permanently, or at least regularly, cultivated. These lands lay on well drained loams of high base status at a height of 250 feet or less 'below the hill' or limestone ridge overlooking the Hendref (Old Settlement) on the coastal lowlands.[2] None of the lands described as lying *desuper collem*, in other words to the south beyond the ridge, were rented at 1s. per acre and most were leased at 6d. per acre and less. Since they lay at a height of 400 feet, or more, on loams of low base status, these lands, to judge from sixteenth-century conditions, were probably only temporarily or intermittently cultivated, even in times of need. Some 70 local acres (89 statute acres) of escheat land were deemed to be worth 1s. per local acre and, since the total escheat area amounted to about a quarter of the township, it follows that by 1334 some 280 local acres (356 statute acres) of land of this quality are likely to have been in regular cultivation. This figure is so far in excess of the statute equivalent of 480 'acres' (*erwau*) that the 'acre' (*erw*) assessment seems to have been ancient, though the actual imposition of $\frac{1}{4}d.$ per *erw* probably occurred after the mid-tenth century, for the laws record that there were no farthings in the time of Hywel Dda.[3] In Hendregyda, at least, the assessment seems to have included the oldest nuclei of arable land as well as the homesteads, for the theoretical 'homestead' equivalent of 480 'acres' would give 120 households, which is about three times the number of resting-place proprietors recorded for the township in 1334. Even with this qualification the evidence for Hendregyda suggests a considerable increase in the cultivated area between the time of the 'acre' assessment and 1334.

A similar impression is gained for wider areas when the commotes of the lawbooks, each with 12,800 'acres' (3,809 statute acres), are compared with the known commotes of North Wales. The two commotes of Arfon (western Snowdonia) together contained over 110,000 statute acres, and even the six commotes of Anglesey each contained on average some 29,000 acres. Here in particular, given Gerald's twelfth-century description of the island as the granary of Wales, we can safely postulate a considerable enlargement of

[1] P.R.O., L.R. 2/238, fos. 61–2, 69.
[2] G. R. J. Jones, 'Some Medieval Rural Settlements in North Wales', *Trans. Inst. Brit. Geogr.*, XIX, 1953, pp. 62–3.
[3] Owen, *Ancient Laws and Institutes of Wales*, II, 596–7.

the cultivated area after the initial imposition of the 'acre' assessment.[1]

Nevertheless, even in the most productive part of Anglesey some temporary cultivation of the kind suggested by the laws appears to have been practised.[2] Thus the demesne lands of Llanfaes (Ang.) in 1305 included not only the 'best land' (terra meliore) in the open fields (campi) of the township but also 'mountain land' (terra montana). The former consisted of lowland brown earths of high base status, worth 6d. per acre, whereas the mountain land, some two miles distant at an altitude of just over 300 feet, consisted of brown earths of low base status, worth only 1d. per acre.[3]

Terra montana was also to be found on the mainland of North Wales, alike on bond and free ground.[4] These lands appear to have been the same as Tir mynythe, Tir mane or 'wilde grownd' which George Owen described in 1593 as ground 'suche as yeldeth corne but once in xx or xxiiii yeeres by beating and burning for rie or otes and at all tymes ells lieth grownd with small fursse or heathe and serveth for pasture for sheepe or yong cattell'.[5] Significantly three bond resting-places in Trawsfynydd (Mer.) in 1636 contained 'arable land, meadow, pasture, woods, underwoods and mountain bond ground'. Since the nuclei of these resting-places lay at 750 feet, the outfield implied by 'mountain bond ground' is likely to have attained a height of 1,000 feet or more.[6]

(b) Upland pastures and wastes

Extensive tracts of the uplands were unsuited even for temporary cultivation. Some of these were used as the pastures and wastes of the king, among them the waste of Bishopswall which contained nearly 1,400 acres in Mynydd Hiraethog (Denb.), and the hafod (summer dwelling) of Cwm Clorad near Capel Curig (Caerns.). As the name hafod implies, these upland pastures were usually grazed only in summer but, somewhat exceptionally, Bishopswall was stated in 1334 to be capable of sustaining 8 bulls and 192 cows in winter as in summer.[7]

[1] Giraldi Cambrensis, Opera VI, J. F. Dimock (ed.), Rolls Series, 1868, p. 127.
[2] G. R. J. Jones, 'The Distribution of Medieval Settlement in Anglesey', Anglesey Antiqu. Soc. Trans., 1955, pp. 41, 52–3.
[3] P.R.O., S.C. 11/767; G. R. J. Jones, 'Rural Settlement in Anglesey' in Geography as Human Ecology, S. R. Eyre and G. R. J. Jones (eds.), 1966, p. 214.
[4] P.R.O., L.R. 2/240, fo. 200, C. 143/74/22; National Library of Wales, Liber Ruber Asaphensis, fo. 80; Wynnstay Ms. L. 1279, Bachymbyd Mss. 664, 665, 708.
[5] N.L.W., Vairdre Book, fo. 137, cited by B. E. Howells, 'Pembrokeshire Farming circa 1580–1620', National Library of Wales Journal, IX, 1956, p. 325.
[6] Jones, Welsh Hist. Rev., II, 1964, p. 20.
[7] Survey of Denbigh, p. 25; Record of Caernarvon, pp. 11, 292.

Conversely, in the case of some Merionethshire examples we are told in 1563 that the pastures were grazed in the summer 'for in winter by reason of the coldness of it and long continuance of snow there, the same can maintain no cattle'.[1]

The considerable upland areas which remained were at the disposal of lowland communities of freemen and bondmen from the Kalends of May onwards. Accordingly the large waste of Mynydd Hiraethog was said in 1334 to be common to all the tenants of the five commotes in the Honour of Denbigh.[2] By providing summer grazing for lowland townships, these 'out commons' enabled the common pastures within the townships to be preserved as much as possible for use in winter and the lean months of Lent.[3] Thus it was that an occupant of the west coast township of Llanaber (Mer.) was fined in 1326 for keeping his animals in the common pasture of the Old Settlement (in communi pastura del hendreve) after the community of the township, which included both freemen and bondmen, had moved early in May of that year with its animals to the mountains.[4] It is not surprising therefore that one text of the Book of Iorwerth describes the bondman's winter residence as one of his three 'nets' or sources of profit. The others were his herd of cattle and his herd of swine, so that for every beast found among them from the Kalends of May to the month of August the bondman received compensation. These provisions for the period from May until August suggest that the bondman tended his own herds in summer; hence the scattering of summer dwellings implied by surviving material remains of huts in rocky upland areas, and confirmed by specific references to isolated summer dwellings in Llanwrin (Mont.) in 1573.[5]

Such is the general backcloth against which the evolution of the field systems of North Wales must be viewed. In tracing this evolution it is desirable to distinguish between the main customary tenures already described, a consideration completely overlooked by H. L. Gray in his studies of field systems in Wales.[6]

[1] E. A. Lewis and J. C. Davies (eds.), Records of the Court of Augmentations relating to Wales and Monmouthshire, 1954, p. 442; Jones, Welsh Hist. Rev., II, 1964, pp. 27–9.
[2] Survey of Denbigh, p. 96.
[3] P.R.O., L.R. 2/240, fos. 197–8.
[4] P.R.O., S.C. 2/225/28; Record of Caernarvon, pp. 277–8.
[5] Wiliam, Llyfr Iorwerth, p. 22; compare however Evans, The Chirk Codex, p. 29 and Lewis, The Black Book of Chirk, p. 50. See also Jones, Welsh Hist. Rev., II, 1964, p. 64 and B. M. Evans, 'Settlement and Agriculture in North Wales, 1536–1670', Ph.D. thesis, University of Cambridge, 1965, pp. 126–7.
[6] H. L. Gray, English Field Systems, Cambridge, Mass., 1915, pp. 171–87, 199–205.

(c) Tir gwelyog (hereditary land)

Since hereditary land was subject to partible succession it is to be expected that the arable land outside the home croft should have lain in open field. That such was the case is clearly confirmed by the reply given to a petition in 1305 concerning the holding of escheat land. In the reply to the petition, which had been made to the Prince of Wales on behalf of the Welsh communities in Gwynedd, the petitioners were assured that such lands should not be held *in defenso*, or in any way separated other than was customary in the time of the former tenants. The lands were to be held openly and not otherwise (*aperte et non aliter*), presumably because their enclosure would have interfered with the system of husbandry.[1] Likewise escheat land in Abergele township (Denb.) in 1334 was described as being made up of parcels *de acris campestribus* or *de terris campestribus*.[2] In the Honour of Denbigh, hereditary land was by far the most characteristic and it is significant therefore that customary payments for fencing – probably temporary – were recorded in every commote of the lordship in 1334. In the Denbigh commote of Ceinmeirch these fences were sometimes used by individuals around their own corn.[3] Further east in Chirkland in the late fourteenth century one resting-place (*gwely*), and a great many 'holdings' (*gafaelion*), were said to be held by groups of heirs 'in common'.[4]

(i) *The ground-plan of medieval Llwydfaen.* A clear insight into the actual disposition of lands within such 'holdings' was first provided by Jones Pierce in his admirable diagrammatic reconstruction of part of Llwydfaen in the Conway valley as it was in the mid-fifteenth century (Fig. 10.1).[5] Llwydfaen was part of the township of Castell which, according to an extent of 1352, contained free holdings. In Castell, as in Hendregyda, 'holding' (*gafael*) meant a subdivision of a resting-place (*gwely*), for these two terms were sometimes used interchangeably.[6] It was appropriate therefore that in Castell 20 'holdings' were said to be held by groups of co-heirs and only two

---

[1] *Record of Caernarvon*, p. 213, cited by A. E. Lewis in 'The Decay of Tribalism in North Wales', *Trans. Hon. Soc. Cymmrodorion*, 1902–3, pp. 29, 64.

[2] *Survey of Denbigh*, pp. 254–6.

[3] *Ibid.*, pp. 8, 59, 150, 270, 314.

[4] G. P. Jones (ed.), *The Extent of Chirkland (1391–1393)*, 1933, pp. 13–15, 23, 25–6, 34, 36, 51, 54, 57, 67, 74; cf. T. P. Ellis (ed.), *The First Extent of Bromfield and Yale A.D. 1315*, 1924, pp. 24–5.

[5] T. Jones Pierce, 'The Gafael in Bangor Manuscript 1939', *Trans. Hon. Soc. Cymmrodorion*, 1942, pp. 158–88.

[6] *Record of Caernarvon*, pp. 5–7; P.R.O., L.R. 2/250, fos. 55–60; *Survey of Denbigh*, p. 211.

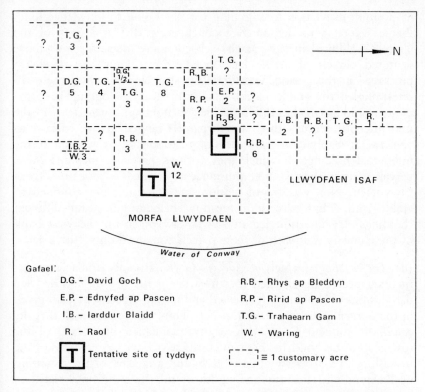

Fig. 10.1 The shareland of Llwydfaen (Caernarvonshire) during the mid-fifteenth century.
Sources. Slightly modified from Jones Pierce's reconstruction which was based on U.C.N.W., Bangor Ms. 1939.

by single heirs. Eight of the 'holdings' were confined to the neighbourhood of the hamlet of Castell proper and the remainder had offshoots in one or more of the remaining four administrative hamlets into which the township was divided. Using the rental of an estate belonging to one Bartholomew Bolde in the mid-fifteenth century,[1] Jones Pierce was able to show that at least 8 of the 22 'holdings' (*gafaelion*) had offshoots in the peripheral subdivision of Castell known as Llwydfaen. Many of the component parcels of individual holdings within these *gafaelion* had been acquired by Bolde when he was building up his estate between 1420 and 1453. Fortunately the 'holding' (*gafael*) affiliation of each parcel was given in the rental along with

---

[1] For details see 'The Bolde Rental (Bangor Ms. 1939)', C. A. Gresham (ed.), *Trans. Caernarvonshire Hist. Soc.*, XXVI, 1965, pp. 31–49.

its position in relation to adjoining parcels. Using this evidence Jones Pierce was able to demonstrate conclusively that at least 5 of the Castell 'holdings' in Llwydfaen each contained there three or more scattered parcels of arable land or meadow. Thus Llwydfaen, as portrayed in this period, was literally a shareland in which there lay intermingled the arable parcels and homesteads belonging to component holdings within different lineage 'holdings' (*gafaelion*). In the mid-fifteenth century these arable parcels ranged in size from 2 to 12 acres, probably customary acres of 3,240 square yards. Some of the individual holdings of which they formed part also included other parcels lying in sharelands at a distance of as much as four miles from Llwydfaen. Nor was fragmentation and intermingling confined to arable land. Thus parcels of meadow belonging to four different 'holdings' lay intermingled in Morfa Llwydfaen on the west bank of the Conway, but each of these parcels contained only 1 or 2 acres.

(ii) *The 'holding'* (gafael) *of Audoeni Gogh'*. Broadly similar arrangements appear to be implied for an earlier period by the less detailed descriptions of 'holdings' (*gafaelion*) and resting-places (*gwelyau*) given in the *Survey of the Honour of Denbigh*. Thus we are informed that the *gafael* of Audoeni Gogh' before 1283 contained the whole of the township of Llwyn, half the hamlet of Casyth, five-eighteenths of the townships of Garthserwyd and Llech, and a quarter of the township of Bachymbyd.[1] In 1334 one-eighth of this 'holding' was stated to be escheat 'everywhere' (*ubique*). In other words all the members of the progeny of Audoeni Gogh' who had forfeited their land – because they had fought against the English in 1282–3 – were deemed to have held arable lands and appurtenant pasture rights in every one of these administrative units. The same was undoubtedly true of the twenty-five kinsmen who held seven-eighths of this 'holding' in live tenure in 1334. Thus each one of the twenty-five kinsmen would have exercised proprietorship over a share of Llwyn where the rights of the lineage survived over 121 local acres of 'land, wood and waste', a share of the 351 acres in Casyth, a share of the 184 acres in Bachymbyd, a share of 39 acres in Garthserwyd and a share of 35 acres in Llech. In brief, the twenty-five appear together as proprietors of every one of the five estates so that the combined holding of each individual was 29 local acres (37 statute acres) of 'land, wood and waste'. In the small township of Llech, though two out of every three acres were here deemed to be cultivable, there must have been a considerable fragmentation of the permanent arable lands. Nor was this fragmentation narrowly circumscribed, for the core of Llwyn was about three miles

[1] *Survey of Denbigh*, pp. 9, 33–7, 40–3, 45.

distant from that of Bachymbyd. Throughout the whole 'holding' of Audoeni Gogh' the tenure appears to have been strictly communal. Since the same was true of another 'holding' (*gafael*) which embraced part of Garthserwyd, Llwyn, Bachymbyd and, in addition, the township of Garthennwch, where the progeny of Audoeni Gogh' was *not* represented, this communal tenure cannot be readily attributed to the kind of re-sharing among kinsmen permitted by law.[1] Instead it was probably due to a deliberate decision to retain undivided shares of arable land in a joint holding.

(iii) *The fragmentation of individual holdings.* Usually by this date a greater individual consciousness of possession had developed. Such appears to have been the case with Gwely Bleth' ap Edred which contained land in Abergele, in Llwytgoed and its hamlets of Gwlypdref and Dinerth some seven miles to the west, as well as Cilcen some six miles to the southwest where Gwely Bleth' was further subdivided into three resting-places.[2] The thirty-three proprietors in Gwely Bleth' in 1334 held some 586 local acres of 'land, wood and waste' giving an average holding of $17\frac{3}{4}$ local acres. Only eight of these proprietors however held land in all the five administrative units where the lineage was represented. In other words, a conscious effort appears to have been made to apportion rights to many proprietors only in certain localities, presumably so as to limit the incidence of the fragmentation of holdings brought about by the operation of partible succession.

How necessary such steps were is indicated by the suggestion in a wide variety of sources that the typical holding of arable land in the early fourteenth century contained some 5 to 10 acres of arable land, made up of parcels dispersed over a number of open field sharelands.[3] In Hendregyda, for example, in 1334 the average individual holding of hereditary land comprised only 28 local acres even when the wood and waste within the township was included with the arable land. On a holding of this size in Hendregyda only about 7 local acres are likely to have been regularly cultivated. Appropriately, the regularly cultivated lands were more fragmented than those apparently used only for temporary cultivation. Thus the average size of 26 parcels of various escheat holdings specified as lying 'below the hill' on the most valuable land in Hendregyda was just over half

[1] *Ibid.*, pp. 17–18, 40–3, 45. See above, p. 433.
[2] *Ibid.*, pp. 248–50, 262–4, 301.
[3] Jones, *Anglesey Antiqu. Soc. Trans.*, 1955, pp. 38–40, 87; C. Thomas, 'The Evolution of Rural Settlement and Land Tenure in Merioneth', Ph.D. thesis, University of Wales, 1956, pp. 119–25; Jones Pierce, *Agrarian History*, p. 360.

a local acre; and the four smallest parcels contained on average only a quarter of an acre. On the other hand the 30 escheat parcels specified as lying beyond the ridge, on less valuable land, each contained on average an acre and a quarter.[1]

On first impression these findings seem to be at variance with those of Jones Pierce for Llwydfaen, where some of the parcels recorded for the mid-fifteenth century contained more than 4 acres. In this instance however it must be borne in mind that Llwydfaen was not a primary shareland of Castell, nor even a secondary one, and may have been appropriated by the freemen of Castell at a relatively late date. Moreover the relatively large size of some of the parcels in the shareland of Llwydfaen was probably due to an earlier consolidation of at least some of the parcels within any one 'holding' (gafael) there, for the Bolde rental itself suggests that Bartholomew Bolde was not the first to have acquired parcels belonging to the occupants of different 'holdings'.[2]

A more representative impression of the effects of partible succession on the pattern of landholding is provided by an early fourteenth-century concession concerning the attendance of Welsh freeholders at the shire courts of the Principality of North Wales. This obligation, imposed on all Welsh freeholders after the Edwardian conquest of 1282–3, had proved to be particularly burdensome especially when holdings were subdivided. After a struggle the English authorities, therefore, were obliged to limit the obligation to freeholders with 4 bovates, or 16 acres, each probably containing 3,240 square yards.[3] It was probably for similar reasons that, in 1305, the Welsh communities of Gwynedd had petitioned that their members be allowed to buy and sell land.[4] Shortly afterwards the free tenants of North Wales recited the damaging effects of two practices: one was partible succession; the other was the procedure whereby lands were secured by means of vifgage conveyances for successive periods of four years. The latter was presumably a palliative, albeit an unwieldy one, for the adverse effects of the former. Its employment had probably been stimulated by the complete commutation of joint dues and services into cash rents after the Edwardian conquest, thus eliminating the need for one of the more important collective functions of the lineage, and permitting cash rents to be apportioned to recognisable units of

[1] Survey of Denbigh, pp. 235–9.
[2] University College of North Wales, Bangor Ms. 1939; Gresham, Trans. Caernarvon-shire Hist. Soc., XXVI, 1965, pp. 34, 37, 46.
[3] Record of Caernarvon, pp. 213–14.
[4] J. B. Smith, 'Crown and Community in the Principality of North Wales in the Reign of Henry Tudor', Welsh Hist. Rev., III, 1966, pp. 145–71.

land.[1] To judge alike from these petitions and from surviving vifgage conveyances of the early fourteenth century, this palliative was widely used at an early date.[2] Hence the request of the freeholders that they might be permitted to sell and convey their lands in accordance with English custom. Their representations were not rewarded and so leasing by means of vifgage continued, gradually spreading outwards from the small areas of desirable land where it seems to have been first used.

To judge from contemporary records it was in the late fifteenth and early sixteenth centuries that the morcellation of holdings became pronounced.[3] Sir John Wynn of Gwydir, writing in the fifteenth century, could comment retrospectively on the descendants of certain well-known lineages in North Wales who had been brought 'by the division and subdivision of *gavelkind* (the destruction of Wales) to the estate of mean freeholders'.[4] In similar vein, the writer of a fifteenth-century legal tract could assume quite incidentally, in dealing with an entirely different matter, that an inheritance of land could descend 'in small shares among forty or sixty co-inheritors'.[5] Thus the average size of individual holdings subject to alienation, or falling in by way of escheat, was much lower in the fifteenth century, when aggregates of one or two acres were frequent, than in the fourteenth century.[6] But unless demographic trends in North Wales were very different from those in other parts of western Europe – and if only because of plagues and the Glyn Dŵr rebellion this does not appear to have been the case – then it would be wrong to ascribe this morcellation in the late fourteenth and early fifteenth centuries solely to population pressure. The smaller average size of holding in the fifteenth century may equally be due to the reconversion of arable land to pasture. This is known to have occurred on some lands because of declining fertility.[7] Given the climatic deterioration known to have taken place in the later Middle Ages, this is likely to have occurred on a significant scale with 'mountain land' subject to temporary cultivation.

(iv) *The evolution of some typical lowland resting-places.* Only rarely does the record evidence permit an insight into the way in which the

[1] Jones Pierce, *Agrarian History*, p. 363.
[2] Smith, *Welsh Hist. Rev.*, III, 1966, pp. 148–9; *Survey of Denbigh*, pp. 227, 297, 309; U.C.N.W., Mostyn Mss. 1, 5, 95, 98.
[3] Jones Pierce, *Agrarian History*, pp. 360–1.
[4] Sir John Wynn, *The History of the Gwydir family*, ed. J. Ballinger, 1927, pp. 14, 35.
[5] Owen, *Ancient Laws and Institutes of Wales*, II, 430–3.
[6] Jones Pierce, *Agrarian History*, p. 311.
[7] *Survey of Denbigh*, pp. 2, 230.

resting-place (*gwely*) and the kind of 'holding' (*gafael*) already described could have evolved and ultimately broken down. There are however a few rentals of the sixteenth and seventeenth centuries which record in tolerable detail the affiliations of parcels of arable land to their parent resting-places. They do so in order to facilitate calculation of the rights over joint land (*cytir*) appurtenant to these parcels, and also to simplify the collection of ancient quit rents. Such was the case with a rental of 1549 which records the territorial bases of the seven medieval resting-places of the township or vill of Llysdulas in northeast Anglesey.[1] By this date resting-place affiliations were recorded in Llysdulas essentially for mnemonic purposes. The kind of estate consolidation practised by Bolde at Llwydfaen had long since disrupted the traditional tenurial pattern of the township of Llysdulas. So far indeed had engrossment proceeded that the components of the resting-places described in the rental were in the main the holdings of individuals rather than constituent parcels of land. Nevertheless the locations of these components were described in considerable detail in Welsh. The use of the vernacular, rare in administrative documents, suggests that the rental was well founded on local knowledge. As a result it can be used to locate with a considerable degree of accuracy the actual sites of nearly all the components of the seven Llysdulas resting-places (Fig. 10.2). There is moreover a striking consistency between the rentals imposed on each of the seven resting-places in 1549 and those imposed in 1352.[2] The rent of 10*d.* and the increase of 5*s.* levied in 1352 on the escheat land of Grono Gogh, which then contained three bovates, was still levied in 1549 on the lands described as the escheat land of Grono Gogh in Llysdulas. Again the combined rental of the seven resting-places in 1352 is virtually identical with that recorded for the township of Llysdulas in 1294. Accordingly, our reconstruction of Llysdulas (Fig. 10.2), though based on the 1549 rental, gives some insight into tenurial dispositions within the township at the close of the thirteenth century.[3]

The seven free resting-places with their appurtenant rights of joint land (*cytir*) embraced almost the whole of the parish of Llanwenllwyfo and a large part of the parish of Amlwch (Fig. 10.2). The exceptions were the lands of numerous other vills and hamlets, within the parish of Amlwch, and the small bond resting-place known as Twrllachied in the northwestern corner of Llanwenllwyfo.[4] Within those parts of

[1] T. Jones Pierce, 'An Anglesey Crown Rental of the Sixteenth Century', *Bulletin of the Board of Celtic Studies*, X, 1939–41, pp. 156–76. P.R.O., S.C. 12/21/13.
[2] U.C.N.W., Baron Hill Ms. 6714, fo. 43; P.R.O., L.R. 2/250, fo. 25d.
[3] P.R.O., S.C. 11/769; S.C. 6/1154/5; DL. 29/633/10, fo. 312.
[4] Jones, *Geography as Human Ecology*, p. 207.

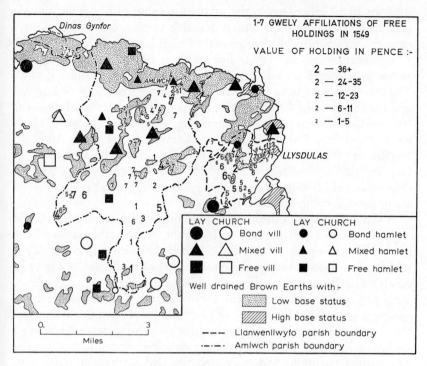

Fig. 10.2 The ramifications of the seven lineages of Llysdulas township
(Anglesey) in 1549.

Sources. Compiled from: P.R.O., S.C. 11/769, S.C. 12/21/13, S.C. 6/11/1154/5,
D.L. 29/633/10,312, E. 178/5052, L.R. 2/237, L.R. 2/250; N.L.W., Powys Castle
Ms. 16724, Welsh Church Commission Ms. 1; U.C.N.W., Baron Hill Ms. 6714,
Llysdulas Mss. 4, 6, 12, 13, 37, Tynygongl Mss. 11, 47, 775; *The Record of Caernarvon*,
'An Anglesey Crown Rental of the Sixteenth Century'; the tithe maps and awards
for Amlwch, 1841, and Llanwenllwyfo, 1843; published and unpublished Anglesey
maps of the Soil Survey of England and Wales.

the two parishes and their outliers which formed the township of
Llysdulas the distribution of the arable parcels of the seven resting-
places was far from even. All seven were represented in the vicinity
of the modern mansion of Llysdulas in the northeastern corner of
Llanwenllwyfo, where place names, like *Hendref* (Old Settlement) and
Cae hen (Old Field) recorded in the 1549 rental, point to an old-
established settlement. Nowhere else in the township were all the
resting-places represented in contiguous parcels, so that *Llysdulas Old
Settlement*, in northeastern Llanwenllwyfo, must have been the primary
settlement of the seven lineages. For agricultural purposes this site was

superior to all other sites in the whole township of Llysdulas, since it occupied a sheltered slope with a desirable southeastern aspect; moreover the soils were well drained and of high base status.[1]

Significantly all the seven lineages can be traced back to two ancestors named Karwed and Gryffri who lived in Llysdulas *c.* 1170. The seven lineages were in fact named after the three sons of Karwed and the four sons of Gryffri. Thus, in the numerical order adopted for Fig. 10.2, they were, Gwely Tygeryn ap Karwed (1), Gwely Hoell ap Karwed (2), Gwely Dolfyn ap Karwed (3), Gwely Adda ap Gryffri (4), Gwely Denawel ap Gryffri (5), Gwely Vrochwel ap Gryffri (6), Gwely Bledrws ap Gryffri (7). Accordingly the tenurial dispositions in Llysdulas townships may be envisaged as having evolved along the following lines.

In the mid-twelfth century Karwed and Gryffri acquired, either as their shares of a wider estate or by grant, some arable lands in the pre-existing township of Llysdulas. These lay near the court (*llys*), which gave its name to the whole township of Llysdulas. On Karwed's death his lands were divided equally among his three sons in accordance with partible succession; likewise Gryffri's lands were divided equally among his four sons. In the case of Llysdulas the seven agnatic lineages, thus initiated, maintained their unity over succeeding centuries, though within each lineage partible succession *per stirpes* continued to operate. The earliest partitions had converted the Old Settlement arable into a shareland and made necessary new appropriations, which were probably chosen after an initial phase of temporary outfield cultivation. With the continued operation of partible succession these newer appropriations appear to have been made progressively further afield within the joint land (*cytir*) over which each lineage exercised rights of pasture, and in due course these too were partitioned into sharelands. Such was the desire for an equiponderance of rights between brothers, especially on the best soils, that the lands of any kinsman would have lain scattered through a number of sharelands. Links of sentiment, reinforced by a shrewd awareness of the superior quality of the Old Settlement lands, led most heirs to retain a share here, at least in the early partitions. With the newer appropriations a conscious effort appears to have been made to forestall the incidence of fragmentation by permitting the participation of only a few of the seven lineages. In the secondary sharelands nearest to Llysdulas Old Settlement not more than four lineages were represented, though these were drawn from the stocks both of Karwed and of Gryffri. In the outermost sharelands not more than three lineages were represented and all were

---

[1] *Memoirs of the Soil Survey of Great Britain*: E. Roberts, *The County of Anglesey*, 1958.

from the stocks of either Karwed or Gryffri. Thus the southern extremity of Amlwch parish was shared only by Gwely Tygeryn ap Karwed (1) and Gwely Dolfyn ap Karwed (3). In the outlier of Amlwch near the promontory fort of Dinas Gynfor only Gwely Adda ap Gryffri (4), Gwely Vrochwel ap Gryffri (6) and Gwely Bledrws ap Gryffri (7) were represented; but, since the promontory fort could have been the retreat in time of stress for the former court of Llysdulas, these particular dispositions may owe something to early military considerations.

Given the lesser fragmentation of the secondary sharelands, and in particular the outermost, it became convenient for many an heir, on first inheriting, to establish his homestead not at the Old Settlement but instead in the vicinity of a newer shareland. To economise on good arable land, the scarce factor of production, these homesteads were often sited on the outer edges of the newer sharelands thus giving rise to what may be best described as girdle patterns of dispersed dwellings.[1]

To judge from the rentals of the Llysdulas resting-places, which ranged from 8s. 2d. to 43s. 9d., some lineages had a greater propensity, or need, for expansion than others but, ultimately, there were obvious geographical and technical limits to this process. Once this stage was attained the continued operation of partible succession reduced the shares of some heirs below the economic minimum. Thus opportunities opened up for some – the avaricious, the industrious, or those blessed with privileged but none too fecund ancestors – to acquire the shares of less fortunate neighbours. By means of vifgages they contrived to build up estates from the components of a number of resting-places. They patiently added quillet to quillet so as to create compact arable blocks which in turn were enclosed within quickset hedges. New enclosures for pasture were carved out of adjoining parts of the joint land (cytir) in lieu of some of the appurtenant rights of pasture; and parcels of meadow, whether adjoining the sharelands or lying at a distance, were likewise consolidated.[2] Gradually, therefore, compact hedged holdings took the place of the hitherto open arable sharelands, the meadows, and the unenclosed pastures of joint land.

By 1549, concentration of arable parcels and appurtenant rights of pasture in the hands of large proprietors had eliminated from direct ownership of the soil of Llysdulas most of the descendants of the seven lineages. Altogether thirty-one proprietors then held the 125 holdings of resting-place land in live tenure recorded for the township. But, of these, only six proprietors held land in more than one resting-

[1] Jones, *Anglesey Antiq. Soc. Trans.*, 1955, p. 33.
[2] P.R.O., S.C. 12/21/13; E. 178/5052.

place and between them these six controlled no less than 94 holdings whose rental value amounted to some two-thirds of that of the seven resting-places. Among the six was William Gruffudd of Penrhyn (Caerns.), with 29 holdings principally in the central part of Amlwch parish, and Thomas Lloyd with 27 holdings, most of them grouped around his residence of Llysdulas in the former Old Settlement of the township.

The perpetuation of such estates was facilitated by the adoption of *primogeniture* instead of *gavelkind* and the frequent use made of entail to prevent any would-be irresponsible heir from disposing of his estate. To the satisfaction of estate-building proprietors these English practices acquired the full force of law in 1542 when it was also enacted that all impediments on freedom to part with land be swept away, and that Welsh vifgages would no longer be valid.[1] Inevitably older usages like partible succession lingered on among freeholders in some parts of Wales but among estate consolidators the new order prevailed. On consolidated estates the unified control thus achieved permitted the further modification of the rural pattern. Already by the late sixteenth century some holdings of 50 or even 100 acres, with additional appurtenances, had emerged on the former Llysdulas sharelands, as for example in the central part of Amlwch parish or in the southern part of Llanwenllwyfo.[2] Near the oldest centres of settlement like Amlwch or Llysdulas Old Settlement, however, there were still some small-holdings which, even with their appurtenances, contained 10 acres or less. These reminders of the older order have survived near Amlwch but in the vicinity of the enlarged mansion of Llysdulas they ultimately disappeared with the continued progress of estate consolidation.[3] In the case of Llysdulas the discovery of copper beneath appurtenant pasture on Parys mountain enabled the Rev. Edward Hughes, the then owner, to make his fortune and thus accelerate this process of estate consolidation in the late eighteenth century.[4] As a result the nucleus of consolidation at the Old Settlement was transformed by landscape gardening and on the home farm large regular fields were laid out anew since, in the interests of improved crop rotations, field size had become a function of farm size.[5] Thus by 1843, when a map was made of the parish, Llysdulas proper was a compact ring-fence unit with large enclosed fields betraying no trace of the former Old Settlement shareland.[6]

[1] Jones Pierce, *Agrarian History*, p. 363; I. Bowen, *The Statutes of Wales*, 1908, pp. 75–93, 101–33, 122–3.
[2] N.L.W., Powys Castle Ms. 16724.   [3] U.C.N.W., Tynygongl Mss. 11, 47.
[4] U.C.N.W., Llysdulas Mss. 4, 6, 12–13, 27; Tynygongl Ms. 775.
[5] Jones, *Geography as Human Ecology*, p. 207.
[6] P.R.O., Tithe Apportionment and Map, Llanwenllwyfo Parish, 1843.

Similar transformations took place on the sites of most of the sharelands which had formed part of the resting-places (*gwelyau*) of North Wales. Although change was sometimes hindered by the continued operation of partible succession,[1] the process of estate consolidation ultimately proved triumphant over the greater part of North Wales and especially in the vicinity of family seats like Clenennau (Caerns.) and Peniarth (Mer.).[2]

It is for reasons bound up with a broadly similar tenurial evolution that so many of the sites of former medieval sharelands are now occupied by farms which are among the largest and the best organised in the lowlands of North Wales.[3]

(v) *Tenurial change in the uplands.* Similar developments took place in the uplands, where many secondary sharelands and some primary sharelands had emerged in the Middle Ages.[4] Here, however, where the joint land (*cytir*) and the waste (*cydwyllt*) were very extensive, the arable sharelands tended to be smaller and the home crofts correspondingly larger than in the lowlands, so that few traces of sharelands survived the sixteenth century and then only on the fringes of the uplands.[5]

Among the few upland sharelands to survive to a late date were those in the interior township of Pennant (Mer.). Already a populous unit in 1293, Pennant contained a number of free 'holdings' (*gafaelion*) which by 1389 had been divided into fractional shares.[6] Even in 1840, because the process of consolidation had been arrested locally, relics of these 'holdings' were very evident in five contiguous enclosures (Fig. 10.3). Only two of these enclosures bore the name *maes*, which meant open field, but all five contained quillets divided merely by turf balks. This patch of 'open field arable', containing some 12 acres, was shared by a number of owners and formed part of no less than

---

[1] U.C.N.W., Mostyn Ms. 786; E. D. Jones, 'Rhannu Tir Rhys ab Elise', *National Library of Wales Journal*, III, 1943–4, pp. 23–7.

[2] T. Jones Pierce (ed.), *Clenennau Papers and Letters in the Brogyntyn Collection*, *N.L.W. Journal*, Supplement, 1947, pp. v–xxi; Thomas, Ph.D. thesis, pp. 124–6; Smith, *Welsh Hist. Rev.*, III, 1966, pp. 149–50.

[3] T. Rowlandson, 'The Agriculture of North Wales', *Jnl. R. Agric. Soc. Engl.*, VII, 1846, pp. 553–88; Jones, *Geography as Human Ecology*, pp. 222–5.

[4] Jones, *Welsh Hist. Rev.*, II, 1964, pp. 24–8.

[5] Jones, *Trans. Inst. Brit. Geogr.*, 1953, pp. 62–3; G. R. J. Jones, 'Medieval open fields and associated settlement patterns in North-West Wales', *Géographie et Histoire Agraire, Actes du Colloque International de Nancy*, 1957, *Annales de l'Est*, Memoire XXI, 1959, pp. 316–17.

[6] P.R.O., E. 179/242/53; N.L.W., Peniarth Mss. 236, pp. 141–3; 403, pp. 309–10; Rûg Ms. 251; A. D. Carr, 'The Barons of Edeyrnion, 1282–1485', *Jnl. Merioneth Hist. Rec. Soc.*, 1964, pp. 291–2.

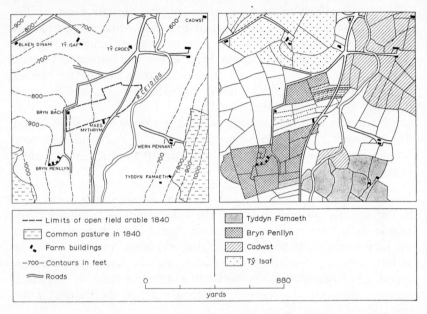

--- Limits of open field arable 1840

[---] Common pasture in 1840

🖤 Farm buildings

—700— Contours in feet

Roads

▒ Tyddyn Famaeth

▓ Bryn Penllyn

▨ Cadwst

⠂ Tŷ Isaf

0   880

yards

Fig. 10.3 Late surviving sharelands at Pennant (Merionethshire) in 1840.
Sources. Based on the tithe map and award for Llandrillo, 1840.

eight distinct farms.[1] The homesteads of two of these farms lay in the adjoining township of Garthian which, like Pennant, had contained free 'holdings' in 1389. The remaining six were in Pennant township. Tyddyn Famaeth and Wern Pennant were to the east of the River Ceidiog, but Bryn Penllyn, Bryn Bâch, Tŷ Croes and Tŷ Isaf all to the west of the river, formed a girdle of farmsteads roughly adapted to the contour. This girdle encompassed the surviving sharelands of Pennant, one of which had been established at a height of about 800 feet on the favoured east-facing slope near Bryn Bâch. Earlier there had been more sharelands within the girdle but, because of the fragmentation of the 'holdings', many of these had come to be consolidated and enclosed. By 1840, only field names and right-angle bends in trackways remained to give any hint that many an enclosed field within the girdle had once been a shareland consisting of bundles of small quillets.[2] As the example of Bryn Penllyn shows, the first sharelands to be enclosed had been those nearest the homesteads but, to these older enclosures, outlying bundles of enclosed quillets and even

[1] P.R.O., Tithe Apportionment and Map, Llandrillo Parish, 1840.
[2] Cf. G. R. J. Jones, 'Early Settlement in Arfon; the setting of Tre'r Ceiri', *Trans. Caernarvonshire Hist. Soc.*, XXIV, 1963, pp. 5–8.

single quillets were added, some as late as the First World War. Outside the girdle of farmsteads, fringing enclosures of pasture were carved out of the common pastures. Thus, over the centuries, progressively more compact farms came to be established in Pennant. Nevertheless sufficient of the medieval ground-plan remained in 1840 to prove that even in the uplands of North Wales open field could well be the precursor of enclosed holdings.

With the growing demand for Welsh cattle and wool in England during the sixteenth and seventeenth centuries large numbers of encroachments were made in the uplands, as for example in eastern Snowdonia where they reached an altitude of 1,400 feet.[1] Much of this colonising activity was an outgrowth of the custom of transhumance. In Montgomeryshire it was the custom to have a 'deiry' or summer house with two folds for beasts and sheep on the mountain or waste ground where the freeholders dwelt during the summer time.[2] Many of these summer dwellings became permanent rearing or 'dairy' farms worked in severalty and carrying cattle and sheep throughout the year.[3]

Detailed analysis of the encroachments made in Merionethshire has shown that the majority were plots of less than 10 acres but that there were not a few exceeding 100 acres. Unlike the small encroachments made by the lesser freeholders, the really large encroachments of several hundred acres were made by landowners of standing, often within a convenient distance of their mansion houses.[4] But there were many proprietors, large and small, who, to protect themselves from overstocking of the wastes by unscrupulous neighbours, withdrew areas of mountain from communal use and converted them into permanent enclosures.

In western Montgomeryshire, as in westernmost Shropshire, it was asserted that these encroachments were justified since the wastes were *cyd-tir* (*sic*), literally joint land rather than 'commons'. In 1561 the jurors of Arwystli and Cyfeiliog maintained that their commotes were 'divided into *gavell* as well the wastes as also the lands now

---

[1] R. E. Hughes, 'Environment and Human Settlement in the Commote of Arllechwedd Isaf', *Trans. Caernarvonshire Hist. Soc.*, 1940, pp. 1–25; Hughes, 'Possible Human Historical Factors Determining the Distribution of *Eriophorum latifolium* in the north-west Conway Valley', in *The Changing Flora of Britain*, J. E. Lousley (ed.), 1953, pp. 40–5.

[2] N.L.W., Powys Castle Ms. 11785.

[3] F. Emery, 'The Farming Regions of Wales' in *The Agrarian History of England and Wales: IV, 1500–1640*, J. Thirsk (ed.), 1967, pp. 137–8.

[4] C. Thomas, 'Encroachment on to the Common Lands in Merioneth in the Sixteenth Century', *Northern Universities Geogrl. Jnl.*, v, 1964, pp. 33–8; Thomas, Ph.D. thesis, pp. 167–70.

severed', and that 'the chief rent...is payed as well for the one as for the other'.[1] As late as 1637 it was asserted that Bryncoch *cyttir* (*sic*) was not 'common' but land enjoyed by five adjoining landowners as 'coparceners in gavellkind'; that the same five landowners had distinct and several holdings on Bryncoch *cyttir* according to the yearly value of their tenements; and that the land was 'enjoyed by the five places among themselves partly by plowing and manuring thereof and partly by depasturing'.[2] In other words this joint land (*cytir*) embraced not only rough pasture but also land used for temporary outfield cultivation; it therefore resembled the 'mountain land' of the Middle Ages. Though officials insisted on treating the 'frivolous terme Kyttyr' as no more than the Welsh equivalent of 'common',[3] the claim of Welshmen that this was 'inheritance undevided' finds warrant alike in medievallaw and in records dealing with hereditary land (*tir gwelyog*). In *Llyfr Colan*, a text of the thirteenth century, the only hereditary land which could be divided after a final partition (*gorffenran*) was joint land (*cytir*).[4] The better parts of joint land (*cytir*) probably became the enclosed *ffridd* or 'inbye-land' of later centuries; for the term *ffridd* was used not only of common pasture, and of 'forest' in the sense of a game preserve, but also of ploughed land taken out of a mountain.[5]

(d) Tir cyfrif (*reckoned land*)

On hereditary land held by bondmen there normally occurred the kind of tenurial evolution already described for the free *gwely*. Indeed the small size of many bond townships facilitated morcellation and thus early consolidation except occasionally where a township was held of the Church and such consolidation deliberately prevented.[6]

On reckoned land a different course of events was characteristic. Few of the hamlets or girdle settlements on such land survived the later Middle Ages, for reasons closely bound up with the conditions whereby the land was held. Just as the lands in a reckoned township

---

[1] E. Evans, 'Arwystli and Cyfeiliog in the Sixteenth Century: An Elizabethan Inquisition', *Montgomeryshire Collections*, LI, 1951, pp. 23–37.

[2] P.R.O., E. 134/13. Ch. 1./M. 55 cited by E. Evans in 'Arwystli and Cyfeiliog in the Sixteenth Century', M.A. thesis, University of Wales, 1939, pp. 66–9. Cf. also Powys Castle Mss. 11785, 11788, 16757, 12104, 12494.

[3] John Norden, *Survey of Oswestry in 1602*, in *The Lordship of Oswestry, 1393–1607*, W. J. Slack (ed.), 1951, p. 59.

[4] Jenkins, *Llyfr Colan*, pp. 149–50.

[5] M. Richards, 'Ffridd/Ffrith as a Welsh Place-name', *Studia Celtica*, II, 1967, pp. 29–31; Palmer and Owen, *A History of Ancient Tenures of Land*, pp. 77–80; N.L.W., Rûg Ms. 78.

[6] Jones, *Geography as Human Ecology*, pp. 207–11, 221–5.

were shared out equally *per capita*, so the rents and services were a communal obligation. Consequently, if but one tenant survived he was to have the whole township in return for all the rents and services imposed on the township. Commutation of customary obligations into cash payments had been introduced on a very small scale into the bond townships under the Welsh Princes but an immediate result of the Edwardian conquest was a composition of tributary renders and labour services into cash rents. Many bondmen must therefore have been driven to distraction by the effort required to find the necessary *denarii*, especially in those townships where the bond population had declined.[1] They experienced difficulties even before the plagues of the middle years of the fourteenth century caused a substantial reduction in the bond population. Such a reduction caused a further increase in the burdens of the survivors and not unnaturally therefore many bondmen took advantage of the Glyn Dŵr rebellion to escape their obligations by flight.[2] Thus many bond lands and demesnes, whether owned by the Crown or by Lords Marcher, fell into decay. As a result such lands provided opportunities for the activities of estate-consolidators who, by means of legitimate leases or even illegal encroachments from adjoining free resting-places, converted bond land, or demesne land, into compact holdings. But occupation of bond land could bring the occupant by prescription to bond status, hence the concern of freemen with the emancipation of bondmen. Manumission was granted however in Ceri and Cydewain in 1447, and elsewhere in north Wales in the early sixteenth century, thus facilitating the exploitation of bond land.[3] As a result, most of the bond hamlets in north Wales shrank in size or became single farmsteads. Nucleated settlements survived only where local circumstances were particularly favourable. Among such circumstances were the rivalries of grasping estate-builders or the existence of opportunities for the descendants of the bondmen to engage in supplementary activities like trading or fishing.[4]

(i) *Aberffraw*. Both extremes are well illustrated at Aberffraw (Ang.), the traditional capital of North Wales.[5] To judge from the royal inscription of the seventh century at Llangadwaladr, whose church was dedicated to St Cadwaladr Rege, the ancient royal estate of

---

[1] T. Jones Pierce, 'Some Tendencies in the Agrarian History of Caernarvonshire during the Later Middle Ages', *Trans. Caernarvonshire Hist. Soc.*, I, 1938, pp. 1–27.

[2] Smith, *Welsh Hist. Rev.*, III, 1966, pp. 152–71.

[3] Jones Pierce, *Trans. Caernarvonshire Hist. Soc.*, I, 1938, pp. 26–7; Smith, *Welsh Hist. Rev.*, III, 1966, pp. 155–71.

[4] Jones, *Welsh Hist. Rev.*, I, 1961, pp. 121–3.

[5] Seebohm, *The Tribal System in Wales*, pp. 1–27.

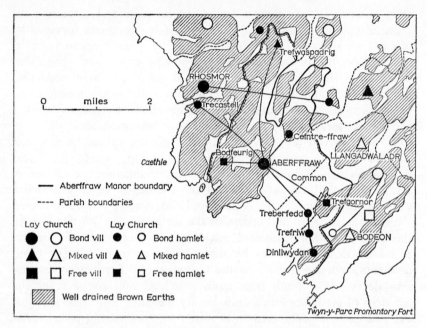

Fig. 10.4 The manor of Aberffraw (Anglesey) during the
mid-fourteenth century.

Sources. Compiled from: P.R.O., S.C. 11/769, S.C. 6/1154/5, S.C. 6/1180/3, S.P. 1/236, D.L. 29/63310,/312, E. 178/3307, L.R. 2/250; N.L.W., Welsh Church Commission Ms. 1; U.C.N.W., Baron Hill Ms. 6714, Bodorgan Mss. 862, 871–80, 1579, 1588, 1625, Penrhyn Ms. 68, Tynygongl Ms. 775; *The Record of Caernarvon*, 'The Aberconwy Charter'; the tithe maps and awards for Llangwyfan, 1839, and Aberffraw, 1843; published and unpublished Anglesey maps of the Soil Survey of England and Wales.

Aberffraw had at one time been sufficiently extensive to include the retreat provided by the promontory fort of Twyn-y-Parc.[1] Donations to the Church in the Dark Ages and to Aberconwy Abbey in the thirteenth century had reduced its area but nevertheless the 'manor' of Aberffraw as described in the extent of 1294 was a substantial multiple estate embracing several distinct settlements (Fig. 10.4).[2] Chief among these was Aberffraw proper on the site of the modern village of that name at the tidal limit of the River Ffraw. Here in 1294 were two juxtaposed hamlets, *Maerdref* (Reeve's Settlement), a reckoned-

---

[1] *Record of Caernarvon*, pp. 46–50; *Royal Commission on Ancient and Historical Monuments in Wales and Monmouthshire: Anglesey*, 1937, pp. 87–8.

[2] P.R.O., S.C. 11/769; *Record of Caernarvon*, pp. 48–50; C. A. Gresham, 'The Aberconwy Charter', *Arch. Camb.*, XCIV, 1939, pp. 142–4.

land unit inhabited by at least one group of nine bondmen, and *Garthau* (Gardens) with its 14 gardens, 9 of which were then occupied by nine bondmen.

In addition there were numerous outlying hamlets. Like Maerdref–Garthau they all occupied sites which were well-drained until a later influx of blown sand caused a deterioration in the coastal area. Cefntreffraw, Treberfedd, Trefriw and Dinllwydan were all reckoned-land hamlets but within the manor there were also a number of free tenants. As the more detailed extent of 1352 reveals, these freemen occupied four resting-places and one 'holding'.[1] There was one resting-place in Bodfeurig, another alongside some bond holdings in Trefwaspadrig, and a third in Trefgornor.[2] The occupants of the remaining resting-place, that of the Gate-keepers, were responsible for making and repairing a length of wall on either side of the gateway into the Prince's court. Since the court was a complex of buildings in the southern part of the main settlement, this resting-place must have adjoined Maerdref–Garthau, and the same was probably true of the 'holding' which was ascribed to the Carpenters.

The freemen of Aberffraw manor appear in the main to have been officials with duties at the court. Bondmen of local and outlying hamlets also served the court and before the conquest had been responsible together with freemen for erecting the buildings of the court. But their main duty was the cultivation of the demesnes (*tir bwrdd*), the mensal land or board land of the court, which amounted to 5 carucates (in theory 300 acres). One of these carucates was in an outlier of Aberffraw at Trecastell but the remainder were in the main part of the manor to the north and southwest of Maerdref–Garthau (Fig. 10.4).

Despite the commutation of labour services, the dismantling of the hall before 1317, and the farming out of the manor throughout the later Middle Ages,[3] much of the medieval pattern survived into the sixteenth and seventeenth centuries. Lawsuits brought by rival members of the gentry provide evidence that the demesnes of the Crown, the tenants' lands, and the glebe land for the support of the parish incumbent still lay intermingled in open field.[4] The arable parcel named *y dalar gam* (the crooked headland), which lay well to the north of Aberffraw 'within a bowe shute of the said towne', was still bounded by turf

[1] *Record of Caernarvon*, pp. 48–9.
[2] P.R.O., S.C. 6/1154/5.
[3] Seebohm, *The Tribal System in Wales*, App. A e; P.R.O., *Black Prince's Register*, I, 1930, p. 130; P.R.O., D.L. 29/633/10,312; S.C. 6/1180/3; 1154/5; S.P. 1/236/fo. 325.
[4] E. G. Jones (ed.), *Exchequer Proceedings (Equity) Concerning Wales*, 1939, pp. 17–26; Lewis and Davies (eds.), *Records of the Court of Augmentations*, pp. 12–14.

balks and 'mearestones'.[1] There was still opportunity therefore for ploughmen to practise illegal intrusions on behalf of their gentle-born employers. By 1608, some 687 acres of the manor were in the hands of the free tenants but Sir Hugh Owen held over a third of these and also claimed to hold all the bond and demesne lands of Maerdref–Garthau by letters patent.[2] Yet his triumph was not complete, for among his tenants in the village itself was Sir Richard Meyrick; and in *Maes y Maerdref* (the Open field of the Reeve's Settlement), which then contained almost 65 acres, one of Sir Hugh's three tenants was a landed gentleman.

By this date, over a third of the lands of Maerdref–Garthau had been enclosed in fields of up to 36 acres and, as a result, some large farmhouses had been established outside the village. Nevertheless Maerdref–Garthau, still the setting for a market and fair, remained an important nucleation. A mere three acres of free land with a capital messuage had come to be occupied by 14 houses, 6 other buildings and 12 gardens, and further infilling of settlement had occurred on some former bond gardens. Some of the outlying settlements had also survived. Treberfedd, occupied by nine bondmen in 1294, contained eleven dwellings in 1608, and Trefriw which was occupied by at least four families in 1294, still supported three households in 1608. Already however Sir Richard Meyrick exercised sole rights in the southern bond hamlets. Here at Dinllwydan and Treberfedd tenant holdings of over 100 acres had already emerged, though Trefriw still contained only small-holdings. Characteristically, by the mid-nineteenth century all three settlements were compact ring-fence farms of over 100 acres.[3] In Maerdref–Garthau on the other hand the rivalries between the gentry continued. Thus quillets in intermingled ownership as well as a small area of open field survived near the village down to the late nineteenth century, and to this day the manorial common to the east of the village remains unenclosed.[4]

Since there were 400 acres of common in the manor in 1608 the greater part of the land within the hamlets of Aberffraw could be used for cultivation. Of the total area of 688 acres of bond and demesne land in Maerdref–Garthau no less than 533 acres were arable and

---

[1] P.R.O., E. 178/3307; U.C.N.W., Penrhyn Ms. 68.

[2] P.R.O., L.R. 2/205, fos. 45–55.

[3] Jones, *Trans. Inst. Brit. Geogr.*, XIX, 1953, pp. 66–9: P.R.O., Tithe Apportionment and Map, Aberffraw Parish, 1843; U.C.N.W., Bodorgan Mss. 862, 1579.

[4] Jones, *Anglesey Antiqu. Soc. Trans.*, 1955, pp. 81–4; Jones, *Geography as Human Ecology*, pp. 209, 211–14; D. R. Denman, R. A. Roberts and H. J. F. Smith, *Commons and Village Greens*, 1967, pp. 110–13; U.C.N.W., Tynygongl Ms. 775; Bodorgan Mss. 871–80, 1625; Bodorgan Estate Office: Bodorgan Ms. 1588; Aberffraw Manor Court Book; Manor Court Correspondence 15/3.

a further 130 acres, described as 'arable and pasture', were probably used for temporary cultivation. In the thirteenth century also, to judge from the customary renders of the bondmen and the assessments to a lay subsidy of 1293, arable farming had loomed quite large in the manorial economy.[1] But although winter and spring cereals were cultivated they were not in equal proportion, and in the evidence for Aberffraw there is no hint of a field system with a communally organised rotational sequence.

(ii) *The Dinorben estate*. Despite the Edwardian conquest only in a few places in North Wales was any attempt made to develop and systematise demesne farming.[2] Among these was the Welsh demesne vill of Dinorben Fawr (Denb.), focus of an ancient multiple estate dating possibly even from the Late Bronze Age when the local hill fort was first constructed.[3]

When the manor was surveyed in detail in 1334 there were 201 local acres (255 statute acres) of demesne arable land 'converted into three seasons', with 67a. or. 15p. in the first season, 64a. 1r. 30p. in the second, and 69a. 2r. 31p. in the third. The first season was '*in ij culturis*' in the 'Spitelfeld' The second season, as the diagrammatic reconstruction (Fig. 10.5) shows, was in two pieces to the west of Spitelfeld and '*in ij forlongis*' to the south as far as the 'king's highway' below *Pendinas*, as the hill fort was then known. The third season was partly to the north of the king's highway and partly to the south.[4] All this arable land to the north of the highway was worth 1s. 3d. per acre whereas that to the south was worth only 1s. per acre.

In addition there were 40a. 2r. *de veteri frisco* in the *cultura* called the *Maerdref* (Reeve's Settlement). These were deemed not to be worth 'converting' into seasons because they were barren, possibly as a result of an exhausting 'infield' system of cultivation. Valued at only 6d. per acre, they were used instead for the pasturing of sheep. Of the demesne arable there remained 1a. 3r. 39p. which could be sown every year and were valued at 1s. 8d. per acre.

The demesne meadows, amounting to some 23 local acres worth 60s. 8d., lay partly in the large meadow, partly in the Spitelfeld, and partly among the arable lands below the Spitelfeld. The several pasture in demesne amounted to about 72 acres. Of this area 66a. 1r. 30p.

[1] P.R.O., S.C. 11/769: E. 179/242/49 printed in App. A to Seebohm, *The Tribal System in Wales*.
[2] W. Rees, *South Wales and the March, 1284-1415*, 1924, p. 31.
[3] G. R. J. Jones, 'The Pattern of Settlement on the Welsh Border', *Agric. Hist. Rev.*, VIII, 1960, pp. 76-8; Willoughby Gardner and H. N. Savory, *Dinorben*, 1964.
[4] *Survey of Denbigh*, pp. 230-3; P.R.O., L.R. 2/235, fos. 21-2; N.L.W., Lordship of Ruthin Ms. 1704.

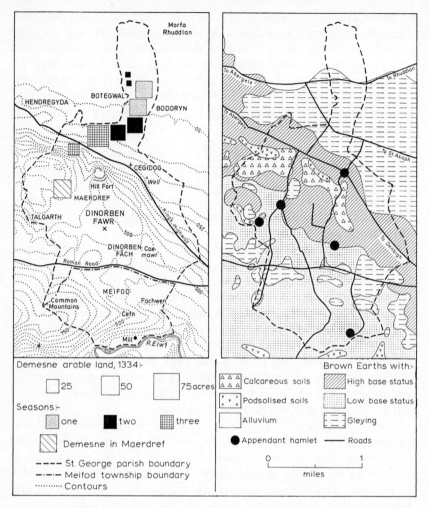

Fig. 10.5 The Dinorben district, Denbighland, in 1334.

Sources. Compiled from: *Survey of the Honour of Denbigh, 1334*; P.R.O., C. 134/22, S.C. 6/1182/1, D.L. 29/1/2, E. 178/5929, L.R. 2/235, L.R. 2/238, L.R. 2/240; N.L.W. Ms. 12647F, Lordship of Ruthin Ms. 1764; U.C.N.W., Kinmel Mss. 38, 600, 615, 619, 690; the tithe maps and awards for Meifod, 1840, and St George, 1840; published and unpublished Denbighshire maps of the Soil Survey of England and Wales.

worth 1s. 3d. per acre lay in the marsh – to the north of Spitelfeld – called *le Frith*; the remainder, which was less valuable, lay in various places including the field (*campus*) above Spitelfeld, the area below Pendinas, and the wood extending from Pendinas, along either side of *le longe clogh*, to the door of the manor. Pendinas wood, extending over some 34 acres, then consisted of weak underwood which could be coppiced every twelve years and was also used for pasture.

Apart from some 28 acres of land arrented to individuals at the will of the lord, the only other component of the manor was the 'hamlet' of Maerdref (Reeve's Settlement). This was inhabited by *nativi* who contributed to the lord a joint render of 35s. 10d. for all rents, customs and works. In return they held communally (*inter se hereditarie*) the hamlet, which seems to have contained about 287 local acres (241 statute acres). Of this, 40a. 2r. 30p. in the *cultura* had been converted into demesne and 38a. 2r. worth 8d. per acre were arrented. These arrented lands were part of the lord's share of escheat, possibly the holding of a former *maer* (reeve). The community of the vill (*communitas ville*) held 22 acres of arable from this share and, in addition, rented 18 acres of 'land and waste' for use as herbage.

The survey of 1334 records that in the time of the Welsh Princes the *nativi* of the Maerdref had performed various customs and works at the manor of Dinorben. In their tasks they had been aided by the *nativi* of Cegidog, Dinorben Fach and Meifod (Fig. 10.5) who, by 1334, paid a cash rent in lieu of ploughing and harrowing. The incidence of ploughing and harrowing varied according to the numbers of *nativi* possessing ploughs. To judge from the rate and payment recorded in 1334, the 44 *nativi* of the three townships at this date possessed between them only nine ploughs so that they themselves were obliged to practise co-aration.[1] In addition the tenants of Talgarth, which consisted of a bond resting-place, had at one time performed the services appropriate for half a plough team, but later they had left because of need, and their tenements had been let to others. By 1334, Talgarth lay vacant for lack of tenants and, for want of other pasture, was grazed by the sheep of the manor of Dinorben.

This manor, which had been granted after the Edwardian conquest to Henry de Lacy, Lord of Denbigh, was retained in direct exploitation, a policy in keeping with the creation within the lordship of new manors at Denbigh, Cilffwrn and Wigfair.[2] In 1305 the revenue from the manor was nearly nine times that expected in 1297, when the manor appears to have been suffering from the depredations of a

---

[1] *Survey of Denbigh*, pp. 223, 270.
[2] D. H. Owen, 'The Lordship of Denbigh; 1282–1425', Ph.D. thesis, University of Wales, 1967, pp. 209, 214.

Welsh revolt. Despite difficulties reflected in increasing expenses, manorial activities had expanded considerably and substantial revenues came from the sale of wheat and oats.[1] A grange and other buildings had been improved in the previous year and a new grange for hay constructed. In the northward projection of the manor, towards the ill-drained lands of Morfa Rhuddlan, 94 perches of ditch had been cut (Fig. 10.5).[2] A continuation of such drainage activities probably accounts for the discrepancy between the 120 acres of arable demesne recorded for 1311 and the much larger figure for 1334.[3] Certainly by 1334 the area of arable demesne had been extended, from the most desirable brown earths of high base status below the limestone ridge, northwards on to imperfectly drained brown earths now subject to gleying.[4] The disproportion between oats and wheat in the manorial account of 1305 suggests that there was no systematically organised rotation at that date. It was probably the subsequent extension of the arable lands which made possible the organisation of three seasons by 1334.

Already by 1305 however the demesne was being worked in severalty, hence a marked reliance on hired labour in place of the commuted customary services of the *nativi*. Demesne farming on this basis was still practised in 1331 and probably also in 1334.[5] But references to demesne lands notwithstanding, the concentration in the 1334 *Survey of Denbigh* on land values signifies that Dinorben was considered as a rent-contributing unit rather than a centre for demesne agriculture, an impression confirmed by the ruined state of a dovecote and of one of the two granges.[6] The manor, though still functioning in 1334, was evidently in a state of decline and by 1356 had been granted to a burgess of Denbigh.[7] Later in the century Dinorben experienced the kind of population decline that occurred in many bond settlements,[8] and after the Glyn Dŵr rebellion 'decayed rents' were prominent in official accounts.[9]

Despite subsequent recovery, the leasing of the manor and of neighbouring escheat lands contributed to the consolidation of private

[1] P.R.O., D.L. 29/1/1; 29/1/2.
[2] P.R.O., D.L. 29/1/2.
[3] P.R.O., C. 134, File 22, m. 23(d).
[4] *Memoirs of the Soil Survey of Great Britain*: D. F. Ball, *The Soils and Land Use of the District around Rhyl and Denbigh*, 1960, pp. 33–4, 55–7.
[5] P.R.O., S.C. 6/1182/1.
[6] Owen, Ph.D. thesis, pp. 210–11.
[7] G. A. Holmes, *The Estates of the Higher Nobility in Fourteenth-Century England*, 1957, pp. 96–7, 129.
[8] P.R.O., S.C. 6/1182/4.
[9] Owen, Ph.D. thesis, pp. 214–16.

estates in the district.[1] It was by such means that a branch of the prolific Holland family came to dominate at Dinorben. By the end of the fifteenth century the demesne farm of Fardre (*Maerdref*) was occupied by Griffith ap David Holland who built the massive house which still remains.[2] The Holland family then acquired a firm foothold by leasing the manor of Dinorben at least from 1534. In Elizabethan times the manor, still called *tir y llys* (court land), consisted of some 50 acres of arable, 219 acres of 'arable and pasture', 4 acres of meadow, and 9 acres of underwood. It was divided into some very large parcels. Thus, between the road leading from Abergele to Denbigh and that from Abergele to St Asaph, one parcel of arable contained 30 acres, and in the area to the north of the road to St Asaph was a parcel containing no less than 65 acres of 'arable land and pasture' (Fig. 10.5).[3] The same manor, containing only 276 acres and valued at nearly £54 per annum, was held by David Holland for a mere £8 per annum in 1608. Finally, in 1614, he purchased it from the Crown, along with six tenements and 144 acres of land in the township of Cegidog.[4]

Meanwhile the Holland family had acquired by lease or purchase numerous holdings in the vicinity of Dinorben,[5] and, as compared with 1334, a significant transformation of the tenurial scene had already been effected. Of the 245 acres of 'land, wood and waste' in the township of Cegidog in 1334 some 98 acres were escheat and farmed out to individuals and, in part, to the township community.[6] By Elizabethan times the escheat was reduced, probably by encroachment, to about 75 acres but all of these were in the hands of Piers Holland.[7] His escheat or 'divisible lands' were fragmented like the components of a typical resting-place holding and the constituent parcels ranged in size from half a rood, near the village, to 4 acres at Cae Mawr and 18 acres nearby (Fig. 10.5). Intermingled with this escheat and the lands of some freeholders were a further 137a. 2r. of lordship lands in eight parcels and again held by Piers Holland.[8] Near the church hamlet of Cegidog (alias St George) these parcels contained only two or three acres and were described as 'good arable ground' valued at 40d. per acre. The largest parcel contained 92a. 2r. valued in 1583 at 20d. per acre – as compared with 6d. per acre in 1334. It extended southwards over the ridge and the greater part was described

[1] P.R.O., E. 178/5929; N.L.W., Ms. 12647F.
[2] E. G. Jones (ed.), U.C.N.W., *Schedule of Kinmel Manuscripts and Documents*, 1953.
[3] P.R.O., L.R. 2/235, fos. 21–2.
[4] P.R.O., L.R. 2/240, fo. 14; U.C.N.W., Kinmel Mss. 615, 619.
[5] P.R.O., E. 178/5929; Kinmel Mss. 38, 600, 690.
[6] *Survey of Denbigh*, pp. 225–7.
[7] P.R.O., L.R. 2/235, fo. 22.
[8] P.R.O., L.R. 2/238, fos. 61–2; N.L.W., Lordship of Ruthin Ms. 1704.

as 'barren arable grounde bearinge corne by means of burninge but
not otherwise'. This was presumably the practice, described by
Camden for west Denbighshire shortly afterwards, whereby turves
were pared and burnt to ashes, 'which being throwne upon the
ground so pared, and flayed, causeth the hungrey barrainnesse therof
so to fructifie that the fields bring forth a kinde of Rhie or Amel
corne'.[1]

Tenurial changes had also taken place in neighbouring Meifod, a
township of 360 acres of 'land and waste'. This in 1334 was shared
by two bond lineages and one privileged free lineage. In that year the
escheat amounted to 81 acres of 'land and waste' with the greater
part valued at 6d. per acre or less and presumably therefore used only
for temporary cultivation.[2] By Elizabethan times the escheat had
increased to 103 acres. It then comprised the following: two messuages
with a parcel of 46 acres 'arable and pasture' adjoining the 'comon
mountaynes'; four messuages and a parcel of 42 acres 'arable and
pasture' likewise adjoining the common; and one messuage with 15
acres 'arable and pasture' near Fachwen (Fig. 10.5).[3] This escheat
was in the hands of 'divers tenants'. Among them was the above-
mentioned Piers Holland who in 1583 also held here no less than
187 acres of the lordship lands, an area about ten times larger than the
average individual holding of 'land and waste' in the Meifod resting-
places in 1334. These lordship lands lay in three parcels separated by
the lands of other freeholders but divided into 'several closes and fields'
and occupied by various under-tenants. The parcel by the River Elwy
contained some 63 acres of 'very barren arable grounde' valued in
1583 at only 12d. per acre so that 'for the moste parte after two or
three yeares cropes being had will beare no more grayne in ten or
twelve yeares after'.[4] Nevertheless it was 'mownded very well' and
had 'some scatteringe trees in the hedgerows'. The second parcel
contained 10 acres in two closes at Cefn; valued at 12d. per acre, it
was considered to be little better than the first though 'well mounded
for ye moste parte with quicksett' and having 'more store of trees
for ye quantitie than ye other'. The third parcel, again for the most
part 'mounded with quicksett', extended to the northern edge of the
township and contained 114 acres valued at 24d. per acre. Some 5 or
6 acres were 'course medoe' and the rest 'all arable and pasture' with,
significantly, a distinction drawn between the arable ground, which
was 'indifferent good for a great part', and the rest, which bore corn

[1] William Camden, Britannia, 1607 (translated by Philemon Holland, 1637), p. 575.
[2] Survey of Denbigh, pp. 222–5.
[3] P.R.O., L.R. 2/235, fo. 28; L.R. 2/238, fo. 1.
[4] P.R.O., L.R. 2/238, fo. 61.

only by burning. Yet it was 'a far better soyle than the firste parte of this farme'.

The estates patiently built up in this fashion by the Hollands was retained in the family until the eighteenth century. It was then sold three times, finally in 1786 passing into the possession of the Rev. Edward Hughes, the wealthy father of the first Lord Dinorben. By 1840 Lord Dinorben owned more than nine-tenths of Meifod. His sixteen farms in the township as would be expected were all enclosed and, with only one exception, formed compact units. In the remainder of the parish Lord Dinorben's predominance was even more marked, for less than a twentieth of the land was in the possession of other landowners. Near the hamlet of St George some fragmented small-holdings and intermingled quillets of glebe still retained something of their medieval dispositions but elsewhere ring-fence farms were characteristic. Among them was Fardre, a compact enclosed farm of 133 acres, where only the names *Cae henllan* (Field of the old church) and *Cae popty* (Kiln field) remained to give any hint of the presence in the Middle Ages of a hamlet community at Maerdref.[1]

(e) Tir corddlan (*nucleal land*)

The fate of the 'gardens' of nucleal land appears to have been determined by that of the surrounding expanses of reckoned land or hereditary land. At Aberffraw the hamlet known as Garthau was probably nucleal land, with the 'gardenmen' as the Welsh equivalents of the cottars sometimes recorded in the Domesday manors of England as living around the hall of the lord.[2] Two gardens still adjoined the ruins of the capital messuage of Aberffraw in 1608,[3] and since the court was sited near the southwestern end of the village, where open field quillets survived in 1827, it is possible that some at least of these quillets were originally nucleal land. Similarly the small area of arable land in the manor of Dinorben Fawr which could be sown every year was probably nucleal land, but it disappeared with the consolidation of the township; and the same appears to have been true of the *due crofte incluse* around the court of Ystrad Owain.[4]

The best opportunities for the survival of nucleal land existed in the older nuclei of settlement around important churches, where the glebe land used for the maintenance of the parish incumbent has often

---

[1] P.R.O., Tithe Apportionments and Maps: Meifod, 1840; St George, 1840; Tithe Files: 14292, 14248.
[2] *Domesday Book*, fos. 163, 175; P.R.O., S.C. 11/789; *Record of Caernarvon*, pp. 48–50.
[3] P.R.O., L.R. 2/205, fo. 51; Jones, *Geography as Human Ecology*, pp. 209, 211–15.
[4] *Survey of Denbigh*, pp. 2, 230.

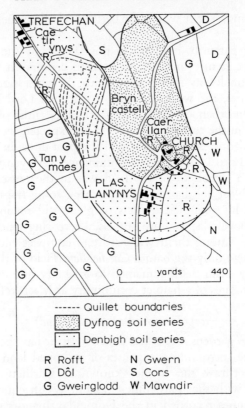

Fig. 10.6 The setting of the sharelands at Llanynys, Vale of Clwyd, in 1841.
Sources. Compiled from the tithe map and award for Llanynys, 1841; unpublished
Denbighshire maps of the Soil Survey of England and Wales.

remained fragmented and intermingled with the lands of laymen.[1]
In many parishes the glebe parcels lay not only in outlying 'fields' but
also near the church hamlet on land named *Maes y llan* (Open field
of the church). Such was the case in lowland parishes like Ruabon
(Denb.) or Llandrinio (Mont.), and also in upland parishes like
Gwytherin (Denb.) or Hirnant (Mont.).[2]

The best example of a late-surviving *Maes y llan* (Open field of the
church) – which still contains fast-disappearing traces of arable quillets
though no glebe land – is that on either side of the road from Llanynys
to Trefechan (Fig. 10.6) in the Vale of Clwyd (Denb.). Since the
core of the church hamlet of Llanynys also contains some rare

[1] Cf. M. W. Beresford, 'Glebe Terriers and Open Field, Yorkshire', *Yorkshire Arch. Jnl.*, XXXVII, 1951, pp. 325–68.
[2] N.L.W., Welsh Church Commission Mss., St Asaph Terriers 512, 144, 224, 162.

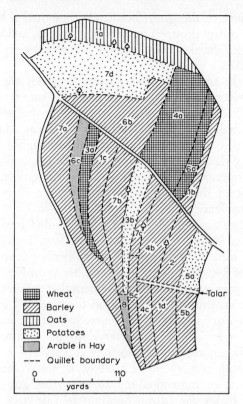

Fig. 10.7 *Maes isa* (Lower open field) and *Maes ucha* (Upper open field),
Llanynys, in 1841.
Sources. Based on the tithe map and award for Llanynys, 1841.

surviving traces of nucleal land (*tir corddlan*) this example merits
close examination.

In *Maes isa* (Lower open field), to the west of the road, and *Maes ucha* (Upper open field), to the east, there were until 1971 quillets in divided ownership delimited only by means of turf balks. Until they were ploughed out in 1970 and 1971 most of these were about 18 inches wide, the width stipulated in the Welsh laws. An old oak tree on a balk in *Maes isa*, the sole survivor of seven trees on the balks in 1841 (Fig. 10.7), served as a reminder of the high value placed on the oak in the laws and provided some measure of the antiquity of the local open field. Further evidence of long-continued cultivation was provided until 1971 by the long quillets on the western side of *Maes isa*, for these bore some resemblance to strip lynchets formed by soil creep. Moreover, the elevation of the headland (*talar*) known as *Erw dalar green* (Acre of the green headland) suggested a long-continued accumulation of soil dropped by turning ploughs, and the deposition, along the slight barrier thus formed, of dust blown from freshly ploughed quillets.

Even now the ancient 'kings highway' between *Maes isa* and *Maes ucha* is little wider than the 12 Welsh feet (9 statute feet) stipulated in the lawbooks but, over recent years, access to the quillets was provided along the roadside hedgerows. The occupants arranged the cultivation of their quillets so as to facilitate access for their neighbours, but within living memory there were no communal arrangements for cultivation or even for common of shack. Thus, when the quillets were grazed, farmers restricted their animals to their own quillets by means of temporary wire fences.

In 1841, *Maes isa* and *Maes ucha* were divided into more quillets and were shared by more owners than at present. Together containing 15a. or. 34p. they then comprised 21 quillets of arable land which formed part of 8 distinct holdings as numbered on Fig. 10.7.[1]

For earlier periods it is perhaps no accident that the precise antecedents of this pattern are difficult to determine, for it was alleged in the early seventeenth century that most of the records of the manor had been deliberately cut into 'taylors measures' to the disinheritance of the Crown.[2] Sufficient records however have survived to show that in the mid-sixteenth century many holdings of free tenants of the king in this locality were fragmented in much the same way as the holdings of 1841, and that some fifteen holdings in Llanynys *and* Trefechan were held in 'free tenure by gavelkind'.[3] These records confirm the occasional hint in records of the fourteenth and fifteenth centuries that there was a considerable amount of hereditary land (*tir gwelyog*) in the district.[4] Entries on court rolls of the fifteenth century reveal that there was at least some hereditary land in *Maes isa* and *Maes ucha*. Thus a vifgage (*tir prid*) holding in the township was described in 1441 as 'the hedges of Yokkyn and two lands in the fields of Llanynys' (*clothia Yokkyn et duas seliones in campis de Llanenys*); and in 1444 a parcel of hereditary land on either side of the way from Llanynys to Trefechan was exchanged for the hereditary lands of some co-heirs lying in the fields (*in campis*) called *Maes y llan*.[5]

---

[1] P.R.O., Tithe Apportionment and Map, Llanynys Parish, 1841.
[2] T. I. J. Jones (ed.), *Exchequer Proceedings Concerning Wales*, 1955, p. 165.
[3] N.L.W., Lordship of Ruthin Ms. 1593; N.L.W., Ms. 86; P.R.O., L.R. 2/239, fos. 180–2.
[4] N.L.W., Bachymbyd Mss. 51, 482, 483, 519; P.R.O., S.C. 12/23/42: 24/1; Wales 15/8.
[5] P.R.O., S.C. 2/222/4, ms. 1, 20.

Some of the land in Llanynys was bond, and four bond holdings were recorded for the township in 1484. There is evidence, moreover, to suggest that the original core of the church hamlet consisted of bond tenements.[1] At an early date some of these appear to have been alienated for the support of the Celtic *clas* (church community) of Llanynys, formerly one of the richest in North Wales.[2] It is appropriate therefore that some late surviving elements of the field pattern in the immediate vicinity of Llanynys church should resemble nucleal land as described in the laws.

Among the parcels of glebe land scattered in various parts of Llanynys parish were formerly some quillets arranged in radial fashion around the roughly circular churchyard.[3] One was the croft (*rofft*), of the 1841 survey, on the southwest of *Cae'r llan* (Enclosure of the Church) and extending northwestwards from the lane around the northwestern edge of the churchyard (Fig. 10.6). This radial parcel had its end virtually 'to the churchyard' as in the laws. In the glebe terriers it was well named as *Clwtt yn y gerddi duon* (Piece in the black gardens), for constant cultivation and manuring has long since darkened its naturally reddish-brown soils of the Dyfnog series. The terriers also reveal that the part of *Cae'r llan* to the northeast of this parcel was likewise once known as *Gerddi duon* (Black gardens). To judge from the ancient cottage gardens to the immediate east of *Cae'r llan* these former black gardens had also been disposed radially around the northwestern side of the churchyard.

Before an exchange of land which took place in the early nineteenth century there had been two further parcels of glebe on *Bryn castell* (Castle hill). One was *Gardd llidiard y bengam* (Garden at the gate of the crooked head), which flanked the road; the second, named *Cefn ym mryn y castell* (Ridge or butt in Castle hill), was bounded on the south by *Gardd llidiard y bengam* but, as the terrier of 1808 recorded, 'inter-runs from thence Northward *c.* 119 yards to a stone in the ground within the said *Bryn y castell*'. If, as seems likely, the black gardens were part of the regularly manured and cultivated nucleal land, or infield, of Llanynys then the parcels in *Bryn castell* probably represent a secondary extension. Hence perhaps the contrast between *Clwtt yn y gerddi duon*, which like the 'acre' of the south Welsh lawbooks was about 75 yards in length, and *Cefn ym mryn y castell*

---

[1] P.R.O., S.C. 12/24/1; 23/42; G. R. J. Jones, 'The Llanynys Quillets; A measure of Landscape Transformation in North Wales', *Denbighshire Hist. Soc. Trans.*, XIII, 1964, pp. 148–50.

[2] P.R.O., *Calendar of Papal Letters: IV (1362–1404)*, 1902, p. 349; G. Williams, *The Welsh Church from Conquest to Reformation*, 1962, pp. 17–18, 158, 168.

[3] Llanynys Glebe Terriers: 1671, 1697, 1749, 1808, 1811.

which, with 119 yards, was but one yard shorter than the legal 'acre' of north Wales. Many of the quillets in *Maes isa* and *Maes ucha* were even longer and probably represent the result of a still later transition from temporary outfield cultivation to the permanent cropping of resting-place land.

In Llanynys township the first lands to be cultivated were undoubtedly the well-drained sandy loams of the Dyfnog series occupying the relatively elevated island site near the church. Only later was cultivation extended on to the heavier, though still well-drained, silty clay loams of the Denbigh series; but even these, as the name *Cae tir ynys* (Enclosure of island land) near Trefechan implies, were raised above the floor of the vale (Fig. 10.6). The meadow (*dôl, gweirglodd*), on the other hand, to judge from field names, was located on the floor of the vale, often, as in *Tan y maes* (Below the open field), on the edge of the arable land; while the common pasture with its alder marsh (*gwern*) bog (*cors*), and turbary (*mawndir*), occupied the most poorly drained land.[1] There were therefore obvious physical limits to the extension of cultivation in Llanynys, hence the ultimate breakdown of hereditary land (*tir gwelyog*) tenure. The land nearest the church, the first to be settled, was the earliest to be fragmented by partible succession, and thus became the scene of the earliest estate-consolidation in the township. Already by the mid-sixteenth century some of the original nucleal land to the southwest of the church appears to have been absorbed into the capital messuage, Plas Llanynys, with its 120 acres of 'divers lands, appurtenances and pastures'.[2] The same was true of some butts (*kefne*) in *Maes y llan*, but, unlike the nucleal land, these retained much of their original character. This persistence of the old order in *Maes y llan* was probably due in part to its later colonisation but, since the Denbigh soils are inherently richer than the Dyfnog soils, conservatism here may also reflect an awareness of subtle variations in soil quality on the part of peasant proprietors.[3]

(f) The later general evidence of enclosure

As the example of Llanynys suggests, estate-builders operated wherever opportunity offered, seizing on the distinctions between customary tenures only when it served their advantage. Indeed, mere-stones and

---

[1] N.L.W., Rûg Ms. 289.

[2] N.L.W., Ms. 1593E; Bachymbyd Ms. 520; Crosse of Shaw Hill Collection, no. 708; Rûg Ms. 910; Jones, *Denbighshire Hist. Soc. Trans.*, XIII, 1964, pp. 151–6.

[3] N.L.W., Wynnstay (1952) Mss. 9/10; 91/5; Memoirs of the Soil Survey of Great Britain: Ball, *The Soils and Agriculture of the District around Rhyl and Denbigh*, pp. 39–45. I am particularly indebted to Mr D. F. Ball for his comments on the soils of *Maes y llan*.

bounds were often deliberately removed to facilitate their activities. With the formal abolition in the sixteenth century of the Welsh customary practices of land inheritance, and the continued progress of consolidation, now accelerated by the frequent leasing of Crown bond land and the purchase of monastic land, the distinctions between hereditary land, reckoned land and nucleal land had become increasingly blurred.[1] The erection of quickset hedges or walls accelerated the process. Glebe terriers of some thirty parishes in the uplands and lowlands of eastern North Wales in the 1630s confirm that open field arable had once been widespread.[2] The same sources and, less frequently, maps of the eighteenth and nineteenth centuries, record the existence of open fields which had once been extensive.[3] Multiple open fields are sometimes recorded for each settlement, as for example at Gwaenysgor (Flint.) or Llandrinio (Mont.), though there is nothing to suggest a communally organised rotational sequence for these fields.

With the progress of enclosure, parcels of arable bounded only by 'meares of earth' or 'lynchards' became much less characteristic, though hedgerows were not always successful.[4] Thus in Maes y Cae (Denb.) the 'mounds' were 'very bad and chargable to mayntayne' apparently because of the burning necessary to make the barren soil bear corn.[5] Again, as John Leland was informed in the sixteenth century, 'in tyme of mynde menne usid not in Termone [i.e. Anglesey] to separate their grounde, but now stille more and more they digge stony hillokkes yn theyre groundes, and with the stones of them *rudely congestid* [my italics] they devide theyre groundes after Devonshire fascion'.[6] But in parts of Anglesey the transformation must have been gradual for in 1704 Henry Rowland could write that cattle were constantly treading or eating corn 'lying open or very weakly fenced'; so that the 'every way necessary assistance and defence of husbandry consists chiefly in good fences and inclosures'. He added that 'if the fields be cleared of stones which lie dispersed and in rows as are the old boundaries or *terfynau*, in many places upon them, there accrues

---

[1] T. Jones Pierce, 'Notes on the History of Rural Caernarvonshire in the Reign of Elizabeth', *Trans. Caernarvonshire Hist. Soc.*, II, 1940, pp. 1–23; W. Ogwen Williams (ed.), *Calendar of the Caernarvonshire Quarter Sessions Records*, I, 1956, pp. lix–lxxvi; G. R. J. Jones, 'Die Entwicklung der ländlichen Besiedlung in Wales', *Zeitschrift für Agrargeschichte und Agrarsoziologie*, x, 1962, pp. 191–4.
[2] B. M. Evans, Ph.D. thesis, pp. 162–73.
[3] D. Sylvester, 'The Rural Landscape of Eastern Montgomeryshire', *Mont. Coll.*, LIV, 1955, pp. 14–26.
[4] N.L.W., Welsh Church Commission Mss., St Asaph Terriers, 211, 496, cited in Evans, Ph.D. thesis, pp. 162–73.
[5] L.R. 2/238, fo. 74.
[6] John Leland, *The Itinerary in Wales*, L. T. Smith (ed.), 1906, p. 90.

thereby a double benefit, viz., good clear ground and securely fenced'.[1] Nevertheless the 'conveniences' attributed by Rowland to consolidated lands were not always satisfied, for even in the nineteenth century there were still 26 Anglesey parishes whose glebe lay scattered.[2]

By this date the enclosure of arable land in the lowlands had been virtually consummated, save in a few restricted localities easily overlooked by any save the most careful observer. Thus the only 'commonfields, or fields in run-rig' specifically recorded in the Board of Agriculture Reports for North Wales in the period 1794–6 were those which lay between Flint and St Asaph.[3] On the other hand vast tracts of upland pasture and smaller areas of coastal and valley waste remained open.[4] In the period from about 1733 to 1869, but especially during the Napoleonic Wars when food prices were high, the lowland wastes and also large parts of the uplands were enclosed.[5] As the population grew in numbers, particularly during the eighteenth and nineteenth centuries, the pressure on the land became considerable. The large enclosures created in the uplands from the sixteenth century onwards came to be leap-frogged in many places by squatters. It was believed, albeit mistakenly, that if a cottage could be erected on the common in one night by a newly-wed couple and their well-wishers, so that smoke was emitted from the chimney at daylight, then the couple acquired the freehold of the site in perpetuity. Hence the erection on the common pastures of many a *tyunnos* (house of one night) or hastily constructed *clodhall*. Each was set within its own roughly circular enclosure for it was considered that the area which the squatter–bridegroom could claim was determined by the distance he could throw an axe in various directions from his new abode. By the mid-nineteenth century however many of these curvilinear enclosures, laboriously reclaimed by the squatters, had come to be engulfed by large new rectangular enclosures. Often too the squatters' encroachments had been absorbed into the large landed estates of which the rectangular enclosures all too frequently formed a part, thus furthering

[1] Henry Rowland, *Idea Agriculturae* (written by 1704, published 1764), reprinted in *Anglesey Antiqu. Soc. Trans.*, 1936, pp. 54–93.

[2] Jones, *Anglesey Antiqu. Soc. Trans.*, 1955, pp. 31–2.

[3] G. Kay, *Flintshire*, 1794–6, p. 4; Jones, *Zeitschr. f. Agrargeschicte u. Agrarsoziologie*, x, 1962, pp. 186–8.

[4] D. Thomas, *Agriculture in Wales during the Napoleonic Wars*, 1963, pp. 58–9, and especially Fig. 15, p. 64.

[5] A. H. Dodd, 'The enclosure movement in North Wales', *Bulletin of the Board of Celtic Studies*, III, 1926–7, pp. 216–38; Dodd, *The Industrial Revolution in North Wales*, 1933, pp. 53–88; W. L. Davies, 'The Henllan enclosure award', *Bulletin of the Board of Celtic Studies*, IX, 1937–9, pp. 247–71, 367; T. I. J. Jones (ed.), *Acts of Parliament concerning Wales*, 1959, pp. 276–99.

in North Wales that pluralism of society which owed so much to the many-faceted dichotomies between the powerful landlord and his humblest tenants.[1]

With the enclosure of large tracts of the uplands traditional trans-humance finally disappeared. No longer was the *hafod* (summer dwelling) used only during the more genial months of the year when the deciduous grasses of the uplands flourished. Indeed, by an inversion of the old order, many of the new permanent farms established on the hills came to depend on the enclosed pastures of lowland farms for the wintering of sheep. Nevertheless most farmers occupying the lower fringes of the hill country continue to summer their stock in the uplands, either on enclosed pastures or still-unenclosed sheepwalks.[2]

To this day there remain in North Wales large areas of upland 'common', some, like joint land (*cytir*) in the seventeenth century still of uncertain status, an abiding reminder of an ancient agrarian econ-omy. [3]These alone are the only obvious relics of the communal basis of the old order. Thanks to consolidation and enclosure the arable fields once to be found, alike on hereditary land, on reckoned land, and on nucleal land, have disappeared. With the breakdown of local self-sufficiency there gradually developed an increased specialisation in stock farming, so that much of the land formerly used for grain cultivation is now under grass, and large tracts of North Wales are used almost exclusively for pastoral purposes. The resulting pastoral scene may well appear to be an original and obvious response to the local humid climate and broken terrain, but the record of the past provides only limited justification for such an assumption. Many of our best pastures occupy the sites of ancient, and formerly unenclosed patches of grain-land whose appearance has been transformed by changes patiently wrought over the centuries.

[1] *Report of the Royal Commission on Land in Wales, 1894*, pp. 576–97; *Minutes o, Evidence*, v, 1896, pp. 339, 393; U.C.N.W., Mostyn Mss. 2141–2; J. G. Thomas, 'The Distribution of Commons in Part of Arwystli at the Time of Enclosure', *Mont. Coll.*, LIV, 1955, pp. 27–33; Thomas, 'Some enclosure patterns in central Wales', *Geography*, XLII, 1957, pp. 25–36; Thomas, *Agriculture in Wales during the Napoleonic Wars*, pp. 120–41; C. Thomas, 'Enclosure and the Rural Landscape of Merioneth in the Sixteenth Century', *Trans. Inst. Brit. Geogr.*, XLII, 1967, pp. 153–62.

[2] E. Davies, 'Sheep farming in Upland Wales', *Geography*, XX, 1935, pp. 97–111.

[3] *Report of the Royal Commission on Common Land, 1955–1958*, 1958, pp. 251–8.

11

Field Systems of South Wales

BY MARGARET DAVIES

A. INTRODUCTION

In 1578 Rice Merrick described the Vale of Glamorgan as 'a Champyon and open country, without great store of inclosures; for in my time old men reported that they remembred in their youth, that Cattell in summer time, for want of shade, have from the Port Way runne to Barry, which is four miles distant'.[1] The Portway (A48) is now bordered by walls and hedges and is so heavily trafficked that a common through which it passes is no longer grazed; but four and a half centuries ago, cattle, tormented by flies and heat, could escape from children who were herding them on the fallows and common pastures and make their way southwards, unimpeded by fences, to the woods around Barry and to the Bristol Channel shore. Piecemeal enclosure was proceeding in the sixteenth century, but before 1500, the greater part of the low coast plateaux of the Vale of Glamorgan south of the Portway was champion. Other coastal lowlands in South Wales had similar common field patterns and their farmsteads were and are largely clustered in nucleated villages.

The counties of Brecon, Monmouth, Glamorgan, Carmarthen, Pembroke and Cardigan still bear many traces in their lowland landscapes of arable fields which were formerly tilled in common and divided into strips. At Rhosili in Gower, Laugharne in Carmarthenshire and Llan-non in Cardiganshire, large numbers of arable strips separated by balks still exist. Extensive common pastures still cover the hills of South Wales. Breconshire has 151,019 acres of common rough grazings, by far the highest total of any Welsh county. Although strip fields can clearly be seen fossilised into the field patterns of many South Wales lowlands, it has often been claimed that there were no common fields there. Other authors found what were thought to be rare examples.[2] The documentary evidence for the existence of English

---

[1] R. Merrick, *A Booke of Glamorganshire's Antiquities*, ed. J. A. Corbett, 1887, p. 10. Rice Merrick lived near the Portway at Cottrell, 7 miles west of Cardiff.

[2] H. L. Gray, *English Field Systems*, Cambridge, Mass., 1915, p. 186, examined Jacobean surveys and concluded that there was 'only a relatively slight extent of open arable field in which the parcels of tenants were intermixed in Wales'. C. S. and C. S. Orwin, *The Open Fields*, 1954, p. 65, noted that 'there were still

forms of manorial tenure, and of accompanying medieval field systems was set out in detail and analysed by Rees in 1924.[1] This work, and later manorial and tithe surveys, estate maps and enclosure awards, point to the widespread survival of common fields in South Wales until Tudor times, and in some cases until the eighteenth and nineteenth centuries. In view of their persistence it has been thought useful to give a detailed account of their occurrence in each of the six south Welsh counties.

Neither the common fields nor the settlements of the South Wales lowlands were on the same scale as those of the plains of the English Midlands. They were modified by adaptation to a more broken landscape and, in some cases, by contact with Welsh forms of land tenure. The mountain cores of the south Welsh counties remained largely pastoral and were only indirectly exploited by the Anglo-Norman conquerors. But a broad strip of relatively good land, lying mostly below 600 feet, extends from the Gloucestershire border to south Pembrokeshire and from there stretches, narrower and more broken, northwards along the Cardigan Bay coast. Relatively broad valleys of rivers like the Wye, Usk, Towy and Teifi penetrate the hill core of South Wales. Like the coastal lowlands they have provided belts of country along which Anglo-Norman armies, settlers and manorial tenure were diffused. Hoskins has pointed out that 'the topography of the greater part of Devon presented not the slightest obstacle to the development of the open fields'.[2] Neither did the South Wales lowlands, but they are not a level unbroken plain. Undulating dissected coast plateaux, shelves of raised beach, and eroded limestone and sandstone ridges produce great variety of scene. They also produced very varying common fields, ranging from large common arable fields with very numerous selions to small bundles of strips which may have been enclosed from the outset by hedges. This range was paralleled in Normandy, where varying terrain gave rise to the contrasting common fields noted by Marc Bloch.[3]

Common arable fields were widespread in the manors of South Wales by the thirteenth century. Large common fields comparable with those of Mercia are as rare as they are in Devon, but even the small-scale common fields and lowland villages contrast markedly with tenure and settlement patterns in the hilly hinterland.

Open Fields in four townships of Monmouthshire, on the Severn, in the eighteenth century' but could trace no others in the county.
[1] W. Rees, *South Wales and the March, 1284–1415: A Social and Agrarian Study*, 1924.
[2] W. G. Hoskins, *Devon*, 1954, p. 21.
[3] M. Bloch, *Les Caractères Originaux de l'Histoire Rurale Française*, I, Oslo, 1931, p. 57 and plates III, X, XVI.

Communal tenure and cultivation was a feature of the pre-Norman Welsh as it was of English and other peoples who had to tame a difficult environment. Modified Mercian systems of husbandry may have spread across the lower Wye into Monmouthshire well before the Norman invasion of Wales. The manor of Tidenham, which became part of the Norman lordship centred on Chepstow, had common fields around its five hamlets in 956 and they are unlikely then to have been newly laid out.[1] Pre-Norman field systems in the plains of south Monmouthshire could have been modelled on those which existed across the Wye or on others found on intervisible lowlands across the Severn estuary. Contacts between arable lands fronted by marshes in Monmouthshire and Somerset have existed since Neolithic times and cultural ties have often been stronger than those with their respective upland hinterlands.

After England was subdued, William I established his earls at Chester, Shrewsbury and Hereford and invasions of Wales began from these bases. Using the Severn valley the Normans thrust across to Cardiganshire and southward to Pembrokeshire. Advancing up the Wye, they crossed to the Usk valley at Brecon. The Bristol Channel lowlands, and the Channel itself, were used in the conquest of South Wales. By 1135 the lowlands of South Wales were securely held and Marcher lords had founded their largely independent lordships and were building castles and establishing boroughs, amassing demesnes and imposing their manorial pattern on the older system. Little is known in detail of the early phases of anglicisation of land tenure. The thirteenth century saw the full flowering of the manorial system in South Wales. In the fourteenth century the manors began to decay; their decline was accelerated in the fifteenth century by plague and by the Glyn Dŵr revolt during which many manors were devastated.

Welsh land tenure in the lowlands of South Wales had features in common with the Anglo-Norman system which would facilitate the metamorphosis of a Welsh leader's land after it passed to a Norman lord. In both systems the demesne was worked by bondsmen who lived in a cluster of dwellings near the lord's hall and home farm. Communally tilled arable land and meadows lay on the better land around both settlements. Giraldus Cambrensis did not, as has been suggested, describe the late twelfth-century Welsh as wholly pastoral. They laid down the greater part of their land in pasture but on their arable 'they seldom yoke less than four oxen to their ploughs' and they ploughed in March and April for oats and in winter for wheat.[2]

[1] H. P. R. Finberg, *Gloucestershire*, 1955, p. 44.

[2] W. Ll. Williams (ed.), *The Itinerary through Wales and the Description of Wales*, 1908, pp. 166 and 184.

Welsh freemen lived upslope from the bondsmen's village in scattered farms on the lower hillsides. Here there was naturally a greater emphasis on cattle and sheep rearing but arable patches were tilled where soil and slope were favourable. These scatters of upland farms, running along the hillsides and varying in site with aspect, exposure and soil, were characteristic of the Welshries of Norman lordships. The larger lowland bond villages could readily be adapted as Anglo-Norman manors and the Welsh bondsmen incorporated into the manorial system. In the Welshries the freemen continued, throughout the Middle Ages, both their forms of tenure and farming, but paid their tribute of cattle, or sheep, or honey, or oats to the Norman lord who had displaced their Welsh chief. The Domesday renders for unhidated lands west of Offa's Dyke, such as the eastern slopes of the Black Mountains, include many honey rents.[1]

The Englishries and Welshries of Marcher lordships were most readily demarcated from each other in areas where hills rise sharply from the lowlands. The Englishry of Hay centred on the castle and manor in the broad Wye valley; its Welshry was in the Black Mountains. Some Glamorgan lordships included a southern Englishry and a northern Welshry in what became the South Wales coalfield. Others in the Vale of Glamorgan, and in south Pembrokeshire, had large Englishries whose castles, boroughs, and Anglo-Norman manorial pattern could be matched in western England. The field systems discussed below are largely those of the manorialised lowlands which the conquerors considered to be fit for exploitation. The people of the Welshries paid their tribute from the produce of small arable plots and much larger common pastures. Hillsides in many of the Welshries were more densely peopled in the fourteenth century than they now are. Commutation of services was accelerated after the Statute of Wales of 1284. Cash payments became associated with definite holdings and there was no longer a need for the tribal cooperation which had produced tributes of cattle. By the fifteenth century enclosed upland arable fields, farmed in severalty, were more usual than communally cultivated fields. Few of the latter were extant in the eighteenth century. Examples of remnants of common fields are given below.

Throughout South Wales piecemeal enclosure accounted in the main for the disappearance of common fields. A study of widely distributed manors suggested that, by the early seventeenth century, at least half of them were enclosed.[2] Progressive piecemeal enclosure

---

[1] C. W. Atkin in H. C. Darby and I. B. Terrett (eds.), *The Domesday Geography of Midland England*, 1954, p. 69.

[2] T. I. J. Jones, 'The Enclosure Movement in South Wales in the Tudor and Early Stuart Periods', M.A. thesis, University of Wales, 1936, National Library of Wales.

left only a few common fields, mainly in Monmouthshire and Breconshire, to be dealt with by Parliamentary enclosure in the mid-nineteenth century.

B. BRECONSHIRE

More than half of Breconshire is over 1,000 feet high and only the Wye and Usk basins have land lying below 500 feet. The county lends itself to the development of extensive common pastures rather than large common arable fields and meadows. But the lower hillsides and valleys are sheltered and are often underlain by well-drained red or brown soils derived from Devonian rocks, or by alluvium which has been improved by drainage. The middle valleys of the Wye and Usk, and that of the Llynfi which forms the Talgarth Gap between them, proved attractive to the Norman conquerors for both invasion and occupation.

In 1088 Bernard Neufmarché moved up the Wye from Hay into the Welsh territory of Brycheiniog and, through the Talgarth Gap, reached Brecon in 1091. The first castles at Hay, Bronllys and Talgarth were built in 1088 and that at Brecon in 1091–3. The middle Usk valley was occupied after an advance southeastwards from Brecon. Manors within Neufmarché's lordship of Brecon were granted to knights: Ystradyw, focussing on Tretower, went to Picard, Crickhowell to de Turberville. The manorial pattern which gradually evolved displaced the Welsh lowland systems of tenure. At Hay, Brecon and Crickhowell, boroughs soon grew in the shelter of the castles. In the Welshries the hill people slowly adjusted their way of life and their tribute to the new order. A large area between the Brecon Beacons and the Carmarthenshire border was preserved as the Great Forest of Brecknock, a hunting ground for the Norman lords of Brecon. These moorlands became a vast common pasture and were not wholly disafforested until 1815–19.[1]

On the undulating lowlands and lower hillsides of the Wye, Llynfi and Usk valleys, wheat, rye, barley, oats and buckwheat were grown on the common arable fields. The bishop of St David's had a medium-sized manor at Llanddew. The small nucleated village of Llanddew lies 1½ miles north of Brecon at a height of c. 730 feet and is surrounded by land which slopes gently by Breconshire standards; most slopes look into the sun. In 1326, when David Francis, Chancellor of St David's, made his extent, five freeholders and twenty-two copyholders held land in the manor.[2] Some of the twenty-nine cottars also held a little

[1] W. Rees, *The Great Forest of Brecknock*, Brecon, 1966.
[2] J. W. Willis-Bund (ed.), *The Black Book of St David's*, Cymmrodorion Rec. Ser., 5, 1902, pp. 293–306.

land. Money rents and boon works were required of the tenants; land rented by copyholders at 3*d*. an acre varied from 2 to 16 acres. The lord bishop's demesne lay in the common arable fields of Pengaer (32¼ acres), Hasfeld (34½ acres) and Lowefeld (20 acres). These fields were sown with wheat and buckwheat (4½ truggs to the acre), barley (6 truggs) and oats (8 truggs). Oats were expected to yield double and other crops thrice the amount sown. The bishop had two small common meadows of 4 and 2½ acres. His pastures included 9 acres near the village and a larger common pasture at Garthbrengy 2 miles north of Llanddew. On these 6 oxen and 201 sheep could be kept.

Many tenants bore English names in 1326 though Welsh families had been absorbed into the manorial system here as elsewhere. All were required to carry produce to the nearest bishop's vill, Trallwng, up the Usk valley, *en route* to his palace at Llawhaden, in Pembrokeshire, which was then his administrative centre. They would pass *en route* Fenni Fach wood, 2 miles west of Brecon, the common wood of its inhabitants.

The last remnants of the common fields of Llanddew appear on the tithe map of the parish. A few unenclosed 2- or 3-acre pieces are grouped under the names Maes Llanddew Isha and Maes Llanddew Ucha, i.e. Lower and Upper Fields of Llanddew.

Many of the Norman manors of the Usk basin became the estates of progressive Tudor and later squires. Common arable fields and common meadows, like those used by Crickhowell farmers between the town and the Usk or those similarly placed at Brecon, disappeared. By the eighteenth century piecemeal enclosure had completely changed the landscape and given the Usk lowlands their present pattern of well-kept hedges. A mid-eighteenth-century survey of an estate which lay between Brecon and Talybont-on-Usk shows the valley lands as wholly enclosed.[1] On the southward-facing slopes of the Usk valley, the small cluster of farms at Llechfaen, 2 miles east of Brecon, had attenuated common fields as late as the tithe survey of 1839. An estate survey of 1776 shows two small groups of unenclosed strips there.[2] One was east of the village, sloping southwards from an upper margin at 750 feet. The other group lay on the southward facing slope of a knoll 1,000 feet high. Its strips had been reduced to sixteen, some of half an acre, by the enclosure of peripheral strips. One such enclosure was still called Maes Newydd in 1839. Strips in both groups are

[1] M. Jones (surveyor), *An Exact Survey of Abercynrig Estate in the County of Brecon*, 1749, N.L.W., Ms. Maps, vol. 17.
[2] E. Thomas (surveyor), *A Book of Survey of the Estates of the Hon. George Venables Vernon*, 1776, Glamorgan R.O., D/DBF.

described as parts of the *maesydd* or parts of the common fields. Between them and the village, intermixed holdings with some strip fields survived in 1839, but with one exception they were enclosed. Two tenants held alternating strips in the upper field and one of them similarly shared the lower arable strips with a third tenant.

These are relics of common fields which developed well upslope where soils were good and aspect favourable and they probably owed as much to Welsh as to Anglo-Norman forms of land tenure. Llechfaen lay in the Welshry of Pencelli manor. Adjustment to terrain must also be taken into account: small commonable fields, one or two to each hamlet, were a feature of the uplands of northern England and of anglicised areas on the Welsh border.[1]

The most extensive area of mixed farming in present-day Breconshire and the farms with the highest proportion of arable land lie in the triangle between Hay, Talgarth and Llys-wen, i.e. in the Wye and Llynfi basins. It was here that the Normans first entered Breconshire and around the strongpoints which they set up at Bronllys, Llys-wen and Talgarth, considerable manors developed. Remnants of their systems of husbandry survived until the mid-nineteenth century. At Llys-wen 50 acres of commonable fields were enclosed in 1856; the Bronllys award is dated 1860 and relates to 105 acres. South of Talgarth, on the gentle slopes which cradle Llangorse Lake, relics of common fields were revealed by the tithe survey; there was and is a common on the north side of the lake. Between Talgarth and Hay small blocks of strip fields could be found in the mid-nineteenth century on the lower hillsides of the Englishry of Hay, around Llanigon and Oakfield.

Bronllys was a prosperous medieval manor which flourished throughout the plague-ridden fourteenth century. In 1372 it produced good hay and corn crops but, because of the Black Death, parts of the demesne were let and its outlying sheep farm at Bryndu was sold and dismantled.[2] Early enclosure was also facilitated by the Glyn Dŵr revolt of the early fifteenth century; the neighbouring settlement of Court Llaca was destroyed then and its arable, meadow and pasture were let. When the tithe survey was made in 1840 two remnants of common arable fields still adjoined Bronllys village and larger groups of strips lay half a mile northwest and northeast of it. Behind the northern margin of the village closes lay the Maes Bach, whose ten unfenced strips had five tenants. An adjoining enclosure larger than the Maes Bach had the significant name of Close Newydd (New

[1] J. Thirsk (ed.), *The Agrarian History of England and Wales: IV, 1500–1640*, 1967, p. 101.
[2] Rees, *South Wales and the March*, p. 255.

Enclosure). Across the road leading into the west end of the village a formerly minutely fragmented field was almost entirely rearranged, though eight tenants still had intermixed holdings there. One of the small unfenced strips in it was glebe land. Enclosure of the Minfield had also progressed, but there were still twenty-six fenced or unfenced strips in it and six tenants each held from one to nine pieces there. Three pieces were glebe land and one tenant held sixteen pieces in two ownerships, thereby farming some pairs of contiguous strips.

The largest common arable field farmed by Bronllys farmers in 1840 was Colebrook Common Field. It lay northeast of the village, from which it was separated by the large fields north of Bronllys Castle. These appear to be early enclosed demesne land. At the village end, Colebrook Field was divided into West Shoot and East Shoot, each lying on either side of the central access road which bisected the field. Strips northeast of the two shoots, across another access road lying at right-angles to the first, were grouped as the Lowest Shoot. These names appear in an estate survey of c. 1770.[1] In 1840 there were forty-seven unfenced and two enclosed strips in this common arable field and ten tenants each held from one to eighteen disparate pieces there. Some regrouping of selions had produced wider strips in the East Shoot but the Lowest Shoot still lay in one acre or half acre strips. On the enclosed lands north of Colebrook Common Field, holdings of fenced strips and fields were also intermixed.

Colebrook Field was separated from the Llynfi River by narrow water meadows. Around Talgarth, across the Llynfi, the Ashburnham estate survey shows a Lowest Common Field in ten unfenced strips and Brier Common Field in twelve strips, each averaging an acre, south of it. North of Talgarth was a Red Common Field, with six strips, which had formerly extended northwards. Between c. 1770 and the tithe survey further consolidation and enclosure of strips occurred, though remnants named Common Field are found on the tithe map both northwest and southwest of the town. The Brecon and Hay tramroad, opened in 1816, would have disrupted the farming pattern, hastening enclosure of residual field systems around Talgarth.

The village of Llys-wen lies by the Wye at a point where its valley broadens noticeably. The foothills of Mynydd Epynt rise steeply west of the village, sheltering it and formerly providing it with common pasture. A large area of fairly flat land lies above flood level between the village and the meandering Wye. On this land, at a little over 300 feet, the main common field of Llys-wen extended until 1856. In 1840 seven tenants farmed fifty-three strips there. Enclosure of

[1] Book of Survey of the Estates of the Earl of Ashburnham in the County of Brecknock, N.L.W., Ashburnham Welsh Estates, Dep. Mun. 7a.

groups of as many as eight strips into a Close Newydd or Cae Newydd had occurred in four sectors of the field and single strips had also been fenced, but the original pattern of groups of quarter and half acre strips is discernible on the tithe map. Two tenants who farmed sixteen and seventeen strips appear to have led in enclosing. This common field adjoined the farm cluster of Llys-wen on its east side. Southwest of the village the former common field of Maes Megan, though described as commonable, was reduced to three unfenced strips. Tenancies of the fenced strips which surrounded them were intermixed. On the north side of the village, between the hill foot and the Wye, lay the largely fenced strips which are grouped in the tithe apportionment under the names Maeslan Cafn (Boat field), Boatside Field, and Cae Rhyd (Ford Field). These three fields formed a continuous elongated block of twenty-eight strips in which eight tenants had disparate holdings. Strips of glebe land were distributed over all the fields of Bronllys which were, or had been, commonable.

In the three lowland manors of Llys-wen, Bronllys and Talgarth the late evidence is inadequate to determine the original number of common arable fields. There may originally have been three common fields around Llys-wen. A three-course rotation is likely to have been the medieval practice; throughout South Wales three large fields are seldom found. Local differences, varying with relief features, in number and size of common fields are encountered in all the former manorial lands of South Wales.

C. MONMOUTHSHIRE

When the Normans began to occupy the Monmouthshire lowlands in 1067 they entered a long-settled area which Camden later singled out, in contrast to leaner lands to westward, as productive of surplus crops for export.[1] From Neolithic to Iron Age times prehistoric farmers tilled the lower hillsides of south Monmouthshire; it supported the Roman legionary fortress of Caerleon and, at Caerwent (Venta Silurum) the only Roman market town west of Offa's Dyke. The Domesday Survey gives details of many villages between Chepstow and Caerleon, of the holdings of Durand the sheriff around Caldicot, of Gochelin the Breton at Caerwent, of Thurstan Fitzrolf around Caerleon and William Fitzbaderon at Monmouth. Around Monmouth Castle in 1086 lay the king's demesne of four carucates, three mills, the lands of Welshmen who had twenty-four ploughs and paid their old honey dues and money rents, and two carucates held by the

[1] *Camden's Britannia*, ed. R. Gough, 1806, p. 105.

Benedictine priory of Monmouth.[1] Chepstow (Strigoil) became an equally important control point and manorial focus. Strigoil Lordship included Tidenham, across the lower Wye, and extended westwards to the western margins of Wentwood and southwards, around Caldicot, to the Severn. Caerleon Lordship stretched from the Bristol Channel to the hills near Pontypool. Usk Lordship, founded after 1086, included the valleys of the Usk and its tributaries in central Monmouthshire. The lowland west of the lower Usk was conquered by Robert Fitzhamon in 1093 and became Newport Lordship. Much of Bergavenny Lordship, in north Monmouthshire, was upland. The Anglo-Norman imprint was strongest in the southern lowlands of Monmouthshire and common fields were extant there in the mid-nineteenth century (Fig. 11.1).[2] The coastal strip between Cardiff and Chepstow is occupied by polders known as the Wentloog and Caldicot Levels and locally as the Moors. This fenland lies behind sea walls which were probably initiated by the Romans.[3] From the sea walls, where the land is comparatively firm, meadowland underlain by heavy marine clays extends for from one to two miles to the solid land whose margin is demarcated by the 25-foot contour on Fig. 11.1. At this junction, drainage is particularly difficult, and much of this shallow trough on the north side of the Moors was used as common pasture. Outside the sea walls are saltings which have varied greatly in width over the centuries. They are known locally as warths and provided additional common pasture. The land north of the polders has undulating and relatively gentle southward-facing slopes underlain by soils which are well drained. Here the common arable fields were situated. Parishes and manors were for the most part aligned roughly north–south and many of the villages developed at the junction of arable and meadow land.

Drainage of the polders was and is by high-level watercourses which carry the upland water to outlets or pills on the coast.[4] The meadows drain into ditches of varying width which often replace hedges between fields. Main drains (reens) take water from the field ditches to sluices or gouts whence it is discharged through the sea wall. Both walls and sluices need frequent repair. Breaches in the sea walls have resulted in disastrous floods and the water level of the winter floods of 1606–7

[1] Darby and Terrett, *The Domesday Geography of Midland England*, p. 110.
[2] D. Sylvester, 'The Common Fields of the Coastlands of Gwent', *Agric. Hist. Rev.*, VI, 1958, p. 9 and M. Davies, 'Common Lands in Southeast Monmouthshire', *Trans. Cardiff Nat. Soc.*, LXXXV, 1955–6, p. 5.
[3] V. E. Nash-Williams, 'New Roman Site at Redwick', *Bull. Board Celtic Stud.*, XIV, 1951, p. 254.
[4] Welsh Agricultural Land Sub-Commission, *Monmouthshire Moors Investigation Report*, 1955, pp. 32–40 and App. B.

490

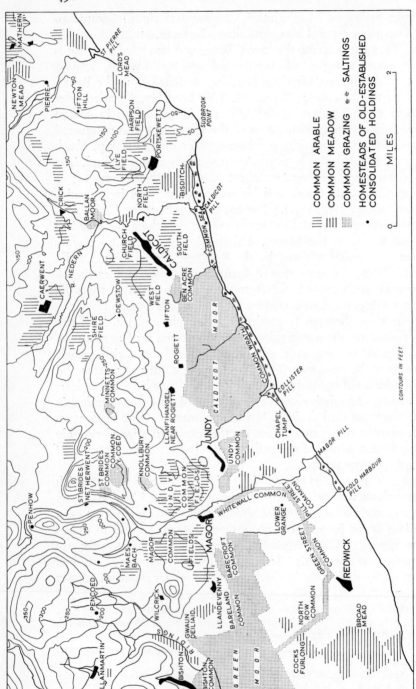

Fig. 11.1 Land held in common in southeast Monmouthshire, 1750–1850.

Sources. Compiled from manorial records, tithe maps and estate maps, notably J. Aram (surveyor), *Badminton Ms, maps, II and IX, 1763–4*, Nat. Lib. Wales, Badminton Dep. Man. Rec.; J. Aram (surveyor), *A Book of Survey of the Estates of Morgan Lewis of St Peer, 1765–77*, Mon-is indicated on several church towers. The rich meadowland demanded communal effort for its conservation, and responsibility for repairing and scouring reens and gouts is detailed in many documents.[1]

The pattern of field drains often makes the meadowland appear to lie in ridge-and-furrow. Arable patches have been scattered over firmer parts of the levels and immediately behind the sea wall in many periods, but the Moors are not ploughlands. In South Wales ridge-and-furrow cannot be correlated with common arable fields; these lay in flat selions separated by narrow balks or landshares. One occurrence of old ridge-and-furrow, on arable land which early reverted to pasture, is found in the former manor of Runston, 2½ miles southwest of Chepstow. This hillside village was finally deserted in the eighteenth century.

The Roman and Norman stronghold of Usk lies at the confluence of the flat-bottomed valleys of the Usk and Olway Brook. Though their flood plains may be as much as a mile wide, their slopes are often abrupt and broken. The manorial pattern imposed here made concessions to terrain. Common arable fields were often small and numerous. Sharing of the limited rich valley meadows persisted until a late date. In 1765 several owners held small intermixed patches of bottom land south of Tredunnock where, halfway between Caerleon and Usk, the Usk valley is flanked by steep slopes.[2] On a 150–200 foot slope 2½ miles east of Usk, remnants of a common arable field in the former Gwernesney manor existed in 1778. By then only two owners held alternating strips described as 'parcels of the common field'.[3]

Where the Usk valley is at its widest, and its eastern slopes open out into a sheltered embayment lying below Wentwood, lies Llan-trissent village, former centre of the manor of Llantrissent Parva. Professor Rees has shown how a three-course rotation was applied to the numerous arable fields of this manor in 1323–6 (Table 11.1).[4] The acreage in oats for these four years exceeds that in wheat, as might be expected in maritime Britain, but a considerable area was under wheat. The surplus sold off the Llantrissent demesne in 1323–6 was 109 quarters of wheat and 174 quarters of oats; there was also a small surplus of beans.

The lordship of Monmouth was granted to Edmund earl of Lancaster

[1] T. B. Pugh, *The Marcher Lordships of South Wales, 1415–1536*, Cardiff, 1963, p. 265 and N.L.W., Badminton Man. Rec. 2198 (1601).
[2] J. Wise (surveyor), *Maps of the Several Farms in the Parishes of Tredunog, Magor and Redwick belonging to William Nicholas Esq.*, Monmouthshire R.O., M436, fol. 3.
[3] J. Willcock (surveyor), *Map of Three Step and Tir y Ffynnon Farms*, 1778. Newport Ref. Lib., Ms. maps.
[4] Rees, *South Wales and the March*, pp. 190–4, based on P.R.O., Min. Acc. 923/29, 30; 924/1, 2, 3.

Table 11.1. *Cultivation of the demesne of Llantrissent 1323–6*

Year	Wheat		Barley		Peas		Oats		Beans	
17 E II 1323	*Overmarsh*	17			Sladacre	3½	Longfield	19½		
	Overeyland	2	Overeyland	1			Wautonscroft	2	Overeyland	—
							Helles	14	Garden	2½
							Tredenauksmore	9		
							Sladacre	13		
							Nethermarsh	20		
							Nethereyland	16		
		19						93½		
18 E II 1324	*Maestiriog*	33	Overeyland	1	Sladacre	4	Sladacre	13	Overeyland	2
	Benecroft	4					Marsh	29	Overeyland	2½
	Gilberdscroft	4					*Coppredegrove*	6½	Garden	3
	Old Orchard	5					Helles	4½	Wautonscroft	1
	Coppredegrove	10								
		56						53		8½
19 E II 1325	*Long field*	10	Old Orchard	2½			Maestiriog	33	Old Orchard	2½
	Wautonscroft	11	Overeyland	3			Gilberdscroft	4	Garden	1½
	Nethereyland	17			Wyneegrue	—	?---grew	12	Benecroft	4
	Tredenauks-more	16½					Longfield	5		
		54½		5½				54		8
20 E II 1326	Maestiriog	33	*Marsh*	2	Sladacre	4	*Marsh*	37		
	Coppredegrove	7	Croft near	½			*Sladacre*	7½		
	Gilberdscroft	3	Court				*Coppredegrove*	8		
	Garden	5					Garden	3		
	Benecroft	4								
		52		2½				55½		

Based on Rees, *South Wales and the March*, pp. 192–3. The figures show the acreages sown. Fallow of the previous year is indicated in italic.

after the de Montfort rebellion. The Monmouth tenants farmed a large, fairly flat area around the confluence of the Wye and Monnow. Surrounded by hills and spread with warm soils, it is the most productive enclave in north Monmouthshire. In 1610 four arable fields, Williams (32¼ acres), Castell (14 acres), Leviattes (37¾ acres) and Marrettes (Margaret's: 19½ acres) were being farmed by ten, six, ten and six tenants respectively.[1] Holdings ranged from 1 to 13 acres. Strips in the first two fields were rented at 13*d.* and in the other two at 8*d.* an acre. No holding was spread over all four fields and only two tenants (members of the Herbert and Somerset families) had holdings in three fields. There was common of shack for Monmouth tenants in the four fields. The common meadows included Chippenham (43¼ acres) between the town and the rivers, which was rented to fourteen

[1] W. Rees, *A Survey of the Duchy of Lancaster Lordships in Wales, 1609–13*, Cardiff, 1953, p. 3.

tenants who paid 20d. for each acre. After the hay harvest Chippenham was common pasture until 2 February and the same right was claimed for Humfreys Meade where one of the three tenants appears to have disputed it. Commons of estover, timber and pannage existed in Hadnock Wood, on the hills which overlook Monmouth from the north.

Eight of the fourteen Chippenham tenants held 2 acres or less in 1610. After that date some holdings were amalgamated; in 1765 there were twelve tenants[1] and in 1844 eight. The area at the time of the tithe survey was nearly 40 acres, laid out in eighteen strips whose merestones are clearly indicated. Leviatts Field survived northwest of the town in 1844 when 34 acres were occupied by eleven tenants. Castle field, which lay across the Rockfield road from it, was reduced to large enclosed strips approached by a sharply angled access road. The other common arable fields had disappeared.

In the Duchy of Lancaster lordships of Grosmont, Skenfrith and White Castle, northwest of Monmouth, field systems adapted to a more broken landscape existed in the Middle Ages.[2] The survey of 1610 shows that, although shared holdings existed, the greater part of the land was farmed in severalty by Welsh tenants who then had equal rights with the descendants of English settlers and zealously maintained them, particularly on common pastures.

Fig. 11.1 covers an area where there is abundant evidence of the anglicisation of land tenure and of extensive common fields. Caldicot manor extended from the Common Sea saltings and the Bisditch common meadow, on the coast, northwestwards to the arable Shire Field and to the boundaries of Caerwent manor. Here there were also extensive common arable fields. Ballan Moor was Caldicot's small northeastern common and Caldicot Moor a much larger common pasture for Caldicot cattle *sans nombre*. In an early report to the Board of Agriculture this practice is described as 'promiscuously depasturing the motley herds of six parishes'.[3] In the detached Newton portion of the manor, north of Caerwent, tenants had housebote, heybote, pannage and pasture rights in the large Earlswood Common. On Newton's lower, southern slopes 621½ acres were in closes in 1574 and 433½ acres lay in common fields.[4]

Fig. 11.2 shows the common arable fields which adjoined Caldicot

[1] N.L.W., Badminton Dep. Man Rec., Badminton Maps, IX, fol. 5.
[2] A. J. Roderick and W. Rees, 'Ministers' Accounts for the Lordships of Aber-gavenny, Grosmont, Skenfrith and White Castle', *S. Wales and Monmouth Rec. Soc.*, II, 1950, p. 67; III, 1954, p. 21; IV, 1957, p. 5.
[3] G. Hassall, *General View of the Agriculture of the County of Monmouth*, 1812, p. 68.
[4] P.R.O., Duchy of Lancaster, 43/13/6 (1574).

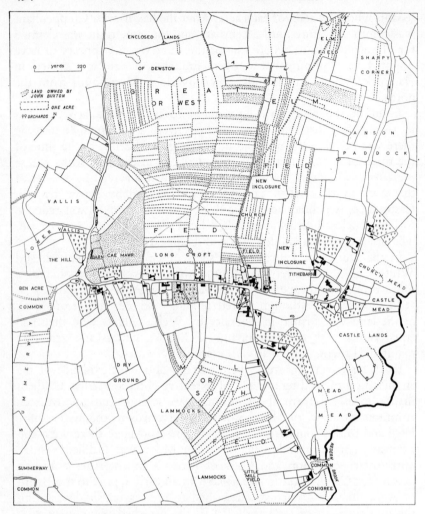

Fig. 11.2 Farmsteads, common arable, meadow and pasture in Caldicot (Monmouthshire) in 1842. *Sources.* Based on the tithe map and award.

village in 1842. The results of piecemeal enclosure are obvious, especially south of the village. North of it, beyond the former ecclesiastical manor of Dewstow, lay the Shire Field and its detached remnants. The common arable fields of Caldicot (243 acres) were enclosed in 1858; the enclosure award relating to 1,300 acres of common pasture in Caldicot and Newton is dated 18 December 1849. The South Field of Caldicot, fringed by water meadows, would never have been very large. It covered $31\frac{1}{2}$ acres in 1842. The common arable

land shown north of the village closes on Fig. 11.2 extended over
nearly 136 acres situated on both sides of the main access road, Sandy
Way. Paths running diagonally across the Great Field suggest that the
arable was thrown open for grazing after harvest. Disparate holdings
were still usual in 1842. One tenant farmed 46 acres held in forty-nine
pieces when the Duchy of Lancaster survey was made in 1613.[1] In
1842 another Caldicot farmer held 45 acres in forty-two pieces which
included nineteen scattered over the Great Field.

The common meadow of Caldicot, the Bisditch, lay immediately
behind the Warth and extended eastwards from Caldicot Pill to the
closes around Portskewett village.[2] In 1613 customary tenants each
paid 1d. towards a total of 4s. for grazing the Bisditch after the hay
had been carried. This common meadow was minutely fragmented;
in 1613 holdings were often in ¼-acre strips for which 2d., or twice
the rent of a comparable arable strip, was paid. The retention in
common until 1858 of so large a proportion of the arable land would
reduce the acreage available for fodder crops. Hay from the Bisditch
so retained its usefulness that many of the meadow strips were, at
the time of their enclosure, still the ¼-acre fardels of 1613. In 1613
several tenants had holdings in meadows such as Wellmoor and the
significantly named Ridges in the valley of the Nedern Brook. These
meadows were not thrown open after the hay harvest and had all
been enclosed when the tithe survey was made.

Durand the sheriff's tenement of Caldicot, with its three carucates
in 1086, became a Duchy of Lancaster manor c. 1521 and so remained
until 1857. Communal tillage on this manor could still have been
seen by passengers on the Gloucester–Cardiff line, opened in 1850.
This railway altered the drainage pattern and restricted access between
village farms and fields in south Monmouthshire. It runs close to the
farm clusters of which the villages then consisted and its construction
coincided with the enclosure of the common grazings like Caldicot
Moor which it separates from nearby villages. Further west, Undy,
Magor and Llandevenny villages had common arable fields north of
the railway and common meadows between it and the coast. At
Llandevenny the railway cut through the unenclosed strips of Waun
Deiliaid (Tenants' Meadow); the name still appears on modern large-
scale maps.

Undy and Magor manors contained several freehold consolidated
holdings. Manorial boundaries cannot now be delineated but both
appear to have had one common arable field. Records dating from

[1] Rees, *Duchy of Lancaster Lordships*, p. 135.
[2] Davies, *Trans. Cardiff Nat. Soc.*, LXXXV, 1955–6, has maps of Caldicot Bisditch and
Shire Field, and the field systems of Magor, Undy and Redwick.

the fourteenth to eighteenth centuries refer to Undy's Field and Magor's Field. By 1842, at Undy, the fencing of access roads had produced five blocks of strips with different names north of the village. The strips lie on an undulating ridge and are much less regular than those at Caldicot. Magor's Field, laid out in more uniform strips on flatter land adjoining the village, appears on the tithe map of 1847 as Lower, Middle and Upper Fields. These too are separated by fenced roads. In the mid-eighteenth century unfenced arable strips extended from the west side of Magor's 'General Common Field' towards Llandevenny village.[1] Enclosure awards relating to both field systems were made in 1854.

Common grazings used by the occupiers of old-established farms in Undy and Magor lay south of the villages where the sloping arable land meets the polders. Beyond these commons, meadows extended to the sea wall. At Undy groups of unenclosed meadow strips were still in being in 1842, notably in Monkey Mead and Hencroft. The common meadows of Magor parish had all been enclosed by 1847, but the lands of Magor manor lay partly in Redwick parish which lies wholly on the Caldicot Level. Redwick consisted almost entirely of meadowland in 1846. There were a few enclosed arable patches behind the sea wall, where shell sand lightens the heavy clay, and near the roads. Roadside encroachments had reduced Redwick's street commons to 113 acres but there was grazing on the aftermath of the extensive common meadows to offset this loss.

The fenland of Redwick and other manors was greatly valued for fattening. Scattered holdings are still characteristic of the Levels and farmers rent meadows at considerable distances from their farms. In 1846 a large number of meadow strips of varying width were laid out parallel to each other west of Redwick village and they extended a mile northwards from the sea wall to Kimney Pool, a junction of reens. Immediately northeast of Kimney Pool, Cock's Furlong included a large group of narrow meadow strips. Other smaller unenclosed meadows lay northeast of Cock's Furlong across North Row Common. Between these small groups of meadow strips and Redwick village other common meadows existed in the seventeenth century. Most strips covered a half to one acre (fardels are detailed in court rolls) and their collective names are old-established.[2] In 1846 holdings were still largely disparate and three strips in Broadmead were held by their two occupiers only in alternate years. Changeable acres are a feature of other common meadows in South Wales. The enclosure

[1] N.L.W., Lockwood Dep. Coll. Ms. maps, vol. IX.
[2] Many appear in seventeenth-century court rolls cited by J. Bradney, *History of Monmouthshire*, 1929, IV, pt. I, pp. 236ff.

award for Redwick common meadows, dated 1 January 1850, lists fifty-eight interested parties.

The field name 'furlong', though used in early documents like one dated 1245 concerning Sladfurlong, owned by Runston church, largely disappeared from the nomenclature of South Wales common fields. It was retained in the common arable lands between Redwick and Chepstow where it was used for, *inter alia*, common arable fields such as the Upper and Lower Furlongs of Pwllmeurig, near Chepstow, and for the Cliffurlong of Portskewett in 1502. In the latter area Harpstones or Harpson common arable field and common meadow are often recorded, as are arable strips in Sudbrook Southfield. Furlong was also used in Mathern manor, near Chepstow, where much land lay intermixed. Hardwick common field, in what is now the Hardwick suburb of Chepstow, was probably in one of the three Domesday hardwicks of Strigoil.[1]

The southwestern portions of both the Caldicot Level, near Newport, and the Wentloog Level, near Cardiff, provide evidence of early enclosure of meadowland. Their ditches and hedges are far more irregular than those of the remainder of the Levels. Further inland, in the manors of Newport Lordship, on the Wentloog Level, common fields occurred in Dowlais manor, near Marshfield village, and in Stow manor, now engulfed by Newport. Stow's medieval manor house was flanked by the usual oxhouse, columbarium and fishpond, and 150 acres of the demesne lay on the arable land around the lower Ebbw and Usk rivers. Although Newport did not receive its charter until 1384, its gradual expansion could have influenced the enclosure of most neighbouring common fields well before its rapid late eighteenth- and nineteenth-century growth. Unenclosed meadow strips near the Usk were still in use in the mid-nineteenth century. The Marshes common meadow, north of the town, on to which Newport burgesses turned their cattle after the hay was auctioned, was part of the Marshes estate on which considerable profits were then being made.[2] Similar common meadows, all liable to flooding, and not until recently used for housing, could be found in the mid-nineteenth century surrounded by the increasing sprawl of other south Wales coal ports.

D. GLAMORGAN

The Norman conquest of Morgannwg was accomplished in 1090–1 by Robert Fitzhamon, earl of Gloucester. Fees were granted in the Vale of Glamorgan (Bro Morgannwg) to Norman knights; the high

[1] W. Rees, 'Medieval Gwent', *Br. Arch. Ass. Jnl.*, xxxv, 1930, p. 197.
[2] D. Williams, *John Frost: A Study in Chartism*, Cardiff, 1939, p. 28.

hills (Blaenau Morgannwg) were retained by Welsh lords answerable to their Norman overlord in Cardiff. The Vale was productive, the lean hills nurtured guerilla bands. Norman policy was 'this to be wonne by gentilness, the other kept under with feare'.[1]

The occupation of the Vale of Glamorgan and the spread of manors and manorial custom resulted in a very wide distribution of common fields there. All the land south of a line between the medieval boroughs of Cardiff and Kenfig had strip fields in its manors. It is low coast plateau, mainly underlain by Lias limestones and clays, and rises at varying levels to the higher Carboniferous Limestone ridge along which the Portway runs from Cardiff to Kenfig. Rivers such as the Thaw, Colhugh and Ogmore have bitten deeply into the relatively soft Lias limestones, leaving few extensive blocks of flat plateau top on which to lay out large arable fields. Where the plateau surface is largely unbroken, as it is around Llantwit Major, large demesnes developed. The silt-filled valley bottoms are relatively narrow and the rich grass of their meadows was and is highly valued. There is still a common meadow in the Thaw valley. Between Cardiff and the mouth of the Ogmore River cultivation extends to the tops of high cliffs, but beyond the Ogmore extensive sand dunes, initiated in Bronze Age times, gradually spread inland over many medieval fields; they finally overwhelmed the borough of Kenfig in the seventeenth century.

Common field patterns, formerly universal in the Vale, still leave their mark on the landscape both north and south of the Portway. Many strips were walled or hedged by their owners in the course of the piecemeal enclosure which was responsible for the disappearance of nearly all the Vale field systems. They can be seen fossilised in the modern field pattern, around a resort like Porthcawl or on the valley sides near Bridgend Industrial Estate. In Cardiff, where common meadows existed around the estuaries of the Ely, Taff and Rhymney rivers, districts of the city retain names like Portmanmoor and Splott. Now dominated by a steel works, this was 'the Splott, parcel houlden of the Lord of Landaph' which supplied hay to the large dairy farm which developed on the medieval manor of Roath.

The manor of Llantwit stretched inland from a coastal frontage three miles long which is cleft by the Colhugh River. It included the village of Boverton and the small market town of Llantwit Major. In 1262, 565 acres of arable on the demesne were let at 6d. an acre, 14 acres of meadow at 18d. and 147 acres of pasture at 4d.[2] The pasture of the scrub woodland on the steep slopes of the Colhugh valley was

---

[1] Merrick, *Booke of Glamorganshire's Antiquities*, p. 12.
[2] J. S. Corbett, *Glamorgan*, Cardiff, 1925, p. 193.

let at 10s. The customary tenants held 2,116 acres and their rents and services were valued at £42 18s. 0d. Ten acres of the lord's arable and 14 of his meadows in Llantwit were worked by bond cottars and 18½ acres of the Taff's Mead in Cardiff were mown and gathered by Llantwit customary tenants. Fifteenth-century accounts relating to Llantwit manor provide evidence of increased rents (including those for strips in the Southfield), tenements burnt during the Glyn Dŵr revolt, and the subsequent migration of the tenantry and sale of demesne land. Intermixed ownerships became characteristic on the former demesne land. In 1766, immediately west of Llantwit Major, the gently sloping arable land between the Llantwit–St Donat's road and the lip of the Colhugh gorge was held in scattered parcels by at least a dozen owners.[1] South of Llantwit Major, where the Odnant joins the Colhugh, was the Commonhey, which was still fragmented in 1766. Llanmaes manor, immediately east of Llantwit manor, still contained several blocks of acre strips which were not wholly enclosed at the time of the tithe survey (1843). The common arable fields of Llanmaes included Butts, Slade and Middle Fields.

The Taffs Mead, which was once worked by Llantwit tenants, adjoined the west end of Cardiff Bridge and still lay in twenty-seven unfenced strips in 1840. West of it were the Salt Mead, whose thirty strips had eight owners, and Leckwith Moors which extended to the Ely River and, on their northern side, passed into Ely Moors. Strips in the common meadow on Leckwith Moors provided pasture for 100 oxen and 400 sheep in 1492.[2] Ely Moor had twenty tenants on its strip holdings in 1840.[3] There are memories in many Cardiff families of the grazing of cattle, sheep and geese on these meadows and on Canton and Llandaff commons. The common meadows on the east side of Cardiff, between the Taff and Rhymney rivers, included West Moor and Portmansmoor. In West Moor, meadow parcels are described in 1558 as lying in the East and West Furlongs and in the Tenants' Moor.[4] Extensive common meadows existed, then, throughout the seaward fringe of Cardiff. One of the common arable fields is described as the Town Field. All the land west of the little cathedral city of Llandaff, now a suburb of Cardiff, was still partly unenclosed in the late eighteenth century when the intermixed strips were intensively tilled by the marketmen of Llandaff.[5]

[1] Glamorgan R.O., Plymouth Estate Plans, I, p. 28, D/D Pl₁.
[2] P.R.O., Min Acc. 10334.
[3] M. Davies, 'Field Patterns in the Vale of Glamorgan', *Trans. Cardiff Nat. Soc.*, LXXXIV, 1954–5, Fig. 6, p. 14.
[4] J. H. Matthews, *Cardiff Records*, 1898–1911, II., 50.
[5] E. Thomas (surveyor), *A Book of Maps of the Estates of Thomas Edwards*, 1776, N.L.W., Ms. maps, vol. 28, p. 2.

Southwest of Cardiff, tenants in the manors of Wenvoe, Wrinstone and Dinas Powis were still farming the relics of common arable fields in the late eighteenth century and ownerships were often scattered over widely separated strips.[1] These strips, now fenced, are prominent on the slopes of Pop Hill, south of Dinas Powis. Below the arable are the bottom lands of the Wrinstone Brook and its tributaries, which drain down into Pablin, Dinas Powis and Cog Moors and today, through saltings, into Barry Docks.[2] In 1798, 130 strips and a number of larger parcels in these moors had seventeen owners. Many strips were of half an acre or less. Cattle were stinted according to acreage and the names of the surrounding farms, such as Westra and Eastbrook, from which the cattle came, were given to the strips. The common meadows in the northern basin of the Wrinstone Brook were South Moor and Hen Forfa (Old Moor). Here Wrinstone and Wenvoe farmers held strips. Their partly enclosed arable strips, upslope from the moor, were described as furlongs.[3]

Barry, Fonmon, Llancadle and Penmark manors occupied Leland's 'principal good corn land' between Barry and the Thaw estuary. Surveys of these manors, made in 1622–4 by Evans Mouse for Sir Anthony St John, reveal formerly extensive common fields undergoing piecemeal enclosure.[4] Barry manor was wholly enclosed in 1622 except for two strips, one being glebe land. Around Penmark village the Towncroft lay in unfenced strips. Six tenants in the hamlet of Treduccon held intermixed and partly unfenced arable strips in Treduccon Field; landsets or lancets was then the local term for the strips. The sharply angled access roads around Treduccon were hedged in 1624 and appear to have once served larger common fields.

In Fonmon manor the demesne was enclosed in large pastures which still retain the boundaries shown on Fig. 11.3. Fairly compact holdings existed in 1622 around the outlying farms, but the farmers of Aberthaw tilled strips in the remnants of four common arable fields on the flat plateau which terminates in low cliffs above the Thaw estuary. The larger unfenced strips in the Chapel Field were acre strips and those in the North Field were of half an acre. That the

[1] E. A. Lewis and J. Conway Davies (eds.), *Records of the Court of Augmentations Relating to Wales and Monmouthshire*, Cardiff, 1954, pp. 414 and 422.

[2] Davies, *Trans. Cardiff Nat. Soc.*, LXXXV, 1954–5, Fig. 6.

[3] *A Survey of the Estates of Robert Jones*, Glamorgan R.O., D/D F, vol. XXVI, p. 30 and *An Exact Survey of the Freehold Estate of Sir Edmund Thomas*, 1762, Glamorgan R.O., D/D We Map VII.

[4] The maps of the first three manors are in Cardiff Reference Library (Ms. 4. 672). The Penmark map and copies of the other three maps are in Glamorgan R.O., as are copies of the manorial rolls (D/D F, vol. XLI). The maps are printed as Figs. 1–4 in Davies, *Trans. Cardiff Nat. Soc.*, LXXXIV.

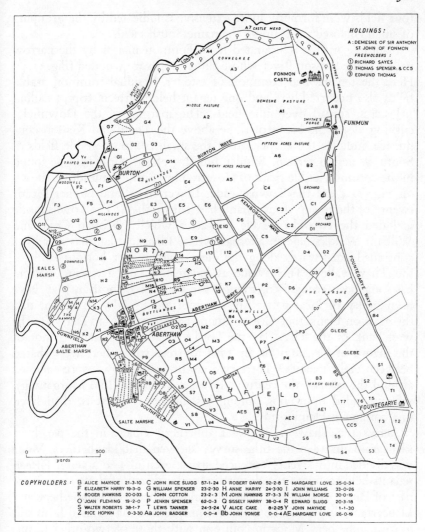

Fig. 11.3 Fonmon manor (Glamorgan) in 1622.

Sources. Based on a map showing The Mannor of Funmun, 1622, as it was surveyed by Evans Mouse. Glamorgan R.O., D/D F, Vol. XII. On Figs. 11.3–11.4 asterisks indicate pieces of the lord's waste. Sizes of parcels and fields on Figs. 11.3–11.7 are stated in acres, roods and perches.

four fields were formerly more extensive is indicated by the grouping of small enclosed fields under the name South Field.

Llancadle manor is separated from Fonmon manor by the narrow valley of the Kenson River whose cliffed slopes are wooded (Fig. 11.4). Here the tenants had common of estover. Residual common arable fields also occurred here and one tenant held fourteen strips, totalling 13¼ acres, spread over nine fields. The margins of the Downfield, curving along the break of slope above the Thaw and Kenson confluence, indicate the adaptation of the small common arable fields of South Wales to terrain. Similar bundles of strips can still be found in the common arable fields of Gower. The common meadows shown on Fig. 11.4 are the Townsmeade, Lower Mead and Higher Mead; twenty of the twenty-four tenants had strips in them. The Townsmeade included the two changeable half-acres which Christian Coxe and William Walters held in alternate years. Llancadle lammas meadows continued northwards along the increasingly wider bottom lands of the Thaw valley. Their value as hayground and fattening pasture has long been recognised, though the vicar of Llancarfan may have been guilty of local patriotism in reporting to Edward Lhuyd that the grass on Llanbethery Moor attained a height of 9–10 feet.[1] On the west bank of the Thaw lay the Lord's Mead and Tenants' Moor of the manor of Flemingston. In 1778 fourteen strips there were shared between eight tenants.[2] These two common meadows were enclosed around the turn of the century. Edward Williams (Iolo Morganwg), who included improving among his numerous interests, then lived in a cottage in Flemingston.

Across the Thaw valley lies Llanbethery village in the parish of Llancarfan. In 1840 the tithe survey showed that Llanbethery Moor was divided into seventy unfenced strips, each of ¾ to 2 acres. Fifteen tenants held scattered meadow strips and a dozen of these strips were part of Pancross farm whose arable land lies between Llanbethery and Llancarfan villages. Cattle from this progressive modernised farm still graze Llanbethery Moor in common with those of two other farms. This holding belonged to the Church in Wales until its disestablishment in 1919, and it has been a feature of South Wales that, where corporate bodies, and especially ecclesiastical bodies, shared in common fields, they were among the last to be enclosed. Holdings on Llanbethery Moor are not now demarcated on the ground. The three farmers meet each spring and agree on the date and numbers of cattle to be turned on to the moor when it has dried out after winter waterlogging.

[1] E. Lhuyd, *Parochialia*, ed. R. H. Morris, *Arch. Camb.*, Supp. Pt. III, 1911, p. 22.
[2] N.L.W., Dunraven Dep. Coll., Map 18.

Herds are stinted according to acreages held. Hay crops have not been taken off Llanbethery Moor for many years.

The tithe survey shows groups of unfenced arable strips on the plateau top around Llanbethery village and an enclosed strip sloping into the sun which was a vineyard. Lansetts and lancets are replaced as names of strips by landshares; tithe surveyors used this term in many South Wales parishes which had remnants of common fields. The name is also given to the balk which separated the strips and in existing common arable fields in South Wales it is used only for the balk.

East of Llancarfan, around the Moulton group of farms, groups of fenced strips with the general name Furlong existed in 1840. Throughout the large parish of Llancarfan holdings were scattered and the largely fenced strips of former common arable fields were widely distributed throughout the south of the parish.

Further up the Thaw valley, in Penlline parish, there was a common meadow with twenty-nine strips, many of an acre, in 1839. This lammas meadow, part of which was called Tenants' Moor, was enclosed in 1858. By the Ewenny River, tenants shared a common meadow on former monastic property and encroached considerably on it in the seventeenth century.[1] Aberavon borough, with a charter dating from 1350, lies below steep hills and behind coastal marshes and dunes. In 1841 its burgesses still owned hundreds of acres of mountain, marsh and dune land. The latter provided scanty pasture, the wet meadows, in this narrow strip below the coalfield hills, yielded valuable hay and their aftermath was available for grazing. The tithe survey of Baglan meadows shows seven of the Aberavon burgesses' marsh pieces extending as a line of enclosed fields below the Aberavon–Neath road. Much of their common meadow and pasture between Baglan and Averavon had been sold to the recently formed Port Talbot Dock Company. The remainder of Baglan meadows lay in Clawdd Coch Ycha and Clawdd Coch Isha and in adjoining smaller groups of unfenced meadow strips. There were seventy-four unfenced landshares, varying from a half to two acres in area and farmed by sixteen tenants of various owners. Unfenced parcels of meadow on the flats of the lower Neath valley also had a scarcity value. In early nineteenth-century rentals three cases occur of the hay of such parcels going to one hill farm and the aftergrass to another.[2]

Another nascent coal port, Porthcawl, appears on the Newton Nottage tithe map of 1846. It was then a group of beerhouses, ware-

[1] N.L.W., Ewenny Coll. 11 (1634).
[2] Glamorgan R.O., D/D BF 32.

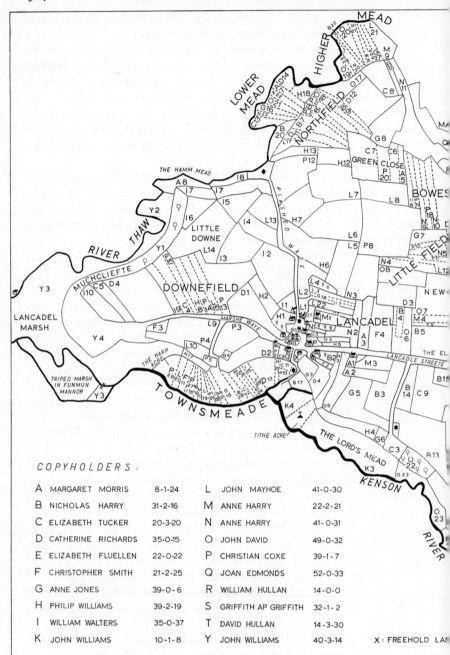

COPYHOLDERS:

A	MARGARET MORRIS	8-1-24	L	JOHN MAYHOE	41-0-30
B	NICHOLAS HARRY	31-2-16	M	ANNE HARRY	22-2-21
C	ELIZABETH TUCKER	20-3-20	N	ANNE HARRY	41-0-31
D	CATHERINE RICHARDS	35-0-15	O	JOHN DAVID	49-0-32
E	ELIZABETH FLUELLEN	22-0-22	P	CHRISTIAN COXE	39-1-7
F	CHRISTOPHER SMITH	21-2-25	Q	JOAN EDMONDS	52-0-33
G	ANNE JONES	39-0-6	R	WILLIAM HULLAN	14-0-0
H	PHILIP WILLIAMS	39-2-19	S	GRIFFITH AP GRIFFITH	32-1-2
I	WILLIAM WALTERS	35-0-37	T	DAVID HULLAN	14-3-30
K	JOHN WILLIAMS	10-1-8	Y	JOHN WILLIAMS	40-3-14

X : FREEHOLD LAN

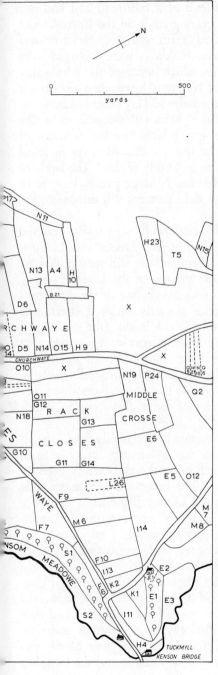

Fig. 11.4 Llancadle manor
(Glamorgan) in 1622.
Sources. Based on a map showing
The Mannor of Lancadel, 1622, as it
was surveyed by Evans Mouse.
Glamorgan R.O., D/D F, Vol. XLI.
The Triped Marsh appears as
Triparte Marsh in a Fonmon
manorial roll.

houses and cottages at the seaward end of a tramroad and had not begun to spread over the common grazing lands on the Burrows and on Backs Common. Two nucleated farm clusters, Newton and Nottage villages, dominated the area. Holdings were scattered over a mass of largely parallel fenced strips which occupied the whole area between the sea and the scarp foot of Newton Down, then a common of 744 acres. Only one group of fifteen strips still lay unfenced between Lock's Common and Nottage village. Manorial documents of the seventeenth and eighteenth centuries give a large number of names of fields in which strips lay and suggest that bundles of strips in small fields were characteristic, as elsewhere in South Wales.[1] The lands of three manors were intermixed in Newton Nottage parish. In spite of the growth of Porthcawl the former field patterns still impose themselves on the lands around it.

Evidence of former common fields can also be seen today near the northern margin of the Vale of Glamorgan. Treoes and Llangan villages, which lay in the manor of Penlline, are still surrounded by narrow strip fields. Treoes lies on the margin of the Ewenny valley which, in 1840, was occupied by Treoes Moor, one of the commons of the Penlline tenants, and by a series of partly enclosed intermixed meadow strips. Field names are mainly Welsh in the tithe survey and the $\frac{1}{4}$ to 2 acres arable strips around both villages are grouped, as at Llechfaen in Breconshire, under the name 'Maesydd'. An access road is described as Heol y Maesydd and strips are frequently referred to as 'two acres in the maesydd'. Strips of this size are well-fossilised into the field pattern of the gentle slopes of the embayment in which Treoes lies.

Most of the Gower peninsula is composed of relatively flat Carboniferous Limestone plateaux. They are cut by streams and rise from the sea in rugged cliffs. On the north coast the cliffs are fronted by extensive salt marshes and sand spits. The limestone surfaces provide good arable land; the inner marshes and a few valley bottoms produce hay. Natural meadows were scarce in Gower and extensive common pastures, on which there is a long grazing season, compensated for this deficiency. The Gower commons are on Devonian ridges which protrude through the limestone plateau (e.g. Rhosili Down, Cefn Bryn) or, in the east of the peninsula, they are on drift-covered Coal Measures (e.g. Clyne and Fairwood Commons). Herds from the Gower manors intercommoned on them without restriction and they are still used as common grazing. The only large common underlain by well-drained soils derived from limestone, Porteynon Moor, was enclosed in the seventeenth century. The peninsula, and the Loughor

[1] Glamorgan R.O., D/D Wi 206 (Newton Nottage).

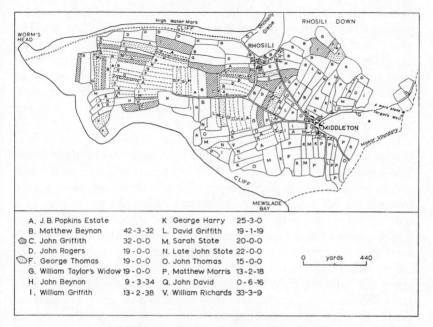

A. J.B. Popkins Estate
B. Matthew Beynon 42-3-32
C. John Griffith 32-0-0
D. John Rogers 19-0-0
F. George Thomas 19-0-0
G. William Taylor's Widow 19-0-0
H. John Beynon 9-3-34
I. William Griffith 13-2-38

K George Harry 25-3-0
L. David Griffith 19-1-19
M. Sarah Stote 20-0-0
N. Late John Stote 22-0-0
O. John Thomas 15-0-0
P. Matthew Morris 13-2-18
Q. John David 0-6-16
V. William Richards 33-3-9

0   yards   440

Fig. 11.5 Rhosili manor (Glamorgan) in 1780.
Sources. Based on a survey by John Williams of the Estates of Thomas Mansel Talbot of Penrice. Glamorgan R.O., D/D P.821. The area of the Popkins estate is not given because it lay largely outside the area shown on the map.

area north of it, formed the Englishry of Gower. The Welshry was in the thinly peopled mountains between the Loughor and Tawe valleys and here there were very large common pastures.

Gower terminates in the fine fragmented limestone ridge which forms Worms Head. Between it and Rhosili and Middleton villages lies Rhosili Vile. Land y vile was used as a strip name in the Oyster-mouth area of Gower. The name vile is probably derived from O.E. *gefilde*, a field or plain (*maes* in Welsh), and shows the softening of the initial *f* characteristic of southwest Britain. Gower received many settlers from Somerset. The strip fields of Rhosili Vile are still communally occupied (Fig. 11.5).[1] The strips average $1\frac{1}{2}$ acres in area and are enclosed within limestone walls near the cliffs, or earth banks near the villages. The unenclosed bundles of strips are separated by narrow low balks, made up of earth and field stones, and known as landshares. Disparate holdings are still a feature and are spread

[1] M. Davies, 'Rhosili Open Field and Related South Wales Field Patterns', *Agric. Hist. Rev.*, IV, 1956, p. 80.

over bundles of strips which have distinctive names. Stonyland, adjoining Rhosili village, is on the southern limit of drift deposits. The unenclosed strips are intensively farmed, producing vegetable crops, especially new potatoes and spring cabbage. Peripheral enclosed strips have partly served as pasture for many years and are increasingly so used as tourist pressures restrict grazing on the narrow cliff commons. Fig. 11.5 shows encroachments by squatters on Rhosili Down, but 900 acres were available there as common pasture.

In 1780 the six farmers of Rhosili village (B–H on Fig. 11.5) held nearly 142 acres in the Vile and in meadow closes around their farms. The seven farmers of Middleton (I–P) had nearly 130 acres in the Vile and in enclosed fields sloping up to Rhosili Down or more gently towards the Mewslade valley. Strips were handed over as part of a holding when tenancies changed and some Rhosili and Middleton families have farmed them for many generations. Although the strips are owner-occupied since the post-war sale of this part of the Penrice estate, little enclosure has occurred. A few wire fences have been run along the balks, or they have occasionally been ploughed out. Balks are preferred to hedges because they occupy little space and cast no shade. The farmers say that the sea winds sweep in evenly over them to ripen the corn. Communal grazing of stubbles is not remembered at Rhosili, though grazing of strips by supervised cattle was a feature a generation ago.

Existing field patterns, tithe surveys and manorial records show that other manors in peninsular Gower Anglicana were formerly communally tilled and that holdings were intricately intermingled.[1] East of Rhosili small groups of unfenced strips, or enclosed strips grouped under the same name, are revealed by the tithe surveys of all the manors behind the south coast of Gower. Porteynon's Middle Field was still in seven unfenced acre strips; the Underhill meadow between the dunes and the cliff foot, east of Porteynon, was in six landshare pieces. Pennard, with its besanded demesne lands, had small groups of strips named Forge Field, Great Field and Bush Moor. Lunnon, north of Pennard, had the remains of Middle, Great and High Grove Fields in fenced or unfenced landshares. The five Lunnon farmers also had large and small disparate landshares in Llethrid Common Meadow. This lies up Parc le Breos Cwm, 2 miles north of

[1] Davies, *Agric. Hist. Rev.*, IV, 1956, pp. 88–92. The manorial surveys appear in G. G. Francis, 'The Lordship of Gower', *Arch. Camb.*, Supp. vols., 1861 and 1864 and (ed. C. Baker) 1870. They are analysed by F. V. Emery in 'West Glamorgan Farming *c.* 1580–1620', *Nat. Lib. Wales Jnl.*, IX, 1956, p. 1 and X, 1957, p. 17. In 1764, Gabriel Powell, Steward to the Duke of Beaufort, made a *Survey of the Seignories of Gower and Kilvey* which is largely unpublished. The manuscript is in the Royal Institution of South Wales in Swansea.

Lunnon. Common pasture was available on Lunnon Moor (Pengwern Common) between Llethrid Common Meadow and Lunnon's arable fields. In the southern half of Bishopston manor the numerous narrow strips which covered the arable area in 1844 are still noticeable and their balks have not entirely disappeared. The field patterns here would have resembled those of Rhosili Vile.

In the north of English Gower, common arable fields extended inland from the cliffs. Common meadows lay below them. Between the meadows and the Burry estuary lay huge common grazings spread over saltings which have increased in area since the medieval period. Centres of former manors, like Llanrhidian, Leason, Llandimore, Llanmadoc and Llangennith, all villages on or just above the spring-line, were all flanked by arable fields 'lying in landshare' in the late eighteenth or early nineteenth centuries. West of Llangennith the meadows behind the dunes lay in intricately intermixed holdings of $\frac{1}{2}$ to 2 acres which were still partly unenclosed in 1844.

The medieval borough of Loughor was established on the eastern shore of the Loughor estuary where the solid land meets the saltings. It surrounded the castle mound which rises above a field still communally occupied in 1839. It was known as Pen Bailey and was divided into sixteen small strips occupied by eight tenants. Its northern strips were unfenced. This field had formerly continued beyond the Loughor–Swansea road but here, in 1839, only two unfenced landshares survived alongside a glasshouse and zinc works. Between Loughor and the Lliw estuary the former burgess lands lay partly in unenclosed strips described as landshares; the saltings here had formerly been divided into the Lord's Marsh and the Townland. Below Pen Bailey five tenants each held a landshare in the Boro' common meadow and a sixth held two pieces.

Swansea's charter of 1306 made the lord's meadows of Portmead and Crows Wood Mead commonable to the burgesses. These meads, like the woods in which burgesses could pasture their herds as far as they could go in a day and return the same night to their homes, were distant from the borough. They lay on ill-drained gentle slopes northwest of Swansea between Fforest Fach and the River Llan. The Cromwellian survey of 1650 shows that the Portreeve collected rents totalling seven guineas from the Portmead and from the Redmead or Reedmarsh in the Tawe valley.[1]

The Lliw valley, which flows down to Loughor from the Welshry of Gower, leaves the high hills (the Supraboscus of Gower) at Felindre. The village takes its name from the mill of the Bishop of St David's manor of Llangyfelach. It lay in Sub boscus, the lower division of the

[1] Francis, *Arch. Camb.*, Supp. vol., 1861, p. 30.

Welshry, which occupied the Swansea–Loughor isthmus, a routeway on which English and Welsh traditions met and merged. It did not attract English settlers as did peninsular Gower, nor is it so well suited to arable farming. Llangyfelach manor had large common pastures and tenants had rights of estover in the Bishop's woods.[1] In 1326 the free tenants were grouped as seven *gwelyau* with one tenant named to represent the co-sharers. Their names and those of other tenants were largely Welsh. The lord's demesne included 26 acres of arable on which oats were grown. Holdings ranged from a half to eight acres let at $1\frac{1}{2}d$. an acre. The lord's meadows covered $6\frac{3}{4}$ acres each let at 2d. Common meadows near the bishop's mill at Felindre still lay in landshares in 1839, disparate landshares went with dispersed farms. The largest common meadow is named as Waun Garwen. It extended over half a mile of fairly flat land southeast of Felindre and lay in twenty-five unfenced pieces. East of it unfenced landshares were grouped under other meadow names. This more open and better quality land, set among extensive hilly common pastures was, then, attractive to the medieval Church and, corporately held, some of its field systems survived until well on into the nineteenth century.

E. CARMARTHENSHIRE

Anglicisation of land tenure affected only the southern fringe of Carmarthenshire. For over two hundred years after the Norman conquest the greater part of the county was held by Welsh princes and Welsh customs were maintained there. Their hold was firm on both the hills and the broad vale of Towy east of Carmarthen. Here their influence spread from their royal castle of Dinefwr near Llandeilo. By Edward I's settlement of 1284, the north of the county was attached administratively to the small 'county of Carmarthen'. This was the region north of the town which was already held by the Crown, but there had been few changes in its land tenure. South of the 'county' of Carmarthen were the Marcher Lordships of Laugharne, St Clears, Llanstephan and Kidwelly. These had existed since the twelfth century and all had castellated boroughs and communally tilled burgess lands on lower hillsides open to the sun or on limited pockets of valley land. Their lords, de Brian at Laugharne and de Camville at Llanstephan, gave them charters and burgess lands and introduced field systems whose traces contrast markedly with field patterns in the Carmarthenshire hinterland.

Kidwelly became a Duchy of Lancaster lordship in the fourteenth

[1] Willis-Bund (ed.), *Black Book of St David's*, p. 285.

century. When surveyed in 1609 the borough was described as decayed. Its lands were rented to burgesses who paid money and pepper rents. Many of them had English names.[1] The demesne land consisted of marshes, closes, and pieces in the Portcrofte and an arable parcel 'betwene the waye and the North Lanchard', i.e. the northern borough boundary. The tithe survey of 1840 shows that the salt marshes were still owned by the Corporation of Kidwelly and that some of the field names used in 1609 and many largely enclosed strip holdings survived. South of the Gwendraeth Fach River, on firm ground above the quay, was a field which may have been part of the Portcroft. Its thirteen unfenced strips had seven tenants and it appears to have extended over twice its 1840 area before partial enclosure. Access roads to former common arable fields snaked upslope north of the town.

In the lordship of Llanstephan the demesne lay around the castle which lay apart from the borough within the ramparts of an Iron Age fort. The town was fronted by common pastures along the Towy estuary and its arable extended upslope. There were about 120 burgages. As in other Carmarthenshire lordships, small groups of burgesses also lived in outlying nucleated settlements. In Llanstephan lordship the outlier was Morbrichurch (Llanybri), a former bond village. Enclosed strips grouped under the same name existed in the nineteenth century around both settlements and many of them can still be seen there.

New Carmarthen received its charter from Henry II and was walled off from Old Carmarthen which lay around St Peter's church. In 1302 New Carmarthen had 172 burgages totalling 458 acres.[2] Its demesne was at Llanllwch, southwest of the borough. This appropriated land of Welsh lords lay around a former bond village; tenants' services on the demesne arable were commuted to rents of 6d. an acre. Other tenants of field systems at Llanllwch included the lepers who lived in the Tawelan valley west of the town. The common meadows of New Carmarthen included 34 acres at Rhydygors and 5 acres at Dokehoke (common meadows in medieval Cardiff also had the suffix-*hoke*). These and other meadows lay in the broad trough west of the main Towy valley. Although there was much enclosure by the seventeenth century, common arable fields are still recorded then near Carmarthen town.

The borough of St Clears was aligned above the Tâf at its tidal limit and lay at the southeastern tip of St Clears Lordship. Its residual common fields and common pastures were enclosed in 1810. The borough had common meadows, including the Portreeve's Meads, corporation property until 1889, the Gors Fach and Morfa Bach.

[1] Rees, *Duchy of Lancaster Lordships*, p. 175.
[2] A. J. Richard, *A History of Carmarthenshire* (ed. J. E. Lloyd), Cardiff, 1935, I, 319.

A St Clears court record of 1857 refers to a common arable field called Danygors.[1] The map which illustrates the 1810 award shows some unfenced acres of arable land west of the town, sloping down to a minutely fragmented narrow meadow along the Tâf. The enclosure award was preceded by much piecemeal enclosure of common pastures and by the renting out of the common meadows and the sale of their standing hay to pay the corporation's debts.

The burgesses of Laugharne, three miles south of St Clears, have been more successful in preserving the corporation's land since it was granted to them by Guy de Brian early in the fourteenth century. In 1871 their lands were valued at £20,000. Much of the land within the boundaries detailed in their charter has been enclosed, but 312 acres of common fields are still held by the corporation and are organised as two common arable fields and as a common meadow.[2]

Laugharne burgesses, and a few in the adjoining parish of Llan-sadurnen, which has shared Laugharne's common meadow since medieval times, hold seventy-six shares in the common fields. They pay rents of 6d. for their shares in the Lees, 1s. for a share in the Hugdon, and 2s. for a Whitehill Moor share. Shares are allocated, as they were in 1842, as follows: Lees, 40; Hugdon, 20; Whitehill Moor, 16. It is not known when this allocation began. Shares on the Hugdon (Fig. 11.6) average 7–9 acres made up of five to twelve strips and include a 3 to 4 acre strip which runs up and over the ridge. A hedge has been thrown along its crest since 1842. Not all the 150 strips on the Hugdon's 171½ acres are now ploughed. The Hugdon, a rounded Devonian hump, drops sharply towards Laugharne and on this slope the small strips form lynchets and are gradually reverting to scrub.

The sixteen shares on Whitehill Moor run smoothly upslope from the Tâf and are typically of 5 to 10 acres held in three strips distributed over the 100 acres there. Whitehill Moor has fifty-three strips and its soils, derived from Silurian rocks, are heavier than those of the Hugdon. Enclosed pieces allocated to officers of the Corporation, like the Herds-piece by the Tâf, are scattered throughout the arable lands around Laugharne. Strips on both the Hugdon and Whitehill Moor are separated by very narrow low balks, here called 'landscars' or 'land-skers', which must not be touched by the ploughshare.

The Lees meadow is ridged to facilitate drainage. On the eastern half of its 39½ acres, which lies in Laugharne township, there are twenty shares of ½ to 2 acres, made up of one to five strips (Fig. 11.7). The western, drier half of the Lees (Le Wester Leaze under Clyff) lies

[1] T. I. J. Jones, 'The Court Leet Presentments of the Town, Borough and Liberty of St Clears', Bull. Board Celtic Stud., XIII, 1948, p. 28.
[2] M. Davies, 'The Open Fields of Laugharne', Geography, XL, 1955, p. 169.

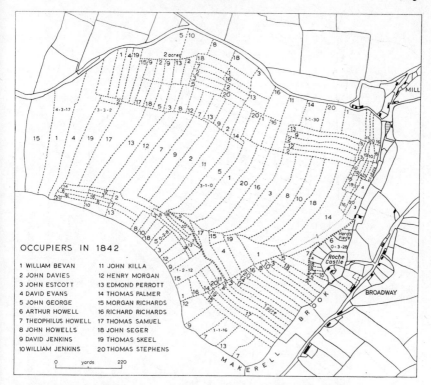

Fig. 11.6 Laugharne, the Hugdon (Carmarthenshire) in 1842.
Sources. Based on the tithe map and award. The one-acre strip left blank on the northwest of the Hugdon was wrongly entered by the tithe commissioners as privately owned and occupied by a man whose name is not included in the list of shareholders.

in Llansadurnen parish and here, in 1842, nineteen burgesses each held one arable strip. The twentieth share was in two strips. The fifty-one strips on the Lees are bordered by the largest of the borough's former common pastures, Laugharne Marsh. This was appropriated by Sir John Perrott during the reign of Elizabeth I.

The tithe award of 1842 indicates that eight burgesses occupied a share in one of the arable fields and a second share of pasture on the Lees. Only one burgess held shares in each of the three fields. This grouping of shares into one arable field, and the balanced distribution of strips in respect of area, gradient and aspect, has facilitated the persistence of common fields in Laugharne. In the mid-nineteenth century burgesses who were not farmers had their strips worked by a neighbour to whom they paid half the produce of their share.

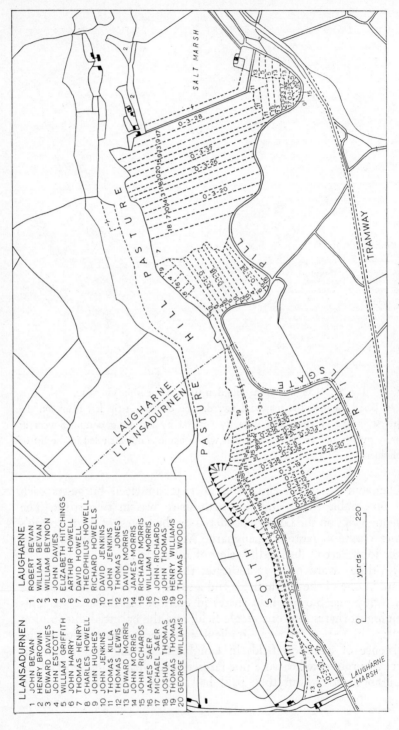

Fig. 11.7 Laugharne, the Lees (Carmarthenshire) in 1842.

Sources. Based on the tithe map and award. The tramway led to a limestone quarry.

Normal rack rents now prevail. The early nineteenth-century crop-system was three years in corn followed by three in grass. The chief control on cropping today is the throwing open of the arable fields for grazing for two winter months, usually November and December, when the cattle are stinted according to the acreage of the shares.

Laugharne Corporation own about a hundred properties, including many enclosed fields, in addition to the common fields. The Recorder and Portreeve organise the beating of the bounds (the Common Walk) every third year; the boundaries then walked are those of Guy de Brian's fourteenth-century charter.

F. PEMBROKESHIRE

Most of south Pembrokeshire lies below 300 feet. It is a region of eroded ridges and silt-filled valleys, which have a generally west–east trend. South of Haverfordwest and Narberth, well-drained soils overlie its limestones and sandstones. The St David's peninsula has a flat plateau surface, around 200 feet in height, from which intrusive igneous monadnocks rise like steep islands. Similar country extends northeastwards behind the north coast of Pembrokeshire. The northern half of the shire is dominated by the pointed peaks of Presely, which culminate in Foel Cwmcerwyn (1,760 ft) and pass eastwards into the Carmarthenshire hills. The Presely ridge falls sharply down to undulating plateau country about 600 feet high, and bogs and common grazings occur around and below the break of slope. Mynydd Presely, with its acid soils and heavier rainfall, did not attract Anglo-Norman and Flemish settlers. They occupied south Pembrokeshire, tamed lands which were never far from salt water, and administered their manors from numerous castles. In north Pembrokeshire Anglo-Norman outposts, sustained by the produce of relatively fertile coastlands, were set up at Newport, Fishguard and St David's.

To St David's, renowned as a Celtic Christian centre, came its first Norman bishop, Bernard (1115–48). He and his successors acquired extensive lands and gradually modified tenures, customs and services on them until their larger lowland manors resembled those of England. The bishops of St David's obtained early recognition as Marcher Lords of Pebidiog and their inheritance was inviolate until the Reformation.[1] Among lands lost then was the large manor of Lamphey, in south Pembrokeshire, where, as at St David's and Llawhaden, Bishop Gower (1328–47) had built a splendid castellated palace, but many of the bishops' lands and manorial rights were held by the

[1] G. Williams, *The Welsh Church from Conquest to Reformation*, Cardiff, 1962, p. 273.

Welsh Church until its disestablishment in 1919. A century before this, improvers noted that *c.* 15,000 acres were open or common in the bishop's manors and that they could be enclosed for £1 an acre and let at 5s. But the land was likely to remain commonable as no bishop could be expected to see the completion of enclosure whose expenses he had borne.[1] Some commons were enclosed in the mid-nineteenth century, but there are still many small lowland common grazings near St David's. The little cathedral city, like many other Pembrokeshire nucleated settlements, is set in a mosaic of enclosed strip fields.

Accounts by George Owen of the Tudor common fields of both south and north Pembrokeshire, of common of shack, and of children employed in herding, have often been quoted.[2] Enclosure of common arable fields came as late as the mid-eighteenth century in many parts of the county. The arable at Roch, at the northwest end of the landsker between English and Welsh-speaking Pembrokeshire, and that in the adjoining manor of Nolton, then lay in common.[3] Walter Davies reported in 1815 that 'between 1750 and 1760 whole parishes were enclosed by common consent in Pembrokeshire'.[4] Eighteenth-century improvers like the Cawdors effected large enclosures in southwest Pembrokeshire.

In 1326 an extent of his lands was made for Bishop Martin of St David's. One of his most productive manors was at Lamphey.[5] This south Pembrokeshire village, and the bishop's palace and fish-ponds, lie at 80 feet in a sheltered valley. The low flat coast plateau runs seaward for 1½ miles from it. Here, in 1326, the bishop's demesne lay in six fields which, with his park and 'land already let below the town', covered 526 acres. Twenty-seven tenants grew autumn and spring sown wheat, barley, oats, peas, beans and vetches on it, and the fallows supported 300 sheep in winter and 200 in summer. Both the fields and most of the tenants had English names.

Around St David's the bishop had 73 acres of demesne land in several fields and 15½ acres in three meadows. His arable was let in parcels of ½ to 1½ acres to thirteen tenants, and in 2 to 8 acre holdings to fourteen tenants. Walter Orliens, a free tenant, held 18 acres 'in a field called Emeleth'. The Emlych holding, half a mile north of St David's, was scattered over several strips in 1838. Beyond the St David's

[1] N.L.W., Welsh Church Comm. Coll., 14229⁶.
[2] G. Owen, *The Description of Penbrokeshire*, Cymmrodorion Rec. Ser., 1, pt. 1, 1892, pp. 55, 178 and 193.
[3] R. Fenton, *A Historical Tour through Pembrokeshire*, 1811, p. 156.
[4] W. Davies, *General View of the Agriculture and Domestic Economy of South Wales*, 1, 1815, p. 221.
[5] Willis-Bund (ed.), *Black Book of St David's*, pp. 169–91.

demesne land, small groups of farms, sometimes clustered in the shelter of igneous monadnocks, housed Welsh tenants who worked the surrounding land in common. Settlements in the Welshry of St David's, which are recorded in 1326 and still had unenclosed strip fields in the eighteenth and nineteenth centuries, on the evidence of estate or tithe surveys, include Treleddyn, Treswni and Clegyrvoia (west of St David's), Treleidir, below Penbiri (north of St David's) and Caerfarchell and Harglodd (northeast of St David's). The latter area, near Dowrog Common, on the Fishguard road, had many of the intermixed church lands to which the improvers drew attention.

There was a small common field by the bishop's mill in the Solva valley in 1840 and seven small adjoining fields were then in unenclosed strips by his mill at Felindre in the manor of Villa Camerarii, west of Fishguard. His mill at Tre-fin, beautifully placed where a colourful valley slips into the sea, ground the corn of a considerable community. Tre-fin, a street-village which was granted a weekly market and annual fair in 1290, lies at 100 feet on the coastal plateau. The bishop's demesne lay in Stepilhull (55$\frac{1}{2}$ acres) and Northfield (97$\frac{1}{2}$ acres), and wheat, barley, oats, buckwheat, beans and peas were grown on it. It was let to thirty-nine copyholders at 3d. an acre and 17$\frac{1}{2}$ acres in three meadows were each let at 1s. Numerous fenced groups of arable strips lay between Tre-fin village and the cliff top in 1840 and holdings were still widely dispersed among them. Nineteenth-century villagers called the manor house ruins 'Bishop Martin's Palace'.[1] East of Tre-fin, at Castle Maurice, similar crops were grown in 1326 on 176 acres of demesne arable lying in three fields. Bovate holders rented holdings in it, as at Tre-fin; there were twenty-six of them at Castle Maurice. This village is on the upper reaches of the Western Cleddau. Downstream from it, at Wolf's Castle, 64$\frac{1}{2}$ acres of the bishop's arable lay in twelve fields and fourteen bovate holders farmed an additional 262$\frac{1}{2}$ acres. The bishop had quillets in three meadows; in 1840 'moor' by the river was still jointly held. Fourteenth-century tenants had both English and Welsh names in these three manors.

Strip fields are today fossilised into many parts of the Pembrokeshire landscape. Perhaps those most readily seen are around Robeston Wathen on the A40 road, and the Fishguard 'slangs'. Robeston (Roberts Vill), Narberth, and the Templars' manor of Templeton, all lie in the western half of Narberth lordship in undulating country which occasionally rises to 350 feet. At Robeston and Templeton parallel lines of strip fields still slope down the gentler hillsides. Around Narberth town, enclosure and rearrangement of the common fields was already well advanced in the seventeenth century and only five

[1] Fenton, *Historical Tour through Pembrokeshire*, 1811, p. 31.

common fields can be identified in 1609.[1] Two were at Flimstone and
Coxhill, west of the town. At Robeston thirty groups of strips are
named in the 1609 survey and seventeen of these included between
four and thirteen strips. In half of them – in Upper Hook (9 strips),
Castle Croft (11), Blind Well (4), Above the Hayes (8), Narberth
Way (11), Longstone (6), Linacre (5) and Shortlands (4) – holdings
of $\frac{1}{4}$ to $1\frac{1}{4}$ acres were still in what is likely to have been their original
form. In Hooks Mead, north of Robeston, four of the six meadow
holdings were of $2\frac{1}{2}$ roods. In 1282 'the meadow of Robert's Vill' had
been rented at 1s.; 3s. an acre was charged in 1609. At Templeton the
survey names large holdings of enclosed ground and a few shared
lands such as Jackshill in which there were ten holdings varying from
$\frac{1}{2}$ to $1\frac{1}{2}$ acres, and a holding in Headland which was in enclosed strips
in 1842; disparate holdings were then still a feature.

The villages between Templeton and the south Pembrokeshire
coast, such as East Williamston and Jeffreston, are medieval foundations
which, by 1840, numbered coal miners among their people. But
ploughlands still dominated the landscape. The knot of farmsteads at
East Williamston was surrounded by blocks of partly enclosed strips
known as South Field, Kittle Park, Watershill and Middle Hill and
the pattern of ownerships and tenancies formed an intricate patch-
work in them.

South of Milford Haven the fine land of south Pembrokeshire lay
in the Lordship of Pembroke and was administered from that town.
It included the medieval borough of Tenby, large manors like St
Florence and Manorbier, and many smaller medieval farming communities. It is an area of light soils, where strong winds and light
rainfall restrict the growth of forest trees.

Kingswood manor lay north of Pembroke Pill and grew wheat,
barley, oats and peas and reared stock to sustain the garrison and
borough of Pembroke. Founded late, for this purpose, it had no
bondsmen. The early fourteenth-century accounts of its reeves detail
the sums paid to men who ploughed, weeded and harvested the corn.[2]
One man's hire for pitching corn into the carts in the common field
was $13\frac{1}{2}d$. The hay from five meadow acres was sent to Pembroke
Castle. In contemporary Tenby, 61 acres of the demesne arable was
let at 1s. an acre. William de Valence, earl of Pembroke, had granted
the burgesses of Tenby common of shack from 'the casting down of
the corn' to 2 February. In 1840 the lands of Tenby Corporation,
outside the dignified Regency town, the Charity Land, the Poors Land

[1] P.R.O., L.R. 2/206, fos. 124–58.
[2] H. Owen (ed.), *A Calendar of the Public Records Relating to Pembrokeshire*, Cymmrodorion Rec. Ser., 7, pt. III, 1918, p. 118.

and the glebe were intermingled with the lands of twenty private owners. The majority of both arable fields and meadows were in small strips which had not wholly been enclosed.

In St Florence manor, between Tenby and Pembroke, the demesne extended over 478 acres and twenty-eight tenants each held from 2½ to 28 acres at 8d. an acre. By 1609 the arable lay in West Field, East Field, Ladyland and Middle Hill.[1] The latter is described as a close. In it were 5½ acres 'not enclosed'. Half the holdings in the Ffoord Meadow of St Florence were still half-acre strips in 1609; the others had been consolidated into a two-acre enclosed parcel. St Florence, one of the finest nucleated villages of Pembrokeshire, was still flanked by enclosed half-acre and acre strips in the mid-nineteenth century. Some of them shared names like Honeyland and Ladyland.

Manorbier manor included four nucleated settlements. The largest was Manorbier, dominated by the castle in which Giraldus Cambrensis was born c. 1147. Jameston, Manorbier Newton, and Penally were also in Manorbier manor. By Tudor times, considerable enclosure of common fields had occurred and in 1611 there were complaints of depopulation because of engrossing. But common arable fields still persisted then, as did a considerable number of farmers with arable holdings of up to 20 acres, and common pasture behind the cliff tops. By 1840 the coastal strip both east and west of Manorbier village lay in consolidated holdings. The remainder of the large parish, i.e. the relatively flat area northeast of Manorbier village, and that between Jameston and Manorbier Newton, was covered with long parallel strip fields laid north–south. Holdings of farmers from the three nucleated villages were widely scattered in them. Only around Newton were four arable strips of 1 to 2½ strips unenclosed; their total area was similar to that of most of the enclosed strips. Newton Mead, in one of the few valleys, adjoined Manorbier Newton village. Seven of the nine holdings in it were each occupied by two tenants.

Angle and Marloes, set on promontories south and north of Milford Haven, showed similar field patterns in 1840. Long parallel strip fields ran north–south from both street villages and holdings were not consolidated. Piecemeal enclosure of bundles of very narrow strips had produced largely enclosed strip fields which were adequate for non-mechanised farming. Marloes Mere, which provided 60 to 70 acres of summer grazing, had been enclosed since Fenton described it.[2] The land round Cosheston street village, near Pembroke, was and is similarly disposed. Strips there were grouped under names like Headland and Upper and Lower Furlong.

[1] P.R.O., L.R. 2/206 (1609).
[2] Fenton, *Tour through Pembrokeshire*, p. 162.

Between St Bride's Bay and Haverfordwest lies the Rhos (Roos) area where Flemish craftsmen and farmers, as well as English settlers, were brought in by Henry I. The mixed and thriving community which developed at Haverfordwest zealously guarded its rights. In 1514 the demesne of Haverford was leased to the mayor and burgesses. It included the meadows by Gundwynesditch and at Froghole, Black Meadow, Goosemead and Millmead.[1] Haverford's considerable arable lands lay in 'Aillardishulle', Tirellisholm and Austerslade where 166 acres were let to tenants at will in 1358 at 5d. an acre. The common grazing land lay on Portfield Common, west of Haverford. The 1624 survey of Haverford Lordship, quoted by Gray,[2] notes that some landshares have been broken when tenants have exchanged pieces for convenience and an amendment has been 'straightly required'. It urges that, because lands throughout Haverford Lordship lie 'in small parcels lying intermixedlie', and tenants cannot make full profit of their tenements, the King as lord should exchange and enclose by jury in every manor, but that, 'notwithstandinge the exchaunge the auncient landshares and meares betwixt the pieces be preserved'. Gray also quotes evidence of the enclosure in 1593 of small bundles of strips at Carew and Sageston, which lie across Milford Haven in Pembroke Lordship. Part of this lordship lay west of Milford Haven in the large manor of Burton. Here, in 1541, the Westfield was rented to four tenants, as were lands lying in divers parcels at Houghton, another village in the lordship.[3] All the land west of Houghton village lay in blocks of partly enclosed strips in 1840. They included the contiguous blocks called Hayguard Meadow, Greenway, Middle Hill, Oxland and South Field, each in groups of eight strips of about an acre.[4] There were also larger strips on the north side of Middle Hill which are described as Undivided Land.

In Rosemarket manor, in Haverford Lordship, piecemeal enclosure was replaced by high-handed action on the part of Morris Walter, an ancestor of the Duke of Monmouth, who, in 1581, put his sheep flocks on to his enclosures and deprived fifty to sixty householders of their rights in the common arable fields.[5]

George Owen, Lord of Cemaes, lived near Newport in north Pembrokeshire. Its Marcher Lords were descended from Martin de

[1] H. Owen (ed.), *Pembrokeshire Records*, I, 1911, 143.

[2] P.R.O., LR 2/206; Gray, *English Field Systems*, p. 174.

[3] Owen, *Pembrokeshire Records*, III, 1918, 183.

[4] Sizes of Pembrokeshire oxlands are discussed in B. E. Howells, 'The Distribution of Customary Acres in South Wales', *Nat. Lib. Wales Jnl.*, XV, 1967, p. 231.

[5] P.R.O., E/112/62/2. Quoted in full by B. E. Howells, 'Pembrokeshire Farming, 1580–1620', *Nat. Lib. Wales Jnl.*, IX, 1956, pp. 327–8. See also B. E. Howells, 'Open Fields and Farmsteads in Pembrokeshire', *Pembrokeshire Historian*, III, 1971, p. 12,

Tours; like Guy de Brian, who later gave Haverford and Laugharne their charters, Newport's twelfth-century lord also held lands in Devon. In his account of Pembrokeshire, George Owen attributes the growing of summer wheat by the Welsh of the north of the county to the intermixture of holdings 'so as in every five or sixe acres you shall have ten or twelve owners'.[1] He argued that the country remained champion because of gavelkind. It is doubtful whether gavelkind explains the remnants of common fields which survived in the eighteenth century around the old borough of Newport, whose charter dates from c. 1240. Its medieval people reaped and carried the lord's hay from the marshes by the Nevern estuary and paid a shilling rent for their burgages in the fifteenth century. By 1758 part of the town and its lands were owned by the Bowens of Llwyngwair, a mile east of Newport. Their lands sloped seaward from the Fishguard road to Newport Bay in long parallel arable strips.[2] The access road to the shore through them was the King's Way. The strips of at least five other owners, and of the church, were intermingled with those of the Bowens. This pattern, and the field name burgage, survive on the Newport tithe map.

Farming of holdings scattered over the remnants of common arable fields, by the inhabitants of another old-established trading borough, is revealed by the Fishguard tithe map. A survey of 1653 divides Fishguard into English and Welsh manors. The tithe map of 1838 shows that a large percentage of Fishguard folk still had a share in the surrounding land, hence the outrage of the topographer Malkin: 'It is the only town I ever met with from which dunghills, I do not mean mere heaps of dirt, but literal and bona fide dunghills, are not excluded.'[3] Middens are no longer a feature of Fishguard streets but the long narrow fields which run gently upslope south of Fishguard are still prominent in the landscape. In 1838 Welsh names were given to the blocks of enclosed strips. One strip in Parc Bigney, southwest of the town, was used as a ropewalk. The remainder of Bigney Field, the equivalent of about six strips, formed the only large field near the town. On it, in February 1797, a small French force battled with the Pembrokeshire militia before an audience of scarlet-cloaked women who were aligned along field walls and other vantage points.[4]

George Owen and later writers make it clear that common fields existed throughout the coastlands of north Pembrokeshire. John Evans notes that the country between St David's and Fishguard had few

[1] Owen, *Penbrokeshire*, I, 61.
[2] H. John (surveyor), N.L.W., Llwyngwair Dep. Coll., Map 8.
[3] B. H. Malkin, *The Scenery, Antiquities and Biography of South Wales*, 1807, II, 240.
[4] E. H. S. Jones, *The Last Invasion of Britain*, Cardiff, 1950, pp. 115–21.

enclosures and was formerly grazed in common from harvest to Lady Day.[1] In 1804 it was more usual to tether horses, cattle, sheep, pigs, and even geese on the strips. Cattle were still herded in the hilly, unenclosed hinterland. Here, in northeast Pembrokeshire, there is neither evidence of field systems nor nucleated villages.

G. CARDIGANSHIRE

North Cardiganshire, north of the Aeron valley, came into English hands in 1277; the southern half of the county was conquered in 1284. Much of coastal Cardiganshire and the slopes of major valleys like that of the Teifi, are suitable for arable crops. Around the main villages of the Welsh lords of Ceredigion, and on the Cardiganshire lands of the bishops of St David's, a manorial system which resembled that of anglicised South Wales was in being before the Edwardian conquest. Customary tenants of Lampeter maerdref, on the Teifi, each paid a rent of 1d. for their share of about 24 acres, performed agricultural and transport services and did suit at court. The Welsh lord's mill, meadow and wood, and his house, lay within the maerdref.[2] Similar arrangements, modified by commutation of services, are found in the fourteenth-century manors of the bishops of St David's in Cardiganshire. The partitioning of land among Welsh bondsmen in lowland Cardiganshire resulted in a number of long-lived common fields. They are features of the best land of the county, adjoin nucleated settlements, and provide a sharp contrast with the field patterns of the upland hinterland. There, for example, upslope from Llanddewibrefi, in the Teifi valley, the *patria* was held in 1326 by eight kindreds who tended cows and pigs and paid commorth.[3] Their equal shares of land were each rented at 3s. 4d., but these upland pastoralists left on the landscape no traces of their communal tenure. Much of the land appears to have been distributed among the kindreds later in the fourteenth century and farmed as consolidated holdings.

Llanddewibrefi was a Celtic monastic settlement. St David's foundation was reconstituted as a collegiate centre by Bishop Bek in 1287 and endowed with land. In 1326 it had an annual fair and a weekly market. It was lost to St David's between 1650 and the Restoration, and sold in the eighteenth century to John Johnes of Dolaucothi, near Lampeter. In 1780 Llanddewibrefi went to his son-in-law, Thomas Johnes, best known as the improver of the Hafod estate in the Ystwyth

[1] J. Evans, *Letters written during a tour through South Wales*, 1804, pp. 300–1.
[2] Rees, *South Wales and the March*, p. 200.
[3] Willis-Bund (ed.), *Black Book of St David's*, p. 197.

valley. Fig. 11.8 is based on a survey made for him in 1791.[1] Before his death in 1816, Thomas Johnes had effected the consolidation of the numerous intermixed quillets in his lordship by an enclosure act of 1812.

Llanddewibrefi village lies at a height of 570 feet at a point where the River Brefi trenches the steep western front of the high plateau of Mid-Wales. It is separated from the River Teifi by a rounded hill, the Garth, which is flanked by relatively large areas of flat land. Most of this hill and valley land lay in intermixed strips in 1791 and Rhosgarfan, a 'moory meadow' of 185 acres, on one of the less steep slopes of the plateau front, was shared by eleven tenants. They mainly held northern farms and had no shares in Y Ddôl Fawr (the big meadow). Johnes did not own Garth and Llwyn farms, which appear to have been enclosed well before 1791. Garth nevertheless rented four strips in Dôl Fawr and nine of Johnes' quillets on the Garth. Llwyn farmed one on Dôl Fawr, three on the Garth and one in Rhosgarfan.

Dôl Fawr was in arable on its northern margin; its meadowland contained many acre or half-acre strips. Most of the remaining intermixed quillets were also arable. Further intermixed meadow strips, grouped under the name Pen y ddôl, extended southwards in the valley bottom beyond Dan y ffordd. Thirty of Johnes' tenants held shares in his 673 acres at Llanddewibrefi. The 82 acres of Dôl Fawr were held by fifteen tenants, three of whom had two holdings. Dan y ffordd ($42\frac{1}{2}$ acres), also partly meadow, was farmed by seven tenants, one having two holdings. On the slopes and rounded summit of the Garth hill, 104 acres of intermixed lands had thirteen tenants and on the flat open Ystrad eight tenants farmed nearly 259 acres. The village end of Ystrad had already been enclosed. The greater part of the unenclosed land at Llanddewibrefi was worked in 1791 by occupants of farms situated outside the main village cluster. The bishop's low-lying lands covered the same area east of the River Teifi in 1326. Some of the fourteen burgages then rented at 1s. may have lain at some distance from the village, but in the intervening centuries there must have been partial rearrangement of holdings as an adaptation to the pattern of scattered farms which are more usual in the area. The tenants of hill farms east of Llanddewibrefi had no part of the intermixed lands. The one exception was Foelallt, an old farm half a mile up the Brefi valley, which held one strip of $1\frac{1}{2}$ acres in each of the Dôl Fawr, Garth and Ystrad fields, and 35 acres on Rhosgarfan. The land called 'Vaynallt', and a plot and curtilage in the vill of Llanddewibrefi which went with it, had been bought by the bishop before 1326.

[1] Nat. Lib. Wales, Ms. Maps, vol. 36.

524

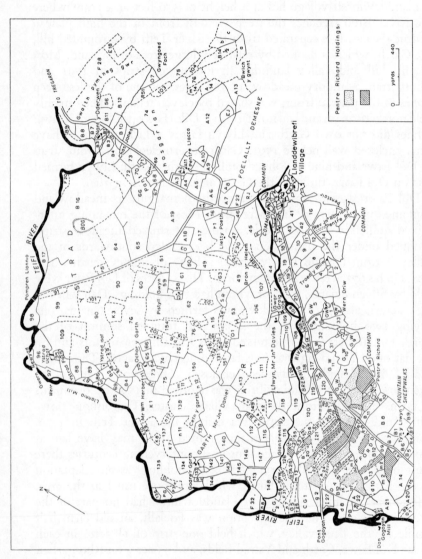

Fig. 11.8 Intermixed lands in Llanddewibrefi (Cardiganshire) in 1791. The Pentre Richard holdings are designated in two ways on the original map, indicating the amalgamation of adjoining parcels of land. Source: Based on maps of the Llanddewibrefi Estate of Thomas Johnes of Hafod, N.L.W. Ms. Maps, Vol. 26.

Between the mouths of the Teifi and the Aeron, Cardiganshire has a cliffed coast. Six and a half miles northeast of Aberaeron lies Llan-rhystyd, and along five miles of the intervening coast there is a raised beach. It has an average width of half a mile and its soils are well-drained. Some of it has probably been lost to the sea since it was first occupied. It proved attractive to medieval leaders with an eye for good land and this low coastal shelf was more intensively developed than any other part of Cardiganshire. The bishops of St David's held Llanddewi Aber-arth and its hilly hinterland and the land unit known as Rhandir Llan-non, which had been granted to Bishop Iorwerth (1215–29) by Rhys ap Gruffydd. The bishop's holding on the Llan-non raised beach became known as Morfa Esgob (Bishop's Moor). It was flanked on its south side by Morfa Mawr, a grange of the Cistercians of Strata Florida. Land at Llanrhystyd, at the north end of the raised beach, was held by the Knights Hospitallers and was probably granted by Rhys ap Gruffydd to the Slebech commandery.

Morfa Mawr was granted after the dissolution to Sir Richard Devereux. The lands of this large farm were enclosed at an early date and now produce Aberystwyth pedigree seeds. On the remaining former ecclasiastical lands on the raised beach, Morfa Esgob is still in partly unfenced quillets, and others which were in existence until the mid-nineteenth century were noted by the first reporters to the Board of Agriculture. 'The only tract like a common field is an extent of very productive barley land reaching on the coast from Aberaeron to Llan-rhystyd. This quarter is much intermixed and chiefly in small-holdings.'[1] Walter Davies noted numerous very small unfenced strips, some of which were consolidated by an act of 1812, and a field which could be found adjoining several parish churches in Cardiganshire.[2] Although the remainder of the parish might be enclosed, this Maes y llan was in inconvenient quillets of varying size which had several owners. Maes yr Eglwys and Banc yr Eglwys were alternatives to Maes y llan at Llansanffraid, the parish church of Llan-non (Fig. 11.9), and at Llanddewi Aber-arth, where Banc yr Eglwys had four un-enclosed strips in 1840.

At Llanddewi Aber-arth four groups of freemen shared the land in 1326 and paid the usual rent of one mark for it to the bishop. In 1840 the slopes behind the village, apart from Banc yr Eglwys, were covered by consolidated holdings. A small common arable field existed between the village and the sea. The unfenced strips, of from ¼ to 2 acres, were demarcated by merestones. They had several owners and twelve tenants. At the seaward ends of five adjoining strips were

[1] T. Lloyd, *General View of the Agriculture of the County of Cardigan*, 1794, p. 29.
[2] Davies, *Agriculture and Domestic Economy*, pp. 222–3.

the lime kilns of five different tenants. Only two strips went with an outlying farm; the remainder were held by the people of the cluster of farms and cottages which faced the mill across the mouth of the Arth.

Llanrhystyd lies in the east–west valley of the Wyre which from time to time functioned as a frontier between the de Clares and their Welsh adversaries. The village lies around the Wyre bridge under the slopes of a hill which shelters it from westerly gales. Enclosed strip fields still lie along the lower slopes. In 1840 a block of a dozen unfenced arable quillets here were occupied by seven villagers. This land adjoined Llanrhystyd church; disparate ownerships were a feature of the enclosed land around the village.

In 1326 the Llan-non land of David Martin, Bishop of St David's, was rented by one group of kinsmen for half a mark.[1] In 1841, Morfa Esgob, stretching from the sea to the inner limit of the raised beach, had seventy owner-occupiers or occupiers who lived in the villages of Llan-non and Llansanffraid. They included craftsmen, tradesmen and captains of trading schooners. A typical scattered holding is shown on Fig. 11.9; the tithe map does not use the normal convention of broken lines for unfenced strips. The strips and the roads across them were largely unfenced and then, as now, landshares separated them from each other. Today, especially near the villages, where they are in pasture, the balks are surmounted by post and wire fences. Morfa Esgob was largely arable in 1841 and the farmers shared storehouses at its southwest corner. It still produces good cereal and root crops. During the second half of the nineteenth century a ribbon of cottages spread between the two villages. On Morfa Esgob a southern access lane was made parallel to the River Clydan and two links were made between this lane and the central access road along the strip margins shown on Fig. 11.9. The 25-inch Ordnance Survey map of 1905 shows the strips regrouped into 108 largely linear blocks. Some consisted of a single strip, and many of two strips, but one holding of two acres included seven strips. The area occupied by the 108 linear holdings was 108.45 acres. Morfa Esgob still provides work for smallholders or supplementary income for the villagers. There is no memory of common of shack on it. Abundant pasture, some of it former common pasture, is available on hillsides behind Llan-non.

[1] Willis-Bund (ed.), *Black Book of St David's*, p. 211.

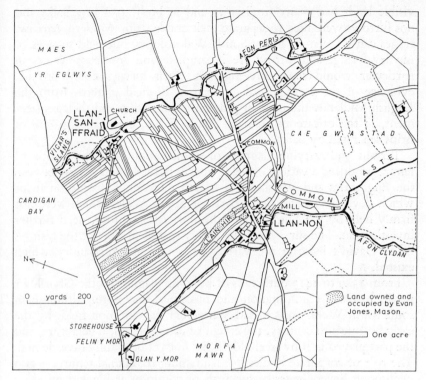

Fig. 11.9 Llan-non, Morfa Esgob (Cardiganshire) in 1841.
Sources. Based on the tithe map and award. Broken lines showing unfenced strips, not used in this case by the tithe surveyors, appear on subsequent Ordnance Survey maps.

H. CONCLUSION

The field patterns introduced by the Normans into the border and coastal lowlands of South Wales, and laid out by laymen for knights or bishops, were modelled on those of English manors. Terrain was the all-important factor in their layout and if relatively large areas of flat land were available, this, rather than proximity to the English border, produced common arable fields and meadows similar to those of the English Midlands. South Monmouthshire's common arable fields were large by Welsh standards but so, too, were those of south Pembrokeshire.

The coastlands of South Wales front on to the Bristol Channel and for centuries there has been an exchange of peoples, products and customs with southwest England. The field patterns of these intervisible lands had many similarities and in both areas low balks and not furrows were used to separate their arable strips. Modern, narrow, ridges can be seen on many South Wales slopes, but field surveys of medieval ridge-and-furrow are incomplete and southeast Wales in particular would repay investigation. Such surveys could provide evidence of the early spread and extent of field patterns from the English Midlands and of their gradual modification and their replacement, in the calcareous areas of South Wales, by smaller groups of strips separated by balks.

Terrain and varying degrees of anglicisation of older forms of tenure produced a variety of field patterns in the border zones between the Englishries and Welshries of Marcher lordships. Common fields which developed here, or in parts of South Wales which were not firmly held by the English until the thirteenth century, need further investigation. The surveys of the widely spaced manors of the bishops of St David's indicate the variety of tenure and husbandry which existed.

From 1349 to 1413 outbreaks of bubonic plague and the Glyn Dŵr revolt hastened commutation and piecemeal enclosure. Although in some south Welsh areas it had obliterated the common fields by the early seventeenth century, the extent of early piecemeal enclosure, and the part played in it by freeholders, has not yet been fully investigated. The role of corporate bodies in maintaining traditional tenures is also of interest. Several cases of survivals of common arable and meadow until the nineteenth century, or the present day, have been attributed above to ownerships or part-ownership by ecclesiastical bodies. Further cases could no doubt be found where the existence of glebe strips, or larger acreages of church property, slowed down enclosure.

Many common meadows persisted until the mid-nineteenth century or, at Laugharne and on Llanbethery Moor, until today. These, and the changeable acres which formerly existed in south Monmouthshire and the Vale of Glamorgan, suggest that the limited meadowlands of the narrow valleys and coast plains of South Wales had a considerable scarcity value. These meadows, and common grazings which were often extensive and distant from the nucleated villages, may be partly responsible for the erratic and often slow adoption of clover and root crops in South Wales.

The above account has attempted no more than a description of common lands in a variety of manors in the lowlands which fringe the south Welsh hills from Bronllys round to the Cardiganshire coast. Local variations in tenure, in the application of three-course rotations in dissimilar demesnes and in rates of enclosure within this large area all need to be investigated in relation to local history and geography.

The modern rural scene in the south Welsh lowlands will often yield vestigial clues which will facilitate reconstruction of the medieval landscape. Hedged strips and small fields in this mixed farming area have not yet disappeared as they have from some English landscapes which are rapidly becoming 'champyon and open country, without great store of inclosures'.

12

Field Systems of Scotland

BY G. WHITTINGTON

A. INTRODUCTION

A comprehensive review of the field systems of Scotland is at once both difficult and necessary. H. L. Gray's attempt in the early part of this century was an extremely courageous and important one and there has been no really comparable study.[1] Since his work appeared other books have been published which have treated the subject incidentally – either while dealing with the overall development of Scottish farming or with the evolution of the Scottish economy. There has however been no study which has attempted to examine critically Gray's suggestions and conclusions. The time has arrived for this task to be undertaken; many may consider it to be long overdue. The suggestions and conclusions of various authors may now be brought together, and the detailed work undertaken for small areas placed in a wider context.

At the outset, it is perhaps necessary to point out that the views of Gray are largely discredited as far as the existence of a 'Celtic' system of land organisation is concerned. Work by E. E. Evans and D. McCourt in Ireland, and by H. Uhlig and P. Flatrès in Europe,[2] has shown that the former agricultural patterns of Scotland were part of a system which pertained most probably to the whole of the Atlantic fringe of Europe. It is also possible that this system was the first to be developed over a wide area of England, being an early predecessor of the more sophisticated two- and three-field systems. It must be made quite quite clear, however, that only the surface of the problems associated with the development of the Scottish field systems has been scratched. Something of their development pattern is known, and it is possible to indicate the lines along which further enquiry

---

[1] H. L. Gray, *English Field Systems*, Cambridge, Mass., 1915.

[2] E. E. Evans, 'Survivals of the Irish Openfield System', *Geography*, XXIV, 1939, pp. 24–36, and 'Donegal Survivals', *Antiquity*, XIII, 1939, pp. 207–22; D. McCourt, 'Infield and Outfield in Ireland', *Econ. Hist. Rev.*, VII, 1955, pp. 369–76, and 'The Rundale System in Donegal: its Distribution and Decline', *Jnl. Co. Donegal Hist. Soc.*, III, 1955, pp. 47–60; H. Uhlig, 'Old Hamlets with Infield and Outfield Systems in Western and Central Europe', *Geogr. Annlr.*, XLIII, 1961, pp. 285–312; P. Flatrès, *Géographie Rurale de Quatre Contrées Celtiques; Irlande, Galles, Cornwall et Man*, Rennes, 1957.

should move, but it is not possible to make any greater claim than that. The progress of studies of Scottish fields and their patterns is not comparable with that in Ireland, England, and many of the countries of Europe. This chapter reviews the known facts, considers the possible evolution of the field systems, and outlines outstanding problems.

The continued existence of archaic forms of agricultural organisation well into the nineteenth and even into the twentieth centuries in Scotland has been a mixed blessing. It has in many ways harmed the study of field systems in that many workers have been content to consider the patterns described by the authors who wrote the county reports for the Board of Agriculture in the early part of the ninteenth century as being representative of the whole spectrum of Scottish agrarian systems. Perhaps more misleading has been the attention given to the agricultural systems of the northwest of Scotland and in particular to the Outer Isles. The patterns found there were frequently responses to environmental factors which did not operate on the mainland, and in most cases these patterns are of comparatively recent development.

The lack of pre-eighteenth-century maps and associated documents in Scotland also conspires to make the task of deciphering the development of field patterns much harder than it is for example in England, and the evidence obtained from the hard toil of field excavation, such as that carried out in pioneering fashion by H. Fairhurst,[1] is therefore of great value. It also means that the worker in Scotland is denied an absolute chronology for most of his statements. He has to rely on supposition and logical deduction to provide working hypotheses. These could in certain areas be supported or modified by material available in legal documents, as work by G. W. S. Barrow and R. A. Dodgshon has shown.[2]

While perhaps overmuch attention has been given to some areas of Scotland and while the contributions of certain writers have been given undue prominence, it must be admitted that without the spark of enquiry that was kept alive in the northwest, and without the great flood of writing on agricultural matters which appeared in the late eighteenth and early nineteenth centuries, our present state of

[1] H. Fairhurst, 'Scottish Clachans', *Scott. Geogr. Mag.*, LXXVI, 1960, pp. 67–76; H. Fairhurst and G. Petrie, 'Scottish Clachans: II. Lix and Rosal', *Scott. Geogr. Mag.*, LXXX, 1964, pp. 150–63.

[2] G. W. S. Barrow, 'Rural Settlement in Central and Eastern Scotland', *Scott. Stud.*, VI, 1962, pp. 123–44; R. A. Dodgshon, 'The Nature and Development of the Infield–Outfield System in Scotland: a Contribution', Paper read to Section H of the British Association for the Advancement of Science: Dundee Meeting, August 1968.

knowledge would be quite meagre. It is from these twin sources that we are able to comprehend fairly clearly the terms used to describe the component parts of the past agrarian landscapes. Before turning to an evolutionary study of the field systems in Scotland it is necessary to provide the bases for such a discussion. Field patterns are the product of a multiplicity of factors and attention will therefore be given in the following sections to the different types of land exploited, to settlements and farm sizes, to tenancy systems and types of tenants, and to inheritance practices and land use.

B. THE COMPONENT PARTS OF THE INFIELD–OUTFIELD SYSTEM

I. THE INFIELD

The basic features of the field systems in Scotland were the infield and outfield. The infield was an area of land close to the farmsteads while the outfield was usually, but not always, to be found at a far greater distance. Neither of these parts of the field system was more important than the other, for they played complementary roles. The infield, variously referred to as 'croftland', 'inbyland' and 'mukked land', was permanently cultivated. Its area, layout and method of cropping varied with time, location and population density. In one respect however there was no variation in the treatment of the infield, namely that it was never in any part of Scotland allowed to go out of cultivation. There was no such thing as a period of fallow in the use of the infield. This area received all of the manure that was available to the farmer. The cultivation of the infield must not be regarded as the most important part of the agrarian system but rather as a vital adjunct to the cattle-keeping sector. During the winter it was necessary to keep the cattle indoors in byres and thus an accumulation of manure became available. This was augmented in different ways. The houses of the farmers were in almost every case either thatched or roofed with turf sods and these coverings were frequently stripped from the roof and deposited with their soot coating on the manure heap. In addition, hillsides were often pared of their humic layer and this was added to the compost collected. It was noted by some authors of Board of Agriculture reports that soil was also dug from pits and mixed with the animal manure. The fact that this practice ruined land which could and should have been used for crop-raising appears not to have been considered by the farmers. These various and often insufficient manures were spread on to a portion of the infield. The area of the infield which received this fertiliser varied according to the number of different crops grown there and this in turn varied through time. Originally, one half of the infield may have received all the manure but the commonest known method was to place it on one-third of the permanent arable land. On this third was sown the barley or bere. The other two-thirds of the infield received no manure and were only ploughed once, as distinct from the bere land which received three ploughings; after this single ploughing the land was put under oats. The infield therefore was involved most commonly in a one-third-manured–barley and a two-thirds-unmanured–oats rotation.

2. THE OUTFIELD

The other basic feature of the system was the outfield. The area of outfield associated with any settlement varied enormously not only in time but also from place to place. Often it was an area of land poorer in fertility and drainage, although this was not always the case. To a certain extent it may be regarded as the equivalent of the fallow land of some English field systems. The outfield lands lay in irregular patches around the settlement and were broken up and cropped on a shifting system. The amount of land broken up each year varied greatly from area to area but its treatment, once having been broken up, was usually the same. Before it was ploughed the cattle belonging to the settlement were 'folded' on it during the nights of the summer months. The cattle were herded into a fold made of turf sods and the land thus received a rudimentary fertilising. Ploughing then took place and the land was planted with oats. This crop was grown continuously without further fertilisation until the land was incapable of returning the amount of seed necessary to sow the land the following year. When this state of affairs was reached the land passed out of cultivation and was allowed to regenerate a natural vegetation cover. The period of rest allowed to this portion of the outfield would of course vary, depending upon local soil conditions, the amount of outfield available and in more recent times more significantly upon population pressure and land hunger. Usually however the outfield portion was cropped for about three or four years and then allowed to rest for five years. A further distinction between the infield and the outfield land was the purpose for which the crops they produced were grown. The infield crops were mainly food grains or brewing grains. The outfield crops however were seen in a different context. The poorer preparation which the land received before the sowing of the crop and the often inferior drainage conditions of the outfield meant that the grain produced was usually of a poor quality. In the first year or two of production, the oats would provide a very welcome addition to the grain crop of the infield. After this however the returns not only got smaller but the grain actually produced became increasingly inferior. The crop of the outfield was primarily grown in fact for straw, for Scottish field systems developed in a zone in which animal husbandry was a dominant occupation and in which natural pasture was minimal and the technique of cultivating fodder crops was very late in developing.

3. HAUGH, LAIGH AND BRUNTLAND

The infield and the outfield were not the only types of cultivated land that existed but they did comprise the basic cultivation units of practically every settlement. In some areas however other land was available for cultivation, some on a fairly permanent basis and some on a very temporary one. Over much of Scotland settlements are located close to rivers and streams which vary greatly in their rate of flow. Many of these water courses also occur in valleys cut by streams of greater volume than those found at the present time. It is common therefore to find areas of land along the courses of rivers and streams which are often less wet in the summer period and which are kept fertilised to a certain extent by an accretion of silt deposited during the winter spates. This land, known as *haugh* land, was used by the farmers as a welcome addition to the arable land found in the infields and outfields. In other areas land was to be found which flooded during the winter months due to its low-lying nature. This land also received silt and was therefore kept in quite good heart. This so-called *laigh* land was also put under the plough.

The final type of land added to the basic unit was that known as *brunt* land. This land was of frequent occurrence in Scotland due to the large spreads of boulder clay and the considerable areas of upland. Either or both of these features led in many instances to the growth of a heather-dominated vegetation, usually on a strongly humic soil. In areas such as these a zone would be cleared of the vegetation and the top layer of the soil would be pared. The vegetation and the turves were burned and the ashes were then mixed in with the soil and a crop of oats was grown. This land, like the outfield, was cropped until it was incapable of returning even the amount of seed needed to plant it. It was then abandoned and allowed to return to its former cover and another clearing would then be made elsewhere. This shifting agricultural feature was probably a remnant form of the earliest attempts at arable farming in Scotland.

4. MEADOW

In addition to the arable land already described there was also a variety of pasture land which differed strongly in type and especially in amount from locality to locality. In most cases the infield–outfield complex was held together in a matrix of natural hay meadows. These were not fields in the organised sense but were merely areas of land near the settlement which were either too boggy to be cultivated as part of the outfield or else had so poor a soil that they were left as scrubby woodland. Patches of similar land intervened between most of the outfields and in many cases between the infields. Such areas however played a comparatively minor part in the agrarian unit, although before the seventeenth or eighteenth centuries they held a much more important position.

5. THE HEAD DYKE

The various parts of the field system described above, with the exception of the brunt lands, were in many circumstances enclosed by what was known as the head dyke. This varied in type and construction from area to area. It was of stone in some zones but in others was merely of an earthen nature, suggesting an interesting parallel with that at Wheldrake described by J. A. Sheppard.[1] How widespread the use of the head dyke was is not clearly known but in an agrarian system where unenclosed arable and free-ranging cattle were involved it seems most likely that it was a very common occurrence. Above or outside the head dyke lay the *muir* lands. The use of these lands again varied from area to area but basically they provided a zone for the pasturing of cattle. The method by which the cattle were pastured varied from an elaborate system of transhumance to a simple journey from the outfield in the morning to the muirlands and then a return at night to the temporary fold. The muirland area was used until the weather conditions were such that the keeping of cattle outside was no longer possible. The cattle then returned permanently to the cattle byre in the settlement, grazing the stubble and the uncultivable areas around and between the infields while the weather was reasonable, and thereafter being kept in the byre on an inadequate food supply until spring.

[1] J. A. Sheppard, 'Pre-enclosure Field and Settlement Patterns in an English Township', *Geogr. Annlr.*, XLVIII, Ser. B, 1966, pp. 69–71.

6. THE SETTLEMENT

It is proposed here to confine this consideration of the form of the settlement to what was undoubtedly the earliest and most widespread form of occupance associated with sedentary agriculture. The village as it is known from quite an early period in England did not exist in Scotland until a comparatively recent time. Even then it came into existence only in a Lowland context where quite different environmental conditions obtained from those which marked off the Highlands.

The basic form of settlement was the often formless group of houses which are most readily classified by the term *clachan*. The farmsteads which made up the settlement were frequently placed at the edge of the infield, but this depended upon the nature of the terrain in which the settlement occurred. Wherever possible the clachan was placed on a declivity to promote drainage of the site. Sometimes this would be a piece of unimprovable moor, a river terrace, or merely a piece of land that was better drained than any other in the neighbourhood. In most instances care was taken not to site the houses on land that was of first class agricultural potential for in many areas the sterilisation of land by buildings could not be afforded. The houses usually stood altitudinally above the infield thus allowing a natural drainage of effluent from the cow-byre or bestiary on to the infield during the winter months. The clachan, or township, as it was often called, was occupied by differing numbers of tenants, but four to six was the usual minimum where the working of the land was done on a communal basis. In such instances each of the cultivators supplied at least one animal to the plough-team, for until the eighteenth century, due to the cumbrous nature of the Scots plough, six or eight animals were often necessary to plough the land and agriculture was frequently a joint concern. The difficulty of keeping enough animals to plough the land on an individual basis was probably a far more compelling reason for joint-farming than the desire for defence in an uncertain political era.

C. LAND TENURE

I. RUNRIG AND THE 'RUNRIG SYSTEM'

The basic elements of the infield–outfield system were described in the last section. No account was given there of the land division pattern in which the various tenants and occupiers of the associated settlements were involved. In the cultivation process the land was divided into a series of high-backed ridges, often as high as six feet from crown to foot and up to twenty feet in width. They were sinuous in form, with balks in-between, and ran parallel to one another within any one unit of the infield or seeded outfield. The ridges held by individual cultivators were not usually grouped in a block but dispersed in a fragmented form. This, together with a lack of well-documented, detailed information for a large area of Scotland regarding the length of time each cultivator farmed a particular piece of ground before it was changed for another piece, has caused the infield–outfield system frequently to be called the 'runrig system'.

It is true to say that considerable confusion exists over the word 'runrig' and yet it was runrig and the imagined existence of a 'runrig system' which Gray made one of the underpinnings of his 'Celtic' system of land organisation. He must therefore have had a clear idea of what the 'runrig system' involved.[1] But the contention held here is that the basic conceptions of Gray and some other writers concerning this term are wrong. It is easiest to illustrate their errors by first describing what appears to be their notion of the system.

Because of the communal nature of farming in the infield–outfield system they claim that an even or as near even division as possible of the different qualities of land amongst all the cultivators was necessary. Thus came about the system known as runrig in the Scottish Lowlands and *roinn ruith* in the Gaelic-speaking areas. This led to the infield, the cultivated outfield, the haugh, laigh and bruntland and the turf-cutting area being divided into a system of strips. Each cultivator, depending upon his status in the community, took a varying number of alternate strips in the fields and received the produce of those strips. Thus good soil, poor soil and badly drained soil could be divided out amongst all the cultivators. Furthermore Gray at least took it for granted that redistribution of the strips occurred annually throughout the whole of Scotland and that this practice was of great age.[2]

Before examining further the ideas put forward by Gray and others, it is necessary to try to establish the meaning of the term 'runrig'. Definitions given by dictionaries are usually very broad but they provide a convenient starting point for discussion. One such definition runs:

'a system of land tenure in which each tenant was allocated several detached portions and rigs of land each year by lot and rotation, so that each would share in turn in the more fertile areas; a portion of land thus cultivated.'[3]

[1] Gray, *English Field Systems*, p. 202.
[2] *Ibid.*, p. 171.
[3] *Scottish National Dictionary*, 1968.

Here then is agreement with the ideas put forward by Gray. But elsewhere, different ideas and a less categoric assertion may be found:

> '*run-rig*, noun. In Scotland and Ireland, a form or system of holding land or of distribution of lands among tenants or owners, by which the land is apportioned so that a single tenant's or owner's holding consists of strips lying between those of others. Also, the order or arrangement of the strips so held.'[1]

Here there is no mention of annual rotation, no mention of all sharing in the fertile land. Moreover there appears in this definition the idea that runrig affected proprietors as well as tenants. It seems that not only did the tenants' lands lie fragmented among those of other tenants but that those of the proprietors, or heritors as they were known, were similarly affected. The statement in Webster is therefore more cautious and also more informative. It is also more readily acceptable until there is a greater wealth of *established* evidence from areas in which runrig was known to operate.

Perhaps the most important implication of the Webster definition is that the frequent assumption that runrig merely involved the intermixture of land occupied by tenants may be wrong. Tenant runrig was apparently the commonest occurrence within this type of land holding. Its existence can be established for many parts of Scotland and it is known to have operated for example on the estate of Pitkellony in Perthshire, which is the subject of detailed examination below. There, one half of the lands of Westertown of Drumaquance (Figs. 12.2 and 12.3) was in runrig with the lands of Eastertown of Drumaquance (Figs. 12.2 and 12.4). But the land of the proprietors was also involved in runrig, a feature which called for an act of the Scots Parliament in 1695. The text of this act is given here because it is frequently assumed that it applied to all lands lying in runrig whereas from the text it is quite clear that it only applied to proprietary runrig.

'Act anent Lands lying in Run-rig

> Our Sovereign Lord and the Estates of Parliament Taking into their Consideration the great Disadvantage arising to the whole Subjects from Lands lying run-rig, and that the same is highly prejudicial to the Policy and Improvement of the Nation, by planting and inclosing, conform to the several Lawes and acts of Parliament of before made thereanent: For remeid whereof His Majesty with the Advice and Consent of the said Estates Statutes and Ordains that wherever Lands of different Heretors ly run-rig,

---

[1] *Webster's International Dictionary*, 1959.

it shall be leisum to either party to apply to the Shirriffs, Stewarts, and Lords of Regality or Justices of the Peace of the several Shires where the Lands ly; to the effect that these Lands may be divided according to their respective interests, who are hereby appoynted and authorised for that effect; And that after due and lawfull Citation of all parties concerned, at an certain day to be prefixed by the Judge or Judges. It is always hereby Declared that the said Judges, in making the forsaid Division, shall be, and are hereby restricted, so as special regaird may be had to the Mansion houses of the respective Heretors, and that there may be allowed and adjudged to them the respective parts of the Division, as shall be most commodious to their respective Mansion houses and Policy, and which shall not be applicable to the other adjacent Heretors: As also it is hereby Provided and Declared that their presents shall not be extended to the Burrow and Incorporat Acres but that notwithstanding hereof, the same shall remain with the Heretors to whom they do belong, as if no such Act had been made.'[1]

Thus fragmented holdings of both a proprietary and tenant nature did exist in the infield–outfield system but there is no proof for Gray's suggestion that this occurrence was *initially* due to a wish for an equitable division of differing land qualities or that there was an annual distribution. On this latter point opinions vary from: 'Sometimes each tenant would occupy the same bundle of strips in perpetuity; but more commonly the whole arable ground would be periodically (often annually) re-allocated among the different tenants',[2] to: 'But we have not sufficient evidence to enable us to draw definite conclusions, and there is no evidence that annual re-allotment of the rigs was customary.'[3] These quotations present opposite ends of the spectrum. What in fact do earlier writers say and what evidence do documents and maps give on this matter? In some instances the land was re-allocated every year but among the very few areas where this practice is actually described are Perthshire,[4] Inverness-shire,[5] Arran,[6] Lewis, St Kilda and Islay.[7] Reallocation also occurred in Argyllshire but no specific period is mentioned. Certainly in some areas, documented for a late period of agrarian history (late seventeenth and eighteenth

---

[1] *Acts of the Parliaments of Scotland*, IX, 421 (1695).
[2] M. Gray, 'The Abolition of Runrig in the Highlands of Scotland', *Econ. Hist. Rev.*, V, 1952, pp. 46–7.
[3] W. C. Dickinson, *Scotland from the Earliest Times to 1603*, 1963, p. 64.
[4] J. Robertson, *General View of the Agriculture of Perthshire*, 1799, p. 61.
[5] J. Rae, 'The Scotch Village Community', *Fortnightly Rev.*, XLIV, 1855, p. 661.
[6] W. Aiton, *General View of the Agriculture of Bute*, 1816, p. 79.
[7] T. Pennant, *A Tour of Scotland*, 1772, p. 274.

centuries), strips were allocated on a three-yearly basis. At the end of three years the strips were pooled and the whole of the land was divided into the number of strips according to the number and standing of the tenants. Lots were drawn for the shares. In this way a third of the townland was redivided every year. Such a practice is however only definitely recorded in Inverness-shire,[1] the Outer Isles,[2] and Arran[3] (where obviously there were either two systems operating or there had been a change between the report made by Headrick and that made by Aiton, or perhaps more likely the two commentators were making general statements about isolated or restricted occurrences of the phenomena they were describing).

In some areas prior to the eighteenth century the division of the land into shares did not take place until harvest time so that no man knew which was to be his share of the land and its produce until the work of cultivation was done. It would appear most likely that this was the fundamental share system from which the pre-cultivation share-out of the land developed. In other instances it seems that the lottery system was never adopted at all but the whole crop after harvesting was divided among all the co-joint tenants.

A system did exist therefore which required that the ridges be divided among the various cultivators. What seems to be uncertain is whether the shares were permanently allocated to the tenants at the beginning of new tenancy arrangements or whether they were frequently reallocated. The answer seems to be that in some areas reallotment did not take place but that by the time documentation became available the system had broken down, or that some areas had never known it. A way in which reallocation could have been abandoned is suggested by a practice quoted by J. Robertson for Perthshire. He writes that

'...the first deviation from runrig was by dividing the farms into Kavels or Kenches, by which every field of the same quality was split into as many lots as there were tenants in the farm...The tenants cast lots (or Kavels in the Scottish dialect) for their particular share...This was an improvement in as far as it went; every farmer has his own lot in each field...reaping the benefit of his industry, which by runrig husbandry he could not enjoy, owing to the exchange of ridges every year.'[4]

[1] J. Robertson, *General View of the Agriculture in the County of Inverness*, 1808, p. 334.
[2] A. Carmichael, 'Grazing and Agrestic Customs of the Outer Hebrides', *Celt. Rev.*, x, 1914, p. 256; W. F. Skene, *Celtic Scotland*, 1880, III, 380.
[3] J. Headrick, *View of the Agriculture of the Isle of Arran*, 1807, p. 307.
[4] Robertson, *Agriculture of Perthshire*, p. 61.

Such a system is also known to have operated in Moray and Nairn.[1]

It is noticeable here that Robertson does talk of 'runrig husbandry' and it is perhaps this and similar expressions involving runrig that served to confuse later workers. Certainly land was divided among the various cultivators in some areas and in some periods, but there is no proof that it was an essential part of the infield–outfield system. Recent work by I. M. Matley on the origin of infield–outfield agriculture in Scotland,[2] based on a linguistic approach, has helped to confirm this view. He examined the provenance of the term runrig and came to the conclusion that it is not only non-Celtic in origin but is certainly associated from at least 1437 with the Scottish Lowlands. There it could have meant quite simply a 'run of ridges' and there is no certain proof that periodic allocation or reallocating of the ridges was inevitably involved.

It is best therefore to regard 'runrig system' as something which came into existence as an agrarian term due not only to a misunderstanding of the original meaning of runrig but also to an unclear idea of the area over which redistribution of land holdings actually operated. 'Runrig system' is not a synonym for infield–outfield and as proof of a 'Celtic' agrarian system the existence of runrig has no value. First, as Matley believes, *roinn ruith* is a translation of a Lowland Scots word into Gaelic and not vice versa; the Gaelic word for ridge is *iomair* and is used in the vernacular but there is no documentary or indeed spoken proof that any Gaelic-speaking cultivator used or uses the term *roinn ruith*. Secondly, Gray took it for granted that annual redistribution of shares (i.e. his runrig) occurred throughout the whole of Scotland and that this system was of great age; this has already been demonstrated to be false. Thirdly, he considered the existence of runrig to be the cause of a basic difference between the English and his 'Celtic' field systems – the lack of fields.[3] Even disregarding his misconceptions about the nature of runrig, it is still necessary to dispute his assertion that it was responsible for the difference between the two- and three-field system of England and the infield–outfield system of Scotland. On the one hand, the latter system made a fallow field on the English pattern unnecessary. On the other, the planting of one field with a winter grain and another with a spring grain did not occur in Scotland. Thus two distinct fields for grain-growing were unnecessary as all grains were spring-grown.

[1] W. Leslie, *General View of Agriculture in the Counties of Nairn and Moray*, 1811, p. 459.
[2] I. M. Matley, 'The Origin of Infield–Outfield Agriculture in Scotland: the Linguistic Evidence', *Prof. Geog.*, XVIII, 1966, pp. 275–9.
[3] Gray, *English Field Systems*, p. 171.

Runrig can be regarded as an agrarian term which underwent an evolution of meaning during the period in which infield–outfield agriculture was operating. To begin with it perhaps meant 'ridges running in parallel within the same agrarian unit'. Then it became associated with a system whereby the land in each agrarian unit (either after harvest or, possibly at a later date, before cultivation) was shared between the total number of cultivators involved. Thus came into existence an intermixture of land belonging to different tenants. Whether this was based upon a desire for an equitable share of land of different qualities is still open to debate. But at this stage of the evolution of the term runrig this possibility seems to be quite likely. Certainly Dodgshon presented a good case for this from an examination of land division in southeast Scotland.[1] He showed that great emphasis was placed in the eighteenth-century land division proceedings on the equality of proportions within individual husbandlands (see below, p. 543). But this equality was not to be only of quality of land but also of quantity, and while emphasis on one or other could still lead to compact holdings, an equal division with regard to both quality and extent almost invariably would lead to some form of intermixture – to this term runrig was applied. At a later date than this application of the term, and only in some areas of Scotland possibly, runrig was also recognised as involving an exchange or reallocation of the fragmented areas, either annually or at longer intervals.

Furthermore the development of runrig should not be divorced from the system of land leasing. In Scotland there were two forms commonly employed. First, there was the system of co-joint tenancy where all the tenants on one farm were equally responsible for its running and for the payment of its rent. In such a situation the land would most sensibly have been cultivated in common and its produce divided after harvest. In such a case runrig would simply have referred to ridges lying in parallel. This system was probably the older of the two. Under a second system, several cultivators on one farm each had a separate lease or standing and were only responsible for the cultivation and rent of the land involved in the lease agreement – the multiple tenancy farm. In such an arrangement, allocation of the shares of lands would have involved the dividing of the ridges before cultivation and hence runrig would have taken on another connotation. Where runrig is used as an agrarian term on maps and in documents it is necessary to bear the tenancy arrangement in mind. Thus it can be considered that runrig meant different things in differing contexts and at differing periods. Certainly in the period of the eighteenth

[1] R. A. Dodgshon, 'Runrig in Southeast Scotland', Paper presented to Institute of British Geographers Conference on Runrig, Musselburgh 1969.

century it always referred to intermixed holdings, both of a proprietary and of a tenantry variety, but reallocation was not necessarily a part of the practice.

The existence of intermixed holdings and of the redistribution of strips within the infield–outfield system in some areas of Scotland would not have caused any differences to appear in the rural landscapes of those areas in contrast with areas where infield–outfield occurred without any operation of runrig. The lack of enclosure and difficulties of drainage meant that land was cultivated in exactly the same way everywhere. The high ridges and their dividing balks have already been referred to. The latter were sometimes of grass but were more usually a zone of unploughed land between the ridges on to which were thrown the stones frequently turned up by the plough. The balks in fact were the drainage lines into which the crowns of the ridges shed their water. More often than not however the water stood stagnant in the balks during the winter while during the summer the water level dropped and they became infested with weeds, supplementing those allowed to grow amongst and strangle the grain crop. In some instances the balks provided additional pasture land for cattle.

2. FARM SIZE AND TENURE

The size of the farms varied greatly. The ploughgate was the usual areal designation given to a southeastern Scottish farm. It was divided into four husbandlands or eight oxgates (oxgangs) but the size of these units varied from area to area depending to a large extent upon the emphasis placed on grain-growing. The most common size of the husbandland was twenty-six acres but this must not be considered as anything but a nominal size. A large number of terms were used to designate land units in the north, especially to the northwest of the Central Lowlands, among which are *davoch, rath, auchten, merkland, pennyland, farthingland, ounceland* and *boll.* The fact that these terms had no precise areal connotation causes a great deal of confusion when trying to interpret earlier writings. It is impossible to be absolutely sure of the actual unit being described. Furthermore, the differences in terms used in the north has been taken as evidence of a different agrarian organisation in the north from that which operated in the south. But on close examination of the terms used in both areas it appears that there were used in the north terms which did have equivalence in concept with those used in the south. Thus quarter-davoch seems to equate with the ploughgate or carucate (nominally 104 acres), rath with husbandland (nominally 26 acres) and auchten with oxgate, bovate or horsegate (nominally 13 acres). Thus once again the question of Anglian or Celtic occupance seems to have little relevance to the study of Scottish agrarian forms. Further discussion of this subject is unnecessary here but a study of the whole problem leads to the belief that Barrow's treatment[1] of the topic is sound and especially so in his rejection of the ideas proposed by A. McKerral in 1960.[2]

In all this however it must be emphasised that land in the earliest period was not measured but was estimated in units and proportions either as in the north (where fractions of the davoch were used), or as in the south (where the ploughgate was used) according to the amount that could be ploughed in a certain period by a plough-team.

However as far as the actual *appearance* of the field pattern and field system of Scotland is concerned the importance of the various unit names used is not great. As Barrow has so well expressed it, using the example of the southern area,

'...the largest visible, physical unit of the agrarian exploitation was the field, sometimes divided into furlongs, everywhere divided into rigs or acres, equally visible and physical...Alongside and overlying these visible, physical units of field and rig were the semi-tangible or wholly intangible units of ploughgate and oxgang. Originally, no doubt, the ploughgate and the oxgang would have been as tangible and concrete as the field and acre...But in this period (twelfth and thirteenth centuries), as a rule ploughgate and oxgang (and similarly fractions of the davoch) were essentially abstract concepts, expressions used to denote an approximate area, or rather, approximate capacity.'[3]

The proportions of infield to outfield also varied on each farm. A very common arrangement however was one of infield to three of outfield. Thus in areas as different as Forfar, Argyllshire and Ayrshire farms were often of ninety to one hundred acres in size and their infield occupied twenty to twenty-five acres. In certain circumstances, such as the type and nature of soil and climate, and at certain periods, this arrangement did not apply. This whole subject will be discussed in a later section.

The land held by the cultivator varied not only in amount but also in the manner of holding. It has been suggested that in quite an early period individual tenure did occur. Such an arrangement however is difficult to place in an accepted agricultural context. One of the main

[1] Barrow, *Scott. Stud.*, VI, 1962, pp. 123–44.
[2] A. McKerral, 'The Lesser Land and Administrative Divisions in Celtic Scotland', *Proc. Soc. Antiq. Scotl.*, LXXXV, 1960, pp. 52–64.
[3] Barrow, *Scott. Stud.*, VI, 1962, p. 128.

reasons for cultivation in a group and by the group was the problem of owning enough cattle for the extremely large plough-team that was necessary with the old heavy Scots plough.[1] It is difficult to imagine any single-tenure unit being operable without a large number of cottars and also without the tenant being of considerable means. The large farms in the Lothians referred to by J. Handley[2] were worked with hired labour and they were probably a fairly recent innovation.

The suggestion made by Fairhurst that single-tenant units existed in the north of Scotland is more puzzling.[3] He found isolated dwellings and noted that such settlements would have had little arable land due to the limited and discontinuous nature of land that could be cultivated. Fairhurst suggests that this settlement would have been occupied by the tacksman class, but how did they cultivate? Was their arable farming achieved by the *caschrom* or the *casghirach* and lazybeds? It is perhaps more likely that these single dwellings represent the occupations of mailers (an early class of cultivator to emerge, being referred to in an act of 1568[4] – see also p. 549). Clearly this is a problem which needs much more attention. In the early period unless spade cultivation or a complex system of shared plough-teams operating over a large area were the norm then individual tenure and isolated settlement without cottar help was out of the question. However the more normal system of land holding was in runrig whether this involved reallotting or not. Within the long strips into which the infields were divided each cultivator held a certain amount of land. When considering land holding it is possible to find two extremes: the individual form of tenure with compact holding or the scattered strip system with in many cases fragmentation of a severe nature. In the latter case it is interesting to compare land holding situations in Scotland with those in Ireland for both had large areas of runrig within an infield–outfield arrangement. As Gray showed[5] it was quite possible for land divisions in runrig associated with extreme fragmentation to occur at quite a late date (the eighteenth century, for example), and to replace in fact what was formerly a consolidated holding. In Scotland the re-emergence of runrig also occurred after a period of consolidation, as shown by Carmichael for the Outer Hebrides.[6] J. Symon also quotes instances at a much earlier

---

[1] R. Jirlow and I. Whitaker, 'The Plough in Scotland', *Scott. Stud.*, I, 1957, pp. 71–94.
[2] J. Handley, *Scottish Farming in the 18th Century*, 1953, p. 50.
[3] H. Fairhurst, 'The Surveys for the Sutherland Clearances 1813–20', *Scott. Stud.*, VIII, 1964, p. 8.
[4] *Acts of the Parliament of Scotland*, III, 45 (1568).
[5] Gray, *English Field Systems*, pp. 191–2.
[6] Carmichael, *Celt. Rev.*, X, 1914, p. 260.

date for the monastic lands.[1] But there the complicating factor of the attitude of the monasteries to runrig is involved. However in all these cases it is noticeable that the severe fragmentation of holdings which occurred in Ireland did not take place in Scotland. The holdings in the strip fields were often scattered but they were not wildly fragmented. Why this difference between Ireland and Scotland? In Scotland is this situation connected with the development of the emergence of the complicated groups of sub-tenants – the cottars, the pendiclers, the acremen and the crofters?

Subdivision of the land is of course bound up with two features – the growth of population and social customs. In the earliest period group settlement was vital. At this time the multiplication of settlement units would have been slow; general but especially infant mortality rates would have been high. Furthermore, as Fairhurst has shown at Lix,[2] whole settlements could disappear and this would lead to a new availability of land. Famine must have been a frequent occurrence in Scotland causing large numbers to die and the survivors to desert their settlements. In such instances land would have been available for reconsolidation and in the earliest period for resettlement. Thus for a long time there would have been no pressure on land. As time passed new settlement units would have appeared. Why this occurred is not clear. Why did the existing ones not grow to a greater size as did the English nucleated village? R. A. Gailey has investigated this problem but much more information is needed because it is fundamental to the question of settlement distribution and growth which in turn has a strong bearing on field patterns and land holdings. As the years went by the largely landless classes appeared. Were they victims of a social system or, more likely in the Scottish context, did they come into existence as a result of population growth and a reluctance to subdivide land? It is noticeable that there was no great growth of clachan populations comparable with that of Ireland.

Is the difference between fragmentation in Ireland and Scotland due to social custom? Gailey suggested that the existence of a multiplicity of clachans and the minute subdivision of land in Ireland and the absence of these features in Scotland was due to 'a different attitude by the proprietor in the two countries'.[3] The attitudes of proprietors are and have been a powerful factor in the countryside – for such a reason it is impossible in England to equate directly the period of enclosure with the form of husbandry. But how did this factor operate

[1] J. Symon, *Scottish Farming Past and Present*, 1959, p. 70.
[2] Fairhurst, *Scott. Geogr. Mag.*, LXXVI, 1960, pp. 74–6.
[3] R. A. Gailey, 'The Evolution of Highland Rural Settlement', *Scott. Stud.*, VI, 1962, p. 166.

on a countrywide scale in Scotland or for that matter in Ireland? Furthermore it is necessary to ask whether there is not here a difference in the inheritance system, perhaps associated with the importance held by gavelkind. In Ireland this system was widely adopted whereas in Scotland it seems to have had a very late and limited development. Perhaps this is the reason why over-fragmentation did not occur while also providing the main reason for the appearance of the landless class.

3. LAND TENANTS AND OCCUPIERS

Consideration must now be given to the types of tenants that existed. The literature describing these features reveals that systems of land ownership, land inheritance and land occupancy are exceedingly complex and difficult to decipher. Very few authors agree on the systems that existed and even more confusing are the variations in names that they use for the actual cultivators. Added difficulty is caused by the lack of absolute dates for much of what is known to have existed at some time in the past.

Comparatively little is known of the method of land holding for the period before the early eighteenth century. In time however it becomes obvious that the lands were deemed to be held by superiors[1] and from these they were rented out in a number of different ways. The superiors were lay and religious and this difference sometimes led to variations in agrarian custom. Attention here will be focussed on what came to be the norm in land holding and this occurred on the lay holdings. The superior or, as he later became, the proprietor of the land let his possessions out for a rent, at first in kind and later in money or a mixture of the two. In the full flowering of the system the lands passed from the proprietor either into the hands of a tacksman, often a cadet member of the proprietor's family, or to a group of joint tenants. In either case a rent had to be paid to the superior. The tenants were jointly responsible for this rent and the contribution of each tenant was worked out in relation to his holdings in the common fields. If any one tenant was unable to pay his contribution then the rest of the tenants had to make good the deficit. The tacksman also had to provide a rent and this he achieved in one of two ways. He either farmed the holding himself with the aid of cottars or he sublet the land to other tenants from whom he often extorted rents in excess of what was needed to pay his superior. Sometimes he employed a combination of these systems on the same holding. In southeast Scotland at least, however, there was a tendency by the eighteenth century for multiple tenancy to be replaced by single tenancy. This

[1] The superior was the feudal lord of a vassal, one to whom feu-duty was paid.

has been shown conclusively by an analysis of 144 farms in Roxburgh-shire and Berwickshire where by 1755 only 44 per cent of the farms were in multiple tenancy.[1]

Any land unit could therefore consist of a combination of infield, outfield and moorland which would be divided up among tenants holding directly from the proprietors, sub-tenants holding from the tacksman, and the tacksman himself. Their portions of arable land would often lie in runrig in the various fields involved and they would use the common pasture in proportion to their share of arable land, this system being termed *souming and rouming*. It was also possible for any one settlement and the land associated with it to be worked by any one of the group systems alone – tacksman and cottars or direct tenants or sub-tenants.

The period in which the tacksman first appeared as an important person in the land-holding hierarchy is difficult to assess (I. F. Grant states that it was *developing* during the fifteenth and sixteenth centuries).[2] It is not possible to relate this to the rate of population growth which would have made the acquisition of areas of empty land impossible. Under the inheritance system (not one of gavelkind in the early period at least) large holdings were not subdivided among the various sons. The system of the tacksman working the land for himself with the aid of cottars gives no clue either to his appearance on the scene. The cottars could have appeared in two ways: either as bondmen in the days of serfdom or in the period after that due to pressure of population making the provision of new land on an infield–outfield basis to all of the populace out of the question.

The pressure of population eventually led to an occupation of existing wastelands and the development of new settlements to such a degree that it could go no further. Therefore new social classes came into existence and new additions were made to the infield–outfield pattern. It is in this realm that great confusion exists – such names as cottars, cotters, cottagers, acremen, crofters, pendiclers and mailers are frequently met in old literature and it is often difficult to discover their precise meaning. Two names among these are further confused in that mailer and crofter, especially the latter, have taken on quite different connotations in the recent past.

It is quite clear however that the tenants were eventually forced to share their lands in various ways with new groups of people who were often not fully involved in the workings of the traditional agricultural system. One group of these which came into existence due to the non-acceptance of gavelkind were known as acremen or

[1] Dodgshon, *I.B.G. Conference on Runrig.*
[2] I. F. Grant, *The Social and Economic Development of Scotland Before 1603*, p. 98.

crofters. At a much later date they would have become landless persons but at this time, perhaps the period of the twelfth and thirteenth centuries which saw great population growth, they did find a place in the rural society which still gave them a share in the land. They became the sub-tenants of the main occupiers of the clachan and also lived there. They had some infield land but no outfield or muir land. Their arable was cultivated by their superiors and in return they provided them with various services such as cutting and collecting of peat and of the harvest.

A further group, already referred to, was made up of cottars. They can be subdivided according to their function within the rural community. One division comprised landless servants who were early forerunners of the agricultural labourer. Before the division of the commonties the cottar usually lived, often in a compact settlement, on their boundaries. He gave to the farmer a limited number of days of labour in the ploughing and harvest period plus a small rent in money and/or kind. In most instances he also paid a day of labour each week. He had a house and a small kail-yard and in many cases a cow and a few sheep which he pastured on the common. The second division was probably of later evolution. These cottars were specialist workers or tradesmen in the township. They however worked land to supplement their income. It was held in runrig but lay in a block separate from the infield holdings of the rest of the community.

Finally there was a class of cultivators known as mailers and pendiclers. In most communities there came a time when the majority of easily accessible good land would have been occupied for some time and the infield–outfield units had been divided as far as was considered desirable. Thus with increased population there occurred the problem of the livelihood of the people who could not be accommodated on the lands of the clachan and yet who were above the cottars in social standing. Such people were settled in an area of unimproved land, usually of formerly uncultivated moorland, and left to make what they could of their environment. Such cultivators occurred in groups or singly and were known as mailers. If they settled in groups they often created a central clachan attached to which was a field system of the usual kind. If settled singly they were unable to develop this system and more often than not cultivated the land by means of lazybeds. The pendicler also fits into this class but in some respects resembled the cottar–tradesman. He often had a specialist occupation in the community but also occupied land, usually in the normal system of infield, outfield and muirland. During the seventeenth and eighteenth centuries the pendicler frequently became nothing more than a farm labourer, a kind of superior cottar whom in many areas he had displaced.

Mention might be made here too of the confusion of names that can occur. In many areas the mailer was also called a crofter and it is from this type of crofter rather than the one mentioned earlier that the occupier of land on the west coast and islands developed.

D. THE INFIELD-OUTFIELD MODEL

Writing in 1902, J. Wilson produced a model[1] to show the arrangement of fields commonly found on an Aberdeenshire farm unit in the middle of the eighteenth century, that is before enclosure. Although useful, his model is not basic enough to allow a general understanding of the layout of the fields in Scotland as a whole because it incorporates features of a developed system and also some which were peculiar to the farming patterns found only in Aberdeenshire. The value of his model is that it clearly demonstrates the ring structure of the field pattern.

A model which is perhaps more applicable to Scotland as a whole can be produced and such is shown in Fig. 12.1. It shows an inner circle of land surrounding the clachan – an area of land which was known by a variety of names but most commonly as the infield or in-bye land. This land is shown divided into three parts to accord with the practice of manuring a third of it each year. In general the ratio of infield to outfield was one to three and viewed from the clachan it was the outfield which provided the second ring. In the model this is divided into two different units: one, which includes a third of the outfield area, would have been under cultivation at any one time; the second, consisting of the rest of the outfield, lay under natural grass or more accurately varied in its state from bare earth through a cover of sparse weeds and grass which in time provided a full cover of vegetation. One portion of this second area, that which had been released from cultivation the longest, would have been enclosed by a turf wall to provide the cattle fold. The third ring would show, as it did in the model produced by Wilson, the extent of moorland, hill-land or wasteland which was common for pasturage to all the main tenants of the clachan. The ratio of this land to the rest of the farming unit was in most cases more variable than in the case of infield to outfield.

The model shows the basis of the field patterns to be found in Scotland in the period before enclosure and its eventual attendant widespread dispersal of settlement. It agrees in general with the system

[1] J. Wilson, 'Farming in Aberdeenshire Ancient and Modern', *Trans. Highland Agric. Soc. Scotl.*, xiv, 5th Ser., 1902, p. 79.

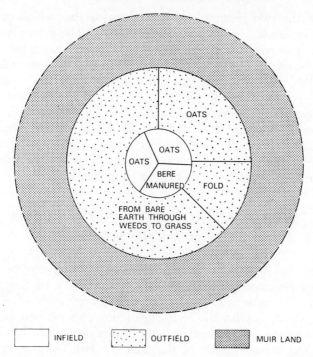

INFIELD □   OUTFIELD □   MUIR LAND ▨

Fig. 12.1 The basic unit of the Scottish field system. The settlement in this situation
would occur at the junction of the three parts of the infield area.

operative in much of England during an equivalent period of agricultural
development. There the nucleated settlement was surrounded by its
arable fields and these in turn were succeeded by the waste lands or
common pasturage. That this system should exist in both areas is not
surprising for it represents a recognition of the economic principles
involved in the differing amounts of work needed by the various
parts of the field system and thereby recognises the value of the rewards
coming from each section of the land. A thorough knowledge of the
location of the parts is the key to the understanding of any field
system.

Apart from the development of the infield-outfield system, the
feature which distinguishes the Scottish pattern of fields from the one
found in association with the nucleated village in England is the
difference in their evolution after the basic settlement was made.
Certainly the infield-outfield pattern existed over much of England.
But it is necessary to ask why the field patterns of England and
Scotland diverged in their development and what this divergence
meant to the developing landscapes of the two countries. The boundary

between the two systems was not of course that which eventually became established in the political sense. As will be shown later, there seems to have been an overspilling of the 'English' system into adjacent areas in Scotland. The continued existence of an infield–outfield system in Scotland and its disappearance in England might be explained by the difference in emphasis placed in the two zones upon the arable as against the pastoral sectors of the rural economy. Furthermore a system of fallowing operated in both field systems. It became more strictly formalised in England due to the less hostile environment found there and where this was also the case in Scotland it can be shown that a system existed similar to that operating in England.

E. THE INFIELD–OUTFIELD SYSTEM IN DEVELOPMENT

The stage has now been reached when examination may be made of the map evidence which is available for a study of Scottish field systems and yet which, apart from the pioneer work of A. Geddes and B. Third, has hardly been explored.[1] This perhaps because so much of it dates from rather late in the history of agrarian development.

Fig. 12.2 shows a map of the estate of Pitkellony in Perthshire. It was drawn from a survey in 1753 by William Winter. It is an extremely interesting document in that it shows the holdings belonging to a Scottish estate typical of the period, but of more interest in the present context is the complex of small settlements or clachans and cotteries with their associated fields. This map deals with an area of land that is neither purely Highland nor Lowland in its physical characteristics due to its location on the border between the two zones. It shows that the countryside was in a state common to much of Scotland at a period before the Improvers had really begun their work in full, although as the holding of Drumduie reveals this period was not too far away. But the process had not gone far enough to wipe away the effects of centuries of gradual evolution of the Scottish agrarian system which had led to the differing field patterns associated with the numerous house groupings to be found in the area.

In this section the map in Fig. 12.2 will be used to illustrate the way in which settlements multiplied, and certain associated field

[1] A. Geddes, 'The Changing Landscapes of the Lothians, 1600–1800, as Revealed by Old Estate Plans', *Scott. Geogr. Mag.*, LIV, 1938, pp. 129–43; B. M. W. Third, 'Changing Landscape and Social Structure in the Scottish Lowlands as Revealed by 18th-century Estate Plans', *Scott. Geogr. Mag.*, LXXI, 1955, pp. 83–9, and 'The Significance of Scottish Estate Plans and Associated Documents', *Scott. Stud.*, I, 1957, pp. 39–64.

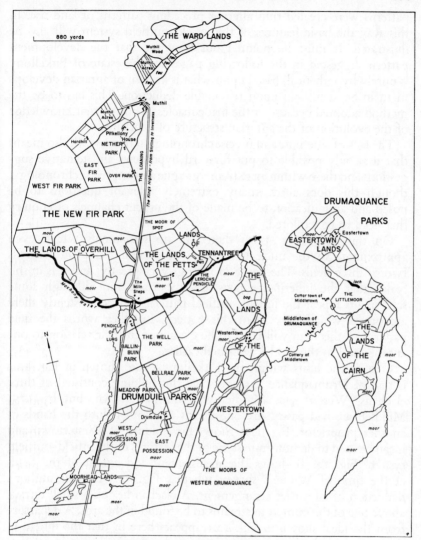

Fig. 12.2 A plan of the estate of Pitkellony in Perthshire.
Sources. Based on a map produced from a survey by William Winter in 1753.
Scottish R.O., R.H.P. 3485.

patterns were created thus altering preceding patterns of land use. In this way the basic features of the infield–outfield system will also be illustrated. It must be pointed out however that the development pattern suggested in the following pages for the estate of Pitkellony is purely hypothetical, based upon what is known of agrarian development in Scotland and upon reasonable deduction. This has to be the method adopted because of the inadequacies of our present knowledge of the evolution of the agrarian structure of Scotland.

The lack of a definite and precise chronological framework also means that it is only possible to put forward hypotheses and tentative suggestions and these within an extremely vague and imprecise chronology, though this does allow many extremely relevant questions to be posed and an indication to be made of the urgent channels of enquiry that need to be explored.

On this map (Fig. 12.2) there are no settlements which even approximate to the nucleated village of the English plain with its two or three fields. The house groupings vary greatly, and it is in this realm that the inheritance laws are important and although some settlements repeat the infield–outfield pattern fairly consistently there are others which vary from this pattern. In other words the field patterns of this map will need to be examined in their relation to one another and to the model described earlier.

One of the units within the Pitkellony estate shown in Fig. 12.2 is that of Drumaquance. At one stage this holding consisted of three clachans, Westertown, Middletown and Eastertown, but by 1753 Middletown had passed, by one means or another, into the hands of another proprietor. Fig. 12.3 shows the holding of Westertown and it can be used to demonstrate some of the features of the infield–outfield system. Fig. 12.3B shows the arrangement and extent of the fields at the time of Winter's survey whereas Fig. 12.3A is the author's deduction of an earlier arrangement. A clachan lies on a small terrace above one of the numerous streams to be found in the area. A departure from the ideal shown in Fig. 12.1 appears here in that the infield in the early period (Fig. 12.3A) only existed as an inner ring in relation to the rest of the field system but not in relation to the clachan; a feature due in large measure to environmental control. The clachan does not occupy the centre of the infield zone because there it would have occupied valuable arable land and also a less well drained site.

The outfields (Fig. 12.3A) lie beyond the infields but mostly only to north and to south. They do not form a single ring for two reasons. The first is the area occupied by moorland to the west of the clachan consists of very heavy boulder clay and therefore its proximity to the clachan could not compensate for the extra labour involved in its

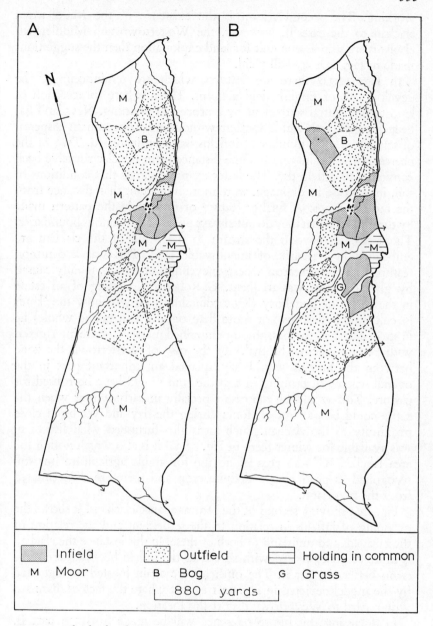

Fig. 12.3 The lands of Westertown, part of the estate of Pitkellony; a postulated earlier stage (A) in the development of the field units known to exist in 1753 (B). *Sources*. Based on a map produced from a survey by William Winter in 1753. Scottish R.O., R.H.P. 3485.

working. The second reason is the existence of the Middletown clachan to the east. If, however, the Westertown and Middletown clachans are seen as one unit for land exploitation then the suggestions made in Fig. 12.1 are still valid.

In Fig. 12.3B there are features which are reminiscent of the development of English field patterns. There is here an accretion of land to the central settlement by a process of assarting. New land has been brought into arable use but without any concomitant dispersal of settlement. The number of infields has been increased. Two of the nearest outfields and one at some distance from the clachan have been converted to infield use. The latter example shows that conditions of soil, in this case its drainage, were more important than distance from the farmsteadings. A further feature of interest in the pattern made by the infields is that they do not always possess coterminous boundaries. Those that lie beyond the stream to the south of the clachan are embedded in a matrix of uncultivable land. This was a common feature, especially in areas where unevenness of terrain, mainly caused by glacial action, was frequent. G. Robertson, writing of an estate in the parish of Banchory (Kincardineshire), showed how the 'lands in cultivation (perhaps not more than one-fortieth of the whole) lie in small detached patches, among undrained marshes, or are intermixed with...unproductive heaths'.[1] In the case of Westertown the zone between the infields would have played an important part in the overall scheme of farming in that the land would have been used for pasture. This would be the case especially in early winter when the cattle could be put out of doors during the day and yet be in close proximity to the clachan. Such areas also furnished what little hay was available for winter feed. In Fig. 12.3B it is also worth noting the area labelled 'G' – an area of no use for arable agriculture but still recognised as producing a definite crop and therefore differentiated from the moorland.

Fig. 12.4 shows a second of the Drumaquance clachans. It shows the grouping of infields in relation to the settlement and the relation of the outfields and muirland to both of these. In this instance the clachan is more centrally placed with regard to the infield because here there is no better site for it. The outfields are again located as suggested by the model depicted in Fig. 12.1 except where the factors discussed with regard to Westertown distort this location.

In discussing this figure reference will be made firstly to part B. It shows the area of land used by Eastertown at a date later than that of part A. By this time new factors have entered into the pattern of land holding and therefore of the pattern of fields of the area. In general

[1] G. Robertson, *A General View of the Agriculture of Kincardineshire*, 1813, p. 64.

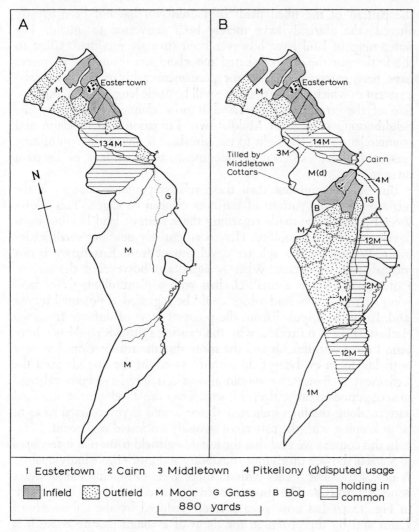

Fig. 12.4 The lands of Eastertown and Cairn, units in the estate of Pitkellony; B shows the known pattern in 1753 and A the deduced arrangement of fields before the intrusion at an unknown date of the settlement of Cairn.

Sources. Based on a map produced from a survey by William Winter in 1753. Scottish R.O., R.H.P. 3485.

the pattern of the tilled fields of Eastertown has not been greatly altered – the outfields have merely been converted to infield. The outer rings of land have however been strongly modified. Close to the settlement the area of shared moorland has shrunk. Two pieces have been extracted entirely for permanent cultivation by cottars – a system to which further reference will be made later. On the southern side of the stream the moorland is now claimed entirely by the neighbouring clachan of Middletown. Litigation due to claim and counterclaim over the right to use muirland is one of the commonest reasons for the existence of documents with content of agrarian interest.

But of more interest than these relatively minor changes is the intrusion into the pattern of the new clachan of Cairn. This allows several points to be made regarding the system of land holding in its development and flexibility. Here is an entirely new but small settlement. Whether it is a splinter development from Eastertown is not immediately important. What is significant however is the size of Eastertown. Here is a small clachan with a plentiful supply of land lying near at hand – land which could be regarded as potential infield land. If this be disputed from the point of view of distance from the clachan, there is no reason why the existing outfields could not have been turned into infields and the more distant area developed as new outfields. In an evolving field pattern system in the English plain the settlement of Eastertown would almost certainly have been enlarged to accommodate the settlers at Cairn. Then the development of a field pattern along the lines indicated above would have occurred so as to be in keeping with the pattern of strongly nucleated settlement.

In this context we find that the infield–outfield pattern *as it developed in Scotland* showed much more flexibility and much more individuality. A new settlement occurs with an inner zone of infields and an outer zone of outfields. The moorland area enjoyed solely by Eastertown in Fig. 12.4A has now been severely reduced by the cultivators of Cairn and by the provision for them of a rough pasture zone. It is interesting to note that the moorlands held solely be Eastertown (1M) and solely by Cairn (2M) are still in an area furthest from the respective settlements. The moorland however which the two settlements share in common lies nearer to the primary settlement.

One piece of land which stands out as quite different from the rest of the field pattern is visible on both parts A and B of Fig. 12.4. This is the area of grassland which Eastertown retained even after the development of and despite its proximity to the Cairn clachan; this reinforces what was said about the importance of grassland when discussing this in the context of Westertown.

Now returning to Fig. 12.4A, it is noticeable that the land shown here was not used exclusively by the farmers of Eastertown. The portion labelled 134M entered into the farming operations of Eastertown but it was also utilised by Pitkellony and Middletown, settlements located at some distance from Eastertown. In the earliest period this land would not have been defined by the boundaries of Eastertown as shown in Fig. 12.4A but would have merely formed part of a further ring of land devoted to less intensive use than the outfields of any of the settlements involved in its use. The location of this land near Eastertown is however interesting. It was noted above while discussing the moorland shared between Eastertown and Cairn that this lay between the extreme outer ring of unshared moorland belonging to Cairn and Eastertown and the outfields of Cairn. In the case under discussion the land shared by Pitkellony, Middletown and Eastertown lies between the unshared moorland of Eastertown and its outfields. This suggests therefore that just as Cairn developed at some time after the establishment of Eastertown, so Eastertown came into existence after the development of Pitkellony and its associated field system. The land is distant from Pitkellony thus suggesting that it was once part of the outer ring of land associated with that settlement and into which the new settlement of Eastertown intruded. This is further attested to by the existence of an area of unshared moorland belonging to Pitkellony to the east of Cairn and thus beyond its shared moorland. Evidence other than that of the field pattern can be marshalled to support this hypothesis. The place-name Pitkellony contains the Pictish element 'pit' and this points to its having considerable antiquity as a settlement site.[1] Here then is an instance of the ring pattern associated with the Scottish field system providing useful clues as to the development of settlement units.

Fig. 12.5 allows further consideration to be made of the evolution of settlements and the field patterns associated with them. Fig. 12.5A shows an area of land associated in general with the two clachans of West and East Pett. Their toponymity indicates their site as having been settled for a considerable period and it is reasonable to infer that once there was a single settlement here called Pett which in time gave rise to two separate units. The date of this and the reason for it are obscure. The existence of these two settlements so close together however does point to a difference in the evolution of settlements and their associated field systems from that widely observed in the English plain. The infields and outfields occur in the recognised pattern with the exception of an area to the south of West Pett and its

[1] See G. Whittington and J. A. Soulsby, 'A Preliminary Report on an Investigation into *Pit*- Place-names', *Scott. Geogr. Mag.*, LXXXIV, 1968, pp. 117–25.

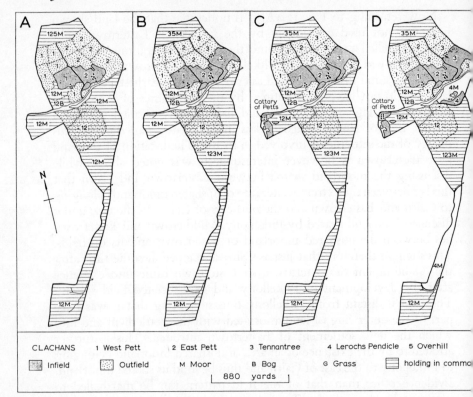

Fig. 12.5 The lands of the Petts and Tennantree, the Pendicle of Lerochs and the Cottary of Petts, units in the estate of Pitkellony; D shows the known arrangement of settlements and land units in 1753 and A, B and C show what are believed to be separate stages in the evolution of this known pattern.

Sources. Based on a map produced from a survey by William Winter in 1753. Scottish R.O., R.H.P. 3485.

adjacent stream. Here is a new feature – an outfield unit (12) worked on a common basis by the two clachans. Is this an indication of the time when the two clachans did not exist as separate entities and if so why have the other outfields become closely identified with one clachan only? More likely, perhaps, is it an indication of joint assarting in an area of formerly common moorland? The amount of cooperation between separate units is still something neither well understood nor even well studied.

In Fig. 12.5B the field patterns have been modified by the appearance of a new clachan, Tennantree. It is possible to see in this situation two features of the tenancy pattern. Conceivably due to its antiquity the settlement of Petts was originally one of joint tenants holding land directly from their superior. In the case of Tennantree are we seeing a settlement of sub-tenants, holding their lands from a tacksman who perhaps by this time had come to have an interest in the Petts holding? The new clachan has been established on the outfield land of East Pett. A part of this has been converted to infield and the clachan sited on its edge. The occupants have been admitted to a portion of the moorland used by the Petts in the zone nearest the clachan. A portion of the moorland, beyond the newly shared area, has however remained solely in the usage of the Petts – a pattern seen already in the study of Eastertown. An interesting question arising here in relation to this occupation of land by another community is how much it changed the agrarian practices of the Petts. Did they hold too much land for a full use to be made of it or did they have to adjust their agriculture to accommodate the setting up of a new clachan necessitated by the growth of population?

Fig. 12.5C shows the common moorland of the Petts further eroded. At this stage there exists here, due to population growth, a settlement of cottars. Their houses are grouped on the edge of the moorland and they occupy blocks of infield land. There are however no areas of outfield or moorland in which they are shown as having a share; their animals would most probably have been pastured on the area of adjacent grassland. The occupants of this cottary would be specialist workers attached to this holding on which there did occur a waulk mill. Only the inner ring of the field system is developed here. While discussing cottars it will be worthwhile to return to Fig. 12.4B. Here are shown two areas of land that were tilled by the cottars of Middletown. Fig. 12.2 shows Middletown as having two cottar establishments. One is called the 'Cottar Town of Middletown'. This was an establishment almost certainly akin to that already discussed which belonged to the Petts. It was established near the edge of the moorland and the occupants tilled fragmented holdings, not with the rest of the arable of Middletown but in their own block fields. The second cottar establishment is described as the 'Cottery of Middletown'. Here were a few houses, this time located on uncultivable land at the margin of a stream, occupied by landless labourers attached to the main clachan. This type of person was often referred to as a cottager.

In Fig. 12.5D is shown the final development in the field patterns in the Petts area prior to enclosure. This is the creation of a separate settlement called Lerochs Pendicle situated near the main stream. It has been established on moorland common to West and East Petts and it has associated with it areas of infield, outfield and moorland. Although called a pendicle there are problems in seeing it as such for normally such a holding did not have this elaborate system of land use, being confined rather to an area of arable and an area of rough grazing land. Lerochs is perhaps best regarded as a settlement of mailers. It is possible however that the small size of the outfield attached to Lerochs is evidence of pendiclers at work. The creation of arable land would have involved the clearing of heathland vegetation and probably the paring and removal of peat and moss. In this case the land would have had a stage between being moorland and permanent arable and would have appeared to the surveyor as outfield although strictly speaking not falling within this category. Here is the establishment of a group of independent cultivators who on second sight appear not to have been involved in what has always been thought to be the typical Scottish agricultural system; furthermore a settlement which stood halfway in the social sense between that of the sub-tenants and that of the cottary.

The postulations of Fig. 12.5 can therefore be regarded as an illustration of the evolution of settlements and fields taking into account the social hierarchies of people found in the rural areas of Scotland. The actual dates and details of the stages must remain obscure and of course there is no certainty that the differences suggested as existing between the Petts and Tennantree were in operation at the time of the survey or even for some considerable time before that. It is quite conceivable that the Petts might also have been a sub-tenant holding at this time. Reference was made earlier to the possible splitting of Petts into two parts from a single clachan. This was not an unusual occurrence and examples of it can be traced well back into history. Sometimes a permanent division would remain while on other occasions one clachan would again completely disappear owing to changes in the leasing arrangements of the land. This impermanence of settlement will be referred to later. What can be stated here is that the creation of a clachan with its attendant rings of different land did not mean that the total pattern of land occupance in that area was firmly established up to the period of change undertaken by the improving landlords.

The unit of land associated with the settlement of Drumduie is examined in the various parts of Fig. 12.6. The occurrence of two small clachans in close proximity has been seen in the study of the Petts. Each clachan there had its own development of the various field units. In the case of Drumduie this same double development of the fields is also found but the duplication of clachans is not. Here, if the cartographic evidence is to be believed, there is only one distinct clachan called Drumduie and yet there are the two distinct field systems designated by the terms East and West. Furthermore it is noticeable that the actual development of infield land by the date

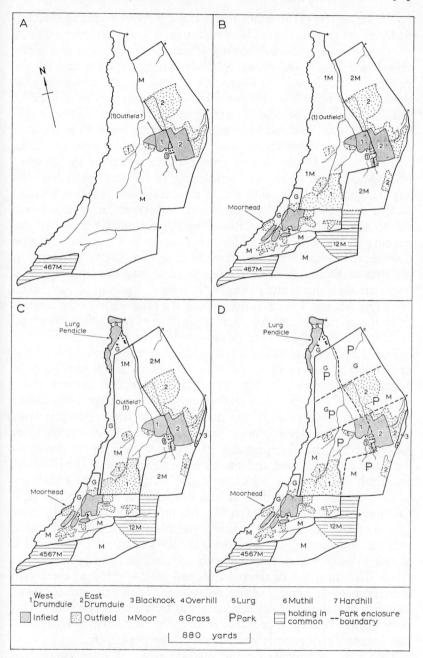

Fig. 12.6 The lands of Drumduie and Moorhead, the Pendicle of Lurg and the mailer settlement of Blacknook, units in the estate of Pitkellony; examples of the changes believed to have occurred in field patterns by movement of settlement to the margin (B and C) and by the first application of enclosure rights (D).

Sources. Based on a map produced from a survey by William Winter in 1753. Scottish R.O., R.H.P. 3485.

of the survey (1753) is rather small. It is conceivable that the clachan of Drumduie was occupied by a tacksman, tenants, either his or those of someone else, and some crofters. There is no indication of a cottar class living here. One group of fields was perhaps worked by the group of tenants and the other was utilised by the tacksman with the aid of crofters. It is also possible that the farm may have been let out to a single tenant who worked it with sub-tenants. Later it could have been subdivided and let to numerous tenants but with the clachan remaining as a single entity. The variations in tenancy possibilities, made very easy by the lack of permanent enclosure and the presence of fragmentation, makes the deciphering of the tenancy systems on any particular unit very difficult. In most instances, as far as the field pattern was concerned, this was of little importance, in that whoever the tenants were they were forced by the communal nature of the farming to follow communal farming practice and thus no landscape differences resulted from variations in type of tenancy. However in the case of Drumduie, features which came into the landscape at a later date do indicate the existence there of one person of more than usual importance. Thus in some respects the presence in or the absence from the clachan of an important land holder could affect the speed at which change came to the infield–outfield pattern.

Figs. 12.6B and 12.6C make possible an examination both of the movement of settlement to the margins and the accompanying field pattern development. In Fig. 12.6B the major new feature is the settlement of Moorhead – a clachan associated with the colonisation of the moorland lying on the margins of the area associated with Drumduie. This development deprived Drumduie of some of its moorland but this was probably no hardship judging by the small extent of its arable land and the continued existence of moorland to the north of the clachan which in similar situations on the Pitkellony lands had been converted to at least outfield. At Moorhead there is the now familiar pattern of fields. An inner zone of infields exists in a matrix of land less favourable for arable use due to its streamside location. An outer ring of outfields is followed by moorland which in this instance was not shared with the clachan from which it was taken. The small size of the outfields and their widespread nature are indications of the poorer environment here. Their existence however indicates that this new development was by a group of mailers who were planted here most probably from the main clachan at Drumduie due to new developments which were taking place there.

Two new settlements on the margins make their appearance in Fig. 12.6C. The larger of these is the Pendicle of Lurg. Here is a small group of houses and associated with them a small area of infield but no outfield. Instead there is an exceptionally large development of grassland. The occupants here would have been pendiclers but in addition to their involvement in their own infields and the lands of Drumduie, it would appear that they had an additional occupation or at least a source of livelihood. This was of frequent occurrence with this class of cultivator. It is interesting to note that their lands are located alongside the main road from Stirling to Inverness along which moved large numbers of cattle from the Highlands to the Lowland markets. The grassland, so much more extensively developed at Lurg, is almost certainly a response to this cattle movement, for it would provide a resting place on the journey south.

The other settlement, Blacknook, is areally the most insignificant encountered yet. Almost without doubt it is the site of the planting of another mailer. No detail at all is given of the pattern of land use here. The area is very small and most probably the cultivation was done in lazybeds. This was a form of cultivation undertaken with a spade. Lazybeds were used mainly in the later period for the growing of potatoes but they were also used for the production of oats. They consisted of covering the strip of earth upon which the seed potatoes or grain had been placed with earth from the adjacent strip. Thus a series of regular and narrow (compared, that is, with those of the open fields) ridges and furrows were brought into existence. Such a method of cultivation was the only one feasible for land occupiers such as the mailers when they lived in single units of settlements and were therefore without the means of forming a plough-team. The lazybed was of course of common occurrence and made a distinctive contribution to the field patterns of Scotland, especially those of the west and the islands.

With the settlements of Lurg and Blacknook the final stage of the infilling of the settlement and associated field patterns is being approached. The subtraction of land from the outer ring of the major clachans would have reached its peak just before the Improver period (approximately 1720–90) affected Scotland. The first manifestation of change in the landscape which resulted from interest in enclosure makes an appearance in two places in Fig. 12.2. It is however best studied in Fig. 12.6D. Before discussing this, something must be said on the subject of enclosure in general as it operated in Scotland, a system differing greatly from that prosecuted in England where frequent recourse had to be made to Parliament.

In 1695 the Scots Parliament passed two acts of great importance in agrarian history. The first, dealing with runrig, has already been discussed (p. 538). By the second[1] it was made possible for proprietors

[1] *Acts of the Parliament of Scotland*, IX, 462, 1695.

who had rights of commonty over the waste pastures to ask in the Court of Session for a division of such land (in Scotland it was not possible to establish a common right by customary usage). Until such times as the landlords began to take an active interest in their estates the provisions of these two acts were rarely utilised. But when they were, they did not completely reorganise the rural landscape as was the case in England. There enclosure led quickly to the appearance of an entirely new field pattern and considerable associated dispersion of settlement. In Scotland the appearance of the landscape changed more slowly. The first type of enclosure will be referred to below but even after this stage had been passed change was slow. Settlement patterns did not automatically change, land was not necessarily physically enclosed although distinct fields of regular shape came into existence, infield–outfield practices still occurred, albeit often within hedged or walled fields, and exaggerated forms of ridge-and-furrow persisted for a long period. There was nothing in Scotland to match the flood of Parliamentary Enclosure Acts witnessed in England. Enclosure in Scotland was a long, drawn-out affair, part of a general evolution of field patterns and systems which started with shifting agriculture and which is still continuing today.

In Fig. 12.6D can be seen the Parks of Drumduie. The earliest enclosures in Scotland, known as Parks, were to be found around the proprietors' houses or the other important houses on their estates. Such enclosures were used in two different ways. In some instances they were the equivalent of the emparking movement in England. An area of land near the large house was allowed to revert to grass and planted with scattered trees, often of an ornamental nature. Thus another dimension, known as the policy, was added to the field pattern. But more frequently, as in the county of Dunbarton, 'around the houses of gentlemen several enclosures are kept constantly in grass'.[1] This is what had occurred at Drumduie by 1753. Three of the Parks were under grass while the old system of infield, outfield and moorland still operated in the other three, despite the occurrence of enclosure. Here then is a transition stage. In time the clachan at Drumduie disappeared and each Park was used completely for grass or a single crop. Where enclosure with parks took place the use of the land was retained in the hands of the occupant of the main house. In Fig. 12.2 a further instance of this enclosure system can be seen. In the northwest lies the house of Pitkellony, the successor to a former clachan. The lands to the south and west of the house are all called Park. The two nearest the house are under grass while the three largest, developed

[1] A. Whyte and D. MacFarlane, *General View of the Agriculture of Dunbarton*, 1811, p. 140.

in areas of either former outfield or moorland, have been used to establish fir plantations. This became a common feature in the eighteenth century due to the general scarcity of woodland in Scotland as a whole.

The creation of the Parks, however, was merely an eighteenth-century fulfilment of an Act of James IV (cap. 74) of 1503 which stated,

> 'It is statute and ordained anent policie to be halden in the countrie, that everlich lord made them to have parkes with deare, stankes, cunningares, dawcattes, orchards, hedges and plant at the least one aiker of woode quhair there is no great woods nor forrestes.'

Thus by dividing the map of the estate of Pitkellony (Fig. 12.2) into its many constituent parts and by reference to the basic infield/outfield/moorland ring structure shown in Fig. 12.1 it is possible to postulate the development of some of the features of the field patterns in Scotland. What distinguishes this Scottish pattern from the English development from a similar base into the two- or three-field system was the lack of evolution beyond the pattern shown in Fig. 12.1. In Scotland additions to the infield was not the normal response to population growth, although this did happen as will be shown later, but more usually this response took the form of the development of further settlement centres which remained small and still maintained the pattern shown in Fig. 12.1. In a later period, but before enclosure, there took place an infilling of the gaps left between the settlements, i.e. where the outer rings of each unit met, by other settlement with a system of fields which reflected the social status of the people involved in their tillage. Thus the Scottish system differed from that developed in England and accommodated changes in the composition of society and agrarian practice without having to suffer the drastic upheaval which occurred with enclosure south of the border. The actual appearance of the landscape under the Scottish system differed, however, from area to area due to variations in physical environment and in the policy of land proprietors in certain localities. It is to the differences which occurred in certain locations and at certain periods that attention must now be turned.

F. DEPARTURES FROM THE INFIELD-OUTFIELD MODEL

I. THE SHIELING

One feature of agrarian practice in Scotland led to a departure from the close association of land with the settlement as shown in Fig. 12.1. This was the development of the shieling, a zone of hill grazing on

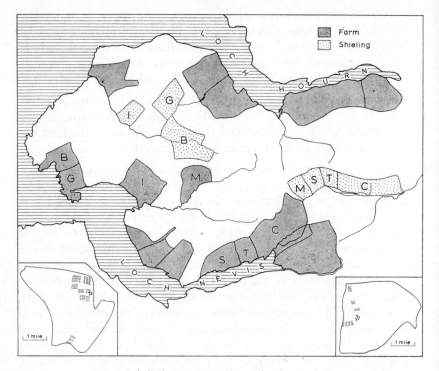

Fig. 12.7 Farms and shielings in Knoydart, Glenelg Parish, Inverness-shire, belonging to the Forfeited Estate of Barrisdale.

Sources. Based on an extremely inaccurate scale plan which is a copy made in 1805 of an original by William Morrison dated 1771. Scottish R.O., R.H.P. 112. Farms possessing shielings have been identified by the initial letter of their name and the individual farm/shieling relationship is indicated by the shieling unit carrying the same initial as the farm. The two insets (corrected for scale and area) are of the farms G (left inset) and B (right inset). They show the clachan and its arable land, a very small part of the total farmland and almost certainly worked in lazybeds.

which was located a temporary or seasonal dwelling. This unit was situated at some distance from the farm by which it was exploited. The actual distance depended to a great degree upon the actual location of hill-land which would provide summer grazing, but up to seven miles was quite common. The area of land forming the shieling was carefully demarcated (see Fig. 12.7), forming a unit complementary to the outer ring of the township's land and therefore as such part of the overall field pattern. The grazing was frequently divided into two parts. The dwelling was placed in close proximity to the area which had the greatest grazing potential in that its vegetation cover was almost exclusively of grass. This was reserved for the milch cows which went with varying numbers of men and women to the upland zone usually in late May or early June. There they remained until August or such time as the pasture gave out. On their return to the township, the young cattle and horses which had been grazing the rest of the area were allowed the complete freedom of the shieling until such time as deterioration in the weather forced them back to the township also. In spring this latter group returned to the shieling but was excluded from the inner area from the first or second week of April so as to allow a full vegetative growth before the arrival of the milch cattle. The distribution of shielings is not well understood although a recent paper by R. Miller[1] has indicated the way that investigations in this area should proceed. As M. D. MacSween has pointed out,[2] it is clear that the whole question of transhumance in Scotland has been little examined. Not every settlement unit, even where the environment permitted it, possessed a shieling. Where the extent of the outer ring of land allowed it there would be a common pasturing of cattle at some distance from the settlement but unless this involved the movement of milch cattle shieling development cannot be considered to have occurred. This point is well illustrated by Barrow by reference to a charter in the Arbroath Cartulary dating from late in the twelfth century.[3] Moreover some townships did not possess a shieling although as can be seen from Fig. 12.7 there was one being exploited in close proximity to them.

This system did, however, occur widely throughout Scotland. It was not confined to the Highlands but was also found in the Southern Uplands, especially in the Lammermuirs (Fig. 12.8) and Cheviots. A comprehensive study of this whole subject is badly needed and until it is done an integral part of the infield–outfield system is missing. One thing is clear however. The collapse of the shieling system was not mainly a change brought about by enclosure. It is true that the shieling areas were often disjoined from the township lands which exploited them. But the most important reason was the introduction of potatoes and flax which demanded labour in the township area in the only period when the shieling area could be used.

2. THE BURGHS

The infield–outfield distinction in field patterns and the fragmentation that often accompanied it was also to be found in the lands belonging

[1] R. Miller, 'Land Use by Summer Shielings', *Scott. Stud.*, XI, 1967, pp. 193–219.
[2] M. D. MacSween, 'Transhumance in North Skye', *Scott. Geogr. Mag.*, LXXV, 1959, p. 87.
[3] Barrow, *Scott. Stud.*, VI, 1962, p. 138.

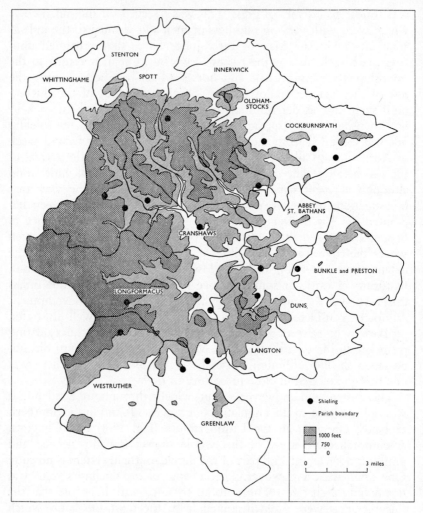

Fig. 12.8 Features of the former distribution of shielings
in part of the Lammermuirs.

Sources. Compiled by reference to the Ordnance Survey six-inch maps which reveal
several place-names containing the element *shiel*. The map makes no claim to
comprehensiveness but points a way of approach as well as revealing interesting
features of altitudinal association.

to the emerging urban areas. As Grant has said, 'the embryonic Scots burghs...were largely, perhaps mainly, agricultural communities. In their charters all the Scots burghs received considerable grants of land, which the burgesses cultivated.'[1] The operation and appearance of the zone around the towns cannot however be considered as distinct from that of the rest of the agricultural land in Scotland. The infield, or burgh acres, was divided into shares, as was the infield of the farms, but could be sold or inherited (Fig. 12.9). As a result much of this land was feued or sold as building plots for the growing settlements. This had occurred in the burgh acres of Muthil, a settlement shown in Fig. 12.2. The outfield land was noted for the persistence of its existence, remaining for a long period as undivided common. The acts of 1695 quoted earlier expressly excluded common belonging to royal burghs from their provisions. Unless complete agreement could be reached among the right-holders, and this was almost impossible due to minorities or intransigence, the commonty had to remain undivided. Thus long after outfield had disappeared in the rural context it remained as periodically cropped land or stinted pasture in association with the royal burghs.

G. CONJECTURES AND CONCLUSIONS

The infield–outfield distinction has been shown to lie at the heart of Scottish field patterns. But was this always the case? The earliest reference Grant found to an infield–outfield division was in the Register of Sasiness for Edinburgh for August 1606.[2] This is not to say that such a distinction did not exist before but Barrow, who has initiated a long overdue search for agricultural and settlement evidence in documents of the period 1100 to 1300, states that 'there is no indication in early documents of any system of infield and outfield cultivation, although the texts are not incompatible with the existence of such a system'.[3]

In Fig. 12.1 the infield is shown as supporting two parts of oats and one of bere. But in the eighteenth century this did not obtain everywhere. In some instances where the soil was poor and the climate wet only oats were grown on the infield – a practice which was paralleled in the *Geest* area of the North European Plain in the concentration on rye.[4] In other areas, especially those of the climatically

[1] Grant, *Development of Scotland*, p. 111.
[2] *Ibid.*, p. 287.
[3] Barrow, *Scott. Stud.*, VI, 1962, p. 127.
[4] Uhlig, *Geogr. Annlr.*, XLIII, 1961, p. 288.

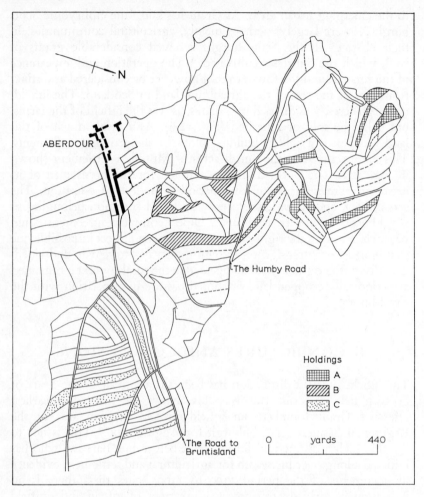

Fig. 12.9 The Town Lands or Burgh Acres of Aberdour, Fife.

Sources. Based on part of a plan drawn *c.* 1750. Scottish R.O., R.H.P. 1022. The Lands lie in three distinct blocks: (i) north of the Humby Road; (ii) between the Humby Road and the Bruntisland Road; (iii) south of the Bruntisland Road. The holdings of one man are shown for each of the three blocks. The two most northerly blocks have undergone much more consolidation of parcels than has the third. In the block to the south of the Bruntisland Road the parcels are all of the order of one acre; the zone at the extreme east of this block is so badly damaged that it is impossible to decipher the size of the parcels.

more favoured east coast of Scotland, the infield was divided into four or more parts due to the addition after 1740 of potatoes to the field crops. Does the more sophisticated use of the infield point to an evolution of the infield–outfield system and was there perhaps a time when a distinction of the two parts did not exist? One piece of evidence which might further this idea can be found in a description of the agriculture of Galloway in the period about 1750.

'About forty years ago, the whole agricultural operations were confined to oats after oats, so long as the ground would carry any; and it was afterwards allowed to remain for grass. The only exception to this plan was a small bit of land near the house, called the Bear Fay, which was kept perpetually in tillage, received the whole dung of the farm, and was regularly sown with bear or barley. Little dependence was placed on this crop; while the failure of the oats was looked to with horror, being considered the next thing to a famine in the country.'[1]

Is the Bear Fay in this instance the first step towards an infield development in an area where, due to heavy rainfall and poor soil drainage, oats was the most feasible crop and where due to a mono-culture it was unnecessary to differentiate between infield and outfield? Unless this development is occurring why waste the manure on what appears to be a small zone of little consequence? If the Scottish agrarian system is seen as a progression from shifting arable farming associated with cattle-keeping to a sedentary form in which cattle remained more important in the wetter west and grain in the drier east, then a stage must have occurred when a more extensive type of arable was changed into a mixture of intensive and extensive. Due most probably to a growing population there would be a stimulus towards the develop-ment of an inner ring (infield or intensive zone) and an outer (outfield or less intensive zone) ring; an arrangement forced into existence by the paucity of manure in an area with generally leached, acid soils. As Barrow has pointed out, 'the twelfth and thirteenth centuries were a period of steadily growing population'.[2] Was this the period in which the infield–outfield distinction started to develop in a country-wide sense? Were, as Uhlig has hinted,[3] the areas which became known as the outfield an older agrarian form than the infield which came to hold the dominant position in a later period? This is an attractive hypothesis but one which needs much more investigation before any final assessment can be made.

[1] J. Webster, *General View of the Agriculture of Galloway*, 1794, p. 12.
[2] Barrow, *Scott. Stud.*, VI, 1962, p. 127.
[3] Uhlig, *Geogr. Annlr.*, XLIII, 1961, p. 305.

Further evidence of the non-existence of the infield–outfield distinction comes from Moray and Nairn at the beginning of the nineteenth century; Leslie, writing of the field pattern and associated crops, asserted that 'except where the remiss arrangement into croft (infield) and outfield has been adopted, one general rotation seems, for many centuries, unwisely to have prevailed'.[1] Here is corroboration of the idea suggested by the evidence from Galloway. What this does not make clear however is whether, unlike Galloway, the distinction *once* existed here but had been eliminated. This introduces another development in the Scottish field pattern which can now be discussed. In some areas there appears to have been a gradual and in some instances complete elimination of the outfield. In areas which had higher summer temperatures, due mainly to longer hours of sunshine and lower rainfall, grain-growing became the more important branch of agricultural activity. As Dickinson has written, 'The "tilling of the land" is said to have been urged and encouraged by the kings of the twelfth and thirteenth centuries; and in the fertile parts arable gradually became more and more important.'[2] There is evidence from the Laigh of Moray and the Lothians that this did take place. Thus Leslie indicates the lack of outfield in certain areas of Moray:

'Each farm was divided into four nearly equal allotments, one of which was in succession, annually prepared by two or three ploughings, and the applications of the whole manure of the farm for barley [surely an indication of the former existence here of the infield/outfield distinction]; the other three allotments were under a crop of oats, raised by one ploughing, varied in some cases by a crop of rye, where the soil was suited to that grain; sowing occasionally a small quantity of peas on a few only of the earlier farms, was probably the first deviation from this system. The *whole* (my italics) of every farm was under corn by the first of June.'[3]

A map recently discovered in Fife can perhaps make a contribution here. Fig. 12.10 shows a plan of the estate of Bandon and Pilmuir in 1762. The layout of the fields is normal for such a late period in Lowland Scotland and both infield (mukked land) and outfield are shown as separate units. But what is unique here as far as the present author has been able to establish are the fields designated 'infield and outfield by turn'. Twenty per cent of the land of Wester and of Easter Bandon falls into this category. How did this system work?

---

[1] Leslie, *Moray and Nairn*, p. 143.
[2] Dickinson, *Scotland from the Earliest Times*, p. 63.
[3] Leslie, *Moray and Nairn*, p. 143.

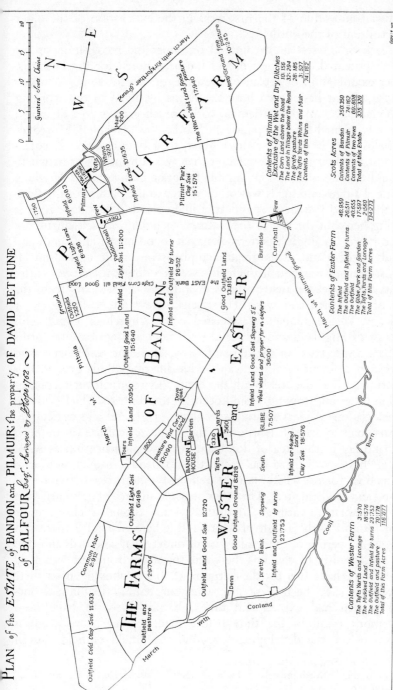

Fig. 12.10 A plan of the estate of Bandon and Pilmuir in the parish of Markinch, Fife.

Sources. Drawn from a survey by J. Hope in 1762 and reproduced here by permission of Mrs J. C. Balfour.

Is this an indication of the first steps in the extirpation of the older agrarian unit of the outfield?

A lack of interest in an outfield or rather the recognition of the greater potential of a larger infield has been noted for the Lothians. In her examination of a plan of Newton, drawn following a survey in 1754, Third has shown how the farms involved in the working of the land around the settlement had a much greater area of infield than was normal for that period in Scotland as a whole.[1] Moreover the fields were larger and more regular, their boundaries were coterminous and their ridges were larger than was common in areas where soil and climate were less favourable for grain cultivation. The whole layout of ridges and fields was much nearer to the pattern of the two- and three-field system as it appeared in England. The fallow zone is missing here but the rest of the features, including the settlement, are much nearer an English pattern than that found in the Highlands and Islands of Scotland. This greater emphasis on arable agriculture as against grazing was one of the features which differentiated the settlements and associated field patterns of southeastern Scotland from the area of the north and west. The clachan grew into a fermtoun or nucleated village frequently associated with a church or a mill. This contrast of Highland and Lowland settlement and agricultural forms is not a resurrection of the ideas of Gray, Skene or A. Meitzen who associated different rural landscapes with differing ethnic groups. It is unfortunate that the areas with the better environment for a concentration on grain-growing should occur in the contexts which allowed an association of ideas relating to culture in general and agriculture in particular to arise. It is true that the arable agriculture of southeast Scotland lay in the area of dominant Anglian influence but as R. A. Butlin[2] has shown there was in Northumberland a distinction in land occupation forms which largely reflected differences between the upland and lowland areas. The other outstanding area of grain growing and movement towards an 'all infield system' is one which is remote from 'Anglia' – the Laigh of Moray. But here of course there was a strong flowering of the feudal system under alien landlords and thus the protagonists of the link between social environment and field system type have fuel for their argument. But as shown earlier there appears to have been a period when an unmodified infield–outfield pattern had existed and this is hardly likely to have been a memory recall of the time before feudalisation. More proof is needed before the development beyond the infield–outfield pattern

[1] Third, *Scott. Stud.*, I, 1957, pp. 44–6.
[2] R. A. Butlin, 'Northumberland Field Systems', *Agric. Hist. Rev.*, XII, 1964, pp. 99–120.

can be considered to have sprung from the social as against the natural environment.

The basic assertion here is that in the fermtoun area an evolution beyond the infield–outfield development was occurring or had already occurred by the end of the eighteenth century. In 1952 H. P. R. Finberg put forward the hypothesis that all open field types were 'a genus, of which the two-field system and its probable derivative, the three-field system form one species, and the infield–outfield another. The two probably evolved side by side, moulded by the contrasting qualities of highland and lowland landscape.'[1] This finds much support here. If for 'landscapes', environment is substituted and if the infield–outfield system is regarded merely as the dominant theme over a particular period in the evolution of field systems in Scotland then the hypothesis is even more valuable.

Thus by an examination of field systems in Scotland and of the derivations from the infield–outfield pattern it is quite clear that the view of Grant that

'what we should look for in Scots agriculture is a gradually evolved system, in process of development during the great changes of the historic period, rather than a cut-and-dried "Celtic" system such as certain writers have postulated'[2]

is viable and is the most valuable approach to the study of field systems in Scotland. Where in the Lowland environment the infield–outfield theme evolved into something nearer to a modern concept of land use, so in the Highlands and Islands the social environment caused a change in the co-joint tenancy and brought into existence the fore-runner of the present crofting landscape pattern. This latter subject has been well aired and it will suffice here to point out that in their occupation of the transhumance and fishing sites, the crofters did bring into existence a new form of field pattern. Cut out of former uncleared and uncultivated moorland, the farms were laid out in a series of squared fields with dispersed settlement thus creating the pattern which in Ireland is known best by the term 'ladder farms'.

This pattern produced regularity within the field patterns in some areas of the north and west. Indeed regularity of appearance in field shape was something which occurred over most of Scotland in the post-Improver period. This was due to a desire by the land-owners to share in the new agricultural prosperity; but the desire could not be consummated until the land surveyors had been active. But this

[1] H. P. R. Finberg, 'The Open Field in Devon', in W. G. Hoskins and H. P. R. Finberg, *Devonshire Studies*, 1952, p. 286.
[2] Grant, *Development of Scotland*, p. 99.

regularity is not to be seen as a revolutionary change. It is obvious from Roy's Map (1747–54)[1] that the Scottish agrarian landscape was already undergoing great changes. Progress towards enclosure varied over Scotland depending on the one hand upon the physical environment and on the other upon the desire of the individual proprietors. Thus in Ayrshire the wetter areas above 400 feet which were well suited to pastoral activities demanded enclosure to prevent depredations of the crops by cattle. Interest in cattle was always dominant here and thus enclosure occurred at an early date before the land surveyor's work had reached its full flowering. As a result the enclosures, as J. H. G. Lebon has shown,[2] were of a 'spider's web' variety. The former infield was enclosed in small fields and the outfield in units of a larger size. An analysis of field patterns in Galloway where similar environmental conditions occur would also be of interest here.

Where enclosure depended upon the desire of the landlord a more regular geometrical pattern of fields emerged. This began, as shown when discussing the holding of Drumduie on the Estate of Pitkellony, with the delineation of Parks around the larger houses. Then as agriculture became a fashionable occupation the activities of the land surveyors spread widely over Scotland. Farm sizes and the actual field pattern however varied from area to area depending upon the physiography of the area involved, the actual desires of the proprietor and the methods of the individual land surveyors.

Thus great change was wrought in the Scottish landscape, change which stemmed from the provisions of the acts of 1695. The methods of enclosure – gradual consolidation, individual planning, private agreement and legal action – brought about a change more rapid than any other which had occurred within Scottish agrarian development. But, as Roy's Map shows, even by the middle of the eighteenth century, before the main period of the land surveyors' activity, enclosure could be found over a wide regional range – in Ayrshire and Galloway, around Glasgow, in the Lothians along the Forth coast, in the Merse and up the East Coast. The rapid changes in the latter part of the eighteenth century were a recognition of the advantages of the enclosures already carried out but which could not be implemented everywhere until that time when the economic climate became favourable. The rapidity of the change must not however be allowed to cloud the main attribute of the Scottish agrarian landscape – it is the product of an evolutionary and not a revolutionary process. Change

---

[1] A. C. O'Dell, 'A View of Scotland in the Middle of the Eighteenth Century', *Scott. Geogr. Mag.*, LXIX, 1953, pp. 58–63.

[2] J. H. G. Lebon, 'The Process of Enclosure in the Western Lowlands', *Scott. Geogr. Mag.*, LXII, 1946, p. 107.

was always occurring within the system at work at any one time. Changes in individual field units, localised consolidation and re-organisation of settlements all occurred long before the activities of the land surveyors. The so-called revolution which affected the Scottish agrarian landscape was merely a rapid consummation of the changes which had been slowly evolving over a very long period. A total system was not overthrown as is demanded in the term revolution. This could not be, for there was never one total and all-embracing field system. There was never such a thing as '*a* Scottish field system', but merely a continually evolving pattern which even today is still being modified and being added to. To talk of 'a Scottish field system' is like using the term 'Neolithic Period' – without qualification with specific times and locations they are both just useless and potentially misleading labels.

13

Field Systems of Ireland

BY RONALD H. BUCHANAN

A. INTRODUCTION

Many features of Irish life and landscape can be understood only in relation to the island's geographical position on the western margins of Britain and the European mainland. Its field systems are no exception, for their evolution reveals close parallels with the systems developed in neighbouring lands across the Irish Sea, especially in Wales and Scotland. Yet there are important contrasts, which may be partly explained by distance from the main centres of agricultural innovation in eastern Britain, and partly by the circumstance of Ireland's colonial relationship with England. The effect of these cultural links, operating through space and time, has been to accentuate internal regional contrasts, based on the environmental distinction between the lowlands of the east and the mountain areas of the west. This east–west dichotomy is a persistent theme in the evolution of field systems in Ireland, and its bases will be outlined briefly in terms of environment and cultural history. Existing field patterns will then be described, and their antecedents traced back through time by examining the characteristic field systems in existence at different periods.

From Donegal in the north to Kerry and Cork in the south, much of western Ireland is dominated by mountain ranges, each differing in age, structure and topography, but all providing conditions of soil and climate which make farming difficult (Fig. 13.1). The weathering of their schists, quartzites and sandstones produces thin mountain soils, but drift and glaciofluvial deposits thickly mantle the valley floors and coastal lowlands. Here good drainage is essential for farming, since waterlogged soils encourage peat formation in a climate where heavy and consistent rainfall is matched by mild winter temperatures. Peat-bog covers nearly one-third of Ireland's land surface, and although the most extensive tracts are found in the lowlands, blanket bog is ubiquitous on the western hills and encroaches on reclaimed land in the valley bottoms unless drainage is carefully maintained. High rainfall, mean summer temperatures of between 14°C and 16°C, and relatively few sunny days provide poor conditions for cereal cultivation: the western farmer 'wins' his harvest and 'saves' his hay, and finds that grass is the crop best suited to his particular environment.

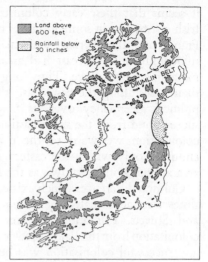

Fig. 13.1 Ireland: some administrative divisions and physical features.
U = Ulster, C = Connaught, L = Leinster, M = Munster.

Similar conditions prevail in the eastern mountains, in Wicklow, Down and Antrim; but in the lowlands of Ulster and Leinster rainfall is lower than in the west and summer brings more sunshine, especially to coastal districts. Differences in glacial deposition are mainly responsible for regional contrasts in these lowlands, particularly between those developed on Palaeozoic rocks in Ulster and on Carboniferous Limestones farther south. In the former, the drift is moulded into drumlins, forming a rolling surface of medium loam soil with intervening marshy hollows; but south of a line from Dundalk in the east to Clew Bay in the west, the topography changes. To the east in Meath, the limestones are masked by thick deposits of heavy boulder clay which form some of the richest pasture in Ireland, but westward the drift becomes thin, and drainage deteriorates among the lakes and bogs which mark the course of the River Shannon.

In some areas, the alignment of bog and mountain along the western margins of the central lowlands has inhibited contact between east and west, especially as possibilities for agriculture are localised in valleys and along the coasts. The western areas have thus tended to be relatively isolated, their scattered communities maintaining a cultural identity different in many respects from that of the eastern lowlands, where cultural innovations derived from Britain first gained a foothold and were diffused slowly westward. Only during the Neolithic was this east–west drift of culture markedly reversed, for it seems that these early colonists made many landfalls around the Irish coasts, and in some instances came direct to the west by sea from France and the Iberian peninsula. Yet by the middle of the first millennium B.C. the east had assumed a dominant role which it has maintained ever since. Thus long before the Norsemen established their bases along the east coast, the Kingdom of Meath had sought political ascendency over its neighbours with varying degrees of success; and from the same bastion the Anglo-Normans pushed their colonisation westward to the coast, although their power proved enduring only within the eastern half of the central lowlands, in the area around Dublin known as the Pale.

Cultural differences which existed between east and west in medieval times were accentuated by subsequent immigration under the Tudors and Stuarts. Plantation schemes were devised to extend English colonisation from the Pale westward to Munster, but the most thorough and successful colonisation was begun in Ulster in 1610. Except for Donegal, none of these immigrations affected the west directly, but as a result of war and rebellion the estates of native landowners were steadily confiscated, and even in the west English landowners were numerous by the close of the seventeenth century. With the change in land-ownership, east–west differences were now expressed more in terms of economic development than in regional contrasts of folk culture. The prospect of expanding trade with England stimulated the new landlords to develop the agricultural potential of their estates, and lowland farmers were quick to adapt their husbandry to the needs of commercial agriculture. But the west was less well endowed with natural resources, its landowners were often absentee, and the demands of the new agrarian economy undermined traditional subsistence farming with disastrous results as population steadily increased in the early nineteenth century. Widespread destitution, and the ultimate catastrophe of the Great Famine of 1845–7, finally forced landlords and government to undertake a drastic programme of land reform, designed to bring western agriculture into line with contemporary practices. In these events, vestiges of older field systems were largely erased from the landscape, but enough evidence survives to establish their characteristic features (Fig. 13.2).

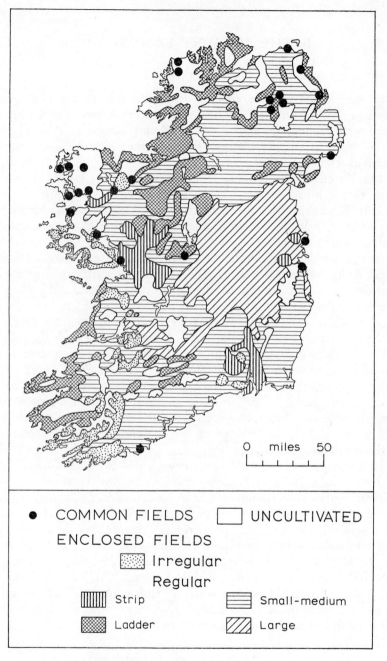

Fig. 13.2 Ireland: field types.
Source. P. Flatrès, *Géographie Rurale de Quatre Contrées Celtiques*, Rennes, 1957.

B. THE PRESENT LANDSCAPE

I. COMMON FIELDS

Professor Evans was the first to draw attention to the continued existence of an Irish common field system when he discovered a small community living on the slopes of Mount Errigal in the isolated mid-section of County Donegal in the 1930s.[1] Here he found three families with shares in a joint-farm, living in a small cluster of houses set on the edge of an unenclosed arable field (Fig. 13.3a). There were also two compact farms, whose dwellings were separate from the others. The arable in this townland, known as Meenacreevagh, amounted to 38 acres, held by individual farms in a number of scattered plots which were demarcated by low earthen banks, some two to three yards in width. In addition, each farmer had a small enclosed field next to his house which he cropped for hay and later used to stack his oats; he also had a stone-walled garden for potatoes and cabbage. Finally he had a share in 300 acres of hill land, divided in long strips and roughly outlined by stone markers, which he used for grazing and peat-cutting. Plots on the arable were cultivated with the spade in lazybeds,[2] and cropped in a ten-year successsion of oats and potatoes, after which they were allowed to revert to grass for between five and seven years. Manure was applied only before the potato crop, but winter grazing of the arable in common provided a continuous supply of dung. Two cows were kept and between ten and thirty sheep on each farm, grazing on the mountain slopes in summer where they were herded to prevent their wandering on the arable land.

According to tradition, Meenacreevagh had been reclaimed from the surrounding bog by herders some two hundred years before, but by the 1930s this community was an anachronism, its farming based solely on hand implements and providing little more than subsistence. It might seem to be a case of marginal existence, yet the system of farming followed here found parallels in similar communities discovered by D. McCourt during an extensive field survey he undertook during the late 1940s. McCourt's unpublished thesis, 'The Rundale System in Ireland',[3] is the definitive work on Irish common fields, its title based on the term used by nineteenth-century writers and possibly derived from the Irish *roinn*, meaning to make a division or share, and

---

[1] E. E. Evans, 'Some Survivals of the Irish Openfield System', *Geography*, XXIV, 1939, pp. 24–36.   [2] E. E. Evans, *Irish Folk Ways*, 1957, pp. 140–51.

[3] D. McCourt, 'The Rundale System in Ireland', Ph.D. thesis, Queen's University, Belfast, 1950.

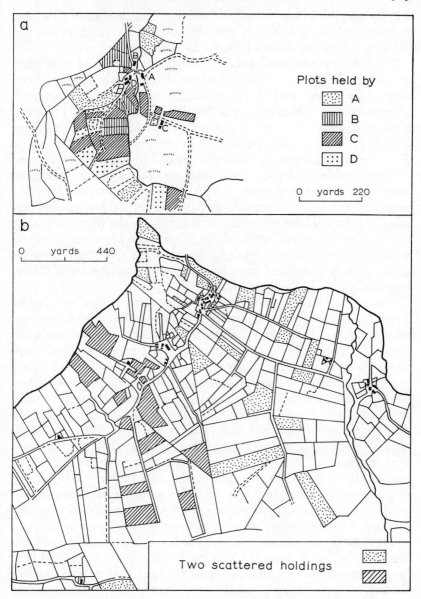

Fig. 13.3 Common Fields: (a) Meenacreevagh, Townland of Beltany Mountain, Co. Donegal; (b) Corick, Co. Londonderry.

Sources. E. E. Evans, 'Some Survivals of the Irish Openfield System', *Geography*, XXIV, 1939, pp. 24–36. D. McCourt, 'Surviving Openfield in County Londonderry', *Ulster Folklife*, IV, 1958, p. 26.

dail, an assembly. From a study of existing rundale communities and their oral tradition, McCourt was able to establish the main features of the system as it existed within the last century.

Twenty years ago, rundale communities rarely included more than nine or ten farmers, but tradition relates that formerly they had been very much larger. Their land lay mainly within a single townland, a territorial unit whose mean size for the country is about 325 acres. If the townland was large, it was sometimes divided among several rundale groups, each holding its land in lots separate from the others. The system varied greatly in detail, but had five main components: common arable or infield, an outfield used for pasture and periodic cultivation, common meadow, rough grazing which usually included peat-bog, and small enclosures near the farmhouse for gardens and haggards. Finally, the settlement was usually in the form of a loose cluster of dwellings and outbuildings. There is no common colloquial word in either Irish or English to describe such settlements, but the term *clachan*, a loan word from Irish formerly used in parts of Ulster, is generally used in the literature.[1]

The infield was normally held in rectangular strips, varying in length from 50 to 250 yards according to slope and soil conditions, and not more than 20 yards in width. Most were cultivated with the plough, and where the spade was used, the plots tended towards a square shape. Plots were demarcated by low, earthen banks, known by such terms as *mearings, ribs, roddens, keelogues* or *bones*;[2] and a higher earthen bank frequently bounded the infield. Individual plots were widely scattered throughout the infield to ensure equality in the share of different qualities of soil, and they varied in size (Fig. 13.3b). Cropping tended to conform to prevailing farm practice, and this, together with the use of improved grasses, meant that livestock had to be tethered in winter when they grazed the stubble. The older practice of common winter grazing was still followed in several communities, with a continuous oats/potatoes cropping cycle, usually without any fallow and an application of manure annually or one year in two.

The infield was the core of the rundale system, and was usually accompanied by an outfield.[3] This rarely survives as unenclosed land in existing examples, but is represented by a girdle of enclosed pasture fields around the infield, usually on poorer quality land. These are now used for grazing and are rarely cropped, but in each instance they are said to have been reclaimed to supplement the infield for

---

[1] V. B. Proudfoot, 'Clachans in Ireland', *Gwerin*, II, 1959, p. 110.
[2] D. McCourt, 'Infield and Outfield in Ireland', *Econ. Hist. Rev.*, II, 1954, p. 373.
[3] D. McCourt, 'The Dynamic Quality of Irish Rural Settlement', in R. H. Buchanan, E. Jones and D. McCourt (eds.), *Man and His Habitat*, 1971, p. 130.

potato cultivation. The cropping cycle was several years of potatoes followed by a period of fallow without application of manure. Where natural meadows existed along river or lake their use was carefully regulated to give each farmer a share of hay and grazing, calculated according to his share of the infield. Sometimes the land was divided into plots scattered as in the infield, worked in severalty and grazed by herding the animals, each on its own plot. Occasionally the hay was mowed by communal labour and then divided in shares, with common grazing. But most of the grazing had to be found elsewhere in summer, and especially in mountain districts there are traditions of moving livestock long distances to seasonal pasture. In Achill Island, County Mayo, for example, milch cows were driven from coastal townlands to graze on Slievemore mountain, where they were tended by girls who lived on the hill pastures from early May until Hallowe'en.[1] Booleying, as it was termed in English, has disappeared but grazing rights on unenclosed hill lands are still reckoned in units known as *sums* or *collops*, calculated according to the amount of grass needed to feed a cow, with appropriate equivalents for other livestock. Finally, farmers with rights in common fields usually lived in clachans, groups of houses and farm buildings whose layout is most aptly described by the countryman as 'throughother'. Often the farm families were related, bearing the same patronym, and cooperating in field-work. Clachan dwellers might include landless cottiers or craftsmen as well as farmers, but shops, churches or schools were rarely located in this type of settlement.

Few common fields survived in the 1960s, and even at the time of McCourt's survey they were confined mostly to the mountains and lowlands of the west, with a few examples in Ulster, around Lough Neagh and the Antrim coast (Figs. 13.2 and 13.3). Clearly they occupied areas which are marginal for modern farming, and it is possible they represent a system evolved in a difficult environment by a people living at subsistence level and possessing the simplest of hand implements. Tradition might seem to support this view, for none of the surviving communities appears to date back more than two centuries,[2] originating probably during the period between 1781 and 1841 when Ireland's population rose from an estimated 4,048,000 to 8,175,000 at the 1841 census.[3] As all available land was brought into cultivation, rundale developed through the subdivision of holdings among heirs under the traditional system of customary inheritance.

[1] J. M. Graham, 'Transhumance in Ireland', *Advmt. Sci.*, x, 1953, pp. 74–5.
[2] D. McCourt, 'Surviving Openfield in County Londonderry', *Ulster Folklife*, IV, 1958, pp. 20 and 27.
[3] K. H. Connell, *The Population of Ireland, 1750–1845*, 1950, p. 25.

Through the operation of this process, large individual holdings could become rundale farms within a few generations.[1] An alternative explanation is that rundale is a survival of an archaic field system, now found only in the west but more widely distributed in former times. In support of this view it can be noted that rundale is concentrated in the classic survival areas of earlier folk cultures, although it is absent in the southwest. Whichever explanation is correct, the answer lies beneath the network of regular enclosed fields which covers the present landscape with a deceptive uniformity.

2. ENCLOSED FIELDS

In the 1950s, P. Flatrès made a significant contribution to the study of field systems in the western British Isles and Brittany, concentrating on field patterns visible in the present landscape.[2] He found that enclosed fields could be grouped in two major categories, according to whether their shape was regular or irregular. In Ireland, the latter rarely formed more than a small proportion of fields in any area and were usually small, while the former could be subdivided according to their size and shape. Most regular fields are straight-sided, roughly quadrilateral and with a length one and a half times their breadth. Large enclosures he found are mainly associated with large farms, and since these have a restricted distribution in Ireland, small and medium sized fields predominate. Among the latter he noted a special category of long, narrow and slightly curved fields which resembled the common field strips of the English Midlands.

The distribution of these field types reveals some major regional contrasts which provide clues to their origin (Fig. 13.2). Irregular fields have a sporadic distribution, mainly in the mountain areas of the southwest, and seem to represent piecemeal enclosure of marginal land by farmers using the spade as their principal implement (Fig. 13.4c). Presumably many were formed at the height of population pressure in the early nineteenth century, but others may be very much older, perhaps even prehistoric in origin. Elsewhere the distribution reveals a core area of large, regular fields in the eastern half of the central lowlands, with a peripheral belt of small and medium fields, most prevalent in Ulster where there appears to be a remarkable uniformity of field type. The large field area today is associated with large farms specialising in the rearing of store cattle, but these enclosures are not necessarily of recent origin (Fig. 13.4a). This area was the heart of Anglo-Norman colonisation in Ireland, suggesting a link with

---

[1] D. McCourt, Ph.D. thesis, pp. 178, 180, 186.

[2] P. Flatrès, *Géographie Rurale de Quatre Contrées Celtiques*, Rennes, 1957.

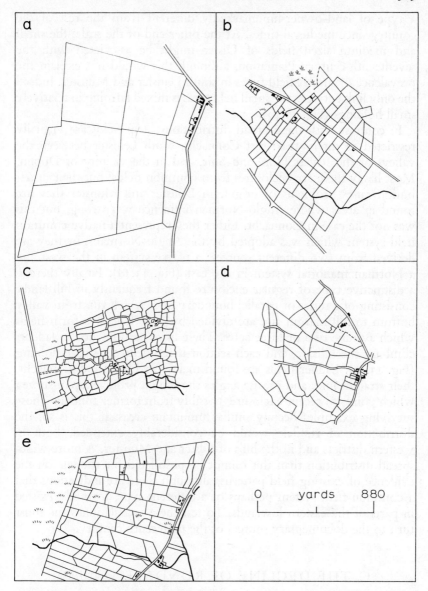

Fig. 13.4 Present-day enclosed fields: (a) large, regular fields – Jordanstown, Co. Meath; (b) small, regular fields – Ballykine Lower, Co. Down; (c) small, irregular fields – Glinsouth, Co. Kerry; (d) curved strip fields – Nicholastown, Co. Kilkenny; (e) ladder farms – Foriff, Co. Antrim.

a type of land-ownership markedly different from the rest of the country since medieval times. At the other end of the scale, the small and medium sized fields of Ulster might be associated with the seventeenth-century Plantation, although this would not explain the prevalence of similar field types in south Leinster and Munster. Indeed the only link between the small field areas is mixed farming in relatively small holdings (Fig. 13.4b).

In contrast with these broad distributions, strip fields are virtually restricted to three areas: east Connacht, south Leinster between the valleys of the Rivers Nore and Suir, and in the vicinity of Dublin. Most likely these are enclosures from common fields, but their distribution raises problems of origin. In Leinster and Munster they are found in areas where Anglo-Norman influence was strong, but this was not the case in Connacht. Either they represent a native common field system which was adopted by the Anglo-Normans, or they are derived from two different sources: a native system in the west and a Norman manorial system in the east (Fig. 13.4d). Finally there is a distinctive type of regular enclosure found frequently in hill lands, consisting of a series of parallel boundary lines which run from valley bottom to hill margin and are divided by cross fences to form fields which average two or three acres. These have been likened to ladders climbing the hillside, and each section is frequently a single holding (Fig. 13.4e). Ladder fields are found mainly in Ulster and Connacht, their straight lines and precise angles showing a proficiency in survey which points to recent enclosure, possibly from former rundale whose surviving examples occupy similar mountain areas. If this is so, the distribution of rundale would be considerably extended, both in western districts and in the hills of Ulster and Munster. A more widespread distribution than this cannot be postulated for rundale on the evidence of existing field patterns, although there are indications that a common field system perhaps of a different type, formerly existed in parts of the eastern lowlands. To test these speculations, one must turn to the documentary sources of the ninteeenth century.

C. THE DECLINE OF RUNDALE 1780–1900

Fortunately this period is adequately documented, beginning with the publication of Arthur Young's *Tour in Ireland* in 1780.[1] A notable volume in itself, Young's example may also have stimulated the Royal Dublin Society to sponsor a remarkable series of county statistical accounts on agriculture which appeared between 1802 and 1832. The

[1] A. Young, *A Tour in Ireland made in the years 1776, 1777 and 1778*, 1780.

main purpose of these volumes was to propagate new methods of husbandry, but in doing so their authors provide invaluable insights on the state of Irish agriculture at this time. In many counties the picture was not encouraging. Landowners were wealthy, and there was a ready market in England for the produce of Irish agriculture, but farming in general was ill-adjusted to meet the needs of commercial agriculture, and there was widespread destitution even before the Great Famine. Government reports on the condition of the rural poor provide much information on the west in the aftermath of the Famine, and this may be supplemented by the published accounts of the many travellers who visited Ireland at this time. They were mostly attracted to western areas, so information on the more prosperous farmlands of the east is rather less detailed. But in the 1830s the Ordnance Survey began to publish its 6-inch maps, beginning in the northern counties in 1832 and gradually extending southward. Unfortunately field fences were not mapped at first, but by the time the Survey reached County Monaghan all permanent field boundaries were mapped, although plots in common fields were not included. Estate maps and documents can be used to overcome this deficiency in specific areas, but so far only a few studies[1] have used the material which is slowly accumulating in the national archives in Dublin and Belfast.

These sources provide additional information on the working of the rundale system. They confirm that it was based on infield cultivation, the arable held in plots whose shape seems to have depended on local methods of ploughing. Squarish plots resulted when cross-ploughing was made necessary by use of the light wooden ard – 'a log of wood sharpened and shod with iron' which 'merely scratched the land with furrows'.[2] It seems to have been widely used until the more manoeuvrable swing plough was introduced early in the nineteenth century, with a consequent change to a long, narrow strip. Heavy ploughs, probably descendants of those used on the Anglo-Norman manors, were also known in some counties, producing the 'curved and waved ridges' which William Tighe described in Kilkenny.[3] Oats were the principal crop, together with some barley; and the infield was kept in continuous cultivation, a practice condemned by many writers who commented on the resulting loss of fertility and lower

---

[1] McCourt, Ph.D. thesis; R. H. Buchanan, 'The Barony of Lecale, County Down', Ph.D. thesis, Queen's University, Belfast, 1958; I. Leister, *Das Werden der Agrarlandschaft in der Grafschaft Tipperary (Irland)*, Marburg, 1963.

[2] Evans, *Irish Folk Ways*, pp. 131, 129.

[3] W. Tighe, *Kilkenny: Statistical Observations, County of Kilkenny*, Dublin, 1802, p. 294.

yields.[1] This may be one reason why periodic cultivation of poorer quality land in oats and potatoes was normal at this time, although cropping practices varied considerably. In Tyrone, for example, the *Ordnance Survey Memoirs* state: 'the land was immediately thrown into pasture when it was no longer capable of bearing a crop, in which state it was suffered to lie until there was some prospect of profitable return in making it up again'.[2] In contrast, a definite succession of cropping and fallow was followed in Londonderry, Roscommon and Kilkenny, varying from three to eight years according to soil quality, and followed by a similar number of years ley.[3] There is no record of the size of plot normally worked in the outfield, but cultivation was mainly with the spade or the foot plough known as the loy.[4]

In twentieth-century rundale, the infield strips were demarcated by permanent boundaries and held by individuals who had right of inheritance, subject only to common rights of winter pasturage. But McCourt has shown that in the previous century farmers often held shares rather than specific portions of land, and the plots they cultivated varied from time to time. In Mayo in 1841 for example:

'in the land appropriate to tillage, each head of the family casts lots every year for the number of ridges he is entitled to...and moreover the ridges change ownership every third year, a new division taking place. The head of the village...makes the division, requiring each tenant to cast lots for his ridge, one in a good field, another in an inferior, and another in a worse.'[5]

A yearly change of plots, known as 'changedale', was recorded by Arthur Young as far apart as Antrim and Limerick,[6] while twenty years later other writers noted that reallotment took place at two or three year intervals in Galway and Kilkenny.[7] The main reason behind this practice seems to have been the overriding concern for equality of shares which permeated every aspect of the rundale system. In Mayo it reached extreme porportions: 'the arable is divided into lots, even including the cabbin. It may occur that a man changes his habitations, his cornfields, his potato patches and his pasture ground

[1] For example, A. Young, *Tour*, I, 113.
[2] McCourt, Ph.D. thesis, p. 67.
[3] G. V. Sampson, *Statistical Survey of the County of Londonderry*, Dublin, 1802, p. 218; I. Weld, *A Statistical Survey of County Roscommon*, Dublin, 1832, p. 493; Tighe, *Kilkenny*, p. 278.
[4] Evans, *Irish Folk Ways*, pp. 132–9.
[5] C. Otway, *Sketches in Erris and Tyrawley*, 1841, p. 35.
[6] Young, *Tour*, I, 215–16, 371.
[7] McCourt, *Econ. Hist. Rev.*, II, 1954, pp. 373–4.

all to situation remote to each other.'[1] Wakefield, writing of Donegal in 1812, notes the effect of changedale on soil fertility: 'as the fields pass from one hand to another every year, no occupier takes the least pains to ameliorate the land'.[2] Nonetheless, this procedure meant that some increase in population could be accommodated without causing undue hardship to any one individual, since additional shares were created through periodic lottery. But once the plots came into fixed ownership, subdivision of holdings under gavelkind inheritance resulted in extreme fragmentation of holdings as population increased. In the early 1840s in Donegal for example, a case was reported in which 'one man (a tailor by trade) had his land in 42 different places and gave it up in despair, declaring it would take a very keen man to find it'.[3]

The use of common meadows and mountain grazing was much the same in the early nineteenth century as in recent times, but there are more frequent references to booleying, i.e. the use of seasonal pastures grazed in summer, both in the west and in mountain districts in the east. There are also hints of a more complex movement. 'It often happens', wrote Sir William Wilde with reference to Donegal in 1836, 'that a man has three dwellings – one in the mountains, another upon the shore, and the third upon an island, he and his family flitting from one to another of these habitations.'[4] Yet J. M. Graham has shown that booleying was not so important in the nineteenth century as it had been earlier. Pressure of population meant that former booley land was being brought into permanent use, for cultivation if the land was fertile, or for common pasture if it lay near newly established farms. Here herds were employed by the community to manage the livestock, which included young cattle, goats and sheep as well as milch cows.[5]

Finally, rundale farmers lived mainly in clachans, of which the following is a typical description:

'There is no row of houses…but each cottage is stuck independently by itself, and always at an acute, obtuse or right angle to the next cottage as the case may be. The irregularity is curious; there are no two cottages placed in a line, or of the same size, dimensions or build. As this is the largest village I ever saw, so it is the poorest,

[1] McCourt, Ph.D. thesis, p. 76.
[2] E. Wakefield, *An Account of Ireland, Statistical and Political*, 1812, I, 372.
[3] D. McCourt, 'The Rundale System in Donegal, its Distribution and Decline', *Donegal Annual*, III, 1955, p. 48.
[4] Evans, *Irish Folk Ways*, p. 35.
[5] J. M. Graham, 'Transhumance in Ireland', Ph.D. thesis, Queen's University, Belfast, 1954, chap. 2.

the worst built and most strangely irregular and most completely
without head or centre, or market or church or school of any village
I ever was in. It is an overgrown democracy. No man is better or
richer than his neighbour. It is in fact, an Irish rundale village.'[1]

Clachans of the early nineteenth century were much larger than
modern surviving examples, for as population increased and holdings
were subdivided, houses were usually added to the existing nuclei.
In 1802 for example, McParlin notes that Donegal clachans averaged
between thirty and forty houses,[2] while a decade later in Clare some
had two hundred dwellings.[3] Subdivision of holdings through gavelkind ensured that clachan families were often closely related, and
cooperation in farmwork, the sharing of implements and sometimes
even livestock, was based on ties of kinship. This could lead to tension,
as clachans grew in size and fragmented holdings could scarcely meet
subsistence needs: 'The co-partnerships which they have in their
farms', wrote one visitor, 'give frequent opportunities for indulging
this litigious disposition, as well as numerous contentions about the
number of horses with which they plough, or the quantity of work
done in the day.'[4] To help resolve such disputes some communities
had a headman, known as 'The King' in Tory Island, Donegal, and
the 'Raigh' in the Mullet of Mayo.[5]

Rundale farming had the drawbacks of all common field systems,
but the main reason for its decline was its inability to increase
production of crop and livestock both for cash sale and subsistence, on
holdings which became progressively smaller and less fertile as population increased. Initially crop production could be increased by more
careful management of the outfield and increasing dependence on the
potato as the main subsistence crop. Indeed as K. H. Connell has
shown, the ability of the potato to produce good yields on poor
quality land was mainly responsible for sustaining population growth.[6]
But reclamation of land for cropping led to curtailment of grazing,
and a reduction in the number of livestock meant less manure for the
infield when animals grazed the stubble. Livestock numbers could be
maintained if alternative winter fodder was available, and root crops
were an obvious solution, used in combination with a green fallow
which in turn would help maintain the fertility of the infield. If this

[1] T. C. Foster, *Letters on the Condition of the People of Ireland*, Dublin, 1846, pp. 292–3.
[2] J. McParlin, *Statistical Survey of the County of Donegal*, Dublin, 1802, p. 64.
[3] W. Shaw Mason, *Parochial Survey: A Statistical or Parochial Survey of Ireland*,
    Dublin, 1814, I, 485.
[4] *Ibid.*, p. 106.
[5] McCourt, Ph.D. thesis, p. 88.
[6] Connell, *The Population of Ireland*, p. 135.

was adopted however, livestock would have to be denied access to the infield in winter. There were two possibilities: to provide enclosed pasture for the livestock, or to enclose the infield strips. The former was often achieved by enclosing the individually owned plots on the outfield, or on the edge of the common grazing; but the latter required common agreement since it denied rights of common grazing. This was impossible to achieve where changedale was practised, and it became increasingly difficult as subdivision progressed.

Between the census of 1821 and 1841, Ireland's population rose by 1,373,000. The degree of subdivision implied by this growth-rate in rundale areas helps to explain the poverty encountered wherever the system was practised; but the landlords also contributed through rising rents. This arose mainly through the renting of property on long leases to middlemen, who in turn sub-let to farmers on short leases or sometimes at will. Many tenants meant good incomes for the middlemen and landlords, and also votes, for an Act of 1793 extended the franchise to Roman Catholic tenants who held leases worth 40s. or more. This was a further encouragement to subdivision, increasing competition for land and resulting in rising land values, for leases on renewal passed to the highest bidder. Since rents were paid in cash, the farmer had to adjust his production to suit the demands of the market, and this was largely determined by trade with England. Prior to the mid-eighteenth century livestock had dominated Anglo-Irish trade, but grain became increasingly important as towns grew in Britain, and especially during the Napoleonic Wars when the continental markets were closed to English trade. The Irish rundale farmer was in no position to adapt his farming from livestock to tillage. Winter-sown wheat could not be grown on the infield without enclosure, nor was it a suitable crop for the western environment, although barley was grown for market sale. Thus as his arable acreage declined through subdivision, the rundale farmer had to concentrate on livestock sales, despite the difficulties of providing pasture and winter fodder. Not surprisingly, the pig rather than the cow began to pay the rent.

Eventually, the effect of these changes was to encourage consolidation and enclosure, either through the initiative of individual farmers or as a result of landlord intervention. If subdivision had not reached extreme proportions, it was sometimes possible to arrange an exchange of strips to form more compact holdings which could then be enclosed. Emigration and eviction aided this process, both before and after the Famine. The resultant field pattern is often characterised by a series of narrow strips enclosed from the former infield, surrounded by a girdle of small rectangular fields occupying the outfield. Such farms are rarely compact, but consist of scattered blocks of fields interspersed with those of neighbouring holdings, and often with clachans surviving amidst dispersed farmsteads.

Reorganisation by landlords came later, stimulated by increasing poverty which not only lowered estate income, but also became a major financial liability following the passing of a new Poor Law in 1838. Consequently, as leases of middlemen and tenants fell due, holdings were repossessed increasingly during the 1830s, and plans made for consolidation. On an estate in southwest Donegal for example, square fields were laid out and arranged in compact holdings which were then allocated to tenants by drawing lots. New farmhouses were built and subsidised by the estate, which also bore half the cost of fencing. Tenants who could not be accommodated on existing farmland were provided with mountain land, where holdings were surveyed and allocated, and reclamation encouraged by payment of a nominal rent for the first three years.[1] Not all landlords followed this procedure: many made no provision for displaced tenants, some provided passage money to assist emigration, and others simply left things as they were, with disastrous results in the famine years of the 1840s.

Later in the nineteenth century, when government assumed responsibility for consolidation, this 'squared' farm was most commonly adopted in schemes undertaken both by the Congested Districts Board and its successor, the Land Commission.[2] Sometimes, however, the ladder farm or 'striped holding' was preferred by tenants, since it preserved the rundale principle of equal shares of good land and bad in holdings which extended from valley bottom to hill margin. The idea of grouped settlement was retained in this scheme, by placing farmsteads on their holdings to form a linear pattern, connected by a road running along the valley side. As a compromise between old and new the ladder farm was widely adopted, but it could be inefficient, especially if subdivision persisted – as it frequently did, despite an act of 1826 which prohibited the practice unless the landlord gave his permission. Consolidation and enclosure spread quickly in the decades after 1830, and after 1850 rundale was to be found only on the most isolated and worst managed estates. These were mostly in Connacht and west Ulster, and here the Land Commission was still working on the consolidation of rundale as late as the 1920s.

From the available evidence it is certain that rundale was widely practised in western Ireland at the beginning of the nineteenth century,

[1] McCourt, *Donegal Annual*, III, 1955, p. 56.
[2] B. O. Binns, *The Consolidation of Fragmented Agricultural Holdings*, Washington, 1950, chap. 3.

extending from Donegal and Londonderry in the north, through Sligo, Mayo and Galway to Kerry and west Cork. Compact farms and enclosed fields were also found throughout the west, especially in Clare, Galway and Limerick, but they were mainly associated with large stock farms, and the greater proportion of small farmers seem to have held their land in common fields. The eastern boundary of rundale is difficult to determine, but there seems to have been a broad transition belt, west of a line from the cities of Londonderry and Cork, where enclosed fields were common and rundale was found only in the mountain valleys and on isolated patches of fertile land among the bogs and lakes of the central lowlands. To the east of this line enclosure was normal, and the field pattern in Leinster and Ulster was little different from that of the present day. Rundale communities, however, were found in several areas. In Kilkenny, for example, Tighe states it was the 'universal custom' in hilly tracts of that county,[1] and this was also true in Wicklow.[2] In eastern Ulster rundale was common on the north coast of Antrim and the northern fringe of the Mourne Mountains in Down,[3] and as late as 1834, seventeen rundale farms were to be found along the southeast coast of the same county.[4] No rundale is recorded in Meath, Westmeath and Dublin counties by contemporary writers, and there is doubtful evidence of its existence in Louth, Laois, Offaly and Carlow.

The fact that rundale existed at all in the east suggests that it may have been more widely distributed in earlier times, and some evidence for this may be found in the writings of the period. For instance, enclosures were sometimes little better than those which surrounded the infield, and were of similar construction: 'The fences of common farmers', wrote Arthur Young of County Limerick, 'are making banks and sowing furze seed.'[5] Thorn hedges were still uncommon in many districts, and were mainly associated with the estates of improving landlords. Subdivision of holdings in the rundale manner was also widely practised in compact holdings, leading to a steady decline in average farm size and increasingly small fields. In one County Down district in 1807, an agent wrote to his employer:

'I have endeavoured to prevail on the tenants to send their sons early to trade that they may be able to provide for themselves without depending on their father's farm, which would put a stop to the present bad practice of farmers dividing their small holdings

[1] Tighe, *Kilkenny*, p. 48.
[2] R. Frazer, *A Statistical Account of the County of Wicklow*, Dublin, 1801, p. 91.
[3] McCourt, Ph.D. thesis, chap. 3.
[4] Buchanan, Ph.D. thesis, p. 190.   [5] Young, *Tour*, I, 369.

among their three or four sons, thereby cutting up their farms into cabbage gardens.'[1]

This type of inheritance need not necessarily be derived directly from rundale, but it was sometimes linked with farm practices very reminiscent of husbandry in the common fields. In County Londonderry, Sampson notes that some farmers continued to use a three year oats/two year fallow rotation similar to that used on the outfield, and he records one 40-acre farm which was managed like an infield, with a five-year cropping cycle uninterrupted by fallow or green crop. Collectively these features suggest that the tradition of rundale was strong in some districts of the east, indicating that the system may have preceded the existing pattern of regular, enclosed fields and scattered farmsteads.

D. COMMON FIELDS AND ENCLOSURE: THE SEVENTEENTH AND EIGHTEENTH CENTURIES

In Arthur Young's time, the landscape of eastern Ireland was similar in many respects to that of the present day. Yet this was clearly a period of economic growth and change, for Young comments with approval on the improvements being made by many landowners, in land reclamation, planting and building, both farmhouses and in estate towns and villages. A century earlier, many English visitors were less flattering in their comments: 'Enclosures are very rare amongst them, and then no better fenced than an old wife's toothless gums... as for the arable gound it lies almost as much neglected and unmanured as the sandy deserts of Arabia.'[2] Admittedly this description relates to the period following the Williamite wars, but at the beginning of the seventeenth century other commentators refer to the absence of enclosure and to the extensive woodlands. E. McCracken has calculated that in 1600 about 12 per cent of the country was under forest, the most extensive tracts occurring in Ulster and west Munster, yet by the end of the century most of this had been cleared.[3]

This transformation of the landscape, which broadly signifies a change from subsistence to commercial farming, was mainly due to the replacement of native Irish and the old Anglo-Norman families

[1] Buchanan, Ph.D. thesis, p. 184.
[2] Quoted in G. O'Brien, *The Economic History of Ireland in the Seventeenth Century*, 1919, p. 143.
[3] E. McCracken, 'The Woodlands of Ireland *c.* 1600', *Ir. Hist. Stud.*, XI, 1959, pp. 271–96.

by newcomers from Britain during the seventeenth century. Under the Tudors, 'Plantations' had been made in parts of Leinster and Munster, but the most enduring colonisation was that undertaken in Ulster after 1610. Here native landowners were dispossessed, and the Planters were required to settle their properties with English and Scottish farmers, to establish villages and market towns, and to require their tenants to 'use Tillage and Husbandry after the manner of the English Pale'.[1] These instructions were complied with in varying degree, but the Ulster colony was able to withstand the Irish uprising of 1641, and subsequent immigration meant that by the end of the century a substantial body of colonists were established as tenant farmers in the north. In the remainder of the country, land confiscations occurred in two main phases: in the mid-century following the 1641 rebellion, and again after the war of 1689-90. Following the first, a great number of Irish and Anglo-Irish landowners were evicted from their estates and provided with small grants of land in Connacht and Clare, their places being taken mainly by ex-officers of the Cromwellian army. After 1690 less than one-fifth of the total country remained in the hand of native landowners,[2] and even this proportion was reduced under the Penal Laws enacted at the turn of the century which made it increasingly difficult for Roman Catholics to hold land except on lease. But despite the change in ownership, native farmers continued to occupy the land; only in Ulster were wholesale clearances contemplated, and even here they were rarely completed.

Changes in land-ownership affected agriculture mainly because most of the new landowners had acquired their estates essentially as a business speculation. To profit from their investment it was necessary that agriculture be reorganised on a commercial basis, and this had to await the return of more peaceful conditions. The latter was largely achieved by the third quarter of the century, but it took longer to introduce changes in farming. Ireland had long produced a surplus of livestock, exported either as live cattle or as 'provision' to England and the continent. This trade expanded quickly in the second half of the century, despite embargoes imposed by the English Parliament, and livestock rearing for export soon dominated Irish farming. Later the emphasis shifted to tillage, mainly after 1760 in response to changes in the English market to which Irish agriculture was now firmly committed. But the changes required by the new commercial interests were not uniform in their effect on agriculture, for the initiative for change and improvement depended entirely upon the interest and ability of the individual landlord. As a result, there were considerable

[1] G. Hill, *The Plantation of Ulster*, Belfast, 1877, p. 87.
[2] J. C. Beckett, *A Short History of Ireland*, 1952, p. 104.

differences in the rate and extent of consolidation and enclosure between different estates and regions.

For the seventeenth century it is possible to gain only a very generalised impression of the nature of Irish field systems. The contemporary landscape is well portrayed in surviving small-scale maps, and military surveys such as those of Richard Barthelet.[1] For the country as a whole important data on rural life are contained in the mid-century Civil Survey[2] and the later Books of Survey and Distribution,[3] which list in detail changes in land-ownership. Literary sources are less satisfactory, for visitors to Ireland at this time were mainly officials concerned with military and political affairs, and with few exceptions, their accounts lack the detailed descriptions of the countryside so valuable in later writings. Relevant estate documents are not numerous for the first half of the century, and even the surveys undertaken for the Ulster Plantation give few details on fields and their ownership. Not until the first half of the eighteenth century do estate maps, surveys and rentals become readily available, and by then the transformation of the landscape had already begun. Even with this material it is harder to follow the development of enclosure than in England, for in Ireland no act of Parliament was necessary to enclose estates.

The few surviving accounts of common fields show that rundale farming had changed little between the seventeenth and early nineteenth centuries. For example, a 1684 description of County Westmeath[4] shows that the arable was worked in a single field and held in shares which were reallocated by periodic ballot. Work was undertaken by ploughteams, and the partnership group consisted mainly of relatives. Here and in other areas where rundale can be identified, the clachan was the normal form of settlement, although in Lecale, County Down, a manorial survey indicates that partnership groups might sometimes live in dispersed farmsteads.[5] In Lecale five or six families was the normal partnership unit, and this agrees with McCourt's findings elsewhere in Ireland.[6] However larger groups are also recorded, as in the eighteen tenants who held a joint-tenancy in Tipperary at the time of the Civil Survey. L. O'Buachalla suggests that such large groups may have developed through eviction by landlords enclosing land for grazing farms, for under Irish customary law displaced families might be given shares in other farms held by members of

[1] G. A. Hayes-McCoy, *Ulster and other Irish Maps c. 1600*, Dublin, 1964.
[2] For example, see R. C. Simington, *The Civil Survey, A.D. 1654–56, County of Tipperary*, Dublin, 1931–4.
[3] R. C. Simington, *Books of Survey and Distribution*, Dublin, 1949.
[4] C. Vallency, *Collectanea de Rebus Hibernicis*, Dublin, 1770, pp. 115–19.
[5] Buchanan, Ph.D. thesis, chap. III.
[6] McCourt, Ph.D. thesis, p. 92.

the same sept or extended family group.[1] Apart from these special circumstances, rundale holdings were larger than at the end of the eighteenth century. Most of the Lecale joint-farms had between 50 and 100 acres of arable in the 1730s, and here, as in Westmeath, there is no evidence for outfield cultivation.[2] At the beginning of the seventeenth century however, outfield was a concomitant of rundale in north County Down, but the farms here were held by Scottish immigrants.[3] In many areas it is possible that outfield cultivation was adopted only during the course of the eighteenth century under conditions of marginal farming, and in response to changes in cropping practices and rising population. Throughout the seventeenth century, oats was the main cereal grown on rundale farms, but by the early eighteenth century barley had become an important cash crop both in the drier east and in the west.[4] Its cultivation in the infield, together with the adoption of the potato, may have been responsible for the development of the outfield as a normal rundale feature, especially in those areas of the north where Scottish influence was strong.

The relative distribution of enclosed and common field systems at the beginning of the seventeenth century is largely a matter of conjecture. Writing of Laois in 1600, for example, Fynes Moryson comments: 'It seemed incredible, that by so barbarous inhabitants, the ground should be so manured, the fields so orderly fenced, the Townes so frequently inhabited, and the high waies and paths so well beaten as the Lord Deputy here found them.' Significantly, he adds the reason: 'the Queenes forces, during these warres, never till then came among them'.[5] Laois may be an exception, for most writers took the opposite view and stress the absence of enclosure in the country as a whole. It is possible, of course, that this was because the traditional manner of fencing was both unfamiliar and unobtrusive, consisting either of earthen banks without hedgerows, or wattle fences. Both these types, which are specified in the eighth-century Brehon Laws, are clearly illustrated in a view of Cahir Castle, County Tipperary, in 1599,[6] where the landscape is divided into small, rectangular fields but still has the 'open and champain' appearance so frequently mentioned by eighteenth-century writers on eastern Ireland. It is possible that in some areas the only permanent enclosures were those which delimited

[1] L. O'Buachalla, 'Tenant Farmers of the Barrymore Estate, 1768', Jnl. Cork Hist. Arch. Soc., LI, 1946, p. 32.

[2] R. H. Buchanan, 'Common Fields and Enclosure: an Eighteenth Century Example from Lecale, County Down', Ulster Folklife, XXV–VI, 1970, pp. 99–118.

[3] McCourt, Ph.D. thesis, p. 65. [4] Buchanan, Ph.D. thesis, p. 156.

[5] F. Moryson, The Commonwealth of Ireland: The Itinerary, Glasgow, 1907, II, 330.

[6] J. O'Loan, 'Land Reclamation Down the Years', Jnl. (Irish) Dept. Agric., LV, 1959, Fig. 3, p. 9.

townlands, as was the case in Armagh.[1] Sometimes the 'outbounds' of farms were permanently enclosed, but internal divisions were made by temporary fences. There are several references to this practice in the seventeenth century, and it is recorded in both north and south in the first half of the eighteenth. By then tenants on many estates were being required to 'separate their arable, pasture and meadow with ditch and quickset'.[2] Although its use had been advocated from the early sixteenth century, the hedge was still a rarity in Ireland in 1700, except for certain districts like the Baronies of Forth and Bargy in County Wexford,[3] and around towns such as Downpatrick in the north, or Dublin.

The absence of enclosure, then, does not mean that the land was held entirely in common fields. In the west for example, there is reason to suppose that compact holdings and dispersed farmsteads were intermixed with common fields and clachans. Under Irish custom the land was held from chiefly families by men of the same sept but of lower social rank, who might be likened to the freeholder in England. Their holdings varied greatly in size: some were small, and Graham suggests that these were probably worked as compact farms; but the larger holdings were often composed of discrete units of varying size which must have been worked by under-tenants, presumably in rundale.[4] At this time cattle dominated the economy, and tillage was of secondary importance, a characteristic reflected in the disposition of the land units known as 'quarters'. In seventeenth-century County Clare and Donegal, these were aligned inland from the coast, to provide tracts of mountain grazing for farmers whose permanent settlements were on the coastal plain.[5] Booleying, often involving the entire family, was the means by which cattle belonging to freeholders and their tenants could be maintained over the summer months. This seasonal movement was different from that practised by *creaghts* in Ulster, where it was said: 'The Irish...doe not dwell together in any orderly forme, but wander with thyr cattle all the sommer in the mountaynes, and all the winter in the woods.'[6] The explanation for this apparent nomadism lies in the land forfeitures of the Ulster Plantation. Dispossessed Irish landowners and some of their followers simply extended the traditional practice of booleying throughout the year,

---

[1] W. H. Crawford, 'The Woodlands of the Manor of Brownlow's-Derry, North Armagh, in the Seventeenth and Eighteenth Centuries', *Ulster Folklife*, x, 1964, p. 62.   [2] *Ibid.*
[3] F. H. A. Aalen, 'Enclosure in Eastern Ireland', *Ir. Geogr.*, v, 1965, p. 32.
[4] Graham, Ph.D. thesis, p. 175.
[5] J. M. Graham, 'Southwest Donegal in the Seventeenth Century', *Ir. Geogr.*, vi, 1970, p. 139.
[6] J. T. Gilbert (ed.), *A Contemporary History of Affairs in Ireland from 1641 to 1652*, Dublin, 1879, i, 341.

until eventually they were forced to resume a more settled life towards the end of the century.

The booleying system described by Graham began to break down in the west following the land forfeitures which brought many dispossessed landowners and their more substantial tenants to Connacht and Clare after 1650. As a result of this immigration, former booleys were gradually settled, and the grazing of common mountain restricted, with herds of sheep and young cattle taking the place of the milch cows of the older system. By the beginning of the nineteenth century commercial grazing had largely replaced booleying except in a few remote areas. More subsistence crops were also needed as population began to rise during the eighteenth century, and this was achieved partly by reclamation of marginal land formerly used for grazing. The proportion of tillage on existing farmland was also increased through the subdivision of compact holdings, held by native freemen who were reduced to tenant status under the new English landlords. Formerly thcsc farms were mainly in pasture, but as subdivision gradually transformed them into joint-holdings,[1] the land was gradually brought into arable cultivation.

As a result of this process it is possible that in the west the proportion of land in rundale actually increased for a time during the eighteenth century, but in the east the trend was towards consolidation and enclosure. Here a more complex field pattern was already in existence by the mid-seventeenth century. In Ulster this had resulted from British immigration, but in Leinster and parts of Munster it was in part a legacy of the Anglo-Norman occupation. Here examples of common fields were to be found in several counties in addition to those worked in rundale. Most were enclosed during the eighteenth century,[2] but at Dalkey, County Dublin, three common fields survived into the nineteenth century.[3] Tenants, who lived in a centrally located village, held strips in each of three fields, and a meadow. Each had a share in the common grazing, and a few held enclosed fields which formed a girdle around the common land, though most of these were retained by the lord of the manor (Fig. 13.5a).

In Ulster, the acreage held in compact farms and enclosed fields increased markedly in the Planted counties. The Articles of Plantation required the colonists to live in villages for their mutual protection,

[1] McCourt, Ph.D. thesis, pp. 40-4, 180; J. Anderson, 'The Decay and Breakup of the Rundale System in the Barony of Tirhugh', *Donegal Annual*, VI, 1964, p. 12.
[2] Aalen, *Ir. Geogr.*, V, 1965, p. 31; F. H. A. Aalen, 'The Origin of Enclosures in Eastern Ireland', in N. Stephens and R. E. Glasscock (eds.), *Irish Geographical Studies*, 1970, pp. 213 and 220.
[3] J. Otway-Ruthven, 'The Organisation of Anglo-Irish Agriculture in the Middle Ages', *Jnl. R. Soc. Antiqu. Ir.*, LXXXI, 1951, pp. 7-8.

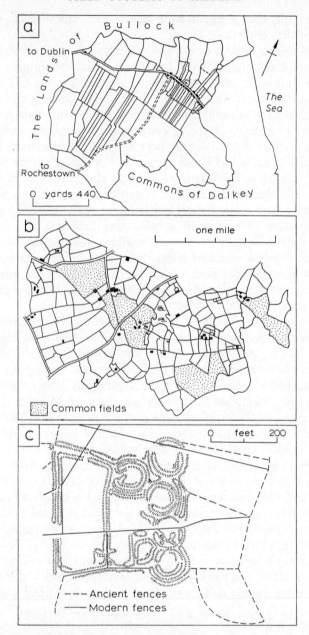

Fig. 13.5 Historic field systems: (a) three-field system – Dalkey, Co. Dublin, *c.* 1830; (b) enclosure from rundale – Bright, Co. Down, 1768; (c) raths and enclosure – Cush, Co. Limerick.

Sources. (a) J. Otway-Ruthven, 'The Organisation of Anglo-Irish Agriculture in the Middle Ages', *Journal of the Royal Society of Antiquaries of Ireland*, LXXXI, 1951, p. 7; (b) B.M., Add. Ms. 15,646; (c) S. P. O'Riordain, 'Excavations at Cush, County Limerick', *Proceedings of the Royal Irish Academy*, XLV, *c.* 1940, pp. 88–181.

but since each tenant held his land under separate title, they preferred to build dwellings on their farms. As the then Lord Deputy complained: 'They lie not in townrids together as they were appointed, but lie scattered up and down upon their proportions.'[1] They also enclosed their farmland, a change lamented in a contemporary Irish poem: '...the mountain (allotted) all in fenced fields...the (open) green... crossed by girdles of twisting fences'.[2] The 1641 rebellion interrupted colonisation for more than a decade, but when immigration resumed, farmers and military pensioners received land in compact grants like their predecessors, contributing substantially to the amount of land enclosed by the end of the seventeenth century. In the Barony of Lecale, County Down, for example, about 30 per cent of the farmland was enclosed by the 1730s, mostly on farms held in severalty by British settlers.[3] Some colonists, however, may have held land in common from the beginning, and certainly during the seventeenth century there are cases of compact farms held by settlers being subdivided into rundale holdings.[4] This may represent a reversion to earlier tradition, or simply the adoption of Irish customs of inheritance, sometimes arising through intermarriage.

In Ulster the immigrants provided an initial stimulus to enclosure, but the main period in which the present pattern of small, regular fields evolved was during the second and third quarter of the eighteenth century. For example, estate documents show that in southeast County Down enclosure was largely completed by individual farmers between 1730 and 1770,[5] and on the Brownlow estate in north County Armagh between 1760 and the end of the century.[6] In Leinster and Munster, detailed studies of enclosure have yet to be undertaken, except in Tipperary where Leister has shown that there were two main periods: during the second half of the seventeenth century, especially after 1695; and between 1760 and the end of the century.[7] These two periods represent major phases in the adaptation of Irish agriculture from subsistence to commercial farming, which affected the eastern lowlands much earlier than the west. The first was related to the expansion of commercial grazing and mainly affected those parts of the eastern lowlands where large farms were developed in medieval times by Anglo-Norman landowners and their freeholders. The second phase came with the resurgence of arable farming in the later eighteenth century.

[1] R. D. Edwards, 'Letter-book of Sir Arthur Chichester, 1612–14', *Analecta Hibernica*, VIII, 1938, p. 74.
[2] C. Maxwell, *Irish History from Contemporary Sources*, 1923, p. 291.
[3] Buchanan, Ph.D. thesis, p. 99.   [4] McCourt, Ph.D. thesis, p. 186.
[5] Buchanan, Ph.D. thesis, chap. 3.
[6] McCourt, Ph.D. thesis, pp. 208–12.
[7] Leister, *Der Agrarlandschaft*, pp. 88–203.

Cattle rearing had long dominated Irish farming, but much of the medieval trade in fat cattle was derived from the manorial farms, native farmers being mainly concerned with milch cows. This trade continued during the early seventeenth century, but after about 1650, it developed as a specialist enterprise, stimulated by market demand and made possible by changes in land-ownership. Initially the prospects seemed bleak, for the Cattle Acts of 1663-6 prohibited the import of fatstock into Britain, and Irish woollen goods were similarly excluded by high tariffs enacted in 1660. Yet the wool trade thrived by developing alternative markets on the continent, until in the last decade of the century, Parliament in Britain forbade Ireland to export wool except to Britain. Meantime the cattle trade had revived, for the Cattle Acts did not apply to dead meat. Consequently a trade in provisions, tallow and hides was developed with the continent and with the American colonies, increasing steadily in volume during the second half of the eighteenth century.

Livestock rearing on the scale demanded by rising exports meant that more land had to be found for commercial grazing, and this was easily accomplished following the mid-century land confiscations. For the new landlords, livestock represented a profitable return on invested capital in times of political unrest; and for much the same reason, substantial Roman Catholic farmers turned increasingly to livestock when their security of tenure was threatened by the Penal Laws. In some districts, it was comparatively easy for the landlords to convert into pasture farmland which had been abandoned after the mid-century rebellion. This happened in Tipperary for example, where there was already a long tradition of sheep farming. In 1686 Lord Clarendon reported that population here was small and little of the land was in arable; some years later, estates confiscated after the Williamite wars were often advertised as good sheep pasture.[1] As demand for livestock increased, some landlords also began to enclose common land which had provided grazing for rundale farmers. Often these attempts were successfully opposed, but eviction was made easier under a tenant law of 1695 which made Irish customary tenure equivalent to tenancy at will, and through the operation of the Penal Laws.[2] Civil disturbances directed against enclosure became more frequent as grazing became more profitable following the remission of tithes on pasture in 1735, leading in Munster to the foundation of the secret society known as the Whiteboys. Parts of Leinster were also affected by clearances, with results which were described by Viscount Taaffe, writing in 1767: 'The sculoag race [i.e. the peasant farmers]...who in my time cultivated the lands everywhere till...some rich grazier took their

[1] *Ibid.*, p. 120.   [2] O'Brien, *Economic History*, p. 218.

lands over their heads...has been broken and dispersed in every quarter and we have nothing in lieu but...the cottagers.'[1] From then on cattle rearing was the dominant enterprise in the large farm areas of Leinster and Munster, and most of the large regular fields of eastern Ireland were formed during this time.

Enclosure for livestock rearing was preceded by consolidation undertaken by landlords and their more substantial tenants; but where it developed in response to tillage it was mainly the work of the small farmer. The background here was one of increasing shortage of home-grown grain for the domestic market as grazing steadily increased in importance. By 1720 English grain was cheaper than the Irish product in the Dublin market, and although disturbed by the trend, the Irish Parliament did not act effectively until 1757 when it provided a subsidy on domestic grain transported to Dublin. In 1784 it passed a further act, subsidising grain exports and placing tariffs on imports, but by then Britain itself was beginning to import grain. Under the stimulus of rising rents, small farmers in the eastern counties found that tillage had become more profitable for them than cattle rearing. For those holding in severalty it was comparatively easy to devote more of the farm to cash crops, mainly barley before 1760, and thereafter wheat. But for the rundale farmer, spring-sown wheat disrupted traditional practices by preventing wintering of stock on the infield. For them enclosure was necessary. In Tipperary, Leister shows that this began on rundale farms in the late 1750s, and accelerated after 1780 wherever common fields had survived enclosure for grazing. But in other areas, for example in County Down and probably in parts of south Leinster, enclosure began earlier. In Lecale for example, barley was the main commercial crop by the early eighteenth century, and by the 1730s it accounted for 40 per cent of the crop area on rundale farms. Continuous cropping was maintained by a liberal use of marl, but the effort to sustain yields was only achieved by encroachment of arable on common pasture. Marling practices apparently stimulated enclosure of infield plots, for this had already progressed a long way when wheat became the principal crop in the late 1760s (Fig. 13.5b). A new rotation was introduced about this time to replace marl, based first on peas and later on clover, giving a final stimulus to enclosure which was virtually completed by the end of the century.[2]

In these ways, Ireland moved from common fields to enclosure in a process which in the east was spread over nearly two centuries, but in the west came later and had to be compressed into little more than fifty years. Throughout the country as a whole, the initiative to

[1] Viscount Taaffe, *Observations on Affairs in Ireland*, Dublin, 1757, p. 12.
[2] Buchanan, Ph.D. thesis, chap. III.

change came from a new class of alien landowners, just as three
centuries earlier the Anglo-Normans also sought to introduce to
Ireland methods of farming then current in England.

E. NORMAN AND NATIVE: THE MEDIEVAL
PERIOD AND THE DARK AGES

The Norman colonisation of Ireland which began in 1171 was never
as complete or as effective as in England. At its maximum extent in
the early fourteenth century, the Norman colony covered some two-
thirds of the country, but within this territory many areas remained
in the hands of native chiefs; and as early as the thirteenth century
complaints were made about the 'degenerate English' who assumed
Irish customs on the more remote estates. Acculturation to Irish ways
became more marked in the second half of the fourteenth century, for
political events in England had repercussions in Ireland, and quarrels
between the barons were quickly exploited by the Irish. By the
fifteenth century, effective military control was virtually confined
to the Leinster Pale, and many Anglo-Norman families in Munster
and Connacht had become little different from their Irish neighbours.
    Wherever the barons acquired land, they established manors and
tried to attract settlers from England, offering favourable leases and
founding new settlements, many of which were given charters.[1] In
addition, large grants of land were made to English ecclesiastical
orders. The success of this policy is reflected in the predominance of
English names among the free tenants in manorial records, whereas
Irish form a majority among the lower social grades. Along with the
burgesses of chartered settlements, the free tenants held in fee and
inheritance, and formed the top of the social hierarchy. On the smaller
manors they were often obliged to perform labour services, and their
holdings might be as little as one or two acres. But grants of between
250 and 500 acres were more normal, and they could extend to several
thousand acres.[2] Next to them in status came the *firmarii*, who were
mostly of Irish origin and rented land for a fixed term often of seven
years. On a typical manor in County Kildare, their holdings varied
from 2 to 100 acres.[3] A much smaller group were the *gavellarii*, whose
tenancy was said to be similar to that of copyholders in England. They

---

[1] Otway-Ruthven, *Jnl. R. Soc. Antiqu. Ir.*, LXXXI, 1951, p. 1.
[2] J. Mills, 'Tenants and Agriculture near Dublin in the fourteenth century', *Jnl.
R. Soc. Antiqu. Ir.*, XXI, 1890–1, pp. 58–9.
[3] J. O'Loan, 'The Manor of Cloncurry, County Kildare', *Jnl.* (Irish) *Dept. Agric.*,
LVIII, 1962, pp. 1–23.

were mainly English, their farms were small and held at will, but apparently they could be inherited though not necessarily in gavelkind as the name suggests. Next came the *betaghs*, invariably Irish but of lower status than the firmarii. There are indications that they were bondsmen to the free classes of native society, and certainly under the Normans their status was enacted to be the same as that of the English villein.[1]

According to Curtis, the Normans made every effort to reduce the firmarii to near-servile status, with the result that there was little distinction between the two groups of Irish tenants by the fourteenth century.[2] The betaghs paid rent for their land and were required to labour on the demesne, although their customary services were not as onerous as in England;[3] apparently they could always escape to the unconquered Irish areas, and they frequently did. Much of the demesne labour seems to have been provided by the *cotagii*, a group of mixed Irish and English origin, whose holdings were usually less than an half an acre, and who were mainly paid for their work. On the Manor of Cloncurry, County Kildare, the tenant composition in 1304 was: forty free tenants, forty-eight firmarii, eleven gavellarii, sixty-five betaghs, forty-two cotagii and an unspecified number of burgesses.[4]

This social stratification influenced the organisation of manorial land and its field systems, but it is difficult to establish the pattern in detail, for most of the available evidence is in the form of charters. Analysis of these by Otway-Ruthven suggests that each social group among the tenants often held land in separate parts of the manor. Land held in burgage and the demesne were nearly always separate entities, but that of the free tenants was usually scattered, sometimes held in large blocks and sometimes in individual parcels of between a quarter acre and an acre in size. For example, a free tenant holding 69 acres at Callane, County Kilkenny, had 52 parcels in seventeen separately named locations.[5] Sometimes the firmarii held individually in compact lots or in parcels intermixed with those of the free tenants, sometimes in a joint-tenancy with other firmarii, and occasionally with betaghs. The betaghs' holding was always a joint-tenancy and usually segregated from other land on the manor. Often they are listed as holding specific townlands, and it is likely that they held and worked land in common as extended family groups. Sometimes the townland is identified with

[1] Mills, *Jnl. R. Soc. Antiqu. Ir.*, XXI, 1890–1, p. 54.
[2] E. Curtis, 'A Rental of the Manor of Lisronagh, 1333', *Proc. R. Ir. Acad.*, XLIII, 1935–7, pp. 63–72.
[3] Otway-Ruthven, *Jnl. R. Soc. Antiqu. Ir.*, LXXXI, 1951, p. 9.
[4] O'Loan, *Jnl. Dept. Agric.*, LVIII, 1962, pp. 3–7.
[5] Otway-Ruthven, *Jnl. R. Soc. Antiqu. Ir.*, LXXXI, 1951, p. 4.

their name, as in the townland of 'Balikenachy' on the Manor of Youghal, County Cork, named after the betaghs O'Kenachi who lived there in 1288.[1]

There is no indication in the documents of the betaghs' method of farming, except that their chief produce seems to have been cattle. It has been suggested that they may have worked their land on an infield system by analogy with the seventeenth-century farmers in Westmeath,[2] and it is possible that those firmarii who held land in a joint-tenancy followed the same practice. But on the rest of the manor, on the demesne and the land both of free tenants and burgesses, it seems clear that a three-course rotation was followed, both in common fields and in compact holdings. On Dublin manors in the fourteenth century, this was winter corn, either wheat or rye, oats and fallow, although there are indications that a two-course rotation may have been followed by the first colonists.[3] Small quantities of barley, peas and beans were also grown, together with cows and sheep, but cattle rearing seems to have been hazardous in border areas due to the Irish propensity for cattle-raiding – there are some references to pasture being unused for this reason.[4] Nevertheless, cattle, hides and wool formed the staple exports to England throughout the medieval period, and the value of manorial produce could be quite substantial: it is estimated that the Priory of Llanthony in Gloucestershire received £80 per annum from its manor in County Meath, to cite one example.[5]

It seems likely that field and settlement patterns in the Norman territories were more varied in medieval times than at any other period, before or since. Besides common fields worked presumably in a three-field system, there may have been infield; and if it was the only system followed by the betaghs it formed a sizeable proportion of land on each manor. The betaghs also contributed diversity to the settlement pattern, for they lived in separate nucleated settlements, probably similar to clachans and designated *baile* in the documents – a word later anglicised as 'bally' and a common element in place-names. These settlements are normally distinguished from manorial villages in contemporary documents. The latter were often located near the landlord's residence to house demesne employees and cottagers, and some were dignified by the grant of a charter which gave tenurial

[1] Mills, *Jnl. R. Soc. Antiqu. Ir.*, XXI, 1890–1, p. 58.
[2] *Ibid.*, p. 57.
[3] Otway-Ruthven, *Jnl. R. Soc. Antiqu. Ir.*, LXXXI, 1951, p. 9.
[4] Mills, *Jnl. R. Soc. Antiqu. Ir.*, XXI, 1890–1, pp. 60–1.
[5] E. St John Brooks, 'Fourteenth century Monastic Estates in Meath', *Jnl. R. Soc. Antiqu. Ir.*, LXXXIII, 1953, p. 147.

privileges to the burgesses. The demesne itself formed the largest compact holding, sometimes surviving into modern times as the home farm of a landlord's country estate. Surviving documents give little clue to the settlement of other social groups. Some of the smaller free tenants who held land in common fields probably lived in the manor villages, but others who had large compact holdings probably lived in dispersed farmsteads, such as the example excavated by Waterman at Lismahon, County Down.[1] The firmarii also probably lived in scattered dwellings, some of them in raths, a settlement form of the first millennium A.D. which continued in occupation during this period.

From the charters of the period, it seems that most of the free tenants and firmarii held their land in scattered and unenclosed parcels in common fields. Some free tenants, however, held in compact farms and enclosed fields, the result perhaps of individual land clearance and reclamation which was taking place as early as the mid-thirteenth century. Fields and 'parks' as they were termed, resulting from consolidation of unenclosed strips in the common fields, do not become numerous until the fifteenth century, although consolidation without enclosure was taking place as early as the thirteenth century.[2] This was mostly undertaken by free tenants, but by the mid-fourteenth century some betaghs were holding large, compact farms.[3] Their status had gradually improved during this century, first with a limitation of customary services and then by their commutation, and by 1500 actual serfdom was rare.[4] Apparently the passage of time had blurred ethnic differences originally formalised in tenurial status, but the *status quo* was also affected by depopulation following the Black Death and the political unrest which increasingly undermined Norman political power during the fourteenth and fifteenth centuries. At present it is impossible to show the way in which these events affected rural life, but the development of enclosure at this time clearly marks the beginning of the breakdown of the Norman common field system, a process which was largely completed during the seventeenth century.

Outside Norman territory, in Ulster, most of Connacht and west Munster, native custom prevailed in a system which may have comprised both common fields and compact farms, held mainly by

[1] D. M. Waterman, 'Excavations at Lismahon', *Medieval Archaeology*, III, 1959, pp. 139–76.
[2] Otway-Ruthven, *Jnl. R. Soc. Antiqu. Ir.*, LXXXI, 1951, p. 2.
[3] R. Caulfield et al., 'The Pipe Roll of Cloyne', *Jnl. Cork Arch. Hist. Soc.*, XIX, 1913, p. 162.
[4] Curtis, *Proc. R. Ir. Acad.*, XLIII, 1935–7, p. 74.

bondsmen and free farmers respectively. There is no direct evidence about the organisation of native farming in medieval times, but it is unlikely to differ greatly from that of the previous millennium. For this earlier period some information is available in literary texts such as the Brehon Laws, and in material derived from archaeological excavation. Both sources indicate that agriculture was based on mixed farming, with the rearing of milch cows the dominant activity.[1] Considerable numbers of livestock were raised, to judge from the sixteenth-century comment on Sorley Boy MacDonnell of Antrim who 'was Lord over 50,000 cows (and now) has but 1,500 to give him milk'.[2] This is a reference to the national pastime of cattle-raiding practised by chiefly families, for whom cattle represented wealth, the medium of exchange and the basis for evaluating land. The same emphasis on livestock is also apparent in the inventory of a typical large farm presented in the eighth-century document *Críth Gablach*. According to J. O'Loan, this farm was about 100 acres in size, with 12–14 acres of arable in oats, rye and flax. The stock included: 'twenty cows, two bulls, six oxen, twenty pigs, twenty sheep, four domestic boars, two sows and a riding horse'.[3]

The system of farming described in the Laws required land for arable and pasture, with access to rough grazing. Ploughing of the arable was begun in March after manuring, and the corn was sown broadcast and harrowed. The Laws also specify four standard types of fence for enclosing cultivated land: the earth-bank and ditch familiar in later centuries and known as the *cas*, the dry stone wall (*cora múr*), post and rail (*dair múr*), and post and wattle (*nochtaile*).[4] Mountain grazing, referred to as 'the unenclosed above all', was used in the familiar pattern of booleying, the movement beginning in May and returning to 'the hay loft belonging to the old winter residence at Allhallow-tide'.[5] If there was sufficient pasture close to the cultivated land, this was used instead, the cattle being herded by boys and herdsmen. At night they were driven into the rath farmsteads or nearby enclosures as a protection against wolves and human predators. A special type of enclosure known as the *tuar* is mentioned, into which the cattle were driven specifically to collect their manure, which was then used for bleaching, but also presumably for fertiliser.[6]

[1] A. T. Lucas, 'Cattle in Ancient and Medieval Irish Society', *O'Connell School Union Record, 1935–7*, Dublin, 1958.
[2] *Calendar of State Papers, Ireland: 1574–85*, p. 532.
[3] J. O'Loan, 'A History of Early Irish Farming', *Jnl. (Irish) Dept. Agric.*, LX, 1963, pp. 165–7.
[4] O'Loan, *Jnl. Dept. Agric.*, LIV, 1959, pp. 6–7.
[5] Graham, Ph.D. thesis, p. 193.
[6] A. T. Lucas, *O'Connell School Record*, p. 6.

Pasture seems to have been held in common, but the form of holding in arable is not clear. Sometimes it may have been common land, but holding in severalty must have been normal too, judging from the references to the fencing of property following subdivision on inheritance, and to the letting of land for short periods, rather like modern conacre.

Archaeological evidence tends to support the view that holding in severalty was common. From 300 B.C. until well into the Norman period, the principal form of settlement was the rath, a circular earthwork comprising one or more banks and ditches: when built of stone it is termed a 'cashel'. Raths rarely occur in groups of more than two, and a solitary structure is by far the most common, forming a pattern of dispersed settlement. Excavation has shown that some were simply cattle enclosures, but the great majority were farmsteads, inhabited by single families whose economy was similar to that described in *Críth Gablach*. As Proudfoot has pointed out,[1] raths are found mainly in lowland areas, suggesting that farmers were engaged in pioneer forest clearance – the presence of red deer among faunal remains on excavated sites indicating an environment partly forested, but with frequent clearings for agriculture. At Cush and Caherguilla-more, both in County Limerick, it has been shown that raths were associated with small rectangular fields, enclosed with the *cas* type of fence, and about an acre in size (Fig. 13.5c).[2] Similar associations have yet to be demonstrated where raths are embedded in the modern field pattern, but it seems likely that enclosed fields were a normal feature of the rath farm economy.

The literary evidence suggests that raths represent the farmsteads of free farmers who held one of the three categories of land mentioned in the Law. This was *sept* land, belonging to an extended family group and held under the local chief in payment of an annual tribute. Their status was similar to that of freeholders, but under the Normans they were treated as tenants, with the title of firmarii. Land belonging to the sept was allocated in smaller proportions to groups known as the *derbfhine*, in theory comprising a four-generation family whose head was recorded as the occupier under the sept. Each nuclear family in the derbfhine had a share of this land, subject to customary inheritance by which a man's share was divided among his sons on death.[3] Derbfhine

---

[1] V. B. Proudfoot, 'The Economy of the Irish Rath', *Mediaeval Archaeology*, v, 1961, p. 113.

[2] S. P. O'Riordain, 'Excavations at Cush, County Limerick', *Proc. R. Ir. Acad.*, XLV, 1940, pp. 83–181; S. P. O'Riordain and J. Hunt, 'Mediaeval Dwellings at Caherguillamore, County Limerick', *Jnl. R. Soc. Antiqu. Ir.*, LXXII, 1942, pp. 37–63.

[3] O'Buachalla, *Jnl. Cork Hist. and Arch. Soc.*, LI, 1946, p. 32.

land could thus be regarded as common land, although there is some evidence to suggest that shares could be enclosed. Individual nuclear families may also have held some land privately, presumably through forest clearance, and Binchy suggests that by the twelfth century they had replaced the joint-family as the basic social unit.[1]

The remaining land categories were *private* land, held in inheritance by the chiefly families and distinct from sept land; and *official* land, set aside for the maintenance of specific offices such as the king, and the professions. These lands and some of the larger holdings belonging to freemen were worked by bondsmen. These comprised both servile tenants, bound to the soil, and tenants-at-will, whose bond status had been acquired either by criminal conviction or through falling into debt. The bondsmen formed the bulk of the population, but they appear as shadowy figures in the Laws which are basically concerned with the rights of freemen, and there is little specific information about their way of life. Circumstantial evidence suggests that like the Norman betaghs, they may have lived in hut clusters and farmed in common fields.[2] For example, settlements comprising several huts grouped near cashels and contemporary with them, are known at such sites as Lissachiggel, County Louth, and Twomile Stone, near Ballyshannon, County Donegal, their disposition suggesting the homes of bondsmen and freemen respectively.[3] The *Annals of Ulster* in 1010 make a specific reference to this type of association, in recording that the *dun* (i.e. rath) of Duneight and its *baile* were burnt. Excavation of this County Down site revealed traces of an undefended settlement outside the rath,[4] quite possibly the baile which was the term used to describe betagh settlements in manorial documents. S. MacAirt considered that baile was a specific type of settlement, common during the first millennium, and he believed the word itself might be of pre-Goidelic origin,[5] perhaps originally referring to settlements of farmers in the Bronze Age. No habitation site of this period has yet been traced in Ireland, but almost certainly they were hut clusters such as are recorded in the Neolithic at Lough Gur, County Limerick.[6]

[1] D. A. Binchy (ed.), 'Críth Gablach', *Mediaeval and Modern Irish Series*, XI, 1941, p. 75.

[2] V. B. Proudfoot, 'Clachans in Ireland', *Gwerin*, II, 1959, pp. 113–15.

[3] O. Davies, 'Excavations at Lissachiggel', *Jnl. Louth Arch. Soc.*, IX, 1939–40, pp. 209–43; O. Davies, 'The Twomiles Stone, A Prehistoric Community in County Donegal', *Jnl. R. Soc. Antiqu. Ir.*, LXXII, 1942, pp. 98–105.

[4] D. M. Waterman, 'Excavations at Duneight, County Down', *Ulster Jnl. Arch.*, XXVI, 1963, pp. 55–78.

[5] S. MacAirt, 'County Armagh: Toponymy and History', *Proc. Ir. Catholic Historians*, 1955, pp. 1–5.

[6] S. P. O'Riordain, 'Lough Gur Excavations: Neolithic and Bronze Ages Houses on Knockadoon', *Proc. R. Ir. Acad.*, LVI, 1954, pp. 297–459.

MacAirt suggested that where *baile* was a common element in place-names, the pre-Celtic population may have remained in occupation of the land, becoming bondsmen to the Celtic immigrants who formed an overlord group, rather like the Anglo-Normans.

Proudfoot has shown that in County Down this could well be the case, for raths, the homes of immigrant freemen, are most densely distributed in wooded areas which were largely unoccupied before the beginning of the first millennium A.D., and are least common in the eastern peninsulas of the Ards and Lecale where there is evidence of a well-established population by this time.[1] Here *baile* is common in place-names, and the population must have lived in settlements other than raths. At national level a similar distribution is apparent, for raths are least common in the uplands and hill margins, and in lowland areas of free-draining light soil which are known to have been occupied during the Neolithic and Bronze Ages.[2] Assuming that the bondsmen were descendants of Bronze Age farmers, it is likely that they practised a system of common field farming, for unlike their Neolithic predecessors, there is reason to believe that the Bronze Age population were mainly sedentary farmers. The advent of the ard plough during this period may have encouraged the change from shifting cultivation, for it can have been of little use except on land already broken for cultivation. Settled farm communities were already established on the hill margins and lowland areas of light soil when the Celtic-speaking peoples arrived in the last centuries of the first millennium B.C. It is possible that they practised an infield type of cultivation, based on animal manure and utilising hill pasture for their sheep and cattle; but they may also have cleared forest for periodic cultivation in the manner of their Neolithic predecessors.[3] Where farmland was already occupied, it seems unlikely that the Celtic immigrants altered the existing system in any radical way; but they were free to develop new methods of farming and land use on the heavy lowland soils where they were the first to undertake forest clearance, using the iron tools and the heavy plough they themselves had introduced.

Unfortunately the evidence available so far permits no firm conclusions about Irish field systems during the first millennium A.D. It is possible that the bondsmen worked in a common field system analogous to the rundale of historic times; but it is difficult to interpret the type of field systems which developed under the derbfhine method of land-holding which was followed by most of the freemen. If they

[1] Proudfoot, *Gwerin*, II, 1959, p. 115.
[2] L. J. Symons (ed.), *Land Use in Northern Ireland*, 1963, pp. 26–7.
[3] E. E. Evans, 'The Peasant and the Past', *Advmt. Sci.*, LXVIII, 1960, p. 4.

cultivated in common as the evidence seems to imply, an outfield system, involving shifting cultivation in long ley, would be more appropriate than infield to rath farmers, living in woodland clearings and practising an economy based on cattle rather than tillage. There is some evidence that this was the case in a literary source cited by Leister[1] and Uhlig has reviewed the parallels to this practice which may be found both in Britain and northwest Germany.[2] There is also clear evidence of enclosure, in small regular fields such as those at Cush, suggesting that individual occupancy of arable land was combined with common pasture for livestock. Most likely the pattern varied, for flexibility was required of a society which combined ownership of land on which farm communities had been established in earlier periods, with pioneer colonisation of extensive forest land. At any rate, it is clear that common fields and enclosure coexisted in Ireland at the time of the Anglo-Norman colonisation in the twelfth century.

F. FIELD SYSTEMS IN IRELAND

The trend towards more intensive use of land in Ireland over the last 2,000 years has been accompanied by a gradual shift from partnership farming in common fields to farms held in severalty and enclosure. It has not been an even progression, but has varied according to the emphasis placed on livestock rearing and arable farming at different periods, and with the type of land-holding introduced by successive immigrant groups. For the formative years of Irish farming, one must turn to the Neolithic colonists who had begun the clearance of upland forests during the third millennium B.C., raising cattle, sheep and pigs, and growing crops of wheat and barley in a system of shifting cultivation. Further immigration during the Bronze Age added little in the way of new crops or animals, except perhaps the horse, but evidence of continued occupation from this time onwards in many areas suggests an improvement in farming methods and food production. The innovations which had the greatest significance for the development of later field systems were introduced by Celtic-speaking peoples during the last few centuries B.C. They had a new technology based on iron implements and a heavy plough, they introduced new crops of which oats was the most important, and

---

[1] I. Leister, 'Zum Problem des Keltischen Einzelhofes in Irland', *Annales de l'Est*, XXI, 1957, p. 376.
[2] H. Uhlig, 'Old Hamlets with Infield and Outfield Systems in Western and Central Europe', *Geogr. Annlr.*, XLIII, 1961, pp. 294–6.

they began forest clearance on the lowland soils. The system of farming and land holding established during this period formed the basis of agriculture for many centuries, unaffected by further colonisation until the coming of the Anglo-Normans, and even then surviving in many areas until the seventeenth century.

Further research on the literary texts and manorial documents of Anglo-Norman times may provide further evidence on the field systems of the first millennium A.D. and help resolve some of the problems relating in particular to farming on common land. There can be little doubt that a common field system analogous to rundale was practised during this period, but it is uncertain whether it included both infield and outfield. Both were integral parts of rundale in the eighteenth century when detailed evidence becomes available, but this may represent modifications of an earlier system caused by increasing population and the opportunities for cultivating poorer land which was afforded by the potato. The infield formed the core of the system in the eighteenth century, and a tradition of continuous cropping of common arable may well date back to the Bronze Age. Assuming that infield cultivation developed at this time, it may have become a normal practice during the first millennium A.D., as rising population restricted land available to the Celtic bondsmen, and later, as cereal cultivation was encouraged by the native monastic foundations.[1] But periodic cultivation of outfield may also have been practised, either in association with infield, or as a separate system. As an extensive use of land, outfield cultivation represents a continuation of Neolithic shifting cultivation, and in some respects was better suited to Irish conditions of soil and climate than continuous cropping in infield. Whatever its early form may be, rundale as it appears in the eighteenth century was well adjusted to the ecological conditions and economic needs of its time, though its failure to cope with fast-rising population had tragic consequences in the Great Famine of the 1840s.

As the indigenous field system, rundale contrasts with the three-field system introduced by the Anglo-Normans. This was established wherever manors were organised, and must have been widely distributed in Leinster and Munster by the end of the thirteenth century. Yet its importance lasted for little more than four hundred years, and consolidation and enclosure seem to have been well advanced by the beginning of the sixteenth century. Only in the vicinity of some manorial villages and on ecclesiastical properties did the three-field system survive into the eighteenth century. The reason for this is that the system was identified primarily with colonists, while native tenants, who formed the majority of the population, continued to

[1] Duignan, *Jnl. R. Soc. Antiqu. Ir.*, LXXIV, 1944, pp. 144–5.

follow their traditional practices, often on land reserved to them on the manor. The three-field system survived as long as it could provide for the subsistence and commercial needs of the Norman free tenants, especially in grain. But the internal market for cereals was limited by the absence of large urban settlements, and the diet of the native population at least, was based on milk, butter and cheese, with limited quantities of oatmeal. Trade possibilities lay in livestock, and the export trade which developed in cattle, hides and wool during the fourteenth and fifteenth centuries must have been largely derived from the manorial free tenants. This trade must have been a major incentive to consolidate and enclose holdings from the common fields.

From the beginning of the sixteenth century, enclosed fields became steadily more common in the Irish landscape, although the major period of enclosure did not come until the second half of the eighteenth century. Yet enclosure in Ireland is as old as farming itself, for the earliest fields belong to Neolithic times, known at such sites as Beaghmore, County Tyrone; and at Ballygroll, County Londonderry, a system of enclosed fields, varying from 3 to 12 acres in size, was covered by advancing peat probably by the middle of the first millennium B.C.[1] Archaeological evidences of small enclosed fields become more numerous from the early centuries A.D., confirming the impression gained from the Brehon Laws that holding in severalty was not uncommon among the rath dwellers, and was probably made necessary by their specialisation in cattle. These early enclosures are difficult to distinguish in the existing field pattern, and many must have been obliterated in the farm consolidations of the eighteenth and nineteenth centuries which spread a uniform pattern of small fields over so much of the country. Today it is the large fields of the Anglo-Norman Pale, and the ladder farms of the peripheral uplands which reveal their origin most clearly, but there are few parts of the country where some trace of earlier field systems cannot be found in the existing landscape. This is especially true of western districts, where prehistoric fields and rundale survivals may yet exist alongside enclosures laid out by twentieth-century surveyors of the Land Commission.

[1] V. B. Proudfoot, 'Ancient Irish Field Systems', *Advmt. Sci.*, LVI, 1958, pp. 369–70. Since this paper was written, pre-bog field systems have been identified at thirty new sites in western Ireland, the most notable being in north Mayo. The fields are mostly regular in shape, averaging three to four acres, though some are as small as half an acre. Some fences are particularly straight and up to a mile long, suggesting to the excavator that they may be boundaries between family holdings. M. Herity, 'Prehistoric Fields in Ireland', *Irish University Review*, 1971, pp. 258–65.

14

Conclusion: Problems and Perspectives

BY ALAN R. H. BAKER AND R. A. BUTLIN

A. PROBLEMS OF GENERALISATION

I. REAL DIFFERENCES IN FIELD SYSTEMS

Studies of field systems in the British Isles and on the continent of Europe have endeavoured to steer a safe course between the Scylla of gross generalisation and the Charybdis of parochial particularisation. Broad syntheses have been both based upon and in turn stimulated local analyses. A handful of generalising studies – those, most notably, of H. L. Gray, R. Dion, M. Bloch, C. S. and C. S. Orwin, P. Flatrès, E. Juillard, G. Duby and J. Thirsk – are paralleled by a host of detailed studies of the field systems of particular localities.[1] As the number of local studies has increased, so to some extent has the difficulty of attempting generalisations and it becomes increasingly clear that no single interpretation will exactly fit all the known facts. As recently as 1966 M. M. Postan wrote: 'It is even more dangerous to generalise about the organisation of medieval agriculture than about its physical and demographic background. The rules and institutions which regulated medieval agriculture and ordered rural society differed in almost every particular from place to place and from generation to generation. So great were the variations that no student of medieval agriculture would nowadays dare to assemble all the medieval agrarian institutions into a portmanteau model capable of accommodating the whole of England during the whole of the Middle Ages.'[2] Countless local studies provide verification for this statement, itself paradoxically a generalisation. But this is not to undermine the truth of M. Bloch's

---

[1] H. L. Gray, *English Field Systems*, Cambridge, Mass., 1915; R. Dion, *Essai sur la Formation des Paysage Rural Français*, Tours, 1934; M. Bloch, *Les Caractères Originaux de l'Histoire Rurale Française*, Oslo, 1931, rep. Paris 1952, Engl. tr. London, 1966; C. S. and C. S. Orwin, *The Open Fields*, 1938; P. Flatrès, *Géographie Rurale de Quatre Contrées Celtiques*, Rennes, 1957; E. Juillard *et al.*, 'Structures agraires et paysages ruraux', *Annales de l'Est*, XVII, 1957; G. Duby, *L'Economie Rurale et la Vie des Campagnes dans l'Occident Médiéval*, Paris, 1962; Engl. tr. London 1968; J. Thirsk, 'The Common Fields', *Past and Present*, XXIX, 1964, pp. 3–25. A selected bibliography on British field systems follows this present chapter.

[2] M. M. Postan, 'Medieval Agrarian Society in its Prime. 7. England', being pp. 548–632 of M. M. Postan (ed.), *The Cambridge Economic History of Europe: I, The Agrarian Life of the Middle Ages*, 2nd edn, 1966. The quotation comes from p. 571.

conviction that there are moments in the development of a subject when a synthesis, however premature it may appear, can contribute more than a host of analytical studies; in other words, there are times when the formulation of problems is more urgent than their solution.[1]

Undoubtedly there were considerable spatial and temporal variations in the field systems of the British Isles. Local, regional and national variations in the complex of factors – physical, socio-economic, cultural and technological – influencing field systems inevitably resulted in contrasts in rural settlement patterns and farming systems. Consequently, difficulties of generalisation about field systems exist at all scales. In addition to these spatial differences were twofold temporal complexities. First, the history of farming systems within the British Isles is by no means one of continuous and uninterrupted progression towards increasing sophistication, commercialisation and specialisation. On the contrary, it is marked by years, decades and even perhaps centuries of retardation and recession, the incidence of which again varied from place to place. Second, the process of the diffusion of agricultural innovations over space and through time meant that, in respect both of individual innovations and of entire farming systems, there existed time-lags in agricultural development from one region to another. The resultant patterns of farming being practised at any one moment in time throughout the British Isles were, not surprisingly, very varied, and the problems of generalising about their organisations and origins are certainly substantial, perhaps intractable.

2. PERCEIVED SIMILARITIES AMONG FIELD SYSTEMS

Some of the differences in field systems within the British Isles might be more apparent than real, while some might be more real than they seem. Reasons for this state of affairs are to be found in the spatial, temporal and topical variations in the quality and quantity of the surviving sources and in the quality and quantity of the analyses made of those sources. The evidence is very uneven from place to place, from period to period and from topic to topic, while the research so far undertaken varies in the same ways. Our models of field systems within the British Isles are, in consequence, far from being equally defined along each of these three axes. For example, if we consider the end of the thirteenth century, there is much information on, and many views about, field systems in Kent and East Anglia, considerably less for Northumberland and Durham and hardly anything for much of Scotland. If we wish to consider the field systems of any one area, then the sources available and the studies undertaken vary considerably

[1] Bloch, *French Rural History*, p. xxiii.

from period to period. For example, for the Midland counties there is much more for the seventeenth and eighteenth centuries than there is for the seventh and eighth centuries, or even for the twelfth and thirteenth centuries. It is hardly surprising but nonetheless a limitation that many views about medieval field systems have been based on evidence from later periods. The classic work of C. S. and C. S. Orwin on the open fields of Laxton (Notts.), for example, was woven around sources which are for the most part seventeenth-century and later in date.

It is also true that sources from different periods have been utilised to very differing degrees. For example, whereas the documents relating to the enclosure of open fields and commons by Parliamentary acts have received considerable attention, the probate inventories of farmers remain a relatively neglected source on regional variations in agricultural systems and changes between about 1550 and 1750. Furthermore, surviving documents provide only limited information. For the medieval period, for example, the informational bias is towards landlord rather than peasant farming, towards ecclesiastical rather than lay estates. Direct information on population totals and trends is for many places and periods harder to obtain than information on, say, prices of livestock or yields of crops. Much of the extant evidence, then, is fragmentary and equivocal. There exists considerable room for several interpretations of the same body or piece of evidence. Views on medieval field systems in particular have changed considerably over the last fifty years or so. Historical interpretation depends upon an assessment of the balance of probabilities indicated by the available evidence. Assessment is likely to change as more and more evidence is sifted and sorted, and as new questions are asked of old sources.[1] Such revaluations are possible in relation to generally accepted ideas about field systems, including notions about the 'Midland' field system, and to particular terms, such as 'open' and 'common' fields.

A central tenet of Gray's work was the plurality and regional variety of English field systems. He offered as one of his principal conclusions a rejection of the then current view, that the two- and three-field system was ubiquitous in England. He argued instead that it was restricted to a large irregular area lying chiefly in the Midlands.[2]

---

[1] E. Barger, 'The Present Position of Studies in English Field Systems', *Engl. Hist. Rev.*, LVIII, 1938, pp. 385–411; H. P. R. Finberg, 'Recent Progress in English Agrarian History', *Geogr. Annlr.*, XLIII, 1961, pp. 75–9; A. R. H. Baker, 'Howard Levi Gray and *English Field Systems*: an Evaluation', *Agric. Hist.*, XXXIX, 1965, pp. 86–91.

[2] Gray, *English Field Systems*, p. 403.

Gray's view was rejected in turn by C. S. Orwin who suggested 'wherever you find evidence of open-field farming and at whatever date, it is sufficient to assume that you have got the three-field system at one stage or another'. Orwin could not see the necessity for supposing the great variety of field systems which Gray described.[1] Since the Orwins' book *The Open Fields* was published, in 1938, there have been two particularly notable developments: first, the regional and temporal diversity of open field systems has again been stressed, an emphasis on differentiation again coming to the fore; second, the so-called 'Midland' field system has been shown to have been much more complex and varied in its operation than was once believed. It has been demonstrated, for example, that the unit of rotation was often not the field but the furlong, so that from the point of view of agrarian practice it was of little moment whether a village was organised on a two- or three-field system. As rotations were based upon furlongs, a three-course rotation was possible in a two-field township; strips of fallow and pasture-ley occurred within fields under arable cultivation; complex rotations developed at an earlier date than was once supposed. Some of the relatively simple generalisations made by some of the pioneers of field system studies have had to be abandoned.

It is nevertheless true that the 'Midland' model has been too readily and too widely used as a basis for the study of the field system of areas outside the Midlands. It is perhaps surprising and certainly paradoxical that only in the last few years have the limitations of our knowledge about field systems in the English Midlands become explicit. In his essay on the West Midlands, Roberts is able to point out in relation at least to south Warwickshire that the impact of seigneurial control, systems of inheritance, technological innovations and the action of the land market on the development of open field systems and the parallel emergence of common field practices are topics which await further research.[2] The ideas recently advanced by Thirsk on the origin of the common fields require us – whether accepting the ideas or not – to re-examine earlier work on field systems and in particular to look again at the evidence for Midland England. Old generalisations about the distribution of common fields need thorough revision, because much that was once accepted as evidence of common fields merely illustrates the presence of intermingled strips: it does not necessarily follow that such strips were part of a common field system.[3]

[1] C. S. Orwin, 'Observations on the Open Fields', *Econ. Hist. Rev.*, VIII, 1938, pp. 125–35 on p. 127.
[2] See above, pp. 221–30.
[3] J. Thirsk, 'The Origin of the Common Fields', *Past and Present*, XXXIII, 1966, pp. 142–7; J. Thirsk, 'Preface to the Third Edition', being pp. v–xv of C. S. and

Changing perceptions of field systems in general are mirrored in the changing interpretations of particular terms and phrases. The terminology of British field systems shows considerable variation both spatially and temporally. Such terms as 'furlong', 'shott', 'flatt' and 'wong' all usually related to a bundle of unenclosed parcels but the terms in predominant usage varied from one part of the country to another.[1] Within a single locality, a particular term might be used in a number of ways: for example, in Devon 'landscore' only became deeply rooted in local terminology after the sixteenth century, being used to denote a boundary of an unenclosed parcel, an unenclosed parcel itself, and open field land in general.[2] Through time, the meaning attached to a particular term could change. The original meaning of the word 'lynchet' was very different from the one it conveys today.[3] The existence of dialect terminologies and the changing meaning of terms through time make their interpretation in contemporary documents doubly difficult. Seemingly inexplicable anomalies and features of agrarian systems recorded in a document might reflect the inability of the compiler correctly to perceive and describe what he saw. Inappropriate terms might have been applied by 'alien' commentators to features they did not fully understand.[4] This could be particularly true of English observers in 'Celtic' areas, especially in Ireland and Scotland. The interpretative problems associated with the term 'runrig' illustrate these general points and they have been discussed in the essay by Whittington.[5] Perhaps the greatest difficulties, however, have been encountered with the more familiar terms 'open field' and 'common field'. There is much to be said in support of Thirsk's view that fields comprised of unenclosed parcels not definitely known to have been cultivated or grazed in common are best described as 'open fields', the term 'common fields' being preserved for fields over which common rules of cultivation and grazing are known to have operated.[6] This distinction between a

C. S. Orwin, *The Open Fields*, 3rd edn, 1967. Dissenting views have been forcefully expressed in J. Z. Titow, 'Medieval England and the Open-Field System', *Past and Present*, xxxii, 1965, pp. 86–102. See also J. Z. Titow, *English Rural Society 1200–1350*, 1969, pp. 19–23.

[1] R. A. Butlin, 'Some Terms Used in Agrarian History: a Glossary', *Agric. Hist. Rev.*, ix, 1961, pp. 98–104.

[2] R. A. Butlin, 'Recent Developments in Studies of the Terminology of Agrarian Landscapes', *Agric. Hist. Rev.*, xvii, 1969, pp. 141–3.

[3] G. Whittington, 'Towards a Terminology for Strip Lynchets', *Agric. Hist. Rev.*, xv, 1967, pp. 103–7.

[4] A. R. H. Baker, 'Some Terminological Problems in Studies of British Field Systems', *Agric. Hist. Rev.*, xvii, 1969, pp. 136–40.

[5] See above, pp. 536–43.

[6] Thirsk, *Past and Present*, xxxiii, 1966, p. 144.

formal and a functional definition is well worth making in order to avoid the fallacy of assuming that from a similarity of agrarian form may be inferred a similarity of function and even of genesis. J. Z. Titow's insistence on regarding the terms 'open field' and 'common field' as synonyms confuses rather than clarifies the problems involved.[1] But it also emphasises the important role of interpretation in attempts to elucidate regional histories of field systems in Britain.

3. THEORETICAL NOTIONS ABOUT FIELD SYSTEMS

Given the complexity of real differences in field systems and the problems involved in the interpretation of the available evidence, it is hardly surprising that conclusions are virtually inseparable from conjectures. Given also the traditionally inductive approach of historical scholarship, it is not surprising to find that there are very few theoretical notions about British field systems. Nonetheless, there have been a number of major attempts at generalisation against which these present studies have to be considered.

Gray, claiming that the two- and three-field system was most widespread and characteristic in central England, distinguished different systems in East Anglia, the Lower Thames Basin, and Kent, as well as the Celtic system. Gray claimed that, in spite of the development over time of regional differences, the unique origin of the Midland system distinguished it from other systems.[2] From the outset of his views in 1915, Gray failed to secure general consent when dealing with origins.[3] Gray offered two sets of explanations for the differing field systems which he described. Primary differences were ascribed to ethnic factors, secondary differences to physical environmental factors. He regarded the common field system as a method of husbandry imported to England from the continent by Anglo-Saxons. But the evolution of the common field system in Germany is now thought to have been a prolonged process. German scholars now argue that the first complete common field system developed during a period of growing population, some time between the tenth and thirteenth centuries.[4] It can therefore no longer be claimed that in the fifth and sixth centuries the Anglo-Saxons brought with them to England

[1] Titow, *Past and Present*, XXXII, 1965, p. 86.
[2] Gray, *English Field Systems*, p. 156.
[3] J. Tait, review note, *Engl. Hist. Rev.*, XXXI, 1916, pp. 626–8.
[4] A. Krenzlin, 'Zur Genese der Gewannflur in Deutschland', *Geogr. Annlr.*, XLIII, 1961, pp. 190–204; A. Krenzlin and L. Reusch, *Die Entstehung der Gewannflur nach Untersuchungen in nördlichen Unterfranken*, Frankfurt, 1961; H. Mortensen and H. Jäger (eds.), 'Kolloquium über Fragen der Flurgenese am 24–6 Oktober, 1961, in Göttingen', *Berichte zur deutschen Landeskunde*, XXIX, 1962.

a ready made and matured two- or three-field system. Ethnic explanations of the origins of the other regional differences in field systems, while developed further by some, such as G. C. Homans and J. E. A. Jolliffe, are no longer particularly convincing:[1] first, because greater emphasis has been placed upon the dynamic aspects of field systems; second, because the role of ethnic influences has come to be set in a wider context of the multivariate factors shaping rural settlement patterns and farming systems.

Among these factors are those relating to the physical environment. Gray was fully aware of the significant influence of physical factors on the development of field systems. He stressed three aspects in particular. First, the influence of extensive wastes upon the development of irregular field arrangements – 'if in any township the waste was extensive in comparison with the open-field arable, utilization of the latter for pasturage might be a matter for little moment, the former sufficing for cattle and sheep. In consequence, deviation from a strict two- or three-field system in the cultivation of the arable and in the rotation of crops became relatively easy'.[2] Second, physical factors were influential in the development of irregular field arrangements in the area within which Gray considered the Midland system to have predominated. River valleys, 'frequently fertile and abounding in meadows', and other localities which, for reasons of situation and soil, were favourable to agricultural improvement Gray expected to develop irregular field systems and to undergo early enclosure.[3] Third, relatively late reclamation of forested areas, peopled less densely than the earlier settled areas and characterised by hamlets rather than large villages, often gave rise according to Gray to irregular field arrangements, notably a multiplicity of usually small open fields and numerous enclosures.[4] On all of these points Gray's ideas have been confirmed and extended.

The views of the Orwins were based as much upon imaginative reconstruction as upon hard evidence but are nonetheless worthy of attention. The Orwins thought themselves into the situation of those first farmers faced with the problem of clearing wood and scrub for cultivation of crops and grazing of livestock. The open field system, they suggested, was a sensible method of insuring against hunger and famine, a product of the practical cooperation of pioneer peasant farmers. Parcels were long because no ploughman wanted to turn

[1] G. C. Homans, 'The Rural Sociology of Medieval England', *Past and Present*, IV, 1953, pp. 32–43; J. E. A. Jolliffe, *Pre-Feudal England: The Jutes*, 1933.
[2] Gray, *English Field Systems*, p. 47.
[3] *Ibid.*, pp. 83 and 88–97.
[4] *Ibid.*, pp. 83–8.

his plough more often than necessary, drawn as it was by a slow and cumbrous team of oxen; each parcel was narrow because the team could plough no more in a day's work; the animals, men and equipment needed to make an effective plough-team were beyond the resources of individual peasants and so families had to cooperate; and having done so in this way, they naturally apportioned the units of ploughed land equally among themselves. A day's work was allotted to each contributor to the team, and so each peasant received a share of the good and bad lands, with his parcels scattered throughout the fields of the village.[1] Perhaps because this is such a plausible and common-sense argument, it remains one which has been passively accepted but not often actively verified. It is also an argument which assumes that all of the elements of the common field system – strip fields, common cultivation and common pasturing – were present at the time of the earliest colonisation.

An alternative model has been formulated by Thirsk who considers that the classic common field system represented an intensive system of farming for corn which was characteristic of all well-populated villages in plain and valley locations. In pastoral areas, arable fields were a subsidiary element in a farming system based on the rearing of livestock. Those fields which were parcelled into strips were some-times subject to common rules of cultivation, sometimes not. Pasture farming, Thirsk believes, was practised over much of highland England and in all forests and fens in the lowlands.[2] The distinction between open field systems and common field systems was spatial but Thirsk further suggests that it was also temporal, with an open field system being, as it were, an immature common field system, the latter developing slowly in response to the changing needs of the community and not reaching maturity in England until about the middle of the thirteenth century. Thirsk places much importance on the study by T. A. M. Bishop which showed that in twelfth-century Yorkshire some consolidated farms newly carved out of the waste became subsequently divided into many parcels and strips of land in succeeding generations and emerged two hundred years later as villages with a common field system. Fields were partitioned among heirs. If this is a typical example of the way in which settlement proceeded in virgin territory, then it is not difficult, in Thirsk's view, to see why the common field system eventually emerged. When the land became divided into hundreds of parcels, and when this process was accom-panied by a rise in total population, acute problems arose of providing

[1] Orwin and Orwin, *The Open Fields*, pp. 1–63.
[2] J. Thirsk, 'The farming regions of England' being pp. 1–112 of J. Thirsk (ed.), *The Agrarian History of England and Wales: IV, 1500–1640*, 1967.

access to the many small pieces of land, of ensuring water for stock, and of enabling stubble to be eaten by livestock without damage to the crops of neighbours. Inescapably they called for some agreement and co-operation.[1]

Our knowledge of the regional variations in field systems in, say, about 1600 has in recent years become much clearer than hitherto, thanks to the syntheses of Thirsk, Kerridge and Emery.[2] But our knowledge of the processes at work in the formation of medieval field systems remains less certain. As Thirsk has stated, 'the debate about the origin of the common-field system turns at present upon whether the common-field system was a gradual growth, co-ordinated and systematized by practical necessity as populations grew and land became more and more subdivided, or whether it was in full working order before our documents begin. If the latter, then its origin cannot be documented, but only guessed at on the basis of practical probability. If the former, then a review of the old evidence and a search for new may yield more support for these speculations.'[3] Crucial to the entire debate are the processes which can be shown to have resulted first in a pattern of intermingled and unenclosed parcels of land and second in a set of regulations which linked these parcels into a field system.

B. PERSPECTIVES ON PROCESSES

I. A SYSTEMS APPROACH TO FIELD SYSTEMS

Studies of field systems have often lacked precision – the terminology employed has been ambiguous, and the relationships investigated have been loosely described rather than carefully analysed. In many instances, of course, the nature of the sources precludes any precise measurement of the processes shaping rural settlement patterns and field systems. Nonetheless, there probably are benefits to be derived from a more explicit endeavour to apply some of the concepts of a systems approach to the study of field systems. If it does no more, such an approach points clearly to the limitations of the simpler conceptualisations of process often employed in historical agrarian studies by making explicit

---

[1] Thirsk, *Past and Present*, XXIX, 1964, pp. 10–25; T. A. M. Bishop, 'Assarting and the Growth of the Open Fields', *Econ. Hist. Rev.*, VI, 1935–6, pp. 13–29.

[2] Thirsk, *Agrarian History of England and Wales*, pp. 1–112; E. Kerridge, *The Agricultural Revolution*, 1967, pp. 41–180; F. V. Emery, 'The Farming Regions of Wales' in Thirsk, *Agrarian History of England and Wales*, pp. 113–60. See also F. V. Emery, 'England c. 1600' and R. E. Glasscock, 'England c. 1334' in H. C. Darby (ed.), *An Historical Geography of England* (forthcoming).

[3] Thirsk, *The Open Fields*, p. xv.

the nature of the change-producing mechanisms which they omit and of the consequences of their omission.

A systems approach to the study of field systems requires a search for answers to questions about the basic properties common to all systems: structure, function, equilibrium and change. It is necessary to ask of each system: what was its structure; how did it function; what degree of stability did it have; how did it evolve through time; how might it be expected to develop in the future?[1] Such an approach, with its emphasis as much upon processes of change as upon the original forms, could overcome some of the limitations of earlier studies of field systems which, in their search for ultimate origins, have been forced to place too much emphasis on the stability and continuity of field systems through time and have tended also to stress monocausal explanations. Morphogenetic studies of field systems, frequently inferring the processes which might have operated principally from a study of settlement and field forms, often ignored the circularity of any such argument. The principle of equifinality, an integral element of systems theory, indicates that very different processes can result in very similar forms. An emphasis in field system studies on settlement and field forms was in part an inevitable consequence of the nature of much of the evidence, which is most abundant and easy to use in relation to the structures of field systems. A growing emphasis on the functional aspects and on the change-producing mechanisms of field systems is certainly encouraging but there are difficulties involved: first, the evidence often allows only a qualitative approach to rather than a quantitative analysis of the processes which operated; second, the principle of indeterminacy – that similar processes can result in different structures – has to be recognised. A systems approach has the merit of stressing the importance of all aspects of a field system – form, function and flexibility over time – rather than any one at the expense of the others. It should finally dispense with any attempt to establish a single explanation for the origin of, say, open fields and indeed with any notion of a single open field system or even common field system. General notions about field systems can be no more than models against which the actual farming arrangements of individual communities may be compared.

The structure of a field system may usefully be conceptualised in hierarchical terms. At the base of the hierarchy was the parcel, the smallest functional unit of land within a township, and above it organisationally lay successively furlongs, fields, and farm holdings. In turn these were integrated into field systems and, more widely,

[1] D. Katz and R. L. Kahn, 'Common Characteristics of Open Systems', being F. E. Emery (ed.), *Systems Thinking*, 1969, pp. 86–104.

land-use systems. In different places at the same time and at different times in the same place the key functional unit – the basis of the rotation – might be the parcel, the furlong, or the field, so that a crucial need in relation to particular field systems is to identify the structure and function of each of these units together with the nature of their connections. This requires specification of the customs, practices, rules and regulations whereby this hierarchy of agrarian units was integrated into an operational system of fields. The structure, function and degree of stability of each of these elements in a field system was dependent upon many factors and it might serve to emphasise the complexity of the problem by itemising briefly some of the main inputs into a field system. No attempt will be made to be comprehensive, because there are already available some useful general surveys of the factors affecting field systems.[1] But rural settlement patterns and farming systems may usefully be seen as adjustments to a complex of physical, social, economic and technological inputs, so that a change in one or more of the inputs may be expected to lead to a readjustment within the system. Particular attention will be paid here to changes in the inputs into a field system.

Within historic time, some aspects of the physical environment within which field systems developed may be regarded as constants rather than variables, for example, altitude and slope of the ground. A catena of land use with altitude and slope was a common enough feature throughout the British Isles at almost every period, although boundaries between particular land uses fluctuated over time, as studies of the varying height of the moorland edge have indicated.[2] In detail, local topographic variations influenced the anatomy of individual fields and rural settlements. But it is probably more realistic to regard most aspects of the physical environment as variables, either changing themselves in actuality, in part because of the impact of colonisation in altering, for example, soils and vegetation, or else changing perceptually as settlers came to alter their evaluations of particular features of their physical environment. Changes in climate of any consequence for agriculture over the last millennium have perhaps too often been discounted but evidence is now accumulating that in certain periods a deterioration in the climate – notably a succession of years with above-average rainfall – could seriously affect harvests and thus the amounts of seed available for sowing. Some at least of the agricultural setbacks observed within the British Isles must be

[1] A. Meynier, *Les Paysages Agraires*, Paris, 1958; B. H. Slicher Van Bath, *The Agrarian History of Western Europe A.D. 500–1850*, 1963, pp. 7–25.
[2] For example, see S. R. Eyre, 'The Upward Limit of Enclosure on the East Moor of North Derbyshire', *Trans. Inst. Br. Geogr.*, XXIII, 1957, pp. 61–74.

attributable in part to such climatic changes and it might be that this is to minimise their importance, particularly in relation to the climatic changes of the later Middle Ages.[1]

Changes in soil fertility and thus in harvest yields have received more attention and it has recently been argued convincingly that declining cereal yields at the end of the thirteenth century reflected the fact that some of the long-cultivated soils were becoming exhausted and that many of the relatively newly-cultivated soils were thin and hungry, the fertility of these marginal soils soon being mined out.[2] The restoration and maintenance of soil fertility was an important goal of farming practice, achieved in a variety of ways: by letting the arable land lie fallow for a period of time; by convertible husbandry; by manuring with free-ranging, tethered, shepherded or folded live-stock; by turf manuring, i.e. putting on the land a layer of humus from uncultivated land, such as moorland and rough pasture, mixed with farmyard manure; and ultimately by the cultivation of nitrogenous crops and by the application of purchased organic and inorganic fertilisers. Many of the structural as well as the functional aspects of field systems are linked to the different ways, both over space and through time, in which this particular farming objective was realised.

In conjunction, the physical inputs of topography, climate, soils and vegetation have exercised two significant broad influences. First, spatial variations in the physical environment were important in influencing the pace of settlement and colonisation. This is the case whatever the scale of analysis adopted, be it the individual township or a region such as the Chilterns or the British Isles as a whole. The 'best' sites and situations were usually the ones to be occupied and exploited by the earliest colonists, the 'worst' sites and situations those occupied and exploited by the latest colonists. Contrasts in field systems detectable in, say, 1300 are thus in part a reflection of the differential colonisation of varied physical environments. Areas of thick forest and watery fen, for example, were usually exploited for many years by communities living outside them, settlement and colonisation within them coming later. The most intensive forms of farming were to be found in the 'lowland' districts, a generalisation which remains valid when applied to such different areas as Kent, the Midlands, and Scotland. Second, spatial variations in the physical

[1] For examples see W. G. Hoskins, 'Harvest Fluctuations and Economic History', *Agric. Hist. Rev.*, XII, 1964, pp. 28–46; H. H. Lamb, 'Britain's Changing Climate', *Geogrl. Jnl.*, CXXXIII, 1967, pp. 444–66; G. Manley, 'Climate in Britain over 1000 Years', *Geogrl. Mag.*, XLIII, 1970–1, pp. 100–7; P. F. Brandon, 'Late-Medieval Weather in Sussex and its Argicultural Significance', *Trans. Inst. Br. Geogr.*, LIV, 1971, pp. 1–17.

[2] Postan, *Cambridge Economic History of Europe*, pp. 556–9.

environment were important in influencing the amount and quality of waste or rough pasture available within particular townships or areas. Where such pasture abounded and was always plentiful there was never any necessity to utilise the arable land for grazing livestock, although it might have been regarded as desirable in the interests of soil fertility. But where pasture was in short supply or where, because of the spread of reclamation for cultivation, it came to be in short supply – as was the case in most areas of mixed farming in the lowland districts of England by the beginning of the thirteenth century – pressures to utilise the arable for pastoral purposes were considerable and the variety of regulations and arrangements for controlled grazing which emerged may be seen in practice as a general response to these pressures.

Over time there is a cumulative recognition of the devices for organising the life of a community and a deliberate extension of the use of these devices. An awareness of changes in social attitudes, customs, laws, practices and regulations thus becomes fundamental to studies of the processes at work in transforming field systems. Methods of land measurement and of land evaluation, for example, have not only varied from place to place but also become increasingly sophisticated through time, so that they find themselves reflected in particular field systems to varying degrees.[1] Regional differences among field systems have often been argued as being a consequence of the contrasting cultures of the particular ethnic groups who laid their imprint most firmly upon the lands they colonised.[2] But perhaps the most important single set of social inputs into field systems was the procedure whereby land in all its forms – parcels and fields, farms and estates – passed from one generation to the next. As A. Meynier has observed, 'le grand facteur de modifications du dessin agraire réside dans l'héritage'.[3] The practice of partible inheritance, whether by law or by custom, would tend towards instability in field systems, while that of impartible inheritance would tend towards stability. The divisive role of inheritance practices will be examined in more detail later but for the moment three limitations to the generalisation just made must be noted. First, inheritance practices varied not only from region to region and from time to time but also from social class to social class, so that their impact on field systems and rural settlement

[1] See, for example, S. Göransson, 'Regular Open-Field Pattern in England and Scandinavian *Solskifte*', *Geogr. Annlr.*, XLIII, 1961, pp. 80–104; H. C. Darby, 'The Agrarian Contribution to Surveying in England', *Geogrl. Jnl.*, LXXXII, 1933, pp. 529–35.

[2] G. C. Homans, 'The Explanation of English Regional Differences', *Past and Present*, XLII, 1969, pp. 18–34.

[3] Meynier, *Paysages Agraires*, p. 85.

patterns is complex and not easy to determine. Second, practices recorded in laws must be seen as statements of objectives and as such they may idealise the process, concealing or distorting some essential practical aspects of the functioning of land devolution in reality. Third, the effects of inheritance practices have to be matched against the consequences of a market in land. Marriage settlements, exchanges of land, leasing, buying and selling of land could accentuate or mitigate the influence of inheritance laws and parctices. It might be worth adding a fourth limitation: surprisingly few detailed studies have yet been made of the role of land inheritance in the history of field systems and many more are necessary.[1]

Closely linked to these social factors were an especially important set of economic inputs. Changes in the pattern of demand for agricultural products were fundamentally important in the modification and even transformation of field systems. Basic to these changes, of course, were fluctuations in population levels. Population pressure is a fundamental condition of agricultural growth, resulting in both the extension of the cultivated area and the more intensive use of the land already being cultivated.[2] The primary need, of course, was to feed people but a secondary need of considerable importance was to feed livestock, the source both of power and of manure. In periods of acute population pressure, more land was brought into cultivation and that already occupied was subdivided into smaller units, i.e. into smaller farms, smaller fields, smaller furlongs and smaller parcels, although not all of these forms of subdivision necessarily happened everywhere simultaneously. But population pressure is clearly to be seen as a divisive and change-producing mechanism. As the demand for cereals grew so did the need to substitute arable for pasture land and hence arose the necessity of making arrangements for using the arable for feeding livestock, whose manure was indispensable to the maintenance of soil fertility. So the growth of more intensive forms of husbandry, the emergence of more explicit rules and regulations about fallowing, cropping and grazing, was closely linked to the growth of demand.

Demand might expand simply at local or regional levels and populations, while growing, might remain principally agricultural. But levels of demand could obviously also increase as populations became more urbanised and industrialised, as they certainly did in England in, say, the twelfth and thirteenth centuries and again in the sixteenth

[1] R. J. Faith, 'Peasant Families and Inheritance Customs in Medieval England', *Agric. Hist. Rev.*, XIV, 1966, pp. 77–95.

[2] E. Boserup, *The Conditions of Agricultural Growth. The Economics of Agrarian Change under Population Pressure*, 1965.

century. The growth of non-agricultural populations seems to have been particularly important in stimulating not only the market-orientation of agriculture in particular areas but also in encouraging their specialisation on a particular range of products. The role of the London market for food, for example, was repeated at lower levels throughout the urban hierarchy. One other aspect of the growth of demand needs to be emphasised. Its impact was uneven from place to place and from time to time, so that population pressure and the growth of demand can most usefully be viewed as change-inducing processes of a general nature. In this light, agricultural changes in, say, Cumberland in the sixteenth century when open and common fields were being actively created, find close parallels in, say, Leicestershire in the thirteenth century.

The spatial time-lags involved in population growth may be incidental or at most only tenuously related, but there were other spatial time-lags which were closely related. The diffusion process taken together with the learning process may be adequate on their own, especially in essentially subsistence economies, to account for spatial contrasts in farming practices.[1] Given the basically constant nature of the physical environment and a finite limit to the cultivable area, the acquisition of knowledge about and the adoption of new farming techniques was essential to the whole process of agricultural improvement, whether that be understood as higher productivity per unit of land or per unit of labour. Differential rates of adoption of agricultural innovations result in spatial contrasts in farming practices. The precise application of concepts of spatial diffusion to changing field systems in the British Isles has as yet made little headway, even in relation to the agricultural changes after, say, 1600 when documentary sources are sufficiently abundant to make such application especially worthwhile. But even a more general use of diffusion concepts may throw light on some of the changes seen in field systems before 1600. On *a priori* grounds, the diffusion of agricultural innovations in Britain before this period would have taken two forms. First, a process of contagious diffusion, with an innovation spreading spatially from one or more centres. Second, a process of hierarchical diffusion, with innovations spreading through chains of land ownership and seigneurial jurisdiction, and perhaps from social class to social class.[2] These two processes could, of course, operate in conjunction as well as independently. The spread of new crops and rotations, the adoption of new

---

[1] D. Harvey, 'Theoretical Concepts and the Analysis of Agricultural Land Use Patterns in Geography', *Ann. Ass. Am. Geogr.*, LVI, 1966, pp. 361–74.
[2] G. Duby, 'The Diffusion of Cultural Patterns in Feudal Society', *Past and Present*, XXXIX, 1968, pp. 3–10.

systems of farming organisation and the acceptance of enclosure are just some of the changes in field systems which may be viewed as part of a diffusion process. Regional concentrations of a distinctive farming practice, such as the 'Norfolk' foldcourse, may perhaps be considered in this way as an innovation spreading contagiously from a few centres, while the similar cropping systems adopted on the widely separated estates of Canterbury Cathedral Priory provide a good example of the spatial impress of a particular organisation, an example of hierarchical diffusion.

While the diffusion of innovations is clearly one important mechanism of change in field systems, this process needs to be set alongside the others. It cannot validly be argued, for example, that the development of the classic common field system was related to the diffusion of the heavy wheeled plough, as was argued by the Orwins and more recently by White. The coming into general use of the heavy wheeled plough in the Frankish heartland in the seventh century resulted, in White's view, in the emergence of triennial rotations in a common field system, because the heavy plough necessitated joint plough-teams which in turn had as a consequence the allocation of ploughed strips according to the size of each peasant's contribution to the plough-team. As far as Britain is concerned, White argued that the heavy plough and its associated field system did not reach this country until the Norse invasions of the ninth century.[1] Hilton and Sawyer have shown in detail the weaknesses of this argument[2] and it will suffice to say here that there is good evidence that the heavy plough was in use in Britain in the first century B.C.[3] It is fallacious to argue that field systems were determined by the existing ploughing technology, although of course this was one of the many inputs into a field system. In detail, the shapes and sizes of the units of cultivated land must have reflected the process of ploughing[4] but, as White has himself also pointed out, 'in plough structure and field arrangement there are many elements, no two of which have any consistent and necessary relationship'.[5]

Given the range of technological, economic, social and physical inputs into field systems, it would be surprising if any single one

[1] L. White, *Medieval Technology and Social Change*, 1962, pp. 39–78.
[2] R. H. Hilton and P. H. Sawyer, 'Technical Determinism: the Stirrup and the Plough', *Past and Present*, XXIV, 1963, pp. 90–100.
[3] F. G. Payne, 'The British Plough: Some Stages in its Development', *Agric. Hist. Rev.*, V, 1957, pp. 74–84.
[4] M. Nightingale, 'Ploughing and Field Shape', *Antiquity*, XXVII, 1953, pp. 20–6; H. C. Bowen, *Ancient Fields*, 1961; A. G. Haudricourt and M. J-B. Delamarre, *L'Homme et la Charrue à travers le Monde*, 3rd edn, Paris, pp. 329–36 and 353–7.
[5] White, *Medieval Technology*, p. 48.

could be selected as having been of greatest importance in changing field systems.[1] But perhaps two further general points may be made. First, fundamental to the process of change was the question of whether the units of cultivation were being divided or fused, whether parcels, fields and farms were being subdivided or consolidated. Each of these two processes tended to operate simultaneously but at some periods division was dominant, at others fusion. Second, and also fundamental to the process of change, was the question of whether the operations of farming were becoming more or less closely controlled by the community as a whole. These specific processes would seem to be especially crucial to the debate about British field systems, and their operation will now be examined more closely.

2. SOME SPECIFIC PROCESSES IN PRINCIPLE AND IN PRACTICE

It has already been demonstrated that fundamental to an understanding of field systems are the specific processes which can be shown to have resulted first in a pattern of intermingled parcels and second in a set of regulations linking these parcels into a field system. Each of these groups of processes will now be considered in turn.

The formation of patterns of parcels in intermingled ownership and occupation results from at least three distinct processes: first, some strips resulted from the communally organised colonisation of wasteland, followed by the allocation of the cleared land among the assarters and the maintenance of the pattern of strips by the need for co-aration; second, some strips resulted from the partitioning of land among sons in accordance with the practice of partible inheritance or as a response to the pressure of population; third, some strips were formed when demesnes were parcelled among lessees, when manorial lords gave up farming themselves.

The practice of co-aration is well-documented and beyond dispute. The livestock required to draw the plough were rare in medieval England, the supplies of fodder being limited and imposing constraints on the number of livestock which could be kept throughout the winter. The bulk of villagers possessed on the average very few oxen and horses and even the wealthiest agricultural holdings had insufficient stabled livestock to meet the needs of tilling the fields. Many peasant families possessed no animals at all: on some manors of the bishop of Winchester in the thirteenth century one-half of the tenants had no working stock at all.[2] Land was ploughed by teams made up from

[1] H. S. A. Fox, 'The Study of Field Systems', *Devon Historian*, IV, 1972, pp. 3–11.
[2] Postan, *Cambridge Economic History of Europe*, p. 555.

oxen in different ownerships. On some manors it was the duty of some tenants to combine their resources to make up a plough-team for tilling the demesne, but it is equally clear that neighbours co-operated in making up plough-teams to till their own lands.[1] Co-aration was a widespread feature of medieval farming in England and, as Whittington points out, was a continuing feature of Scottish agriculture until the eighteenth century.[2] It can, perhaps, be regarded as one of the most basic forms of agrarian cooperation.

But, as Roden indicates, co-aration would have been necessary on land in both enclosed and open fields[3] and it need not necessarily have been peculiarly associated with the latter. It is now almost a century since Seebohm, in his *The English Village Community* (first published in 1883), suggested that co-aration produced strip fields, strips being allotted in rotation, as they were ploughed, to the individual owners of the oxen making up the team. Thus, if a team consisted of eight oxen, each contributed by a different owner, each owner would have one of every eight strips ploughed by the team, a strip being the result of a day's work. Or if one partner contributed two oxen, his share would be two strips, and so on. According to Seebohm, 'this, and this alone, would give the requisite elasticity to the system, so as to allow, if necessary, of the admission of new-comers into the village community, and new virgates into the village fields. So long as the limits of the land were not reached, a fresh tenant would rob no one by adding his oxen to the village plough teams, and receiving in regular turn the strips allotted in the ploughing to his oxen. In the working of the system, the strips of a new holding would be inter-mixed with the others by a perfectly natural process.'[4] This view was elaborated upon by the Orwins[5] and has come to be tacitly accepted by many as an explanation of the origin of strip fields. But it needs to be remembered that, while there is ample evidence of co-aration, there is slender evidence for the actual allocation of strips as a direct consequence of this process. Seebohm regarded as 'very significant' the evidence of the Welsh lawbooks, which he interpreted as specifically stating that the acre strips were to be shared out, in numerical order, to the contributors to the plough-team.[6] But as Jones has emphasised, the rules were frequently, though probably not invariably, applied to strips already in the occupation of the partners to a co-tillage

[1] W. O. Ault, 'Open-Field Husbandry and the Village Community: a Study of Agrarian By-Laws in Medieval England', *Trans. Am. Philosophical Soc.*, LV, part 7, 1965, pp. 31–2.
[2] Above, p. 536.   [3] Above, p. 362.
[4] F. Seebohm, *The English Village Community*, 1883, 3rd edn, 1890, pp. 111–17.
[5] Orwin and Orwin, *The Open Fields*, pp. 5–12 and 40–3.
[6] Seebohm, *English Village Community*, pp. 121–4.

contract. Had the strips been distributed to the partners only after the ploughing, it would not have been necessary to have the rule that a defaulter who sold his ox should nevertheless 'maintain the yoke'. Further confirmation on this point is provided by the rules for settling disputes, whereby one partner wanted distant lands ploughed in return for the ploughing of nearby lands, or to have fresh soil ploughed in return for land already in cultivation. Jones concludes that there is no warrant whatsoever in the laws proper for the assumption made by Seebohm and repeated by the Orwins that the strips were allocated only *after* the ploughing. This assumption, often invoked as a general explanation for the scattering of strips in open fields, was based on the Triads of Dyvnwal Moelmud which were codified only in the eighteenth century and cannot safely be used as evidence of conditions in the tenth century.[1] Furthermore, since the laws refer to 'whoever shall engage in co-tillage with another' and to 'tillage between two co-tillers', it is, as Thirsk has argued, reasonable to interpret them as referring to partnerships among a few cultivators and not to a system of cultivation involving an entire township.[2]

If a connection between the subdivision of arable land into strips as a direct consequence of the process of ploughing remains to be proved beyond reasonable doubt, there is better evidence in support of the other aspect of this long-held view – that some strips were a product of the process of reclamation by communities and groups of people, newly reclaimed land being divided into unenclosed parcels and shared among those who had participated in the effort. In the Chilterns, for example, Vollans and Roden have both noted clear examples of the creation of unenclosed strips during the twelfth and thirteenth centuries by lords allocating freshly cleared lands to their tenants,[3] while Hallam has shown that some fenland reclamation in Lincolnshire between 1230 and 1250 involved partitioning the new land first among the seven Hundreds involved, then among the villages and finally among the individual colonists who came to hold unenclosed parcels of land in severalty.[4] The process of communal reclamation was not confined to the medieval period, for it can be seen operating in the northern counties of England in the sixteenth

---

[1] Above, p. 436.
[2] Thirsk, *Past and Present*, XXIX, 1964, pp. 11–12.
[3] E. C. Vollans, 'The Evolution of Farm Lands in the Central Chilterns in the Twelfth and Thirteenth Centuries', *Trans. Inst. Br. Geogr.*, XXVI, 1959, pp. 197–241, especially p. 233; for Roden, see above, p. 329.
[4] H. E. Hallam, *Settlement and Society. A Study of the Early Agrarian History of South Lincolnshire*, 1965, pp. 31–5.

and seventeenth centuries. In Northumberland, for example, tired furlongs in the common fields were allowed to revert to pasture and waste and new furlongs were brought into cultivation, the strips in these being allocated to tenants who had held land in the abandoned furlongs.[1]

It is, of course, also the case that much assarting resulted not in parcellated but compact holdings. Land was brought into cultivation not only by groups of peasants and divided up among themselves but also by individuals. These would mostly be lords but could also include the more substantial free tenants. Land assarted by them would, at first at any rate, be held as one piece: in individual ownership as far as arable cultivation was concerned (even if subject to common grazing rights after the harvest). But it could later become subdivided as a result of some process of alienation by inheritance, sale, lease or gift, and then become indistinguishable from other furlongs of a common field system. Hilton cites a case at Swannington (Leics.), where an assart, *Godebertes Ryding*, held in severalty by Roger Godeberd in the thirteenth century, was later found subdivided among several tenants and incorporated in the common fields.[2] Roberts draws attention to a piece of assart land in Coleshill (War.) which was granted to Simon March in the mid-thirteenth century and which during the latter half of the century became increasingly subdivided until by 1300 eleven different tenants were holding strips within *Marchesfeld*, which was part of the common arable fields enclosed in the eighteenth century.[3] There are many examples from widely separated parts of the country of assarts bearing the names of individuals but coming in the course of time to contain parcels of a number of tenants. The process itself would seem to have been a fairly general one but its end product was not everywhere the same. In some places subdivided assarts came to be incorporated as furlongs into a common field system, but in other places they did not.

One especially interesting study of assarting and the growth of common field systems was that undertaken by Bishop in the Ouse basin of central and eastern Yorkshire.[4] Although this study was published in 1935, it did not receive at that time the attention it deserved, being most surprisingly not referred to in the text or even listed in the bibliography of the Orwins' *The Open Fields* when this book appeared in 1938. Yet Bishop's study demonstrates the process

[1] See above, pp. 117–20 and 133–4.
[2] R. H. Hilton, 'Medieval Agrarian History', *V.C.H.* (*Leics.*), II, 1954, p. 158.
[3] Above, p. 228.
[4] T. A. M. Bishop, 'Assarting and the Growth of the Open Fields', *Econ. Hist. Rev.*, VI, 1935–6, pp. 13–29.

whereby a pattern of farms held in severalty could be transformed into an open field system. The open field system of the typical Yorkshire vill at the end of the thirteenth century 'has not the appearance of having simply survived from some period when it was created by a large group of settlers; it seems, on the contrary, to be the result of successive accretions of freshly cleared land, and to have expanded with the expanding numbers of the village community'.[1] From the mid-twelfth century assarts were cleared and cultivated by individuals, and tenants occupied farms held in severalty. But in the course of time they provided for their heirs by dividing up their lands and, when necessary and where possible, clearing more land which in turn became subdivided. Assarts bore the names of those individuals who first cleared the land and by the end of the thirteenth century they were divided among several occupiers, often heirs of the original tenant. Sales and grants of parcels of land as well as the division of land among heirs gave considerable fluidity and flexibility to the pattern of land holdings. Farms held in severalty and made up of individually cleared land could, in the course of a few generations, be transformed into an open field system as holdings were partitioned among heirs.

The partitioning of land among heirs might have been a requirement of the customs and laws of inheritance but it might equally have been a response to the need to accommodate increasing numbers of tenants at times of rapidly expanding populations. The creation of assarts in the first instance may be regarded as a form of external colonisation of the waste land, while the subdivision of assarts subsequently may be viewed as a form of internal colonisation of the already cultivated land. With the growth of population, the expansion of settlement and the multiplication of farm holdings could take a number of forms. First, secondary colonisation which would have required the migration of one set of tenants to some outlying part of the estate or to an altogether new place of abode. This would have created a dispersed settlement pattern of compact farms and would only have been possible in an area of relatively low population density where there remained sufficient waste to allow expansion of the cultivated area. Second, fragmentation or morcellation of holdings into minor yet still compact parts. This would have created a dispersed settlement pattern only if a new farmstead were also erected, but it would certainly have led to a lowering of the average size of farm holdings, unless some additional lands were also cleared and incorporated into the existing holdings in order to bring the holdings up to what was regarded as a reasonable size. Third, subdivision or parcellation of

[1] *Ibid.*, p. 19.

a holding into intermixed parcels, tending to equalise advantages and disadvantages in the distribution of land on soils of differing qualities. This would have tended to favour the existing settlement pattern, because of the locational advantages to be derived from a more or less central position in relation to scattered parcels of land. A new farmstead, if built, would have entailed enlarging the existing settlement cluster.[1]

Now, these different solutions to the problem of accommodating a growing population have been variously adopted at particular times and in particular places. But the underlying principle, the role of population pressure in stimulating changes in rural settlement patterns and field systems, is beyond dispute. It would have made little difference in practice whether land was acquired by new generations by legal inheritance or by simple succession, for the impact on the field system would have been much the same. Attempts to determine regional variations in the laws of inheritance do indeed throw light on some aspects of spatial contrasts in field systems but as this particular problem is investigated more closely so the boundary lines between different forms of inheritance become increasingly blurred, both in principle and in practice.[2] The fragmentation of holdings subject to rules of partibility could be prevented by the buying out of younger sons, while in areas of legally impartible succession younger sons could acquire land by a variety of methods, including leasing, buying, marriage and gift. The operation of the land market could both mitigate and accentuate the impact of particular laws of inheritance. How active the market in land was clearly depended to a considerable extent upon the pressure of demand and this was likely to be especially acute in periods when growing populations had few opportunities for making a living outside of farming. Without exception, all of the essays presented here stress the role of the growth of population – in a variety of time periods – as a fundamental mechanism of change in rural settlement and field systems. By no means all of them stress equally the role of partible inheritance.

Indeed, Roden makes the point that there is little evidence of the legal partibility of land holdings in the Chiltern Hills and their environs and argues instead that it was more usually population pressure coupled with the operation of the land market which resulted in the successive divisioning of tenements.[3] Similarly, H. S. A. Fox in a recently completed study of the field systems of Devon and Cornwall was able to put forward considerable evidence for the former existence of strip

[1] P. Vinogradoff, *English Society in the Eleventh Century*, 1908, pp. 273–4.
[2] Homans, *Past and Present*, IV, 1953; Faith, *Agric. Hist. Rev.*, XIV, 1966.
[3] Above, pp. 356–7.

fields but absolutely no evidence for the operation of partible inheritance. Fox argues that the emergence of strip fields in these two counties is to be associated rather with the growth of population and the practice of communal assarting.[1] It would, then, clearly be fallacious to argue that partible inheritance was peculiarly responsible for the growth of strip fields. But one must at the same time accept the fact that there are some well-documented instances of partible succession to land resulting in the subdivision of farm holdings and of individual fields. The Irish cases cited by Buchanan for the seventeenth, eighteenth and nineteenth centuries would seem to mirror cases noted for much earlier periods in parts of England, such as East Anglia and Kent.[2]

Strip fields, then, may perhaps most usually be seen as products of communal assarting and of the subdivision, in response to the growing pressure of population, of assarts and innings originally cleared and held in severalty. But a third process needs to be mentioned briefly, for some strip fields were a consequence of the fragmentation of all or parts of a lord's demesne. In Kent, for example, while demesne fields were being directly cultivated by manorial lords and their agents, they were frequently sown in sections with more than one kind of crop in any given year. And as the fields had often been sown in sections with different crops, so in some places they came to be leased out in parcels to different tenants when the demesne was no longer farmed by the lord.[3] As Thirsk has pointed out, demesne lay open to fragmenting influences like all other land, though these influences were slower in operation on demesnes than elsewhere. Demesnes were at times divided among the heirs of a lord and occasionally a lord granted a piece of land to the church or to a favoured individual. The process of fragmentation was accelerated when the demesne ceased to be farmed by the lord and was divided among tenants, as happened on many manors in the Midlands and elsewhere during the second half of the fourteenth century.[4] The subdivision of a compact demesne could lead to the creation of what were later regarded as common fields, as happened, for example, at Sherington (Bucks.) and Wrotham (Kent).[5] While this process of strip formation must not be ignored, it would seem to be relatively less important in its contribution to the overall picture of strip fields than the other two processes already considered.

[1] H. S. A. Fox, 'A Geographical Study of the Field Systems of Devon and Cornwall', Ph.D. thesis, University of Cambridge, 1971, pp. 65–73.
[2] Above, pp. 593, 597–8, 294–5, 311 and 403–4.
[3] Above, pp. 411–12.   [4] Above, pp. 266–7 and 412.
[5] A. C. Chibnall, Sherington. Fiefs and Fields of a Buckinghamshire Village, 1965, pp. 107–8; A. R. H. Baker, 'Field Systems in the Vale of Holmesdale', Agric. Hist. Rev., XIV, 1966, pp. 1–24.

Having discussed the ways in which patterns of open fields could be created, it now becomes necessary to examine the ways in which the myriad strips were welded into a functioning system. Clearly the subdivision of arable land into unenclosed parcels in intermingled ownership and occupation posed problems relating to their cultivation. Where the degree of subdivision was small and few farmers were involved, private agreements about how their lands were to be cropped and pastured would have been adequate. Moreover, they would often have been verbal agreements rarely entering into the written record. But where – and when – the degree of subdivision was great and many farmers were involved, more formal agreements would have been required and these might well have been written down. It therefore becomes very instructive to search the surviving historical record for evidence of the rules and procedures which provided the framework for farming operations.[1] In this search, it is crucial to attempt to determine for different times and places the character of the agrarian organisation (the single family, a group of neighbouring families, the farming community of an entire township) and the basis of its decision-making. It is also important to try to discover the nature of the basic land unit (parcel, furlong, field) and the way in which it was articulated by the agrarian organisation into a system of husbandry. Furthermore, fundamental to any consideration of the evolution of field systems is an assessment of the extent to which field patterns and farming practices were from time to time deliberately and consciously reorganised more or less as a whole, as opposed to their constantly being modified in detail to meet changing circumstances.

A number of the essays in this present book make it clear that on occasions it is misleading to refer to the farming practices of particular places as 'field systems' because furlongs rather than fields were the bases of crop rotations. Groups of furlongs were bundled together to make up the acreage prescribed for sowing in different courses of a rotation in any given year. Medieval cropping practices in many areas of England, for example, seem to have been remarkably flexible, with more intensive rotations being adopted during the thirteenth and early fourteenth centuries in response to the rising pressure of population on the land. Given the existence of bundles of unenclosed strips, some common routine would have been followed in their husbandry out of practical necessity. There could not, for example, have been much variation possible in the time of sowing the strips in a furlong. Winter wheat, where sown, and rye were the chief

[1] W. O. Ault, 'Open-field Husbandry and the Village Community: a Study of Agrarian By-laws in Medieval England', *Trans. Am. Phil. Soc.*, LV, part 7, 1965.

bread crops and the seed had to be broadcast in the ploughed field and harrowed in when conditions were favourable, between Michaelmas and Christmas. In the spring there took place the sowing of oats, barley, peas, beans and vetches. These crops, largely fed to the live-stock, would ripen about the same time as the autumn-sown wheat and rye, so that all the furlongs of the open fields could be cleared for pasturing purposes at about the same time. But with the furlong as the basic unit of rotation, the amounts of land devoted to particular crops could vary from year to year, and the grouping of particular furlongs into winter-sown, spring-sown and fallow areas was similarly flexible. In many instances, the distinction between furlong and field was extremely blurred and, in the documents, the two terms are frequently used interchangeably. It thus becomes more important to discover whether in any particular township a two- or three-course rotation was practised than whether its lands lay in two or three or any other number of fields. This was the case, for example, in medieval East Anglia. There was a close correlation between a 'field' and a course or season in a rotation in western and central Cambridge-shire and even where the number of fields exceeded the number of cropping shifts or seasons a relatively simple field system was achieved by the combination of two or more 'fields' for cropping purposes. Elsewhere in East Anglia, however, 'fields' were very numerous and of varying sizes within individual townships, so that a pattern of shifts had to be superimposed on to them in order to ensure what was considered to be an appropriate ratio of sown to fallow land.[1] Considerable flexibility is also to be seen in cropping arrangements practised in the Chilterns where, in an individual township, the many common fields were loosely organised into three divisions, the fields of each group being subject to the same cultivation sequence and lying fallow every third year. In effect, Roden argues, these combi-nations were the Chiltern equivalent of the large units of the typical two- and three-field Midland township, the role of the 'fields' of the Chilterns being closer to that of the furlongs of the Midlands. But whereas the individual seasons of the Midlands were usually simple geographical units – i.e. fields – each Chiltern season comprised a number of fields lying throughout the common arable, not necessarily adjacent to each other.[2] Within the Midlands during the Middle Ages, the large areas designated as 'fields' might individually be groups of contiguous 'furlongs' and in some cases be identical with the courses of a rotation, but there is similarly evidence here that cropping systems were very flexible and based upon furlongs. It is not until the sixteenth century and later that the most clear-cut examples become available

[1] Above, pp. 296–305. [2] Above, pp. 337 and 344–5.

of whole communities utilising entire fields as the basic units in the
rotation and even then there were deviations, most often prompted
by the need to increase the amount of forage available and involving
the use of some furlongs as pasture–leys within the arable. But for the
medieval period one thing at least is certain: as Postan has emphasised,
the variations in field systems considered in detail were far more
numerous than the conventional distribution of two- and three-field
systems would indicate. Some villages had different sequences of crops
on different parts of the village arable; some had a three-course
rotation on some lands, a two-course rotation or no recognisable
rotation at all on others; some varied the size and composition of
their spring-sown and winter-sown areas from year to year; some
dovetailed arable with pasture and one system of rotation with another
to suit the lay of the land and its physical properties, the vagaries of
seasons, the changing qualities of old land and the progress of
reclamation.[1]

But whatever the local variant, some form of communally agreed
rotations would have been practised on almost all arable land which
comprised holdings composed of strips too numerous, too small and
too dispersed to be cultivated and pastured separately. Open fields
must almost always have been cultivated in common even if they
were not pastured in common. There would seem to be little doubt
that regulated cropping on the basis of two- or three-course rotations
was practised in strip fields in England from at least the twelfth
century onwards.[2] Whether or not strip fields were also pastured in
common from this early period remains somewhat equivocal.

The practice of pasturing in common the stubble of the arable fields
after harvest and during the fallow season would have had a twofold
purpose, for in addition to providing forage at times when and in
places where pasturage was in short supply it would also have manured
the land and contributed considerably to the maintenance of soil
fertility. The tethering, folding or shepherding of livestock on the
arable lands was an essential element of good husbandry and the
variety of arrangements made testify to its generally recognised
importance. What is still questionable, however, is Thirsk's thesis that
rights of grazing over arable land were still being shared by neighbours
in the twelfth century, but that before the middle of the thirteenth
century there were villages in which all tenants shared common rights
in all fields. Thirsk believed the earliest unmistakable statement about
commoning by a whole village to date from 1240 although she of

---

[1] Postan, *Cambridge Economic History of Europe*, p. 573.
[2] Thirsk, *Past and Present*, XXIX, 1964, pp. 19–20; Titow, *Past and Present*, XXXII,
1965, pp. 96–8.

course admitted that further search might well produce evidence from the twelfth century. For this reason, together with the fact that the earliest case of regulated cropping by a whole village is dated 1156-7, Thirsk argued that the twelfth and first half of the thirteenth century were possibly the crucial ones in the development of the first common field systems.[1] Within this present book, Roden cites the 1240 Bedford-shire case of common grazing referred to by Thirsk but also an earlier one, of 1226, relating to a Buckinghamshire village in which there was 'common of pasture in the field of Westleg...in every year in which the field lies fallow or uncultivated', and Thirsk herself also draws attention to examples of vills in Lincolnshire sharing common rights of pasture over each other's fields in c. 1162, and communal organisation for grazing is referred to in a Welsh text of the early thirteenth century.[2] But only a few additional early instances of common pasturing of fields by whole villages have thus come to light so far.

On the other hand, it is becoming increasingly clear that common pasturing – like common cultivation – might well have been practised by owners and occupiers of neighbouring strips in furlongs and subdivided closes, and that this practice might well have preceded the organisation of common grazing practices over wider areas and involving larger numbers of farmers. Subdivided closes in the Chiltern Hills, for example, were sometimes pastured in common by the live-stock of co-tenants, while by 1300 stints rationing the number of animals allowed on the common arable fields had been introduced in the northeast of the Hills, no doubt reflecting a growing shortage of fodder.[3] There is evidence from Yorkshire that grazing rights in assarts were sometimes limited to those who cultivated them, although in other cases more widely based common grazing of the fallows and stubble seems to have been the practice.[4] It is certainly not difficult to imagine, with the amalgamation of furlongs into a coordinated field system, the merging not only of cropping but also of grazing practices on the larger group of furlongs. Fortunately this process does not have to be left entirely to the imagination. A sequence of bylaws at Newton Longville (Bucks.), as Ault has observed, portrays a community struggling with this problem. In 1290 it was provided that no one could pasture his beasts in any furlong until the grain of one selion adjacent, at least, had been completely harvested. This bylaw was re-enacted from time to time. In 1329 it was repeated, adding the words 'one selion on both sides'. In 1331 it was stated that 'no one shall cause his beasts to pasture next to rye, mixed corn

---

[1] Thirsk, *Past and Present*, XXIX, 1964, pp. 16–18 and 23.
[2] Above, pp. 349, 243 and 437.   [3] Above, pp. 334-5.   [4] Above, p. 172.

or oats before a space of two selions wide has been cleared of grain'. In 1387 it was declared that a space of 10 selions must be cleared unless the beasts were tethered. In 1388 the space cleared had to be 14 selions in the case of the larger livestock and 20 selions in width in the case of sheep or hogs. In 1406 'no one this autumn shall pasture beats, sheep or pigs on his own grain by a space of 10 selions'. Finally, in 1608, '...the beasts shall not be kept uppon any furlong of stubble ...untill all the corne of the same furlong be all carried from the same furlong'.[1] The practice of tenants pasturing their own strips in the common fields before the end of harvest is perhaps itself an indication that common cropping became a necessity before common grazing. Eventually this practice gave way to a more rigid control of common grazing, in which no livestock were allowed to pasture on the stubble until the harvest of the entire community had been brought in. Very clear and rigid rules of this sort, controlling communal cropping and grazing practices, are seen in quantity in the sixteenth and seventeenth centuries in, for example, Northumberland, Yorkshire and the East Midlands, when the numbers of population and the pressure upon scarce grazing resources both increased. Where, by contrast, there remained plenty of good grass available, as in the fenland villages of Lincolnshire, such common grazing practices did not emerge. Clearly the timing of the sort of developments discussed here varied from place to place depending upon local circumstances but the process of an increasingly sophisticated control by expanding communities of their cultivation and pasturing practices may be seen to be a general one with a relative rather than an absolute chronology.

This kind of argument requires consideration of the evidence relating to the ability of these primitive agricultural communities to plan their activities and to reorganise their farming structures and operations. Many modifications to field systems would have been of a piecemeal and evolutionary nature, as attempts were made to increase the efficiency of a particular system. But some alterations to field systems might well have been of a general and revolutionary nature, as attempts were made by village communities to rationalise their farming arrangements, as it were 'at the stroke of a pen'. Both sets of solutions to the basic problem of improving the efficiency of agriculture are to be expected. Thus Thirsk has envisaged the casual development of a field system which arrived at its most systematic form at varying dates in different villages between about the thirteenth and eighteenth centuries. She did not consider that the emergence of the common field system necessarily involved a major reallocation of holdings, although she

[1] Ault, *Trans. Am. Phil. Soc.*, LV, part 7, pp. 21–2.

did not exclude the possibility that this happened in some cases.[1] Titow, on the other hand, has argued that if it is accepted that the common field system only emerged during the twelfth and thirteenth centuries, then it becomes necessary to discover wholesale and general reallocations of land over this crucial period to explain the regular distribution of the parcels of an individual, an arrangement too orderly to have arisen by some haphazard process of natural selection. Titow considered there to be no evidence of widespread and all-embracing reshaping of holdings, arguing instead that the more or less equal distribution of the parcels of a holding throughout the strip fields of a village was a very early feature.[2] Each of these two aspects of the problem – the evidence for the remodelling of field systems and the evidence concerning the distribution of an individual's strips within a township – merits closer attention.

There is, of course, abundant evidence from the sixteenth century and later of the more or less complete reorganisation of field and even rural settlement patterns within townships. Surviving maps of common field systems illustrate field arrangements which, with their symmetrical division into two or three equal fields comprising the entire village arable and with strips regularly distributed among the common fields, are – as Postan has emphasised – 'perhaps too orderly to have spontaneously grown up in the course of centuries. They bear every sign of a relatively late tidying-up process by landlords or village communities.'[3] In Northumberland, for example, there existed some extremely 'tidy' common field systems at the end of the sixteenth century and maps and surveys of the period make it clear that schemes to rationalise field systems were being put into practice, involving the divisioning of the arable land of townships into three or more fields and the reallocation of holdings more or less equally among them.[4] Some townships in Yorkshire experienced a rearrangement of holdings during the seventeenth and eighteenth centuries known as 'flatting'. An exchange of lands gave each tenant fewer but larger parcels than in the traditional layout.[5] Much of the remodelling of field systems in the sixteenth and later centuries involved, of course, the reorganisation of holdings as a prelude to enclosure. All of this is well documented and beyond dispute.[6] But what remains debatable is the extent to which such *remembrement* operations were significant

[1] Thirsk, *Past and Present*, XXIX, 1964, p. 22; XXXIII, 1966, p. 146.
[2] Titow, *Past and Present*, XXXII, 1965, pp. 90–4.
[3] Postan, *Cambridge Economic History of Europe*, p. 572.
[4] Above, pp. 111–24.   [5] Above, p. 155.
[6] The literature on enclosure is vast but a useful survey is J. D. Chambers and G. E. Mingay, *The Agricultural Revolution 1750–1880*, 1966, pp. 77–105.

in the development of field systems during the Middle Ages. There were, of course, many minor changes in farming practices during this period which involved a readjustment of field systems, such as the expanding cultivation of fodder crops, the growing practice of cultivating parcels of land lying within the fallow season and the development of leys within the arable fields. There is also evidence that the substitution of a two-course rotation by a three-course or even more complex rotation involved the redrawing of 'field' boundaries in many townships during the Middle Ages and later.[1] Such rotational changes could involve a number of alterations to the field system. In Great Corringham (Lincs.) in 1200 the holdings of tenants were divided between two halves of the village: some strips lay in the West Field and some in the East Field. Some time between 1200 and 1600 the fields were redivided into four. Later documents suggest that this was done by dividing each field (not necessarily equally) into two. In 1601 a new agreement was reached to reduce the four fields of Corringham to three, achieved by leaving East and West Fields as before but counting the third and fourth fields as one field, even though they were physically separated from each other by East (now called Middle) Field. By 1758 yet another arrangement was in operation: part of the third field was now united with West Field, its nearest neighbour, while the rest of the third field survived separately.[2]

This example serves to emphasise the flexibility of field systems through time and should lead us to expect, rather than to be surprised by, evidence of the remodelling of field systems even in the early Middle Ages. In particular, it is reasonable to hypothesise that such reorganisations would have been responses by expanding village communities to their growing needs. There does exist, even for the early Middle Ages, some evidence of the remodelling of field systems. Postgate argues that in southeast Cambridgeshire the superimposition of shifts on to a haphazard pattern of irregular field plots was the most important step in the development of a mature open field system there in the thirteenth century.[3] Roden emphasises the disruption of traditional cropping systems by the change from two- to three-field arrangements that took place along the scarp-foot loams and in the clay vales to the northwest of the Chilterns: a significant number of townships had become organised on a three-field basis by about 1250. At South Stoke (Oxon.), for example, the switch from a double to a triple divi-

---

[1] Above, p. 297.
[2] I. Beckwith, 'The Remodelling of a Common Field System', *Agric. Hist. Rev.*, xv, 1967, pp. 108–12.
[3] Above, p. 324.

sion of the common arable was probably in progress in 1240, while details of the reorganisation at Mursley and Dinton (Bucks.) survive in an agreement of 1345.[1] The old field system at Laughton (Sussex) seems to have come under considerable pressure from an expanding population during the thirteenth century and to have been largely abolished in the late thirteenth century by a redistribution and rearrangement of holdings.[2] By the later twelfth century some holdings in Lincolnshire had land that was more or less evenly divided between two halves of the village, which Thirsk interprets as implying that a substantial group of tenants in these villages had agreed upon a field course and had divided their arable accordingly. Similarly, common grazing of the stubble – a commonsense solution to the problem of controlling animals which were grazing narrow strips of land – was being practised, in some cases by neighbours, in others by the whole community, from the late twelfth century. The systematisation of field arrangements here was closely linked with the rise of population.[3] The impact of planning and control in the early development of some rural settlements and field systems is emphasised by Sheppard in relation to Yorkshire. Very regular village, furlong and strip layout are interpreted as the result of a planned reorganisation of a revolutionary rather than evolutionary nature, a change which most probably took place between the late eleventh and the mid-twelfth century in many townships, possibly not until the late twelfth or early thirteenth century in others.[4] On the other hand, it has to be noted that, in his survey of the West Midlands, Roberts concludes that while the possibility of some degree of regularisation of field systems in the early Middle Ages must not be excluded, there were no major agricultural developments in the area between 1086 and 1279.[5]

It would, nonetheless, seem both theoretically possible and – in some instances – practically proven that field systems have been remodelled at varying dates in different villages between the eleventh and eighteenth centuries. Field systems can be seen to have evolved slowly, with the land market being operated by farmers in order to overcome the disadvantages of having parcels distributed unevenly throughout a township's arable lands. But field systems can also be seen to have been changed rapidly, with planned regularisation of farmsteads, farm holdings and fields. In this latter context, the distribution of the parcels of an individual's holding within a township becomes particularly significant.

The problem here is to decide whether the more or less equal

[1] Above, p. 350.
[2] Above, p. 424.
[3] Above, pp. 279–80.
[4] Above, pp. 183–6.
[5] Above, p. 224.

distribution of strips of a holding among the fields was a characteristic of the original settlement or whether it was more usually a later feature consequent upon the reorganisation of holdings. Titow, for example, has argued that we should envisage an original settlement which created the nucleus of the regular elements – the standard holdings, the strips, the even distribution among the rotational fields – and which was expanded in a rational way by succeeding generations of villagers. The original settlement and holdings must, he argues, have been added to in an organised and coordinated fashion to account for the strong pattern of regularity so clearly present in the earliest relevant documents.[1] This view – that holdings originated as bundles of scattered selions allotted to peasants by some orderly system of allocation – is based on documents of the thirteenth and fourteenth centuries which show scattered selions with the same neighbours in many cases. On the other hand, Thirsk has argued that in the light of our knowledge about the operation of the land market it is impossible to believe that such order can have survived from several centuries before.[2] And Seebohm suggested long ago that the fact that around some villages the strips of one holding were adjacent to the same neighbours throughout the furlongs might have reflected a recent rearrangement of land holdings.[3] Given the demonstrable flexibility of field systems after 1300, it becomes on *a priori* grounds alone somewhat dubious to postulate their inflexibility before 1300 and since the time of the original settlement.

But not all parcel patterns which portray regularity in the distribution of parcels among holders necessarily emerged as products of a reorganisation of land holdings. Some might well have been a consequence of the partitioning of one holding among heirs or other claimants which involved the division of every parcel. An example of this is provided by the history of the holding of Richard Priest's-son in Chippenham (Cambs.) during the thirteenth century. Richard had inherited his tenement from his father, also Richard Priest's-son, who had divided his land between his son and daughter Beatrice, wife of Ralph le Porter. All three relations made grants to a Hospital and in one case Beatrice granted 3 roods, lying end to end, next to 3 roods granted by her brother, also lying end to end. It seems quite clear that division of the father's holding had been accomplished by the physical division of strips longitudinally, which explains their small size. In the circumstances, as Spufford points out, it is highly suggestive that nearly half of the strips granted by Richard Priest's-son lay next to

---

[1] Titow, *Past and Present*, XXXII, 1965, p. 94.
[2] Thirsk, *Past and Present*, XXIX, 1964, p. 21.
[3] Seebohm, *English Village Community*, pp. 24–6.

those of his brother-in-law, Ralph le Porter. Spufford concludes: 'This concrete example of the workings of inheritance means that caution must be employed in interpreting the fact that in many of the cases in which one man granted land away, a significant proportion of his strips had the same neighbour on one side. At first sight, this looks like a much battered survival from the original allotment of strips; in fact it may not be the product of co-aration, but of the division of holdings between heirs.'[1] Only a good deal of further research will enable us to determine the relative importance of this particular process in contributing towards a regularity of parcel distribution among holders.

An orderly arrangement of parcels might, then, be a product of at least three processes: communal assarting, with parcels being allocated in some prescribed order among the assarters; partitioning of holdings; and the remodelling of holdings, an act of *remembrement*. Which of these processes was the most significant requires an assessment of probabilities, and this in turn requires an examination of the evidence for orderly arrangements of parcels. The annual reapportionment of meadows by lot was customary in many English villages and the reallotment of arable parcels occasionally (though not necessarily annually) would not have involved entirely alien notions about the utilisation of land. There is good evidence that, in some parts of the British Isles, a more or less regular distribution of the parcels of an individual holder throughout the fields of a township was, in the seventeenth and eighteenth centuries, a consequence of reorganisation and reapportionment. This seems to have been especially the case in some parts of northern England and of Scotland. In many Northumberland townships in the sixteenth and seventeenth centuries, for example, holdings were distributed throughout the fields in proportions which reflected the sizes of the fields and the reallotment of arable land was a frequent feature.[2] In Scotland considerable emphasis was placed in the eighteenth-century land division proceedings on the equality of portions within individual sectors, an equality of both quality and quantity which necessitated a pattern of strips in intermixed ownership. In some instances in Scotland the land was reallocated annually, in others the allocation was on a three-yearly basis. In some areas prior to the eighteenth century the division of the land into shares did not take place until harvest time so that no man knew which was to be his share of the land and its produce until the work of cultivation

---

[1] M. Spufford, 'A Cambridgeshire Community. Chippenham from Settlement to Enclosure', *Occasional Papers, Dept. of Engl. Local Hist., Univ. of Leics.*, xx, 1965, p. 22.

[2] Above, pp. 111–24.

was done. Whittington considers that most likely this was the fundamental share system from which the pre-cultivation share-out of the land developed.[1] In parts of Ireland in the nineteenth century reallotment of parcels at one, two or three yearly intervals was practised, a procedure which meant that some increase in population could be accommodated without causing undue hardship to any individual, since additional shares were created through periodic lottery.[2]

There is, then, evidence in some areas in the early modern period of regular arrangements of parcels resulting from processes of land redistribution. It is certainly possible to argue that an analogous process could account for similar parcel arrangements observed in parts of England during the early Middle Ages. In the northern and eastern districts of Yorkshire, for example, a regular disposition of parcels throughout the fields was even more common in medieval times than in the seventeenth and eighteenth centuries. Here the repetitive layout of parcels was in detail related to the process of sun-division, but this seems to have been a specific solution to the need to reallocate parcels rather than the underlying reason for it. It seems to have been a method rather than a philosophy of land divisioning. Sheppard postulates that furlongs termed 'Wandales' saw agreed shares measured out, which then formed the model for the subdivision of other furlongs. Reallocation could then have been achieved simply by measuring out 'Wandales' anew. The principle of sun-division could thus, as Sheppard argues, have been an inherent part of the new layout, even though the precise distribution of holdings that appears in the thirteenth-century records may not have been established until the twelfth century.[3] There is some evidence cited within the chapters on the West and East Midlands for a more regular distribution of the parcels of an individual holding by about 1300 than had previously been the case, although even this regularity was being disrupted by the operation of the land market.[4] A somewhat similar situation is to be seen in western and central Cambridgeshire and in the area to the north of the Chiltern Hills at about the same time.[5] The regularity of field arrangements observable in many townships of England in the thirteenth century would seem to be explicable in terms of their remodelling relatively recently.

If this is so, then the converse of this explanation – the absence of any remodelling – might explain the situation in those townships in which the parcels of an individual holding were concentrated within one part of the township rather than scattered throughout it.

[1] Above, p. 540.
[2] Above, pp. 592-3.
[3] Above, p. 184.
[4] Above, pp. 223, 258-60, 267-73 and 279.
[5] Above, pp. 294-5, 312, 348 and 350.

Thus in much of East Anglia, the Chilterns and southeast England the land holdings of individuals in about 1300 tended to be located preferentially within one part of a township rather than being equally distributed throughout all of a township's fields and furlongs. The expansion of cultivation in these areas seems to have been undertaken from a large number of relatively small clustered settlements and from isolated farmsteads, so that the individual tenements were concentrated around these in one part of a township rather than being held from a central village and dispersed throughout its entire lands. The pattern of multiple fields and furlongs, of unevenly distributed holdings, had not in these cases been reorganised on a village basis into a system of common fields. Why some townships underwent reorganisation while others did not would thus seem to be a crucial problem requiring further investigation. The nature of the decision-making unit – whether it was the farming household or the farming community, the individual or the group, the freeholder or the seigneurial lord – would in turn seem to be as significant in the development of regional and temporal variations in field systems as the intensification of agricultural practices under the stimulation of population pressure.

Both the developmental processes and the structural patterns of British field systems retain something of their enigmatic character and – given the fragmentary nature of the evidence about them – they are always likely to do so. Much of the research completed during the last fifty or so years has emphasised both the regional diversity and the temporal complexity of field systems in Britain. Increasingly detailed analyses have resulted in a heightened awareness of differences between field systems from place to place and from to time time, which makes it all the more necessary to attempt a general synthesis which tries to discern similarities as well as differences, both of form and of process. There is, of course, a considerable danger – faced by any who attempt generalisation in historical geography – of producing a synthesis which does violence to the 'facts'. But one of the roles of synthesis and generalisation in historical geography is to direct further enquiries. Generalisation can usefully be seen as a means towards an end as much as an end in itself. Provided it is accepted that generalised notions about field systems can be no more than models against which the actual farming arrangements of individual communities developed, then they serve a useful purpose.

A model of the evolution of field systems in the British Isles might well be based on the assumption that population growth is the main force by which agrarian change is brought about. This is an argument which has been advanced by Boserup recently in relation primarily to modern agricultural communities but the approach is also seen as being 'conducive to a fuller understanding of the actual historical course of agriculture, including the development of patterns and techniques of cultivation as well as the social structures of agrarian communities'.[1] Boserup points out that in primitive types of agriculture there is no sharp distinction between cultivated and uncultivated land and that it is impossible to distinguish clearly between the creation of new fields and a change of farming methods in existing fields. She places emphasis instead on the frequency with which land is cropped, recognising a continuum of types of land use as follows:

1. *Forest-fallow cultivation* with 20 to 25 years fallow after one or two years of cultivation.
2. *Bush-fallow cultivation* with cultivation for two to as many as eight years followed by six to ten years fallow.
3. *Short-fallow cultivation* with one to two years fallow in which only wild grasses can invade the fallow land.
4. *Annual cropping*, a system in which the land is left fallow for several months between the harvesting of one crop and the planting of the next. In this category are included systems of annual rotation in which one or more of the successive crops is a grass or other fodder crop.
5. *Multi-cropping*, the most intensive system of agriculture with the same plot bearing several crops a year with little or no fallow.

Now, most or all of the land added to the sown area as population increased in a particular township was being used already, as fallow land, pasture, hunting ground or for some other purpose, such as the provision of timber to meet the varied demands for wood. So when a given area of land came to be cropped more frequently than before, the purposes for which it was used hitherto had to be taken care of in a new way and this might have created additional activities for which new tools, investment and methods of organisation were required. Thus technological and organisational changes in agriculture are likely to have resulted from population changes. In a very general way, Boserup herself suggested that by combining the results of archaeological and historical research we get the picture of a successive change in Europe from neolithic forest-fallow to systems of shifting cultivation on bush and grass land followed first by short-fallow systems and in recent centuries by annual cropping. Boserup's classification of types of land use is more than an attempt to identify various types of agriculture existing today and in the past in terms of the frequency of

---

[1] Boserup, *Conditions of Agricultural Growth*, p. 12.

cropping. It is also intended broadly to describe the main stages of the actual evolution of primitive agriculture.[1]

It has not been the purpose of this present book to examine prehistoric field systems within the British Isles but the evidence presented here about historic field systems may usefully be interpreted in the light of Boserup's thesis. The general tendency towards more intensive field systems – and in particular towards the association of these tendencies with periods of population growth – is, in our view, clearly demonstrated. Of course, not all parts of the British Isles developed their agricultural systems at the same rate. The pressure of population was by no means felt uniformly throughout the whole area and agricultural systems developed more rapidly in some areas than in others so that by, say, 1300 or 1600 – dates which had seen considerable population growth in some areas in preceding decades – there were significant local and more especially regional differences in the intensity of farming practices. In detail, of course, the particular response to the general pressure of population varied from one locality and region to another, depending upon a whole range of variables other than population. There were many differing responses to this basic condition of agricultural growth. It could, indeed, be argued in general that British field systems after, say, 1086, became increasingly varied, both in terms of the regional contrasts in intensity of land use and in terms of the farming methods and systems of organisation being practised.

To argue thus is also to invite speculation about the nature and degree of uniformity, both structurally and functionally, of field systems in the eleventh century and earlier. Conjectures here outweigh conclusions, and there is considerable room for differences of opinion as well as for further research, particularly perhaps of an archaeological nature for which most historical geographers and economic historians are ill-equipped. But on theoretical grounds it is possible to consider what form one might expect these early field systems to have taken and on an empirical basis to examine to what extent the surviving evidence and interpretations provide confirmation of these expectations. Both lines of enquiry converge towards the view that an early form of settlement and agrarian organisation was the hamlet and its associated infield–outfield system. A small cluster of farmsteads of kinship groups constituted the settlement. Nearby lay a plot of intensively cultivated and manured arable, perhaps as undivided block fields or perhaps as subdivided strip fields. In addition, a number of plots in the surrounding area were brought into cultivation for short periods of two to eight years and fallowed for periods of six to twenty-five years. Considerable areas of pasture land – grasslands, heathlands, woodlands – were used

[1] *Ibid.*, pp. 13–18.

only extensively, not being brought into cultivation. Because of the great importance attached to the intensively cultivated infield, this system is sometimes referred to as a 'one-field system' but this is perhaps misleading because it ignores both the existence of temporarily cultivated outfields and the possibility of flexibility and complex rotations being used on the infield – sowing the infield in sections with different crops at different seasons. With the growth of population small hamlets developed into large villages, more land was brought into intensive cultivation – the 'infield' area was enlarged – and the subdivision of block fields promoted, of strip fields intensified. As land came to be cropped more frequently than before, so the pasture lands diminished and provision had to be made to utilise the arable lands for pastoral purposes. With the increasing intensity of agricultural practices developed a greater diversity of solutions to the basic problem of augmenting the food supplies, both for people and for livestock. This evolutionary model is one which in outline seems applicable throughout much of the British Isles. The infield–outfield system, a primitive form of agrarian organisation, persisted in almost perfect form until quite late in areas of relatively low population pressure, such as much of Scotland and parts of highland England. But it soon evolved into more intensive field systems in areas of relatively high population pressure, such as the vales and plains of many areas of lowland England. In these areas, elements of the earlier system often survived into the Middle Ages – such as the permanent cultivation of some plots and the intermittent cultivation of others – but by the end of the thirteenth century short-fallow systems were already well advanced. Nonetheless, both on *a priori* grounds and on the basis of the surviving evidence it is now possible to argue that a form of infield–outfield system was at some time practised throughout the British Isles. Such an argument would find much support in the growing view of continental scholars that it was once practised throughout much of western and central Europe.[1]

[1] H. Uhlig, 'Old Hamlets with Infield and Outfield Systems in Western and Central Europe', *Geogr. Annlr.*, XLIII, 1961, pp. 285–312; H. Uhlig, 'Fields and Field Systems' in R. H. Buchanan, E. Jones and D. McCourt (eds.), *Man and his Habitat. Essays Presented to Emyr Estyn Evans*, 1971, pp. 93–125.

Select Bibliography

A. GENERAL REFERENCES

Adams, I.H. 'Large-scale Manuscript Plans in Scotland', *Jnl. Soc. Archivists*, III, 1967.

Allison, K.J. *Deserted Villages*. 1970.

Applebaum, S. 'Agriculture in Roman Britain', *Agric. Hist. Rev.*, VI, 1958.

Ashmore, O. 'Inventories as a Source of Local History. II – Farmers', *Amat. Histn.*, IV, no. 5, 1959.

Ault, W.O. 'Some Early Village By-laws', *Engl. Hist. Rev.*, XLV, 1930.
  The Self-Directing Activities of Village Communities in Medieval England. Boston, 1952.
  'Village By-laws by Common Consent', in: *Medieval Representation in Theory and Practice, Speculum*, XXIX, 1954.
  'By-laws of Gleaning and the Problems of Harvest', *Econ. Hist. Rev.*, XIV, 1961.
  'Open-field Husbandry and the Village Community: a Study of Agrarian By-laws in Medieval England', *Trans. Am. Phil. Soc.*, LV, part 7, 1965.

Aurrousseau, M. 'Neglected Aspects of the Enclosure Movements', *Econ. Hist.*, I, no. 2, 1948.

Baker, A.R.H. 'Howard Levi Gray and *English Field Systems*: An Evaluation', *Agric. Hist.*, XXXIX, 1966.
  'Some Terminological Problems in Studies of British Field Systems', *Agric. Hist. Rev.*, XVII, 1969.

Barger, E. 'The Present Position of Studies in English Field Systems', *Engl. Hist. Rev.*, LVIII, 1938.

Bath, B.H. Slicher Van. *The Agrarian History of Western Europe, A.D. 500–1850*. 1963.

Beckwith, I. 'The Remodelling of a Common-field System', *Agric. Hist. Rev.*, XV, 1967.

Beecham, H. 'A Review of Balks as Strip Boundaries in the Open Fields', *Agric. Hist. Rev.*, IV, 1956.

Beresford, M.W. 'Lot Acres', *Econ. Hist. Rev.*, XIII, 1943.
  'Commissioners of Enclosure', *Econ. Hist. Rev.*, XVI, 1946.
  'Ridge and Furrow and the Open Fields', *Econ. Hist. Rev.*, I, 1948.
  'Maps and The Mediaeval Landscape', *Antiquity*, XCV, 1950.
  The Lost Villages of England. 1954.
  History on the Ground: Six Studies in Maps and Landscapes. 1957.
  and St Joseph, J.K.S. *Medieval England: an Aerial Survey*. 1958.

Blanchard, I. 'Population Change, Enclosure, and the Early Tudor Economy', *Econ. Hist. Rev.*, XXIII, 1970.

Bloch, M. *Les Caractères Originaux de l'Histoire Rurale Française*. Oslo, 1931. Vol. 2, supplement, Paris, 1956. Translated by Sondheimer, J. as *French Rural History*. London, 1966.

Bowen, H.C. *Ancient Fields*. British Association for the Advancement of Science, 1962.

Bradley, H. *The Enclosures in England: an Economic Reconstruction*. Columbia University Studies in History, Economics and Public Law, No. 186, LXXX, no. 2, New York, 1918.

Brewer, J.G. *Enclosures And The Open Fields: A Bibliography*. The British Agricultural History Society, 1972.

658 SELECT BIBLIOGRAPHY

Butlin, R.A. 'Some Terms used in Agrarian History: A Glossary', *Agric. Hist. Rev.*, IX, 1961.
'Recent Developments in Studies of the Terminology of Agrarian Landscapes', *Agric. Hist. Rev.*, XVII, 1969.
Campbell, M. *The English Yeoman under Elizabeth and the Early Stuarts.* New Haven, 1942.
Chaloner, W.H. 'Bibliography of Recent Work on Enclosure, the Open Fields, and Related Topics', *Agric. Hist. Rev.*, II, 1954.
Chambers, J.D. 'Enclosure and the Small Landowner', *Econ. Hist. Rev.*, X, 1940.
Laxton: the last English Open Field Village. 1964.
and Mingay, G.E. *The Agricultural Revolution 1750–1880.* 1966.
Clark, H.M. 'Selion Size and Soil Type', *Agric. Hist. Rev.*, VIII, 1960.
Coppock, J.T. 'Changes in Farm and Field Boundaries in the Ninteeenth Century', *Amat. Histn.*, III, no. 7, 1958.
Crone, G.R., Campbell, E.M.J., and Skelton, R.A. 'Landmarks in British Cartography', *Geogrl. Jnl.*, CXXVIII, 1962.
Curtler, W.H.R. *The Enclosure and Redistribution of Our Land.* 1920.
Curwen, E.C. 'The Plough and the Origin of Strip Lynchets', *Antiquity*, XIII, 1939.
Darby, H.C. 'The Agrarian Contribution to Surveying in England', *Geogrl. Jnl.*, LXXXII, 1933.
(ed.). *An Historical Geography of England Before 1800.* 1936.
The Domesday Geography of Eastern England. 1953.
'Some Early Ideas on the Agricultural Regions of England', *Agric. Hist. Rev.*, I, 1954.
and Terrett, I.B. (eds.). *The Domesday Geography of Midland England.* 1954.
and Maxwell, I.S. (eds.). *The Domesday Geography of Northern England.* 1962.
and Campbell, E.M.J. (eds.). *The Domesday Geography of South-East England.* 1962.
and Welldon Finn, R. (eds.). *The Domesday Geography of South-West England.* 1967.
Davidson, T.D. 'The Untilled Field', *Agric. Hist. Rev.*, III, 1955.
Donaldson, G. 'Sources for Scottish Agrarian History before the Eighteenth Century', *Agric. Hist. Rev.*, VIII, 1960.
Emmison, F.G. 'Estate Maps and Surveys', *History*, XLVIII, 1963.
Types of Open-Field Parishes in the Midlands. Historical Association. 1937. Reissued as: *Some Types of Common Field Parish.* The Standing Conference for Local History, 1965.
Erixon, S. 'The Age of Enclosures and its Older Traditions', *Folk Life*, IV, 1966.
Eyre, S.R. 'The Curving Plough-strip and its Historical Implications', *Agric. Hist. Rev.*, III, 1955.
Faith, R.J. 'Peasant Families and Inheritance Customs in Medieval England', *Agric. Hist. Rev.*, XIV, 1966.
Finberg, H.P.R. 'Recent Progress in English Agrarian History', *Geogr. Annlr.*, XLIII, 1961.
Flatrès, P. *Géographie Rurale de Quatre Contrées Celtiques.* Rennes, 1957.
Fowler, P.J., and Evans, J.G. 'Plough-Marks, Lynchets, and Early Fields', *Antiquity*, XLI, 1967.
Fox, H.S.A. 'A Geographical Study of the Field Systems of Devon and Cornwall'. University of Cambridge Ph.D. thesis, 1971.
Franks, J.W. 'Pollen Analysis: a Technique for Investigating Early Agrarian History', *Agric. Hist. Rev.*, V, 1957.
Fussell, G.E. 'Ploughs and Ploughing before 1800', *Agric. Hist.*, XL, 1966.
Gay, E.F. 'The Inquisition of Depopulation in 1517 and the Domesday of Inclosures', *Trans. R. Hist. Soc.*, XIV, 1900.
'Enclosure in England in the Sixteenth Century', *Q. Jnl. Econ.*, XVII, 1903.

Gonner, E.C.K. *Common Land and Inclosure*. 1912.
Göransson, S. 'Regular Open-Field Pattern in England and Scandinavian *Solskifte*', *Geogr. Annlr.*, XLIII, 1961.
Gras, N.S.B., and Gras, E. *The Economic and Social History of an English Village (Crawley, Hampshire), 909–1428*. Cambridge, Mass., 1930.
Gray, H.L. *English Field Systems*. Cambridge, Mass., 1915.
Green, E.R.R. 'On Open Town Fields', *Agric. Hist. Rev.*, IX, 1961.
Harley, J.B. 'Maps for the Local Historian: a Guide to British Sources. 2: Estate Maps', *Amat. Histn.*, VII, no. 7, 1967.
'Maps for the Local Historian: a Guide to British Sources. 3: Enclosure and Tithe Maps', *Amat. Histn.*, VII, no. 8, 1967.
'The Evaluation of Early Maps: Towards a Methodology', *Imago mundi*, XXII, 1968.
and Phillips, C.W. *The Historian's Guide to Ordnance Survey Maps*. The Standing Conference for Local History. 1964.
Harris, A. 'A Note on the Ridge-and-furrow Controversy', *Amat. Histn.*, VII, 1966.
Harrison, M.J., Mead, W.R., and Pannett, D.J. 'A Midland Ridge-and-Furrow Map', *Geogrl. Jnl.*, CXXXI, 1965.
Helmfrid, S. (ed.). *The Morphogenesis of the Agrarian Cultural Landscape*. Reprinted from *Geografiska Annaler*, XLIII, 1961.
Henderson, H.C.K. 'Agriculture in England and Wales in 1801', *Geogrl. Jnl.*, CXVIII, 1952.
Herlihy, D. 'The Carolingian *Mansus*', *Econ. Hist. Rev.*, XIX, 1906–1.
Hilton, R.H. 'The Content and Sources of English Agrarian History before 1500', *Agric. Hist. Rev.*, III, 1955.
Homans, G.C. 'Partible Inheritance of Villagers' Holdings', *Econ. Hist. Rev.*, VIII, 1937–8.
English Villagers of the Thirteenth Century. Cambridge, Mass., 1940.
'The Rural Sociology of Medieval England', *Past and Present*, IV, 1953.
'The Explanation of English Regional Differences', *Past and Present*, XLII, 1969.
Hoskins, W.G. 'Regional Farming in England', *Agric. Hist. Rev.*, II, 1954.
Fieldwork in Local History, 1967.
and Stamp, L.D. *The Common Lands of England and Wales*. 1963.
Jackson, J.C. 'Fossil Field Boundaries', *Amat. Histn.*, IV, no. 2, 1958–9.
'The Ridge-and-furrow Controversy', *Amat. Histn.*, V, no. 1, 1961.
John, E. *Land Tenure in Early England*. 1960.
Johnson, A.H. *The Disappearance of the Small Landowner*. 1909.
Jones, E.L. (ed.). *Agriculture and Economic Growth in England, 1650–1815*. 1967.
Jones, G.R.J. 'Early Territorial Organisation in England and Wales', *Geogr. Annlr.*, XLIII, 1961.
Keil, I. 'Interpreting Medieval Measurements', *Amat. Histn.*, VI, no. 4, 1964.
Kerridge, E. 'A Reconsideration of Some Former Husbandry Practices', *Agric. Hist. Rev.*, III, 1955.
'The Manorial Survey as an Historical Source', *Amat. Histn.*, VII, 1965.
Agrarian Problems in the Sixteenth Century and After. 1969.
Kirbis, W. *Siedlungs – und Flurformen germanischer Länder, besonders Gross-Britanniens, im Lichte der deutschen Siedlungsforschung*. Gottingen, 1942.
Kosminsky, E.A. *Studies in the Agrarian History of England in the Thirteenth Century*. Trans. R.H. Hilton. 1956.
Lambert, A. 'Early Maps and Local Studies', *Geography*, LXI, 1956.
Leadam, I.S. *The Domesday of Inclosures, 1517–1518*. 1897.
Lennard, R. *Rural England, 1086–1185. A Study of Social and Agrarian Conditions*. 1959.

Leonard, E.M. 'The Inclosure of Common Fields in the Seventeenth Century', *Trans. R. Hist. Soc.*, XIX, 1905.

McCourt, D. 'Infield and Outfield in Ireland', *Econ. Hist. Rev.*, VII, 1955.

MacNab, J.W. 'British Strip Lynchets', *Antiquity*, XXXIX, 1965.

Mead, W. R. 'Ridge and Furrow in Buckinghamshire', *Geogrl. Jnl.*, CXX, 1954.

'The Study of Field Boundaries', *Geogr. Z.*, LIV, 1966.

Miller, A.A. 'The Mapping of Strip Lynchets', *Advmt. Sci.*, XI, 1954.

Minchinton, W.E. 'Agricultural Returns and the Government during the Napoleonic Wars', *Agric. Hist. Rev.*, I, 1953.

Mingay, G.E. *English Landed Society in the Eighteenth Century*. 1963.

Enclosure and the Small Farmer in the Age of the Industrial Revolution. 1968.

Munslow, F.W. 'Field Names in Village and Parish History in England', *Amat. Histn.* II, no. 2, 1956.

Nightingale, M.D. 'Ploughing and Field Shape', *Antiquity*, XXVII, 1953.

Oldfield, F. 'Pollen Analysis and the History of Land Use', *Advmt. Sci.*, XXV, 1969.

Orwin, C.S. 'Observations on the Open Fields', *Econ. Hist. Rev.*, VIII, 1938.

and Orwin, C.S. *The Open Fields*, 1938; 2nd edn, 1954; 3rd edn, 1967.

Oschinsky, D. 'Medieval Treatises on Estate Management', *Econ. Hist. Rev.*, VIII, 1956.

Parker, R.A.C. *Enclosures in the Eighteenth Century*. 1960.

Pitkin, D.S. 'Partible Inheritance and the Open Fields', *Agric. Hist.*, XXXV, 1961.

Pocock, E.A. 'The First Fields in an Oxfordshire Parish', *Agric. Hist. Rev.*, XVI, 1968.

Postan, M.M. (ed.). *The Cambridge Economic History of Europe. Vol. I: The Agrarian Life of the Middle Ages*. 2nd edn, 1966.

Scrutton, T.E. *Commons and Common Fields*. 1887.

Seebohm, F. *The English Village Community*. 1883.

Customary Acres and their Historical Importance. 1914.

Slater, G. *The English Peasantry and the Enclosure of Common Fields*. 1907.

'The Inclosure of Common Fields Considered Geographically', *Geogrl. Jnl.*, XXIX, 1907.

Steensberg, A. 'Plough and Field Shape', *Selected Papers of the Fifth Intern. Congr. of Anthrop. and Ethnol. Sciences*, Philadelphia, 1956.

Steer, F.W. 'Short Guides to Records. 3. Probate Inventories', *History*, XLVII, 1962.

Tate, W.E. *The English Village Community and the Enclosure Movements*. 1967.

Tawney, R.H. *The Agrarian Revolution in the Sixteenth Century*. 1912.

Taylor, C.C. 'Strip Lynchets', *Antiquity*, XL, 1966.

Taylor, E.G.R. 'The Surveyor', *Econ. Hist. Rev.*, XVII, 1947.

Thirsk, J. 'The Content and Sources of English Agrarian History after 1500', *Agric. Hist. Rev.*, III, 1955.

English Peasant Farming. 1957.

Tudor Enclosures. Hist. Assoc. Pamphlet, General Ser. 41, London, 1959.

'The Common Fields', *Past and Present*, XXIX, 1964.

'The Origin of the Common Fields', *Past and Present*, XXXIII, 1966.

(ed.). *The Agrarian History of England and Wales, IV: 1500–1640*. 1967.

'Preface to the Third Edition', in Orwin, C.S. and Orwin, C.S. *The Open Fields*. 3rd edn, 1967.

'Seventeenth Century Agriculture and Social Change', *Agric. Hist. Rev.*, XVIII, 1970.

Supplement: *Land, Church and People. Essays presented to Professor H.P.R. Finberg*.

Thomas, A.C. (ed.). *Rural Settlement in Roman Britain*. 1966.

Thomas, C. 'Estate Surveys as Sources in Historical Geography', *Nat. Lib. Wales Jnl.*, XIV, 1966.

Thomas, D. *Agriculture in Wales during the Napoleonic wars: a Study in the Geographical Interpretation of Historical Sources.* 1963.

Thompson, F.M.L. *English Landed Society in the Nineteenth Century.* 1963.

Titow, J.Z. 'Medieval England and the Open-Field System', *Past and Present*, XXXII, 1965.

English Rural Society 1200–1350. 1969.

Trow-Smith, R. *A History of British Livestock Husbandry to 1700.* 1957.

Uhlig, H. 'Old Hamlets with Infield and Outfield Systems in Western and Central Europe', *Geogr. Annlr.*, XLIII, 1961.

'Fields and Field Systems', in: Buchanan, R.H., Jones, E., and McCourt, D. (eds.). *Man and His Habitat.* 1971.

Vinogradoff, P. *The Growth of the Manor.* 1905.

English Society in the Eleventh Century. 1908.

White, K.D. *Agricultural Implements of the Roman World.* 1967.

White, L.J. 'Enclosures and Population Movements in England, 1700–1830', *Expl. in Entrep. Hist.*, 2nd ser. VI, 1969.

White, L.T. *Medieval Technology and Social Change.* 1962.

Whittington, G. 'The Distribution of Strip Lynchets', *Trans. Inst. Br. Geogr.*, XXI, 1962.

'Towards a Terminology for Strip Lynchets', *Agric. Hist. Rev.*, XV, 1967.

Williams, M. 'The Enclosure and Reclamation of Waste Land in England and Wales in the Eighteenth and Nineteenth Centuries', *Trans. Inst. Br. Geogr.*, LI, 1970.

Wilson, D.M. 'Anglo-Saxon Rural Economy: a Survey of the Archaeological Evidence and a Suggestion', *Agric. Hist. Rev.*, X, 1962.

Wood, P.D. 'Strip Lynchets Reconsidered', *Geogrl. Jnl.*, CXXVII, 1961.

B. ENGLAND

1. Northwest England

Bailey, W., and Culley, G. *General View of the Agriculture of the County of Cumberland.* 1794.

Bainbridge, T. H. 'Eighteenth Century Agriculture in Cumbria', *CW2*, XLII, 1942.

Bean, J.M.W. *The Estates of the Percy Family 1416–1537.* 1958.

Bouch, C.M.L., and Jones, J.P. *A Short Economic and Social History of the Lake Counties 1500–1830.* 1961.

Chapman, V. 'Open Fields in West Cheshire', *Trans. Hist. Soc. Lancs. and Ches.*, CIV, 1952.

Clarke, J. *A Survey of the Lakes of Cumberland, Westmorland and Lancashire.* 2nd edn, 1789.

Cunliffe Shaw, R. *Royal Forest of Lancaster.* 1956.

'The Townfields of Lancashire', *Trans. Hist. Soc. Lancs. and Ches.*, CXIV, 1962.

Davies, C.S. *The Agricultural History of Cheshire 1750–1850.* Chetham Soc., X, 1960.

Dickens, B. (ed.). *The Place-Names of Cumberland.* English Place-Name Society, XX–XXII, 1950.

Dickenson, W. 'The Agriculture of Cumberland', *Jnl. R. Agric. Soc.*, XIII, 1853.

Dickson, R.W. *General View of the Agriculture of Lancashire.* 1815.

Dilley, R. 'The Cumberland Court Leet and Use of Common Lands', *CW2*, LXVII, 1967.

Elliott, G. 'The System of Cultivation and Evidence of Enclosures in the Cumberland Open Fields in the 16th Century', *CW2*, LIX, 1959.

'The Enclosure of Aspatria', *CW2*, LX, 1960.

Ellwood, T. 'The Reanns of High Furness', *CW1*, XI, 1891.

Fair, M.C. 'The Townfields of Drigg', *CW2*, XXXIV, 1934.

Farrer, W. (ed.). *Lancashire Inquests and Extents*, Lancs. and Ches. Rec. Soc., LIV, part 2, 1907.

and Brownhill, J. (eds.). *V.C.H. Lancashire*, III, 1914.

Fletcher, T.W. 'The Agrarian Revolution in Arable Lancashire', *Trans. Lancs. and Ches. Antiqu. Soc.*, LXXII, 1962.

Fussell, G.E. 'Four Centuries of Cheshire Farming Systems, 1500–1900', *Trans. Hist. Soc. Lancs. and Ches.*, CVI, 1954.

Garnett, W. *History of Westmorland Agriculture 1800–1900*. 1912.

Giles, S. 'Stockport Enclosure', *Trans. Lancs. and Ches. Antiqu. Soc.*, LXII, 1953.

Graham, T.H.B. 'The Townfields of Cumberland', *CW2*, X, 1910.

(ed.). *The Barony of Gilsland, Lord William Howard's Survey, taken in 1603*. 1934.

Grainger, F., and Collingwood, W.G. *Register and Records of Holm Cultram*. 1929.

Harris, A. 'A Note on Common Fields in North Lancashire', *Trans. Hist. Soc. Lancs. and Ches.*, CXIX, 1968.

Hesketh Hodgson, T. 'The Village Community in Cumberland as instanced at Halltown near Rockliff', *CW1*, XII, 1891.

Hewitt, H.J. *Medieval Cheshire – An Economic and Social History*. Chetham Soc., LXXXVIII, 1929.

Husain, M.B. 'Delamere Forest in Late-medieval Times', *Trans. Hist. Soc. Lancs. and Ches.*, CII, 1952.

Jones, G.P. 'Some Population Problems Relating to Cumberland and Westmorland in the Eighteenth Century', *CW2*, LVIII, 1958.

Kirby, D.P. 'Strathclyde and Cumbria: a Survey of Historical Development to 1092', *CW2*, LXII, 1962.

Marshall, J.D. *Furness and the Industrial Revolution*. 1958.

Maxwell, R. *The Practical Husbandman, A Collection of Miscellaneous papers on husbandry*. 1757.

Millward, R. *The Making of the English Landscape – Lancashire*. 1955.

Nicholson, I., and Burn, R. *The History and Antiquities of the Counties of Westmorland and Cumberland*. 1777.

Parker, F.H.M. 'Inglewood Forest – Part IV', *CW2*, IX, 1909.
'Inglewood Forest – Parts V and VI', *CW2*, X, 1910.

Pearson, G.H. 'The Town Books of Biggar', *CW2*, XI, 1911.

Porter, R.E. 'The Townfields of Coniston', *CW2*, XXVIII, 1928.

Pringle, A. *General View of the Agriculture of Westmorland*. 1797.

Sanderson, R.P. (ed.). *A Book of the Survey of the Debatable and Borderlands, 1604.* 1891.

Simpson, G.M. 'Townfields at Threlkeld, Mardale, Wet Sleddale and Langdale', *CW2*, XXVIII, 1928.

Singleton, F.J. 'The Influence of Geographical Factors on the Development of the Common Fields of Lancashire', *Trans. Hist. Soc. Lancs. and Ches.*, CXV, 1963.

Stamp, L.D. (ed.). *Land Utilisation Survey of Britain*, part 49, *Cumberland*. 1943.

Stewart-Brown, R. 'The Townfields of Liverpool 1207–1807', *Trans. Hist. Soc. Lancs. and Ches.*, LXVIII, 1917.

Sylvester, D. 'The Open Fields of Cheshire', *Trans. Hist. Soc. Lancs. and Ches.*, CVIII, 1956.
'A Note on Medieval Three-course Arable Systems in Cheshire', *Trans. Hist. Soc. Lancs. and Ches.*, CX, 1958.
The Rural Landscape of the Welsh Borderland. 1969.

Tate, W.E. 'A Handlist of English Enclosure Acts and Awards', *CW2*, XLIII, 1943.

Tupling, G. *The Economic History of Rossendale*. Chetham Soc., LXXXVI, 1927.
Tyrer, F. 'The Common Fields of Little Crosby', *Trans. Hist. Soc. Lancs. and Ches.*, CXIV, 1962.
Wordsworth, W. *A Guide through the District of the Lakes in the North of England*. 5th edn, 1835.
Youd, G. 'The Common Fields of Lancashire', *Trans. Hist. Soc. Lancs. and Ches.*, CXIII, 1961.

2. *Northumberland and Durham*

Bailey, J. *A General View of the Agriculture of Durham*. 1794.
and Culley, G. *A General View of the Agriculture of Northumberland*. 1794.
Bain, J. (ed.). *The Border Papers: Calendar of Letters and Papers relating to the Affairs of England and Scotland*. 1894–6.
Batho, G.R. 'The Finances of an Elizabethan Nobleman: Henry Percy, Ninth Earl of Northumberland', *Econ. Hist. Rev.*, IX, 1957.
(ed.). *The Household Papers of Henry Percy, ninth Earl of Northumberland*. Camden Soc., XCIII, 1962.
Bean, J.M.W. *The Estates of the Percy Family 1416–1537*. 1958.
Beresford, M.W. 'The Lost Villages of Northern England', in: *Studies in Architectural History*. 1954.
Blair, P.H. *The Origins of Northumbria*. 1948.
'Baronies and Knights of Northumberland 1166–1266', *Arch. Ael.*, XXX, 1952.
Bradshaw, F. 'Social and Economic History', *V.C.H. Durham*, II, 1907.
'The Lay Subsidy Roll of 1296 – Northumberland at the End of the Thirteenth Century', *Arch. Ael.*, XIII, 1916.
Butlin, R.A. 'The Evolution of the Agrarian Landscape of Northumberland, 1500–1900'. University of Liverpool M.A. thesis, 1961.
'Northumberland Field Systems', *Agric. Hist. Rev.*, XII, 1964.
'Enclosure and Improvement in Northumberland in the Sixteenth Century', *Arch. Ael.*, XLV, 1967.
Chapman, V.C. 'The Fields of Bolam', *Trans. Archit. and Arch. Soc. of Durham and Northumberland*, XI, parts 5 and 6, 1965.
'Barnard Castle: the Enclosures', in: *History Field Studies in the Durham Area*. 1967.
Conzen, M.R.G. *Alnwick, Northumberland: A Study in town-plan analysis*. Institute of British Geographers, 1960.
Dendy, F.W. 'The Ancient Farms of Northumberland', *Arch. Ael.*, XVI, 1894.
Dickenson, P. 'The Historical Geography of County Durham during the Middle Ages'. University of Durham Ph.D. thesis, 1957.
and Fisher, W.B. *The Medieval Land Surveys of County Durham*. 1959.
Hadcock, R.N. 'Map of Medieval Northumberland and Durham', *Arch. Ael.*, XVI, 1939.
Hodgson, J. *A History of Northumberland*. 1820–58.
Hodgson, J.C. (ed.). *Percy Bailiffs Rolls of the Fifteenth Century*. Surtees Soc. Publ., CXXXIV, 1921.
Hogg, A.H.A. 'Native Settlements of Northumberland', *Antiquity*, XVII, 1943.
Hughes, E. *North Country Life in the Eighteenth Century: the North East, 1700–1750*. 1952.
Isaac, P.C.G., and Allan, R.E.A. (eds.). *Scientific Survey of North-Eastern England*, 1949.
James, M.E. *Estate Accounts of the Earls of Northumberland*. Surtees Soc., CLXIII, 1955.
Change and Continuity in the Tudor North. Borthwick Papers No. 27, 1965.
A Tudor Magnate and the Tudor State. Borthwick Papers No. 30, 1966.
Jolliffe, J.E.A. 'Northumbrian Institutions', *Engl. Hist. Rev.*, XLVI, 1926.

Mackenzie, E. *A Historical, Topographical and Descriptive View of the County of Northumberland.* 2nd edn, 1825.

Mawer, A. *The Place-Names of Northumberland and Durham.* 1920.

Middlebrook, S. *Newcastle upon Tyne, its Growth and Achievement.* 1950.

Northumberland County History Committee. *A History of Northumberland.* 15 vols., 1839–1940.

Raine, J. *The History and Antiquities of North Durham.* 1852.

Ridpath, G. *The Border History of England and Scotland from the Earliest Times to the Union of the Two Crowns.* 1810.

Smailes, A.E. *North England.* 1960.

Tate, W.E. 'A Handlist of English Enclosure Acts and Awards: Part 26, Northumberland', *Proc. Soc. Antiqu. Newcastle,* x, no. 1, 1942.

'A Handlist of English Enclosure Acts and Awards: Part 26. Durham', *Proc. Soc. Antiqu. Newcastle,* x, no. 3, 1943.

Thorpe, H. 'The Green Villages of County Durham', *Trans. Inst. Br. Geogr.,* xv, 1949.

Tough, D.L.W. *The Last Years of a Frontier. A History of the Borders during the Reign of Elizabeth.* 1928.

Trevelyan, G.M. *The Middle Marches.* 1934.

Uhlig, H. *Die Kulturlandschaft Nordostengland.* Cologne, 1956.

Young, A. *A Six Months' Tour through the North of England.* 1770.

3. Yorkshire

Allerston, P. 'Field and Village in the Pickering District of North Yorkshire'. University of London M.Sc. thesis, 1966.

Allison, K.J. 'Enclosure by Agreement at Healaugh (W.R.)', *Yorks. Arch. Jnl.,* xl, 1961.

Barley, M.W. 'East Yorkshire Manorial By-Laws', *Yorks. Arch. Jnl.,* xxxv, 1943.

Beresford, M.W. 'Glebe Terriers and Open Field Yorkshire', *Yorks. Arch. Jnl.,* xxxvii, 1948–51.

Bishop, T.A.M. 'Assarting and the Growth of Open Fields', *Econ. Hist. Rev.,* vi, 1935–6.

'Monastic Granges in Yorkshire', *Engl. Hist. Rev.,* ccii, 1936.

'The Norman Settlement of Yorkshire', in Hunt, R.W., Pantin, W.A., and Southern, F.W. (eds.). *Studies in Medieval History presented to Frederick Maurice Powicke.* 1948.

Darby, H.C., and Maxwell, I.S. (eds.). *The Domesday Geography of Northern England.* 1962.

Donkin, R.A. 'Settlement and Depopulation on Cistercian Estates during the Twelfth and Thirteenth Centuries, especially in Yorkshire', *Bull. Inst. Hist. Res.,* xxxiii, 1960.

English, B.A. (ed.). *Handlist of West Riding Enclosure Awards.* 1965.

Fowler, J.T. (ed.). *Coucher Book of Selby Abbey.* Yorks. Arch. Soc. Rec. Soc., xiii, 1893.

Gamble, G.G. 'A History of Hunslet in the Later Middle Ages', *Thoresby Society Transactions,* xli, 1943–51.

Harris, A. 'Pre-Enclosure Agricultural Systems in the East Riding of Yorkshire'. University of London M.A. thesis, 1951.

'"Land" and Oxgang in the East Riding of Yorkshire', *Yorks. Arch. Jnl.,* xxxviii, 1952–5.

'The Agriculture of the East Riding of Yorkshire before Parliamentary Enclosures', *Yorks. Arch. Jnl.,* xl, 1959–62.

The Open Fields of East Yorkshire. E. Yorks. Local Hist. Ser., ix, 1959.

The Rural Landscape of the East Riding of Yorkshire, 1700–1860. 1961.

Holt, J.C. *The Northerners.* 1961.

Jones, G.R.J. 'Basic Patterns of Settlement Distribution in Northern England', *Advmt. Sci.*, XVIII, 1961.

Lancaster, W.T. (ed.). *Chartulary of Bridlington Priory.* 1912.

(ed.). *Chartulary of the Cistercian Abbey of Fountains.* 1915.

Leatham, I. *General View of the Agriculture of the East Riding of Yorkshire.* 1794.

Linton, D.L. (ed.). *Sheffield and its Region.* 1956.

Loughbrough, B. 'An Account of a Yorkshire Enclosure – Staxton 1803', *Agric. Hist. Rev.*, XIII, 1965.

Palmer, J. 'Landforms, Drainage and Settlement in the Vale of York', in Eyre, S.R., and Jones, G.R.J. (eds.). *Geography as Human Ecology.* 1966.

Purvis, J.S. *Bridlington Charters, Court Rolls and Papers.* 1926.

Raistrick, A. *Malham and Malham Moor.* 1947.

(ed.). *The North York Moors.* National Park Guide No. 4, 1966.

Rodgers, W.S. 'The Distribution of Parliamentary Enclosures in the West Riding of Yorkshire, 1729–1895'. University of Leeds M.Comm. thesis, 1952.

Ruston, A.G., and Witney, D. *Hooton Pagnell: The Agricultural Evolution of a Yorkshire Village.* 1934.

Sheppard, J.A. *The Draining of the Marshlands of South Holderness and the Vale of York.* E. Yorks. Local Hist. Ser., XX, 1966.

'Pre-Enclosure Field and Settlement Patterns in an English Township: Wheldrake, near York', *Geogr. Annlr.*, XLVIII, 1966.

Siddle, D.J. 'The Rural Economy of Medieval Holderness', *Agric. Hist. Rev.*, XV, 1967.

Smith, A.H. *The Place-Names of the North Riding of Yorkshire.* English Place-Name Society, V, 1928.

The Place-Names of the West Riding of Yorkshire. English Place-Name Society, XXXVI, 1962.

Tuke, J. *General View of the Agriculture of the North Riding of Yorkshire,* 1st edn, 1794; 2nd edn, 1800.

Waites, B. *Moorland and Vale-Land Farming in North-East Yorkshire: the Monastic contribution in the Thirteenth and Fourteenth Centuries.* Borthwick Papers No. 32, 1967.

Wightman, W.R. 'Some Aspects of the Historical Geography of the Vale of Pickering Area, 1086–1350 A.D.'. University of Durham Ph.D. thesis, 1964.

Wilkinson, O. *The Agricultural Revolution in the East Riding of Yorkshire.* E. Yorks. Local Hist. Ser., V, 1956.

Yorkshire Inquisitions, I. Yorks. Arch. Soc. Rec. Ser., XII, XII, 1892.

Yorkshire Inquisitions, II, Yorks. Arch. Soc. Rec. Ser., XXIII, 1898.

4. The West Midlands

Barratt, D.M. 'The Enclosure of the Manor of Wasperton in 1664', *University of Birmingham Hist. Jnl.*, III, 2, 1952.

(ed.). *Ecclesiastical Terriers of Warwickshire Parishes.* Dugdale Soc., I, 1955.

Beresford, M.W. 'Lot Acres', *Econ. Hist. Rev.*, XIII, 1941–3.

'The Economic Individualism of Sutton Coldfield', *Trans. Birm. Arch. Society*, LXIV, 1941–2 (1946).

'The Deserted Villages of Warwickshire', *Trans. Birm. Arch. Soc.*, LXVI, 1945–6 (1950).

Harley, J.B. 'Population Trends and Agricultural Developments from the Warwickshire Hundred Rolls of 1279', *Econ. Hist. Rev.*, XI, 1958.

'Population and Land Utilisation in the Warwickshire Hundreds of Stoneleigh and Kineton, 1086–1300'. University of Birmingham Ph.D. thesis, 1960.

'The Settlement Geography of Early Medieval Warwickshire', *Trans. Inst. Br. Geogr.*, XXXIV, 1964.

Harrison, M.J., Mead, W.R., and Pannett, D.J. 'A Midland Ridge-and-furrow Map', *Geogrl. Jnl.*, CXXXI, 1965.

Hebden, R. 'The Development of the Settlement Pattern and Farming in the Shenstone Area', *Lichfield and Staffs. Arch. and Hist. Soc.*, III, 1961–2.

Hilton, R.H. *The Social Structure of Rural Warwickshire in the Middle Ages.* Dugdale Soc. Occasional Papers, 1950.

'Old Enclosure in the West Midlands', *Annales de l'Est*, XXI 1959.

(ed.). *The Stoneleigh Leger Book.* Dugdale Society, 1960.

A Medieval Society: the West Midlands at the End of the Thirteenth Century. 1966.

Hollings, M. 'The Red Book of Worcester'. *Worcs. Hist. Soc.*, 1934.

Marshall, W. *Rural Economy of the Midland Counties.* 1790.

Murray, A. *General View of the Agriculture of the County of Warwickshire.* 1813.

Pelham, R.A. 'The Agricultural Geography of Warwickshire during the Napoleonic Wars'. *Trans. Birm. Arch. Soc.*, LXI, 1952.

Pitt, W. *General View of the Agriculture of the County of Worcestershire.* 1813.

Plot, R. *Natural History of Staffordshire.* 1686.

Roberts, B.K. 'Settlement, Land Use and Population in the Western Portion of the Forest of Arden, Warwickshire, between 1086 and 1350'. University of Birmingham Ph.D. thesis, 1965.

'A Study of Medieval Colonisation in the Forest of Arden, Warwickshire', *Agric. Hist. Rev.*, XVI, 1968.

Skipp, V.H.T. *Discovering Sheldon.* Dept. of Extra-Mural Studies, University of Birmingham, 1960.

'Economic and Social Change in the Forest of Arden, 1530–1649', *Agric. Hist. Rev.*, XVIII, 1970.

and Hastings, R.P., *Discovering Bickenhill.* Dept. of Extra-Mural Studies, University of Birmingham, 1963.

Tate, W.E. 'Enclosure Acts and Awards relating to Staffordshire'. *Staffordshire Historical Collections*, 1942.

'Enclosure Acts and Awards Relating to Warwickshire'. *Trans. Birm. Arch. Soc.*, LXV, 1943–4 (1949).

'Worcestershire Field Systems', *Trans. Worcestershire Hist. Soc.*, XX, 1943.

Thomas, H.R. 'The Enclosure of the Open-Fields and Commons in Staffordshire', *Staffordshire Historical Collections*, 1931 (1933).

Thorpe, H. 'The Lord and the Landscape', *Volume Jubilaire M. A. Lefèvre.* Paris, 1964.

Yelling, J. 'Open-Field, Enclosure and Farm Production in East Worcestershire, 1540–1870'. University of Birmingham Ph.D. thesis, 1966.

'Common Land and Enclosure in East Worcestershire, 1540–1870', *Trans. Inst. Br. Geogr.*, XLV, 1968.

'The Combination and Rotation of Crops in East Worcestershire', *Agric. Hist. Rev.*, XVII, 1969.

Young, A. 'Vale of Evesham Husbandry', *Annals of Agriculture*, XXXVII, 1801.

5. The East Midlands

Barley, M.W. (ed.). 'The Barrow on Humber Town Book', *L.A.A.S.*, II, 1958.

Beckwith, I. 'The Remodelling of a Common Field System', *Agric. Hist. Rev.*, XV, 1967.

Beel, M. 'Bylaws of Ulceby, Yarborough Wapentake, 1677', *Lincs. Historian*, II, 1961.

Boulton, H.E. (ed.). *The Sherwood Forest Book.* Thoroton Soc. Rec. Ser., XXIII, 1965.

Brooke, C.N.L., and Postan, M.M. *Carte Nativorum. A Peterborough Abbey Cartulary of the Fourteenth Century*. Northants. Rec. Soc., xx, 1960.

Chambers, J.D. *Laxton: The Last English Open Field Village*. 1964.

Chibnall, A.C. *Sherington. Fiefs and Fields of a Buckinghamshire Village*. 1965.

Crutchley, J. *General View of the Agriculture in the County of Rutland*. 1794.

Darby, H.C., and Terrett, I.B. (eds.). *The Domesday Geography of Midland England*. 1954.

Davis, R.H.C. 'East Anglia and the Danelaw', *Trans. R. Hist. Soc.*, v, 1955.

Finberg, H.P.R. *Lucerna. Studies of Some Problems in the Early History of England*. 1964.

Gover, J.E.B., Mawer, A., and Stenton, F.M. *The Place-Names of Northamptonshire*. English Place-Name Society, x, 1933.

Grigg, D.B. *The Agricultural Revolution in South Lincolnshire*. 1966.

Hallam, H.E. 'Some Thirteenth Century Censuses', *Econ. Hist. Rev.*, x, 1958.
'The Fen Bylaws of Spalding and Pinchbeck', *L.A.A.S.*, x, 1963.
Settlement and Society: a Study of the Early Agrarian History of South Lincolnshire. 1965.

Hilton, R.H. *The Economic Development of some Leicestershire Estates in the Fourteenth and Fifteenth Centuries*. 1947.
'Kibworth Harcourt. A Merton College Manor in the Thirteenth and Fourteenth Centuries'. In Hoskins, W.G. (ed.). *Studies in Leicestershire Agrarian History*. 1949.
'Medieval Agrarian History', *V.C.H. Leicestershire*, II, 1954.

Homans, G. C. 'Terroirs Ordonnés et Champs Orientés: une Hypothèse sur le Village Anglais', *Annales d'Histoire Economique et Sociale*, VIII, 1936.

Hoskins, W.G. (ed.). *Essays in Leicestershire History*. 1950.
The Midland Peasant. 1957.

Page, F.M. *The Estates of Crowland Abbey. A Study in Manorial Organisation*. 1934.

Peacock, E. 'Notes from the Court Rolls of the Manor of Scotter', *Archaeologia*, XLVI, 1881.

Pettit, P.A.J. *The Royal Forests of Northamptonshire*. Northants. Rec. Soc., XXIII, 1958.

Sawyer, P.H. 'The Density of Danish Settlement in England', *Univ. Birm. Hist. Jnl.*, VI, 1958.

Stenton, D.M. *The Earliest Northamptonshire Assize Roll, A.D. 1202 and 1203*. Northants. Rec. Soc., v, 1930.

Stenton, F.M. *Types of Manorial Structure in the Northern Danelaw*. Oxford Studies in Social and Legal History, 1910.
Documents Illustrative of the Social and Economic History of the Danelaw from Various Collections. British Academy Records of the Social and Economic History of England and Wales, v, 1920.
Transcripts of Charters relating to the Gilbertine Houses of Sixle, Ormsby, Catley, Bullington, and Alvington. Lincs. Rec. Soc., XVIII, 1920.

Swales, T.H. 'The Parliamentary Enclosures of Lindsey, Parts I and II', *Reports and Papers of the Archit. and Arch. Soc. of Lincs. and Northants.*, XLII, 1935.

Tate, W.E. 'Inclosure Movements in Northamptonshire', *Northants. Past and Present*, I, 1949.

Thirsk, J. 'The Isle of Axholme before Vermuyden', *Agric. Hist. Rev.*, I, 1953.
English Peasant Farming. The Agrarian History of Lincolnshire from Tudor to Recent Times. 1957.

Thomas, C. (ed.). *Rural Settlement in Roman Britain*. C.B.A. Research Report, no. 7, 1966.

Wake, J. 'Communitas Villae', *Engl. Hist. Rev.*, XXXVII, 1932.

6. East Anglia

Allison, K.J. 'The Lost Villages of Norfolk', *Norfolk Archaeology*, XXXI, 1955.
'The Wool Supply and the Worsted Cloth Industry in Norfolk in the Sixteenth and Seventeenth Centuries'. University of Leeds Ph.D. thesis, 1955.

'The Sheep–Corn Husbandry of Norfolk in the Sixteenth and Seventeenth Centuries', *Agric. Hist. Rev.*, v, 1957.

'Flock Management in the Sixteenth and Seventeenth Centuries', *Econ. Hist. Rev.*, xi, 1958.

Almack, B. 'On the Agriculture of Norfolk', *Agricultural Journal*, v, 1845.

Bentham, J. *The History and Antiquities of the Conventual and Cathedral Church of Ely.* 1812.

Blomefield, F. *An Essay towards a Topographical History of Norfolk.* 1739.

Bullock, J.H. (ed.). *The Norfolk Portion of the Chartulary of the Priory of St. Pancras of Lewes.* Norfolk Rec. Soc., xii, 1939.

Burrell, E.D.R. 'An Historical Geography of the Suffolk Sandlings'. University of London M.Sc. thesis, 1959.

Corbett, W.J. 'Elizabethan Village Surveys', *Trans. R. Hist. Soc.*, xi, 1897.

Cunningham, W. (ed.). *Common Rights at Cottenham and Stretham in Cambridgeshire.* R. Hist. Soc., Camden Ser., x, 1910.

Darby, H.C. 'Domesday Woodland in East Anglia', *Antiquity*, xiv, 1934.

'The Domesday Geography of Cambridgeshire', *Camb. Arch. Soc.*, xxxvi, 1936.

The Medieval Fenland. 1940.

The Domesday Geography of Eastern England. 1952.

and Saltmarsh, J. 'The Infield–Outfield System on a Norfolk Manor', *Econ. Hist.*, iii, 1935.

Davenport, F.G. *The Economic Development of a Norfolk Manor, 1086–1565.* 1906.

Dodwell, B. 'Holdings and Inheritance in Medieval East Anglia', *Econ. Hist. Rev.*, xx, 1967.

Douglas, D.C. *The Social Structure of Medieval East Anglia.* Oxford Studies in Social and Legal History, ix, 1927.

Gooch, W. *A General View of the Agriculture of the County of Cambridge.* 1811.

Gross, E.J. *Chronicle of the Estates of Gonville and Caius College.* 1934.

Hamilton, N.E.S.A. (ed.). *Inquisitio Comitatus Cantabrigiensis, subjicitur Inquisitio Eliensis.* Royal Society of Literature, 1876.

Hart, W.H., and Lyons, P.A. (eds.). *Cartularium Monasterii de Rameseia, c. 1350*, Rolls Series, 1884–94.

Howard, H.F. *The Finances of St. John's College, Cambridge 1511–1926.* 1935.

Illingworth, W., and Caley, J. *Rotuli Hundredorum.* Records Commission, 1812–18.

Jonas, J. 'On the Farming of Cambridgeshire', *Jnl. R. Agric. Soc.*, vii, 1947.

Kent, N. *A General View of the Agricultural of Norfolk.* 1796.

Lavrovsky, J. 'Parliamentary Enclosure in the County of Suffolk', *Econ. Hist. Rev.*, vii, 1937.

Lunt, W.E. *The Valuation of Norwich.* 1926.

Maitland, F.W. *History of a Cambridgeshire Manor* (ed. H.A.L. Fisher), 1911.

and Baildon, W.P. (eds.). *Court Baron.* Seldon Soc., iv, 1891.

Marshall, W. *The Rural Economy of Norfolk.* 1795.

Miller, E. *The Abbey and Bishopric of Ely.* 1951.

Neilson, N. *Economic Conditions on the Manors of Ramsey Abbey.* 1898.

Page, F.M. *The Estates of Crowland Abbey.* 1934.

Palmer, W.M. *A History of the Parish of Borough Green.* Cambs. Arch. Soc., liv, 1939.

and Bullock, J.H. (eds.). *Documents Relating to Cambridgeshire Villages.* i–vi, 1926.

Postgate, M.R. 'The Historical Geography of Breckland, 1600–1840'. University of London M.A. thesis, 1960.

'The Open Fields of Cambridgeshire'. University of Cambridge Ph.D. thesis, 1964.

'The Field Systems of Breckland', *Agric. Hist. Rev.*, x, 1962.

Raynbird, H. 'On the Farming of Suffolk', *Jnl. R. Agric. Soc.*, viii, 1847.

Read, C.S. 'Recent Improvements in Norfolk Farming', *Jnl. R. Agric. Soc.*, XIX, 1958.
Riches, N. *The Agricultural Revolution in Norfolk.* 1937.
Simpson, A. 'The East Anglian Foldcourse; Some Queries', *Agric. Hist. Rev.*, VI, 1958.
Spufford, M. 'A Cambridgeshire Community. Chippenham from Settlement to Enclosure', *Occasional Papers, Dept. of Engl. Local Hist., Univ. of Leicester*, XX, 1965.
Stenton, F.M. (ed.). *Documents Illustrative of the Social and Economic History of the Danelaw.* 1920.
    Types of Manorial Structure in Northern Danelaw. Oxford Studies in Social and Legal History, 1910.
Tate, W.E. 'Cambridgeshire Field Systems, with a Handlist of Cambridgeshire Enclosure Acts and Awards', *Cambs. Arch. Soc.*, XL, 1939.
    'A Handlist of Suffolk Enclosure Acts and Awards', *Proc. Suff. Inst. Arch.*, XXV, 3, 1951.
Thirsk, J., and Imray, J. *Suffolk Farming in the Nineteenth Century.* Suffolk Rec. Soc., I, 1958.
Vancouver, C. *A General View of the Agriculture in the County of Cambridge.* 1794.
Wretts-Smith, M. 'Organisation of Farming at Crowland Abbey', *Jnl. Econ. and Business Hist.*, IV, 1932.
Young, A. 'A Fortnight's Tour in East Suffolk', *Annals of Agriculture*, XI, 1784.
    'A Week in Norfolk', *Annals of Agriculture*, XIX, 1792.
    A General View of the Agriculture of the County of Suffolk. 1797.
    A General View of the Agriculture of the County of Norfolk. 1804.

7. The Chiltern Hills and their Environs

Allison, K.J., Beresford, M.W., and Hurst, J.G. *The Deserted Villages of Oxfordshire*, 1965.
Allison, R. 'The Changing Geographical Landscape of South-West Essex from Saxon Times to 1600'. University of London M.A. thesis, 1958.
    'The Changing Landscape of South-West Essex from 1600 to 1850'. University of London Ph.D. thesis, 1964.
Ballard, A. 'The Open Fields of Fritwell'. *Oxfordshire Arch. Soc. Reports for 1907*, 1908.
    'Notes on the Open Fields of Oxfordshire', *Oxfordshire Arch. Soc. Reports for 1908*, 1909.
Beavington, F. 'Early Market Gardening in Bedfordshire', *Trans. Inst. Br. Geogr.*, XXVII, 1965.
Beresford, M.W. 'Glebe Terriers and Open-Field Buckinghamshire', *Records of Bucks.*, XV, 1947–52; XVI, 1953–60.
Burley, K.H. 'The Economic Development of Essex in the Later Seventeenth and Early Eighteenth Centuries'. University of London Ph.D. thesis, 1957.
Chibnall, A.C. *Sherington. Fiefs and Fields of a Buckinghamshire Village.* 1965.
Clark, G.N. 'Enclosure by Agreement at Marston near Oxford', *Engl. Hist. Rev.*, XLII, 1927.
Coles, R. 'Enclosures: Essex Agriculture, 1500–1900', *Essex Naturalist*, XXVI, 1937–8.
Coppock, J.T. 'The Agricultural Geography of the Chilterns, 1870–1951'. University of London Ph.D. thesis, 1960.
    'Farms and Fields in the Chilterns', *Erdkunde*, XIV, 1960.
Cox, E.A. 'An Agricultural Geography of Essex c. 1840'. University of London M.A. thesis, 1963.
Cracknell, B.E. *Canvey Island: the History of a Marshland Community.* 1959.
Cromarty, D. *The Fields of Saffron Walden in 1400.* Essex R. O., XLIII, 1966.
Darby, H.C. *The Domesday Geography of Eastern England.* 1952.
    and Campbell, E.M.J. (eds.). *The Domesday Geography of South-East England.* 1962.

Davies, R. *General View of the Agriculture of the County of Oxford.* 1794.

Elvey, E.M. *A Hand-List of Buckinghamshire Estate Maps.* Bucks. Record Soc. Lists and Indices, II, 1963.

Emmison, F.G. *Types of Open-Field Parishes in the Midlands.* Historical Association, CVIII, 1937.

(ed.), *Catalogue of Maps in the Essex Record Office, 1566–1855.* Essex R. O. III, 1947; *First Supplement,* Essex R. O., XVI, 1952; *Second Supplement,* Essex R. O., XXXIX, 1964.

Erith, E.J. 'The Strip System of Cultivation in Buckhurst Hill in the Thirteenth Century', *Essex Review,* LVII, 1948.

Fisher, F.J. 'The Development of the London Food Market, 1540–1640', *Econ. Hist. Rev.,* V, 1934–5.

Fisher, J.L. 'Harlow in the Middle Ages', *Essex Review,* XLVI, 1937.

Fowler, G.H. *Four Pre-Enclosure Village Maps.* Bedfordshire Hist. Rec. Soc. Quarto Memoirs, II, 1928–36.

Godber, J. (ed.). *The Cartulary of Newnham Priory.* Bedfordshire Hist. Rec. Soc., XLIII, 1963–4.

Gretton, R.H. 'Historical Notes on the Lot-Meadow Customs at Yarnton, Oxon.', *Economic Journal,* XXII, 1912.

Harrison, J., Mead, W.R., and Pannett, D.J. 'A Midland Ridge-and-furrow Map', *Geogrl. Jnl.,* CXXXI, 1965.

Harvey, P.D.A. *A Medieval Oxfordshire Village. Cuxham: 1240 to 1400.* 1965.

Havinden, M.A. 'Agricultural Progress in Open-Field Oxfordshire', *Agric. Hist. Rev.,* IX, 1961.

Household and Farm Inventories in Oxfordshire, 1550–1590. Oxfordshire Rec. Soc., XLIV, 1965.

Head, J.F. *Early Man in South Buckinghamshire.* 1955.

Hull, F. 'Agriculture and Rural Society in Essex, 1560–1640.' University of London Ph.D. thesis, 1950.

Lambert, A.M. 'Oxfordshire about 1800 A.D.: a study in Human Geography'. University of London Ph.D. thesis, 1953.

Mansfield, A.J. 'The Historical Geography of the Woodlands of the Southern Chilterns, 1600–1947'. University of London M.Sc. thesis, 1952.

Marshall, L.M. (ed.). *The Rural Population of Bedfordshire, 1671 to 1921.* Bedfordshire Hist. Rec. Soc., XVI, 1934.

Martin, A.F., and Steel, R. W. (eds.). *The Oxford Region.* 1954.

Mead, W.R. 'Ridge and Furrow in Buckinghamshire', *Geogrl. Jnl.,* CXX, 1954.

Mowat, J. L. G. *Sixteen Old Maps of Properties in Oxfordshire.* 1888.

Munby, L.M. (ed.). *Hertfordshire Population Statistics 1563–1801.* 1964.

Newton, K.C. *Medieval Essex from the Conquest to the Eve of the Reformation.* Essex Record Office, XXXVI, 1962.

Nichols, J.F. 'Custodia Essexae: a Study of the Conventual Property Held by the Priory of Christ Church Canterbury in the Counties of Essex, Suffolk and Norfolk'. University of London Ph.D. thesis, 1930.

'Farming Operations in the Fourteenth Century', *Southend-on-Sea and District Antiqu. and Hist. Soc. Trans.,* II, n.s., 1930.

Prince, H.C. 'Parkland in the Chilterns', *Geogrl. Rev.,* XLIX, 1959.

Reaney, P.H. 'The Face of Essex. A Study in Place-names', *Essex Review,* LVIII, 1949.

Roden, D. 'Studies in Chiltern Field Systems'. University of London Ph.D. thesis, 1965.

'Field Systems in Ibstone, a Township of the South-west Chilterns, during the later Middle Ages', *Records of Bucks.,* XVIII, 1966.

'Inheritance Customs and Succession to Land in the Chiltern Hills in the Thirteenth and Early Fourteenth Centuries', *Jnl. Brit. Stud.*, VII, 1967.
'Woodland and its Management in the Medieval Chilterns', *Forestry*, XLI, 1968.
'Demesne Farming in the Chiltern Hills', *Agric. Hist. Rev.*, XVII, 1969.
'Enclosure in the Chiltern Hills', *Geogr. Annlr.*, LII, 1969.
'Fragmentation of Farms and Fields in the Chiltern Hills in the Thirteenth Century and Later', *Mediaeval Studies*, XXXI, 1969.
'Changing Settlement in the Chiltern Hills Before 1850', *Folk Life*, VIII, 1970.
and Baker, A.R.H. 'Field Systems of the Chiltern Hills and of Parts of Kent from the Late Thirteenth to the Early Seventeenth Century', *Trans. Inst. Br. Geogr.*, XXXVIII, 1966.
Salter, H.E. (ed.). *The Thame Cartulary*. Oxfordshire Rec. Ser., XXV-VI, 1947-8.
Steer, F.W. (ed.). *Farm and Cottage Inventories of Mid-Essex, 1635-1749*. Essex Record Office, VIII, 1950.
Stone, T. *General View of the Agriculture of the County of Bedford*. 1794.
Tate, W.E. 'A Handlist of Hertfordshire Enclosure Acts and Awards', *East Herts. Arch. Soc. Trans.*, XII, 1945-9.
A Hand-List of Buckinghamshire Enclosure Acts and Awards. 1946.
Vinogradoff, P. 'An Illustration of the Continuity of the Openfield System', *Quarterly Journal of Economics*, XXII, 1908.
Vollans, E.C. 'The Evolution of Farm-Lands in the Central Chilterns in the Twelfth and Thirteenth Centuries', *Trans. Inst. Br. Geogr.*, XXVI, 1959.
Walker, D. *General View of the Agriculture of the County of Hertford*. 1795.
Young, A. *General View of the Agriculture of Hertfordshire*. 1804.
General View of the Agriculture of the County of Essex. 1807.
Young, A. 'Bledlow: I. Land Tenure and the Three-Field System', *Records of Bucks.*, XVII, 1961-6.

8. Southeast England

Baker, A.R.H. 'Some Early Kentish Estate Maps and a Note on their Portrayal of Field Boundaries', *Arch. Cant.*, LXXVII, 1962.
'The Field Systems of Kent'. University of London Ph.D. thesis, 1963.
'The Field System of an East Kent Parish (Deal)', *Arch. Cant.*, LXXVIII, 1963.
'Open Fields and Partible Inheritance on a Kent Manor', *Econ. Hist. Rev.*, XVII, 1964
'Field Patterns in Seventeenth Century Kent', *Geography*, L, 1965.
'Some Fields and Farms in Medieval Kent', *Arch. Cant.*, LXXX, 1965.
'The Kentish *iugum*: its Relationship to Soils at Gillingham', *Engl. Hist. Rev.*, LX XXI 1966.
'Field Systems in the Vale of Holmesdale', *Agric. Hist. Rev.*, XIV, 1966.
Bishop, T.A.M. 'The Rotation of Crops at Westerham, 1297-1350', *Econ. Hist. Rev.*, IX, 1938.
Boys, J. *General View of the Agriculture of the County of Kent*. 1796.
General View of the Agriculture of the County of Kent. 2nd edn, 1813.
Brandon, P.F. 'Arable Farming in a Sussex Scarp-foot Parish During the Late Middle Ages', *Sussex Arch. Coll.*, C, 1962.
'The Common Lands and Wastes of Sussex'. University of London Ph.D. thesis, 1963.
'Medieval Clearances in the East Sussex Weald', *Trans. Inst. Br. Geogr.*, XLVIII, 1969.
'Demesne Arable Farming in Coastal Sussex During the Later Middle Ages', *Agric. Hist. Rev.*, XIX, 1971.
Brent, J.A. 'Alciston Manor in the Later Middle Ages', *Sussex Arch. Coll.*, CVI, 1968.
Carlin, M.N. 'Christ Church, Canterbury, and its Lands, from the Beginning of the

Priorate of Thomas Chillenden to the Dissolution (1391–1540)'. University of Oxford D.Phil. thesis, 1970.

Chalklin, C.W. 'The Rural Economy of a Kentish Wealden Parish, 1650–1750', *Agric. Hist. Rev.*, X, 1962.

Seventeenth-Century Kent. A Social and Economic History. 1965.

Churchill, I.J., Griffin, R., and Hardman, F.W. (eds.). 'Calendar of Kent Feet of Fines to the End of Henry III's Reign', *Kent Records*, XV, 1956.

Coleman, D.C. 'The Economy of Kent Under the Later Stuarts'. University of London Ph.D. thesis, 1951.

Cornwall, J. 'Farming in Sussex, 1560–1640', *Sussex Arch. Coll.*, XCII, 1954.

'Agricultural Improvement, 1560–1640', *Sussex Arch. Coll.*, XCVIII, 1960.

Darby, H.C., and Campbell, E.M.J. (eds.). *The Domesday Geography of South-East England.* 1962.

Du Boulay, F.R.H. 'Late-continued Demesne Farming at Otford', *Arch. Cant.*, LXXIII., 1959.

'Denns, Droving and Danger', *Arch. Cant.*, LXXVI, 1961.

Medieval Bexley, 1961.

'Gavelkind and Knight's Fee in Medieval Kent', *Engl. Hist. Rev.*, LXXVII, 1962.

'A Rentier Economy in the Later Middle Ages: the Archbishopric of Canterbury', *Econ. Hist. Rev.*, XVI, 1963–4.

'Who Were Farming the Demesnes at the End of the Middle Ages?', *Econ. Hist. Rev.*, XVII, 1964–5.

The Lordship of Canterbury. An Essay on Medieval Society. 1966.

Elton, C.I. *The Tenures of Kent.* 1867.

Everitt, A.M. 'The County Committee of Kent in the Civil War', *Occasional Papers, Dept. of Engl. Local Hist., Univ. of Leicester*, IX, 1957.

Fisher, F.J. 'The Development of the London Food Market, 1540–1640', *Econ. Hist. Rev.*, V, 1934–5.

Glasscock, R.E. 'The Distribution of Lay Wealth in Kent, Surrey and Sussex, in the Early Fourteenth Century', *Arch. Cant.*, LXXX, 1965.

Gray, H.L. *English Field Systems.* Cambridge, Mass., 1915.

Gulley, J.L.M. 'The Wealden Landscape in the Early Seventeenth Century and its Antecedents'. University of London Ph.D. thesis, 1960.

Hanley, H.A., and Chalklin, C.W. 'The Kent Lay Subsidy of 1334/5', *Kent Records*, XVIII, 1964.

Harrison, E. 'The Court Rolls and Other Records of the Manor of Ightham', *Arch. Cant.*, XLVIII, 1936.

'Some Records of Ightham Parish', *Arch. Cant.*, LIII, 1940.

Hull, F. 'The Custumal of Kent', *Arch. Cant.*, LXXII, 1958.

Jolliffe, J.E.A. *Pre-Feudal England: The Jutes.* 1933.

Jordan, W.K. 'Social Institutions in Kent, 1480–1660', *Arch. Cant.*, LXXV, 1961.

Knocker, H.W. 'The Evolution of the Holmesdale. No. 3. The Manor of Sundridge', *Arch. Cant.*, XLIV, 1932.

Lambarde, W. *A Perambulation of Kent.* 1576.

Lodge, E.C. 'The Account Book of a Kentish Estate, 1616–1704'. *Records of Social and Economic History*, VI, 1927.

Lot, F. 'Le Jugum, le Manse et les Exploitations Agricoles de la France Moderne' in *Mélanges Offerts à Henri Pirenne*, I, 1926.

Marshall, W. *Rural Economy of the Southern Counties.* 1798.

Melling, E. (ed.). 'Aspects of Agriculture and Industry', *Kentish Sources*, III, 1961.

Melville, A.M.M. 'The Pastoral Custom and Local Wool Trade of Medieval Sussex, 1085–1485'. University of London M.A. thesis, 1931.

Mingay, G.E. 'Estate Management in Eighteenth-Century Kent', *Agric. Hist. Rev.*, IV, 1956.

Moore, J.S. 'Laughton: a Study in the Evolution of the Wealden Landscape', *Occasional Papers, Dept. of Engl. Local Hist., Univ. of Leicester*, XIX, 1965.

Muhlfeld, H.E. *A Survey of the Manor of Wye*. Columbia, 1933.

Neilson, N. *The Cartulary and Terrier of the Priory of Bilsington, Kent*. 1920.
 'Custom and the Common Law in Kent', *Harvard Law Review*, XXXVIII, 1924–5.

Nightingale, M.D. 'Some Evidence of Open Field Agriculture in Kent'. University of Oxford B.Litt. thesis, 1952.
 'Ploughing and Field Shape', *Antiquity*, XXVII, 1953.

Pelham, R.A. 'Studies in the Historical Geography of Medieval Sussex', *Sussex Arch. Coll.*, LXXII, 1931.
 'Some Medieval Sources for the Study of Historical Geography', *Geogr.*, XVII, 1932.
 'Some Aspects of the East Kent Wool Trade in the Thirteenth Century', *Arch. Cant.*, XLIV, 1932.
 'The Relations of Soils to Grain-Growing in Kent in the Thirteenth Century', *Empire Journal of Experimental Agriculture*, I, 1933.
 'The Agricultural Geography of the Chichester Estates in 1388', *Sussex Arch. Coll.*, LXXVIII, 1937.

Ray, J.E. 'Life on a Sussex Manor in the Middle Ages', *The South-Eastern Naturalist and Antiquary*, LI, 1946.

Reaney, P.H. 'Place-names and Early Settlement in Kent', *Arch. Cant.*, LXXVI, 1961.

Slater, G. 'Social and Economic History', *V.C.H. (Kent)*, III, 1932.

Smith, A. 'A Geographical Study of Agriculture on the Kentish Manors of Canterbury Cathedral Priory, 1272–1379'. University of Liverpool M.A. thesis, 1961.
 'Regional Differences in Crop Production in Medieval Kent', *Arch. Cant.*, LXXVIII, 1963.
 'Medieval Field Systems on Some Kent Manors' in R.W. Steel and R. Lawton (eds.). *Liverpool Essays in Geography. A Jubilee Collection*. 1967.

Smith, R.A.L. 'Marsh Embankment and Sea Defence in Medieval Kent', *Econ. Hist. Rev.*, X, 1939–40.
 Canterbury Cathedral Priory. 1943.

Tate, W.E. 'A Hand-list of English Enclosure Acts and Awards. Part 17. Open Fields, Commons and Enclosures in Kent', *Arch. Cant.*, LVI, 1943.
 'Sussex Inclosure Acts and Awards', *Sussex Arch. Coll.*, LXXXIII, 1949.

Virgoe, R. 'Some Ancient Indictments in the King's Bench referring to Kent, 1450–52', *Kent Records*, XVIII, 1964.

Ward, G. 'A Note on the Yokes at Otford', *Arch. Cant.*, XLII, 1930.
 The Belgic Britons. Men of Kent in B.C. 55. 1960.

Wilson, A.E. 'Farming in Sussex in the Middle Ages', *Sussex Arch. Coll.*, XCVII, 1959.

Wooldridge, S.W., and Linton, D.L. 'The Loam-terrains of Southeast England and their Relation to its Early History', *Antiquity*, VII, 1933.
 'Some Aspects of the Saxon Settlement in Southeast England Considered in Relation to their Geographical Background', *Geography*, XX, 1935.

Yates, E.M. 'History in a Map', *Geogrl. Jnl.*, CXXVI, 1960.
 'A Study of Settlement Patterns', *Field Studies*, I, 1961.
 'The Nonae Rolls and Soil Fertility', *Sussex Notes and Queries*, XV, 1962.
 'Dark Age and Medieval Settlement on the Edge of Wastes and Forests', *Field Studies*, II, 1965.

C. WALES

1. North Wales

Bowen, I. *The Statutes of Wales*. 1809.

Davies, E. 'Sheep Farming in Upland Wales', *Geography*, xx, 1935.

Davies, R.R. 'The Twilight of Welsh Law', *History*, LI, 1966.

Dodd, A.H. 'The Enclosure Movement in North Wales', *Bull. Bd. Celtic Stud.*, III, 1926–7.

The Industrial Revolution in North Wales. 1933.

Edwards, J.G. *Hywel Dda and the Welsh Lawbooks*. 1928.

'The Historical Study of the Welsh Law Books', *Trans. R. Hist. Soc.*, XII, 1962.

Ellis, T.P. *Welsh Tribal Law and Custom in the Middle Ages*. 1926.

Evans, B.M. 'Settlement and Agriculture in North Wales, 1536–1670'. University of Cambridge Ph.D. thesis, 1965.

Evans, E. 'Arwystli and Cyfeiliog in the Sixteenth Century'. University of Wales M.A. thesis, 1939.

'Arwystli and Cyfeiliog in the Sixteenth Century: an Elizabethan Inquisition', *Montgomeryshire Collections*, LI, 1951.

Hughes, R.E. 'Environment and Human Settlement in the Commote of Arllechwedd Isaf', *Trans. Caernarvonshire Hist. Soc.*, II, 1940.

Jones, G.R.J. 'Some Medieval Rural Settlements in North Wales', *Trans. Inst. Br. Geogr.*, XIX, 1953.

'The Distribution of Medieval Settlement in Anglesey', *Anglesey Antiqu. Soc. Trans.*, 1955.

'Medieval open fields and associated settlement patterns in North-West Wales', *Géographie et Histoire Agraire. Actes du Colloque International de Nancy*, 1957. *Annales de l'Est*, Memoire XXI, 1959.

'The Pattern of Settlement on the Welsh Border', *Agric. Hist. Rev.*, VIII, 1960.

'Settlement Patterns in Anglo-Saxon England', *Antiquity*, XXXV, 1961.

'The Tribal System in Wales: A Re-assessment in the Light of Settlement Studies', *Welsh History Review*, I, 1961–2.

'Die Entwicklung der ländlichen Besiedlung in Wales', *Zeitschrift für Agrargeschichte und Agrarsoziologie*, X, 1962.

'Early Settlement in Arfon: the setting of Tre'r Ceiri', *Trans. Caernarvonshire Hist. Soc.*, XXIV, 1963.

'The Distribution of Bond Settlements in North-West Wales', *Welsh Hist. Rev.*, II, 1964.

'The Llanynys Quillets: a Measure of Landscape Transformation in North Wales', *Denbighshire Hist. Soc. Trans.*, IX, 1964.

'Rural Settlement in Anglesey', in Eyre, S.R., and Jones, G.R.J. (eds.). *Geography as Human Ecology*. 1966.

Jones Pierce, T. 'Some Tendencies in the Agrarian History of Caernarvonshire during the Later Middle Ages', *Trans. Caernarvonshire Hist. Soc.*, I, 1938.

'An Anglesey Crown Rental of the Sixteenth Century', *Bull. Bd. Celtic Stud.*, X, 1939–41.

'Notes on the History of Rural Caernarvonshire in the Reign of Elizabeth', *Trans. Caernarvonshire Hist. Soc.*, II, 1940.

'Pastoral and Agricultural Settlements in Early Wales', *Geogr. Annlr.*, XLIII, 1961.

'The Laws of Wales – The Last Phase', *Transactions Honourable Society of Cymmrodorion*, 1963.

Leland, J. *The Itinerary in Wales*. ed. Smith, L.T. 1906.

Lewis, E.A., and Davies, J.C. (eds.). *Records of the Court of Augmentations relating to Wales and Monmouthshire*. 1954.

Lewis, T. (ed.). 'The Black Book of Chirk', *Zeitschrift für Celtische Philologie*, xx, 1933.

Lloyd, J.E. *A History of Wales*. 1911.

Norden, J. *Survey of Oswestry in 1602* in *The Lordship of Oswestry*. ed. Slack, W.J. 1951.

Owen, D.H. 'The Lordship of Denbigh, 1284–1425'. University of Wales Ph.D. thesis, 1967.

Palmer, A.N. *A History of Ancient Tenures of Land in the Marches of North Wales*. 1885. *The Town, Fields and Folk of Wrexham in the Time of James the First*. 1895.

and Owen, E. *A History of Ancient Tenures of Land in North Wales and the Marches*. 2nd edn, 1910.

Rowlandson, T. 'The Agriculture of North Wales', *Jnl. R. Agric. Soc. Engl.*, VII, 1846.

Seebohm, F. *The Tribal System in Wales*. 1895.

Sylvester, D. 'The Rural Landscape of Eastern Montgomeryshire', *Montgomeryshire Collections*, LIV, 1955.

Thomas, C. 'The Evolution of Rural Settlement and Land Tenure in Merioneth'. University of Wales Ph.D. thesis, 1965.

'Enclosure and the Rural Landscape of Merioneth in the Sixteenth Century', *Trans. Inst. Br. Geogr.*, XLII, 1967.

Thomas, D. *Agriculture in Wales during the Napoleonic Wars*. 1963.

Thomas, J.G. 'The Distribution of Commons in Part of Arwystli at the Time of Enclosure', *Montgomeryshire Collections*, LIV, 1955.

'Some Enclosure Patterns in Central Wales', *Geography*, XLII, 1957.

Vinogradoff, P., and Morgan, F.W. (eds.). *Survey of the Honour of Denbigh, 1334*. 1914.

Williams, G. *The Welsh Church from Conquest to Reformation*. 1962.

2. *South Wales*

Bradney, J. *History of Monmouthshire*. 1929.

Cambrensis, Giraldus (ed. Williams, W.W.). *The Itinerary through Wales and the Description of Wales*. 1908.

Corbett, J.S. *Glamorgan*. 1925.

Davies, M. 'Field Patterns in the Vale of Glamorgan', *Trans. Cardiff. Nat. Soc.*, LXXXIV, 1954–5.

'The Open Fields of Laugharne', *Geography*, XL, 1955.

'Common Lands in South-East Monmouthshire', *Trans. Cardiff Nat. Soc.*, LXXV, 1955–6.

'Rhosili Open Field and Related South Wales Field Patterns', *Agric. Hist. Rev.*, IV, 1956.

Davies, W. *General View of the Agriculture and Domestic Economy of South Wales*. 1815.

Emery, F.V. 'West Glamorgan Farming, circa 1580–1620', *Nat. Lib. Wales Jnl.*, IX, 1956 and X, 1957.

Evans, J. *Letters Written During a Tour Through South Wales*. 1804.

Fenton, R. *A Historical Tour Through Pembrokeshire*. 1811.

Finberg, H.P.R. *Gloucestershire*. 1955.

Francis, G.G. 'The Lordship of Gower', *Arch. Camb.* (Supp. vols.), 1861, 1864, and 1870.

Hassall, G. *General View of the Agriculture of the County of Monmouth*. 1812.

Howells, B.E. 'Pembrokeshire Farming, 1580–1620', *Nat. Lib. Wales Jnl.*, IX, 1955–6.

'The Distribution of Customary Acres in South Wales', *Nat. Lib. Wales Jnl.*, XV, 1967.

Jeffreys Jones, T.I. 'The Enclosure Movement in South Wales in the Tudor and Early
    Stuart Periods'. University of Wales Ph.D. thesis, 1936.
    'The Court Leet Presentments of the Town, Borough and Liberty of St. Clears',
    Bull. Bd. Celtic Stud., XIII, 1948.
Jones, E.H.S. The Last Invasion of Britain. 1950.
Lewis, E.A., and Conway Davies, J. Records of the Court of Augmentations Relating to
    Wales and Monmouthshire. 1954.
Lloyd, T. General View of the Agriculture of the County of Cardigan. 1794.
Malkin, B.H. The Scenery, Antiquities and Biography of South Wales. 1807.
Merrick, R. A Booke of Glamorganshire's Antiquities, 1578. (ed. Corbett, J.A.) 1887.
Nash-Williams, V.E. 'New Roman Site at Redwick', Bull. Bd. Celtic Stud., XIV, 1951.
Owen, G. The Description of Penbrokeshire, 1603. Cymmrodorion Rec. Ser., 1892.
Owen, H. A Calendar of the Public Records relating to Pembrokeshire. Cymmrodorion
    Rec. Ser. I–III, 1911, 1914 and 1918.
Pugh, T.B. The Marcher Lordships of South Wales, 1415–1536. 1963.
Rees, W. South Wales and the March, 1284–1415: A Social and Agrarian History. 1924.
    'Medieval Gwent', Br. Arch. Ass. J., XXXV, 1930.
    A Survey of the Duchy of Lancaster Lordships in Wales, 1609–13. 1953.
    The Great Forest of Brecknock. 1966.
Richard, A.J. 'Castles, Boroughs and Religious Houses', in Lloyd, J.E. (ed.). A History
    of Carmarthenshire. 1935.
Roderick, A.J., and Rees, W. 'Ministers' Accounts for the Lordships of Abergavenny,
    Grosmont, Skenfrith and White Castle', S. Wales and Monmouth Rec. Soc., II,
    1950; III, 1954; IV, 1957.
Sylvester, D. 'The Common Fields of the Coastlands of Gwent', Agric. Hist. Rev., VI,
    1958.
Williams, W. John Frost: a Study in Chartism. 1939.
Willis-Bund, J.W. (ed.). The Black Book of St. David's. Cymmrodorion Rec. Ser., V,
    1902.

D. SCOTLAND

Aiton, W. General View of the Agriculture of Bute. 1816.
Barrow, G.W.S. 'Rural Settlement in Central and Eastern Scotland', Scott. Stud., VI,
    1962.
Caird, J.B. 'The Making of the Scottish Rural Landscape', Scott. Geogr. Mag., LXXX,
    1964.
Carmichael, A. 'Grazing and Agrestic Customs of the Outer Hebrides', Celt. Rev., X,
    1941.
Fairhurst, H. 'Scottish Clachans', Scott. Geogr. Mag., LXXVI, 1960.
    'The Rural Settlement Pattern of Scotland, with Special Reference to the West and
    North', in Steel, R.W., and Lawton, R. (eds.). Liverpool Essays in Geography. 1967.
    and Petrie, G. 'Scottish Clachans II: Lix and Rosal', Scott. Geogr. Mag., LXXVI, 1960.
Fenton, A. 'The Rural Economy of East Lothian in the Seventeenth and Eighteenth
    Centuries', Trans. East Lothian Antiqu. Field Nat. Soc., IX, 1963.
Forsyth, R. The Beauties of Scotland. 5 vols., 1805–8.
Franklin, T.B. A History of Scottish Farming. 1951.
Gailey, R.A. 'The Role of Sub-letting in the Crofting Community', Scott. Stud., V,
    1961.
    'Mobility of Tenants on a Highland Estate in the Early Nineteenth Century', Scott.
    Hist. Rev., XL, 1961.
    'The Evolution of Highland Rural Settlement', Scott. Stud., VI, 1962.

'Agrarian Improvement and the Development of Enclosure in the Southwest Highlands of Scotland', *Scott. Hist. Rev.*, XLII, 1963.

Geddes, A. 'The Changing Landscape of the Lothians, 1600–1800, as Revealed by Old Estate Plans', *Scott. Geogr. Mag.*, LIV, 1938.

Grant, I.F. 'The Highland Openfield System', *Geographical Teacher*, XIII, 1926.
The Social and Economic Development of Scotland before 1603. 1930.

Gray, M. 'The Abolition of Runrig in the Highlands of Scotland', *Econ. Hist. Rev.*, V, 1952.
The Highland Economy. 1956.

Handley, J.E. *Scottish Farming in the Eighteenth Century*. 1953.

Headrick, J. *View of the Agriculture of the Isle of Arran*. 1807.

Jirlow, R., and Whitaker, I. 'The Plough in Scotland', *Scott. Stud.*, I, 1957.

Lebon, J.H.G. 'The Process of Enclosure in the Western Lowlands', *Scott. Geogr. Mag.*, LXII, 1946.

Leslie, W. *General View of Agriculture in the Counties of Nairn and Moray*. 1811.

Loch, J. *An Account of the Improvements on the Estates of the Marquess of Stafford*. 1820.

McKerral, A. 'Ancient Denominations of Agricultural Land in Scotland', *Proc. Soc. Antiqu. Scotl.*, LXXVIII, 1943.
'The Lesser Land and Administrative Divisions in Celtic Scotland', *Proc. Soc. Antiqu. Scotl.*, LXXXV, 1960.

MacSween, M.D. 'Transhumance in North Skye', *Scott. Geogr. Mag.*, LXXV, 1959.

Matley, I.M. 'The Origin of Infield–Outfield Agriculture in Scotland: the linguistic evidence', *Prof. Geogr.*, XVIII, 1966.

Miller, R. 'Land by Summer Shielings', *Scott. Stud.*, XI, 1967.

O'Dell, A.C. 'A View of Scotland in the Middle of the Eighteenth Century', *Scott. Geogr. Mag.*, LXIX, 1953.

Owen, T.M. 'The Role of the Township in an Hebridean Crofting Community', *Gwerin*, II, 1958–9.

Robertson, J. *General View of the Agriculture of Perth*. 1799.
General View of the Agriculture in the County of Inverness. 1808.

Robertson, G. *A General View of the Agriculture of Kincardineshire*. 1813.

Skene, W.F. *Celtic Scotland*. 1880.

Smith, J. *General View of the Agriculture of the County of Argyll*. 1798.

Storrie, M.C. 'Landholdings and Settlement Evolution in West Highland Scotland', *Geogr. Annlr.*, XLVII, 1965.

Symon, J.A. *Scottish Farming Past and Present*. 1959.

Third, B.M.W. 'The Significance of Scottish Estate Plans and Associated Documents', *Scott. Stud.*, I, 1957.

Webster, J. *General View of the Agriculture of Galloway*. 1794.

Whittington, G., and Soulsby, J.A. 'A Preliminary Report on an Investigation into Pit Place-names', *Scott. Geogr. Mag.*, LXXXIV, 1968.

Whyte, A., and MacFarlane, D. *General View of the Agriculture of Dunbarton*. 1811.

Wight, A. *Present State of Husbandry in Scotland*. 1778–84.

Wilson, J. 'Farming in Aberdeenshire Ancient and Modern', *Trans. Highland Agric. Soc. Scotl.*, XIV, 5th Ser., 1902.

E. IRELAND

Aalen, F.H.A. 'Enclosures in Eastern Ireland', *Ir. Geogr.*, V, 1965.

Beckett, J.C. *The Making of Modern Ireland, 1603–1923*. 1966.

Brooks, E.St J. 'Fourteenth Century Monastic Estates in Meath', *Jnl. R. Soc. Antiqu. Ir.*, LXXXIII, 1953.

Buchanan, R.H. 'The Barony of Lecale, Co. Down'. Queen's University Belfast Ph.D. thesis, 1968.

Jones, E., and McCourt, D. (eds.). *Man and His Habitat. Essays Presented to Emyr Estyn Evans.* 1971.

Connell, K.H. *The Population of Ireland, 1750–1845.* 1950.

'The Colonisation of the Waste Lands in Ireland', *Econ. Hist. Rev.*, III, 1950–1.

Crawford, W.H. 'The Woodlands of the Manor of Brownlow's-Derry, North Armagh, in the Seventeenth and Eighteenth Centuries', *Ulster Folklife*, X, 1964.

Curtis, E. 'A Rental of the Manor of Lisronagh, 1333', *Proc. R. Ir. Acad.*, XLIII, 1935–37.

Duignan, M. 'Irish Agriculture in Early Historic Times', *Jnl. R. Soc. Antiqu. Ir.*, LXXIV, 1944.

Evans, E.E. 'Some Survivals of the Irish Openfield System, *Geography*, XXIV, 1939.

'Donegal Survivals', *Antiquity*, XIII, 1939.

Irish Heritage. 1942.

Irish Folk Ways. 1957.

'The Peasant and the Past', *Advmt. Sci.*, LXVIII, 1960.

Flatrès, P. *Géographie Rurale de Quatre Contrées Celtiques.* Rennes, 1957.

Foster, T.C. *Letters on the Condition of the People of Ireland.* 1846.

Frazer, R. *A Statistical Account of the County of Wicklow.* 1801.

Graham, J.M. 'Transhumance in Ireland', *Advmt. Sci.*, X, 1953.

'Transhumance in Ireland'. Queen's University Belfast Ph.D. thesis, 1954.

Hayes-McCoy, G.A. *Ulster and other Irish Maps c. 1600.* 1964.

Hill, G. *The Plantation of Ulster.* 1877.

Johnson, J.H. 'Studies of Irish Rural Settlement', *Geog. Rev.*, XLVIII, 1958.

'The Development of the Rural Settlement Pattern of Ireland', *Geogr. Annlr.*, XLIII, 1961.

Jones Hughes, T. 'Society and Settlement in Nineteenth Century Ireland', *Ir. Geog.*, V, 1965.

Leister, I. *Das Werden der Agrarlandschaft in der Grafschaft Tipperary (Irland).* Marburg, 1963.

McCourt, D. 'The Rundale System in Ireland'. Queen's University Belfast Ph.D. thesis, 1950.

'The Infield–Outfield System in Ireland', *Econ. Hist. Rev.*, VII, 1954–5.

'The Rundale System in Donegal, its Distribution and Decline', *Donegal Annual*, III, 1955.

'Surviving Openfield in County Londonderry', *Ulster Folklife*, IV, 1958.

McCracken, E. 'The Woodlands of Ireland c. 1600', *Ir. Hist. Stud.*, XI, 1959.

The Irish Woods Since Tudor Times. 1971.

McParlin, J. *Statistical Survey of the County of Donegal.* 1802.

Mason, W. Shaw. *Parochial Survey: A Statistical or Parochial Survey of Ireland.* 1814.

Mills, J. 'Tenants and Agriculture near Dublin in the Fourteenth Century', *Jnl. R. Soc. Antiqu. Ir.*, XXI, 1890–1.

Moryson, F. *The Commonwealth of Ireland: The Itinerary* (1600). 1907.

O'Brien, G. *The Economic History of Ireland in the Seventeenth Century.* 1919.

O'Buachalla, L. 'Tenant Farmers of the Barrymore Estate, 1768', *Jnl. Cork Hist. and Arch. Soc.*, LI, 1946.

O'Loan, J. 'Land Reclamation Down the Years', *Journal of the* (Irish) *Department of Agriculture*, LV, 1959.

'The Manor of Cloncurry, County Kildare', *Jnl.* (Irish) *Dept. Agric.*, LVIII, 1962.

'A History of Early Irish Farming', *Jnl.* (Irish) *Dept. Agric.*, LX, 1963; LXI, 1964; LXII, 1965.

O'Riordain, S.P. 'Excavations at Cush, County Limerick', *Proc. R. Ir. Acad.*, XLV, 1940.

'Lough Gur Excavations: Neolithic and Bronze Age Houses on Knockadoon', *Proc. R. Ir. Acad.*, LVI, 1954.

Otway-Ruthven, J. 'The Organisation of Anglo-Irish Agriculture in the Middle Ages', *Jnl. R. Soc. Antiqu. Ir.*, LXXXI, 1951.

'The Character of Norman Settlement in Ireland', *Irish Hist. Stud.*, V, 1965.

Proudfoot, V.B. 'Settlement and Economy in Co. Down from the Late Bronze Age to the Anglo-Norman Invasion'. Queen's University Belfast Ph.D. thesis, 1957.

'Ancient Irish Field Systems', *Advmt. Sci.*, LVI, 1958.

'Clachans in Ireland', *Gwerin*, II, 1959.

'The Economy of the Irish Rath', *Medieval Archaeology*, V, 1961.

Sampson, G.V. *Statistical Survey of the County of Londonderry.* 1802.

Simington, R.C. *The Civil Survey*, A.D. *1654–56, County of Tipperary.* 1931–4.

Stephens, N. and Glasscock, R.E. (eds.). *Irish Geographical Studies. In Honour of E. Estyn Evans.* 1971.

Symons, L.J. (ed.). *Land Utilisation in Northern Ireland.* 1963.

Tighe, W. *Kilkenny: Statistical Observations, County of Kilkenny.* 1802.

Uhlig, H. 'Old Hamlets with Infield and Outfield Systems in Western and Central Europe', *Geogr. Annlr.*, XLIII, 1961.

Vallency, C. *Collecteana de Rebus Hibernicis.* 1770.

Wakefield, E. *An Account of Ireland, Statistical and Political.* 1812.

Waterman, D.M. 'Excavations at Lismahon', *Medieval Archaeology*, III, 1959.

Weld, I. *A Statistical Survey of County Roscommon.* 1832.

Young, A. *A Tour in Ireland Made in the Years 1776, 1777 and 1778.* 1780.

Index

Farnacres (D.), 130, 131
Farnborough (War.), 223
Farrington (Lancs.), 43
Faugh, 148
Faversham (Kent), 390
Feckenham (Worcs.), 220, 226; Royal Forest of, 210
Felindre (Glam.), 509–10
Fen Ditton (Cambs.), 295
Fenton, R., 519
Fenwick, (Nd.), 141
Ferlingate, 333
Ferlings, 393, 423
Fermtoun, 576, 577
Ferthings, 393
Feudalism (see also Manorialism), 28, 29, 211, 306–7, 312, 576
Field names, 87, 180, 181–2, 294, 295; evidence of, 6, 9, 26, 27, 32–4, 35; croft, 179, 182
Field patterns, 32–6, 175–6; regular, 588; irregular, 296, 588
Field systems: in Chilterns and environs, 325–76; in East Anglia, 281–324; in East Midlands, 232–80; in Ireland, 580–618; in New England, 233–4, 279; in Northeast, 93–144; in North Wales, 430–79; in South Wales, 480–529; in West Midlands, 188–231; in Yorkshire, 145–87
  champion field systems: in East Anglia, 285–6; in South Wales, 480, 521; in West Midlands, 194, 195–209, 210, 212, 213, 221–2, 231
  'Midland' system, 94, 144, 145, 161, 187, 188–90, 281, 290, 294–5, 297, 312, 324, 325, 329, 345, 375, 377, 425, 621, 622
  remodelled systems, 647–53; in Chilterns and environs, 350, 372; in East Anglia, 297; in East Midlands, 257–62; in West Midlands, 200, 201, 218, 226; in Yorkshire, 183–5, 187
  woodland field systems, in West Midlands, 209–21, 222, 229, 231
  types of: one-field system, 656; in Northeast, 131, 143; in Yorkshire, 180, 185–6, 187
    two-field system, 530, 541, 567, 577, 621, 624–5, 644; in Chilterns and environs, 337, 347–8, 350, 357, 358, 375; in East Midlands, 257, 296; in Northeast, 130, 131; in Scotland, 576; in West Midlands, 192, 203, 205, 206, 208, 222, 224, 225; in Yorkshire, 161, 176
    three-field system, 530, 541, 567,

577, 621, 622, 624–5, 644; in Chilterns and environs, 336, 337, 356, 358, 372–3; in East Anglia, 295, 296–7, 299; in East Midlands, 257; in Ireland, 610, 617–18; in Northeast, 94, 99, 108, 114, 117, 119, 121, 122, 127–30, 133, 141, 144; in Northwest, 52, 55, 57–9; in Scotland, 576; in Southeast, 425; in South Wales, 488; in West Midlands, 206–9, 212, 218, 219, 222, 225; in Yorkshire, 161, 176
    four-field system, 161; in East Anglia, 297; in East Midlands, 257; in West Midlands, 195–205, 206, 222, 225
  multiple-field systems, in Chilterns and environs, 337; in Southeast, 422; in West Midlands, 20, 203, 205–6, 211, 222, 225
  irregular field systems, 625; in Chilterns and environs, 325, 352–3, 366; in Northeast, 118; in West Midlands, 190, 213, 217, 222, 226, 228
Fiennes, Celia, 19, 84
Finberg, H. P. R., 231, 577
Finchurst (Kent), 407
Fingland (Cumb.), 65
Firmarii, 608–9, 611, 613
Fishguard (Pemb.), 515, 517, 521
Fishponds, 241
Fitzherbert, A., 288
Flamstead (Herts.), 332, 334
Flatrès, P., 530, 588, 619
Flatts, 125, 132, 148, 155, 623
Flaxby (E. Riding), 149, 169
Flemingston (Glam.), 502
Flexmore (Herts.), 329
Flint, 478
Flyford Flavell (Worcs.), 200
Fodder crops, 125, 389, 426, 495, 534, 594–5, 648
Foldcourse, 314–22, 323, 414, 634
Folds, 630, 644; in Chilterns and environs, 335, 344, 349, 354, 358, 371–2, 375; in East Anglia, 313; in East Midlands, 254; in North Wales, 435, 459; in Northwest, 49; in Scotland, 533, 535; in Southeast, 398, 413, 414, 419, 426, 429; in West Midlands, 230; in Yorkshire, 159
  see also Foldcourse
Folkestone (Kent), 414
Folkingham (Lincs.), 277
Fonmon (Glam.), 500–2
Foreland, 170–2, 174
Forest Law, 46, 244
Foriff (Co. Antrim), 589

Sutton cum Lound (Notts.), 268
Sutton in Campsall (Yorks.), 165, 169
Swaffham (Norf.), 282, 321
Swannington (Leics.), 638
Swansea (Glam.), 509
Swathes, 134
Swaton (Lincs.), 256
Swine, in Chilterns and environs, 328; in
    East Midlands, 247, 251, 254; in
    Ireland, 595, 612, 616; in North
    Wales, 445; in Northwest, 60; in
    Southeast, 380, 388, 401, 415–16,
    419–20, 423; in South Wales, 522; in
    Yorkshire, 172
Sydenham (Oxon.), 354
Sylvester, D., 57, 67, 91
Symon, J., 545
Symonson, P., 10
Syresham (Northants.), 275

Tacksman, 545, 547–9, 564
Tadcaster (Yorks.), 176
Talgarth (Brecon.), 484, 486, 487, 488
Talgarth (Denb.), 467
Talybont-on-Usk (Brecon.), 485
Tangmere (Sussex), 420
Tanworth (War.), 226–7, 228, 229, 230
Tarleton (Lancs.), 48
Tate, W. E., 8, 190, 192, 194, 209, 290,
    317, 406
Tathe, 285, 315–17
Tattenho (Bucks.), 353
Technology, impact on field systems, 189,
    224–5, 284, 620, 622
Templeton (Pemb.), 517–18
Tenby (Pemb.), 518–19
Tenements, 173–6, 406
Tenementum, 311–12, 323, 407, 421
Tennantree (Perth.), 560–2
Tenure: in Chilterns and environs, 356; in
    East Anglia, 305–13, 323; in East
    Midlands, 264–71, 274–5, 277; in
    Ireland, 608–12; in Northeast, 138–40;
    in North Wales, 431–2, 434, 470; in
    Northwest, 53–4; in Scotland, 532,
    536–50; in Southeast, 391; in South
    Wales, 481, 484–5, 511, 528
Terling (Essex), 339
Tetsworth (Oxon.), 357
Teversham (Cambs.), 298, 305
Teynham (Kent), 413
Thame (Oxon.), 354
Thame Abbey, 354
Thanet (Kent), 387
Thaxted (Essex), 342
Theberton (Suff.), 304
Thetford (Norf.), 287, 324

Thing, 179
Third, B., 552, 576
Thirsk (Yorks.), 166
Thirsk, J., 199, 203, 216, 227, 358, 619,
    622, 623, 626–7, 637, 641, 644–5,
    646–7, 649, 650
Thistleton (Lancs.), 52
Thomas, H. R., 190, 209, 212, 218, 219
Thorneyburn (Nd.), 103
Thorngrafton (Nd.), 108
Thornley (D.), 99, 129
Thornton Rust (Yorks.), 166
Thorpe Acre (Leics.), 254
Thorpe Arches (Yorks.), 180
Thorpe Satchville (Leics.), 275
Three Houses (Herts.), 329
Threlkeld (Cumb.), 81
Thwaite, 179
Tibberton (Worcs.), 217
Tidenham (Gloucs.), 482, 489
Tidmington (War.), 198
Tighe, W., 591
Tiptree Heath (Essex), 365
Tir corddlan, 435, 471–6, 479
Tir cyfrif, 434, 460–71, 479
Tir gwelyog, 432–4, 441, 446–60, 474,
    476, 479
Tithe Commutation Acts, 5
Titow, J. Z., 624, 647, 650
Tofts, 146, 148, 294
Tonbridge (Kent), 392
Tonge (Leics.), 243–5
Tostock (Suff.), 287, 292
Tottington (Norf.), 300
Townfields, 46, 60, 67, 109, 129, 131, 219,
    422, 428
Townland, 586, 609–10
Towns: influence on field systems, 54, 63,
    91–2, 230, 374, 497, 569–71; impact
    on agriculture, 139, 284, 632–3;
    impact on the landscape, 93
Trallwng (Brecon.), 485
Transhumance: in Ireland, 587, 602; in
    Northeast, 95, 125, 126; in North
    Wales, 444, 459, 479; in Northwest,
    50, 74; in Scotland, 535, 567–9, 577
see also Booleying, Hafod and Shieling
Trawsfynydd (Mer.), 444
Treberfedd (Ang.), 463, 464
Trecastell (Ang.), 463
Tredington (War.), 222
Treduccon (Glam.), 500
Tredunnock (Mon.), 491
Trefechan (Denb.), 472, 474, 476
Trefgornor (Ang.), 463
Tre-fin (Pemb.), 517
Trefriw (Ang.), 463, 464

Trefwaspadrig (Ang.), 463
Treleddyn (Pemb.), 517
Treleidir (Pemb.), 517
Treoes (Glam.), 506
Trescott (Staffs.), 219
Treswni (Pemb.), 517
Tretower (Brecon.), 484
Trimley (Suff.), 289
Troston (Suff.), 322
Trysull (Staffs.), 219
Tuar, 612
Tunstall (Lancs.), 46
Tunstall (Staffs.), 211
Turner, G. J., 405
Turnips, 201, 205–6, 217, 304, 321, 371
Tusser, T., 289
Twrllachied (Ang.), 452
Tymberwood (Kent), 386
Tynemouth (Nd.), 119, 140
Tysoe (War.), 222

Uhlig, H., 530, 573, 616
Ulley (Yorks.), 147
Ulley Cliff Common (Yorks.), 164
Ulverston (Lancs.), 54
Undy (Mon.), 495–6
Uphampton (Worcs.), 217
Upper Heyford (Oxon.), 349
Usk (Mon.), 491

Vifgaged land, 434, 450–1, 455–6
Village communities, 232–3; origin of, 274–5
Vinogradoff, P., 405, 430
Virgates, 249, 267, 271, 272–3, 275, 311, 312, 333, 339, 348, 351, 357, 359, 386, 407, 423, 636
Vollans, E. C., 332, 362, 637

Wackerfield (D.), 128
Waddington (Lincs.), 249
Wakefield, E., 593
Walberswick (Suff.), 287
Walcot near Barnack (Northants.), 277
Walcot near Billinghay (Lincs.), 277
Walcot near Folkingham (Lincs.), 277
Walcot near West Halton (Lincs.), 277
Walcot Lodge, Fotheringhay (Northants.) 277
Walcott (Leics.), 277
Waldhufendörfer, 186
Wales: hereditary land, *see Tir gwelyog*
   nucleal land, *see Tir corddlan*
   reckoned land, *see Tir cyfrif*
Wallasey (Ches.), 91, 92
Wallingfen (Yorks.), 157, 164

Walney (Lancs.), 83
Walsall (Staffs.), 218
Walsingham (D.), 99
Walsingham (Norf.), 292, 308
Waltham Abbey, 342
Walton (Lancs.), 85, 87, 88, 91
Walton (Suff.), 288, 289
Walton (Yorks.), 180
Walton on the Wolds (Leics.), 277
Wandales, 185, 652
Wandon (Herts.), 329
Wangford (Suff.), 293, 299, 300
Warcop (Westmld.), 82
Ward, G., 406
Warden (Beds.), 351
Wark (Nd.), 125
Warkworth (Northants.), 248
Warmington (War.), 223
Warsop (Notts.), 236
Warths, 489
Warton (Lancs.), 47, 66
Warton in Polesworth (War.), 213
Wasdale Head (Cumb.), 46
Wasporton (War.), 194
Waste: intakes from, in Chilterns and
   environs, 342, 350–1, 353, 364; in
   East Anglia, 293, 294; in Northeast,
   106, 138–9, 141–2; in Yorkshire, 163,
   174–5
overstocking of, 459
reclamation of, 637–8; in Chilterns and
   environs, 375; in East Midlands, 234;
   in Northeast, 120, 133, 141, 171; in
   North Wales, 478–9; in Northwest,
   41, 45, 46, 52, 69–72, 84–5; in York-
   shire, 171
see also Brecks
Waterbeach (Cambs.), 319
Waterman, D. M., 611
Water meadows, 387
Waterperry (Oxon.), 349–50
Wath-on-Dearne (Yorks.), 164
Wawne (Yorks.), 184
Weasenham (Norf.), 291, 304
Webster, J., 538
Wednesbury (Staffs.), 218
Wednesfield (Staffs.), 218
Weeting (Norf.), 315
Well (Lincs.), 261
Wellington (D.), 128
Wells (Norf.), 284
Welsh Laws, 30, 430–2, 636–7
Welton (Nd.), 137
Wendlebury (Oxon.), 371
Wenvoe (Glam.), 500
West Boldon (D.), 129
Westerdale (Yorks.), 181